PITAL

Professional Voice
The Science and Art of Clinical Care

Professional Voice
The Science and Art of Clinical Care

Robert Thayer Sataloff, M.D., D.M.A.

Professor of Otolaryngology
Thomas Jefferson University
Director, Jefferson Arts–Medicine Center
Faculty, The Curtis Institute of Music and
The Academy of Vocal Arts
Philadelphia, Pennsylvania
Chairman, The Voice Foundation
Chairman, American Institute
for Voice and Ear Research

Raven Press  New York

Raven Press Ltd., 1185 Avenue of the Americas, New York, New York 10036

Made in the United States of America

Library of Congress Cataloging-in-Publication Data

Sataloff, Robert Thayer.
    Professional voice : the science and art of clinical care / Robert Thayer Sataloff.
        p.   cm.
    Includes bibliographical references.
    Includes index.
    ISBN 0-88167-737-X
    1. Voice disorders—Treatment. 2. Voice culture. 3. Voice.
I. Title.
    [DNLM: 1. Voice. 2. Voice Disorders—therapy. 3. Voice Training.
WV 500 S2525p]
RF510.S28 1991
616.85′5—dc20
DNLM/DLC
for Library of Congress   90-9022
                                                                          CIP

The material contained in this volume was submitted as previously unpublished material, except in the instances in which credit has been given to the source from which some of the illustrative material was derived.

Great care has been taken to maintain the accuracy of the information contained in the volume. However, neither Raven Press nor the editors can be held responsible for errors or for any consequences arising from the use of the information contained herein.

Materials appearing in this book prepared by individuals as part of their official duties as U.S. Government employees are not covered by the above-mentioned copyright.

9 8 7 6 5 4 3 2 1

The author is indebted to WB Saunders for permission to use material from Sataloff RT, Professional singers: the science and art of clinical care, *American Journal of Otolaryngology,* 1981;2(3):251–266; to the Journal of Otolaryngology for permission to use material from Sataloff RT, Physical examination of the professional singer, *Journal of Otolaryngology,* 1983;12(5):277–281; to CV Mosby for permission to use material from Sataloff RT, The Professional Voice, in Cummings CW, Fredrickson JM, Harker LA, Krause CJ, Schuller DA, editors, *Otolaryngology-Head and Neck Surgery;* to Raven Press for permission to use material from Sataloff RT, The professional voice, parts I, II, and III from the *Journal of Voice,* Vol 1, nos. 1, 2, and 3; and to the *NATS Journal* for permission to use materials from his "laryngoscope" articles.

Contents

Contributors

Ronald J. Baken, Ph.D. *Professor of Speech Science, Teachers College, Columbia University, 525 W. 120th Street, New York, New York 10027*

Ronald S. Bogdasarian, M.D. *Clinical Assistant Professor, Department of Otorhinolaryngology, University of Michigan, 5333 McAuley Drive, Suite 2017, Reichert Health Building, P.O. Box 994, Ann Arbor, Michigan 48106*

Linda M. Carroll, B.M., B.S. *Singing Voice Specialist, American Institute for Voice and Ear Research, 1721 Pine Street, Philadelphia, Pennsylvania 19103*

John R. Cohn, M.D., F.C.C.P. *Clinical Assistant, Professor of Medicine and Pediatrics, Thomas Jefferson University Hospital, Suite A4120, New Hospital Building, 111 S. 11th Street, Philadelphia, Pennsylvania 19107*

Kathe S. Darby, M.A. *Certified Speech-Language Pathologist, 311 Buchanan Street, Louisville, Colorado 80027*

Mary Hawkshaw, R.N., B.S.N. *Otolaryngologic Nurse-Clinician, American Institute for Voice and Ear Research, 1721 Pine Street, Philadelphia, Pennsylvania 19103*

Richard Miller, D.H.L. *Professor of Singing, Oberlin College, Conservatory of Music, Oberlin, Ohio 44074*

Bonnie N. Raphael, Ph.D. *Voice and Speech Coach-Teacher, American Repertory Theater and Institute, Harvard University, Loeb Drama Center, 64 Brattle Street, Cambridge, Massachusetts 02138*

Rhonda K. Rulnick, M.A. *Certified Speech-Language Pathologist, American Institute for Voice and Ear Research, 1721 Pine Street, Philadelphia, Pennsylvania 19103*

Dahlia M. Sataloff, M.D. *Clinical Assistant Professor, Department of Surgery, University of Pennsylvania, The Graduate Hospital, Suite 901, Pepper Pavilion, 19th & Lombard Streets, Philadelphia, Pennsylvania 19146*

Joseph Sataloff, M.D., D.Sc. *Professor of Otolaryngology, Thomas Jefferson University, 1721 Pine Street, Philadelphia, Pennsylvania 19103*

Robert Thayer Sataloff, M.D., D.M.A. *Professor of Otolaryngology, Thomas Jefferson University, 1721 Pine Street, Philadelphia, Pennsylvania 19103*

Joseph R. Spiegel, M.D., F.A.C.S. *Assistant Professor of Otolaryngology, Thomas Jefferson University, 1721 Pine Street, Philadelphia, Pennsylvania 19103*

Johan Sundberg, Ph.D. *Professor, Department of Speech Communication and Music Acoustics, Royal Institute of Technology, Box 70024, Stockholm, Sweden S-100 44*

Carol N. Wilder, Ph.D. (Deceased) *Professor of Speech Science, Teachers College, Columbia University, 525 W. 120th Street, New York, New York 10027*

Preface

Professional Voice: The Science and Art of Clinical Care is written for physicians, but it is also intended to be useful to anyone interested in the voice. This book provides a practical understanding of specialized aspects of clinical care of professional voice users. Because voice is such a new subspecialty of otolaryngology, it has been difficult for the interested otolaryngologist to find the necessary information conveniently compiled. This book will facilitate better clinical care and provide a basis from which new ideas and research can develop. It should prove similarly useful to speech-language pathologists since their training programs rarely provide training in professional voice care and include essentially no training in how to work with the speaking voices of professional singers. Interdisciplinary fellowships are also uncommon, and it has been difficult for the interested speech-language pathologist to gather necessary background knowledge. This book is intended to make that process easier.

In collecting information about care of the professional voice, this book naturally includes valuable information to the singer, actor, or other professional voice user. In fact, most of the material presented has been included in the author's courses in voice pedagogy taught at the Academy of Vocal Arts and Curtis Institute of Music during the past decade. Voice students, singing teachers, acting coaches, and others have found this new information helpful in augmenting their traditional teaching approaches and in understanding healthy functioning of the voice. It also appears that students trained with this information appreciate the importance of and techniques for maintaining vocal health, and they seem to spend less time sick, injured, or in physicians' offices (especially for preventable problems) than their colleagues without such training.

The introductory chapter provides an overview of modern voice medicine, and an historical review of its development from the time of Hippocrates. Chapters 2, 3, and 4 crystalize clinically relevant anatomy, physiology, and voice science, in considerable depth but in a language suitable for singers as well as physicians and scientists. Chapters 5 and 6 provide in-depth information on special aspects of the medical history important in caring for singers and actors. Chapters 7 and 8 detail state-of-the-art physical examination and clinical laboratory assessment of patients with voice disorders. Chapters 9 through 25 address specific medical problems of professional voice users, including assessment and treatment. In addition to discussing virtually all of the common entities, several chapters provide information that is particularly difficult to find elsewhere such as the chapters entitled Halitosis, Hearing Loss in Singers, and Bodily Injuries and Their Effect on the Voice. Chapter 24 on surgery of the voice highlights critical details of the most modern microsurgical techniques. Chapters 26 through 32 discuss the importance of and techniques for voice modification, therapy, and training for speech and singing. The chapter entitled Voice Therapy provides detailed information on speaking voice therapy in professional singers, including techniques and exercise lists (Appendix V). The final chapter of the book is a philosophical epilogue emphasizing to physicians the importance of the arts in the practice of medicine. The appendices are also particularly useful, including a summary of the phonetic alphabet in five languages, clinical history and examination forms, and a special history form translated into five languages.

This book is intended as a readable text for students, vocalists, teachers and residents, a practical guide to clinical treatment for practicing physicians and speech-language pathologists, and a ready reference for anyone interested in care of the professional voice.

Robert T. Sataloff M.D., D.M.A.

Acknowledgments

A special word of gratitude goes to each of the colleagues who contributed to the writing of this book. The specialists who were invited to contribute chapters added enormously to the value of the book. Their words of wisdom should prove most illuminating not only to practitioners of their own specialties, but perhaps even more to others looking for interdisciplinary insight.

All specialists in voice, and our patients and students, are indebted to Wilbur James Gould, Chairman Emeritus and Founder of the Voice Foundation and Director of the Vocal Dynamics Laboratory at Lenox Hill Hospital in New York, for inspiring and facilitating most of the voice research and clinical development we have witnessed in the past 20 years. Thanks to his efforts and to those of the Voice Foundation under his guidance, there are now over 80 voice research laboratories in operation. The annual Symposium on Care of the Professional Voice, which he founded, has been the keystone in international interdisciplinary education. Without his contributions as an educator and his support of research, much of what we know about the voice today would still be unknown. The growing clinical competence in the care of professional singers and actors can be attributed to Dr. Gould and to his colleagues, including Hans von Leden, M.D., Van L. Lawrence, M.D., Friedrich Brodnitz, M.D., David Brewer, M.D., Ingo R. Titze, Ph.D., Johan Sundberg, Ph.D., and others. Our debt to these pioneers can be repaid only through continued advances in the voice studies they have held so dear. We hope such advances will be facilitated by making known information more easily accessible through *Professional Voice: The Science and Art of Clinical Care*, drawing new minds and imaginations into the fertile field of voice.

The author is also indebted to Mary Hawkshaw, R.N., B.S.N., for countless hours of editorial assistance, proofreading, suggestions, and support—without her help this book would not yet be finished; to Joseph Sataloff, M.D., Joseph R. Spiegel, M.D., Linda M. Carroll, B.M., B.S., Kathe S. Darby, M.A., and Rhonda K. Rulnick, M.A., for their editorial assistance; to Zaven Jabourian, M.D. for his friendship, time, and outstanding illustrations; to Helen Caputo and Laura E. Zebley for preparation of the manuscript; to Mary Rogers and Wanda Woloszyn at Raven Press for their assistance; and to Van L. Lawrence, M.D. and Hans von Leden, M.D. for their continued advice and support.

Special thanks are also due to James B. Snow, M.D. This book evolved from my first article on care of the professional voice published a decade ago. The article was rejected by several journals before Jim Snow deemed it worthy of publication in the *American Journal of Otolaryngology*. Since then, I have run out of 3,000 reprints, expanded the article on several occasions, and seen it grow into *Professional Voice: The Science and Art of Clinical Care*. If Jim Snow had not had the foresight to recognize the importance of this new specialty and had not published the paper, much of my subsequent work might not have been possible.

Professional Voice

The Science and Art of Clinical Care

Professional Voice: The Science and Art of Clinical Care, Robert T. Sataloff.
Raven Press, Ltd., New York © 1991.

1

Introduction

Robert T. Sataloff

Department of Otolaryngology, Thomas Jefferson University,
Philadelphia, Pennsylvania

The importance of the human voice in modern society cannot be overstated. It is the primary instrument through which most of us project our personalities and influence our compatriots. Professional voice users constitute an ever-increasing segment of our population, and their need for expert care has inspired new interest in understanding the function and dysfunction of the human voice. Professional voice users provide exciting challenges and special responsibilities for physicians and other health care professionals. Professional voice users include not only singers and actors, but also attorneys, politicians, clergy, educators (including some physicians), telephone receptionists, and others. Although they span a broad range of vocal sophistication and voice needs, they share a dependence on vocal endurance and quality for their livelihoods. However, the vocal needs of performing artists are especially great. In this book, we emphasize the problems of professional actors and especially singers, because they are the Olympic athletes of the voice world. Their extreme anatomic, physiologic, and therapeutic demands tax our clinical and research skills; but what we learn from them is applicable to the care of all voice patients. In most cases, mastery of the science and art of caring for professional singers provides the physician with sufficient expertise to treat other professional voice users as well, so long as the physician takes the trouble to really understand the special needs and problems associated with various voice-dependent professions.

Voice problems may arise from laryngeal or systemic disease, trauma, or improper treatment. The consequences of voice dysfunction may be devastating; and, if permanent (or even temporary) vocal problems result from suboptimal medical care, they may result in substantial claims for damages. Possibly spurred by the striking increase in litigation, but largely to provide good medical care for its own sake, a great many physicians have recently turned their attention to professional voice care. Interdisciplinary research has resulted in new understanding and technology that have improved the standard of practice of laryngologists and speech-language pathologists. It is no longer sufficient to glance at a singer's vocal cords with a laryngeal mirror and continuous light and declare, "Your cords are fine. It must be the way you sing." Similarly, it is no longer sufficient to say, "The voice sounds bad," or "The voice sounds better," anymore than we would tolerate such vagueness in describing hearing.

Although physicians are frequently called on to care for singers and other voice professionals, most doctors have little or no training in sophisticated analysis and treatment of subtle problems of the voice. Voice disorders are complex. Initially, voice complaints may seem vague and subjective, especially to health care professionals unfamiliar with the jargon of singers and actors. However, accurate diagnosis and rational treatment may be achieved through systematic inquiry based on understanding of the anatomy, physiology, psychology, and psychoacoustics of voice production. More thorough understanding of voice is valuable not only in caring for voice problems themselves, but also in providing good medical care by recognizing systemic diseases that present with laryngeal manifestations. Just as otologists routinely diagnose diabetes and hypothyroidism that cause dizziness or fluctuating hearing loss, laryngologists should be alert to xerophonia as a sign of diabetes, muffling of the voice from hypothyroidism, fatigue from myasthenia, and many other similar problems. Hypochondriasis is rare among serious singers and most other voice professionals. In general, failure to establish a diagnosis in a professional vocalist with a voice complaint is due to lack of expertise on the part of the physician rather than an imaginary complaint on the part of the singer or actor.

HISTORY

Fascination with the human voice has prompted study and literature for centuries, and an excellent review by Dr. Hans von Leden put the evolution of voice medicine into perspective[1]. In *Corpus Hippocraticum,* Hippocrates in the 5th century B.C. provided some of the earliest medical speculation on the workings of the voice, recognizing the importance of the lungs, trachea, lips, and tongue in phonation. Aristotle expanded knowledge on the scientific workings of the voice and commented on the close relationship between the voice and the soul, recognizing its importance in emotional expression. Claudius Galen, who practiced from 131 to 201 A.D., is hailed as the founder of laryngology and voice science. He wrote an essay on the human voice (among his over 300 books) that is frequently referenced but has, unfortunately, been lost. He recognized the workings of the voice, described the larynx, recognized the importance of the brain in controlling phonation, and, for the first time, distinguished between speech and voice. Galen's work went virtually unchallenged for more than 15 centuries, and some of it is still regarded as correct.

Major advancement did not come until the Renaissance and the writings of Leonardo da Vinci, particularly *Quaderni D'Anatomia* in 1500. Additional important Renaissance writers who advanced knowledge of the voice included Andreas Vesalius, Bartolomeus Eustachius, and Fabricius Ab Aquapendente. Fabricius wrote three books on the larynx, including *De Larynge Vocis Instrumento*. Similar important advances occurred in the east, particularly in the ninth century when Rhazes the Experienced, in Baghdad, described disorders of the voice and hoarseness and recommended respiratory and voice training. There are also excellent descriptions of voice production and disorders in the *Quanun,* written by Avicenna the Persian. The *Quanan* was a standard medical textbook for more than 500 years. Major additional advances occurred in the eighteenth century through the efforts of Giovanni Morgagni, who first related dysphonia to abnormalities in the larynx. Also in the eighteenth century, Antoine Ferrein described physiological experiments on animal and human cadaver larynges and coined the term vocal cords, comparing the vocal folds to the strings of an instrument. Albrecht von Haller described the anatomy of vocal resonance. Later, Johannes Mueller in Germany described the mechanism of vocal fold vibration. In the nineteenth century, Hermann von Helmholtz essentially started the experimental science of acoustics with experiments that are still considered valid. All the scientists mentioned above laid the foundation for the close liaison that has existed between physicians and singers.

However, the clear and widely recognized beginning of arts medicine in the voice world dates from the time of Manuel Garcia, who was born in 1805. Garcia was a world-famous opera singer while in his teens. Although he was the son of an acclaimed singer and director, his probably faulty technique and extensive operatic singing impaired his voice sufficiently to cause him to retire while still in his 20s. Thereafter, he became a thoughtful, effective, and famous teacher and was made Professor of Singing at the Conservatoire de Paris at the age of 30. In 1854, Garcia bought a dental mirror and invented the technique of indirect laryngoscopy. The laryngeal mirror is still the basic tool for visualizing vocal folds and is used daily by otolaryngologists. Garcia observed larynges closely with his new tool and presented his findings before the Royal Society of Medicine in 1855. He was considered the greatest singing teacher of his age, and "on his 100th birthday in 1905 he was honored by physicians, music teachers and scientists from all over the world"[1].

Voice medicine continued to develop slowly throughout the first seven decades of the twentieth century. In the past two decades, increasing interest and new technology have generated unprecedented activity within a number of disciplines. Since 1971, laryngologists, voice scientists, physicists, computer scientists, speech-language pathologists, singing teachers, acting teachers, voice coaches, singers, actors, and other professionals have met at the Voice Foundation's week-long annual Symposium on Care of the Professional Voice. At this unique meeting, formerly held at the Juilliard

School of Music and now located in Philadelphia, experts have gathered to report their research and share their ideas. The resultant interdisciplinary understanding and cooperation have produced great advances and even greater promise for future understanding. These activities have rendered care of the professional voice the most advanced discipline within the new specialty of arts medicine. They have also inspired numerous successful interdisciplinary publications, including the "Journal of Voice." This important journal abandons traditional specialty boundaries and brings together in one peer-reviewed journal, with international distribution, articles of high quality on all subjects relating to the voice.

In many ways, the status of voice care is still analogous to that of otology 30 years ago. Until recently, voice evaluation was reminiscent of ear examinations with a head mirror instead of a microscope, or whispered voice tests instead of audiograms. In many places, it still is. Fortunately, expert research has led to greater understanding of the voice and development of instrumentation for sophisticated assessment and quantitative analysis to facilitate clinical management and research. Although efforts have focused largely on professional singers and actors, the knowledge they have accrued has advanced our understanding of voice in general and has modified substantially the state of the art in clinical care of all persons with voice disorders. Still, the field is new. The first extensive article intended to teach clinicians how to approach professional singers was not published until 1981[2], and the first major general textbook of otolaryngology containing a chapter on care of the professional voice was not published until 1986[3]. In the past few years, many new centers and academic training programs have acquired voice laboratories and begun practicing and teaching modern, advanced voice care; but more time will be required before state-of-the-art care is available in most geographical areas.

At present, new understanding of special aspects of the history and physical examination of professional voice users has been supplemented by technological advances through voice analysis that are readily available to interested clinicians. Flexible fiberoptic laryngoscopy has been indispensable. The development and refinement of laryngeal stroboscopy are a singularly important advancement. Strobovideolaryngoscopic evaluation of vocal fold behavior in slow motion allows diagnoses that are simply missed without it. Spectrography, electroglottography, electromyography, airflow analysis, and other techniques have also enhanced our ability to analyze and treat voice disorders reliably.

The knowledge acquired through medical and basic science research has advanced not only clinical care but also the teaching of voice. Modern singing, acting, and speech teachers have acquired new scientific understanding of the voice and use their new knowledge to augment and refine their traditional approaches to voice training. One hopes this will lead to consistently healthier and more efficient voice training. There are many other fascinating potential implications as well. For example, to sing correctly is essentially an athletic endeavor. In this century, most athletic records have been broken. Often this has been the result of technological advancements, such as computer analysis of a runner's form using high-speed photography or stroboscopy. Through these and other methods, the marathon, pole vault, high jump, and swimming records of 50 years ago are barely qualifying marks for today's high school students. Similar principles have just begun to be applied to the proper training of the voice. It is tempting to speculate about the results. Perhaps, as in other athletic pursuits, we shall find that the healthy limits of human vocal potential are far greater than we think.

DISCRETION

The excitement and glamour associated with caring for a famous performer naturally tempt the physician to talk about his distinguished patient. However, this tendency must be tempered. It is not always in a singer's best professional interest to have it known that he has consulted a laryngologist, particularly for treatment of a significant vocal problem. Famous singers and actors are ethically and legally entitled to the same confidentiality we assure for our other patients.

REFERENCES

1. von Leden H. The cultural history of the human voice. In: Lawrence VL, ed. *Transcripts of the eleventh symposium: care of the professional voice: Part II*. New York: The Voice Foundation, 1982;116–123.
2. Sataloff RT. The professional singer: science and art of clinical care. *Am J Otolaryngol* 1981;2(3):251–266.
3. Sataloff RT. The professional voice. In: Cummings CV, Fredrickson JM, Harker LA, et al., eds. *Otolaryngology-head and neck surgery*. St. Louis, Missouri: CV Mosby, 1986;3:2029–2053.

Professional Voice: The Science and Art of Clinical Care, Robert T. Sataloff. Raven Press, Ltd., New York © 1991.

2

Clinical Anatomy and Physiology of the Voice

Robert T. Sataloff

Department of Otolaryngology, Thomas Jefferson University, Philadelphia, Pennsylvania

ANATOMY

The anatomy of a professional voice user is not limited to the region between the suprasternal notch and the hyoid bone. Practically all body systems affect the voice. The larynx receives the greatest attention because it is the most sensitive and expressive component of the vocal mechanism, but anatomic interactions throughout the patient's body must be considered in treating the professional voice. It is helpful to think of the larynx as composed of four anatomic units: mucosa, intrinsic muscles, extrinsic muscles, and skeleton. The *glottis* is the space between the vocal folds.

Larynx: Mucosa

The vibratory margin of the vocal fold is much more complicated than simply mucosa applied to muscle. It consists of five layers (1) (Fig. 1). The thin, lubricated epithelium covering the vocal folds forms the area of contact between the vibrating vocal cords and acts somewhat like a capsule, helping to maintain vocal fold shape. The epithelium lining most of the vocal tract is pseudo-stratified ciliated columnar epithelium, typical respiratory epithelium involved in handling mucous secretions. The vibratory margin of the vocal fold is covered with stratified squamous epithelium, better suited to withstand the trauma of vocal fold contact. The superficial layer of the lamina propria, also known as Reinke's space, is made up of loose fibrous components and matrix. It contains very few fibroblasts. The intermediate layer of the lamina propria contains more fibroblasts and consists primarily of elastic fibers. The deep layer of the lamina propria is composed primarily of collagenous fibers and is rich in fibroblasts. The thyroarytenoid or vocalis

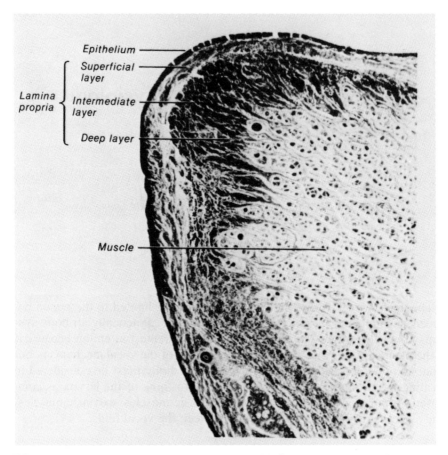

Epithelium

Superficial
layer

Lamina
propria

Intermediate
layer

Deep layer

Muscle

FIG. 1. The structure of the vocal fold. From Hirano M. *Clinical examination of voice.* New York: Springer-Verlag, 1981;5, with permission.

muscle makes up the body of the vocal fold and is one of the intrinsic laryngeal muscles. The region of the intermediate and deep layers of the lamina propria is called the vocal ligament and lies immediately below Reinke's space. Functionally, the various layers have different mechanical properties and act somewhat like ball bearings of different sizes in allowing the smooth shearing action necessary for proper vocal fold vibration. The posterior one-third (approximately) of the vocal fold is cartilaginous, and the anterior two-thirds are membranous (from the vocal process forward) in adults. Most of the vibratory function critical to sound quality occurs in the membranous portion.

Mechanically, the vocal fold structures actually act more like three layers consisting of the *cover* (epithelium and Reinke's space), *transition* (intermediate and deep layers of the lamina propria), and the *body* (the vocalis muscle). Understanding this anatomy is important, because different pathologic entities occur in different layers. Moreover, fibroblasts are responsible for scar formation. Therefore, lesions that occur in the cover (such as nodules, cysts, and most polyps) should permit treatment without disturbance of the intermediate and deep layers, fibroblast proliferation, or scar formation. *Intrinsic muscles* are responsible for abduction, adduction, and tension of the vocal folds. *Extrinsic laryngeal musculature* maintains the position of the larynx in the neck. It includes primarily the strap muscles. Since raising or lowering the larynx may alter the tension or angle between laryngeal cartilages (Fig. 2),* the extrinsic muscles are critical in maintaining a stable laryngeal skeleton so that the delicate intrinsic musculature can work effectively. In the Western classically trained singer, the extrinsic muscles maintain the larynx in a relatively constant position. Training of the intrinsic musculature results in vibratory symmetry of the vocal folds, producing regular periodicity. This contributes to what the listener perceives as a "trained" voice. The vocal folds may be thought of as the oscillator of the vocal mechanism (2).

Larynx: The Intrinsic Muscles

For some purposes, including electromyography and surgery, it is important to understand the function of individual intrinsic laryngeal muscles in greater detail. The muscles of primary functional importance are those innervated by the recurrent laryngeal nerve (thyroarytenoid or vocalis, posterior cricoarytenoid, lateral cricoarytenoid, and interarytenoid or arytenoideus) and superior laryngeal nerve (cricothyroid) (Figs. 3–5).

The *thyroarytenoid (vocalis) muscle* adducts, lowers, shortens, and thickens the vocal fold, rounding the vocal fold edge. Thus, the cover and transition are effectively made more slack, while the body is stiffened. Adduction from vocalis contraction is active, particularly in the membranous segment of the vocal folds. It tends to lower vocal pitch. The thyroarytenoid originates anteriorly from the posterior (interior) surface of the thyroid cartilage and inserts into the lateral base of the arytenoid cartilage from the vocal process to the muscular process.

The *posterior cricoarytenoid muscle* abducts, elevates, elongates, and thins the vocal fold. All layers are stiffened, and the edge of the vocal fold is rounded. It originates from the posterior lamina of the crico cartilage and inserts on the posterior surface of the muscular process of the arytenoid cartilage. The *lateral cricoarytenoid muscle* adducts, lowers, elongates, and thins the vocal fold. All layers are stiffened, and the vocal fold edge takes on a more angular or sharp contour. It originates on the upper border of the crico cartilage and inserts into the anterior surface of the muscular process of the arytenoid. The *interarytenoid muscle* (arytenoideus) primarily ad-

---

* See color plates section that appears following page 14 for Figs. 2–4, 6 and 7.

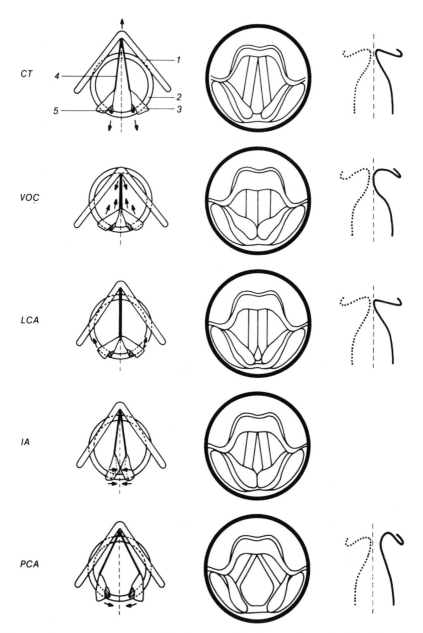

FIG. 5. A schematic presentation of the function of the laryngeal muscles. The **left column** shows the location of the cartilages and the edge of the vocal folds when the laryngeal muscles are activated individually. The *arrows* indicate the direction of the force exerted. 1, thyroid cartilage; 2, cricoid cartilage; 3, arytenoid cartilage; 4, vocal ligament; 5, posterior cricoarytenoid ligament. The **middle column** shows the views from above. The **right column** illustrates contours of frontal sections at the middle of the membranous portion of the vocal fold. The *dotted line* illustrates the vocal fold position when no muscle is activated. CT, Cricothyroid; VOC, vocalis; LCA, lateral cricoarytenoid; IA, interarytenoid; PCA, posterior cricoarytenoid. From Hirano M. *Clinical examination of voice.* New York: Springer-Verlag, 1981;8, with permission.

ducts the cartilaginous portion of the vocal folds. It has relatively little effect on the stiffness of the membranous portion. The interarytenoid muscle consists of transverse and oblique fibers. The transverse fibers originate from the lateral margin of one arytenoid and insert into the lateral margin of the opposite arytenoid. The oblique fibers originate from the base of one arytenoid and insert into the apex of the contralateral arytenoid.

When the superior laryngeal nerve is stimulated, the *cricothyroid muscle* moves the vocal folds into paramedian position. It also lowers, stretches, elongates, and thins the vocal fold, stiffening all layers and sharpening the vocal fold contour. The cricothyroid muscle is largely responsible for longitudinal tension, a very important factor in control of pitch and loudness. Contraction tends to increase vocal pitch. The cricothyroid muscle originates from the arch of the cricoid cartilage and inserts into the inner aspect of the inferior margin of the thyroid cartilage.

Larynx: Extrinsic Muscles

The extrinsic muscles may be divided into those below the hyoid bone (infrahyoid muscles) and those above the hyoid bone (suprahyoid muscles).

The *infrahyoid muscles* include the thyrohyoid, sternothyroid, sternohyoid, and omohyoid (Fig. 6). The thyrohyoid originates obliquely on the thyroid lamina and inserts into the lower border of the greater cornu of the hyoid bone. Contraction brings the thyroid and hyoid closer together, especially anteriorly. The *sternothyroid muscle* originates from the first costal cartilage and posterior aspect of the manubrium of the sternum, and it inserts obliquely on the thyroid cartilage. Contraction lowers the thyroid cartilage. The *sternohyoid muscle* originates from the clavicle and posterior surface of the manubrium of the sternum, inserting into the lower edge of the body of the hyoid bone. Contraction lowers the hyoid bone. The inferior of the *omohyoid* originates from the upper surface of the scapula and inserts into the intermediate tendon of the omohyoid muscle. The superior belly originates from the intermediate tendon and inserts into the greater cornu of the hyoid bone. The omohyoid muscle pulls down on the hyoid bone, lowering it.

The *suprahyoid muscles* include the digastric, mylohyoid, geniohyoid, and stylohyoid. The posterior belly of the *digastric muscle* originates from the mastoid process and inserts into the intermediate tendon, which connects to the hyoid bone. The anterior belly originates from the inferior aspect of the mandible near the symphysis and inserts into the intermediate tendon. The anterior belly pulls the hyoid bone anteriorly and raises it. The posterior belly pulls the hyoid bone posteriorly and also raises it. The *mylohyoid muscle* originates from the inner aspect of the mandible (mylohyoid line) and inserts into a midline raphe with fibers from the opposite side. It raises the hyoid bone and pulls it anteriorly. The *geniohyoid muscle* originates from the mental spine at the mental symphysis of the mandible and inserts on the anterior surface of the body of the hyoid bone. It raises the hyoid bone and pulls it anteriorly. The *stylohyoid muscle* originates from the styloid process and inserts into the body of the hyoid bone. It raises the hyoid bone and pulls it posteriorly. Coordinated interaction among the extrinsic laryngeal muscles is needed to control the vertical position of the larynx, as well as other conditions such as laryngeal tilt.

The Supraglottic Vocal Tract

The supraglottic larynx, tongue, lips, palate, pharynx, nasal cavity (Fig. 7), and possibly the sinuses shape the sound quality produced at the level of the vocal cords by acting as a resonator. Minor alterations in the configuration of these structures may produce substantial changes in voice quality. The hypernasal speech typically associated with a cleft palate and/or the hyponasal speech characteristic of severe adenoid hypertrophy are obvious. However, mild edema from an upper respiratory tract infection, pharyngeal scarring, or muscle tension changes produce less obvious sound alterations. These are immediately recognizable to a trained vocalist or astute critic, but they often elude the laryngologist.

The Tracheobronchial Tree, Lungs, and Thorax

In singing, the lungs supply a constant stream of air that passes between the vocal folds and provides power for voice production. Singers often are thought of as having "big chests." Actually, the primary respiratory difference between trained and untrained singers is not increased total lung capacity, as popularly assumed. Rather, the trained singer learns to use a higher proportion of the air in his/her lungs, thereby decreasing his/her residual volume and increasing his respiratory efficiency (3).

The Abdomen

The abdominal musculature is the so-called support of the singing voice, although singers generally refer to their support mechanism as their "diaphragm." The function of the diaphragm muscle in singing is complex, somewhat variable from singer to singer (or actor to actor), and incompletely understood. The diaphragm generates inspiratory force. Although the abdomen can perform this function in some situations (4), it is primarily an expiratory-force generator. Actually, the anatomy of support for phonation is quite complicated and also not completely understood. Both the lungs and rib cage generate passive expiratory forces under many common circumstances. Passive inspiratory forces also occur. Active respiratory muscles working in consort with passive forces include the intercostal, abdominal wall, back and diaphragm muscles. The principal muscles of inspiration are the diaphragm and external intercostal muscles. Accessory muscles of inspiration include the pectoralis major, pectoralis minor, serratus anterior, subclavius, sternocleidomastoid; anterior, medial and posterior scalenus; serratus posterior and superior, latissimus dorsi, and levatores costarum. During quiet respiration, expiration is largely passive. Many of the muscles used for active expiration (forcing air out of the lungs) are also employed in "support" for singing and acting. Muscles of active expiration either raise the intra-abdominal pressure forcing the diaphragm upward, or lower the ribs or sternum to decrease the dimension of the thorax, or both. They include the internal intercostals which stiffen the rib interspaces and pull the ribs down; transversus thoracis, subcostal muscles and serratus posterior inferior all of which pulls the ribs down; and the quadratus lumborum which depresses the lowest rib. In addition, the latissimus dorsi, which may also act as the muscle of inspiration, is capable of compressing the lower portion of the rib cage and can act as a muscle of expiration, as well as a muscle of inspiration. The above muscles all participate in active expiration (and support). However, the *primary* muscles of active expiration are known as "the abdominal muscles." They include the external oblique, internal oblique, rectus abdominus and transversus abdominus. The external oblique is a flat broad muscle located on the side and front of the lower chest and abdomen. Upon contraction, it pulls the lower ribs down and raises the abdominal pressure by displacing abdominal contents inward. It is an important muscle for support of singing and acting voice tasks. It should be noted that this muscle is strengthened by leg lifting and lowering, and other exercises, but is not developed effectively by traditional trunk curl sit-ups. Appropriate strengthening exercises of the external oblique muscles are often inappropriately neglected in voice training. The internal oblique is a flat muscle in the side and front wall of the abdomen. It lies deep to the external oblique. When contracted, the internal oblique drives the abdominal wall inward and lowers the lower ribs. The rectus abdominus runs parallel to the midline of the abdomen originating from the xiphoid process of the sternum and fifth, sixth and seventh costal (rib) cartilages. It inserts into the pubic bone. It is encased in the fibrous abdominal aponeurosis. Contraction of the rectus abdominus also forces the abdominal contents inward and lowers the sternum and ribs. The transversus abdominus is a broad muscle located under the internal oblique on the side and front of the abdomen. Its fibers run horizontally around the abdomen. Contraction of the transverse abdominus compresses the abdominal contents, elevating abdominal pressure.

The abdominal musculature receives considerable attention in vocal training. The purpose of abdominal support is to maintain an efficient, constant power source and inspiratory-expiratory mechanism. There is disagreement among voice teachers as to the best model for teaching support technique. Some experts describe positioning the abdominal musculature under the rib cage, while others advocate distension of the abdomen. Either method may result in vocal problems if used incorrectly, but distending the abdomen (the inverse pressure approach) is especially dangerous, because it tends to focus the singer's muscular effort in a downward and outward direction, which is ineffective. Thus, the singer may exert considerable effort, believing he/she is practicing good support technique, without obtaining the desired effect. Proper abdominal training is essential to good singing and speaking, and the physician must consider abdominal function when evaluating vocal disabilities.

The Musculoskeletal System

Musculoskeletal condition and position affect the vocal mechanism and may produce tension or impair abdominal muscle function, resulting in voice dysfunction. Stance deviation, such as from standing to supine, produces obvious changes in respiratory function. However, lesser changes, such as distributing one's weight over the calcaneus rather than forward over the metatarsal heads (a more athletic position), alter the configuration of the abdominal and back musculature enough to influence the voice. Tensing arm and shoulder muscles promotes cervical muscle strain, which can adversely affect the larynx. Careful control of muscle tension is fundamental to good vocal technique. In fact, some methods use musculoskeletal conditioning as the primary focus of voice training.

The Psychoneurological System

The psychological constitution of the singer impacts directly on the vocal mechanism. Psychological phenomena are reflected through the autonomic nervous system, which controls mucosal secretions and other functions critical to voice production. The nervous system is also important for its mediation of fine muscle control. This fact is worthy of emphasis, because minimal voice disturbances may occasionally be the first signs of serious neurologic disease.

PHYSIOLOGY

The physiology of voice production is exceedingly complex and will be summarized only briefly in this and the following two chapters. For more

Color Plates

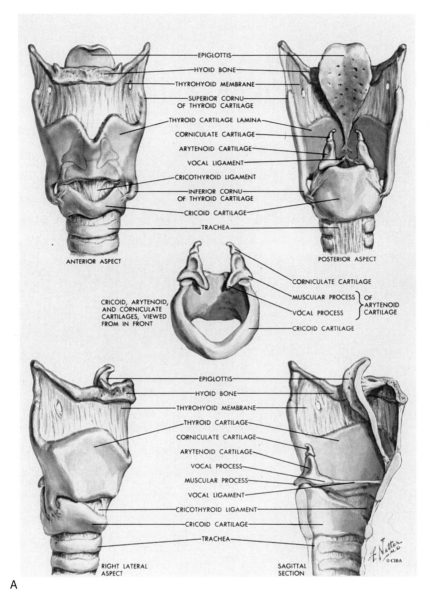

FIG. 2. A: Cartilages of the larynx. From The Larynx. *Clinical symposia.* New Jersey: CIBA Pharmaceutical Company, 1964;16(3): Plate 1, with permission.

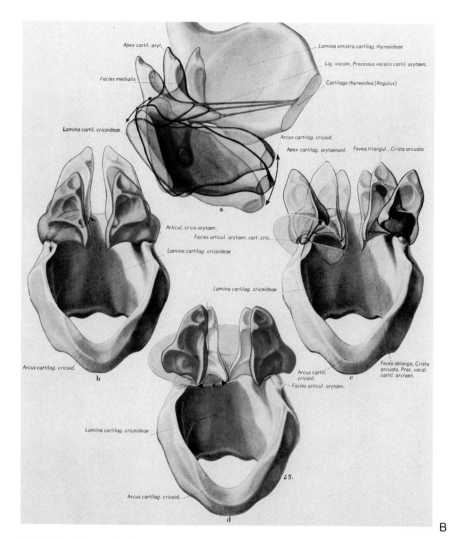

B

FIG. 2. *Continues.* **B:** Schematic representation of position changes of laryngeal cartilages, illustrating the most extreme positions achieved by each., From Pernkopf E. *Atlas of topographical and applied human anatomy.* Munich: Urban & Schwarzenberg, 1963, with permission.

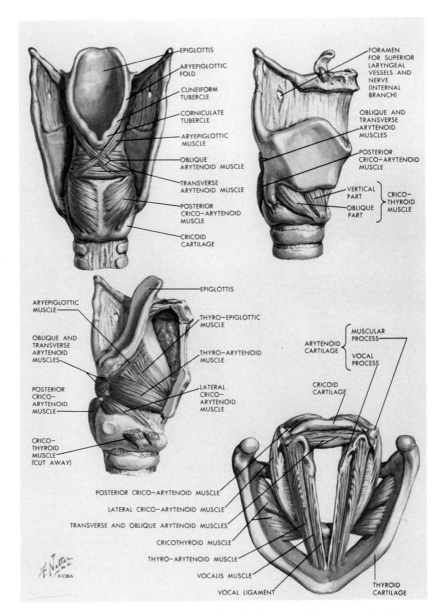

FIG. 3. The intrinsic muscles of the larynx. From The Larynx. *Clinical symposia.* New Jersey: CIBA Pharmaceutical Company, 1964;16(3): Plate 2, with permission.

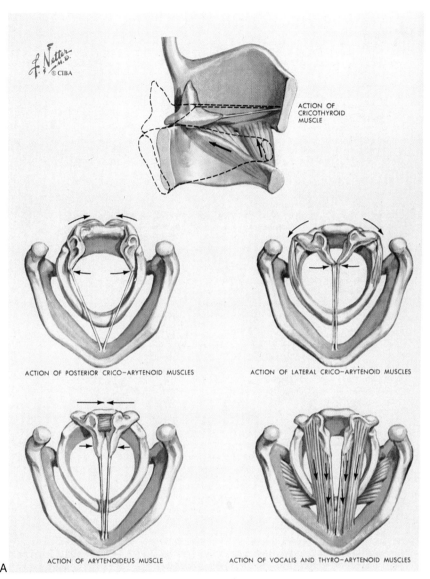

ACTION OF
CRICOTHYROID
MUSCLE

ACTION OF POSTERIOR CRICO-ARYTENOID MUSCLES

ACTION OF LATERAL CRICO-ARYTENOID MUSCLES

ACTION OF ARYTENOIDEUS MUSCLE

ACTION OF VOCALIS AND THYRO-ARYTENOID MUSCLES

A

FIG. 4. A: Action of the intrinsic muscles. From The Larynx. *Clinical symposia.* New Jersey: CIBA Pharmaceutical Company, 1964;16(3): Plate 3, with permission.

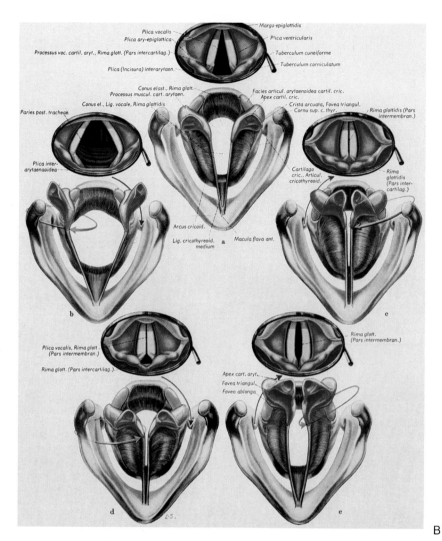

B

FIG. 4. *Continues.* **B:** The shapes of the glottis as seen on mirror examination and on anatomic preparations during rest (a), inspiration (b), phonation (c), whispering (d), and falsetto singing (e). Republished from Pernkopf E. *Atlas of topographical and applied human anatomy.* Munich: Urban & Schwarzenberg, 1963, with permission.

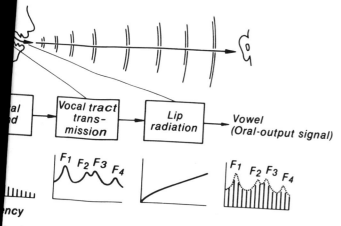

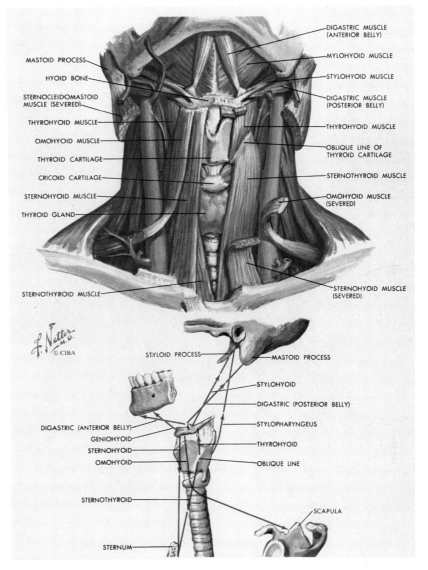

the factors determining the spectrum of a vowel. From Hirano M. *Clinical*
ice. New York: Springer-Verlag, 1981;67, with permission.

is largely responsible for the beauty and variety of the sound
ause of its complexity and importance, vocal tract resonance
Chapter 4.

among the components of the voice are ultimately responsible
al characteristics we produce. Many aspects of the voice still
e understanding and classification. Vocal range is reasonably
d, and broad categories of voice classification are generally
9). Other characteristics such as vocal register are controver-
are expressed as quality changes within an individual voice.
igh, they may include vocal fry, chest, middle, head, falsetto,
though not everyone agrees that all categories exist. The term
used most frequently in speech, refers to the voice quality
by healthy speakers, as opposed to a low, gravelly vocal fry
o. Vibrato is a rhythmic variation in frequency and intensity.
e remains uncertain, and its desirable characteristics depend
and the type of music sung. When variations from the central
ome too wide, we perceive a "wobble" in the voice, and this
eferred to as tremolo. It is not generally considered a good
, and it is unclear whether it is produced by the same mecha-
ible for normal vibrato. Ongoing research should answer many
ng questions.
r and the two that follow provide only enough information on
nd workings of the voice to permit understanding of practical,
nical problems and their solutions. The otolaryngologist,
ge pathologist, singing teacher, singer, actor, or other voice

FIG. 6. Extrinsic muscles of the larynx and their actions. From The Larynx. *Clinical sympo-*
sia. New Jersey: CIBA Pharmaceutical Company, 1964;16(3): Plate 4, with permission.

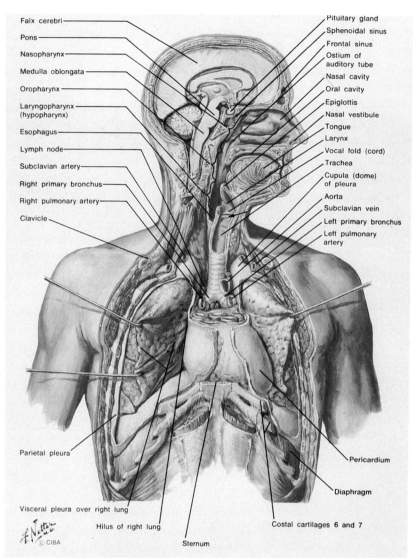

FIG. 7. The respiratory system, showing the relationship of supraglottic and infraglottic structures. The line marking the vocal fold actually stops on the false vocal fold. The level of the true vocal fold is marked by the *arrow*. The diaphragm is also visible in relation to the lungs, ribs, and abdomen muscles. From The development of the lower respiratory system. *Clinical symposia.* New Jersey: CIBA Pharmaceutical Company, 1975;27(4): Plate 1, with permission.

Labels on figure:
Falx cerebri
Pons
Nasopharynx
Medulla oblongata
Oropharynx
Laryngopharynx (hypopharynx)
Esophagus
Lymph node
Subclavian artery
Right primary bronchus
Right pulmonary artery
Clavicle
Parietal pleura
Visceral pleura over right lung
Hilus of right lung
Sternum

Pituitary gland
Sphenoidal sinus
Frontal sinus
Ostium of auditory tube
Nasal cavity
Oral cavity
Epiglottis
Nasal vestibule
Tongue
Larynx
Vocal fold (cord)
Trachea
Cupula (dome) of pleura
Aorta
Subclavian vein
Left primary bronchus
Left pulmonary artery
Pericardium
Diaphragm
Costal cartilages 6 and 7

information, the reader is advised
lications listed as Bibliography at t
ing List near the end of this book.

Volitional voice begins in the
among centers for speech, and mu
command for vocalization. The "i
veyed to the precentral gyrus in th
set of instructions to motor nuclei
areas send out the complicated mes
of the larynx, thoracic and abdomi
lators. Additional refinement of m
pyramidal (cerebral cortex, cerebel
nervous systems. These impulses c
mitted not only to the ears of lister
singer. Auditory feedback is transm
to the cerebral cortex, and adjustm
match the sound produced with th
feedback from the throat and musc
doubtedly helps in fine-tuning voca
role of tactile feedback are not full
the ability to use tactile feedback e
quent interference with auditory fee
environment (such as an orchestra o

The voice requires interaction amc
onator. The power source compress
The vocal folds close and open, perr
tween them. Numerous factors affect
as discussed in greater detail in the ne
the pressure that builds up below th
amount of resistance to opening an ai
tal impedance), volume velocity of
pressure. The vocal folds do not vibr
they separate and collide. The num
second (that is, their frequency) det
escape. The frequency of vocal fold
Other factors help determine loudnes
resistance, and amplitude of vocal fold
each vibratory cycle). The sound cre
similar to the sound produced when
This sound contains a complete set o
in part for the acoustic characteristics
sophisticated interactions in the supra
attenuate harmonic partials, acting as

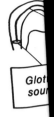

Glott
sou

Intensity

Freque

FIG. 8. Some of
examination of vo

the vocal tract
produced. Bed
is explained in

Interactions
for all the voc
await complet
well understoo
accepted (Fig.
sial. Registers
From low to h
and whistle, a
modal register
used generally
or high falsett
Its exact sour
on voice rang
frequency bed
is generally r
musical soun
nisms respons
of the remain

This chapte
terminology a
everyday cli
speech-langua

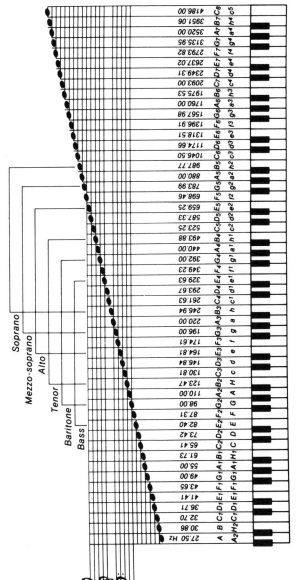

FIG. 9. Correlation between a piano keyboard, pitch names (the lower in capital letters is used in music and voice research, and in this book), frequency, musical notation, and usual voice range. From Hirano M. *Clinical examination of voice.* New York: Springer-Verlag, 1981;89, with permission.

professional would be rewarded well for more extensive study of voice science.

Notation

In speech-language pathology, voice science, and academic music, sounds are designated using the International Phonetic Alphabet (IPA) (Appendix I). This is standard notation and will be used throughout this book. Readers should familiarize themselves with IPA notation and use it, because its meaning is well-defined and widely understood.

REFERENCES

1. Hirano M. Structure and vibratory pattern of the vocal folds. In: Sawashima N, Cooper FS, eds. *Dynamic aspects of speech production*. Tokyo: University of Tokyo Press, 1977;13–27.
2. Sundberg J. The acoustics of the singing voice. *Sci Am* 1977;236(3):82–91.
3. Gould WJ, Okamura H. Static lung volumes in singers. *Ann Otol Rhinol Laryngol* 1973;82:89–95.
4. Hixon TJ, Hoffman C. Chest wall shape during singing. In: Lawrence V, ed. *Transcripts of the seventh annual symposium, care of the professional voice*. New York: The Voice Foundation, 1978;1:9–10.

Professional Voice: The Science and Art of Clinical Care, Robert T. Sataloff. Raven Press, Ltd., New York © 1991.

3

An Overview of Laryngeal Function for Voice Production

Ronald J. Baken

Teachers College, Columbia University, New York, New York

It is common to call the larynx the vocal organ, implying that it is the place where the voice is produced. If by "voice" we mean the sound that reaches our ears, then, in the strict sense, nothing could be further from the truth. The larynx generates only the raw material, the basic waveform of voice, that must be modified and shaped by the vocal tract, the highly adjustable tube of the upper airway. The next chapter will consider that crucial shaping process. In this chapter, we shall concentrate on the laryngeal contribution alone. To keep things as clear and distinct as possible, we refer to it as the "vocal source signal"[1].

Some liken the vocal system to a wind instrument. The analogy is useful if it is clear that the instrument in question is a brass, and *not* a woodwind. That is, despite the fact that we often (inexactly) speak of "laryngeal vibrations," the vocal folds do not vibrate like a reed at all. As we shall see, what they do is "chop" the airstream into short bursts of airflow. Thus, if the vocal system is analogous to a musical instrument, it is more like a trumpet, and the vocal folds correspond to the trumpeter's lips. The *vocal source signal* is similar to the sound a trumpeter would make with only a mouthpiece. The *voice,* in contrast, is the output from the trumpet's bell.

---

[1]An effort has been made to keep this chapter as informal as possible in the conviction that what might be lost in rigor will be more than compensated by what is gained in understanding. When basic principles of physics are crucial, however, they are provided for the novice in interruptions of the main flow of the text that are labeled *Intermezzo.* These can be skipped by those already familiar with the concepts in question. Also, the common scholarly practice of citing references in the text has been abandoned so as to improve the flow of information and lessen the intimidation it might engender. The works listed in the Bibliography, however, will buttress the discussion and help satisfy the curiosity of those who may be encouraged to dig deeper.

THE GLOTTAL WAVE

Before examining the basic mechanisms by which the vocal source signal is produced, it will be worthwhile to take a brief look at the signal itself. In its most fundamental sense, it could be described as a patterned air flow through the glottis (the space between the vocal folds) like the airflow graphed in Fig. 1. Driven by the pressure of the air in the lungs, the flow increases relatively gradually, reaches a peak, and then decreases suddenly until it stops. After a brief pause, the pattern repeats. This flow pattern is called the "glottal wave."

The sharp cutoff of flow is particularly crucial, because it is this relatively sudden stoppage of the air flow that is truly the raw material of voice. To understand why, think of an experience that you may have had with a poorly designed plumbing system. The faucet is wide open, and the water is running at full force. The tap is then quickly turned off. Water flow stops abruptly and there is a sudden THUMP! from the pipes inside the walls. (Plumbers call this "water hammer.") This happens because, in the simplest terms, the sudden cessation causes moving molecules of water to collide with those ahead of them (like the chain-reaction collision caused when a car suddenly stops on a highway). This generates a kind of "shock wave." When the pipe is jolted by this shock, it moves, creating the vibrations in the air that we hear as a thump. The relatively sudden cutoff of flow that characterizes the glottal wave creates very much the same effect in the vocal tract. An impulse-like shock wave is produced that "excites" the vibration of the air molecules in the vocal tract. That excitation is the voice in its unrefined form.

The rate at which the shocks come is the *fundamental frequency* (F_o) of the voice and is measured in hertz (Hz). (One hertz equals one repetition per second.[2]) The time interval from the start of one cycle to the start of the next is called the *period* and is most conveniently measured in milliseconds. The intensity of phonation is related to the magnitude of the impulses. Now, any complex wave (such as the impulses that the larynx delivers into the vocal tract) is composed of a series of pure tones ("harmonics"), so the glottal source signal provides a palette of frequencies among which the rest of the vocal tract can select for creating the final vocal output.

GENERATING THE SOURCE SIGNAL

We are now ready to explore how the glottal source signal is generated. The starring role in that performance definitely belongs to the vocal folds.

---

[2] "Fundamental frequency" and "pitch" are related but not the same. F_o is a physical attribute; pitch is a perception. One does not grow in a lock-step way with the other. The terminological confusion is not helped by the fact that engineers—whose work accounts for a significant fraction of the vocal research literature—typically refer to F_o as "pitch"!

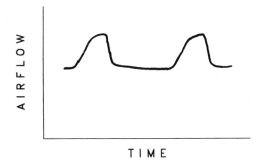

FIG. 1. Two successive glottal waves. Increasing airflow is vertical.

The rest of the laryngeal structures (reviewed in the previous chapter) are, for our present purposes, essentially only stagehands that we can temporarily ignore.

Seen from the top, the vocal folds appear as whitish bands of tissue that stretch across the airway of the larynx. They join together and are attached to the inside of the thyroid cartilage in front, and each is anchored to an arytenoid cartilage at the rear. The arytenoid cartilages are capable of complex movements that cause the vocal folds to be brought into contact with each other along their length (approximated or adducted), or separated (abducted) to open the air passage for breathing. The space between the vocal folds is called the *glottis*. Since the vocal folds are movable, the glottis can be made quite large or can be reduced until its size is zero.

If we use special techniques (such as high-speed filming or stroboscopy) to observe vocal fold motion during phonation, we see the movements schematized in Fig. 2. From an initial condition (Fig. 2A) in which the vocal folds are in complete contact (and the glottal size is, therefore, zero), they increasingly separate until the glottis attains some maximal size (Fig. 2D). The vocal folds then snap back to the midline, closing the glottis once again. In an average male voice, this cycle will repeat about 100 times each second. That is, the F_0 will be about 100 Hz. (Females have a higher F_0, on the order of 220 Hz.) Because the air in the lungs is under pressure, air is forced through the glottis during each glottal opening. The result is the patterned air flow of the glottal wave.

What causes this repeated opening and closing of the glottis, and how is its rate controlled? These have been central questions of voice research. Thanks to very rapid and significant advances in the past few years, we now understand quite a bit about what drives the phonatory process. What we know is derived from empirical studies by a large and international array of voice scientists (several of whom are cited in the Bibliography) and from modern mathematical models of the phonatory process, especially those developed by Titze and by Ishizaka. As with so much in the natural world, the

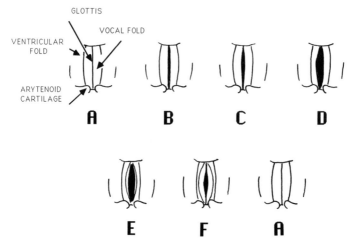

FIG. 2. The glottal cycle as seen from above. Important anatomical landmarks are indicated.

mechanisms turn out to be both elegant (and simpler than we might have feared) and complex (and hence more complicated than we might have hoped). While thorough study of the research literature is clearly essential for anyone intending seriously to pursue voice research, and while examination of the available models is quite rewarding for those who have the advanced mathematical skills to follow them, we shall only be able to undertake a brief nonmathematical summary of the highlights of the vast store of information that is available. Readers who need to know more or who are simply intrigued are urged and implored to delve much deeper.

To understand any of the finer details of the vocal process will require that we view the vocal folds in cross-section (rather than from the traditional viewpoint from above), that we examine a little bit of their fine structure, and that we consider a few things about the nature of air flow and pressure.

Structure of the Vocal Folds

The cross-section of a vocal fold in Fig. 3 shows that it is basically divisible into two zones. Essentially, the vocal fold is built on the supporting mass of the thyroarytenoid muscle that runs along its length. This muscular region, which accounts for most of the bulk of the vocal fold, is referred to as the vocal fold *body*. But it would be a serious mistake to view the body as nothing more than a support for the overlying tissue. Contraction and relaxation of the thyroarytenoid muscle can significantly change its length, thickness, and stiffness. We shall see that these changes play a vital role in determining the characteristics of the vocal source signal.

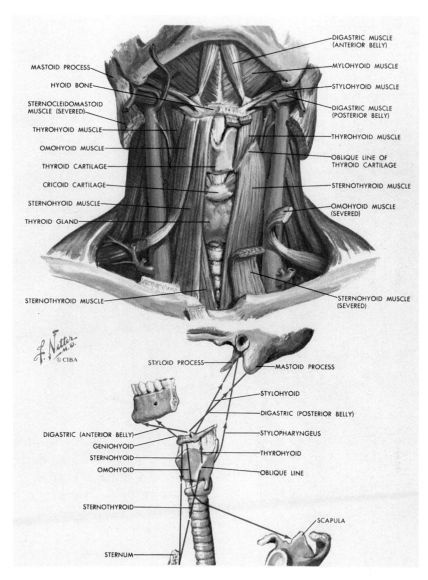

FIG. 6. Extrinsic muscles of the larynx and their actions. From The Larynx. *Clinical symposia.* New Jersey: CIBA Pharmaceutical Company, 1964;16(3): Plate 4, with permission.

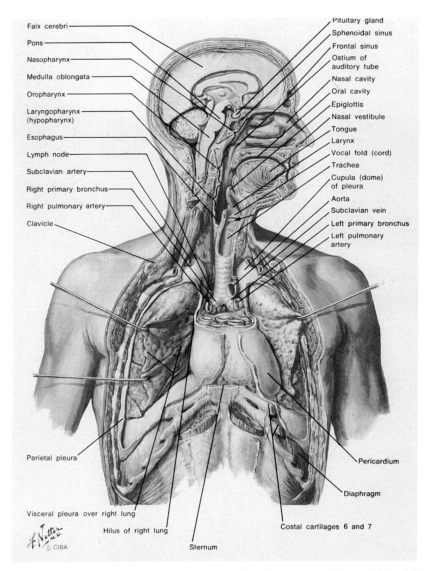

Falx cerebri

Pons

Nasopharynx

Medulla oblongata

Oropharynx

Laryngopharynx
(hypopharynx)

Esophagus

Lymph node

Subclavian artery

Right primary bronchus

Right pulmonary artery

Clavicle

Pituitary gland

Sphenoidal sinus

Frontal sinus

Ostium of
auditory tube

Nasal cavity

Oral cavity

Epiglottis

Nasal vestibule

Tongue

Larynx

Vocal fold (cord)

Trachea

Cupula (dome)
of pleura

Aorta

Subclavian vein

Left primary bronchus

Left pulmonary
artery

Parietal pleura

Pericardium

Diaphragm

Visceral pleura over right lung

Costal cartilages 6 and 7

Hilus of right lung

Sternum

FIG. 7. The respiratory system, showing the relationship of supraglottic and infraglottic structures. The line marking the vocal fold actually stops on the false vocal fold. The level of the true vocal fold is marked by the *arrow*. The diaphragm is also visible in relation to the lungs, ribs, and abdomen muscles. From The development of the lower respiratory system. *Clinical symposia.* New Jersey: CIBA Pharmaceutical Company, 1975;27(4): Plate 1, with permission.

information, the reader is advised to consult other literature, including publications listed as Bibliography at the end of Chapter 3 and Suggested Reading List near the end of this book.

Volitional voice begins in the cerebral cortex. Complex interactions among centers for speech, and musical and artistic expression establish the command for vocalization. The "idea" of the planned vocalization is conveyed to the precentral gyrus in the motor cortex, which transmits another set of instructions to motor nuclei in the brainstem and spinal cord. These areas send out the complicated messages necessary for coordinated activity of the larynx, thoracic and abdominal musculature, and vocal tract articulators. Additional refinement of motor activity is provided by the extrapyramidal (cerebral cortex, cerebellum, and basal ganglion) and autonomic nervous systems. These impulses combine to produce a sound that is transmitted not only to the ears of listeners but also to those of the speaker or singer. Auditory feedback is transmitted from the ear through the brainstem to the cerebral cortex, and adjustments are made to permit the vocalist to match the sound produced with the intended sound. There is also tactile feedback from the throat and muscles involved in phonation that also undoubtedly helps in fine-tuning vocal output, although the mechanism and role of tactile feedback are not fully understood. In many trained singers, the ability to use tactile feedback effectively is cultivated because of frequent interference with auditory feedback by ancillary noise in the concert environment (such as an orchestra or band).

The voice requires interaction among the power source, vibrator, and resonator. The power source compresses air and forces it toward the larynx. The vocal folds close and open, permitting small bursts of air to escape between them. Numerous factors affect the sound produced at the glottal level, as discussed in greater detail in the next chapter. Among others, they include the pressure that builds up below the vocal folds (subglottal pressure), the amount of resistance to opening an airway presented by the vocal folds (glottal impedance), volume velocity of airflow at the glottis, and supraglottal pressure. The vocal folds do not vibrate like the strings on a violin. Rather, they separate and collide. The number of times they do so in any given second (that is, their frequency) determines the number of air puffs that escape. The frequency of vocal fold closing and opening is related to pitch. Other factors help determine loudness (such as subglottal pressure, glottal resistance, and amplitude of vocal fold displacement from the midline during each vibratory cycle). The sound created at the vocal fold level is a buzz, similar to the sound produced when blowing between two blades of grass. This sound contains a complete set of harmonic partials and is responsible in part for the acoustic characteristics of the voice. However, complex and sophisticated interactions in the supraglottic vocal tract may accentuate or attenuate harmonic partials, acting as a resonator (Fig. 8). This portion of

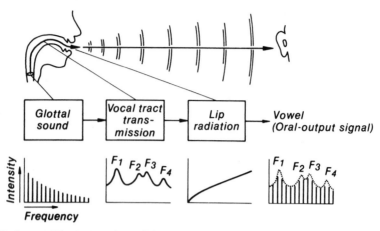

FIG. 8. Some of the factors determining the spectrum of a vowel. From Hirano M. *Clinical examination of voice.* New York: Springer-Verlag, 1981;67, with permission.

the vocal tract is largely responsible for the beauty and variety of the sound produced. Because of its complexity and importance, vocal tract resonance is explained in Chapter 4.

Interactions among the components of the voice are ultimately responsible for all the vocal characteristics we produce. Many aspects of the voice still await complete understanding and classification. Vocal range is reasonably well understood, and broad categories of voice classification are generally accepted (Fig. 9). Other characteristics such as vocal register are controversial. Registers are expressed as quality changes within an individual voice. From low to high, they may include vocal fry, chest, middle, head, falsetto, and whistle, although not everyone agrees that all categories exist. The term modal register, used most frequently in speech, refers to the voice quality used generally by healthy speakers, as opposed to a low, gravelly vocal fry or high falsetto. Vibrato is a rhythmic variation in frequency and intensity. Its exact source remains uncertain, and its desirable characteristics depend on voice range and the type of music sung. When variations from the central frequency become too wide, we perceive a "wobble" in the voice, and this is generally referred to as tremolo. It is not generally considered a good musical sound, and it is unclear whether it is produced by the same mechanisms responsible for normal vibrato. Ongoing research should answer many of the remaining questions.

This chapter and the two that follow provide only enough information on terminology and workings of the voice to permit understanding of practical, everyday clinical problems and their solutions. The otolaryngologist, speech-language pathologist, singing teacher, singer, actor, or other voice

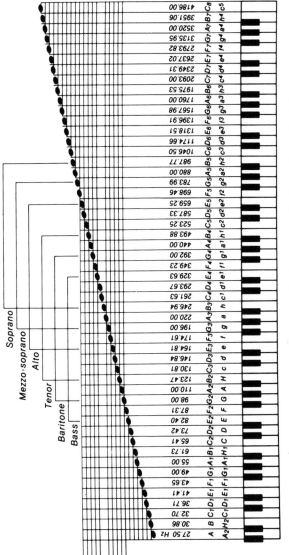

FIG. 9. Correlation between a piano keyboard, pitch names (the lower in capital letters is used in music and voice research, and in this book), frequency, musical notation, and usual voice range. From Hirano M. *Clinical examination of voice*. New York: Springer-Verlag, 1981;89, with permission.

professional would be rewarded well for more extensive study of voice science.

Notation

In speech-language pathology, voice science, and academic music, sounds are designated using the International Phonetic Alphabet (IPA) (Appendix I). This is standard notation and will be used throughout this book. Readers should familiarize themselves with IPA notation and use it, because its meaning is well-defined and widely understood.

REFERENCES

1. Hirano M. Structure and vibratory pattern of the vocal folds. In: Sawashima N, Cooper FS, eds. *Dynamic aspects of speech production.* Tokyo: University of Tokyo Press, 1977;13–27.
2. Sundberg J. The acoustics of the singing voice. *Sci Am* 1977;236(3):82–91.
3. Gould WJ, Okamura H. Static lung volumes in singers. *Ann Otol Rhinol Laryngol* 1973;82:89–95.
4. Hixon TJ, Hoffman C. Chest wall shape during singing. In: Lawrence V, ed. *Transcripts of the seventh annual symposium, care of the professional voice.* New York: The Voice Foundation, 1978;1:9–10.

Professional Voice: The Science and Art
of Clinical Care, Robert T. Sataloff.
Raven Press, Ltd., New York © 1991.

3

An Overview of Laryngeal Function for Voice Production

Ronald J. Baken

Teachers College, Columbia University, New York, New York

It is common to call the larynx the vocal organ, implying that it is the place where the voice is produced. If by "voice" we mean the sound that reaches our ears, then, in the strict sense, nothing could be further from the truth. The larynx generates only the raw material, the basic waveform of voice, that must be modified and shaped by the vocal tract, the highly adjustable tube of the upper airway. The next chapter will consider that crucial shaping process. In this chapter, we shall concentrate on the laryngeal contribution alone. To keep things as clear and distinct as possible, we refer to it as the "vocal source signal"[1].

Some liken the vocal system to a wind instrument. The analogy is useful if it is clear that the instrument in question is a brass, and *not* a woodwind. That is, despite the fact that we often (inexactly) speak of "laryngeal vibrations," the vocal folds do not vibrate like a reed at all. As we shall see, what they do is "chop" the airstream into short bursts of airflow. Thus, if the vocal system is analogous to a musical instrument, it is more like a trumpet, and the vocal folds correspond to the trumpeter's lips. The *vocal source signal* is similar to the sound a trumpeter would make with only a mouthpiece. The *voice,* in contrast, is the output from the trumpet's bell.

---

[1]An effort has been made to keep this chapter as informal as possible in the conviction that what might be lost in rigor will be more than compensated by what is gained in understanding. When basic principles of physics are crucial, however, they are provided for the novice in interruptions of the main flow of the text that are labeled *Intermezzo.* These can be skipped by those already familiar with the concepts in question. Also, the common scholarly practice of citing references in the text has been abandoned so as to improve the flow of information and lessen the intimidation it might engender. The works listed in the Bibliography, however, will buttress the discussion and help satisfy the curiosity of those who may be encouraged to dig deeper.

THE GLOTTAL WAVE

Before examining the basic mechanisms by which the vocal source signal is produced, it will be worthwhile to take a brief look at the signal itself. In its most fundamental sense, it could be described as a patterned air flow through the glottis (the space between the vocal folds) like the airflow graphed in Fig. 1. Driven by the pressure of the air in the lungs, the flow increases relatively gradually, reaches a peak, and then decreases suddenly until it stops. After a brief pause, the pattern repeats. This flow pattern is called the "glottal wave."

The sharp cutoff of flow is particularly crucial, because it is this relatively sudden stoppage of the air flow that is truly the raw material of voice. To understand why, think of an experience that you may have had with a poorly designed plumbing system. The faucet is wide open, and the water is running at full force. The tap is then quickly turned off. Water flow stops abruptly and there is a sudden THUMP! from the pipes inside the walls. (Plumbers call this "water hammer.") This happens because, in the simplest terms, the sudden cessation causes moving molecules of water to collide with those ahead of them (like the chain-reaction collision caused when a car suddenly stops on a highway). This generates a kind of "shock wave." When the pipe is jolted by this shock, it moves, creating the vibrations in the air that we hear as a thump. The relatively sudden cutoff of flow that characterizes the glottal wave creates very much the same effect in the vocal tract. An impulse-like shock wave is produced that "excites" the vibration of the air molecules in the vocal tract. That excitation is the voice in its unrefined form.

The rate at which the shocks come is the *fundamental frequency* (F_o) of the voice and is measured in hertz (Hz). (One hertz equals one repetition per second.[2]) The time interval from the start of one cycle to the start of the next is called the *period* and is most conveniently measured in milliseconds. The intensity of phonation is related to the magnitude of the impulses. Now, any complex wave (such as the impulses that the larynx delivers into the vocal tract) is composed of a series of pure tones ("harmonics"), so the glottal source signal provides a palette of frequencies among which the rest of the vocal tract can select for creating the final vocal output.

GENERATING THE SOURCE SIGNAL

We are now ready to explore how the glottal source signal is generated. The starring role in that performance definitely belongs to the vocal folds.

---

[2]"Fundamental frequency" and "pitch" are related but not the same. F_o is a physical attribute; pitch is a perception. One does not grow in a lock-step way with the other. The terminological confusion is not helped by the fact that engineers—whose work accounts for a significant fraction of the vocal research literature—typically refer to F_o as "pitch"!

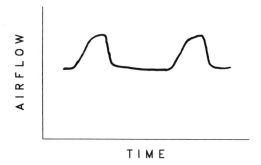

FIG. 1. Two successive glottal waves. Increasing airflow is vertical.

The rest of the laryngeal structures (reviewed in the previous chapter) are, for our present purposes, essentially only stagehands that we can temporarily ignore.

Seen from the top, the vocal folds appear as whitish bands of tissue that stretch across the airway of the larynx. They join together and are attached to the inside of the thyroid cartilage in front, and each is anchored to an arytenoid cartilage at the rear. The arytenoid cartilages are capable of complex movements that cause the vocal folds to be brought into contact with each other along their length (approximated or adducted), or separated (abducted) to open the air passage for breathing. The space between the vocal folds is called the *glottis*. Since the vocal folds are movable, the glottis can be made quite large or can be reduced until its size is zero.

If we use special techniques (such as high-speed filming or stroboscopy) to observe vocal fold motion during phonation, we see the movements schematized in Fig. 2. From an initial condition (Fig. 2A) in which the vocal folds are in complete contact (and the glottal size is, therefore, zero), they increasingly separate until the glottis attains some maximal size (Fig. 2D). The vocal folds then snap back to the midline, closing the glottis once again. In an average male voice, this cycle will repeat about 100 times each second. That is, the F_o will be about 100 Hz. (Females have a higher F_o, on the order of 220 Hz.) Because the air in the lungs is under pressure, air is forced through the glottis during each glottal opening. The result is the patterned air flow of the glottal wave.

What causes this repeated opening and closing of the glottis, and how is its rate controlled? These have been central questions of voice research. Thanks to very rapid and significant advances in the past few years, we now understand quite a bit about what drives the phonatory process. What we know is derived from empirical studies by a large and international array of voice scientists (several of whom are cited in the Bibliography) and from modern mathematical models of the phonatory process, especially those developed by Titze and by Ishizaka. As with so much in the natural world, the

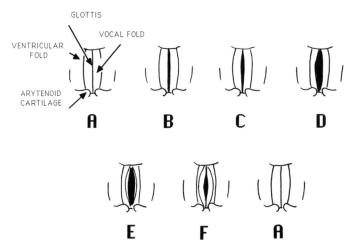

FIG. 2. The glottal cycle as seen from above. Important anatomical landmarks are indicated.

mechanisms turn out to be both elegant (and simpler than we might have feared) and complex (and hence more complicated than we might have hoped). While thorough study of the research literature is clearly essential for anyone intending seriously to pursue voice research, and while examination of the available models is quite rewarding for those who have the advanced mathematical skills to follow them, we shall only be able to undertake a brief nonmathematical summary of the highlights of the vast store of information that is available. Readers who need to know more or who are simply intrigued are urged and implored to delve much deeper.

To understand any of the finer details of the vocal process will require that we view the vocal folds in cross-section (rather than from the traditional viewpoint from above), that we examine a little bit of their fine structure, and that we consider a few things about the nature of air flow and pressure.

Structure of the Vocal Folds

The cross-section of a vocal fold in Fig. 3 shows that it is basically divisible into two zones. Essentially, the vocal fold is built on the supporting mass of the thyroarytenoid muscle that runs along its length. This muscular region, which accounts for most of the bulk of the vocal fold, is referred to as the vocal fold *body*. But it would be a serious mistake to view the body as nothing more than a support for the overlying tissue. Contraction and relaxation of the thyroarytenoid muscle can significantly change its length, thickness, and stiffness. We shall see that these changes play a vital role in determining the characteristics of the vocal source signal.

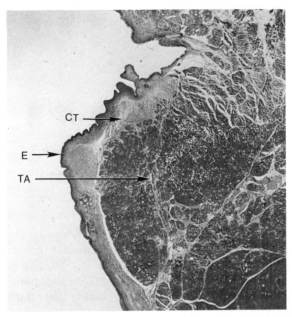

FIG. 3. Cross-section of the human vocal folds. Courtesy of Dr. Joel C. Kahane, Memphis State University.

The body of the vocal fold is wrapped in a layer called the *cover*. Its structure is actually quite complex, but the fine details need not concern us here. It is enough to understand that the cover's outer layer is formed by epithelial tissues (similar to the linings of the rest of the throat and to the upper layers of skin on the surface of the body), and that, under this epithelium, there is a network of fibers that, in some significant ways, resemble rubber bands. The elastic network is particularly well formed near the edge of the upper portion of the vocal fold, where it constitutes the *vocal ligament*. This composite structure has very definite inherent mechanical properties, but, unlike the vocal fold body, those properties cannot normally be altered. The cover is attached only relatively loosely. Like the skin on the back of one's hand, it is partially free to slide over the underlying vocal fold body. This mobility is important in phonation.

The Glottal Cycle

We are finally ready to examine the phonatory cycle in more meaningful detail. We shall assume that there is a supply of air in the lungs and that it has been pressurized (as it must be if phonation is to occur) to a level of

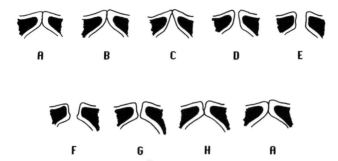

FIG. 4. Movements of the vocal folds during phonation. The vocal folds are seen in cross-section.

perhaps 7 cm H$_2$O (a typical value)[3]. The vocal folds are shown schematically in cross-sectcion in Fig. 4, and we shall consider their changing shape and posture as the vocal cycle progresses.

At the start of the cycle (Fig. 4A), the vocal folds are approximated. Note their cross-sectional shape: each is a wedge, with a fairly flat surface on top and a sloping section below. The glottis at this stage is said to be "convergent"—it narrows from a relatively wide space at the level of the lower surface of the vocal folds to no space at all higher up. The approximation of the vocal folds closes the airway; there is no flow. All the pressure of the air in the lungs acts on the sloping surface of the glottal walls. The pressure tends to push the vocal folds somewhat apart (Fig. 4B), and the separation grows wider and wider as the pressure continues to act (Fig. 4C). Finally, the pressure forces separation all the way to the upper surface of the vocal folds, and a glottal space appears (Fig. 4D). Air flow through the (partially) open glottis begins: the rising part of the glottal flow wave is now under way.

FIRST INTERMEZZO

At this point, it might be useful to pause briefly in order to consider some basic facts about the physics of air flow and air pressure. The mathematical values and formulas will not be important to us, but the *concepts* are crucial to understanding the next events in the vocal cycle.

The energy available in the flow of any gas is stored in two forms. Everyday experience tells us that *pressure* represents one kind of energy storage. (Compressed air, for example, is commonly used to power machinery such as jackhammers.) Pressure represents what the physicist calls *potential en-*

---

[3]cm H$_2$O (read: centimeters of water) is the standard unit of pressure in vocal physiology. One cm H$_2$O is enough pressure to hold up a column of water 1 centimeter high.

ergy, energy waiting to be released to do work. The higher the pressure, the greater the potential energy available. Moving gas molecules have momentum, and that momentum also represents energy. So *motion* is the other form of energy storage. (The force against which one must struggle when walking into a very strong wind is produced by the moving air molecules releasing their momentum energy as they collide with you.) The energy of motion is called *kinetic* energy. The faster the gas molecules are moving, the greater is their kinetic energy.

Consider now the flow of air from the lower airway, through the constriction of the glottis, and into the wider space of the upper larynx just above the vocal folds. The diagram in Fig. 5 represents this flow with the simplifying assumptions that the tract has a uniform size except at the glottis, the shape of which has been made geometrically simpler.

Most basic to what will follow is the fact that the rate of air flow must be the same everywhere in the system. If, for example, 100 ml of air is entering the tube each second, then 100 ml/sec must be leaving it. (If not, the tube would soon either blow up and burst or empty itself of all air and generate a potent vacuum!) If the input and output are the same, it must also be true that 100 ml of air moves past *every* point in the tube each second. Let us also remember that (all other things being equal) a given volume of air represents a given number of air molecules. Therefore, we can say that the same number of air molecules passes every point in the system every second.

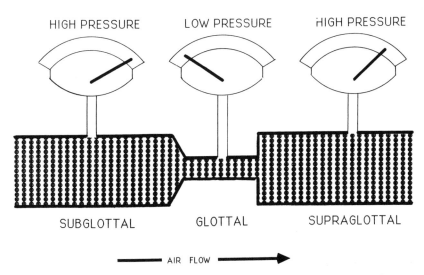

FIG. 5. Pressure changes in the laryngeal airway, showing the Bernoulli effect. Pressure is sensed by gauges connected to the region below the glottis (subglottal), to the glottal space, and to the area just above the glottis (supraglottal). Air pressure within the glottis is lower than in the spaces above or below it.

This does not mean, however, that the *speed* of the air molecules (in meters per second, for example) is the same everywhere. The bottleneck at the glottis poses a special problem. Imagine that the air flow is a parade that fills the street from curb to curb. The marchers are air molecules, arranged in neat rows. Above and below the glottis, the street is quite spacious. In these regions, each row of molecules in the parade is so wide that only a few rows need to pass by every second in order to have a given number of individual marchers pass the spectators, so the rows of molecules do not have to move forward very quickly; just a few rows per second forward movement will do. Now the parade comes to the glottis—a narrowing of the parade route. The rows must become narrower, and fewer marchers can fit in each row, but, every second, the same number of marchers must still pass the parade watchers. (If fewer go by, the marchers to the rear will bunch up on them, creating a major traffic jam.) Since each row holds fewer marchers, and since the same number of marchers must pass every second, there is only one solution: the rows must pass more quickly. All the marchers in the glottal bottleneck have to speed up. When they return to the broader route above the vocal folds, they can all slow down again, but for the moment they must march in quickstep.

The moving air in the lower part of the larynx has a certain amount of energy. It is shared between its potential (pressure) and kinetic (speed of motion) energy, but its energy total is fixed. When the molecules speed up in the constriction, their kinetic energy increases. Such an increase would seem to imply that the total (potential + kinetic) energy would go up, but this cannot be. The total energy cannot increase, because one cannot create energy out of nothing. So, if the total must stay the same, and if the kinetic energy increases, then there is no way around it: the potential energy *must* decrease, which is another way of saying that the pressure must go down. Of course, when the air molecules reach the wider passage of the laryngeal region above the glottis and slow down again, their kinetic energy will decrease, and so their potential energy will be restored. What all of this means is that, if air is flowing through a narrow glottis, the pressure inside the glottal space will be less than the pressure in the wider spaces above the below it. This phenomenon (which is, of course, true for any constricted tube) is called the Bernoulli effect, and it plays an important role in the closing phase of the vocal cycle.

END OF FIRST INTERMEZZO

Now we can return to the vocal cycle, which we left in Fig. 4D with the glottis just barely open. In spite of the small opening, the pressure acting on the underside of the vocal folds is still operative, and so the edges of the vocal folds continue to be blown apart. But now there is an airflow through the narrow glottal constriction, which implies that the air pressure inside the glottis must be less than the air pressure above or below it. This relatively negative pressure has the effect of "sucking" the lower margins of the glottis back toward the midline. Also, having been pushed to the side, the lower walls of the glottis have been compressed, almost like foam rubber. The result is that they will tend to spring back, that is, to return to their original position. Therefore, as the cycle proceeds, the lower margins have begun their return to the midline (Fig. 4E, F), while the upper edges of the vocal folds are still being blown apart.

At this point, a new effect comes into play. Remember that the very edge of the upper portion of the vocal fold contains the highly elastic vocal ligament. As the edge of the vocal fold is pushed farther from the midline, the ligament is stretched more and more. Like a rubber band, the more it is stretched, the stronger is the tendency for it to snap back to its original shape. After a while, this restorative force begins to overcome the outward-pushing force of the air pressure (which, in any case, has been growing weaker as the approximation of lower portions of the folds increasingly pinches off the airflow). The upper portions of the vocal folds, therefore, begin to snap back toward the midline (Fig. 4G, H). Ultimately, the glottis will have been restored to its original closed shape, and the cycle is ready to repeat.

Let us pause again, this time for a few observations on what has happened. One important consideration is that the motion of the vocal folds has been driven by a combination of *aerodynamic* forces (the lung pressure and the Bernoulli pressure) and the elastic (recoil) properties of the tissues. Hence, the mechanism just described is commonly called the *myoelastic-aerodynamic* model of phonation. Another important fact is that the shape of the glottis, and, in particular, its convergence, has played an important role.

Even more interesting is the fact that the upper and lower portions of the vocal folds do not move in synchrony. The lower part is always somewhat ahead of the upper part: It begins to separate earlier, and it begins to return to the midline before the upper portion does. There is, in the more formal language of the vocal physiologists, a *vertical phase difference*. While the reasons are far beyond the scope of our present discussion, it has been demonstrated that this phase difference is critical in maintaining phonation.

Finally, a careful examination of Fig. 4 shows that a great deal of the vocal fold movement is accounted for by displacement of the mobile vocal fold cover and changes in its shape. (In fact, the rippling of the cover creates a "mucosal wave" that can be seen on the upper surface of the vocal fold during stroboscopic observation.) If there were no vocal fold cover (or its equivalent), phonation would not be possible.

CHANGING VOCAL FUNDAMENTAL FREQUENCY AND AMPLITUDE

Several vocal characteristics can be voluntarily altered. The two most significant are F_0 and intensity. Their modification is important in speech and a sine qua non of singing.

Control of Vocal Fundamental Frequency

Changing the vocal F_0 means varying the rate at which the glottal wave repeats. The most efficient way of doing this is by modifying the mechanical properties of the vocal folds (although, as we shall see, it is also possible to change F_0 by altering the pressure of the air supply). The structure of the vocal fold, and its relationship to the rest of the larynx, makes this fairly easy to accomplish by a number of means. We shall look at the most effective.

A reminder of a few anatomical facts is in order. Recall that the vocal folds stretch from the arytenoid cartilages (which are anchored to the back of the cricoid cartilage) at the rear, to the inside of the thyroid cartilage in front. The thyroid cartilage articulates with the cricoid cartilage in such a way that it can pivot, like the visor on a helmet. There is a muscle—the cricothyroid—that spans the gap from the thyroid to the cricoid cartilage in front. When it contracts, it pulls the two closer together. Because of the visorlike relationship of the thyroid and cricoid cartilages, contraction of the cricothyroid muscle causes the thyroid cartilage to pivot. Also, the thyroid cartilage will slide forward a bit. The result of these actions is diagramed in Fig. 6. Note that the net effect is to increase the distance from the arytenoid cartilages to the inside of the thyroid cartilage. Since the vocal folds must span the arytenoid-to-thyroid space, increasing this distance *stretches* the vocal folds and makes them *longer*.

These changes entail important modifications of the glottal cycle. First, if the vocal folds are longer, then they present a greater surface area to the pressure in the airway just below them. That, in essence, makes the pressure more effective in separating the vocal folds during the opening phase of the cycle. The vocal folds, therefore, separate more quickly, shortening the cycle. A greater repetition rate, and hence a higher F_0, will be the result. But there is more. Stretching the vocal fold means that the elastic fibers of the vocal fold cover, and in particular the fibers of the vocal ligament, are stretched. The vocal ligament is like a rubber band, and stretching it has the same effect: The resulting increase in stiffness makes it snap back more quickly after being "plucked." Therefore, once the stretched vocal folds have been blown apart, they return more quickly to the midline, so increasing the stiffness of the vocal fold cover (by contracting the cricothyroid muscle) also shortens the cycle (increasing the repetition rate) and thereby contributes to the rise in F_0.

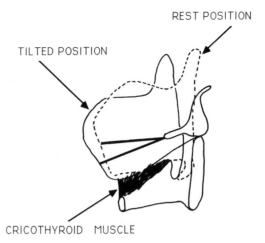

REST POSITION

TILTED POSITION

CRICOTHYROID MUSCLE

FIG. 6. Contraction of the cricothyroid muscle causes the thyroid cartilage to rotate about its point of attachment to the cricoid cartilage. It is also pulled slightly forward. The result is to increase the length of the vocal folds, schematized here by *heavy straight lines.*

It is also possible to increase the stiffness of the vocal fold body by contracting the thyroarytenoid muscle (which, let us recall, *is* the body of the vocal fold) and having it pull against the stretching influence of the contracting cricothyroid muscle[4]. This increased contraction augments the stiffness of the vocal fold cover, and so it, too, helps to shorten the cycle.

Since the phonatory process is governed by aerodynamics as well as by biomechanics, it would be surprising if vocal F_o could not also be changed by modifying the air pressure driving the cycle. Raising the pressure has the effect of increasing vocal intensity (to be discussed shortly), but, as any vocal artist is no doubt aware, there is a strong tendency for F_o to increase as well. (The exact basis of this effect has not been established for certain, but Titze has recently proposed a likely hypothesis, which has to do with the distance to which higher pressure drives the edge of the vocal fold from the midline.) Several experiments have demonstrated that the vocal F_o changes by about 4 or 5 Hz for every 1 cm H_2O change in the pressure operating on the vocal folds. For purposes of ordinary conversational speech, this amount of frequency change is not likely to be significant. But, implying as it does that the pitch of the vocal tone will rise as the loudness does, it is clearly of importance to singers, who will have to compensate their laryngeal mechanics to deal with it.

---

[4]To get a sense of the effect, rest your forearm and elbow on a table, relax your arm, and palpate your biceps muscle. Now (without letting your forearm rise from the table) contract your biceps ("make a muscle") and feel your biceps again. It is now much stiffer.

Control of Vocal Intensity

Vocal intensity[5] is a function of the amount of excitation that the glottal waves deliver to the air in the vocal tract. It is easy to see that, all other things being equal, the greater the amplitude of the glottal wave, the greater the resulting vocal tract excitation and hence the more intense the vocal signal. Raising the pressure of the air supply effectively increases the amount of air that is pushed through the glottis whenever it is open. That translates to a "taller" glottal flow wave. Hence, increased lung pressure translates to greater vocal intensity.

However, we learned earlier that it is the sudden cessation of the flow that bears the primary responsibility for setting the air of the vocal tract into acoustic vibration. The sharper the flow cutoff, the greater the vocal tract excitation will be and the more intense the resulting vocal signal. Greater vocal intensity is, in fact, associated with a much steeper decreasing phase of the glottal wave. This effect is achieved not only by the higher pressure, but also by voluntary changes in the biomechanics of the vocal folds that tend to resist the increase in air flow that the higher pressure would produce. So intensity increases are produced by a carefully regulated interaction of a higher driving pressure and an increased glottal resistance to flow.

REGISTERS

To an outsider, there is probably no concept in the domain of the vocal arts that seems so contentious as that of vocal registers. Dozens and scores of different terms have been coined to describe subjective voice qualities, and the physiologic reality of almost every one of them as a voice register has been both the victim of vehement denial and the object of passionate defense.

Different registers sound different, to be sure. But variant acoustic impressions derive from changes in the way the vocal source signal is molded by the vocal tract as well as from differences in the vocal source signal itself. Because our concern here is solely with the source signal, we can simplify the problem of registers significantly by looking only at variations in laryngeal function. To keep the matter clear, let us agree to call the results of such differences *laryngeal registers*. We shall also impose the following requirements:

1. A laryngeal register must reflect a specific and distinct mode of laryngeal action. Vocal tract contributions are irrelevant.

---

[5]The relationship of vocal intensity and loudness is analogous to that of vocal F_0 and pitch. The former is a physical characteristic, the latter a perception, and the two are not exactly equivalent. We can measure intensity, but only judge loudness, which is influenced by many factors.

2. A laryngeal register is produced across a contiguous range of fundamental frequencies.
3. The F_o range of any given laryngeal register has little overlap with the F_o range of any other register.

With these restrictions, only three distinct laryngeal registers have been verified. To avoid problems due to prior—and, frankly, often confused— terminology, and to reduce the influence of connotations commonly associated with older names, Hollien has suggested that we adopt completely new designations for these narrowly defined registers.

1. *Modal register* describes the laryngeal function in the range of fundamental frequencies most commonly used by untrained speakers (from about 75 to about 450 Hz in men; 130 to 520 Hz in women). The name, in fact, derives from the statistical term for "most common value." This register may include the musical "chest," "head," or "low," "mid," and "high" registers, depending on how these are defined.
2. *Pulse register* occurs in the F_o range at the low end of the frequency scale (25 to 80 Hz in men; 20 to 45 Hz in women). The laryngeal output is perceived as pulsatile in nature. The term is broadly synonymous with "vocal fry," "glottal fry," or the musical term "strohbass."
3. *Loft register* is employed at the upper end of the vocal continuum (275 to 620 Hz in men; 490 to 1,130 Hz in women). The name is intended to convey a sense of "upper reaches." In general, it corresponds to the older term "falsetto."

Modal register phonation is implicitly accepted as the norm, and, in fact, the glottal cycle we have been considering is that which characterizes it. Pulse and loft differ from modal register in the shape and tension to which the vocal folds are adjusted.

Pulse Register

As diagramed in Fig. 7, pulse register phonation is accomplished with vocal folds that are rather massive in cross-section, a configuration that is achieved by freeing them of essentially all tension. (Laminagraphic studies by Allen and Hollien have suggested that the relaxation in the glottal region may be so complete that the ventricular folds may actually lie against the upper surface of the vocal folds. If this occurs, the effective mass of the vocal folds would obviously be increased enormously.) These two conditions—increased mass and reduced stretch—account for the very low fundamental frequencies associated with this laryngeal register. It takes longer for the vocal folds to be blown apart, and, once moving laterally, their increased mass results in greater lateral momentum that sustains the abductory motion longer. The lack of tension implies a reduction of restoring (elas-

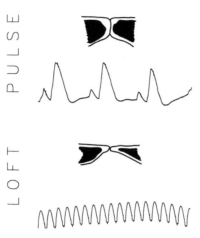

FIG. 7. Vocal fold configuration and resulting waves in the pulse and loft register. The vocal folds are schematized in cross-section.

tic) recoil, so the abductory motion is not opposed as vigorously, nor does closure, once it is finally under way, proceed as fast.

Pulse register phonation is associated with a very interesting pattern of vocal tract excitations, the results of which are also shown in Fig. 7. Modal register glottal waves are relatively uniform in duration and amplitude, a fact that is reflected in the great similarity of the acoustic waves that they generate in the vocal tract. Pulse register, however, typically shows a pattern of weaker, shorter glottal waves alternating with larger and longer ones. The exact mechanisms that account for this behavior have yet to be demonstrated, but the phenomenon is so characteristic that some include its presence in the definition of this laryngeal register.

Loft Register

If pulse register represents an extreme in reduction of vocal fold tension, then loft register is just the opposite: Tension is increased to very high levels. The results are diagramed in Fig. 7. The tension causes the vocal folds to be thinned to such an extent that they take the shape of mere shelves of tissue that may contact each other only over a small vertical distance. (In fact, it is a common observation that loft register phonation may be accomplished with no actual vocal fold contact at all.) A moment's reflection indicates that, under these conditions, vocal fold motion should be rapid but with a small excursion. The increased restorative forces associated with the higher tension cause the opening phase to be terminated early, and the recoil to the midline, driven by greater elasticity, will also be quite fast. On the whole then, loft register adjustment produces high vocal F_o, and the reduction in maximal glottic size generates only weak vocal tract excitations, associated with diminished vocal intensity.

VOCAL SOURCE CONTRIBUTIONS TO VOICE QUALITY

Not all of what we hear in the voice is due to the shaping of the vocal source signal by the resonant and filtering actions of the vocal tract. Any product, after all, is a reflection of the raw material that created it, so some aspects of voice quality are bound to be inherent in the glottal wave itself (and, by inference, in the actions of the vocal folds). The time has now come to examine the vocal source signal in greater detail. To do so, we shall have to consider the *source spectrum*. Some readers may find it useful to pause for the second intermezzo.

SECOND INTERMEZZO

We begin with the somewhat startling statement that there really is no separate and distinct physical entity called sound. What we label by that name is simply our perception of changes in air pressure. The pressure changes must occur within a certain range of rates (about 20 to about 20,000 per second) and must be greater than a certain minimal size before we perceive them, but they are physically no different from the air pressure changes measured by a barometer.

The simplest possible way in which any variable—including air pressure—can change is referred to as "simple harmonic motion" and is depicted at the top of Fig. 8, with pressure on the vertical axis and time on the horizontal axis. The value of the pressure at any given point is proportional to the *sine* of its time location. Hence, this pattern is referred to as a *sine wave*. A sine wave can be almost completely characterized by its F_o (repetition rate) and by the extent of its pressure change (amplitude)[6].

Very few sounds of the natural world are simple sine waves. Almost all are very much more complex, but a physical law known as the *Fourier theorem* tells us that any complex sound is composed of a series of sine waves of different frequencies and amplitudes. The reality of this statement is demonstrated in Fig. 9, in which a complex wave is shown with the four sine wave components, which were added together to create it. (Dissecting a complex wave into its sine wave components is known as *Fourier analysis*.) If the repetition rate of the complex wave is perfectly regular, the wave is

---

[6]There is another descriptor, known as the *phase angle,* that specifies the difference in starting times among two or more waves. When all three parameters—frequency, amplitude, and phase angle—are specified, we know all there is to know about a sine wave. The phase angle is unimportant to the present discussion, however.

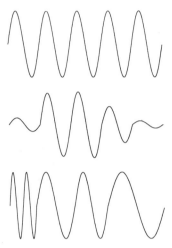

FIG. 8. Sine waves represent the simplest form of pressure change. **Top:** Five sine wave cycles of equal period and amplitude. **Middle:** Waves of constant period but varying amplitudes. **Bottom:** Constant amplitude and variable period.

said to be *periodic*. In that case, all the component sine waves will be integer multiples of the complex wave's F_o. Such components are called *harmonics*. In Fig. 9, the component sine waves have frequencies of 1, 3, 5, and 7 times F_o; they are harmonic frequencies. Notice, however, that they have different amplitudes.

So, any complex wave could be expressed as a tabulation of component frequencies with their respective amplitudes, but such a list would hardly be

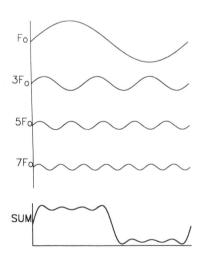

FIG. 9. Any complex repetitive wave is the sum of a series of sine waves of different frequencies and amplitudes. The wave shown at the **bottom** is the sum of the four "harmonics" shown above it.

easy to deal with. A better idea is to produce a graph of the information. We can do this by drawing lines along a frequency dimension wherever there is a component sine wave. The height of the line can represent the amplitude of the component. For the wave of Fig. 10A, such a graph would look like the plot in Fig. 10B. A plot of this type is known as an *amplitude spectrum.* It is nothing but a graphic summary of the components of a complex periodic wave.

Actually, because of the need to begin with simple cases, we have been a bit dishonest. We have behaved as if the wave that we considered as our example is perfectly periodic, that is, it was assumed to repeat with perfect precision and exactitude, each repetition a precise replica of every other. The spectrum of Fig. 10B is called a *line spectrum,* because it is composed of lines separated by empty space on the graph. (There are harmonic frequencies, and nothing else.) But a precisely periodic wave is not to be found in nature. There is always some noise, some irregularity of repetition.

Pure noise—a *totally* random wave, such as is shown in Fig. 10C—has no harmonics. It is composed of sine waves of any and all frequencies (at least within a specifiable range) having unpredictable amplitudes. Its spectrum does not have discrete lines: Since all frequencies are present, the lines fill

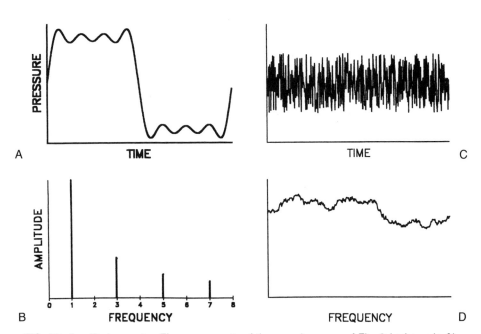

FIG. 10. Amplitude spectra. The components of the complex wave of Fig. 9 (redrawn in **A**) can be indicated in the *line spectrum* shown in **B.** Any purely periodic wave has a line spectrum. A random (noise) wave, such as the one shown in **C,** will have a *continous spectrum,* like that of **D.**

in all available spaces on the graph, forming a *continuous spectrum*, as in Fig. 10D. If a signal is essentially periodic, but also has some noise or irregularity, its spectrum will be a combination of a line and a continuous spectrum: There will be some "fill in" between the harmonic lines.

END OF SECOND INTERMEZZO

The Vocal Source Spectrum

The amplitude spectrum of an ideal (noise free) glottal wave is illustrated in Fig. 11 (top). The regular spacing of the lines tells us that the components are harmonic frequencies. The orderly decrease in their amplitude with increasing frequency is referred to as the spectrum's *roll-off*. For a typical healthy voice, it amounts to an attenuation of approximately 6 dB per octave of frequency increase.

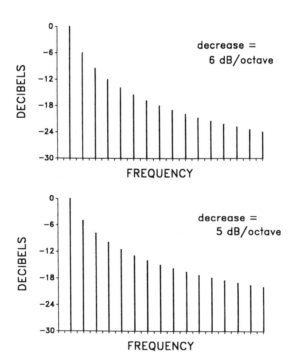

FIG. 11. Spectra of the glottal wave. In the **upper spectrum,** the "roll-off" (decrease) in the amplitudes of the harmonic lines is at the rate of 6 dB/octave. This is typical of the voice at conversational intensity. Increasing intensity (or voluntary adjustment of the vocal folds) can strengthen the higher harmonics, resulting in a roll-off that is less steep, as in the **lower spectrum.**

Let us take a moment and explore where the high-frequency harmonics come from. Consider the waveform we have used as an example (Fig. 9 or 10A). It has a sudden shift at its midpoint. Such a sharp movement represents a fairly rapid rate of change in the acoustic pressure. To generate such a quick change, there must be some among the sine wave components of the waveform that also have rapid change. The higher the frequency of a wave, the faster is its pressure variation, so rapid alterations in a wave translate to stronger high-frequency components in the wave's spectrum.

The sharp cutoff of air flow that is characteristic of the glottal wave now takes on even more significance. It is an important source of the high-frequency components of the glottal source spectrum. The sharper the cutoff becomes, the stronger those high-frequency components should be. It is known that the cutoff becomes sharper as vocal intensity increases. It is also possible to sharpen the cutoff by adjusting the mechanical properties of the vocal folds. Also, of considerable importance to professional voice users, *stronger high harmonics give the voice a perceptually "brighter" sound.* Here, then, is one aspect of voice quality that derives directly from laryngeal adjustment.

Glottal Wave Irregularity

Examination of the amplitude spectrum of a real glottal wave (Fig. 12) shows it to be different in two significant ways from the ideals we have examined so far. The harmonic lines are not nearly so sharp as we have pictured them thus far, and there is continuous energy that fills in part of the space between them. These differences are the result of two phenomena that we have avoided so far, but that are very much part of any real vocal signal: airflow turbulence and vibrational irregularity.

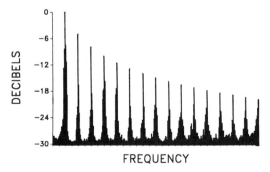

FIG. 12. Amplitude spectrum of a real glottal wave. Note the thickening of the harmonic lines and the "fill" between them. These result from irregularity of the glottal vibration and airflow turbulence.

Turbulence

Airflow through the glottis is not perfectly smooth or (in the language of physics) "laminar." In other words, the air molecules do not all really move in straight lines, like the marchers in a parade. Whenever a flow is forced through a sufficiently narrow opening (like the glottis), there is always a certain amount of random movement or *turbulence*. Also, many individuals do not achieve complete phonatory closure. The arytenoid cartilages may fail to meet at the midline, or they may be angled in such a way that the posterior part of the glottis remains slightly open. In either case, there is often an open pathway by which air can travel around the glottis. This leakage is almost certain to be quite turbulent.

If some of the air molecules are moving in random directions, then there must be randomly oriented pressures acting on them. Since sound is nothing but pressure variation, these erratic pressures contribute randomness to the final acoustic product. That randomness, of course, is noise, and it adds its continuous spectrum characteristics to the line spectrum of the glottal pulsing, partially filling in the spaces between the harmonics.

What is the perceptual effect? Within reasonable limits, added noise in the spectrum produces a sensation of fuzzy softness to the sound, perhaps a velvety quality. A bit more turbulence might be heard as breathiness, or perhaps huskiness, and a lot of turbulence contributes to the perception of hoarseness.

Vibrational Irregularity

Glottal waves are imperfect not only because there are flow turbulences, but also because there is frequency and amplitude *perturbation:* Neither the frequency nor the amplitude of any two successive waves is ever likely to be precisely the same[7] (see Fig. 13). The average differences are quite small: on the order of 40 μsec for period, and about 0.4 dB for amplitude. Still, if the F_0 and amplitude are varying, then the harmonics (which, let us recall, have frequencies that are integral multiples of F_0) must be varying. This results in thickening of the harmonic lines in the spectrum—an indication that the perturbation has introduced an uncertainty about what the exact frequency value of any given harmonic is.

Normal perturbation does not seem to be measurably lessened by attempts to control the voice or by vocal training. Its irreducibility stems from the fact that it reflects inherent instabilities and irregularities in the contractions of the muscles that control the vocal structures. It is not surprising,

---

[7]In the argot of everyday professional communication, frequency perturbation is referred to as *jitter,* amplitude perturbation as *shimmer.*

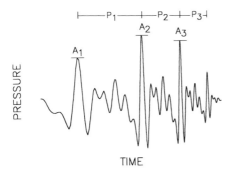

FIG. 13. Perturbation as shown in the acoustic wave of a vowel. The difference between P(*eriod*)$_1$ and P$_2$, and between P$_2$ and P$_3$ is called the *frequency perturbation* or *jitter*. The amplitude difference (A$_1$, A$_2$, A$_3$) is the *amplitude perturbation*, or *shimmer*. (For illustrative purposes, the differences shown here have been made greater than would be expected in a normal voice.)

therefore, that it is one of the factors that give the voice a natural, humanlike quality (a fact appreciated by the creator of the "vox humana" stop on a pipe organ).

CODA

So, at least in outline, we have gone from two flaps of tissue blowing in the pulmonary wind to a palette of acoustic potentials ready to be refined into a baby's cry, a sports fan's cheer, a laborer's grunt, or a Verdi aria.

The voice may be a wondrous thing, but the process of voice production is neither mysterious nor inexplicable. In this chapter, we have been able to explore only the barest outline of the process by which voice is produced, just enough to get the reader started. (There is much that is not understood about laryngeal function, but there is very much that is.) It is obvious, however, that nothing more than perfectly ordinary laws of physics and common principles of physiology are involved.

The mystery, of course, enters with the art.

BIBLIOGRAPHY

Of necessity, but unfortunately, this chapter could only touch on the highest of the high points of what is understood about laryngeal function. There is a great deal that the serious student of voice will want to know. This Bibliography is intended to help in satisfying that desire.

The listing has been divided by topic to facilitate finding a source for whatever specific information is required. We hope readers will also be encouraged to browse, seeking items that strike a chord resonant with their interests.

Despite its length, this Bibliography represents only a very small portion of what is available.

General Introductory Texts

Baken RJ. *Clinical measurement of speech and voice.* Boston: Little, Brown, 1987; pp. 518.

Bunch M. *Dynamics of the singing voice.* New York: Springer, 1982; pp. 156.

Daniloff R, Schuckers G, Feth L. *The physiology of speech and hearing.* Englewood Cliffs, NJ: Prentice-Hall, 1980; pp. 454.

Hirano M. *Clinical examination of voice.* New York: Springer, 1981; pp. 100.

Isshiki N. *Phonosurgery: theory and practice.* New York: Springer, 1989; pp. 233.

Zemlin WR. *Speech and hearing science: anatomy and physiology.* Englewood Cliffs, NJ: Prentice-Hall, 1988; pp. 603.

Anatomy and Tissue Properties

Bach AC, Lederer RL, Dinolt R. Senile changes in the laryngeal musculature. *Arch Otolaryngol* 1941; 34: 47–56.

Baken RJ, Isshiki N. Arytenoid displacement by simulated intrinsic muscle contraction. *Folia Phoniatrica* 1977; 29: 206–216.

Biondi S, Biondi-Zappala M. Surface of laryngeal mucosa seen through the scanning electron microscope. *Folia Phoniatrica* 1974; 26: 241–248.

Gracco C, Kahane JC. Age-related changes in the vestibular folds of the human larynx: a histomorphometric study. *J Voice* 1989; 3: 204–212.

Hast MH. Mechanical properties of the vocal fold muscle. *Practica Oto-Rhino-Laryngologica* 1967; 29: 53–56.

Hirano M. Morphological structure of the vocal cord as a vibrator and its variations. *Folia Phoniatrica* 1974; 26: 89–94.

Hirano M. Phonosurgery: basic and clinical investigations. *Otologia* (Fukuoka) 1975; 21: 239–440.

Hirano M. Structure of the vocal fold in normal and disease states. Anatomical and physical studies. In: Ludlow CL, Hart MO, eds. *Proceedings of the conference on the assessment of vocal pathology.* (*ASHA Reports* No. 11.) Rockville, MD: The American Speech-Language-Hearing Association, 1981; 11–30.

Hirano M, Kurita S, Sakaguchi S. Vocal fold tissue of a 104-year-old lady. *Ann Bull Res Inst Logopedics Phoniatrics* 1988; 22: 1–5.

Hirano M, Matsuo K, Kakita Y, et al. Vibratory behavior versus the structure of the vocal fold. In: Titze IR, Scherer RC, eds. *Vocal fold physiology: biomechanics, acoustics and phonatory control.* Denver, CO: The Denver Center for the Performing Arts, 1983; 26–39.

Kahane JC. Connective tissue changes in the larynx and their effects on voice. *J Voice* 1987; 1: 27–30.

Kahane JC. Histologic structure and properties of the human vocal folds. *Ear, Nose Throat J* 1988; 67: 322–330.

Koike Y, Ohta F, Monju T. Hormonal and non-hormonal actions of endocrines on the larynx. *Excerpta Medica International Congress Series* 1969; no. 206: 339–343.

Mueller PB, Sweeney RJ, Baribeau LJ. Senescence of the voice: morphology of excised male larynges. *Folia Phoniatrica* 1985; 37: 134–138.

Rossi G, Cortesina G. Morphological study of the laryngeal muscles in man: insertions and courses of the muscle fibres, motor end-plates and proprioceptors. *Acta Otolaryngol* 1965; 59: 575–592.

Sellars IE, Keen EN. The anatomy and movements of the cricoarytenoid joint. *Laryngoscope* 1978; 88: 667–674.

F_o and Intensity

Atkinson JE. Inter- and intraspeaker variability in fundamental voice frequency. *J Acoustic Soc Am* 1976; 60: 440–445.

Bowler NW. A fundamental frequency analysis of harsh vocal quality. *Speech Monog* 1964; 31: 128–134.

Coleman RF, Mabis JH, Hinson JK. Fundamental frequency-sound pressure level profiles of adult male and female voices. *J Speech Hearing Res* 1977; 20: 197–204.

Colton RH, Hollien H. Phonational range in the modal and falsetto registers. *J Speech Hearing Res* 1972; 15: 713–718.

Davis SB. Acoustic characteristics of normal and pathological voices. In: Lass NJ, ed. *Speech and language: advances in basic research and practice*, vol. 1. New York: Academic Press, 1979; 271–335.

Dickopf G, Flach M, Koch R, Kroemer B. Varianzanalytische Untersuchungen zur Stimmfeldmessung. *Folia Phoniatrica* 1988; 40: 43–48.

Fairbanks G, Wiley JH, Lassman FM. An acoustical study of vocal pitch in seven- and eight-year-old boys. *Child Dev* 1949; 20: 63–69.

Fitch JL, Holbrook A. Modal vocal fundamental frequency of young adults. *Arch Otolaryngol* 1970; 92: 379–382.

Gramming P, Akerlund L. Phonetograms for normal and pathological voices. In: Gramming P, ed. *The phonetogram: an experimental and clinical study*. Malmö, Sweden: University of Lund, 1988; 117–132.

Gramming P, Sundberg J, Ternström S, et al. Relationship between changes in voice pitch and loudness. In: Gramming P, ed. *The phonetogram: an experimental and clinical study*. Malmö, Sweden: University of Lund, 1988; 87–107.

Hacki T. Die Beurteilung der quantitativen Sprechstimmleistungen: Das Sprechstimmfeld im Singstimmfeld. *Folia Phoniatrica* 1988; 40: 190–196.

Hiki S. Correlation between increments of voice pitch and glottal sound intensity. *J Acoust Soc Jpn* 1967; 23: 20–22.

Hollien H, Jackson B. Normative data on the speaking fundamental frequency characteristics of young adult males. *J Phonetics* 1973; 1: 117–120.

Hollien H, Massey K. A male-female coalescence model of vocal change. In: Lawrence VL, ed. *Transcripts of the fourteenth symposium: care of the professional voice*, part I. New York: Voice Foundation, 1985; 57–60a.

Hollien H, Paul P. A second evaluation of the speaking fundamental frequency characteristics of post-adolescent girls. *Lang Speech* 1969; 12: 119–124.

Hollien H, Shipp T. Speaking fundamental frequency and chronologic age in males. *J Speech Hearing Res* 1972; 15: 155–159.

Linville SE. Maximum phonational frequency range capabilities of women's voices with advancing age. *Folia Phoniatrica* 1987; 39: 297–301.

McGlone RE, Hollien H. Vocal pitch characteristics of aged women. *J Speech Hearing Res* 1963; 6: 164–170.

Michel FJ, Hollien H, Moore P. Speaking fundamental frequency characteristics of 15, 16, and 17 year old girls. *Lang Speech* 1966; 9: 46–51.

Mysak ED. Pitch and duration characteristics of older males. *J Speech Hearing Res* 1959; 2: 46–54.

Pederson MF, Kitzing P, Krabbe S, Heramb S. The change of voice during puberty in 11 to 16 year old choir singers measured with electroglottographic fundamental frequency analysis and compared to other phenomena of puberty. *Acta Otolaryngol* 1982; suppl 386: 189–192.

Ramig LA, Ringel RL. Effects of physiological aging on selected acoustic characteristics of voice. *J Speech Hearing Res* 1983; 26: 22–30.

Ramig LA, Scherer RC, Titze IR. Acoustic correlates of aging. *Recording Res Center Res Rep* 1985; April: 257–277.

Rauhut A, Stürzebecher E, Wagner H, Seidner W. Messung des Stimmfeldes. *Folia Phoniatrica* 1979; 31: 119–124.

Robb MP, Saxman JH, Grant AA. Vocal fundamental frequency characteristics during the first two years of life. *J Acoust Soc Am* 1989; 85: 1708–1717.

Saxman JH, Burk KW. Speaking fundamental frequency characteristics of middle-aged females. *Folia Phoniatrica* 1967; 19: 167–172.

Stone RE Jr, Ferch PAK. Intra-subject variability in Fo-SPLmin voice profiles. *J Speech Hearing Disord* 1982; 47: 123–134.

Stone RE Jr, Bell CJ, Clack TD. Minimum intensity of voice at selected levels within pitch range. *Folia Phoniatrica* 1978; 30: 113–118.

Perturbation

Beckett RL. Pitch perturbation as a function of subjective vocal constriction. *Folia Phoniatrica* 1969; 21: 416–425.

Brown WS Jr, Morris RJ, Michel JF. Vocal jitter in young adult and aged female voices. *J Voice* 1989; 3: 113–119.

Cavallo SA, Baken RJ, Shaiman S. Frequency perturbation characteristics of pulse register phonation. *J Commun Disord* 1984; 17: 231–243.

Deal RE, Emanuel FW. Some waveform and spectral features of vowel roughness. *J Speech Hearing Res* 1978; 21: 250–264.

Higgins MB, Saxman JH. Variations in vocal frequency perturbation across the menstrual cycle. *J Voice* 1989; 3: 233–243.

Horii Y. Fundamental frequency perturbation observed in sustained phonation. *J Speech Hearing Res* 1979; 22: 5–19.

Horii Y. Jitter and shimmer in sustained vocal fry phonation. *Folia Phoniatrica* 1985; 37: 81–86.

Horii Y. Vocal shimmer in sustained phonation. *J Speech Hearing Res* 1980; 23: 202–209.

Iwata S, von Leden H. Pitch perturbations in normal and pathologic voices. *Folia Phoniatrica* 1970; 22: 413–424.

Lieberman P. Perturbations in vocal pitch. *J Acoust Soc Am* 1961; 33: 597–603.

Lieberman P. Some acoustic measures of the fundamental periodicity of normal and pathologic larynges. *J Acoust Soc Am* 1963; 35: 344–353.

Moore P, von Leden H. Dynamic variations of the vibratory pattern in the normal larynx. *Folia Phoniatrica* 1958; 10: 205–238.

Murry T, Large J. Frequency perturbation in singers. In: Lawrence V, ed. *Transcripts of the seventh symposium: care of the professional voice.* New York: Voice Foundation, 1978; 36–39.

Orlikoff RF. Vocal jitter at different fundamental frequencies: a cardiovascular-neuromuscular explanation. *J Voice* 1989; 3: 104–112.

Orlikoff RF, Baken RJ. Fundamental frequency modulation of the human voice by the heartbeat: preliminary results and possible mechanisms. *J Acoust Soc Am* 1989; 85: 888–893.

Ramig LA, Shipp T. Comparative measures of vocal tremor and vocal vibrato. *J Voice* 1987; 1: 162–167.

Sorensen D, Horii Y. Frequency and amplitude perturbation in the voices of female speakers. *J Commun Disord* 1983; 16: 57–61.

Wilcox KA, Horii Y. Age and changes in vocal jitter. *J Gerontol* 1980; 35: 194–198.

Control Mechanisms

Atkinson JE. Correlation analysis of the physiological factors controlling fundamental voice frequency. *J Acoust Soc Am* 1978; 63: 211–222.

Baken RJ, Orlikoff RF. Changes in vocal fundamental frequency at the segmental level: control during voiced fricatives. *J Speech Hearing Res* 1988; 31: 207–211.

Baken RJ, Orlikoff RF. The effect of articulation on fundamental frequency in singers and speakers. *J Voice* 1987; 1: 68–76.

Baken RJ, Orlikoff RF. Laryngeal and chest-wall responses to step-function changes in supraglottal impedance. *Folia Phoniatrica* 1986; 38: 283.

Colton RH. Physiological mechanisms of vocal frequency control: the role of tension. *J Voice* 1988; 2: 208–220.

Erickson D, Baer T, Harris KS. The role of the strap muscles in pitch lowering. In: Bless DM, Abbs JH, eds. *Vocal fold physiology: contemporary research and clinical issues.* San Diego, CA: College-Hill Press, 1983; 279–285.

Faaborg-Andersen K. Electromyographic investigation of intrinsic laryngeal muscles in humans. *Acta Physiol Scand* 1957; 41 (suppl. 140): 1–150.

Faaborg-Andersen K, Sonninen A. The function of the extrinsic laryngeal muscles at different pitch. *Acta Otolaryngol* 1960; 51: 89–93.

Gay T, Hirose H, Strome M, Sawashima M. Electromyography of the intrinsic laryngeal muscles during phonation. *Ann Otol Rhinol Laryngol* 1972; 81: 401–410.

Harvey N, Howell P. Isotonic vocalis contraction as a means of producing rapid decreases in F$_o$. *J Speech Hearing Res* 1980; 23: 576–592.

Hast MH. Physiological mechanisms of phonation: tension of the vocal fold muscle. *Acta Otolaryngol* 1966; 62: 309–318.

Hirano M. Behavior of laryngeal muscles of the late William Vennard. *J Voice* 1988; 2: 291–300.

Hirano M. The function of the intrinsic laryngeal muscles in singing. In: Stevens KN, Hirano M, eds. *Vocal fold physiology.* Tokyo: University of Tokyo Press, 1981; 155–167.

Hirano M, Ohala J, Vennard W. The function of laryngeal muscles in regulating fundamental frequency and intensity of phonation. *J Speech Hearing Res* 1969; 12: 616–628.

Hirano M, Vennard W, Ohala J. Regulation of register, pitch and intensity of voice. *Folia Phoniatrica* 1970; 22: 1–20.

Hixon TJ, Klatt DH, Mead J. Influence of forced transglottal pressure changes on vocal fundamental frequency. *J Acoust Soc Am* 1971; 49: 105.

Hollien H. Some laryngeal correlates of vocal pitch. *J Speech Hearing Res* 1960; 3: 52–58.

Hollien H. Vocal fold thickness and fundamental frequency of phonation. *J Speech Hearing Res* 1962; 5: 237–243.

Hollien H. Vocal pitch variation related to changes in vocal fold length. *J Speech Hearing Res* 1960; 3: 150–156.

Hollien H, Colton RH. Four laminagraphic studies of vocal fold thickness. *Folia Phoniatrica* 1969; 21: 179–198.

Hollien H, Curtis JF. Elevation and tilting of vocal folds as a function of vocal pitch. *Folia Phoniatrica* 1962; 14: 23–36.

Hollien H, Moore GP. Measurements of the vocal folds during changes in pitch. *J Speech Hearing Res* 1960; 3: 157–165.

Holmberg EB, Hillman RE, Perkell JS. Glottal airflow and transglottal air pressure measurements for male and female speakers in soft, normal, and loud voice. *J Acoust Soc Am* 1988; 84: 511–529.

Horii Y. Acoustic analysis of vocal vibrato: a theoretical interpretation of data. *J Voice* 1989; 3: 36–43.

Horii Y, Hata K. A note on phase relationships between frequency and amplitude modulations in vocal vibrato. *Folia Phoniatrica* 1988; 40: 303–311.

Isshiki N. Regulatory mechanism of voice intensity variation. *J Speech Hearing Res* 1964; 7: 17–29.

Isshiki N. Remarks on mechanism for vocal intensity variation. *J Speech Hearing Res* 1969; 12: 665–672.

Isshiki N. Vocal intensity and air flow rate. *Folia Phoniatrica* 1965; 17: 92–105.

Keenan JS, Barrett GC. Intralaryngeal relationships during pitch and intensity changes. *J Speech Hearing Res* 1962; 5: 173–177.

Larson CL, Kempster GB. Voice fundamental frequency changes following discharge of laryngeal motor units. In: Titze IR, Scherer RC, eds. *Vocal fold physiology: biomechanics, acoustics and phonatory control.* Denver, CO: The Denver Center for the Performing Arts, 1983; 91–103.

Leonard RJ, Ringel RL, Daniloff RG, Horii Y. Voice frequency change in singers and non-singers. *J Voice* 1987; 1: 234–239.

Lieberman P, Knudson R, Mead J. Determination of the rate of change of fundamental frequency with respect to subglottal air pressure during sustained phonation. *J Acoust Soc Am* 1969; 45: 1537–1543.

Löfqvist A, Baer T, McGarr NS, Story RS. The cricothyroid muscle in voicing control. *J Acoust Soc Am* 1989; 85: 1314–1321.

Monsen RB, Engebretson AM, Vemula NR. Indirect assessment of the contribution of subglottal air pressure and vocal-fold tension to changes of fundamental frequency in English. *J Acoust Soc Am* 1978; 64: 65–80.

Murry T, Brown WS Jr. Regulation of vocal intensity during vocal fry phonation. *J Acoust Soc Am* 1971; 49: 1905–1907.

Niimi S, Horiguchi S, Kobayashi N. The physiological role of the sternothyroid muscle in phonation: an electromyographic observation. *Ann Bull Res Inst Logoped Phoniatr* 1988; 22: 163–169.

Nishizawa N, Sawashima M, Yonemoto K. Vocal fold length in vocal pitch change. In: Fujimura O, ed. *Vocal physiology: voice production, mechanisms and functions.* New York: Raven Press, 1988; 75–82.

Ohala J, Hirano M, Vennard W. An electromyographic study of laryngeal activity in speech and singing. In: *Proceedings of the sixth international congress on acoustics.* Tokyo, 1968; B-5–B-8.

Rubin HJ, LeCover M, Vennard W. Vocal intensity, subglottic pressure and air flow relationships in singers. *Folia Phoniatrica* 1967; 19: 393–413.

Shin T, Hirano M, Maeyama T, et al. The function of the extrinsic laryngeal muscles. In: Stevens KN, Hirano M, eds. *Vocal fold physiology.* Tokyo: University of Tokyo Press, 1981; 171–180.

Shipp T. Vertical laryngeal position during continuous and discrete vocal frequency change. *J Speech Hearing Res* 1975; 18: 707–718.

Shipp T. Vertical laryngeal position in singers with jaw stabilized. In: Lawrence VL, ed. *Transcripts of the seventh symposium: care of the professional voice,* part I: *The scientific papers.* New York: Voice Foundation, 1979; 44–47.

Shipp T, McGlone RE. Laryngeal dynamics associated with voice frequency change. *J Speech Hearing Res* 1971; 14: 761–768.

Shipp T, Morrissey P. Physiologic adjustments for frequency change in trained and untrained voices. *J Acoust Soc Am* 1977; 62: 476–478.

Sundberg J, Askenfelt A. Larynx height and voice source: a relationship? In: Bless DM, Abbs JH, eds. *Vocal fold physiology: contemporary research and clinical issues.* San Diego, CA: College-Hill Press, 1983; 307–316.

Tanaka S, Tanabe M. Experimental study on regulation of vocal pitch. *J Voice* 1989; 3: 93–98.

Titze IR. Control of voice fundamental frequency. *Nat Assoc Teachers of Singing J* 1988; November/December: pp. 6.

Titze IR. On the relation between subglottal pressure and fundamental frequency in phonation. *J Acoust Soc Am* 1989; 85: 901–906.

Titze IR, Jiang J, Drucker DG. Preliminaries to the body-cover theory of pitch control. *J Voice* 1987; 1: 314–319.

Tizte IR, Luschei ES, Hirano M. Role of the thyroarytenoid muscle in regulation of fundamental frequency. *J Voice* 1989; 3: 213–224.

Registers

Allen EL, Hollien H. A laminagraphic study of pulse (vocal fry) register phonation. *Folia Phoniatrica* 1973; 25: 241–250.

Ametrano Jackson MC. The high male range. *Folia Phoniatrica* 1987; 39: 18–25.

Colton RH. Spectral characteristics of the modal and falsetto registers. *Folia Phoniatrica* 1972; 24: 337–344.

Colton RH. Vocal intensity in the modal and falsetto registers. *Folia Phoniatrica* 1973; 25: 62–70.

Gougerot L, Grémy F, Marstal N. Glottographie à large bande passante. Application à l'étude de la voix de fausset. *J Physiol* 1960; 52: 823–832.

Hirano M, Hibi S, Sawada T. Falsetto, head, chest, and speech mode: an acoustic study with three tenors. *J Voice* 1989; 3: 99–103.

Hollien H. On vocal registers. *J Phonet* 1974; 2: 125–143.

Hollien H. Three major vocal registers: a proposal. In: Rigault A, Charbonneau R, eds. *Proceedings of the Seventh International Congress of Phonetic Sciences.* The Hague: Mouton, 1972; 320–331.

Hollien H, Michel JF. Vocal fry as a phonational register. *J Speech Hearing Res* 1968; 11: 600–604.

Hollien H, Brown WS Jr, Hollien K. Vocal fold length associated with modal, falsetto, and varying intensity phonations. *Folia Phoniatrica* 1971; 23: 66–78.

Hollien H, Damsté H, Murry T. Vocal fold length during vocal fry phonation. *Folia Phoniatrica* 1969; 21: 257–265.

Hollien H, Girard GT, Coleman RF. Vocal fold vibratory patterns of pulse register phonation. *Folia Phoniatrica* 1977; 29: 200–205.

Hollien H, Moore P, Wendahl RW, Michel JF. On the nature of vocal fry. *J Speech Hearing Res* 1966; 9: 245–247.

Kitzing P. Photo- and electroglottographic recording of the laryngeal vibratory pattern during different registers. *Folia Phoniatrica* 1982; 34: 234–241.

McGlone RE. Air flow during vocal fry phonation. *J Speech Hearing Res* 1967; 10: 299–304.

McGlone RE. Air flow in the upper register. *Folia Phoniatrica* 1970; 22: 231–238.

McGlone RE, Brown WS Jr. Identification of the "shift" between vocal registers. *J Acoust Soc Am* 1969; 46: 1033–1036.

McGlone RE, Shipp T. Some physiologic correlates of vocal-fry phonation. *J Speech Hearing Res* 1971; 14: 769–775.

Murry T. Subglottal pressure and airflow measures during vocal fry phonation. *J Speech Hearing Res* 1971; 14: 544–551.

Murry T, Brown WS Jr. Subglottal air pressure during two types of vocal activity: vocal fry and modal phonation. *Folia Phoniatrica* 1971; 23: 440–449.

Rohrs M, Pascher W, Ocker C. Untersuchungen über das Schwingungsverhalten der Stimmlippen in verschiedenen Registerbereichen mit unterschiedlichen stroboskopischen Techniken. *Folia Phoniatrica* 1985; 37: 113–118.

Roubeau C, Chevrie-Muller C, Arabia-Guidet C. Electroglottographic study of the changes of voice registers. *Folia Phoniatrica* 1987; 39: 280–289.

Schutte HK, Seidner WW. Registerabhangige Differentzierung von Elektrogrammen. *Sprache-Stimme-Gehör* 1988; 12: 59–62.

Titze IR. A framework for the study of vocal registers. *J Voice* 1988; 2: 183–194.

Welch GF, Sergeant DC, MacCurtain F. Zeroradiographic-electrolaryngographic analysis of male vocal registers. *J Voice* 1989; 3: 224–256.

Aerodynamics, Vocal Fold Movement, and Models

Baer T. Observation of vocal fold vibration: measurement of excised larynges. In: Stevens KN, Hirano M, eds. *Vocal fold physiology.* Tokyo: University of Tokyo Press, 1981; 119–132.

Baer T, Titze IR, Yoshioka H. Multiple simultaneous measures of vocal fold activity. In: Bless DM, Abbs JH, eds. *Vocal fold physiology: contemporary research and clinical issues.* San Diego, CA: College-Hill, 1983; 227–237.

Biever DM, Bless DM. Vibratory characteristics of the vocal folds in young adult and geriatric women. *J Voice* 1989; 3: 120–131.

Brackett IP. The vibration of vocal folds at selected frequencies. *Annal Otol Rhinol Laryngol* 1948; 57: 556–558.

Broad DJ. The new theories of vocal fold vibration. In: Lass NJ, ed. *Speech and language: advances in basic research and practice.* New York: Academic Press, 1979; 2: 203–257.

Cavagna GA, Camporesi EM. Glottal aerodynamics and phonation. In: Wyke B, ed. *Ventilatory and phonatory control systems.* New York: Oxford University Press, 1974; 76–87.

Childers DG, Alsaka YA, Hicks DM, Moore GP. Vocal fold vibrations: an EGG model. In: Baer T, Sasaki C, Harris KS, eds. *Laryngeal function in phonation and respiration.* Boston: Little, Brown, 1987; 181–202.

Flanagan JL. Some properties of the glottal sound source. *J Speech Hearing Res* 1958; 1: 99–116.

Gauffin J, Liljencrants J. Modelling the airflow in the glottis. *Ann Bull Res Inst Logoped Phoniatr* 1988; 22: 39–50.

Hillman RE, Oesterle E, Feth LL. Characteristics of the glottal turbulent noise source. *J Acoust Soc Am* 1983; 74: 691–694.

Holmes, JN. The acoustic consequences of vocal-cord action. *Phonetica* 1977; 34: 316–317.

Ishizaka K. Equivalent lumped-mass models of vocal fold vibration. In: Stevens, KN, Hirano M, eds. *Vocal fold physiology.* Tokyo: University of Tokyo Press, 1981; 231–241.

Isogai Y, Horiguchi S, Honda K, et al. A dynamic simulation model of vocal fold vibration. In: Fujimura O, ed. *Vocal physiology: voice production, mechanisms and functions.* New York: Raven Press, 1988; 191–206.

Kitzing P, Sonesson B. A photoglottographical study of the female vocal folds during phonation. *Folia Phoniatrica* 1974; 26: 138–149.

Kitzing P, Carlborg B, Löfqvist A. Aerodynamic and glottographic studies of the laryngeal vibratory cycle. *Folia Phoniatrica* 1982; 34: 216–224.

Koike Y. Sub- and supraglottal pressure variation during phonation. In: Stevens KN, Hirano M, eds. *Vocal fold physiology.* Tokyo: University of Tokyo Press, 1981; 181–189.

Matsushita H. The vibratory mode of the vocal folds in the excised larynx. *Folia Phoniatrica* 1975; 27: 7–18.

Monsen, RB, Engebretson AM. Study of variations in the male and female glottal wave. *J Acoust Soc Am* 1977; 62: 981–993.

Rothenberg M. Some relations between glottal air flow and vocal fold contact area. In: Ludlow CL, Hart MO, eds. *Proceedings of the conference on the assessment of vocal fold pathology (ASHA Reports* no. 11). Rockville, MD: American Speech-Language-Hearing Association, 1981; 88–96.

Rothenberg M, Miller D, Molitor R. Aerodynamic investigation of sources of vibrato. *Folia Phoniatrica* 1988; 40: 244–260.

Saito S, Fukuda H, Kitahara S, Kokowa N. Stroboscopic observation of vocal fold vibration with fiberoptics. *Folia Phoniatrica* 1978; 30: 241–244.

Schutte HK. Aerodynamics of phonation. *Acta Oto-rhino-laryngol Belg* 1986; 40: 344–357.

Schutte HK, Miller DG. Transglottal pressures in professional singing. *Acta Oto-rhino-laryngol Belg* 1986; 40: 395–404.

Sonesson B. On the anatomy and vibratory patterns of the human vocal folds. *Acta Otolaryngol* 1960; suppl. 156: 44–67.

Stevens KN. Modes of vocal fold vibration based on a two-section model. In: Fujimura O, ed. *Vocal physiology: voice production, mechanisms and functions.* New York: Raven Press, 1988; 357–371.

Stevens KN. Physics of laryngeal behavior and larynx modes. *Phonetica* 1977; 34: 264–379.

Stevens KN. Vibration modes in relation to model parameters. In: Stevens KN, Hirano M, eds. *Vocal fold physiology.* Tokyo: University of Tokyo Press, 1981; 291–301.

Titze IR. Biomechanics and distributed-mass models of vocal fold vibration. In: Stevens KN, Hirano M, eds. *Vocal fold physiology.* Tokyo: University of Tokyo Press, 1981; 245–264.

Titze IR. The human vocal cords: a mathematical model. *Phonetica* 1973; 28: 129–170.

Titze IR. On the mechanics of vocal fold vibration. *J Acoust Soc Am* 1976; 60: 1366–1380.

Titze IR. Parameterization of the glottal area, glottal flow, and vocal fold contact area. *J Acoust Soc Am* 1984; 75: 570–580.

Titze IR. The physics of flow-induced oscillation of the vocal folds. I. Small-amplitude oscillations. *Record Res Center Res Rep* 1985; April: 1–49.

Titze IR, Talkin DT. A theoretical study of the effects of various laryngeal configurations on the acoustics of phonation. *J Acoust Soc Am* 1979; 66: 60–74.

Neurology

Abo-el-Enein MA, Wyke B. Laryngeal myotatic reflexes. *Nature* 1966; 209: 682–686.

Abo-el-Enein MA, Wyke B. Myotatic reflex systems in the intrinsic muscles of the larynx. *J Anat (Lond)* 1966; 100: 926–927.

Adzaku FK, Wyke B. Innervation of the subglottic mucosa of the larynx and its significance. *Folia Phoniatrica* 1979; 31: 271–283.

Baer T. Reflex activation of laryngeal muscles by sudden induced subglottal pressure changes. *J Acoust Soc Am* 1979; 65: 1271–1275.

Baken RJ. Neuromuscular spindles in the intrinsic muscles of a human larynx. *Folia Phoniatrica* 1971; 23: 204–210.

Bowden REM. Innervation of intrinsic laryngeal muscles. In: Wyke B, ed. *Ventilatory and phonatory control systems.* New York: Oxford University Press, 1974; 370–381.

Kurozumi S, Tashiro T, Harada Y. Laryngeal responses to electrical stimulation of the medullary respiratory centers in the dog. *Laryngoscope* 1971; 81: 1960–1967.

Larson CR. Brain mechanisms involved in the control of vocalization. *J Voice* 1988; 2: 301–311.

Larson CR. The midbrain periaqueductal gray: a brainstem structure involved in vocalization. *J Speech Hearing Res* 1985; 28: 241–249.

Larson CR, Kempster GB, Kistler MK. Changes in voice fundamental frequency following discharge of single motor units in cricothyroid and thyroarytenoid muscles. *J Speech Hearing Res* 1987; 30: 552–558.

Larson CR, Wilson KE, Luschei ES. Preliminary observations on cortical and brainstem mechanisms of laryngeal control. In: Bless DM, Abbs JH, eds. *Vocal fold physiology: contemporary research and clinical issues.* San Diego, CA: College-Hill Press, 1983; 82–95.

Mallard AR, Ringel RL, Horii Y. Sensory contributions to control of fundamental frequency of phonation. *Folia Phoniatrica* 1978; 30: 199–213.

Mårtensson A. Proprioceptive impulse patterns during contraction of intrinsic laryngeal muscles. *Acta Physiol Scand* 1964; 62: 176–194.

Ortega JD, DeRosier E, Park S, Larson CR. Brainstem mechanisms of laryngeal control as revealed by microstimulation studies. In: Fujimura O, ed. *Vocal physiology: voice production, mechanisms and functions.* New York: Raven Press, 1988; 19–28.

Miscellaneous

Abitbol J, de Brux J, Millot G, et al. Does a hormonal vocal cord cycle exist in women? Study of vocal premenstrual syndrome in voice performers by videostroboscopy-glottography and cytology on 38 women. *J Voice* 1989; 3: 157–162.

Dmitriev LB, Chernov BP, Maslov VT. Functioning of the voice mechanism in double-voice Touvinian singing. *Folia Phoniatrica* 1983; 35: 193–197.

Gossett CW Jr. Electromyographic investigation of the relationship of the effects of selected parameters on concurrent study of voice and oboe. *J Voice* 1989; 3: 52–64.

Hamlet SL, Palmer JM. Investigation of laryngeal trills using the transmission of ultrasound through the larynx. *Folia Phoniatrica* 1974; 26: 362–377.

Hicks DM, Childers DG, Moore GP, Alsaka J. EGG and the singers' voice. In: Lawrence VL, ed. *Transcripts of the fourteenth symposium: care of the professional voice.* New York: The Voice Foundation, 1986; 50–56c.

King AI, Ashby J, Nelson C. Laryngeal function in wind instruments: the brass. *J Voice* 1989; 3: 65–67.

Murry T, Caligiuri MP. Phonatory and nonphonatory motor control in singers. *J Voice* 1989; 3: 257–263.

Proctor DF. The physiologic basis of voice training. In: Bouhuys A, ed. *Sound production in man (Annals of the New York Academy of Sciences,* vol. 155). New York: New York Academy of Sciences, 1968; 208–228.

Rosenberg AE. Effect of glottal pulse shape on the quality of natural vowels. *J Acoust Soc Am* 1971; 49: 583–588.

Schutte HK. Efficiency of professional singing voices in terms of energy ratio. *Folia Phoniatrica* 1984; 36: 267–272.

Silverman E-M, Zimmer CH. Effect of the menstrual cycle on voice quality. *Arch Otolaryngol* 1978; 104: 7–10.

Sundberg J. The source spectrum in professional singing. *Folia Phoniatrica* 1973; 25:71–90.

Van Michel C. La courbe glottographique chez les sujects non entrainés au chant. *Comptes Rendus de la Société de Biologie* 1968; 1: 583–585.

Professional Voice: The Science and Art of Clinical Care, Robert T. Sataloff. Raven Press, Ltd., New York © 1991.

4

Vocal Tract Resonance

Johan Sundberg

Royal Institute of Technology, Stockholm, Sweden

The human voice organ consists of three parts (1), as schematically illustrated in Fig. 1. One part is the breathing apparatus, which acts as a compressor: It compresses the air contained in the lungs. The second is the vocal folds, which act as a proper sound generator: They chop the airstream from the lungs into a sequence of air pulses, which is actually a sound. Its sound is a buzz tone and contains a complete set of harmonic partials. The third part is the cavity system—the pharynx and mouth cavity, or the vocal tract: It acts as a resonator, or a filter, which shapes the sound generated by the vocal folds. In producing nasal sounds, the velum is lowered, supplementing the vocal tract resonator by the nasal cavity, called the nasal tract. Of the three parts—the breathing apparatus, the vocal folds, and the vocal tract—it is only the latter two that directly contribute to forming the voice timbre. In other words, the acoustic characteristics of the voice are determined by two factors, (a) the voice source, i.e., the functioning of the vocal folds, and (b) the vocal tract. In this chapter, discussion focuses on the role of the vocal tract resonator.

The voice source passes through the vocal tract resonator, which thus shapes it acoustically. The nature of this shaping depends on the vocal tract configuration. As in phonetics and other voice sciences, the term *articulation* will be used to describe the change in the shape of the vocal tract. Also, the structures that we use in order to arrange the shape of the vocal tract in different ways will be called *articulators*. For example, the tongue is an articulator.

The vocal tract is a *resonator*. What, then, is a resonator? Actually, almost anything is a resonator: every system that can be compressed and has weight. The air column in the vocal tract is one of many examples.

Sound within a resonator decays slowly. If one hits a resonator, it will resound for a little while rather than having the sound disappear immediately. This phenomenon of resounding is called *resonance*. In the vocal tract, the decay is rapid, but still it is possible to hear how a sound in the vocal tract decays. If one flicks one's neck above the larynx with a finger with

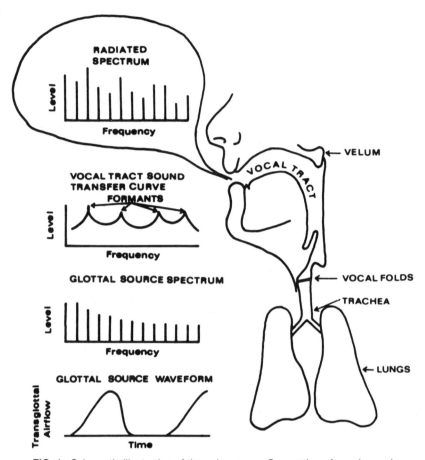

FIG. 1. Schematic illustration of the voice organ. Generation of vocal sound.

closed glottis and open mouth, one can hear a quickly decaying tone; it sounds as when one hits an empty bottle or tin, which, incidentally, are other examples of resonators.

Another aspect of resonance is that a resonator applies very different conditions for sounds that try to pass through it. The frequency of the candidate sound makes all the difference. This is illustrated schematically in Fig. 2. Sounds having certain frequencies pass through the resonator very easily, so that they are radiated with a high amplitude from the resonator. These preferred frequencies fit the resonator optimally, so to speak, and they are called resonance frequencies. It is tones with these resonance frequencies that resound in a struck resonator. In the case of the vocal tract resonator, however, the resonances are called *formants* and the resonance frequencies are called *formant frequencies*. Tones with frequencies in between these for-

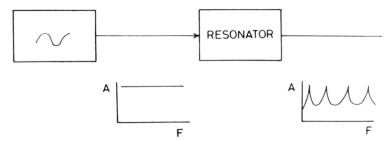

FIG. 2. Schematic illustration of the phenomenon of resonance. If a sine wave of constant amplitude (A) sweeps from low to high frequency (F), the frequency-dependent sound transfer ability of the resonator imposes great variations in the amplitude. The amplitude culminates at the resonance frequencies.

mant frequencies are attenuated more or less when they are transmitted through the resonator. They are not preserved when the resonator is struck.

These formants are of paramount importance to the voice sounds. They totally determine vowel quality, and they give major contributions to the personal voice timbre. In the vocal tract, there are four or five formants of interest. The two lowest formants determine most of the vowel color, while the third, fourth, and fifth are of greater significance to personal voice timbre.

We are very skilled in tuning our formant frequencies. We do this by changing the shape of the vocal tract, i.e., by moving our articulators. In this way, the vocal tract may assume a great variety of shapes. The mandible is one articulator since it may be raised or lowered. The tongue is another one since it may constrict the vocal tract at almost any position from the hard palate to the deep pharynx. The lip opening is a third articulator because it may be widened or narrowed. The larynx can be raised or lowered. Evidently, the latter two variations also affect vocal tract length. Finally, the sidewalls of the pharynx can be moved.

The vocal tract length affects all formant frequencies. Adult males have a tube length of about 17 to 20 cm. Assuming a cylindrical vocal tract shape of length of 17.5 cm, the formant frequencies occur at the odd multiples of 500 Hz: 500, 1500, 2500 . . . Hz. Because of sex differences in vocal tract length, a similar articulatory configuration gives formant frequencies that are about 40% higher in children than in adult males. As adult females have shorter vocal tracts than adult males, their formant frequencies are on the average 15% higher than those of adult males.

The most common way for tuning formant frequencies is by adjusting the vocal tract shape. A reduction of the lip opening and a lengthening of the vocal tract by a lowering of the larynx or by protruding the lips lowers all formant frequencies. Similarly, constricting the vocal tract in the glottal region leads to an increase of the formant frequencies.

Some articulators are particularly efficient in tuning certain formant frequencies. The mandible, which expands the vocal tract in the lip region and constricts it in the laryngeal region, raises the frequency of the first formant. In vowels produced by male adults the first formant varies between approximately 200 and 800 Hz.

The second formant is particularly sensitive to the tongue shape. The second formant frequency in male adults varies within a range of approximately 500 and 2500 Hz.

The third formant is especially sensitive to the position of the tip of the tongue or, when the tongue is retracted, to the size of the cavity between the lower incisors and the tongue. In vowels produced by male adults, the third formant varies between approximately 1600 and 3500 Hz.

The relationships between the vocal tract shape and the fourth and fifth formants are more complicated and difficult to control by particular articulatory means. However, they seem to be very dependent on vocal tract length and also on the configuration in the deep pharynx. In vowels produced by adult males, the fourth formant frequency is generally in the vicinity of 2500 to 4000 Hz, and the fifth, 3000 to 4500 Hz.

It is evident that the formant frequencies must have a great effect on the spectrum, as the vocal tract resonator filters the voice source (see Fig. 1). The spectrum envelope of the voice source is smooth and slopes off at an average of rate, approximately 12 dB/octave, if measured in airflow units, as mentioned. The spectrum of a radiated vowel, however, is characterized by peaks and valleys, because the partials lying closest to a formant frequency get stronger than adjacent partials in the spectrum. In this way, the vocal tract resonances form the vowel spectrum, hence the term formants. Recalling that formants are vocal tract resonances, we realize that it is by means of vocal tract resonance that we form vowels.

Various vowels correspond to different articulatory configurations attained by varying the positions of the articulators as illustrated in Fig. 3. In the vowel /i:/ (as in heed), the tongue bulges so that it constricts the buccal part of the vocal tract. As a consequence of this, the first formant is low, while the second formant is high. In the vowel /u:/ (as in the word who'd), the first and second formant frequencies are both low, and in the vowel /a:/ (as in the Italian word caro), the first formant is high, and the second takes an intermediate position.

Figure 4 shows typical formant frequencies for various spoken vowels as produced by male adults. The "islands" in the figure imply that the vowel marked will result, provided the frequencies of the first and second formants remain within that island. For example, if the first and second formants are between 350 and 500 Hz, and 500 and 800 Hz, respectively, the vowel will be an /o:/. Note that the vowels are scattered along a triangular contour, the three corners of which are the vowels /i:/, /a:/, and /u:/. The vowel /oe:/ (as in heard) is located in the center of the triangle.

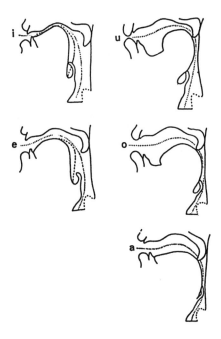

FIG. 3. Tracings of X-ray profiles of the vocal tract showing articulatory configurations for some vowels. From ref. 5.

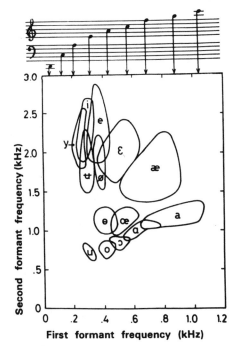

FIG. 4. Typical values for the two lowest formant frequencies for various spoken vowels as produced by male adults. The first formant frequency is given in musical notation at the top. In this figure, the symbol for long vowel, :, has been omitted.

Thus, the formant frequencies determine the vowel quality. Still, different individuals tune their formant frequencies a bit differently for the same vowel. For instance, it would be completely impossible for small children to bring their formant frequencies down to the values typically used by adult males, children's vocal tracts simply not being sufficiently long. This is the reason the vowels are represented by islands rather than dots in the figure. The exact position of the two lowest formant frequencies for a given vowel depends on the individual morphology of the speaker's vocal tract, among other things, and also on the habits of pronunciation.

FORMANT FREQUENCIES IN SINGING

"Singer's Formant"

With regard to the loudest possible tone, it is remarkable that there is no clear difference between a male singer and a nonsinger. This can be seen in Fig. 5, which shows average maximum and minimum sound levels as functions of pitch frequency for professional male singers and nonsingers. Thus, the singers do not sing more loudly than nonsingers. Why, then, can we hear a singer so clearly even when he is accompanied by a loud orchestra?

The answer can be found in the spectral characteristics, which differ considerably between male singers and nonsingers. Moreover, vowels spoken and sung by male singers typically differ with regard to the spectrum characteristics. Figure 6 illustrates the most apparent difference, called the *sing-*

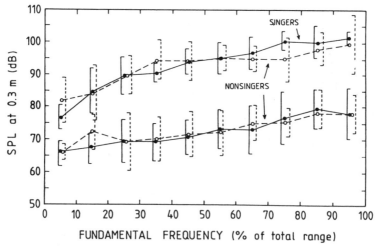

FIG. 5. Average maximum and minimum sound pressure level (SPL) at 0.3-m distance in anechoic room as produced by 10 professional singers and 10 nonsingers. The bars represent ± 1 standard deviation. From ref. 6.

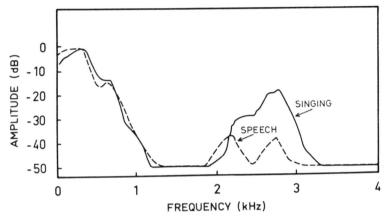

FIG. 6. Illustration of the singer's formant, a prominent peak in the spectrum envelope appearing in the vicinity of 3 kHz in all vowel spectra sung by male singers and also by altos.

er's formant. This is a prominent spectrum envelope peak appearing in the vicinity of 3 kHz in all vowel spectra sung by male singers and also by altos. It belongs to the typical features of sung vowels.

The level of this peak varies depending on the voice classification. It is somewhat lower for a bass and higher for a tenor. Sopranos, on the other hand, have a much lower spectrum level of this peak than the other categories. It appears that, in the case of the soprano, this peak is nothing but a perfectly normal third and fourth formant.

Regardless of voice category, the level of the singer's formant also varies with loudness of phonation, as illustrated in Fig. 7: a sound pressure level (SPL) increase of 10 dB is accompanied by an increase of 12 to 15 dB in the

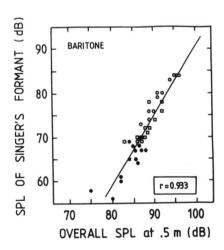

FIG. 7. Level of the singer's formant as a function of loudness of phonation. From ref. 7.

singer's formant. This effect derives from the voice source, the sound generated by the vocal fold vibrations.

The center frequency of the singer's formant varies, depending on the voice category. In bass singers, it centers around 2.2 kHz; in baritones, around 2.7; in tenors, around 3.2; and in altos, around 2.8 kHz. These frequency differences seem to contribute significantly to the timbre differences among these voice categories.

The presence of the singer's formant in the spectrum of a vowel sound has a marked advantage in that it helps the singer's voice to be heard through a loud orchestral accompaniment. In the spectrum of the sound from a symphony orchestra, the partials near 500 Hz tend to be loudest, and above this frequency region, the levels of the spectrum components decrease with rising frequency. This is illustrated by the long-term-average spectrum of orchestral music shown in Fig. 8, where the slope above 500 Hz is about 9 dB/octave. Incidentally, normal speech appears to yield similar long-term-average spectrum characteristics. The perceptual point with a singer's formant is, then, to raise the spectrum envelope in a frequency range where the sound of the accompaniment offers only a moderate acoustic competition, so to speak.

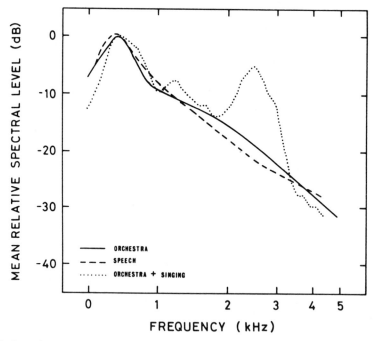

FIG. 8. Long-term-average spectrum of normal speech and of orchestral music with and without a solo singer's voice.

How do singers generate this spectrum peak in all voiced sounds? The answer is "By resonance!" If it is assumed that the third, fourth, and fifth formants are close in frequency, thus forming a formant cluster, the singer's formant peak can be explained as an articulatory phenomenon that can be produced with a normal voice source. In Fig. 9, formant frequency measurements compatible with this assumption for vowels sung by professional singers are compared with those typical for normal speech. As can be seen, the fifth formant in the sung vowels is lower than the fourth formant in the spoken vowels. Thus, five formants appear in the same frequency range as four formants in the spoken vowels. In the vicinity of the singer's formant, the density of formants is high in the sung vowels.

The acoustic consequence of clustering formants is that the spectrum partials in the frequency range of the cluster are enhanced in the radiated

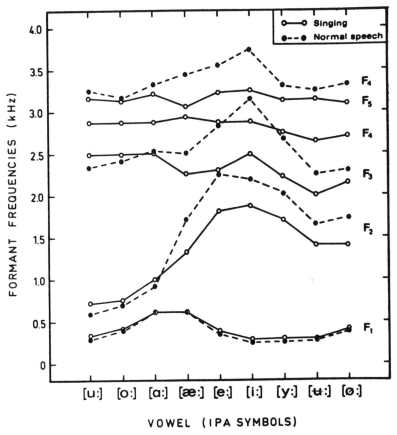

FIG. 9. Average formant frequencies for Swedish vowels spoken normally and sung by professional male singers.

spectrum, as is illustrated in Fig. 10. In other words, the singer's formant is compatible with the normal concept of voice production, provided a clustering of the higher formants is possible.

Experiments with acoustic models of the vocal tract showed that such a clustering of formants can be attained if the pharynx is wide as compared with the entrance to the larynx tube. It seems that, in many singers, this effect is obtained by a lowering of the larynx. In this case, the larynx tube acts as a separate resonator with a resonance in the vicinity of 2.8 kHz (2).

There also may be other, as yet unknown, ways of generating a singer's formant. A Chinese researcher, S. Wang, found that, in Chinese singing and in the type of singing developed for medieval music, a singer's formant was produced without a lowering of the larynx. He hypothesized that the peak was produced by an acoustic interaction between the voice source and the vocal tract resonator. However, Wang's results seem somewhat questionable. For instance, it seems unclear whether there is any singer's formant at all in Chinese classical opera singing.

The particular arrangements of the vocal tract that generate vowels with a singer's formant have certain consequences for the vowel quality, too. This is also illustrated in Fig. 9. We can see that the second and third formants of /i:/ are low, in fact, almost as low as in the German vowel /y:/. This is in accordance with the common observation that vowels are "colored" in singing. This coloring can be seen as a price that the singer pays in order to buy his singer's formant.

Summarizing, we see that resonance is of a decisive relevance to singing, as it creates major characteristics of the singing voice in the case of male voices and altos. It should be observed, however, that all this resonance takes place in the vocal tract. It has not been possible to demonstrate any acoustic significance at all from the vibration sensations in the skull and face that one feels during singing. It seems that they are important to the control

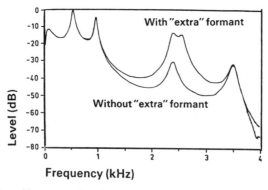

FIG. 10. Clustering of formants when the pharynx is wide as compared with the entrance to the larynx tube.

of articulation and phonation. In any event, they do not contribute directly to the filtering of the sound to any significant extent.

Super Pitch Singing

We just reviewed typical formant (or resonance) frequency differences between speech and singing in male singers and in altos. However, the formant frequency differences between spoken and sung vowels are much greater in the super pitch part of female singers. The reason for this seems to be the exceedingly high fundamental frequencies that occur in female singing. While a bass singer is not required to go higher than 330 Hz fundamental frequency (pitch E_4), the maximum for a high soprano may amount to no less than 1500 Hz (pitch F_6).

Let us now recall Fig. 4, which showed the formant frequencies for various vowels. The scale for the first formant frequency was given in the usual frequency unit Hz, but also, at the top of the graph, in musical pitch symbols. From this, we can see that the super pitches in female singing are very high indeed, as compared with the normal frequency values of the first formant in most vowels. The first formant of /i:/ and /u:/ is about 250 Hz, and the highest value for the first formant in a vowel occurs at 900 Hz for the vowel /a:/.

It is difficult to determine formant frequencies accurately when the fundamental frequency is high. The spectrum partials of voiced sounds are equidistantly spaced along the frequency axis, as shown in Fig. 11, since they

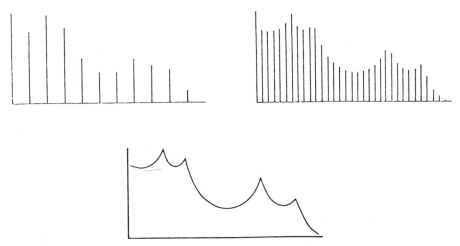

FIG. 11. Illustration of the differing difficulty of determining formant frequencies in spectra with a high (**left**) and a low (**right**) fundamental frequency. Both spectra were generated using the same formant frequencies represented by the idealized spectrum envelope (**below**).

form a harmonic series. This implies that the partials are densely spaced along the frequency axis only when fundamental frequency is low. In this case, the formants can easily be identified as spectrum envelope peaks. In the opposite case, such peaks are often impossible to discern, particularly if there is no partial near the formant frequency. It is certainly for this reason that male voices have been analyzed much more often than female voices, although attempts have also been made to determine the formant frequencies in female singers.

Using various experimental techniques, efforts have been made to estimate the formant frequencies in female singers. One method was to use external excitation of the vocal tract by means of a vibrator while the professional soprano silently articulated a vowel. Another method was to take an X-ray pictcure of the vocal tract in profile while the singer sang different vowels at different pitches. For obvious reasons, the number of subjects in these studies had to be kept low, only one or two. Still the results were encouraging in that they agreed surprisingly well. This supports the assumption that they are typical.

Some formant frequency values for soprano singers are shown in Fig. 12. These results can be idealized in terms of lines, also shown in Fig. 12, relating the first, second, third, and fourth formant frequencies to the fundamental frequency, and to the formant frequencies in speech. The main principle seems to be as follows: As long as fundamental frequency is lower than the normal value of the vowel's first formant frequency, this formant frequency is used. At higher pitches, the first formant is raised with increasing fundamental frequency. In this way, the situation is avoided in which the fundamental goes higher than the first formant. With rising fundamental frequency, the second formant of front vowels is lowered, while that of back vowels is raised to a frequency just above the second spectrum partial; the third formant is lowered and the fourth is raised.

What articulatory means do the singers use in order to achieve these great pitch-dependent rearrangements of the formant frequencies? An articulatory tool that female singers seem to recruit frequently for the purpose of tuning the first formant is the jaw opening. Formal measurements on female singers' jaw opening have shown that, under controlled experimental conditions, it is systematically increased with rising fundamental frequency. This rule is illustrated in Fig. 13, which shows the jaw opening of a professional soprano as a function of fundamental frequency. Within the pitch range covered by Fig. 13, all vowels are produced with a jaw opening that increased with fundamental frequency. Even at the lowest fundamental frequency, the jaw openings are wider than those used for the spoken versions. This system applies to all vowels except /a:/, which is sung with a similar jaw opening throughout this range. However, the first formant frequency of this vowel is higher than the highest fundamental frequency used in this experiment.

The jaw opening is an excellent tool for the purpose of raising the first

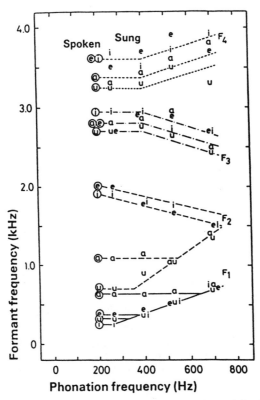

FIG. 12. The vowel symbols show formant frequency estimates of the first, second, third, and fourth formant frequencies for various vowels as sung by a professional soprano. The *circled* vowel symbols represent the corresponding data measured when the vowels were pronounced by the same subject in a speech mode. The lines represent an idealization of how the formant frequencies changed with fundamental frequency.

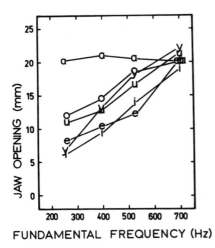

FIG. 13. Jaw opening of a professional soprano singing the vowels indicated at various fundamental frequencies.

formant frequency, as mentioned. There are also other articulators that can be recruited for the same purpose. One is the lip opening: By contracting the mouth corners, the vocal tract is shortened, so the frequencies of all formants will increase. The vocal tract can also be shortened by raising the larynx. At least some professional female singers take advantage of this tool for raising the first formant frequency. Figure 14 gives an example. It is interesting that most singing teachers regard such a pitch-dependent adaptation of larynx height as a mistake from a singing technique point of view. Perhaps these teachers do not mean larynx elevation in general, but rather an elevation that is associated with an audible shift in the mode of phonation and vowel quality; in normal speech, a raised larynx is generally associated with a pressed type of phonation, screaming representing an extreme example.

All the pitch-dependent formant frequency changes illustrated in Fig. 12 are not consequences merely of changes in jaw opening and larynx height. As shown in Fig. 15, there are also considerable changes in tongue shape. It appears that tongue shape changes rather abruptly with pitch. In the subject examined, the vowels /a:/, /i:/, and /u:/ were all produced with very similar tongue shapes only at the fundamental frequency of 960 Hz (pitch B$^b_5$). It is possible that the tongue shape differentiation is influenced by preceding and following consonants at these pitches. Still, with these wide jaw openings, a small difference in tongue shape is not likely to affect the formant frequencies to any appreciable extent.

Even though this principle of tuning formant frequencies depending on the

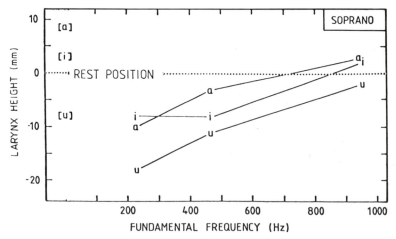

FIG. 14. Vertical larynx position as determined from X-ray profiles of the vocal tract of a professional soprano singing the indicated vowels at various fundamental frequencies. Bracketed symbols refer to vowels spoken by the same subject.

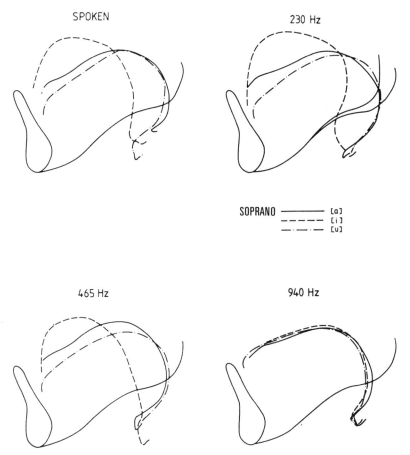

FIG. 15. Midsagittal tongue contours as determined from X-ray profiles of the vocal tract of a professional soprano singing the indicated vowels at various fundamental frequencies shown. From ref. 2.

fundamental frequency has been found to be applied by soprano singers only, it could be used even by other singers; all singers, except possibly basses, can encounter a situation where the first formant is lower in frequency than the fundamental prescribed by the composer. As the first formant frequency varies between vowels, the case depends on the vowel. In the highest range of baritone, the vowels /i:/, /y:/, and /u:/ would need pitch-dependent first formant frequencies. In the top part of an alto's range, all vowels except /a:/ and /æ:/ need modification of the first formant frequency. It is likely that in such cases the other formant frequencies are modified in similar ways as in the case of sopranos.

The benefit of these arrangements of the formant frequencies is great.

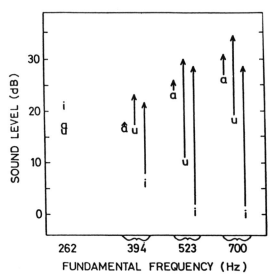

FIG. 16. Gain in sound level at different fundamental frequencies resulting from the pitch-dependent choice of formant frequencies that were represented by the lines in Fig. 11.

They imply that the sound level of the vowels increases enormously in some cases. Figure 16 shows the gain in sound level attained by means of the pitch-dependent choice of formant frequencies that was shown in Fig. 12. The gain is seen to amount to no less than 30 dB in some cases. This is a truly huge increase in sound level that the singer gains by sheer resonance.

Choral Singing

An often discussed question is to what extent choral singing requires the same vocal technique as solo singing. Choir directors tend to maintain that there are no important differences, while many singing teachers see huge differences.

As the singer's formant apparently serves the purpose of helping the individual singer's voice to be heard through a loud orchestral accompaniment, it can be hypothesized that the singer's formant is not indicated in choral singing. This hypothesis was supported by experiments in which male singers, experienced in both choral and soloistic performance, were asked to sing in a choral and in a soloistic framework (3). For solo singing, they heard through earphones the piano accompaniment of a solo song that they were to sing. Similarly, for choir singing, they heard the sound of a choir they were asked to join. As shown in Fig. 17A, the subjects had a singer's formant that was more prominent in solo than in choir singing, while the lowest spectrum partials, below the first formant, were weaker in solo sing-

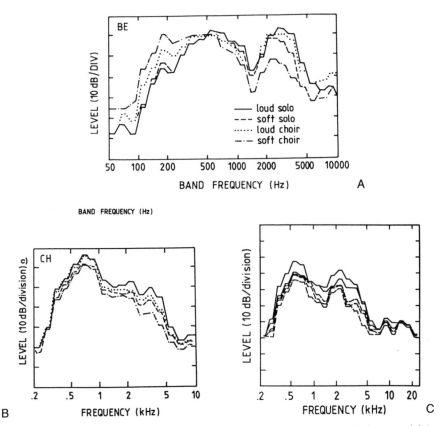

FIG. 17. Long-term-average spectra of male (**A**) and female (**B**) singers singing as soloists and as members of a choir. In **A** and **B** *solid, dashed, dotted,* and *chain-dashed* lines pertain to loud and soft solo, and loud and soft choral singing, respectively. In **C**, the *solid curves* represent the spectra of two opera sopranos of international fame and the *dashed curves* pertain to sopranos who sang professionally both as soloists and as choral singers.

ing. The higher level of the singer's formant in soloistic singing was associated with a denser clustering of the third, fourth, and fifth formant frequencies. Those subjects, unlike average choral singers, were also excellent solo singers. It can be assumed that the differences between soloistic and choral singing are mostly greater than was revealed by this experiment.

The corresponding experiment was also performed with soprano subjects (4). Disregarding the fact that it seems inadequate to speak of a singer's formant in soprano singing, the result was similar, as can be seen in Fig. 17B; the mean spectrum level at 2 to 3 kHz was clearly higher when the singers sang in a solo mode. This suggests that even female solo singers profit from high levels of the higher spectrum partials. This assumption was further supported by the fact that two opera sopranos of world fame were found to sing with a clearly higher level of the partials in the 2 to 4 kHz band than the singers who worked both as choral and solo singers (Fig. 17C). These measurements seem to indicate that solo and choral singing differ slightly with respect to the vocal technique.

Overtone Singing

In some music cultures, a very special type of singing is practiced where the voice pitch remains constant, as in a drone, while the musical interest is caught by the sounding of high overtones. Figure 18 shows an example of a vowel spectrum produced in this type of singing. The pitch perceived in these cases corresponded to the sixth and seventh partial, or a tone two octaves plus a fifth or a seventh above the fundamental. In view of the spectrum, this is not an unexpected finding. These partials are quite outstanding in the spectrum.

The vocal technique behind such spectra seems based on formant tuning. The singers tune the second and third formants so that both are quite close to the partial to be enhanced. The other formants are carefully tuned so as to avoid enhancing any of the other partials. As a result, one single partial becomes much stronger than the others, so that its pitch stands out of the timbral percept. The articulatory tools used seem to be tongue shape and lip opening in the first place. The tongue tip is often raised, while the tongue body is pulled anteriorly or posteriorly. In addition, the voice source char-

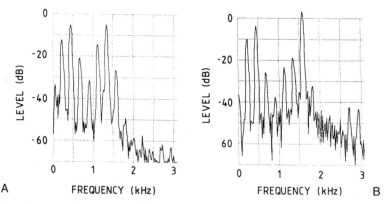

FIG. 18. Vowel spectrum produced in two cases of overtone singing performed by one of the members of The Harmonic Choir. In **A**, the sixth harmonic partial was perceived as an extra tone in the spectrum, two octaves plus a fifth above the fundamental. In **B**, the seventh harmonic partial was perceived as an extra tone, two octaves plus a seventh above the fundamental.

acteristics seem to be adjusted so that the fundamental is suppressed, presumably by shifting the type of phonation toward pressed phonation.

A more modest form of overtone singing is rather simple to practice and learn. The point is to keep the fundamental constant at a rather high frequency, say, 300 Hz, and then to vary articulation while changing the tongue shape and lip opening rhythmically in several steps between the /u:/ and the /i:/ positions. If the rhythmical pattern is repeated, the ear will soon catch individual overtones. Then, it is rather easy to moderate articulation so as to enhance the effect.

HEAD RESONANCE

Above, we have discussed several examples of the enormous significance of resonance in singing. Thereby, the only type of resonance dealt with has been the formants, the resonances of the vocal tract. No mention has been made of face or skull resonances. There is no doubt, however, that the voice sets up forceful vibrations in the structures limiting the voice organ, such as the chest wall, the throat, the face, and the skull. However, these vibrations are much too feeble to compete with the sound radiation from the open mouth. In other words, such vibrations do not contribute acoustically to the formation of vowel sounds. This is not to say that they cannot be used as a sign of a properly used voice organ.

CONCLUSIONS

The vocal tract resonances, called formants, are of paramount significance to voice and vowel quality. The two lowest formants decide what the vowel quality is going to be. The higher formants determine much of the personal voice characteristics, including voice classification. In male singers, the third, fourth, and fifth formants constitute the singer's formant, which helps the singer's voice to be heard through a loud accompaniment. In female high-pitched singing, the two first formants are tuned so that they optimally match the pitch frequency, thereby increasing the loudness of the voice considerably. It is also possible to play small articulatory games with formants and have them "show" individual partials to the listener.

However, the great relevance of vocal tract resonance to singing should not conceal the fact that there are other factors of major importance, too. Thus, the voice source, reflecting the chopped airstream through the vibrating glottis, is as decisive to voice quality as are the formants. On the one hand, the resulting great variability, of course, complicates the work of both singers and singing teachers. There are a great number of control parameters that the singer needs to bring under proper control. On the other hand, the rewards are great. The abundant timbre variability that may result certainly provides the singer with one of the potentially best musical instruments.

REFERENCES

1. Sundberg J. *The Science of the Singing Voice.* DeKalb, Illinois: North Ill. Univ. Press, 1987.
2. Sundberg J. Articulatory interpretation of the "singing formant." *JASA* 1974;55:838–844.
3. Rossing TD, Sundberg J, Ternstrom S. Acoustic comparison of voice use in solo and choir singing. *JASA* 1986;79:1975–1981.
4. Rossing TD, Sundberg J, Ternstrom S. Acoustic comparison of soprano solo and choir singing. *JASA* 1987;82:830–836.
5. Fant G. *Acoustic theory of speech production.* The Hague: Mouton, 1968.
6. Gramming P, Sundberg J, Ternstrom S, et al. Relationship between changes in voice pitch and loudness. *J Voice* 1988;2(2):118–126.
7. Cleveland T, Sundberg J. Acoustic analysis of three male voices of different quality. In: Askenfelt, A, Felicetti S, Jansson E, Sundberg J, eds. *Proceedings of Stockholm Music Acoustics Conference, (SMAC 83) (no. 1).* Stockholm: Royal Swedish Academy of Music, 1983;143–156.

Professional Voice: The Science and Art of Clinical Care, Robert T. Sataloff.
Raven Press, Ltd., New York © 1991.

5

Patient History

Robert T. Sataloff

Department of Otolaryngology, Thomas Jefferson University,
Philadelphia, Pennsylvania

This chapter outlines the historical information collected by a physician in order to adequately evaluate and diagnose a professional voice user with vocal complaints. The chapter discusses primarily singers. Their vocal demands and astute self-analysis in many ways render them the most illustrative voice patients. The principles illustrated in assessing singers are applicable to other professional voice users, although peculiar demands of each voice-dependent professional must be understood and investigated, as discussed in Chapter 6. Although this chapter is directed toward otolaryngologists, the same historical inquiry is appropriate for speech-language pathologists, singing teachers, or voice coaches as they begin work with each new voice professional. This chapter also includes an overview and preliminary discussion of many of the laryngeal and systemic conditions associated with voice dysfunction. Most of them are discussed at greater length in subsequent chapters.

Extensive historical background is necessary for thorough evaluation of the singing voice, and the otolaryngologist who sees singers only occasionally cannot reasonably be expected to remember all the pertinent questions. Although some laryngologists feel that a lengthy inquisition is helpful in establishing rapport with professional singers, many of us who see a substantial number of singers per day within a busy practice need a thorough, but less time-consuming, alternative. A history questionnaire for professional singers can be extremely helpful in documenting all the necessary information, in helping the singer sort out and articulate his problems, and in saving the clinician time writing. During the past few years, the author has developed a questionnaire (1) that has proven helpful (Appendix IIA). The singer is asked to complete the form in the waiting room before seeing the doctor. An alternate questionnaire is used for professional voice users who are not singers (also Appendix IIB).

No history questionnaire is a substitute for direct, penetrating questioning by the physician. However, the direction of most useful inquiry can be determined from a glance at the questionnaire. Obviating the need for extensive writing permits the physician greater eye contact with his/her patient and facilitates rapid establishment of the close rapport and confidence that are so important in treating professional singers. The physician is also able to supplement his/her initial impressions and historical information from the questionnaire with seemingly leisurely conversation during the physical examination. The use of the historical questionnaire has added substantially to the efficiency, consistent thoroughness, and ease of managing these delightful, but often complex, patients.

AGE

Serious vocal endeavor may start in childhood and endure throughout a lifetime. As the vocal mechanism undergoes normal maturation, the voice changes. The optimum time to begin serious vocal training is controversial. For many years, most people advocated delay of vocal training and serious singing until near puberty in the female and after puberty and voice stabilization in the male. However, in a child with earnest vocal aspirations and potential, it is reasonable to start specialized training early in childhood. Initial instruction should teach the child to vocalize without strain and avoid all forms of voice abuse. It should not permit premature indulgence in operatic bravado. Most experts agree that singing during puberty should be minimized or avoided altogether, particularly by the male. Recent studies indicating the contrary are highly controversial. Voice maturation may occur at any age from the early teenage period to the fourth decade of life. The dangerous tendency for young singers to attempt to sound older than their vocal years frequently causes vocal dysfunction.

All components of voice production are subject to normal aging, as discussed in Chapter 9. Abdominal and general muscular tone frequently decrease, lungs lose elasticity, the thorax loses its distensibility, the mucosa of the vocal tract atrophies, mucous secretions change character, nerve endings are reduced in number, and psychoneurologic functions differ. Moreover, the larynx itself loses muscle tone and bulk and may show depletion of submucosal ground substance in the vocal folds. The laryngeal cartilages ossify, and the joints may become arthritic and stiff. The hormonal environment is altered. Vocal range, intensity, and quality all may be modified. Vocal fold atrophy may be the most striking alteration. The clinical effects of aging seem more pronounced in female singers, although vocal fold histologic changes may be more prominent in males. Excellent male singers occasionally extend their careers into their 70s or beyond (2, 3). However, some degree of breathiness, decreased range, and other evidence of aging should be expected in elderly voices.

COMPLAINTS

Careful questioning as to the onset of vocal problems is needed to separate acute from chronic dysfunction. Often an upper respiratory tract infection will bring a singer to the physician's office, but penetrating inquiry may reveal a chronic vocal problem that is the singer's real concern. It is important to identify acute and chronic problems before beginning therapy so that both patient and physician may have realistic expectations and optimum therapeutic selection. The specific nature of the vocal complaint can provide a great deal of information. Just as dizzy patients rarely walk into the physician's office complaining of "rotary vertigo," singers may be unable to articulate their symptoms without guidance. They may use the term "hoarseness" to describe a variety of conditions that the physician must separate. Hoarseness is a coarse or scratchy sound most often associated with abnormalities of the leading edge of the vocal folds such as laryngitis or mass lesions. Breathiness is a vocal quality characterized by excessive loss of air during vocalization. In some cases, it is due to improper technique. However, any condition that prevents full approximation of the vocal cords can be responsible. Such causes include vocal cord paralysis, a mass lesion separating the leading edges of the vocal cords, arthritis of the cricoarytenoid joint, arytenoid dislocation, unilateral scarring of the vibratory margin, and senile vocal cord atrophy. Fatigue of the voice is inability to continue to sing for extended periods without change in vocal quality. The voice may fatigue by becoming hoarse, losing range, changing timbre, breaking into different registers, or by other uncontrolled aberrations. A well-trained singer should be able to sing for several hours without developing vocal fatigue. Fatigue is often caused by misuse of abdominal and neck musculature or "oversinging," singing too loudly too long. Vocal fatigue may be a sign of general tiredness or serious illnesses such as myasthenia gravis.

Volume disturbance may manifest as inability to sing loudly or inability to sing softly. Each voice has its own dynamic range. Within the course of training, singers learn to sing more loudly by singing more efficiently. They also learn to sing softly, a more difficult task, through years of laborious practice. Most volume problems are secondary to intrinsic limitations of the voice or technical errors in singing, although hormonal changes, aging, and neurologic disease are other causes. Superior laryngeal nerve paralysis will impair the ability to sing loudly. This is a frequently unrecognized consequence of herpes infection (K. Adour, *personal communication*) (such as "cold sores") and may be precipitated by an upper respiratory tract infection. Most singers require only about 10 min to half an hour to "warm up the voice." Prolonged warm-up time, especially in the morning, is most often caused by reflux laryngitis. Tickling or choking during singing is associated with laryngitis or voice abuse. Often a symptom of pathology of the vocal fold's leading edge, it should contraindicate singing until vocal cord examination. Pain while singing can indicate vocal cord lesions, laryngeal joint arthritis, infection, or gastric acid irritation of the arytenoids; but it is much more commonly caused by voice abuse with excessive muscular activity in the neck rather than acute pathology on the leading edge of a vocal cord, and it does not require immediate cessation of singing pending medical examination.

DATE OF NEXT IMPORTANT PERFORMANCE

If a singer seeks treatment at the end of his/her busy season and has no pressing engagements, management of the voice problem should be relatively conservative and designed to assure long-term protection of the larynx, the most delicate part of the vocal mechanism. However, the physician and patient rarely have this luxury. Most often, the singer needs treatment within a week of an important engagement, and sometimes within less than a day. Younger singers fall ill shortly before performances, not due to hypochondria or coincidence, but rather from the immense physical and emotional stress of the pre-performance period. The singer is frequently working harder and singing longer hours than usual. Moreover, he/she may be under particular pressure to learn new material and to perform well for a new audience. Furthermore, he/she may be sleeping less than usual because of additional time rehearsing or because of the discomforts of a strange city. Seasoned professionals make their livings by performing regularly, sometimes several times a week. Consequently, *any* time they get sick is likely to precede a performance. Caring for voice complaints in these situations requires highly skilled judgment and bold management.

PROFESSIONAL SINGING STATUS AND GOALS

In order to choose a treatment program, the physician must understand the importance of the singer's voice in his/her long-term career plans, the importance of the upcoming concert, and the consequences of canceling the concert. Injudicious prescription of voice rest can be almost as damaging to a vocal career as can ill-advised performance. Although a singer's voice is his/her most important commodity, other factors distinguish the few successful artists from the multitude of less successful singers with equally good voices. These include musicianship, reliability, and "professionalism." Canceling a concert at the last minute may seriously damage a performer's reputation. Reliability is especially critical early in a singer's career. Moreover, an expert singer often can modify his/her performance to decrease the strain on his/her voice. No singer should be allowed to perform in a manner that will permit serious injury to his/her vocal cords; but in the frequent borderline cases, the condition of the larynx must be weighed against other factors affecting the singer as an artist.

AMOUNT AND NATURE OF VOCAL TRAINING

It is important to establish how long a singer has been singing seriously, especially if his/her active performance career predates the beginning of his/her vocal training. Active amateur singers frequently develop undesirable techniques that are difficult to modify. Extensive voice use without training or premature training with inappropriate repertoire may underlie persistent vocal difficulties later in life. The number of years a singer has been training may be a fair index of vocal proficiency. A person who has studied voice for a year or two is somewhat more apt to have gross technical difficulties than is someone who has been studying for 20 years. However, if training has been intermittent or discontinued for some time, technical problems are common. In addition, methods vary among voice teachers. Hence, a student who has had many teachers commonly has numerous technical insecurities or deficiencies responsible for vocal dysfunction. This is especially true if the singer has changed to a new teacher within the preceding year. The physician must be careful not to criticize the patient's current voice teacher in such circumstances. It often takes years of expert instruction to correct bad habits.

Everyone speaks more often than he/she sings, yet most singers report little speech instruction. Even if a singer uses his/her voice flawlessly while practicing and performing, voice abuse at other times may result in damage that affects singing.

TYPE OF SINGING AND ENVIRONMENT

The "Lombard effect" is the tendency to increase vocal intensity in response to increased background noise. A well-trained singer learns to compensate for this tendency and to avoid singing at unsafe volumes. Singers of classical music usually have such training and frequently perform with only a piano where the balance can be controlled well. However, singers performing in large halls, with orchestras, or in operas early in their careers tend to oversing and strain their voices.

Similar problems occur during outdoor concerts because of the lack of auditory feedback. This phenomenon is seen even more among "pop" singers. Pop singers are often in a uniquely difficult position; often despite little vocal training they enjoy great artistic and financial success and endure extremely stressful demands on their time and their voices. They are required to sing in large halls not designed for musical performance, amid smoke and other environmental irritants, accompanied by extremely loud background music. One frequently neglected key to survival for these singers is the proper use of monitor speakers. These direct the sound of the singer's voice toward the singer on the stage and provide acoustical feedback. In addition to the usual investigation, it is important to determine whether the pop singer utilizes monitor speakers, and whether they are loud enough for him/her to hear.

Amateur singers are often no less serious about their music than are professionals, but generally they have less ability to compensate technically for handicaps produced by illness or other physical disability. It is rare that an amateur suffers a great loss from postponing a performance or permitting someone to sing in his stead. In most cases, the amateur singer's best interest is served through conservative management directed at long-term maintenance of good vocal health. A great many singers who seek physicians' advice are primarily choral singers. They often are enthusiastic amateurs, untrained, but dedicated to their musical recreation. They should be handled like amateur solo singers, educated specifically about the Lombard effect, and cautioned to avoid the excessive volume so common in a choral environment. One good way for a singer to monitor his/her loudness is to cup his/her hand to his/her ear. This adds about 6 dB (4) to his/her perception of his/her own voice and can be a very helpful guide in noisy surroundings. Young professional singers are often hired to augment amateur choruses. Feeling that the professional quartet has been hired to "lead" the rest of the choir, they often make the mistake of trying to accomplish that goal by singing *louder* than others in their sections. Such a singer should be advised to lead his/her section by singing each line as if he/she were a soloist giving a voice lesson to the two people standing beside him/her, and as if there were a microphone in front of him/her recording his/her performance for his/her voice teacher. This approach usually will not only preserve his/her voice but will also produce a better choral sound.

REHEARSAL

Vocal practice is as essential to the singer as exercise is to the athlete. Proper vocal practice incorporates scales and specific exercises designed to maintain and develop the vocal apparatus. Simply singing songs and giving performances without routine studious concentration on vocal technique is not adequate for the performing singer. The physician should know whether the singer practices daily, whether he/she practices at the same time daily, and how long he/she practices. Most serious singers practice for at least 1 to 2 hr per day. If a singer routinely practices in the late afternoon or evening, but frequently performs in the morning (religious services, school classes, teaching voice, choir rehearsals, etc.), one should inquire into his/her warm-up procedures preceding such performances. Singing "cold," especially at unaccustomed hours of the morning, may result in the use of minor muscular alterations to compensate for vocal insecurity due to inadequate preparation. Such crutches can result in voice dysfunction.

Similar problems may occur from instances of voice use other than formal singing. School teachers, telephone receptionists, sales people, and others who speak extensively often derive great benefit from 5 or 10 min of vocalization of scales first thing in the morning. A laryngologist should also be certain that the professional voice user "warms-down" the voice. This involves exercises at the end of a taxing practice session, performance, or day of voice use. Typical warm-down exercises include scales beginning in the middle of the vocal range and going lower with each repetition. Such warm-down exercises are equivalent to stretching down after athletic exercise (such as running), and they are quite important. Although singers rarely practice their scales too long, they frequently perform or rehearse excessively. This is especially true immediately before a major concert or audition, when physicians are most likely to see acute problems. When a singer has hoarseness and vocal fatigue and has been practicing a new role for 14 hr a day for the past 3 weeks, no simple prescription is going to solve his/her problem. However, a treatment regimen can usually be designed to carry him/her safely through his/her musical obligations.

VOICE ABUSE IN SINGING

A detailed discussion of vocal technique in singing is beyond the scope of this chapter. However, the most common technical errors involve excessive muscle tension in the tongue, neck, and larynx; inadequate abdominal support; and excessive volume. Inadequate preparation can be a devastating source of voice abuse, and may result from limited practice, limited rehearsal of a difficult piece, or limited vocal training for a given role. The latter error is tragically common. In many situations, voice teachers are to blame, especially in competitive academic environments. Both singer and teacher must resist the impulse to show off the voice in works that are either too difficult for the singer's level of training or simply not suited to the singer's voice. Singers are habitually unhappy with the limitations of their voices. At some time or another, most baritones wish they were tenors and walk around proving they can sing high Cs in "Vesti la giubba." Singers with other vocal ranges have similar fantasies. Attempts to make the voice something that it is not, or at least that it is not yet, are frequently harmful. Physicians should be aware of the difference between a singing teacher and a voice coach. Singing teachers are responsible for technical and anatomical development of the voice. Voice coaches teach repertoire and style but are not primarily responsible for voice technique. It is common for singers to have both. However, training with only a voice coach is insufficient, especially for the younger singer (classical or popular).

Abuse of the singing voice is particularly common among pop musicians who are required to sing with loud, electric instruments, in concert halls not designed for musical performance, or outdoors. The pop musician may be reluctant to receive voice training, fearing that it will change his/her vocal quality to an operatic sound. To assure compliance, the physician should correct this common misconception, explaining that good singing technique can be applied to any singing style and is designed to prevent injury.

VOICE ABUSE IN SPEAKING

Dissociation of one's speaking and singing voice is probably the most common cause of voice abuse problems in excellent singers. Too frequently, all the expert training in support, muscular control, and projection is not applied to a singer's speaking voice. Unfortunately, the resultant voice strain impacts on the singing voice as well as the speaking voice. Such damage is especially prone to occur in noisy rooms and in cars, where the background noise is deceptively high. Backstage greetings after a lengthy performance can be particularly devastating. The singer usually is exhausted and distracted. The environment is often dusty and dry, and there generally is a noisy crowd. Similar conditions prevail at postperformance parties, where smoking and alcohol worsen matters. These situations should be avoided by any singer with vocal problems and should be controlled through awareness at other times.

Three particularly destructive vocal activities are worthy of note: (a) Cheerleading requires extensive screaming under the worst possible physical and environmental circumstances; it is a highly undesirable activity for anyone considering serious vocal endeavor. This is a common conflict in younger singers, because the teen who is the high school choir soloist frequently turns out also to be student council president, yearbook editor, captain of the cheerleaders, etc; (b) Conducting, particularly choral conducting, can also be deleterious. An enthusiastic conductor, especially of an amateur group, frequently ends up singing all four parts intermittently, at volumes louder than the entire choir, for lengthy rehearsals. Conducting is a common avocation among singers, but must be done with expert technique and special precautions to avoid voice injury. Hoarseness or loss of soft voice control after conducting a rehearsal suggests voice abuse while conducting; (c) Teaching singing may also be hazardous to vocal health. It can be done safely; but it requires skill and thought. Most teachers teach seated at the piano. Late in a long, hard day, this posture is not conducive to maintenance of optimal abdominal and back support. Usually, teachers work with students continually positioned to the right or left of the keyboard. This may require the teacher to turn his/her neck at a particularly sharp angle, especially when teaching at an upright piano. Teachers also often demonstrate vocal materials in their students' vocal ranges, rather than their own, illustrating bad as well as good technique. If a singing teacher is hoarse or has neck discomfort, or his/her soft singing control deteriorates at the end of a teaching day (assuming that the teacher warms up before beginning voice lessons), voice abuse should be suspected. Helpful modifications include teaching when possible with a grand piano, sitting slightly sideways on the piano bench, or alternating student position to the right and left of the piano to facilitate better neck alignment. Retaining an accompanist so that the teacher can stand rather than teach from behind a piano as well as many other helpful modifications are possible.

GENERAL HEALTH

Singing is an athletic activity and requires good conditioning and coordinated interaction of numerous physical functions. Maladies of any part of the body may be reflected in the voice. Failure to exercise to maintain good abdominal muscle tone and respiratory endurance is particularly harmful, in that deficiencies in these areas undermine the power source of the singing voice. Singers generally will attempt to compensate for such weaknesses by using inappropriate muscle groups, particularly in the neck, that result in vocal dysfunction. Similar problems may occur in the well-conditioned vocalist in states of fatigue. These are compounded by mucosal changes that accompany excessively long hours of hard work. Such problems may be seen even in the best singers shortly before important performances in the height of the concert season.

There is a popular but untrue myth that great opera singers must be obese. However, the vivacious, gregarious personality that often distinguishes the great performer seems to be accompanied frequently by a propensity for excess, especially culinary excess. This excess is as undesirable in the vocalist as it is in most other athletic artists, and it should be avoided from the start of one's vocal career. However, attempts to effect weight reduction in an established singer are a different matter. The vocal mechanism is a finely tuned, complex instrument and is exquisitely sensitive to minor changes. Substantial fluctuations in weight frequently result in deleterious alterations of the voice, although these are usually temporary. Weight reduction programs for established singers must be monitored carefully and designed to reduce weight in small increments over long periods of time. A history of sudden recent weight change may be responsible for almost any vocal complaint. In addition, appropriate and attractive body weight is becoming particularly important in the opera world, as this formerly theater-based art form moves to television and film media.

Singers usually will volunteer information about upper respiratory tract infections and "postnasal drip," but the relevance of other maladies may not be obvious. Consequently the physician must seek out pertinent history. Acute upper respiratory tract infection causes inflammation of the mucosa, alters mucosal secretions, and makes the mucosa more vulnerable to injury. Coughing and throat-clearing are particularly traumatic vocal activities and may worsen or provoke hoarseness associated with a cold. Postnasal drip and allergy may produce the same response. Infectious sinusitis is associated with discharge and diffuse mucosal inflammation, resulting in similar problems, and may actually alter the sound of a singer's voice, especially his/her own perception of his/her voice. Futile attempts to compensate for disease of the supraglottic vocal tract in an effort to return the sound to normal frequently result in laryngeal strain. The expert singer compensates by monitoring his/her technique rather than his/her sound, or singing "by feel" rather than "by ear."

Dental disease, especially temporomandibular joint dysfunction, introduces muscle tension in the head and neck, which is transmitted to the larynx directly through the muscular attachments between the mandible and the hyoid bone and indirectly as generalized increased muscle tension. These problems often result in decreased range, vocal fatigue, and change in the quality or placement of a voice. Such tension often is accompanied by excess tongue muscle activity, especially pulling the tongue posteriorly. This hyperfunctional behavior acts through hyoid attachments to disrupt the balance between the intrinsic and extrinsic laryngeal musculature.

Reflux laryngitis is common among singers because of the high intra-abdominal pressures associated with proper support and because of life-style requirements. Singers frequently perform at night. They generally refrain from eating before performances because a full stomach compromises effective abdominal support. They compensate at postperformance gatherings late at night and then go to bed with full stomachs. Chronic arytenoid and vocal cord irritation by reflux of gastric juice may be associated with dyspepsia, but the key features are a bitter taste and halitosis upon awakening in the morning, a dry or "coated" mouth, often a scratchy sore throat or a feeling of a "lump in the throat," hoarseness, and the need for prolonged vocal warm-up. The physician must be alert to these symptoms and ask about them routinely; otherwise, the diagnosis will be missed, often because people who have had this problem for many years or a lifetime do not even realize it is abnormal.

Any condition that alters abdominal function, such as muscle spasm, constipation, or diarrhea, interferes with support and may result in a voice complaint. These symptoms may accompany infection or anxiety.

The human voice is an exquisitely sensitive messenger of emotion. Highly trained singers learn to control the effects of anxiety and other emotional stresses on their voices under ordinary circumstances. However, in some instances, this training may break down, or a performer may be inadequately prepared to control his voice under specific stressful conditions. Pre-performance anxiety, or stage fright, is the most common example; but insecurity, depression, and other emotional disturbances are also generally reflected in the voice. Anxiety reactions are mediated in part through the autonomic nervous system and result in a dry mouth; cold, clammy skin; and thick secretions. These reactions are normal, and good vocal training coupled with assurance that there is no abnormality or disease generally overcomes them. However, long-term, poorly compensated emotional stress and exogenous stress (from agents, producers, teachers, parents, etc.) may cause substantial vocal dysfunction and may result in permanent limitations of the vocal apparatus. These conditions must be diagnosed and treated expertly.

Even minor changes in the hormone environment may affect the voice adversely. Consequently, a thorough history is required, with special attention to symptoms of hypothyroidism and sex hormone dysfunction. Many of the relevant questions are listed in the singer history questionnaire (Appendix IIA and IIC), and specific considerations for singers are discussed in Chapter 16.

EXPOSURE TO IRRITANTS

Any mucosal irritant can disrupt the delicate vocal mechanism. Allergies to dust and mold are aggravated commonly during rehearsals and performances in concert halls, especially older concert halls, because of the numerous curtains, backstage trappings, and dressing room facilities that are rarely cleaned thoroughly. Nasal obstruction and erythematous conjunctivae suggest generalized mucosal irritation. The drying effects of cold air and dry heat may also affect mucosal secretions, leading to decreased lubrication and a "scratchy" voice and tickling cough. These symptoms may be minimized by nasal breathing, which allows inspired air to be filtered, warmed and humidified. Nasal breathing rather than mouth breathing whenever possible is proper vocal technique. While back stage between appearances during rehearsals, aspiration of dust and other irritants may also be controlled by wearing a protective mask such as those used by carpenters or a surgical mask that does not contain fiberglass. This is especially helpful when set construction is going on in the rehearsal area. A history of recent travel suggests other sources of direct mucosal irritation. The air in airplanes is extremely dry, and airplanes are noisy (5). Singers must be careful to avoid talking loudly and to maintain nasal breathing during air travel. Environmental changes can also be disruptive. Las Vegas is infamous for the mucosal irritation caused by its dry atmosphere and smoke-filled rooms. In fact, the resultant complex of hoarseness, vocal "tickle," and fatigue is referred to as "Las Vegas voice." A history of recent travel should also suggest "jet lag" and generalized fatigue, which may be potent detriments to good vocal function.

SMOKE

The deleterious effects of tobacco smoke on mucosa are indisputable. It causes erythema, mild edema, and generalized inflammation throughout the vocal tract. Both smoke itself and the heat of the cigarette appear to be important. Marijuana produces a particularly irritating, unfiltered smoke, which is inhaled directly, causing considerable mucosal response. Smoking should not be permitted by the serious singer. Singers who refuse to stop smoking marijuana should at least be advised to use a water pipe to cool and partially filter the smoke. Some singers are required to perform in smoke-filled environments and may suffer the same effects as the smokers themselves. In some theaters, it is possible to place fans upstage or direct the ventilation system so as to create a gentle draft toward the audience, clearing the smoke away from the stage. "Smoke eaters" installed in some theaters are also helpful.

DRUGS

A history of alcohol abuse suggests the probability of poor vocal technique. Intoxication results in incoordination and decreased awareness, which undermine vocal discipline designed to optimize and protect the voice. The effect of small amounts of alcohol is controversial. Although many experts oppose it because of its vasodilatory effect and consequent mucosal alteration, many singers do not seem to be adversely affected by small amounts of alcohol such as a glass of wine with supper on the day of a performance. However, many singers have mild sensitivities to certain wines or beers. If a singer develops nasal congestion and rhinorrhea after drinking beer, for example, he/she should be made aware that he/she probably has a mild allergy to that particular beverage and should avoid it prior to singing.

Singers frequently acquire antihistamines to help control postnasal drip or other symptoms. The drying effect of antihistamines may result in decreased vocal cord lubrication, increased throat clearing, and irritability leading to frequent coughing. Antihistamines may be helpful to some singers, but they must be used with caution.

When a singer is already taking antibiotics at the time he/she seeks the attention of a physician, it is important to find out the dose and the prescribing physician, if any, as well as whether the singer frequently treats himself/herself with inadequate courses of antibiotics. It is not uncommon for singers to develop "sore throats" shortly before performances and to start themselves on inappropriate antibiotic therapy, which they generally discontinue following their performance.

Diuretics are also popular among singers. They are often prescribed by gynecologists at the request of the singers to help deplete excess water in the premenstrual period. Unsupervised use of these drugs may result in dehydration and consequent mucosal dryness.

Hormone use, especially oral contraceptives, must be mentioned specifically during the physician's inquiry. Women frequently will not mention them routinely when asked if they are taking any medications. Vitamins are also frequently not mentioned. Most vitamin therapy seems to have little effect on the voice. However, high-dose vitamin C (5 to 6 g/day), which is used by some people to prevent upper respiratory tract infections, seems to act as a mild diuretic and may lead to dehydration and xerophonia (6).

A great many other prescribed medications have side effects that may alter the voice. These include common medications such as antihypertensives, diuretics, bronchodilators, antiviral agents, tranquilizers, aspirin, anticoagulants, antitussives (especially if they contain codeine), antipsychotic agents (major tranquilizers), selected antacid medications, antidiarrheal agents, hormones (including birth control pills), belladonna, alkaloid medications (such as scopolamine), central nervous system stimulants, central nervous system depressants, beta blockers, and others. Many of these medications affect the voice by producing dryness, some by causing tremor, and others by different mechanisms. Since many of these side effects are not widely recognized, it is worthwhile for the physician to look up the potential complications of any medications used by a professional voice patient. For further information, the reader is directed to standard pharmacology references and previous literature specifically addressing laryngeal effects of medications (7–9).

Cocaine use is increasingly common, especially among pop musicians. It can be extremely irritating to the nasal mucosa, causes marked vasoconstriction, and may alter the sensorium, resulting in decreased voice control and a tendency toward vocal abuse.

FOODS

Various foods are said to affect the voice. Traditionally, milk and ice cream are avoided by singers before performances. In many people, they seem to increase the amount and viscosity of mucosal secretions. Allergy and casein have been implicated, but no satisfactory explanation has been established. Restriction of these foods in a singer's diet before he/she sings may be helpful in some cases. Chocolate may have the same effects and should be viewed similarly. Singers should be asked about eating nuts. This is important not only because some people feel they produce effects similar to those of milk products and chocolate, but moreover because they are extremely irritating if aspirated. The irritation produced by aspiration of a small organic foreign body may be severe and impossible to correct rapidly enough to permit performance. Highly spiced foods may also be direct mucosal irritants. In addition, they seem to aggravate reflux laryngitis. Coffee and other beverages containing caffeine also aggravate gastric reflux and seem to alter secretions and necessitate frequent throat clearing in some people. In large quantities, they may also cause hyperactivity and tremor. Fad diets, especially rapid weight-reducing diets, are notorious for causing voice problems. Lemon juice and herbal teas are both felt to be beneficial to the voice. Both may act as demulcents, thinning secretions, and may very well be helpful. When inquiring about foods, it is also useful to know whether the singer eats immediately before singing. A full stomach may interfere with abdominal support or may result in reflux of gastric juice during abdominal muscle contraction.

SURGERY

A history of laryngeal surgery in a professional singer is a matter of great concern. It is important to establish exactly why the surgery was done, by whom it was done, whether intubation was necessary, and whether ancillary speech training was instituted if the lesion was associated with voice abuse (vocal nodules). If the vocal dysfunction that brought the singer to the physician's office dates from the immediate postoperative period, significant surgical trauma must be suspected.

Otolaryngologists frequently are asked about the effects of tonsillectomy on the voice. Singers may come to the physician following tonsillectomy and complain of vocal dysfunction. There is no question that removal of tonsils can alter the voice (10, 11). Tonsillectomy changes the configuration of the supraglottic vocal tract. In addition, scarring alters pharyngeal muscle function, which is trained meticulously in the professional singer. Singers must be warned that they may have permanent voice changes following tonsillectomy. These can be minimized by dissecting in the proper plane to lessen scarring. It generally takes 3 to 6 months for the singer's voice to stabilize or return to normal following surgery. As with any procedure for which general anesthesia may be needed, the anesthesiologist should be advised preoperatively that the patient is a professional singer. Intubation and extubation should be done with great care and with nonirritating plastic rather than rubber tubes.

Surgery of the neck, such as thyroidectomy, may result in permanent alterations in the vocal mechanism through scarring of the extrinsic laryngeal musculature. The strap muscles are important in maintaining laryngeal position and stability of the laryngeal skeleton and should be retracted rather than divided whenever possible. A history of recurrent or superior laryngeal nerve injury may explain a hoarse, breathy, or weak voice. However, in rare cases, a singer can compensate even for recurrent laryngeal nerve paralysis and have a nearly normal voice. Thoracic and abdominal surgery interfere with respiratory and abdominal support. Following these procedures, singing should be prohibited until pain has subsided and healing has occurred sufficiently to allow normal support. Frequently, it is advisable to institute abdominal exercises prior to resuming vocalizing. Singing without proper support is worse for the voice than not singing at all. The author requires that his singers be able to do 10 sit-ups before resuming singing following abdominal or thoracic surgery. Other surgical procedures may be significant if they necessitate intubation or if they affect the musculoskeletal system so that the singer has to change his/her stance or balance. For example, balancing on one foot after leg surgery may decrease the effectiveness of the singer's support mechanism.

A comprehensive history frequently reveals the etiology of a singer's problem even before a physical examination is performed. However, a specialized physical examination, often including objective assessment of voice function, is essential (12,13).

REFERENCES

1. Sataloff RT. Efficient history taking in professional singers. *Laryngoscope* 1984;94: 1111–1114.
2. von Leden H. Speech and hearing problems in the geriatric patient. *J Am Geriat Soc* 1977;25:422–426.
3. Ackerman R, Pfan W. Gerotologische untersuchungen zur storunepanfalligkeit der sprechstimme bei berufssprechern. *Folia Phoniat* 1974;25:95–99.
4. Schiff M. Comment at the seventh symposium on care of the professional voice. New York: The Juilliard School, June 15 and 16, 1978.
5. Feder RJ. *The professional voice and airline flight. Otolaryngol Head and Neck Surg* 1984;92(3):251–254.
6. Lawrence VL. Medical care for professional voice (panel). In: Lawrence VL, ed. *Transcripts from the annual symposium, care of the professional voice*. New York: The Voice Foundation, 1978;3:17–18.
7. Lawrence VL. Common medications with laryngeal effects. *Ear Nose Throat* 1987; 66(8):23–29.
8. Martin FG. Drugs and the voice. In: Lawrence VL, ed. *Transcripts of the twelfth symposium: care of the professional voice*. New York: The Voice Foundation, 1984;124–132.
9. Martin FG. The influence of drugs on the voice. II. In: Lawrence VL, ed. *Transcripts of the thirteenth symposium: care of the professional voice*. New York: The Voice Foundation, 1985;191–201.
10. Gould WJ, Alberti PW, Brodnitz F, Hirano M. Medical care preventive therapy (panel). In: Lawrence VL, ed. *Transcripts of the seventh annual symposium: care of the professional voice*. New York: The Voice Foundation, 1978;3:74–76.
11. Wallner LJ, Hill BJ, Waldrop W. Voice changes following adenotonsillectomy. *Laryngoscope* 1968;78:1410–1418.
12. Sataloff RT. The professional voice. II. Physical examination. *J Voice* 1987;1(2):191–201.
13. Sataloff RT. The professional singer: science and art of clinical care. *Am J Otolaryngol* 1981;2(3):251–266.

Professional Voice: The Science and Art of Clinical Care, Robert T. Sataloff. Raven Press, Ltd., New York © 1991.

6

Special Considerations Relating to Members of the Acting Profession

Bonnie N. Raphael

American Repertory Theater and Institute, Harvard University, Cambridge, Massachusetts

Individuals who act for a living are a breed unto themselves. Many of the same attributes that make them exciting and electric onstage—high levels of habitual energy; ability to bring to the surface and communicate a large range of strong emotions; high degree of sensitivity, awareness, and concentration—make them susceptible to functional voice difficulties. Moreover, so many of them are absolutely dependent on the way they sound to do their work that any interference with their vocal effectiveness is both frightening and depressing.

Physicians and speech-language pathologists who work with actors must augment their standard patient histories to include additional information important to both diagnosis and treatment. For example, many young and even older actors who have not yet achieved enough fame in their careers must supplement their income with "survival jobs"; in addition to whatever acting they are doing, many work as waiters and waitresses, taxicab drivers, receptionists, part-time teachers or babysitters, tour guides, or sales personnel. When a stage actor is a member of Actors' Equity Association (AEA), his or her work day is frequently limited to "just" eight hours per day, six days a week (not including learning lines; taking classes in singing, dancing, dialects, acting, fencing; research the actor may have to do on whatever role is being played, etc.). However, semiprofessional stage actors may be working longer hours still *and* may be holding down another job at the same time in order to make ends meet.

It is important to ascertain what kind of acting each actor is doing—proscenium stage, camera work (television and film), voiceover work (often necessitating a number of different voices in quick succession), cabaret or club work, musical acting or "straight" performance, demanding character work, etc. It is also important to know whether the actor has been trained vocally or has learned his/her craft "on the job" by watching other actors and engaging in self-directed trial and error.

When an actor describes his/her symptoms to a physician or voice therapist, he/she may do so in a deceptively beautiful voice. As a result, the physician or speech-language pathologist suspects either hypochondria or pre-opening night nervousness instead of trusting that many actors know their voices well enough and are sensitive enough to the sound and feel of their voices to be the first to know that something is wrong. In a questionnaire study conducted at the Denver Center for Performing Arts, a significant number of professional actors considered the following factors indicative of voice malfunction: general physical fatigue, throat fatigue, tightness or constriction, strain or tension, a greater awareness of the voice and the mechanism, greater effort needed to produce and sustain voice, reduction in functional pitch range, and greater difficulty in producing higher pitches (1). Such factors may not be immediately discernible to either a physician or a speech-language pathologist. In other words, the criteria according to which the voice is evaluated need to be different for the actor than for the average voice patient.

There are a number of special circumstances that make the work and life-style of actors particularly conducive to the development of voice difficulties:

1. Professional actors work hard and long. As stated earlier, a professional actor who is a member of AEA is expected to work an eight hour day during rehearsals (with one or two 10-out-of-12-hour days during technical rehearsals) and could conceivably be rehearsing his or her next show while performing a current show in the evenings. Actors who are doing workshop productions just to be seen by potential agents and producers or who are working at non-union theaters will be paid very little, if anything at all, and are typically holding down other work at the same time.

2. Professional actors often engage in a great deal of travel and in a series of temporary living arrangements. Many will be "jobbed in" for the run of a single show. Many will use their one day off per week to travel from the theater at which they are employed to a number of different places for auditions for their next job. This life-style often necessitates living in hotels or rooming houses. A number of actors who perform in touring companies will do night after night after night of single performances in different theaters as they travel by bus all day to their next destination. Temperature, relative humidity, altitude, and the like are in constant flux as a result.

3. Every actor must adjust vocal production to meet the particular needs of a number of different performance spaces. Theaters can range in size from that of a 99-seat proscenium house to a 2,500-seat stadium, or larger. Certain theaters are wonderfully designed to provide acoustics quite salutary to the

speaking voice, while others provide absolute nightmares for even the best-trained actor. Projection of the voice is a concept that involves certain absolutes and a large number of variables that are related to different playing spaces. Furthermore, many actors change rehearsal spaces, change theaters during the run of a show, or even tour extensively, making these adjustments far more frequent. Technical skill at such changes is essential to the maintenance of good vocal production.

4. Many actors have personalities that a physician or speech-language pathologist might describe as volatile or emotional. In addition to a habitual energy level that is quite high by most standards, actors do plays that involve out-of-the-ordinary life experiences. Plays are most typically written about extraordinary circumstances. Actors are trained to get in touch with their emotions, to give over to the "given circumstances" of the plays they are in (you have just discovered that your wife and both your children have been murdered . . . you have just found your lover in bed with your best friend . . . you must convince your brother not to take his own life). This ability to realize a broad range of emotions in a believable fashion is their stock in trade but may produce volatility not only onstage but offstage as well.

5. Actors often engage in onstage vocal work, which can be potentially abusive to the voice. Even basic, no-frills acting frequently necessitates vocal production that explores a wider than usual range—in terms of loudness, pitch, rhythm, and vocal quality. When one adds to this the demands of characterization (i.e., the character being played by the actor may age during the course of the play from early 20s to late 70s; the character may be suffering from any number of illnesses, disabilities, or psychological aberrations; the character may be a king or a pauper, villain or saint; the actor may be playing two or three or more characters in the same show), the term "transformational actor" or "vocal athlete" becomes aptly descriptive. In order to create the illusion of illness or duress or high emotion, the actor may modify breathing or tighten the shoulders and jaw or constrict the voice, any of which may be harmful to the vocal mechanism. In addition, within the given circumstances of the play, the actor may be required to laugh hysterically or sob or scream or shriek or cough or choke or even "die." Although trained and experienced actors may be able to do this with relative impunity, there is a price to be paid for this extraordinary behavior. Finally, many times, the actor is doing this work over a great deal of aural competition—there may be thunder in the background, a storm raging, music playing underneath spoken dialogue, the sounds of swords hitting shields or battle cries, the march of an approaching army—or even the constant hum and vibration of a theater's ventilation system. The actor must work so that his/her voice is dominant and the competition remains background to the ear of the audience. Interestingly, in the study previously cited (1), actors reported

that the three factors most consistently contributing to vocal strain and fatigue are long working hours, screaming or shouting onstage, and having to speak over high levels of background noise and/or music.

6. A series of potential occupational hazards complicate the actor's work even further. The wearing of certain costumes may restrict the actor's physical mobility so much that vocal production is affected. For example, ruffs, high collars, and heavy capes can produce difficulties, as can artificial beards and artificial moustaches, which are glued to the actor's skin. Actors may be asked to wear half or even full masks while they speak. They may be wearing makeup (e.g., artificial scars), which limits facial mobility, or prosthetic devices (to change the look of the teeth or jawline), which make projection and articulation more difficult. Similarly, the scene may call for the presence of large amounts of onstage smoke, which the actor inhales before and while he or she performs. Add to this the ever-present stage dust (in the canvas on the flats, in the curtains, and in the costumes), the ongoing use of various sprays (to hold the hair in place, to set the makeup, to keep the costumes stain and static free) and it is clear that the hazards are ongoing and plentiful.

7. There is tremendous competition in the acting profession. Actors benefit greatly from being known as cooperative, professional, willing to go the extra mile. Typically, the actor has a real desire to please—an agent, a director, a critic—that will make him or her reticent to "take it easy" during rehearsals or performances. Many fear they will lose their jobs if they refuse to scream or to smoke onstage or to shout over unfair competition. Most do not feel they are in a sufficiently secure position professionally to make demands or even requests for change to a director.

8. The actor who has achieved success or popularity has done so by selling an image very closely connected with a characteristic vocal sound. Even if he/she knows that the sound is not ideal from a physiological or an aesthetic point of view, giving it up may be perceived as career-threatening, foolhardy, or professional suicide. A physician or speech-language pathologist must be clear and communicative with actor-patients, while at the same time being extremely aware of the ramifications of any signficant vocal change in that individual.

Many actors will not seek the services of an otolaryngologist or a speech-language pathologist except as a last resort. They would rather tough it out or wait for this "cold" to pass. Consequently and unfortunately, this often means that they do not set foot in the office until the damage is already quite severe and the poor habits deeply entrenched in their behavior.

Physicians and speech-language pathologists whom actors admire most are those who know about the exigencies of the actor's life and who really care about the actor as a patient and a professional voice user. Such physicians and speech-language pathologists will take the time to come see the actor in action, on location whenever possible. Such physicians and speech-language pathologists will recommend treatment and/or therapy that makes sense to the actor and is compatible with and achievable within the restrictions of his/her professional needs and life-style. Such physicians and speech-language pathologists will communicate with actors in a voice that sounds as if they, too, value a good, healthy, projectable sound, and in language that the actor can understand and embrace rather than fear and reject. Results can be astounding and "dramatic," but only if the actor can be a willing contributor to the healing process rather than a frightened and intimidated victim of medical jargonese, inflexibility, insensitivity, or ignorance. Fortunately, with the rapid advance of voice medicine, more and more interested and specially trained physicians and speech-language pathologists are available, and improvements in quality of care are most gratifying.

REFERENCE

1. Raphael BN, Scherer RC. Repertory actors' perceptions of the voice in relation to various professional conditions. In: Lawrence V, ed. *Transcripts of the fourteenth symposium: care of the professional voice.* New York: The Voice Foundation, 1985;124–130.

Professional Voice: The Science and Art of Clinical Care, Robert T. Sataloff. Raven Press, Ltd., New York © 1991.

7

Physical Examination

Robert T. Sataloff

Department of Otolaryngology, Thomas Jefferson University, Philadelphia, Pennsylvania

As with any of our patients, examination of the professional singer must include an assessment of his/her general physical condition and a thorough ear, nose, and throat evaluation. As with any athletic activity, singing requires stamina and reasonably good physical conditioning. Any physical condition that impairs normal function of the abdominal musculature is suspect as an etiology for dysphonia. Some such conditions are obvious, such as pregnancy. However, a sprained ankle or broken leg that requires the singer to balance himself/herself in an unaccustomed posture may distract him/her from maintaining good abdominal support and may result in voice dysfunction. Any neurologic disorder that results in tremor, endocrine disturbances such as thyroid dysfunction or menopause, the aging process, and other systemic conditions also may alter the voice. The physician must remember that maladies of almost any body system may result in voice dysfunction, and he/she must remain alert to conditions outside the head and neck.

COMPLETE EAR, NOSE, AND THROAT EXAMINATION

Examination of the ears must include assessment of hearing acuity. Even a relatively slight hearing loss may result in voice strain as the singer tries to balance his/her vocal intensity with his/her associate performers'. This is especially true of hearing losses acquired after vocal training has been completed. The effect is most pronounced with sensorineural hearing loss. With conductive hearing loss, singers tend to sing more softly than appropriate rather than too loudly, and this is less harmful.

The conjunctivae should be observed routinely during an ear, nose, and throat examination for erythema suggesting allergy or irritation, for pallor suggesting anemia and sclerae for other abnormalities such as jaundice. These observations may reveal the problem reflected in the vocal tract even before the larynx is visualized.

The nose should be assessed for patency of the nasal airway, character of the nasal mucosa, and nature of secretions, if any. If a singer is unable to breathe through his/her nose because of anatomic obstruction, he/she is forced to breathe unfiltered, unhumidified air through his/her mouth. Pale gray allergic mucosa or swollen infected mucosa in the nose suggests abnormal mucosa elsewhere in the respiratory tract.

Examination of the oral cavity should include careful attention to the tonsils and lymphoid tissue in the posterior pharyngeal wall, as well as to the mucosa. Diffuse lymphoid hypertrophy associated with a complaint of "scratchy" voice and irritative cough may indicate chronic infection. The amount and viscosity of mucosal and salivary secretions should also be noted. Xerostomia (dry mouth) is particularly important. Dental examination should focus not only on oral hygiene, but also on the presence of wear facets suggestive of bruxism (tooth grinding). Bruxism is a clue to excessive tension and may be associated with dysfunction of the temporomandibular joints, which should be assessed routinely. Thinning of the enamel in a normal or underweight patient may be a clue to bulimia. However, it may also occur with excessive ingestion of lemons, which some singers eat to help thin their secretions.

Examination of the neck for masses, restriction of movement, excess muscle tension (anterior or posterior), and scars from prior neck surgery or trauma should be carried out. Particular attention should be paid to the thyroid gland. Laryngeal vertical mobility is also important. For example, tilting of the larynx due to partial fixation of strap muscles cut during previous surgery may produce voice dysfunction. So may fixation of the trachea to overlying neck skin. Examination of the cranial nerves should be included. Finding diminished fifth nerve sensation, diminished gag reflex, palatal deviation, or other mild cranial nerve deficits may indicate mild cranial polyneuropathy. Postviral infection neuropathies may involve the superior laryngeal nerve and cause weakness, fatigability, and loss of range in the singing voice. More serious neurologic disease may also be associated with such symptoms and signs. The otolaryngologist should be alert for signs such as asymmetrical palatal motion, tongue tremor at rest or on protrusion, circumoral tremor, hand tremor, other movement dysfunction, abnormal gait, mood lability, memory or concentration deficits, pathologic muscle fatigue, and other signs of neurologic abnormality.

LARYNGEAL EXAMINATION

Examination of the larynx begins when the singer enters the physician's office. The range, ease, volume, and quality of the speaking voice should be noted. Rating scales to make descriptions of the speaking voice more consistent may be helpful (1,2). The classification proposed by the Japanese

Society of Logopedics and Phoniatrics is probably the most widely used (1). It rates the voice on a scale from 0–3 as rough, breathy, strained and asthenic. 0 is normal; 1 is slight; 2 is fair; and 3 is extreme. For example, a patient's voice might be graded as R2, A1, S1, A0. Technical singing voice classification is beyond the scope of most physicians. However, the physician should at least be able to discriminate substantial differences in range and timbre, such as between bass and tenor, or alto and soprano. Although the correlation between speaking and singing voices is not perfect, a speaker with a low, comfortable bass voice who reports that he is a tenor may be misclassified and singing inappropriate roles with consequent voice strain. This judgment should be deferred to an expert, but the observation should lead the physician to make the appropriate referral. Excessive volume or obvious strain during speaking clearly indicates that voice abuse is present and may be contributing to the patient's singing complaint.

Any patient with a voice complaint should be examined by indirect laryngoscopy at least (Fig. 1). It is not possible to judge voice ranges, quality, or other vocal attributes by inspection of the vocal cords. However, the presence or absence of nodules, mass lesions, contact ulcers, hemorrhage, erythema, paralysis, arytenoid erythema (reflux), and other anatomic abnormalities must be established. Erythema of the laryngeal surface of the epiglottis is often seen in association with frequent coughing or clearing of the throat and is caused by direct trauma from the arytenoids during these maneuvers. The mirror or a laryngeal telescope often provides a better view of the posterior portion of the vocal folds than is obtained with flexible endoscopy. Stroboscopic examination adds substantially to diagnostic abilities. A stroboscopic light source can be directed at the physician's head mirror, permitting good assessment of laryngeal vibration. Such an examination frequently reveals vibratory irregularities that would be missed by routine examination. Another helpful adjunct is the operating microscope. Magnification allows visualization of small mucosal disruptions and hemorrhages that may be significant but overlooked otherwise. This technique also allows photography of the larynx with a microscope camera. Magnification may also be achieved through magnifying laryngeal mirrors or by wearing loupes. Loupes usually provide a clearer image than do most of the magnifying mirrors available. Laryngeal telescopes are also extremely useful and allow photography, magnification, stroboscopy, and excellent visualization.

Fiberoptic laryngoscopy can be performed as an office procedure and allows inspection of the vocal cords in patients whose vocal cords are difficult to visualize indirectly. In addition, it permits observation of the vocal mechanism in a more natural posture than does indirect laryngoscopy. In the hands of an experienced endoscopist, this method may provide a great deal of information about both speaking and singing voices. The combination of a fiberoptic laryngoscope with a laryngeal stroboscope may be especially useful (3). This system permits magnification, photography, and detailed inspection of vocal fold motion. More sophisticated systems that permit fiberoptic strobovideolaryngoscopy are currently available commercially. They are an invaluable asset and are used routinely by this author. The video system also provides a permanent record, permitting reassessment, comparison over time, and easy consultation with other physicians. A refinement not currently available commercially is steroscopic fiberoptic laryngoscopy, accomplished by placing a laryngoscope through each nostril, fastening the two together in the pharynx, and observing the larynx through the eyepieces (4). This method allows excellent visualization of laryngeal motion in three dimensions. However, it is practical primarily in a research setting.

Rigid endoscopy with anesthesia may be reserved for the rare patient whose vocal cords cannot be assessed adequately by other means, or for patients who need surgical procedures to remove or biopsy laryngeal lesions. In many cases, this may be done with local anesthesia, avoiding the need for intubation and the traumatic coughing and vomiting that may occur even after general anesthesia administered by mask. Coughing following general anesthesia may be minimized by using topical anesthesia in the larynx and trachea. However, topical anesthetics may act as severe mucosal irritants in a small number of patients. If a singer has had difficulty with a topical anesthetic in the office, it should be avoided in the operating room. When used, topical anesthetic should be applied at the end of the procedure. Thus, if inflammation occurs, it will not interfere with microsurgery. Postoperative duration of anesthesia is also optimized. The author has had the least difficulty with 4% xylocaine.

OBJECTIVE TESTS

Reliable, valid, objective analysis of the voice is extremely important. Although objective testing is just being developed and has not yet gained wide use in clinical practice, it is as invaluable to the laryngologist as audiometry is to the otologist. Familiarity with some of the measures currently available is extremely helpful. Selected tests and our current methods of using them are discussed in Chapter 8.

EVALUATION OF THE SINGING VOICE

The physician's evaluation of the larynx is aided greatly by examination of the singing voice. This is accomplished best by having the singer stand and sing scales either in the examining room or in the soundproof audiology booth. The physician must be careful not to exceed the limits of his/her expertise; but if voice abuse or technical error is suspected, or if a difficult judgment must be reached on whether to allow a sick singer to perform, a brief observation of the patient's singing may provide invaluable information. The singer's stance should be balanced, and his/her weight should be

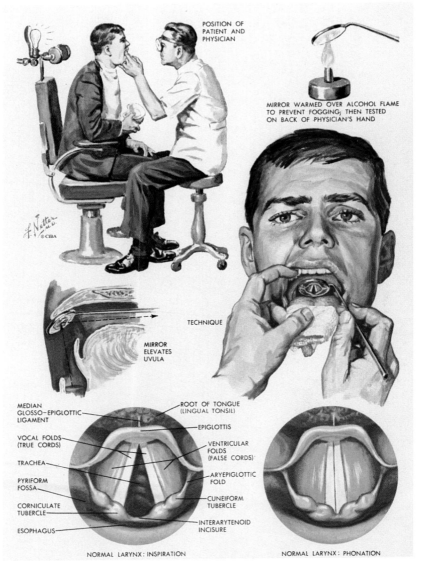

POSITION OF
PATIENT AND
PHYSICIAN

MIRROR WARMED OVER ALCOHOL FLAME
TO PREVENT FOGGING; THEN TESTED
ON BACK OF PHYSICIAN'S HAND

TECHNIQUE

MIRROR
ELEVATES
UVULA

MEDIAN
GLOSSO–EPIGLOTTIC
LIGAMENT

ROOT OF TONGUE
(LINGUAL TONSIL)

EPIGLOTTIS

VOCAL FOLDS
(TRUE CORDS)

VENTRICULAR
FOLDS
(FALSE CORDS)

TRACHEA

ARYEPIGLOTTIC
FOLD

PYRIFORM
FOSSA

CORNICULATE
TUBERCLE

CUNEIFORM
TUBERCLE

ESOPHAGUS

INTERARYTENOID
INCISURE

NORMAL LARYNX: INSPIRATION

NORMAL LARYNX: PHONATION

FIG. 1. Traditional laryngeal examination. The laryngologist uses a warmed mirror to visualize the vocal fold indirectly. The tongue is grasped between the thumb and third finger. The thumb is placed as far posteriorly as possible in the middle third of the tongue (farther back than illustrated). This grip optimizes tongue depression and rotation. If the third finger is held firmly against the lower teeth and used to privot rather than pull, discomfort along the frenulum can be avoided. The mirror is placed against the soft palate while the patient phonates on the vowel /i/. Placing the mirror during the phonation decreases the tendency to gag, and the vowel /i/ puts the larynx in the best position for visualization. From The larynx. *Clinical symposia*. New Jersey: CIBA Pharmaceutical Company, 1964;16(3): Plate V, with permission.

slightly forward. The knees should be bent slightly and the shoulders, torso, and neck should be relaxed. The singer should inhale through his/her nose. This allows filtration, warming, and humidification of inspired air. In general, the chest should be expanded, but most of the active breathing is abdominal. The chest should not rise substantially and the supraclavicular musculature should not be involved obviously in inspiration. Shoulders and neck muscles should not be tensed even with deep inspiration. Abdominal musculature should be contracted before the initiation of the tone. This may be evaluated visually or by palpation (Fig. 2). Muscles of the neck and face should be relaxed.

FIG. 2. Bimanual palpation of the support mechanism. The singer should expand posteriorly and anteriorly with inspiration. Muscles should tighten prior to onset of the sung tone.

Economy is a basic principle of all art forms. Wasted energy, motion, and muscle tension are incorrect and usually deleterious. The singer should be instructed to sing a scale (a five-note scale is usually sufficient) on the vowel /a/, beginning on any comfortable note. Technical errors are usually most obvious as contraction of muscles in the neck and chin, retraction of the lower lip, retraction of the tongue, or tightening of the muscles of mastication. The singer's mouth should be open widely but comfortably. When sing-

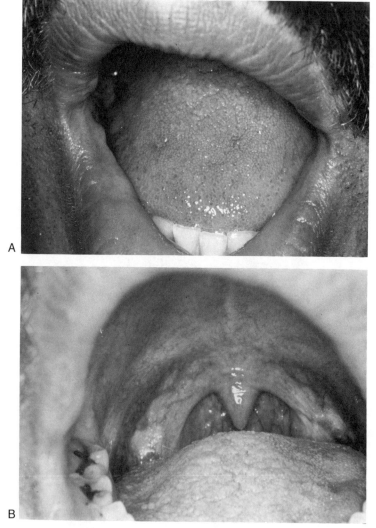

FIG. 3. Proper relaxed position of the anterior (**A**) and posterior (**B**) portions of the tongue.

ing /a/, the singer's tongue should rest in a neutral position with the tip of the tongue lying against the back of the singer's teeth. If the tongue pulls back or demonstrates obvious muscular activity as the singer performs his/ her scales, improper voice use can be confirmed on the basis of positive evidence (Fig. 3). The position of the larynx should not vary substantially with pitch changes, particularly in classical Western music. Rising of the larynx with ascending pitch is also evidence of technical dysfunction in most

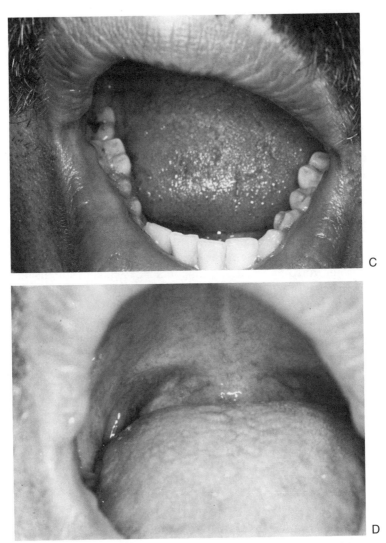

FIG. 3. *Continued.* Common improper use of the tongue pulled back from the teeth (**C**) and raised posteriorly (**D**).

instances. This examination also gives the physician an opportunity to observe any dramatic differences between the qualities and ranges of the speaking voice and the singing voice. A physical examination summary form has proven helpful in organization and documentation (5) (Appendix III).

Remembering the admonition to avoid exceeding his/her expertise, the physician who examines many singers can often glean invaluable information from a brief attempt to modify an obvious technical error. For example, a decision on whether to allow a singer with mild or moderate laryngitis to perform is often difficult. On the one hand, an expert singer has technical skills that allow him/her to sing around adverse circumstances safely. On the other hand, if a singer does not sing with correct technique and does not have the discipline to modify volume, technique, and repertoire as necessary, his/her risk of vocal injury may be increased substantially even by mild inflammation of the vocal cords. In borderline circumstances, observation of the singer's technique may help the physician greatly in making a judgment. If the singer's technique appears flawless, the physician may feel somewhat more secure in allowing him/her to proceed with performance commitments. More commonly, even good singers demonstrate technical errors when they have laryngitis.

In a vain effort to compensate for dysfunction at the vocal cord level, a singer will often modify his/her technique in the supraglottic or subglottic vocal tract. In the good singer, this usually means going from good technique to bad technique. The most common error involves pulling back the tongue and tightening strap muscles in the neck. Although this increased muscular activity gives the illusion to the singer that he/she is doing something to make his/her voice more secure, this technical maladjustment undermines the effectiveness of his/her support and increases vocal strain. The physician may ask the singer to hold the top note of his/her five-note scale; while the note is being held, he/she may simply tell the singer, "Relax your tongue," and at the same time point toward the singer's abdominal musculature. Most good singers will immediately correct to good technique. If they do, and if upcoming performances are particularly important, the physician may be able to allow performance with a reminder that meticulous technique is essential. The singer should be advised to "sing by feel rather than by ear," and to consult his/her voice teacher. He/she should also be told to conserve his/her voice, except when it is absolutely necessary for him/her to use it. If a singer is unable to correct promptly from bad technique to good technique, especially if he/she uses excessive muscle tension in the neck and ineffective abdominal support, it is generally safer not to allow performance in the presence of even mild vocal cord pathology. With increased experience and training, the laryngologist may make other observations that assist him/her in arriving at appropriate treatment recommendations for his/her singer patients. If treatment is to be instituted, at least a tape recording of the voice is advisable in most cases and essential before any surgical intervention. The author routinely uses strobovideolaryngoscopy for diagnosis and documentation in virtually all cases, as well as many objective measures discussed in subsequent chapters. Such testing is extremely helpful clinically and medico-legally.

OTHER APPROPRIATE EXAMINATION

A general physical examination should be performed whenever there is a question as to the patient's systemic health. Debilitating conditions such as mononucleosis may be noticed first by the singer as vocal fatigue. A neurologic assessment may be particularly revealing. The physician must be careful not to overlook dysarthrias and dysphonias characteristic of movement disorders and of serious neurologic disease. Dysarthria is a defect in rhythm, enunciation, and articulation usually resulting from neuromuscular impairment or weakness. It may be seen with oral deformities or illness as well. Dysphonia is an abnormality of vocalization usually originating from problems at the laryngeal level. Physicians should be familiar with the six types of dysarthria, their symptoms, and their significance (6,7). Flaccid dysarthria occurs in lower motor neuron or primary muscle disorders such as myasthenia gravis and tumors or strokes involving the brainstem nuclei. Spastic dysarthria is found in upper motor neuron disorders (pseudobulbar palsy) such as multiple strokes and cerebral palsy. Ataxic dysarthria is seen with cerebellar disease, alcohol intoxication, and multiple sclerosis. Hypokinetic dysarthria accompanies Parkinson's disease. Hypokinetic dysarthria may be spasmodic, as in the Gilles de la Tourette syndrome, or dystonic, as in chorea and cerebral palsy. Mixed dysarthria is seen in amyotrophic lateral sclerosis. The classification above actually combines dysphonic and dysarthric characteristics, but it is very useful clinically. In addition to the articulation dysfunctions described above, the clinician should be familiar with specific voice characteristics associated with various neurologic deficits. They can be elicited through careful examination including a variety of voice tasks (running speech, rapidly varying speech, sustained phonation, and other maneuvers). The voice associated with lesions producing flaccid dysfunction depend upon the site of the lesion. A flaccid paralysis from a problem located high in the vagus nerve typically produces a very breathy, whispered voice with hypernasal resonance. A lower vagus nerve lesion (recurrent laryngeal nerve, below the nodose ganglion) produces no resonance defect, but a hoarse, breathy voice, associated with diplophonia. Spastic conditions due to lesions in the cortico-bulbar region of the brain bilaterally produce hypernasal resonance and a hoarse, strained voice. Combined spastic and flaccid signs occur when bilateral cortico-bulbar lesions are present in addition to tenth nerve paralysis. This combination results in hypernasal resonance, vocal flutter, and a strained voice with hoarseness and crackling from poorly controlled secretions on the vocal folds. Cerebellar lesions associated with ataxia usually do not effect resonance, but they cause vocal tremor and irregularities. Hoarseness and breathiness are not present typically. Parkinson's disease provides the classic example of hypokinetic dysfunction. It is associated with lesions in the basal ganglia and causes a soft, breathy voice with little pitch variability, but fairly normal resonance. Basal ganglia lesions are also responsible for dystonias and choreas. Dystonic disorders are frequently accompanied by a hoarse, strained voice with vocal arrests similar to those seen in adductor spastic dysphonia; and resonance may be hypernasal or normal. In chorea, arrests are the most prominent vocal feature. Brain stem lesions produce two typical voice abnormalities. One is essential (organic) tremor. This condition involves a regular voice tremor occurring at a rate of approximately 4–7 times per second, with interruptions reminiscent of abductor or adductor spastic dysphonia. Visible tremor in the head or neck and elsewhere is common. The other is action myoclonus in which rapid, machine gun-like voice arrests can be heard on sustained vocalization. In contrast, palatopharyngeal myoclonus produces regular voice arrests so slow in rate that they may be missed in running speech without careful examination. They occur at about 1–4 times per second, and are associated with obvious myoclonic contractions of the larynx and related structures. This condition is believed to be due most commonly to lesions in the region of the dentate, red, and inferior olivary nuclei. Recognition of these disordered voice characteristics may lead the astute clinician to an early diagnosis of important and treatable neurological disease. The value of a comprehensive neurolaryngological evaluation cannot be overstated (8,9).

Even "minor" problems may produce disturbing or disabling effects in a professional performer who requires nearly perfect physical function.

REFERENCES

1. Fukazawa T, Blaugrund SM, El-Assuooty A, and Gould WJ. Acoustic Analysis of Hoarse Voice: A Preliminary Report. *J Voice* 1988;2(2):127–131.
2. Gelfer M. Perceptual Attributes of Voice: Development and Use of Rating Scales. *J Voice* 1988;2(4):320–326.
3. Gould WJ, Kojima H, Lambiase A. A technique for stroboscopic examination of the vocal folds using fiberoptics. *Arch Otolaryngol* 1979;105:285.
4. Fujimura O. Stereo-fiberoptic laryngeal observation. *J Acoust Soc Am* 1987;65(Feb): 70–72.
5. Sataloff RT. The professional voice. II. Physical examination. *J Voice* 1987;1(2):191–201.
6. Darley F, et al. Differential diagnosis of patterns of dysarthria. *J Speech Hearing Res* 1969;12:246–249.
7. Darley F, et al. Clusters of deviant speech dimensions in the dysarthrias. *J Speech Hearing Res* 1969;12:462–496.
8. Rosenfeld DB. Neurolaryngology. *Ear, Nose Throat J* 1987;66(8):323–326.
9. Aronson AE. *Clinical Voice Disorders,* 2nd edition. Thieme Inc., New York, 1985;77–126.

Professional Voice: The Science and Art
of Clinical Care, Robert T. Sataloff.
Raven Press, Ltd., New York © 1991.

8

The Clinical Voice Laboratory

*Robert T. Sataloff, *Joseph R. Spiegel, **Linda M. Carroll,
**Kathe S. Darby, **Mary Hawkshaw, **Rhonda K. Rulnick

*Thomas Jefferson University, Philadelphia, Pennsylvania; **American Institute
of Voice and Ear Research, Philadelphia, Pennsylvania

A battery of tests that allows reliable, valid, objective assessment of subtle changes in voice function, a "meter of the voice," is needed. Because convenient instrumentation is still being developed, appropriate equipment is not yet in routine use by many otolaryngologists. Nevertheless, a rapidly increasing number of institutions and private offices are developing clinical voice laboratories. Such sophistication is necessary not only to treat professional voice users, but also in nonprofessional voice patients to assess the results of laryngeal surgery, treatments for spasmodic dysphonia and other conditions, and to help diaganose the many systemic diseases associated with voice change. The otolaryngologic community has recognized in the past several years that reporting that a patient's "voice is better" without objective measures is as unsatisfactory as reporting that a patient's "hearing is better" without an audiogram. Nevertheless, the otolaryngologist who wishes to establish a state-of-the-art voice laboratory is hard pressed to know how to start.

Our clinical voice laboratory includes an ever changing list of instrumentation, but it has been in constant use and evolution for nearly a decade. Colleagues frequently request a written description of our system of patient care, as well as a list of the instrumentation we use. This chapter is written to fill that request; however, it is presented with important reservations, which the reader is urged to bear in mind. First, we have not solved the problem of developing an ideal voice laboratory. We are constantly involved in experimentation to assess the validity and reliability of the equipment we use and to explore new and better ways to accomplish desired tasks. Consequently, by the time this book is printed, certain details will undoubtedly be obsolete. Second, this chapter should not be misconstrued as a commercial endorsement for any specific manufacturer. In some cases, at the time of writing, certain companies produce equipment that is clearly superior to their competitors. However, in this rapidly changing area of technology, competing companies are likely to produce even better equipment soon. The reader is encouraged to investigate the latest developments before purchasing equipment. In addition, some of the equipment that we use is selected on the basis of personal preference, rather than unequivocal advantage. In our hands, the equipment described works well. In many cases, we have supplied manufacturers' names and model numbers for the convenience of colleagues trying to generate an equipment list as a starting point toward the development of a voice laboratory.

PURPOSES OF A CLINICAL VOICE LABORATORY

During the past 20 years, there have been substantial improvements in medical care of voice patients. Nevertheless, this new subspecialty is in a period of rapid evolution, and much remains to be learned. Although voice laboratories can be designed exclusively for clinical diagnosis, or exclusively for basic research, we believe that a good clinical voice laboratory serves both functions. At present, some laboratory procedures clearly provide invaluable diagnostic information that cannot be obtained easily in any other way (e.g., strobovideolaryngoscopy and pulmonary function testing). Other measures are somewhat helpful diagnostically and are particularly useful for following and documenting the results of treatment (e.g., laryngeal airflow and some acoustic analyses). The value of other tests remains to be determined. In structuring our clinical voice laboratory and protocols, we have attempted not only to optimize patient diagnosis and treatment at present, but also to gather research data that will allow development of better technology and even more sophisticated patient care in the future.

As valuable as they are, voice laboratories are still somewhat cumbersome. We undoubtedly gather more information than we need. However, in this way, we hope to be able to determine which information is most valuable, reliable, and clinically important. For example, day-to-day intrasubject variability studies are in progress for several of the measures discussed below, while the value of others has been established. Still other measures have been found not useful and deleted from our protocol. Eventually, this combination of clinical and research analysis should lead to the development of a simple, less time-consuming, less expensive clinical voice laboratory that will be as valuable to the general otolaryngologist as an audiometer.

EXAMINATION SEQUENCE

Ideally, the clinical voice laboratory team should include a laryngologist, speech-language pathologist, singing teacher, nurse, and voice scientist. Daily clinical use of the voice laboratory is understood best when viewed in the context of total voice-patient management. When a patient with a voice complaint enters our office, the patient is asked to complete a specialized history questionnaire. If the patient is not seen emergently, the questionnaire has been mailed to the patient and completed in advance of the visit. Separate questionnaires are used for singers and nonsingers (Appendices IIA and IIB). In most cases, the patient proceeds from the waiting room to the physician's examination room. We have tried other systems, such as having the patient examined first by another member of the voice care team, but alternate approaches have not been satisfactory in our hands.

The laryngologist reviews the professional voice user questionnaire, supplements it with a complete history, and performs a physical examination, as described in previous publications (1). At this point, the larynx is visualized with a mirror using continuous light. Generally, this is done using a head mirror. However, we have recently begun evaluating a Keeler video headlight. This device provides excellent light and visualization, even though the light source is centered over the bridge of the nose rather than being concentric with the line of sight. The video headlight permits easy, excellent video documentation of nasal and oral findings, mouth and tongue movement during speech and singing, and the indirect laryngeal image. It is also extremely valuable as a teaching aid for patients, residents, and visitors. Two monitors are used, one behind the patient and one behind the physician. These monitors allow the patient and other observers to see clearly whatever the examining laryngologist sees. Showing intranasal, oral, and hypopharyngeal lesions to patients in this manner facilitates explanations of the physician's findings and is especially helpful when abnormalities requiring surgery are encountered. In addition, clinical findings can be easily transferred to the chart through use of a video printer discussed below. Although we have worked with the Keeler video headlight for only a short period of time and minor manufacturer's modifications are necessary for otolaryngologic use, the equipment looks most promising.

The physician also performs a limited evaluation of the speaking voice and singing voice, which is recorded on a laryngeal examination form (1) (Appendix III). When indicated, strobovideolaryngoscopy is performed next. If the patient appears to require topical anesthetic, it is applied in the physician's examination room. This determination is made during laryngeal mirror examination. The patient is then escorted to the special procedures room by a nurse, speech-language pathologist, or singing teacher and is prepared for examination. Before the patient enters the special procedure room, the patient's name is entered into the video character generator and the tape is cued to the proper position. After being brought into the room, the patient is seated comfortably, and the electroglottography leads and laryngeal microphone are positioned. Proper function of all three cameras (larynx, face, EGG) and other equipment is confirmed. During this brief interval, the team member with the voice patient explains the procedure again, allays any patient concerns or fears, and has an opportunity to observe behavior or gather information that may not have been volunteered in the physician's presence. The laryngologist then proceeds to the special procedure room and performs the strobovideolaryngoscopy with at least one other member of the team present. Ideally, the speech-language pathologist and singing teacher who will be involved in the patient's treatment are both present. We have found it helpful to use a small room for strobovideolaryngoscopy. A room 10′ × 8′ is more than sufficient (Fig. 1). This small size allows the physician and assistant (usually the nurse clinician) to maintain contact with the patient and still have easy access to all equipment during the procedure. While larger rooms are more elegant, we have found a small room easier to work

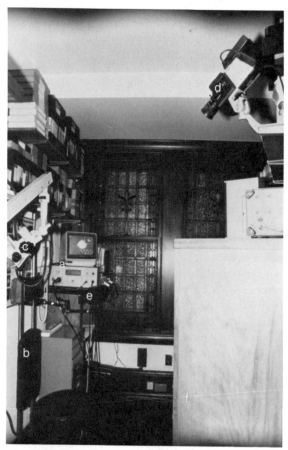

A

FIG. 1. A: Special procedures room containing a stroboscope and monitor (a), examination chair (b), specially modified microscope (c), camera for facial photography (d), endoscopic camera (e), and cabinet housing electronic equipment (f).

in. In addition, the room must be quiet enough so that no extraneous noises are picked up by the recording microphone.

Following strobovideolaryngoscopy, the physician provides the voice team with his preliminary impressions and assures the other team members that it is medically safe to proceed with the rest of the examination (some of which is vocally stressful). In selected instances, it is also helpful to present these preliminary impressions to the patient while reviewing the strobovideolaryngoscopy tape. When the physician's examination has been completed, the evaluation is continued by the speech-language pathologist, voice technologist, or singing specialist.

The next step is objective voice analysis. This is performed in a separate room that should be at least 10' × 10' in size (Fig. 2). When possible, a larger room is preferable. The room should be very quiet or should incorporate a soundproof booth. The voice laboratory includes the equipment for measures of respiratory function, phonatory function, and acoustic analysis. It is essential that this be separate from the strobovideolaryngoscopy room, speech-language pathology treatment rooms (Fig. 3), and singing voice studios (Fig. 4). Otherwise, it will interrupt patient flow and interfere with efficient treatment. Following objective voice analysis, the patient undergoes a 1.5-hr evaluation by the speech-language pathologist, and a 1-hr evaluation

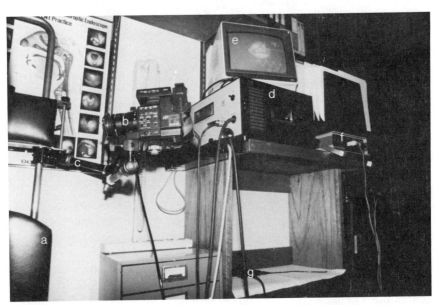

B

FIG. 1. *Continued.* **B:** Closer view of the examining area showing a portion of the examining chair (a), the camera for endoscopy (b), suspended on a magic arm (c), a Bruel & Kjaer stroboscope (d), the monitor viewed by the physician (e), the laryngograph (f), and an Olympus ENFP-2 flexible fiberoptic laryngoscope (g). **FIG. 1.** *Continues.*

C

FIG. 1. *Continued.* **C:** Contents of the electronic storage cabinet facing the examining chair, as pictured in Fig. 1A (g). This figure shows the overall layout for orientation. Equipment is as specified in Figs. 1D and E.

by the singing specialist. The findings of the voice laboratory are documented in two reports. There is a separate report for strobovideolaryngoscopy. Other objective voice analysis is organized in a clinical voice laboratory report. Sample documents are included in Appendix IV. At the conclusion of the examination process, the team members share their findings and the laryngologist provides the patient with a comprehensive, specific treatment plan. A summary report is sent to the referring physician or other voice specialist, including copies of all internal reports and a videotape of the strobovideolaryngoscopy.

FIG. 1. *Continued.* **D:** Equipment directly opposite the examining chair and within easy reach of the endoscopist includes a super VHS recorder (a), multivision (b), editor/controller that links the super VHS recorder with copying decks (c), power sources for cameras (d), special effects generator (e), monitor for the super VHS master deck (f), and monitor for the output of the editing deck (g). These monitors face the patient and may be switched off without disturbing the rest of the system. **FIG. 1.** *Continues.*

Objective Voice Measures

Measure of vocal function may be divided into six categories. (a) Assessment of vibratory function gives us information about the leading edge of the vocal fold. (b) Aerodynamic measures reveal the ability of the lungs and abdomen to provide power to the voice, and the ability of the glottis to release air efficiently. (c) Measures of phonatory function quantify the limits

FIG. 1. *Continued.* **E:** The right section of the electronic equipment cabinet contains the primary copy deck in the editing system, which is linked to the master tape recorder through the controller (a), a second VHS recorder so that the two copies can be made simultaneously (b), a ¾-inch video for copying (lower shelf, not shown), a black and white video printer (c), a color video printer (d), a video switcher (e), a video pointer (f), a character generator (g), two video switchers for multiple camera inputs (h), a hand-held video camera (i) and an oscilloscope (j), a Genlock camera to record the oscilloscope display of the epiglottograph (EGG) (k), the wall mounted camera for facial video (l), and a laryngeal model used for patient education (m).

of vocal frequency, intensity, and duration. (d) Acoustic analysis detects and documents numerous subtleties in the vocal signal. (e) Laryngeal electromyography may confirm the presence or absence of appropriate neuromuscular function. (f) Psychoacoustic evaluation is difficult to quantify in a useful fashion. However, the human ear and brain are still the best equipment we have available; and we have attempted to increase the validity of our team's psychoacoustic assessments.

A

B

FIG. 2. A: The voice laboratory contains a computer work station (a), a voice analysis equipment station (b), airflow equipment (to the left, not shown, see **C**), and a Kay Elemetrics DSP Sona-Graph (c) with electroglottograph. **B:** Voice analysis equipment used routinely includes a Visi-Pitch (a), the PM 100 Pitch Analyzer (b), a Nagra tape recorder (c), a digital pulse code modulator (d), which digitizes the acoustic signal and records it along with the electroglottograph (e) onto high fidelity video tape (f). A computer (g) is essential to this system. **FIG. 2.** *Continues.*

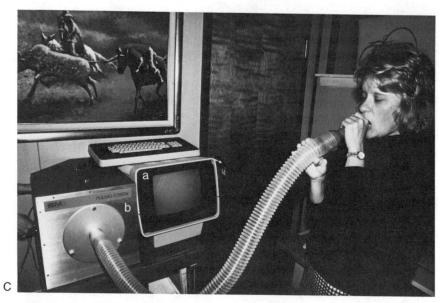

C

FIG. 2. *Continued.* **C:** Computerized pulmonary function machine (a) and spirometer (b) for airflow assessment.

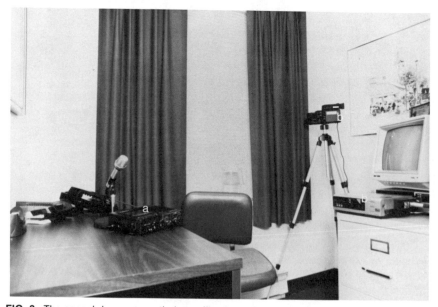

FIG. 3. The speech-language pathology office is equipped with both audio (a) and video (b) equipment.

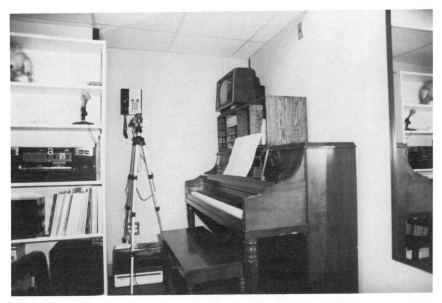

FIG. 4. The voice studio should also be equipped with audio (a) and video equipment (b), in addition to a piano. The audio and video equipment need not be fancy or expensive, but they should be utilized.

Assessment of Vibration

Integrity of the vibratory margin of the vocal fold is essential for the complex motion required to produce good vocal quality. Under continuous light, the vocal folds vibrate approximately 250 times per second while phonating at middle C. Naturally, the human eye cannot discern necessary details during such rapid motion. Assessment of the vibratory margin may be performed through high speed photography, strobovideolaryngoscopy, electroglottography, or photoglottography. Only strobovideolaryngoscopy provides the necessary clinical information in a practical fashion.

Strobovideolaryngoscopy

Strobovideolaryngoscopy is the single most important technological advance in diagnostic laryngology with the possible exception of the fiberoptic laryngoscope. Stroboscopic light allows routine, slow motion evaluation of the mucosal cover layer of the leading edge of the vocal fold. Vocal fold vibration is complex (Fig. 5). This improved physical examination permits detection of vibratory asymmetries, structural abnormalities, small masses, submucosal scars, and other conditions that are invisible under ordinary

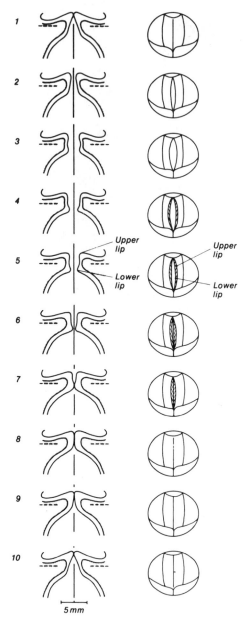

FIG. 5. Frontal view (**left**) and view from above (**right**) illustrating the normal pattern of vocal fold vibration. The vocal fold closes and opens from the inferior aspect of the vibratory margin upward. From Hirano M. *Clinical examination of the voice.* New York: Springer-Verlag, 1981;44, with permission.

light (2). For example, in a patient with a poor voice following laryngeal surgery and a "normal-looking larynx," stroboscopic light reveals adynamic segments that explain the problem even to an untrained observer (such as the patient). In addition, it also permits differentiation between cysts and nodules, allowing better treatment planning and prognostic predictions. Stroboscopy does not provide a true slow motion image, as obtained through high speed photography (Fig. 6). The stroboscope actually illuminates different points on consecutive vocal fold waves, each of which is retained on the retina for 0.2 sec. The stroboscopically lighted portions of the successive waves are visually fused. The slow motion effect is created by having the stroboscopic light desynchronized with the frequency of vocal fold vibration by approximately 2 Hz. When vocal fold vibration and the stroboscope are synchronized exactly, the vocal folds appear to stand still, rather than moving in slow motion (Fig. 7). In most instances, this approximation of slow motion provides all the clinical information necessary.

The stroboscope is also extremely sensitive in detecting changes caused by fixation from small laryngeal neoplasms in patients who are being followed for leukoplakia or following laryngeal irradiation. Coupling stroboscopic light with the video camera allows later reevaluation by the laryngologist, or by other physicians. A relatively standardized method of subjective assessment of video stroboscopic pictures is in wide clinical use (3, 4), allowing comparison of results among various physicians and investigators. Characteristics assessed include fundamental frequency, symmetry of bilateral movements, periodicity, glottal closure, amplitude, mucosal wave, the presence of nonvibrating portions, and other unusual findings (such as a tiny polyp).

Laryngeal stroboscopy is not a new technique. However, poor light limited its use for many years. Recent improvements in laryngeal stroboscopes have provided instrumentation that is practical for clinical use. When nec-

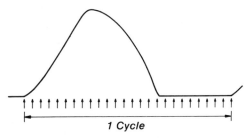

FIG. 6. The principle of ultra high speed photography. Numerous images are taken during each vibratory cycle. This technique is a true slow motion representation of each vocal fold vibration. From Hirano M. *Clinical examination of the voice.* New York: Springer-Verlag, 1981;55, with permission.

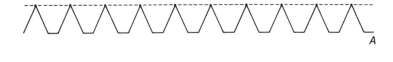

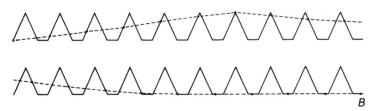

FIG. 7. The principle of stroboscopy. The stroboscopic light illuminates portions of successive cycles. The eye fuses the illuminated points into an illusion of slow motion. If the stroboscope is synchronized with vocal fold vibration (**A**), a similar point is illuminated on each successive cycle and the vocal fold appears to stand still. If slightly desynchronized (**B**), each cycle is illuminated at a slightly different point, and the slow motion effect is created. From Hirano M. *Clinical examination of the voice.* New York: Springer-Verlag, 1981;49, with permission.

essary, it can be supplemented with other techniques, as discussed below. Stroboscopic light was used initially to evaluate the larynx in 1878 (5). Since that time, many investigators have recommended the technique, and numerous equipment designs have been tried (6–99). Stroboscopy has been used much more widely in Europe and Japan than in the United States. Various shortcomings have prevented its routine inclusion in the otolaryngologist's office. Until recently, the only equipment available has been expensive and cumbersome, and it has provided insufficient illumination. In addition, there was no easy way to record the images. In the 1980s, technological improvements have resulted in stroboscopes that provide light bright enough to produce acceptable video recordings through a flexible fiberoptic nasopharyngoscope utilizing inexpensive video equipment. In the past few years, such equipment has been used routinely by several laryngologists who subspecialize in voice disorders.

Since 1985, we have used a Bruel and Kjaer Rhinolaryngoscope type 9414, with minor modifications. The instrument provides adequate light. It has been durable, and in the few instances when it has required service, the company has responded quickly and satisfactorily. Although we make an effort to test every new stroboscope that comes on the market, so far we have not found a comparable instrument. When evaluating stroboscopes, the critical aspect is light during stroboscopic examination. Consequently, the instrument should be evaluated under worst-case light conditions using a flexible fiberoptic laryngoscope with an image that fills the monitor screen. Distance from the vocal folds can be standardized reasonably well for comparative testing by maintaining a predetermined amount of epiglottis and arytenoid apex in the field. The stroboscopes should be compared with all other factors remaining the same, including the "patient." Ideally, comparisons should be done in the physician's office with his/her own equipment.

Our routine stroboscopy protocol has been described in previous publications (100). In virtually all cases, we examine patients with both an Olympus flexible ENFP-3 laryngoscope and with a rigid magnifying telescope. We are not completely satisfied with any of the laryngeal telescopes on the market. At present, we use a telescope designed by the Wolf Company. The optics are excellent, but the scope is rather large, and the angle of observation is 90° from the end of the scope, rather than 70°. It also has other design shortcomings. Consequently, there is a small percentage of patients who are difficult or impossible to examine with this telescope. Examination with the flexible nasolaryngoscope is possible in virtually all cases, and this technique provides good information about vocal habits, vocal fold motion during speech and singing, and vibratory margin characteristics under stroboscopic light in virtually every case. Examination with the telescope provides higher image quality, a larger image with better light, and occasionally reveals subtle abnormalities that are missed with the flexible laryngoscope. When use of the telescope proves impossible and visualization of the vibratory margin is inadequate with the ENFP-3, we have found the Olympus ENF-L3 helpful. This flexible nasolaryngoscope is larger. Consequently, it provides more light and a better image, but it is also less comfortable for the patient, stiffer, and slightly less maneuverable than the ENFP-3.

We use a standardized method of subjective assessment of strobovideolaryngoscopic images, as proposed by Hirano et al. (3, 4). Characteristics that are evaluated include fundamental frequency, symmetry of movements, periodicity, glottic closure, amplitude of vibration, mucosal wave, and the presence of nonvibrating portions of the vocal fold. Other unusual findings such as subglottal cysts or sulcus vocalis may also be observed. The camera stop watch signal is superimposed on the image, allowing frame-by-frame identification. In addition, objective, frame-by-frame computer analysis is possible with inexpensive computer equipment. However, at present, this technique is primarily of interest in research, and we are not using it on a routine clinical basis.

With practice, perceptual judgments of stroboscopic images provide a great deal of information. However, it is easy for the inexperienced observer to draw unwarranted conclusions because of normal variations in vibration. Vibrations depend on fundamental frequency, intensity, and vocal register

(Fig. 8). For example, failure of glottic closure occurs regularly in falsetto phonation. Consequently, it is important to note these characteristics and to examine each voice under a variety of conditions. Fundamental frequency can be influenced by various vocal fold parameters. For example, fundamental frequency is increased with increasing vocal fold tension or stiffness, increased subglottal pressure, or a shortened length of vibrating vocal fold. *Fundamental frequency* is decreased as vocal fold mass increases.

Symmetry is assessed by observing both vocal folds simultaneously. In a trained voice, they are mirror images, opening with the same lateral excursions (symmetry of amplitude) and mirror-image waves (symmetry of phase). In untrained voices, phase asymmetry is common. Clinically significant asymmetries may be due to differences between vocal folds in position, tension, elasticity, viscosity, shape, mass, or other mechanical properties.

Periodicity refers to the regularity of successive vibrations. Regular periodicity requires balanced control of expiratory force and the mechanical characteristics of the vocal folds. Irregular periodicity may be caused by inability to maintain a steady expiratory stream of air, inability to sustain steady laryngeal muscle contraction (as in neuromuscular disease), and marked differences in the mechanical properties of the vocal folds. Periodicity is assessed by locking the stroboscope in phase with vocal fold vibration. This should result in vocal folds that appear to stand still. If they move, vibration is aperiodic. Failure of *glottic closure* may be due to vocal fold paresis or paralysis, an irregular vocal fold edge, a mass (or masses) separating the vocal fold edges, stiffness of a vibratory margin, cricoarytenoid joint dysfunction, falsetto singing, psychogenic dysphonia, and other causes. It is helpful to describe failures of glottic closure more specifically. They may be complete or incomplete, consistent or intermittent, and may involve a posterior glottic chink, specific small portion of the vocal folds, or as much as the entire vocal fold.

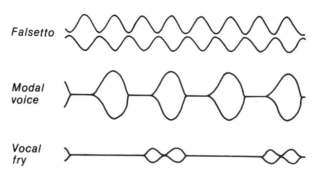

Falsetto

Modal
voice

Vocal
fry

FIG. 8. The normal vibratory pattern of vocal folds. From Hirano M. *Clinical examination of the voice.* New York: Springer-Verlag, 1981;48, with permission.

Amplitude of vibration and *mucusal wave* characteristics are assessed looking at the vocal folds one at a time. Small amplitude is associated with short vibrating segments of vocal fold, increased stiffness, increased mass, and vocal fold masses or other mechanical obstacles to vocal fold motion. Amplitude is increased by increasing subglottal pressure, such as that which occurs with loud phonation. Amplitude is not generally affected very much by soft masses such as cysts and nodules. The mucosal wave is affected by many factors. It is diminished by dryness, scar, mucosal stiffness or edema, epithelial hyperplasia, masses, dehydration, and falsetto phonation. It also varies with pitch. The mucosal wave is also increased with loud phonation (increased subglottal pressure) and altered by hypofunctional or hyperfunctional voice technique. If there is an area of stiffness on the vocal fold, this will impede the traveling mucosal wave. This situation is encountered with small scars, some mass lesions, and sulcus vocalis.

Nonvibrating segments (adynamic) are often signs of serious vocal fold injury involving scar that obliterates the complex anatomy of the lamina propria and mucosa. Adynamic segments are seen only under stroboscopic light or in high speed motion pictures. They are found typically on vocal folds that have undergone previous surgery, hemorrhage, or other trauma. Often the vocal folds look "normal" under continuous light, but the voice is hoarse and breathy. The reason is obvious when the adynamic segment is revealed under stroboscopic light. Hypodynamic segments may also occur temporarily, as seen sometimes in acute vocal fold hemorrhage with submucosal hematoma.

Our strobovideolaryngoscopy room (Fig. 1) permits routine simultaneous imaging with three cameras. The stroboscope is connected to the laryngoscope, which is coupled with a Panasonic Pro-line CCD video camera WV-F2. Unfortunately, this camera is no longer commercially available, and we are currently testing alternatives. Ideally, the camera should have at least 7 lux light sensitivity, a zoom lens, a built-in character generator with a stop watch and internal title–date capability, and a switch for boosting gain. When the gain is boosted, better images can be obtained during flexible stroboscopic examination. However, color is impaired somewhat, and the gain switch should be returned to normal during examination with the rigid telescope.

We have recently added a Toshiba CCD color camera Model No. IK-C30A. This camera has excellent light sensitivity and extremely good color reproduction. For rigid laryngoscopy (telescope), we are now using it exclusively. We tested several lenses and found that the 35-mm lens that has been recommended with it most frequently was fair for use with a telescope but unsatisfactory with the flexible nasolaryngoscope. A 15-mm lens works extremely well with the telescope and is adequate most of the time when using the flexible laryngoscope. However, there are still occasions when the zoom lens is necessary to make the image smaller and brighter. We have continued to use the Panasonic WV-F2, because we have been unable to find a zoom lens for the Toshiba that is reasonably easy to handle and does not decrease light to an unacceptable degree. The Toshiba camera also has the advantage of gen-lock capability, permitting synchronization with other equipment.

A Magnavox Novacon video camera VRA275BK01 is mounted on the wall to provide a full face image of the patient. This is displayed on the screen simultaneously with the laryngeal image. The third camera is a Panasonic TV camera WV-1500X. This camera includes gen-lock, automatic electronic focus control, and a line-locked synchronizing system. It is a black and white camera that is focused on a Leader dual trace oscilloscope LB0523. This is part of the system that permits superimposition of the electroglottographic (EGG) signal. Recalling that strobovideolaryngoscopy provides an illusion of slow motion but does not actually image every cycle, simultaneous EGG display supplies potentially valuable additional information. The stroboscope and oscilloscope are synchronized by connecting the output on the back of the stroboscope to the external trigger input of the oscilloscope, as described by Karnell (101). The three cameras are coordinated using a multivision 1.1 DVC, which permits simultaneous display of the face and laryngeal image, and a Panasonic special effects generator WJ-1600 C, which allows superimposition of the EGG wave on the other video images, as well as numerous other special effects. The cameras are fed into a JVC super VHS editing recorder BR-S810U. We have found ½-inch tapes more convenient and practical than ¾-inch tapes, and super VHS provides adequate quality for editing and copying. The super VHS deck is connected through a controller to a JVC editing recorder BR-8600U, a standard VHS deck. Between the two are a Video Data Systems titling generator T-1024 and a FOR.A video pointer VP-380, which places arrows and markers on the monitor. These devices do not affect the signal on the original super VHS recording, which we leave unaltered, but they appear on all other equipment on the system (copy tapes, video prints).

In addition to the JVC editing recorder, there is a second VHS deck that permits us to make an original video tape and two simultaneous copies during the examination (one for the patient, one for the referring doctor), a Mitsubishi black and white video printer P60-U, and a Mitsubishi color printer. There is also an unused output that can be connected easily to allow copying to other equipment (such as a Beta video recorder or 8-mm system), and a ¾-inch video machine for copying. In addition, there is a fourth camera connected to this system, a Panasonic Novacon video camera WV-3240. This camera is hand-held and used occasionally for full-body photography or other special needs. System versatility and expansion potential are increased through a Vidicraft audio-video switcher and two NECAV centers. For electroglottography, we use the laryngograph marketed by Kay Elemetrics.

As discussed below, we also have a Synchrovoice, Inc. electroglottograph in our voice laboratory. However, because of extremely unsatisfactory service on the Synchrovoice device, we cannot recommend its purchase. The laryngograph available through Kay Elemetrics has worked extremely well and is now the instrument on which we depend for electroglottography. The strobovideolaryngoscopy room is also equipped with a small keyboard to provide pitches for singers and with a Zeiss operating microscope. Both the camera for the laryngoscope and the operating microscope are equipped with C adapters to hold a laryngoscope. The adapters may be obtained through Bruel and Kjaer. A custom-made device on the microscope allows monocular magnification of the flexible fiberoptic image. This is helpful in selected cases, especially patients who will not tolerate examination with the laryngeal telescope.

Other techniques to examine vocal fold vibration are also available, but we have not found them useful enough to incorporate in our office except for electroglottography. Ultra high speed photography provides images similar to stroboscopy. In some ways, the technique is even better because it provides an image of each vibration rather than a slow motion image through optical illusion. However, high speed photography requires expensive, cumbersome equipment, delay in processing, and fairly limited examination time on each reel of film. Photo electroglottography and ultrasound glottography are generally considered less useful clinically than electroglottography. However, photoglottography gives information about the open glottis, while electroglottography documents vocal fold contact. So, combining the two techniques may be useful. We are considering the addition of photoglottography. Information about them may be found in Hirano's excellent book *Clinical Examination of the Voice* (102).

EEG uses two electrodes on the skin of the neck above the thyroid laminae. A weak, high frequency voltage is passed through the larynx from one electrode to the other. Opening and closing of the vocal cords varies the transverse electrical impedance, producing variation of the electrical current in phase with vocal fold vibration. The resultant tracing is called an electroglottogram. It traces the opening and closing of the glottis and can be correlated with stroboscopic images (103) (Fig. 9). EGG allows objective determination of the presence or absence of glottal vibrations and easy determination of the fundamental period of vibration and it is reproducible. It reflects the glottal condition more accurately during its closed phase, and quantitative interpretation of the glottal condition is probably not valid (102). EGG shows increasing promise for clinical usefulness (104). An excellent review of the interpretation of EGG signals is available in the literature (105). Valuable information can also be obtained by studying the air pulses generated by vocal fold vibrations. When the vocal folds are closed, the airstream stops. When the vocal folds open, the airstream increases, peaks, and is

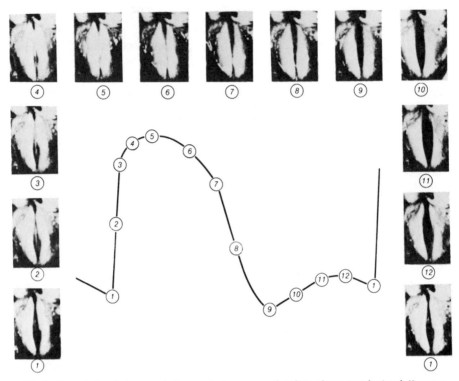

FIG. 9. Correlation between stroboscopic images and points along an electroglottogram. From Hirano M. *Clinical examination of the voice.* New York: Springer-Verlag, 1981;57, with permission; originally appearing in Lecluse, ref. 103.

terminated when the glottis closes. Plotting transglottal airflow in liters per second against time results in a graph called a *flow glottogram.*

Aerodynamic Measures

In our laboratory, we assess pulmonary function and laryngeal airflow. At present, we use an Infomed remote pulmonary function unit, which uses Knudson norms, but we are in the process of switching to new equipment that has greater flexibility. Traditional *pulmonary function testing* provides the most readily accessible measure of respiratory functions. The most common parameters measured include: (a) *tidal volume* (the volume of air that enters the lungs during inspiration and leaves during expiration in normal breathing), (b) *functional residual capacity* (the volume of air remaining in the lungs at the end of inspiration during normal breathing), which may be divided into *expiratory reserve volume* (maximal additional volume that can be exhaled) and *residual volume* (the volume of air remaining in the lungs at the end of maximal exhalation); (c) *inspiratory capacity* (the maximal volume of air that can be inhaled starting at the functional residual capacity); (d) *total lung capacity* (the volume of air in the lungs following maximal inspiration); (e) *vital capacity* (the maximal volume of air that can be exhaled from the lungs following maximal inspiration); (f) *forced vital capacity* (the rate of airflow with rapid, forceful expiration from total lung capacity to residual volume); (g) *FEV*$_1$ (the forced expiratory volume in 1 sec); (h) *FEV*$_3$ (the forced expiratory volume in 3 sec); and (i) *maximal midexpiratory flow* [the mean rate of airflow over the middle half of the forced vital capacity (between 25 and 75% of the forced vital capacity)].

Testing before and after bronchodilator therapy may help establish a diagnosis of asthma. In most established singers, routine pulmonary function testing is not helpful. However, in singers and professional speakers with problems associated with voice abuse, abnormal pulmonary function tests may confirm deficiencies in aerobic conditioning or may reveal previously unrecognized asthma. Either condition can undermine the power source of the voice and cause voice dysfunction. Testing before and after a vigorous 1-hr singing lesson can also be diagnostically revealing. Pulmonary function should not deteriorate substantially following singing. If there is a change, especially in the midexpiratory flow rates, asthma should be suspected. Even in the absence of routine pulmonary function test abnormalities, if asthma is suspected, a methacholine challenge test should be performed by a pulmonologist. Even a mild or moderate obstructive pulmonary disease may have substantial deleterious effects on the voice; and asthma may be present and clinically significant in a professional voice user even in the absence of obvious wheezing. This problem is discussed further in Chapter 11.

The *spirometer*, readily available for pulmonary function testing, can be used for measuring airflow during phonation. However, it does not allow simultaneous display of acoustic signals, and its frequency response is poor. A *pneumotachograph* consists of a laminar air resistor, a differential pressure transducer, and an amplifying and recording system. It allows measurement of airflow and simultaneous recording of other signals when coupled with a polygraph. A *hot-wire anemometer* allows determination of airflow velocity by measuring the electrical drop across the hot wire. Modern hot-wire anemometers containing electrical feedback circuitry that maintains the temperature of the hot wire provide a flat frequency response up to 1 kHz and are useful clinically (106).

The four parameters traditionally measured in analyzing the aerodynamic performance of a voice include *subglottal pressure* (P$_{sub}$), *supraglottal pressure* (P$_{sup}$), *glottal impedance*, and *volume velocity of airflow at the glottis*. These parameters and their rapid variations can be measured under laboratory circumstances. Clinically, their mean value is usually determined as follows:

$$P_{sub}\, P_{sup} = MFR \times GR$$

where MFR is the mean (root mean square) flow rate and GR is the mean (root mean square) glottal resistance.

When vocalizing the open vowel /a/, the supraglottic pressure equals the atmospheric pressure, reducing the equation to

$$P_{sub} = MFR \times GR$$

The *mean flow rate* is calculated by dividing the total volume of air used during phonation by the duration of phonation. The subject phonates at a comfortable pitch and loudness either over a determined period of time or for a maximum sutained period of phonation. *Air volume* is measured by the use of a mask fitted tightly over the face or by phonating into a mouthpiece while wearing a noseclamp. Measurements may be made using a spirometer, pneumotachograph, or hot-wire anemometer. The normal values for mean flow rate under habitual phonation, with changes in intensity or register, and under various pathologic circumstances have been determined (102). Normal values are available for both adults and children. Mean flow rate is a clinically useful parameter for vocal nodules, recurrent laryngeal nerve paralysis, spasmodic dysphonia, and other conditions.

Glottal resistance cannot be measured directly but can be calculated from the mean flow rate and mean subglottal pressure. Normal glottal resistance is 20 to 100 dyne sec/cm^5 at low and medium pitches and 150 dyne sec/cm^5 at high pitches (108). *Subglottal pressure* is less useful clinically, because it requires an invasive procedure for accurate measurement. It may be determined by tracheal puncture, transglottal catheter, or measurement through a tracheostoma using a transducer. Subglottal pressure may be approximated using an esophageal balloon. *Intratracheal pressure,* which is roughly equal to subglottal pressure, is transmitted to the balloon through the trachea. However, measured changes in the esophageal balloon are affected by intraesophageal pressure, which is dependent on lung volume. Therefore, estimates of subglottal pressure using this technique are valid only under specific, controlled circumstances. The normal values for subglottal pressure under various healthy and pathologic voice conditions have also been determined by numerous investigators (102).

The *phonation quotient* is the vital capacity divided by the maximum phonation time. It has been shown to correlate closely with maximum flow rate (106) and is a more convenient measure. Normative data determined by various authors have been published (102). The phonation quotient provides an objective measure of the effects of treatment and is particularly useful in cases of recurrent laryngeal nerve paralysis and mass lesions of the vocal folds, including nodules.

Unfortunately, the only commercially available instrument to measure airflow, frequency, and intensity simultaneously is Nagashima's phonatory function analyzer. Essentially, it consists of a hot-wire anemometer, which does not permit analysis during inspiration, a frequency meter, and an intensity meter. Because of the extraordinary cost and the equipment design, we have removed it from our voice laboratory and cannot recommend it. At present, we are using a spirometer with an X-Y strip chart recorder for analysis of airflow during sustained sounds. Airflow is measured while the patient sustains the vowel /a/. A stop watch is used to measure the time in seconds. The mean flow rate is calculated as airflow volume divided by time. As a measure of glottal efficiency, we expect in normal nonprofessional voice users a mean flow rate of approximately 100 ml/sec in males and 92 ml/sec in females (102). We evaluate these data in conjunction with s/z ratios. However, a new piece of equipment is under development, which should provide all the necessary instrumentation for comprehensive aerodynamic assessment. We hope this device will be available within the next year. Several other potentially useful techniques are also available including flow glottography using a mask and inverse filter, and modifications of body plethysmography.

Measures of Phonatory Ability

Objective measures of phonatory ability are among the easiest and most readily available for the laryngologist, helpful in treating professional vocalists with specific voice disorders, and extremely useful in assessing the results of surgical therapies. *Maximum phonation time* is measured using a stopwatch. The patient is instructed to sustain the vowel /a/ for as long as possible following deep inspiration, vocalizing at a comfortable pitch and loudness. In selected cases, frequency and intensity may be controlled using an inexpensive frequency analyzer and sound level meter. The test is repeated three times, and the greatest value is recorded. Normal values have been determined for nonprofessional voice users (102). We use normal values of approximately 34 sec for males and 26 sec for females. Normal values for professional singers will be published in the future. *Frequency range of phonation* is measured in Hertz and converted to semitones, recording the vocal range from the lowest note in the modal register (excluding vocal fry) to the highest falsetto note. *Physiological frequency range of phonation* (PFRP) disregards the quality of the voice. In nonprofessional voice users, we accept approximately 36 semitones for males and 35 semitones for females as normal. The *musical frequency range of phonation* (MFRP) measures lowest to highest musically acceptable notes. We have found normal MFRP in trained voice users to be 35 semitones for professional voice users.

Tests for maximum phonation time, frequency range, and many of the other parameters discussed below (including spectrographic analysis) may be preserved on a tape recorder for analysis at a later time and used for pretreatment and post-treatment comparisons. High quality tape recorders and microphones are essential to avoid equipment noise or distortion. Frequency limits of *vocal register* may also be measured. The registers are (from low to high) vocal fry, chest, mid, head, falsetto, and whistle, as discussed in previous chapters, although register classification is controversial. Overlap of frequency among registers occurs routinely. Testing the *speaking fundamental frequency* frequently reveals excessively low pitch, an abnormality associated with chronic voice abuse and development of vocal nodules. This parameter may be followed objectively throughout a course of speech therapy. "Normal" must be determined on an individual basis; however, expected approximate normal values are 120 Hz for males and 225 Hz for females, and they vary with age. *Intensity range of phonation* (IRP) has proved a less useful measure than frequency range. It varies with fundamental frequency (which should be recorded) and is greatest in the middle frequency range. It is recorded in sound pressure level (SPL) relative to 0.0002 microbar. For normal adults who are not professional vocalists, measuring at a single, fundamental frequency, IRP averages 54.8 dB for males and 51 dB for females (107). Alterations of intensity are common in voice disorders, although IRP is not the most sensitive test to detect them.

Information from the above tests may be combined in the *fundamental frequency-intensity profile* (102). The maximum and minimum sound level that can be produced at different fundamental frequencies may also be plotted. The resultant graph is called a phonetogram and may be helpful in describing the status of the voice. *Glottal efficiency* (the ratio of the acoustic power at the level of the glottis to subglottal power) provides useful information but is not clinically practical because it is difficult to measure acoustic power at the level of the glottis. *Subglottic power* is the product of *subglottal pressure* and *airflow rate*. These can be determined clinically. Various alternative measures of glottic efficiency have been proposed including the *ratio of radiated acoustic power to subglottal power* (108), *airflow-intensity profile* (109), and ratio of the root mean square value of the AC component (110). Although glottal efficiency is of great interest, none of these tests is particularly helpful under routine clinical circumstances.

Acoustic Analysis

Acoustic analysis of voice signals is particularly important but disappointing. The skilled laryngologist, speech-language pathologist, musician, or other trained listener frequently infers a great deal of valid information from the sound of the voice. Clinically useful technology for analyzing and quantifying acoustic characteristics of voice is under development. Ideally, within the next several years, we shall be able to streamline our process of acoustic analysis into one simple, inexpensive instrument equivalent to an audiometer. At present, although acoustic analysis has become increasingly useful, we still use more equipment and devote more time to each voice patient than is practical for most laryngologists. We are currently involved in studies of intrasubject variability in all of the tests we do as well as validity studies comparing tests on different equipment and different laboratories. We anticipate rapid technological evolution, particularly in this section of the voice laboratory.

In many ways, the tape recorder is still the most valuable and essential tool for acoustic analysis. The patient's voice should be recorded under controlled, repeatable circumstances. High quality microphones should be used. Currently, we are equipped with Beyer dynamic microphone M-88N-C, and a Bruel & Kjaer microphone type 4006. We are currently investigating the effects of microphone design and quality on clinical measures of voice function. The microphone is held at a fixed distance from the mouth. The validity and reliability of voice analysis depend on consistent recording technique from subject to subject and from one recording session to the next. Microphone placement is critical. The intensity of sound decreases in proportion to the square of the distance from the sound source (111). We have overcome this variability in our voice laboratory by using a microphone holder. Like previously proposed devices, it is an imperfect compromise, but we feel it has been more satisfactory than methods described previously. We are currently using a harmonica holder (111) (Hoher International) that can be purchased inexpensively from a music supply house (Fig. 10). The microphone is placed at a 6-inch distance from the mouth for all recordings. Like other methods for maintaining constant distance between the sound source and microphone, this technique involves compromises; however, we have found them preferable to the compromises of other devices.

We record on a Nagra E reel-to-reel tape recorder at 7½ inches/sec. This recording is used for all objective voice analysis except for GLIMPES, which requires digital recording as described below. Most routine voice analysis equipment currently marketed accepts only analog signals. Objective analysis may also be made directly from live voice samples, but high quality recordings are adequate for most purposes and provide many advantages (especially the ability to reanalyze the sample).

Probably the most widely used instrument for acoustic analysis in the United States is a *Visi-pitch,* sold by Kay Elemetrics. We use the Visi-pitch Se-6095, which is interfaced with a microcomputer (IBM-PC). This instrument is an analog fundamental frequency analyzer specially designed for ease of use in clinical practice. It provides an oscilloscopic display of both fundamental frequency (F_0) and relative intensity over time. A digital readout is used with a cursor to determine the exact fundamental frequency of points on the screen's display. A summary of the acoustic analysis is given

FIG. 10. Hohner International harmonica holder with Beyer dynamic undirectional microphone positioned for routine voice recording.

through a two-page report, which may be saved in file management, on a diskette, or sent to a printer for hard copy. The Visi-pitch allows the statistical results of two segments to be compared and summarized. It can both store and display in real time the extracted pitch contour and intensity curves. This statistical analysis calculates average fundamental frequency, extended fundamental frequency, average intensity, frequency perturbation, pitch range, and other useful parameters. Intensity and analog F_0 outputs are provided for optional chart recording. The Visi-pitch is used in our practice to analyze short segments of prerecorded tapes for fundamental frequency, relative intensity, perturbation, voiced/unvoiced percentages, and measurement of physiological low and high frequencies. Numerous segments of /a/ are measured before computation of mean fundamental frequency, mean perturbation (Koike formula), and percent voicing are established. Computed statistics are recorded in the patient's file and compared with normative data.

The Visi-pitch unit has numerous advantages over other equipment including:

1. Operation is easy.
2. Input may be made by microphone or tape recorder.
3. All statistics are available through a single function and are summarized.
4. Comparison of statistics from two samples may be easily compared and summarized.
5. Visualization of input is easy.
6. Analysis of highly disordered voice samples is possible.
7. The program status allows the user to review chosen parameters with one easy step.

Disadvantages of the equipment include:

1. Audio output of the sample is not available.
2. Input is limited to 9 sec.
3. The equipment does not allow for spectrographic analysis.
4. The software is incorrectly marked for analysis ranges. Users should remember that the ranges are: (A) 50–300 Hz, (B) 135–535 Hz, (C) 200–760 Hz, and (D) 450–1,600 Hz. The Visi-pitch does not appear to analyze reliably above 1,300 Hz.
5. Analysis range on hardware and computer must match, making range adjustments a two-step operation.

Nevertheless, the Visi-pitch is an extremely good, reasonably priced, durable instrument. Its advantages outweight its disadvantages by far, and we use it extensively.

The *PM 100 Pitch Analyzer* by Voice Identification is a measurement system the zero-crossing detector functions of which are controlled and enhanced by a built-in microcomputer. Operation of the PM Analyzer takes advantage of the interaction of analog circuits and digital processing. The microprocessor-controlled devices may be used individually or as combinations of two or three programs in a single instrument. The various pitch and intensity traces as well as the digital data are displayed on a TV monitor, which is included as a standard part of the package. All five programs are useful as training and pitch modification devices, and the analysis routines provide voice data with a minimum of effort on the part of the user. Fundamental frequency and intensity curves are shown on a monitor with a split screen. Program 100 allows two speech samples (pre- and post-treatment, therapist's model, and patient's response, etc.) up to nine seconds in length to be displayed simultaneously. The user can manipulate the tracing on the screen, for instance, moving one curve left or right so as to line it up with the other. Program 201 allows display and analysis of fundamental frequency and intensity, with use of cursors to mark differences of the values of fundamental frequency and intensity at point A and point B. Program 300 allows computation of mean frequency, intensity, and percent paused for samples up to 20 min of input. Program 301 is a five-part statistical program for a minimum of 8.5 min input. Mean F_o (and standard deviation), duration of sample, duration of pauses, and percent voice/unvoiced may be analyzed. Program 302 is a four-part statistical program for analyzing up to 30 min of speech. Mean frequency, frequency deviation (pitch segment), cumulative frequency distribution of the pitch periods, and the ratio of voiced/ unvoiced time are displayed in graphic and digital form. The average cycle-to-cycle frequency difference (jitter) can also be computed and displayed.

Some units are equipped with special circuitry designed to handle frequencies that are higher or lower than the normal analysis range of 70 to 1,000 Hz. The special circuitry extends analysis range down to 35 Hz and up to 1,900 Hz.

The PM Pitch Analyzer is used in our practice for analysis of longer speech segments, for mean fundamental frequency (and standard deviation), percent voiced/unvoiced, and jitter (Program 302). It is also used as a therapy tool (Program 100) for modeling the therapist's voice to facilitate improvement/consistency of the patient's voice.

Advantages of the PM Pitch Analyzer include:

1. It allows input up to 30 min.
2. Statistical analysis shows number of samples used to derive fundamental frequency and jitter.
3. Black and white printer (provided) allows hard copy of graphic and digital display for each statistical section.
4. Variety of available programs allows PM Pitch Analyzer to be used as a therapy and statistical tool.
5. Input may be from microphone, tape recorder, or auxiliary.

Disadvantages of the equipment include:

1. Console pushbuttons require direct and sharp pressure to start and stop input signal.
2. Adjustments from the main unit to monitor are made by inserting small tool into unit and blindly finding correct area.
3. Audio output is not available.
4. Percent voiced of shorter segments is not reliable when compared with other analyzers.
5. Spectrographic analysis is not available.

We have found the Pitch Analyzer an extremely useful device, especially when employed in conjunction with the Visi-pitch.

The *Micro Speech Lab* (MSL) by Kay Elemetrics is a speech and signal analysis package designed for processing, measuring, and displaying speech and other signals. The package operates hardwired to an IBM-PC microcomputer or equivalent hardware and is intended to meet the needs of a wide range of speech analysis and display applications, including phonetic and linguistic research and speech analysis, and screening in a clinical setting. Acoustic signals may be input via a microphone, tape recorder, or other ancillary device. These analog signals, consisting of electrical waveform energy, are then converted to digital time series data so they are available for display or analysis. The digital signal can be displayed visually as a waveform, or it can be converted back to analog for audio output. Analysis capabilities include graphic displays of spectra, pitch, and energy, as well as numeric readout of pitch and energy. Graphic cursors enable the user to set apart sections of the data for closer analysis, and graphic and numeric readouts of data and parameters may be sent to a printer for hard copy.

MSL is used in our laboratory for extended analysis of short speech segments, particularly for waveform and energy display. At present, it is not used as primary analysis equipment.

Its advantages include:

1. It contains audio output for listening to marked segment before and after analysis.
2. It is self-contained in IBM-PC computer.
3. Hard copy may be obtained through a printer or saved on diskette.
4. It provides good graphics.

Its disadvantages include:

1. It is complex to operate, with each analysis segment requiring numerous actions.
2. MSL is similar to basic functions of a spectrograph, yet it does not allow analysis of formants, even though energy levels are computed.

MSL SPECT (Kay Elemetrics) is a multifunction spectral analysis program that is designed as a supplementary package to accompany the MSL. Sampled data that have been captured and stored in a file using MSL are used as input data by MSL SPECT. Spectra may be smoothed to emphasize formant characteristics, preemphasized to enhance the upper frequencies, passed through a choice of a hamming or rectangular window, and adjusted in window duration from 32 to 2,048 sampled data points. Spectral data may be moved into "buffers" so that they may be averaged, differenced, or graphically compared, with adjustments to display parameters, including scaling, normalizing, and alignment at a chosen frequency, used to enhance the spectral arrays. It allows speech segments to be analyzed in large or minute segments. MSL SPECT is used in combination with the MSL in our laboratory for extended analysis of short speech segments. At present it is not used as primary analysis equipment.

Its advantages include:

1. Minute analysis of speech segments is possible.
2. It provides audio output to allow the user to hear a segment before and after analysis.
3. It can be combined with MSL.
4. It provides good graphics.
5. It can be self-contained in an IBM-PC computer.

Its disadvantages include:

1. It must be used in conjunction with MSL, forcing the user to continue numerous settings of display/analysis parameters.

At present, the MSL and MSL SPECT have proved modestly useful, primarily for research purposes. They are probably not necessary in a laboratory with a high quality spectrograph.

Spectrography has been readily available for many years. Traditionally, a spectrograph has displayed the frequency and harmonic spectrum of a short sample of voice, and visually recorded noise. In addition to routine spectrographs, other equipment existed to analyze longer voice samples. *Long-time-average-spectrograph* (LTAS) devices analyze spectral distribution of speech amplitude levels over time (112), providing additional information.

The Kay Elemetrics DSP SONA-GRAPH (Model 5500) is an integrated voice analysis system. It is equipped for sound spectrography capabilities. Spectrography provides a visual record of the voice. The acoustic signal is depicted using time (x axis), frequency (y axis), and intensity (z axis, shading of light versus dark). Using the band pass filters, generalizations about quality, pitch, and loudness can be made. These observations are used in formulating the voice therapy treatment plan. Formant structure and strength can be determined using the narrow-band filters, of which a variety of configurations are possible. In those clinical settings where singers and other professional voice users are routinely evaluated and treated, this feature is extremely valuable. A sophisticated voice analysis program (an optional program) has made the Sona-Graph an especially valuable addition to the clinical laboratory. The voice analysis program measures speaking fundamental frequency, frequency perturbation (jitter), amplitude perturbation (shimmer), and harmonics/noise ratio, and provides a breathiness index.

An electroglottograph (EGG) is used in conjunction with the Sona-Graph to provide these voicing parameters. Examining the EGG waveform alone is possible with this setup, but its clinical usefulness has not yet been established. An important feature of the Sona-graph is the long-term-average (LTA) spectral capability. This allows for analyzing longer voice samples

(30–90 sec). The LTA analyzes only voiced speech segments and may be useful in screening for hoarse or breathy voices. In addition, computer interface capabilities (also an optional program) have solved many data storage and file maintenance problems. One important temporary disadvantage of the Sona-Graph is that, currently, normative data with which to compare the voicing parameters are limited. This problem should be solved quickly as this valuable instrument becomes used more widely and additional data are published.

GLIMPES

GLIMPES is an acronym for Glottal Imaging by Processing External Signals (104, 112). GLIMPES is still under development and involves sophisticated computer analysis at a central computer center (the Recording and Research Center of the Denver Center of the Performing Arts), analyzing signals provided by offices in other parts of the country. The intention is to develop a system whereby clinicians can have access to high quality voice analysis with a relatively low equipment investment. The primary disadvantage is the time delay involved in sending data to Denver and waiting for a report. Because the system is still undergoing refinement, GLIMPES is not available commercially; however, it is likely to be available soon. Required equipment includes a high quality microphone [AKG (451-EB) with CK-22 capsule attached to it], a digital audio processor (Sony PCM-501-ES), a high-fi stereo VCR, phantom power supply (AG N-62E), microphone preamplifier (ATI M-100), stereo headphones (Sony MDR-S30), an EGG [Synchrovoice, Inc. (see comments above)], and an oscilloscope with two-channel input display. GLIMPES measures exact real time location of the glottal cycle, fundamental frequency, jitter, opening quotient, closure duration, closure of velocity, closure of focus, shimmer, abduction quotient, and numerous other parameters.

In addition to the equipment described, the voice laboratory includes a standard cassette player for analyzing tapes sent by other institutions or brought by patients. The laboratory also utilizes two IBM-compatible computers to allow for multiple worker capabilities. This permits one team member to analyze data while statistics or reports are being generated on the second computer. One computer is dedicated entirely to analysis. The voice laboratory also includes a video system to permit the laboratory team to view and copy videotapes outside the stroboscopy room without interfering with patient flow.

Usefulness and interpretation of many of the acoustic measures discussed above should be self-evident. Various voice disorders are accompanied by decreased range, intensity, and stability. Acoustic measures allow us to recognize and document such deviations from normal. In addition, they permit quantitative assessment of vocal progress during and following treatment. In order to compare various forms of voice therapy, medications, and different surgical techniques, we need as much objective information as possible about the degree and nature of voice improvement. Restoring or increasing vocal range and intensity, decreasing perturbation, and restoring normal harmonic patterns are important measures of therapeutic success. Since the "sound of the voice" is usually the patient's primary concern, acoustic analysis provides especially relevant information for assessing and modifying nonsurgical and surgical treatments.

Laryngeal Electromyography

Electromyography (EMG) requires an electrode system, an amplifier, an oscilloscope, a loudspeaker, and a recording system. Electrodes are inserted into laryngeal muscles (Figs. 11 and 12). Either a needle electrode or a hooked-wire electrode may be used (102). Because of the invasive nature of the procedure, electromyography is rarely utilized in caring for the customary problems of professional voice users. However, it may be extremely valuable in confirming cases of vocal fold paralysis, differentiating paralysis from arytenoid dislocation, differentiating recurrent laryngeal nerve paralysis from complete vocal fold paralysis, confirming superior laryngeal nerve paralysis or paresis, predicting return of vocal fold movement, guiding botulinum toxin injections, and documenting functional voice disorders.

So far, our EMG has been performed by a neurologist who has developed the appropriate skill at placing laryngeal needle electrodes. However, we recently purchased an Amplaid MK-15 brainstem evoked response audiometer. This instrument is equipped to perform not only brainstem evoked response audiometry, but also electronystagmography, electroneuronography, and EMG. The EMG portion of this instrument works well and is equipped for either surface or needle electrode recording. Surface electrodes can be used on the arm for repetitive stimulation testing when diagnoses such as myasthenia are suspected. Single needle electrode laryngeal EMG can also be performed. One shortcoming of this device for laryngologic purposes is the absence of the second EMG channel. Thus, the Amplaid MK-15 cannot be used to document functional voice disorders, as this requires two electrodes to document simultaneous firing of abductor and adductor muscles. We are, however, investigating its potential use for other clinical purposes such as confirming recurrent or superior laryngeal nerve paralysis. The expense of a high quality multichannel EMG unit is probably not justified for most laryngologists, considering the infrequent need for laryngeal EMG, so long as expert multichannel laryngeal EMG is available elsewhere in the community.

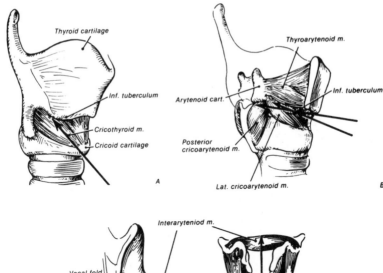

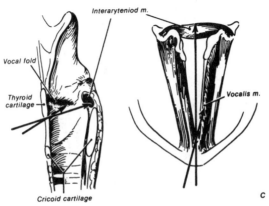

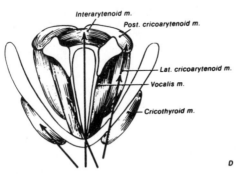

FIG. 11. Position of insertion of electrodes into laryngeal muscles for electromyography. Muscles illustrated include the cricothyroid (**A**), lateral and posterior cricoarytenoid muscles (**B**), the interarytenoid and vocalis muscles (**C**). Also shown is a schematic representation of the positions of insertion into the five major laryngeal muscles (**D**). From Hirano M. *Clinical examination of the voice.* New York: Springer-Verlag, 1981;14, with permission.

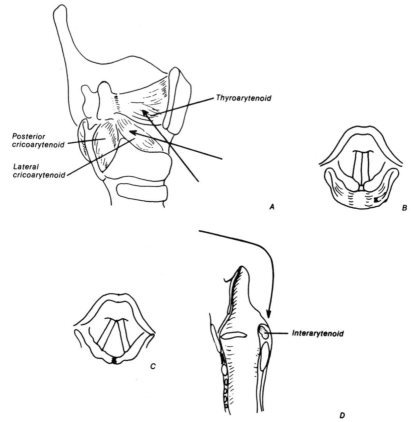

FIG. 12. Alternate method of inserting laryngeal electrodes for electromyography including a modified approach to the vocalis (thyroarytenoid) muscle (**A**), peroral point of insertion into the posterior cricoarytenoid muscle (**B**), peroral point of insertion into the interarytenoid muscle (**C**), and peroral point of insertion into the interarytenoid muscle (**D**). From Hirano M. *Clinical examination of the voice.* New York: Springer-Verlag, 1981;50, with permission.

Psychoacoustic Evaluation

Many researchers have tried to quantify and standardize psychoacoustic evaluation of the voice. Unfortunately, even definitions of such basic terms as hoarseness and breathiness are still controversial. Standardization of psychoacoustic evaluation protocol and interpretation does not exist. Therefore, although subjective psychoacoustic analysis of voice is of great value to the skilled clinician, it remains generally unsatisfactory for comparing research among laboratories or for reporting clinical results. Nevertheless, recognizing that the human ear and brain are still our best tools, we try to optimize the validity and usefulness of our psychoacoustic observations.

Psychoacoustic evaluation is performed independently by three examiners, and their findings are compared. The first evaluation is performed by the physician who records his auditory observations of specific aspects of spoken and sung voice on the laryngeal examination form. Following strobovideolaryngoscopy and objective voice analysis, the speech-language pathologist performs an examination and prepares a report describing vocal quality, vocal habits (such as harsh glottal attacks), resonance, use of vocal fry, audible and visible tension, etc. The speech-language pathologist's office is equipped with a tape recorder and a video recording setup so that observations can be reviewed with the patient and other members of the team. In addition, a one hour evaluation is performed by the singing voice specialist whose office is equipped with a piano, tape recorder, and video camera. The singing teacher also provides a written analysis of voice quality, habits, and techniques of voice production. At the conclusion of these evaluations, the findings of the three examiners are compared, and discrepancies are resolved by reviewing tapes of the examinations. While this system does not solve the need for quantitative psychoacoustic analysis, it has proved useful and thorough for clinical purposes.

COLLATION OF RESULTS

After the laryngologist has completed the examination, reviewed all test results, and received the opinions and recommendations of all team members, the physician provides the patient with the diagnosis (or diagnoses) and treatment plan. Regardless of whether the treatment involves medication, surgery, speech therapy, specialized singing training, or referral to other medical specialists, the laryngologist has primary responsibility for directing and coordinating treatment. In general, most patients with voice abnormalities benefit from comprehensive care involving all members of the clinical voice laboratory team. Such medically supervised collaborative intervention optimizes not only initial clinical care, but also long-term follow-up and acquisition of research data. All members of the clinical voice laboratory team must be expert and committed to high quality voice care, but the importance of a well-informed, active, dedicated physician to the successful establishment of a clinical voice laboratory cannot be overemphasized.

CONCLUSION

Although the ideal clinical voice laboratory has not yet been defined, systematic use of instrumentation has become invaluable in state-of-the-art care of the voice. In establishing a new voice laboratory, an effort should be made to address each of the categories of vocal function. A laryngostroboscope to assess vibratory function is virtually essential. If funds are limited, initially, most of the aerodynamic measures can be performed in a pulmonologist's or hospital's pulmonary function laboratory. Phonatory function measures require extremely inexpensive equipment that can be obtained at a neighborhood electronic store. Equipment for acoustic analysis is important, useful, and elegant and should be included as soon as possible. However, if funds to purchase such equiopment are not available initially, at least a high quality microphone and tape recorder should be acquired. Arrangements can usually be made with other voice laboratories to analyze these recordings as needed, so long as appropriate, standardized recording technique and protocols are used. Laryngeal electromyography can be referred to a neurologist trained in laryngeal electrode placement (usually by the laryngologist). Once a team has begun using even a minimally equipped voice laboratory regularly, its value becomes clear, and additional equipment can be added as dictated by need and resources.

REFERENCES

1. Sataloff RF. The professional voice. II. Physical examination. *J Voice* 1987;1(2):191–201.
2. Sataloff RT, Spiegel JR, Carroll LM, et al. Strobovideolaryngoscopy in professional voice users: results and clinical value. *J Voice* 1988;1(4):359–364.
3. Hirano M. Phonosurgery. Basic and clinical investigations. *Otologia (Fukuoka)* 1975;21:239–442.
4. Bless D, Hirano M, Feder RJ. Video stroboscopic evaluation of the larynx. *Ear, Nose Throat J* 1987;66(7):289–296.
5. Oertel MJ. Das laryngoskopische untersuchung. *Arch Laryngol Rhinol (Berl)* 1895;3:1–16.
6. Alberti PW. The diagnostic role of laryngeal stroboscopy. *Otolaryngol Clin North Am* 1978;11(2)(June):347–354.
7. Barth V, Pilorget J. La stroboscopie laryngee. *Rev Laryngol Otol Rhinol (Bord)* 1983;104(4):359–364.
8. Beck J, Schoenhaerl E. The significance of stroboscopy for the diagnosis of functional voice disorders. *Arch Ohr Nas Kehlkopfheilk* 1959;175:449–452.
9. Bekbulatov GT. Stroboskopiia v otsenke funktsional'nugo vosstanovleniia golosovogo apparata posle operatsii na golosovykh sladkakh. *Vestn Otorinolaring* 1969;31:52–54.
10. Bohme G. The efficacy of electrotherapy in laryngeal diseases as shown in the stroboscopic picture. *Laryngol Rhinol Otol (Stuttgart)* 1965;44(7):481–488.
11. Boudin G, Duron B, Ossart M, Abitbol J. Electromyographie larynge technique—premiers resultats. *J Fr Otorhinolaryngol* 1984;33(1):46–48.
12. Brewer DW, McCall G. Visible laryngeal changes during voice therapy: fiberoptic study. *Ann Otol Rhinol Laryngol* 1974;83:423–427.
13. Cammann RJ, Pahn J, Rother U. Diagnostik der N. -laryngeus - superior -parese. *Folia Phoniatr (Basel)*, 1976;28(6):349–353.
14. Chaplin VL, Iakovleva II. Stroboskopiia detei kapelly mal'chikov. *Nov Med Tekhn* 1964;2:41–44.
15. Cornut G, Bouchayer M, Parent F. Value of videostroboscopy in indicating phonosurgery. *Acta Otorhinolaryngol Belg* 1986;40(2):436–442.
16. Croft TA. Failure of visual estimation of motion under strobe. *Nature* 1971;231(302):397.

17. Eigler G, Podzuweit G, Weiland H. New microphone controlled stroboscope with flashlights for study of vocal cord vibrations. *Ztschr Laryng Rhin Otol* 1953;32(Jan):40–45.

18. Ernst R. Stroboscopic studies in professional speakers. *HNO* 1960;8(March 31):170–174.

19. Ernst R. The stroboscopic recognition of functional voice disorders by means of singing and speaking stress. *Arch Ohr Nas Kehlkopfheilk* 1959;175:452–455.

20. Ertt S, Stein L. History of motorless laryngostroboscopy. *Monatschr f Ohrenh* 1936;70(Dec):1463–1464.

21. Fex S, Elmqvist D. Endemic recurrent laryngeal nerve paresis: correlation between EMG and stroboscopic findings. *Acta Otolaryngol (Stock)* 1973;75(4):368–369.

22. Fulgenicio MS. Laryngeal stroboscopy. *AMB* 1978;24(1):17–18.

23. Gerull G, Gesen M, Mrowinski D, Rudolph N. Laryngeal stroboscopy using a scanning microphone. *HNO* 1972;20(12):369.

24. Gould WJ. The clinical voice laboratory—clinical application of voice research. *Ann Otol Rhinol Laryngol* 1984;93(4, pt 1):346–350.

25. Gould WJ, Kojima H, Lambiase A. A technique for stroboscopic examination of the vocal folds using fiberoptics. *Arch Otolaryngol* 1979;105(5):285.

26. Greiner GF, Dillenschneider E, Conraux C. Stroboscopic and sonographic aspects of the traumatic larynx. *J Fr Otorhinolaryngol* 1968;17(3):237–241.

27. Haas E, Bildstein P. The significance of stroboscopy in the early diagnosis of vocal fold cancer. *Laryngol Rhinol Otol (Stuttgart)*, 1974;53(3):169–172.

28. Hala B, Honty L. Cinematography of vocal cords by means of stroboscope and great speed. *Otolaryng Slavica* 1931;3(Jan):1–12.

29. Hollien H, Coleman R, Moore P. Stroboscopic laminagraphy of the larynx during phonation. *Acta Otolaryngol (Stock)*, 1968;65(Jan–Feb):209–251.

30. Honjo I, Isshiki N. Laryngoscopic and voice characteristics of aged persons. *Arch Otolaryngol* 1980;106(3)(Mar):149–150.

31. Husson R. Principal facts of vocal physiology and pathology gained by laryngostroboscopy. *Rev de laryng* 1936;57(Dec):1132–1145.

32. Husson R. Stroboscopic study of reflex modifications of vibration of vocal cords produced by experimental stimulations of auditory and trigeminal nerves. *Compt Rend Acad Sci* 1951;232(Mar 19):1247–1249.

33. Kallen LA. Laryngostroboscopy in the practice of otolaryngology. *Arch Otolaryngol* 1932;16:791–807.

34. Kallen LA, Polin HS. A physiological stroboscope. *Science* 1934;80:592.

35. Kitzing P. Stroboscopy—a pertinent laryngological examination. *Otolaryngology* 1985;14(3)(Jun):151–175.

36. Koike Y. Diagnosis of voice disorders. *Nippon Jibiinkoka Gakkai Kaiho* 1979; 82(11)(Nov):1434–1437.

37. Krahulec I. Importance of stroboscopy in laryngology. *Cesk Otolaryngol* 1970; 19(1):29–31.

38. Kristensen HK, Zilstorff-Pedersen K. Synchrono-electrostroboscopic examination of the vocal cords. *Nord Med* 1982;68(July 19):927–929.

39. Leitao FB, Morganti AP, Elisabetsky M, Mantoanelli JB. Stroboscopy control of phonetic sound before and after tracheal intubation. *Rev Bras Anesthesiol* 1968;18(2):182–191.

40. Luchsinger R. Stroboscopic symptomatology. *Pract Otorhinolaryngol* 1948;10:209–214.

41. MacKay DM. Fragmentation of binocular fusion in stroboscopic illumination. *Nature* 1970;227(257):518.

42. Maliutin EN. Stroboscopic phenomena in vocal students. *Russk Klin* 1930;13:681–691.

43. Mareev VM, Papshitsky YA. Stroboscopy in hyperplastic and tumour processes of the larynx. *Vestn Otorinolaringol* 1972;34:71–75.

44. Mareev VM, Papshitskii IA. Stroboskopiia pri giperplasticheskikh i opukhdevykh protsessakh gortani. *Vestn Otorinolaringol* 1973;76(April):495–500.

45. McKelvie WB. Stroboscope using grid-controlled neon tube, "strobotron." *J Laryngol Otol* 1944;59(Dec):464–465.

46. Merriman JS. Stroboscopic photography as a research instrument. *Res Quart Am Assoc Health Phys Ed* 1977;48(3):628–631.
47. Milner M, Brennan PK, Wilberforce CB. Stroboscopic polaroid photography in clinical studies of human locomotion. *S Afr Med J* 1973;47(22):948–950.
48. Minnigerode B. The defiguration phenomenon in motion perception and its effect on stroboscopic laryngoscopy. *Laryngol Rhinol Otol (Stuttgart)* 1967;101(1):33–38.
49. Moore DM, Berle S, Hanson DG, Ward PH. Videostroboscopy of the canine larynx: the effects of asymmetric laryngeal tension. *Laryngoscope* 1987;97(5):543–553.
50. Morrison MD. A clinical voice laboratory: videotape and stroboscopic instrumentation. *Otolaryngol Head Neck Surg* 1984;92(4)(Aug):487–488.
51. Musehold A. Stroboskopische und photographische studien uber die stellung der stimmlippen im brust- und falsett-register. *Arch Laryngol Rhinol (Berl)* 1898;7:1–21.
52. Oertel MJ. Ueber eine neue laryngostroboscopische untersuchungsmethode. *Munchen Med Wohnschr* 1895;42:233–236.
53. Padovan IF, Christman NT, Hamilton LH, Darling RJ. Indirect microlaryngostroboscopy. *Laryngoscope* 1973;83:2035–2041.
54. Pakhmilevich AG. Elektonnaia laringostroboskopicheskaia Kartina prinektrorykh. *Vestn Otorhinolaringol* 1981;5(Sept–Oct):58–62.
55. Pantiukhin VP. Stroboscopy in patients after laryngectomy. *Vestn Otorhinolaringol* 1961;23(May–Jun):69–73.
56. Pearlman HB. Laryngeal stroboscopy. *Ann Otol Rhin Laryngol* 1945;54(Mar):159–165.
57. Powell LS. Laryngostroboscope. *Arch Otolaryngol* 1934;19(June):708–710.
58. Powell LS. The laryngo-stroboscope in clinical examination. *Eye Ear Nose Throat Monthly* 1935;14:265.
59. Raes J, Lebrun Y, Clement P. Videostroboscopy of the larynx. *Acta Otorhinolaryngol Belg* 1986;40(2):421–425.
60. Rohrs M. Untersuchungen uber das schwingungsverhalten der stimmlippen in verschiedenen registerbereichen mit unterschiedlichen stroboskopischen techniken. *Folia Phoniatrica (Basel)* 1985;37(3–4):113–118.
61. Russell GO, Tuttle CH. Color movies of vocal cord action aid in diagnosis. *Laryngoscope* 1930;40(Aug):549–552.
62. Saito S, Fukuda H, Kitahara S, Kowawa N. Stroboscopic observation of vocal fold vibration with fiberoptics. *Folia Phoniatrica (Basel)* 1978;30(4):241–244.
63. Salivon LG, Kirina NI. Stroboscopy in malignant tumors of the larynx in the postradiation period. *Zhurnal Ushnykh, no sovkh i Gorlovykh Boleznei (Kiev)* 1972;32(2):74–76.
64. Sawashima M, Hirose H. New laryngoscopic technique by use of fiberoptics. *J Acoust Soc Am* 1968;43:168–169.
65. Schlosshauer B, Timcke R. Stroboscopic studies in hemilaryngectomized patients. *Arch Ohren-Nasen-u Kehlkopfh* 1956;168:404–413.
66. Schonharl E. *Die stroboskopie in der praktischen laryngologie.* Stuttgart: Georg Thieme Verlag, 1960.
67. Schonharl E. Significance of laryngostroboscopy for practicing otorhinolaryngologist. *Ztschr Laryng Rhin Otol* 1952;31(July–Aug):383–386.
68. Schonharl E. Stroboscopic study in myxedema. *Arch Ohren-Nasen-u Kehlkopfh* 1954;165:633–635.
69. Schonharl E. New stroboscope with automatic regulation of frequency and recent results of its application to study of vocal cord vibrations in dysphonias of various origins. *Rev Laryn* 1956;77(suppl)(May):476–481.
70. Sedlackova E. Stroboscopic data in relation to the development of voice in children. *Folia Phoniatrica* 1961;13:81–92.
71. Segre R. Vocal nodules as revealed by stroboscope. *Valsalva* 1933;9(May):380–389.
72. Silberman HD, Wilf H, Tucker JA. Flexible fiberoptic nasopharyngolaryngoscope. *Ann Otol Rhinol Laryngol* 1976;85:640–645.
73. Stern H. Study of larynx and of voice by means of stroboscopic moving picture. *Monatschr f Ohrenh* 1935;69(June):648–652.
74. Szentesi DI. Stroboscopic electron mirror microscopy at frequencies up to 100 MHz. *J Phys Sci Instr* 1972;5(6):563–567.

75. Tarneaud J. Study of larynx and of voice by stroboscopy. *Clinique* (Paris) 1933; 28[Nov(A)]:337–341.
76. Tobin HA. Office fiberoptic laryngeal photography. *Otolaryngol Head Neck Surg* 1980;88:172–173.
77. Tischner H. Vocal cord stroboscopy with automatic adjustment of frequency. *Arch Ohren-Nasen-u Kehlkopfh* 1955;167:524–529.
78. Von Leden H. The electric synchron-stroboscope: its value for the practicing laryngologist. *Ann Otol Rhinol Laryngol* 1961;70:881–893.
79. Voronina EM, Shtumer YF. Strobofaradizator. *Zhur ush nos i gorl boky* 1939;16:258–263.
80. Watanabe H, Shin T, Matsuo K, et al. A new computer-analyzing system for clinical use with the strobovideoscope. *Arch Otolaryngol Head Neck Surg* 1986;112(9):978–981.
81. Welsh AR. The practical and economic value of flexible system laryngoscopy. *J Laryngol Otol* 1982;96:1125–1129.
82. Wendler J. Significance of the strength of the voice in stroboscopic examination. *Folia Phoniatrica* (*Basel*) 1967; 19(2):73–88.
83. Wendler J, Seidner W, Halbedl G, et al. Tele-Mikrostroboskopie. *Folia Phonatrica* (*Basel*), 1973; 25:281–287.
84. West R. A view of the larynx through a new stroboscope. *Q J Speech* 1935;21:355.
85. White JF, Knight RE. Office videofiberoptic laryngoscopy. *Laryngoscope* 1984; 94(9):1166–1169.
86. Williams GT, Farquharson IM, Anthony J. Fiberoptic laryngoscopy in the assessment of laryngeal disorders. *J Laryngol Otol* 1975;89:299–316.
87. Wilson FB, Kudryk WH, Sych JA. The development of flexible fiberoptic video nasendoscopy (FFVN)—clinical-teaching-research applications. *ASHA* 1986;28(11)(Nov): 25–30.
88. Winckel F. Improved stroboscopic technic for examination. *Arch Ohren-Nasen-u Kehlkopfh* 1954;165:582–586.
89. Witton TH. An introduction to the fiberoptic laryngoscope. *Can Anesth Soc J* 1981;28:475–478.
90. Yana D. Stroboscopy of the larynx: apropos of a new stroboscope; the stroborama type L.6. *Ann Otolaryngol Chir Cervicofac* 1969;86(9):589–592.
91. Yanagisawa E. Office telescopic photography of the larynx. *Ann Otol Rhinol Laryngol* 1982;91:354–358.
92. Yanagisawa E, Owens TW, Strothers G, Honda K. Videolaryngoscopy: a comparison of fiberoptic and telescopic documentation. *Ann Otol Rhinol Laryngol* 1983;92(5, pt 1):430–436.
93. Yanagisawa E. Videolaryngoscopy using a low cost home video system color camera. *J Biol Photog* 1984;52(2):9–14.
94. Yanagisawa E, Sullivano J, Carlson RD. Simultaneous video imaging of lip and vocal cord movements for videographic documentation of laryngeal function. *J Biol Photogr* 1986;54(3)(Jul):107–109.
95. Yoshida Y, Koiwa S, Amano M. Comparison between the original and modified NLA methods in stroboscopic laryngomicrosurgery. *Jpn J Anesthesiol* 1976;25(5):497–501.
96. Yoshida Y, Hirano M, Nakajima T. An improved model of laryngo-stroboscope. *Otolaryngology* (*Tokyo*) 1977;49:663–669.
97. Yoshida Y, Hirano M, Nakajima T. A videotape recording system for laryngo-stroboscopy. *J Jpn Bronchoesophagol Soc* 1979;30:1–5.
98. Yoshida Y, Hirano M, Yoshida T, Tateishi O. Strobofibrescopic colour video recording of vocal fold vibration. *J Laryngol Otol* 1985;99(8):795–800.
99. Young KA, Atkins JP Jr, Keane WM, Rowe LD. The role of the voice science center in the otorhinolaryngology practice. *Trans Pa Acad Ophthalmol Otolaryngol* 1982; 35(2)(Fall):141–144.
100. Sataloff RT. Strobovideolaryngoscopy in professional voice users: results and clinical value. *J Voice* 1987;1(4):359–364.
101. Karnell MP. Synchronized videostroboscopy and electroglottography. *J Voice* 1989; 3(1):68–75.

102. Hirano M. *Clinical examination of the voice*. New York: Springer-Verlag 1981;1–98.
103. Lecluse FLE, Brocaar ME, Verschuure J. Electroglottography and its relation to glottal activity. *Folia Phoniatrica* 1975;27:215–224.
104. Scherer RC, Gould WJ, Titze IR, et al. Preliminary evaluation of selected acoustic and glottographic measures for clinical phonatory function analysis. *J Voice* 1988;2(3):230–244.
105. Titze IR. Interpretation of the electroglottographic signal. *J Voice* 1990;4(1):1–9.
106. Hirano M, Koike Y, von Leden H. Maximum phonation time and air usage during phonation. *Folia Phoniatrica* 1968;20:185–201.
107. Coleman RJ, Mabis JH, Hinson JK. Fundamental frequency-sound pressure level profiles of adult male and female voices. *J Speech Hearing Res* 1977;20:197–204.
108. Isshiki N. Regulatory mechanism of voice intensity variation. *J Speech Hearing Res* 1964;7:17–29.
109. Satio S. Phonosurgery, basic study on the mechanism of phonation and endolaryngeal microsurgery. *Otologia (Fukuoka)* 1977;23:171–384.
110. Isshiki N. Functional surgery of the larynx (official report of the 78th annual convention of the oto-rhino-laryngological society of Japan, Fukuoka), Kyoto University, 1977.
111. Price DB, Sataloff RT. Technical note: a simple technique for consistent microphone placement in voice recording. *J Voice* 1988;2(3):206–207.
112. Frokjaer-Jenson B, Prytz S. Registration of voice quality. *Bruel & Kjaer Tech Rev* 1976;3:3–17.

Professional Voice: The Science and Art
of Clinical Care, Robert T. Sataloff.
Raven Press, Ltd., New York © 1991.

9

The Effects of Age on the Voice

Robert T. Sataloff

*Department of Otolaryngology, Thomas Jefferson University,
Philadelphia, Pennsylvania*

THE YOUNG VOICE

Young voices have unique complexities and delicacies that make them exciting, challenging, and hazardous to care for. Their special problems are of interest not only to physicians, but also to voice teachers and speech-language pathologists. Recent arts medicine literature has shown new and welcome interest in aging voices (1–8), but papers on the young voice have been less frequent and less expert than desirable. The subject was addressed in 1984 at the Voice Foundation's Thirteenth Symposium on Care of the Professional Voice (9), and voice development is discussed in numerous standard speech-language pathology textbooks (10–12). However, many basic, practical questions remain unanswered. It is important for all professionals who train and care for singers to understand as much as possible about the growth and development of the voice and to understand clearly anatomic and physiologic differences among children, adolescents, adults, and the elderly. Such knowledge should lead to optimal training and minimal risk of vocal injury.

ANATOMY AND PHYSIOLOGY

Embryologically, the larynx develops most of its anatomical characteristics by the third month of fetal life. At birth, the thyroid cartilage and hyoid bone are attached to each other. The laryngeal skeleton then separates, and the slow process of ossification (cartilages turning to bone) begins. The hyoid bone starts to ossify by two years of age. The thyroid and cricoid cartilages ossify during the early 20s, and the arytenoid cartilages ossify in the latter 30s. Except for the cuneiform and corniculate cartilages, the entire laryngeal skeleton is ossified by age 65. In the infant, the epiglottis is bulky and omega-shaped. It does not open to its normal adult configuration until puberty. The angle of the thyroid cartilage is about 110° in the male and 120° in the female at birth. These relationships also remain fairly stable until puberty. At birth, the larynx is high in the neck, resting at about the level of the third and fourth cervical vertebrae (C_3 and C_4). It descends to about the level of C_6 by the age of five and continues gradual descent, lying at about the level of C_7 between ages 15 and 20. Descent continues throughout life in both sexes. As the larynx descends, vocal tract length relationships change and average voice pitch tends to become lower. In infancy, the membranous (vibrating) and cartilaginous portions of the vocal folds are equal in length. By adulthood, the membranous portion accounts for approximately two-thirds of vocal fold length. Total vocal fold length is six to eight mm in the infant, but increases to 12 to 17 mm in the adult female, and to 17 to 23 mm in the adult male. The dimensions of all other aspects of laryngeal anatomy increase as well.

First vocalizations sometimes occur prior to birth, although the birth cry is normally the first sound uttered. Its frequency averages about 500 Hz (one octave above middle C). At this time, laryngeal mobility is limited primarily to vertical movements, and the appearance of the larynx is very similar to that of primates (monkeys). As the child grows, mean fundamental frequency of speech (the predominant pitch of the speaking voice) drops gradually. By eight years of age, it is approximately 275 Hz. Until puberty, male and female larynges are about the same size. During childhood, the physiologic frequency range (the highest and lowest sounds the child can produce) remains fairly constant. However, musical frequency range increases. That is, the child becomes able to produce musically acceptable sounds throughout an increasing percentage of his frequency range. Thus, between the ages of six and 16, the important developmental change is not absolute range (constant at about 2½ octaves) but rather improved control, efficiency, and quality. Recognizing this principle is helpful in structuring training of young voices to strengthen and take advantage of the natural developmental process, rather than concentrating too heavily and too early on exercises that are designed to stretch the extremes of range. Such exercises may be damaging, especially to fragile young voices.

Puberty provides particularly challenging problems for the young singer, as well as the singer's teacher and physician. In general, puberty begins between age eight and 15 for American females, and between age 9½ and 14 for American males (13). Ordinarily, it is complete by about age 12 to 16½ for females, and by roughly 13½ to 18 years of age for males. Puberty tends to occur earlier in warmer climates. The times of onset and duration of voice mutation vary from study to study and depend somewhat on the techniques used to measure and define voice change. It used to be thought that voice change was completed within three to six months. However, this estimate is probably a function of insensitive measures of voice mutation and is not consistent with clinical observation. As methods of detecting voice mutation become more sophisticated, we will probably find that the period of vocal instability associated with mutation is closer to 1½ years. Even longer periods of voice change have been observed. Some investigators have found voice mutation to last as long as three years (14). Voice changes in girls begin slightly earlier than those in boys, but voice mutation is often complete in both sexes by about age 15.

Voice changes during puberty are caused by major alterations in laryngeal anatomy that occur coincident with the development of other secondary sex characteristics. Male vocal cords grow four to eight mm in length, while female vocal cords grow 1 to 3.5 mm. The angle of the male thyroid cartilage decreases to approximately 90°, while the thyroid cartilage angle in the female remains about 120°. In both sexes, the epiglottis flattens, grows, and elevates; laryngeal mucosa becomes stronger and thicker; and tonsil and adenoid tissues atrophy and partially disappear. The neck itself often elongates, and the chest enlarges. There is somewhat greater thoracic enlargement in the male; consequently, there is a greater increase in vital capacity of the lungs. During puberty, the female voice usually drops about 2½ semitones and averages roughly 220 to 225 Hz when voice change is complete. The male voice drops approximately one octave, averaging about 130 Hz at age 18 years.

VOCAL TRAINING, HEALTH, AND PATHOLOGY

The optimal time to begin vocal training remains controversial. Recently, new trends in education have introduced the concept of ear and voice training in early infancy. As most of the techniques suggested so far involve pitch matching and natural development of ear–voice coordination, they are unlikely to be harmful. The problems of vocal training for young school-aged children are more obvious to many of us who care for vocal disorders. They have been aggravated by the popularity of shows such as "Annie" and by the enthusiasm of preteens for various rock singers with abusive vocal habits. Children have constantly changing voices, with delicate muscles and fragile mucosa. Very few can tolerate the demands of prolonged "belting" or shouting several nights per week over a period of months or years without sustaining vocal injury. Certainly, it is possible and proper to train young voices to sing. Moreover, it is reasonable to begin this training as soon as a youngster shows a serious interest in and aptitude for voice performance. However, the training should be directed toward avoiding voice abuse and toward gradual development of vocal musculature and control. Erroneous technique early in childhood may underlie vocal difficulties throughout a lifetime by improperly developing muscles of singing. Once a muscle is contoured, it is extremely difficult to change its shape. While the demands and opportunities of professional performance (such as "Annie") cannot be ignored, they should be met with compromises other than vocal destruction. For example, proper vocal training, frequent laryngeal examination, and multiple casting (several Annies who alternate appearances) may allow a successful production without injuring the star, or the many youngsters attempting to become the star. Classical musicians have shown greater sensitivity to the needs of young voices, usually limiting school and children's choir performances to appropriate repertoire. However, even among classical musicians, there is a dangerous tendency to ask children to perform works too difficult for their vocal ages. In addition, especially among boys' choirs, damage may be caused by encouraging a boy soprano or alto to maintain his treble voice beyond the initiation of voice change. Trying to force the voice up or down during this unstable period is potentially hazardous.

Voice training during puberty is especially problematic. For generations, voice teachers have believed that heavy voice use during the period of voice mutation and instability should be avoided. Although this tradition was born out of extensive experience rather than scientific experiment, there is much reason to believe its wisdom. Recently, a controversial study proported to show that vigorous vocal training during voice change enhanced vocal development (15). However, although the study raises interesting questions, other investigators who listened to the youngsters studied disagreed with the conclusions of the author and felt that the voices were injured rather than superior. Consequently, although the question remains open, at the present time, the traditional warnings against heavy voice use during mutation should be followed. However, as with the problem of casting lead singers for "Annie," practical considerations must be addressed. For example, a junior high school music teacher is in no position to silence all changing voices. If this were done, there would be no one left to sing in the choir. There are safe ways to permit singing. Most of the abuses of the changing voice come from the youngster (usually male) forcing the voice down or up in order to avoid the embarrassment of voice breaks. If this behavior can be eliminated, safer singing results. One technique that the author has found successful is to begin each rehearsal with exercises in which the youngsters are instructed to allow their voices to break. These exercises can be done as a chorus and individually. For the first few days, everyone laughs. Thereafter, the group is desensitized to the sound of breaking voices and accepts the natural voice change, and the students can be instructed to let their voices break naturally during songs. This produces a tolerable choral sound, and they can continue singing safely in whichever mode is most relaxed for any given note. Other such exercises and appropriate repertoire selection permit limited, safe singing, even during this particularly troublesome period of vocal development.

All the vocal health problems that occur in adults may occur in children. Most of them have been widely discussed in previous literature (16–18). Voice abuse is especially common in children. Screaming may result in vocal nodules, hemorrhages, or other serious vocal cord problems. These habits are often associated with abusive vocal patterns among the child's parents and siblings. This problem is treated best with vocal education and therapy that involves the entire family and, if possible, the child's peer group. While it is true that childhood vocal nodules usually resolve spontaneously at the time of puberty, excellent voice therapy and education may cure them much sooner and simultaneously develop good vocal habits that will last a lifetime.

Gastric reflux laryngitis also occurs in children. In fact, it even occurs in newborns and may be a cause of pneumonia in early childhood. As in adults, morning hoarseness, chronic cough (especially at night), and bad breath are often the most prominent symptoms. However, reflux in children may also present as recurrent vomiting, repeated respiratory infections, intractable asthma, or apnea (cessation of breathing) especially at night. Treatment with elevation of the head of the bed, antacids, and change in eating habits is usually effective.

Many other medical conditions may afflict children's voices. They include birth defects in the vocal cords, paralysis, infections, vocal cord polyps and cysts, asthma, which impairs respiratory support, and numerous other ailments. Hormonal and psychological problems also occur in children and may manifest as abnormal voices. For this reason, any child, adolescent, or young adult with a persistently abnormal voice or failure of voice development deserves the same thorough investigation and diagnosis that we would provide for an adult professional voice user. In fact, it is sobering to remember that we never know which of these children will grow up to be the next bright light at the Metropolitan Opera Company.

Understanding the normal development of the human voice over time is important in recognizing vocal health and disease and in planning vocal training. The voice is complex and dynamic. Its special delicacy and rapid changes during youth warrant extreme care and respect. So long as we remember that children are children, and treat their voices within limits imposed by their bodies and minds, safe, educated singing should be possible at almost any age.

THE ADULT VOICE

Throughout adult life, mean fundamental frequency drops steadily in females from about 225 Hz in the 20- to 29-year-old group to about 195 Hz in the 80- to 90-year-old group (19). In males, fundamental frequency of the speaking voice drops until roughly the fifth decade, after which it rises gradually (20). It is important to be aware of normal changes in the speaking voice, as unskilled conscious or subconscious attempts to alter the quality and frequency of the speaking voice often are abusive and may produce problems reflected in the singing voice.

THE AGING VOICE

Like death and taxes, most people have considered aging changes in the voice inevitable. Indeed, as we get older, there are certainly fundamental changes in the body that often modify the sound of the singing voice. Typically, we are not surprised to hear breathiness, loss of range, change in the characteristics of vibrato, development of tremolo, loss of breath control, vocal fatigue, pitch inaccuracies, and other undesirable features in older singers. While some of these alterations cannot be avoided in specific individuals, not all of them are manifestations of irreversible deterioration. In fact, as our understanding of the aging process improves, it is becoming more and more apparent that many of these changes can be forestalled or even corrected. As physicians and teachers, we need to look closer before concluding: "I can't help your voice; you're just getting older."

Aging

The aging process is being researched extensively because of the importance of aging to the heart, brain, and all other body systems. No natural process has greater impact on our lives. Much of the pioneering work is being performed by scientists who have dedicated their lives to this subject, such as Drs. Robert L. Ringel and Wojtek Chodzko-Zajko of Perdue University who discussed this subject at the Fifteenth Symposium: Care of the Professional Voice in 1986 (21). We are beginning to learn much more about the aging voice by combining general knowledge about the aging process with specific knowledge about laryngeal aging, such as that provided through microscopic studies by scientists such as Dr. Joel Kahane at Memphis State University. This interdisciplinary approach helps us understand our perceptions of voices over the years and helps explain our recent observations that some "old" voices can be made "young" again.

Aging is a complex conglomeration of biological events that change the structure and function of various parts of the body. There are many theories of aging that focus on processes of individual cells, on molecules responsible for the genetic transmission of our characteristics, and on changes in various organ systems. The details of specific theories are beyond the scope of this chapter. However, their principles and solutions show great promise for clinical application not only in the doctor's office, but also in the voice studio. All theories and approaches to study of the aging process recognize well-established and predictable changes throughout the body. Although there are various mechanisms involved in causing these changes, the effects are remarkably similar among various organ systems. As body structure changes, so does performance. Aging is associated with deteriorating bodily functions. Among them are accuracy, speed, endurance, stability, strength, coordination, breathing capacity, nerve conduction velocity, heart output, and kidney function. Muscle and neural tissues atrophy (deteriorate), and the chemicals responsible for nerve transmission change. Ligaments atrophy and cartilages turn to bone (including those in the larynx). Joints develop irregularities that interfere with smooth motion. The vocal folds themselves thin and deteriorate, losing their elastic and collagenous fibers. This makes them stiffer and thinner and may correlate with voice changes often noted with aging. The not-so-cheery picture is one of inevitable decline for all of us. The vocal fold edge also becomes less smooth. However, the notion that this decline occurs gradually and progressively (linear senescence) is open to challenge. It appears possible that many of these functions can be maintained at a better level than expected until very near the end of life, perhaps allowing a high quality singing career to extend into or beyond the seventh decade.

We have not yet stated how old "old" is. One cannot simply categorize people on the basis of how long they have lived—their chronological age. Biological age is a more useful measure, taking into account the condition and functioning of each individual's body. The desired result is to slow biological aging while chronological age advances inexorably. Although the aging process is inevitable, there are great differences among individuals in the rate and extent of its bodily changes. Although more study is needed, physicians and voice teachers already have some tools for intervention to slow the effects of aging.

Intervention

Certain aspects of the aging process are relatively easy to control medically. For example, as female singers reach menopause, estrogen deprivation causes substantial changes in the mucous membranes that line the vocal tract, the muscles, and throughout the patient's body. These are frequently reflected in the voice but can be forestalled for many years with estrogen replacement therapy. Generally, estrogens should not be used alone but rather sequentially in combination with progestens. This provides a more natural hormonal environment. The effects of hormonal change have been recognized for a long time and are among the easiest aging effects to combat.

Systematically attacking the aging process in other areas is more novel and controversial. The bodily changes characteristic of aging are not unique. In many ways, they are identical to those seen in disease, and in disuse such as prolonged bed rest or immobilization of a leg. In particular, muscle disuse causes loss of muscle fibers indistinguishable from that seen with advanced age. Exercise avoids or reverses many of these changes in the young, and initial observations suggest it may have the same effect when the changes are caused by aging. Appropriate exercise may not only help maintain muscle function and coordination, but it should also help elsewhere in the vascular system, nervous system, and especially in the respiratory system. Proper nutrition and weight control are also important. Respiratory function normally decreases with advancing age. In particular, residual volume increases, with a consequent decrease in vital capacity, tending to undermine the primary respiratory improvements resulting from earlier voice training. So, as a singer's respiratory potential diminishes, it is essential that he/she remain as close as possible to his optimum respiratory conditioning.

This author finds it helpful to think of each individual as having a performance range from his/her poorest performance to his/her absolutely optimal performance. Audiences have established a certain level of performance that is acceptable for a professional singer. At the age of 18, a singer with an excellent voice may perform at only 50% of his current potential. Yet, he/she may get away with it, because the condition of his/her body is above the acceptable performance standard. However, as he/she ages, his/her physical abilities deteriorate. If he/she still performs at only 50% of his/her new ability, he/she will fall below the acceptable performance standard. However, if, through appropriate training, exercise, medication, and other factors, he/she is able to get to 70, 80, or 90% of his/her potential performance level, he/she may well maintain professionally acceptable performance standards for many decades.

We are accustomed to thinking of older people as having greater latitude in most things by virtue of experience and in deference to their age. When we hear a 60-year-old tenor develop a "wobble," we write it off as "getting old" and are reluctant or embarrassed to challenge him/her, because, after all, he/she cannot help aging. We also often do not think of prescribing exercises such as swimming, walking, jogging, or aerobics for people with gray hair and a little extra weight. However, this reticence is unfair and unproductive. To the contrary, as lungs lose their elasticity and distensibility and abdominal muscle mass begins to deteriorate, it is all the more important for a singer to be in peak physical condition. A singer whose respiratory and abdominal conditioning is not good enough to allow him/her to walk up a few flights of stairs without becoming winded probably is unable to maintain good abdominal support throughout a recital or opera. When the power source of the voice is undermined in this way, excess muscle use in the neck and tongue usually supervenes. Conditioning muscles gradually in a disciplined fashion under medical supervision restores good support. Regular vocal technical training can eliminate the tremolo and improve agility, accuracy, and endurance in the older singer just as it can in the beginner.

Other age-related medical changes may also be significant to vocal function in some people. *Personality* is now most commonly described in terms of a five-factor model: neuroticism, extraversion, openness, agreeableness, and conscientiousness. In general, personality traits are quite stable after approximately age 30. It is useful for the physician to understand personality traits and their tendency for stability. These may be helpful in interpreting other psychological changes associated with aging. Certain *mental disorders* are more common in the elderly, including Alzheimer's Disease and paraphrenia. In addition, elderly people have a higher incidence of risk factors associated with mental illness including poverty, bereavement, isolation, sensory deficits and physical illness. It should also be noted that older people perform differently on psychodiagnostic tests than younger people, and such studies need to be interpreted with caution, especially when one is trying to distinguish between early dementia, and expected mental changes such as benign senescent forgetfulness. Many of these conditions may impair a person's ability to concentrate, consistently perform vocal tasks, and cooperate with voice rehabilitation.

Sexual dysfunction is also common among the elderly. It is important to recognize that this is associated with alterations in the hormonal environment that may also affect vocal function. For example, in males, serum levels of testosterone decline along with sexual function. In women, postmenopausal levels of estrogen and progesterone are also low, although their effect upon sexual function is less predictable. However, they are associated with changes in mucosal secretions and structure, and in mood. Physicians should be aware that estrogen-androgen combinations are prescribed for sexual dysfunction in women. The androgens may cause irreversible masculinization of the voice, and their use should be avoided whenever possible.

In addition to the endocrine problems discussed above, thyroid disease in the elderly deserves special mention. Both hyperthyroidism and hypothyroidism are notoriously difficult to diagnose during advanced age. The elderly patient with hyperthyroidism frequently does not display the "typical" features encountered in younger people. In addition, elderly patients often have other problems to which their difficulties are ascribed in the absence of clear diagnostic clues to hyperthyroidism. The diagnosis of hypothyroidism in the elderly is often missed because many of the symptoms of hypothyroidism may be inaccurately attributed to age. These include mental slowing, loss of energy, neurotic behavior, hearing loss, weight gain, musculoskeletal discomfort, dry skin, changes in facial appearance, and other problems. Alterations in thyroid function frequently produce substantial changes in vocal quality including loss of range, efficiency, and muffling of the voice. These vocal derangements generally resolve when the thyroid abnormality is treated.

Oral cavity changes associated with aging may be particularly troublesome to singers. Loss of dentition may alter occlusion and articulation causing especially disturbing problems for professional voice users and wind instrumentalists. These difficulties may be avoided to some extent by having impressions made while dentition is still normal. Dentures can then be fashioned that are more similar to the person's natural teeth. Although salivary glands lose up to about 30% of their parenchymal tissue over a lifetime, salivary secretion remains adequate in most healthy, non-medicated people throughout life. However, changes in the oral mucosa are similar to those occurring in the skin (thinning and dehydration). They render oral mucosa in the elderly more susceptible to injury, and the sensation of xerostomia may be especially disturbing to singers. Oral cancers also comprise about 5% of all malignancies, and 95% of oral cancers occur in people over 40 years of age. Cancers in the head and neck may result in profound voice dysfunction.

Many other factors must also be taken into account in diagnosis and treatment of elderly patients. These include *coronary artery disease, cerebrovascular disease, hypertension, obesity, stroke, diabetes, cancer, diet, osteoporosis, hearing loss, vision loss, swallowing dysfunction, anemia, arthritis, neurological dysfunction* including *tremor, incontinence, gastrointestinal disorders* and other conditions. All of these may have adverse effect on the voice either through action on the larynx, or through impairment of the voice producing mechanism at another anatomical site.

Because older singers have considerably less natural reserve and resilience, we need to be particularly demanding with them. They cannot compensate for or tolerate weaknesses like a teenager, nor can they recover quickly from injuries to their vocal apparatus. However, with optimal physical and vocal conditioning, proper medical supervision of cardiac and respiratory function, and appropriate medication, weight control, and nutrition, it appears likely that a great many singers may enjoy extra years or decades of performance that are gratifying both to them and to their audiences.

REFERENCES

1. Sataloff RT. The aging voice. *NATS J* 1987;44(1)(Jan/Feb):20–21.
2. Hollien H. Old voices: what do we really know about them? *J Voice* 1987;1:2–17.
3. Chodzko-Zajko WJ, Ringel RL. Physiological aspects of aging. *J Voice* 1987;1:18–26.
4. Kahane JC. Connective tissue changes in the larynx and their effects on the voice. *J Voice* 1987;1:27–30.
5. Ringel RL, Chodzko-Zajko WJ. Vocal indices of biological aging. *J Voice* 1987;1:31–37.
6. Morris RJ, Brown WS. Age-related voice measures among adult women. *J Voice* 1987;1:38–43.
7. Linville SE. Acoustic-perceptual studies of aging voice in women. *J Voice* 1987;1:44–48.
8. Huntley R, Hollien H, Shipp T. Influences of listener characteristics on perceived age estimates. *J Voice* 1987;1:49–52.
9. Lawrence VL, ed. *Transcripts of the thirteenth symposium: care of the professional voice.* New York: The Voice Foundation, 1985;441–480.
10. Aronson AE. *Clinical voice disorders,* 2nd ed. New York: Thieme, 1985;43–55.
11. Wilson DK. *Voice problems in children,* 3rd ed. Baltimore: Williams & Wilkins, 1986; 2–341.
12. Andrews ML, Summers A. *Voice therapy for adolescents.* Boston: College-Hill Publication, 1988;1–202.
13. Lee PA. Normal ages of pubertal events among American males and females. *J Adoles Health Care* 1980;1(1):26–29.
14. Hagg U, Tarranger J. Menarche and voice change as indications of the pubertal growth spurt. *Acta Odontal Scand* 1980;38(3):179–186.

15. Blatt IM. Training singing children during the phases of voice mutation. *Ann Otol Rhinol Laryngol* 1983;92(5, part 1):462–468.
16. Sataloff RT. The professional voice. I. Anatomy and history. *J Voice* 1987;1(1)92–104.
17. Sataloff RT. The professional voice. II. Physical examination. *J Voice* 1987;1(2): 191–201.
18. Sataloff RT. The professional voice. III. Common diagnoses and treatments. *J Voice* 1987;1(3):283–292.
19. McGlone R, Hollein H. Vocal pitch characteristics of aged women. *J. Speech Hear Res* 1963;6:164–170.
20. Hollein H, Shipp T. Speaking fundamental frequency and chronologic age in males. *J Speech Hear Res* 1972;15:155–159.
21. Special issue on vocal aging. *J Voice* 1987;1(1)(March):2–67.

Professional Voice: The Science and Art of Clinical Care, Robert T. Sataloff. Raven Press, Ltd., New York © 1991.

10

Allergy

*Joseph R. Spiegel, **Mary Hawkshaw, and *Robert T. Sataloff

*Department of Otolaryngology, Thomas Jefferson University, Philadelphia, Pennsylvania; and **American Institute of Voice and Ear Research, Philadelphia, Pennsylvania

Mild allergies are more incapacitating to professional voice users than to others because of their effect on the mucosal cover layer. If a singer has a short period of annual allergy and is able to control the symptoms well with antihistamines that do not produce disturbing side effects, this approach is reasonable. When used, mild antihistamines in small doses should be tried. It is often necessary to "experiment" with several antihistamines before finding a suitable balance in a singer between therapeutic effect and side effects. The adverse side effects may be counteracted to some extent with iodinated glycerol (Organidin, Wallace). This mucolytic expectorant helps liquify mucus and increases the output of thin respiratory tract secretions. Entex-LA (Baylor) is a useful expectorant and vasoconstrictor that increases and thins mucosal secretions. Guaifenesin (Robitussin, Robins) is also an excellent mucolytic expectorant. However, medications may produce disturbing side effects in professional voice users. Such problems justify allergic evaluation and hyposensitization therapy in many patients who might not need to go through this process if they were in other professions.

About one of every five persons in America has an allergy. Allergy, in simple terms, is an abnormal response to substances that ordinarily do not adversely affect the majority of people. An allergy is a reaction to something an individual inhales, ingests, has contact with, or is injected with, and their symptoms range from being very mild to severe (even fatal). Individuals may suffer seasonal bouts with their allergies or may be ill perennially, depending on what in their environment causes their hypersensitivity.

The focus of this chapter is limited to a discussion of inhalant allergies (those that produce hay fever–like symptoms) and the current modalities in diagnosis and treatment. The major inhalant allergies are pollens, dust, molds, and animal dander.

Understanding allergies is a complex and important medical issue. For those of us caring for the professional voice user, it is a crucial issue, since most of the symptoms caused by inhalant allergies affect the mucous membranes of the nose, eyes, ears, and throat. As stated by Sataloff in his article "Professional Singers: The Science and Art of Clinical Care," "any mucosal irritant can disrupt the delicate vocal mechanism" (1). It is easy to see how problematic undiagnosed and or untreated allergies can be in the life of a professional voice user.

An explanation of what allergy is begins with the basic understanding of the immune system, the body's system of defense. Dr. Joseph A. Bellanti in his book *Immunology* has defined the process of immunity as "all those physiologic mechanisms which endow the animal with the capacity to recognize materials as foreign to itself and to neutralize, eliminate or metabolize them with or without injury to its own tissues." Allergies occur because this process does injure the hypersensitive person's tissues (2).

The mechanism of an allergic reaction involves four components: the allergen, the antibody, mast cells, and the body's organs that are affected. Allergens are the substances that elicit an allergic response. Simply summarized, an allergen enters the body and reacts with an antibody (immunoglobin E, IgE) that is fixed to the surface of mast cells, which are found in the nose, lungs, and skin. This allergen–antibody binding triggers the release of mediators, which are responsible for the symptoms of allergy. Histamine is the most well-recognized mediator of the immediate allergic response. The mechanisms of the mediators cause contraction of smooth muscles, dilatation of blood vessels, and the stimulation of mucous glands to produce increased quantities of mucus. The allergic symptoms are a response of the organ being affected by this process (3).

Hay fever is an old English term used to describe an array of allergic symptoms that involve the eyes, ears, nose, and throat. These symptoms include nasal congestion, sneezing, clear drainage of the nose; watery, itchy eyes; throat soreness and a sensation of constantly needing to clear one's throat (from postnasal drip); pain and/or pressure in the ears; headaches; and fatigue. These symptoms are most commonly seasonal, when the grasses, trees, and weeds are pollinating; however, they may occur year-round in some individuals.

Pollinating seasons vary significantly across the United States, as does the allergen that is most problematic in each region. For example, ragweed is a major problem in the east at the end of the summer. Grass is the most problematic allergen in the west, especially during the months of May and June. Dust and molds are the inhalant allergens that generally produce symptoms year-round. "Allergies to dust and mold are aggravated commonly during rehearsals and performances in concert halls, especially older concert halls, because of the numerous curtains, backstage droppings and dressing room facilities that are rarely cleaned thoroughly" (4). Since many singers travel extensively, location is important to bear in mind when attempting to elicit an allergic history.

The symptoms of allergy are similar to those of other diseases that must be ruled out by the physician before the diagnosis of allergy is made. A clue to allergy is that the symptoms are generally chronic and vary in severity. The steps a physician takes in evaluating a person for allergic disease include: history taking and physical examination, followed by skin testing and/or a RAST (radioallergosorbent test) blood test.

Accurate and thorough history taking is the first step in diagnosing allergy. The physician or nurse that he/she may designate takes a very detailed in-depth history of the patient's life, which includes assessment of present symptoms; where the individual lives and works; what he/she eats, drinks, and takes as medication; and his/her personal and family medical history. The questioning is often long and tedious, but the patient must remember that the goal of such extensive interviewing is to uncover clues as to what allergens in his/her environment may be causing the problems.

The physician then performs a physical examination not only to confirm the diagnosis of allergy but also to rule out all other medical conditions that may be stimulating or aggravating the symptoms of allergy. On completion of a history and physical examination, when allergic disease is strongly suspected, the physician then proceeds with skin testing and/or RAST blood testing to confirm the diagnosis.

Skin testing has been the "state of the art" in allergy testing for many years and is still used by most physicians. The two most common types of skin testing are the scratch test and the prick test. In this type of testing, the skin (generally on the arms) is scratched or pricked, and a drop of extract of the allergen being tested is placed on the site. Evaluation of the site after 20 min is made to determine if an allergic reaction has occurred. A positive response is a small, red, raised spot (similar to a mosquito bite), which is sometimes associated with itching at the site. No local reaction at the site of testing is considered a negative result. Skin testing is time-consuming and generally takes four to eight hours to perform, since each allergen is tested separately with at least 20 min between each test. Skin testing is traditional, and proponents of skin testing argue that this is the most sensitive and reliable means of determining the presence of allergy. The RAST blood test is rapidly becoming the state of the art in diagnosing allergy in many physicians' offices across the country. This is an *in vitro* test, performed outside the body in a test tube. The details of this assay are beyond the scope of this review; however, in basic terms, the test is a measurement of the patient's IgE antibody response to the various allergens being tested. The test results are scored in classes, which reflect an individual's degree of hypersensitivity to each allergen. This type of testing is far more time efficient for the patient, as it only requires five minutes to have one's blood drawn in the doctor's office.

Once the diagnosis of allergy is made, a plan of treatment is determined. "The allergy sufferer can and must learn to treat themselves with the help and advice of a physician" (5). The three modalities of treatment are avoidance, medications, and immunotherapy (allergy shots). Avoidance of what one is allergic to seems like common sense; however, it is often impossible to achieve. Individuals with dust allergies may be able to keep their homes relatively "dust-free," but they have no control over the homes they may visit, hotels they may stay in, or where they work or perform. In our practice, we see many patients who suspect that they might be allergic to their dog or cat, and they refuse to be tested for such an allergy. They simply do not want to know if they are allergic to their pet, because they would rather suffer with allergies than consider being without the animal. These examples illustrate the variance of compliance in modifying one's environment to help treat the symptoms of allergy. The patient must be a willing participant in his/her care.

When avoidance and/or environmental control are not sufficient to control the allergic symptoms, the physician will then prescribe medication to help relieve the suffering. Antihistamines, decongestants, and nasal sprays comprise the armamentarium of medications universally used to treat allergies.

Antihistamines block the release of histamine and thus prevent activation of the allergic response. Two side effects of antihistamines, drowsiness and excessive drying of the nose and mouth, are often bothersome in most individuals and almost always are intolerable in the professional voice user. Decongestants are used to help treat the allergic symptoms by decreasing the swelling of mucous membranes that cause congestion. Depending on the severity of allergic symptoms, antihistamines and decongestants are often prescribed in combination.

Nasal sprays (Beconase [Allen and Hanburys], Vancenase [Schering], and Nasalide [Syntex]) are topical steroids whose function is to decrease swelling of mucous membranes and thus promote easier breathing. This type of steroid is not absorbed by the bloodstream, thus eliminating the fear of long-term steroid use, which has received a great deal of media attention over the past few years. This type of nasal spray is only available with a doctor's prescription, and its use and effectiveness need to be monitoried by the doctor at regular intervals.

When antihistamines, decongestants, and nasal sprays in some combination fail to control the allergic symptoms, allergy shots are the next line of treatment. Allergy shots are injections of the allergens to which the patient is allergic. The goal of therapy is to increase the individual's immunity to the allergen by desensitization to that allergen. Individuals are initially given minute amounts of the allergen which are gradually increased to a maximally tolerated dose, one in which the allergic symptoms no longer manifest themselves. This desentization takes several months, since injections cannot be given more than twice weekly. This type of therapy dictates compliance on the part of the patient, since a requirement is a visit to the doctor's office at least once a week for several months.

SUMMARY

Allergic disease is a common problem and must not be overlooked in the evaluation of the professional voice user who seeks medical attention for complaints of changes in his/her voice. Even complaints of mild nasal congestion or dry scratchy throat, which may not alter the voice primarily, can cause chronic irritation that may impair vocal performance. Important to remember is that symptoms of allergy are generally chronic, vary in severity, and sometimes have seasonal variation. Understanding allergy and its diagnosis and treatment is essential for providing comprehensive care to the professional voice user. An appreciation for allergy and its special implications for performers is important not only for physicians, but also for professional voice users and their teachers.

REFERENCES

1. Sataloff RT. Professional singers: the science and art of clinical care. *Am J Otolaryngol* 1981;2:251–266.
2. Frazier C. *Coping and living with allergy.* Englewood Cliffs, New Jersey: Prentice-Hall, 1980.
3. Manji RJ. Allergy skin tests: an overview. In: Lee KJ, ed. *The otolaryngologic clinics of North America.* Philadelphia: W.B. Saunders, 1985;719–724.
4. Nalebuff DJ. PRIST, RAST and beyond. In: Lee KJ, ed. *The otolaryngologic clinics of North America.* Philadelphia: W.B. Saunders, 1985;725–744.
5. Fadal RG, Nalebuff DJ. A study of optimum dose immunotherapy in pharmacological treatment failure. *Arch Otolaryngol* 1980;106:38–43.

Professional Voice: The Science and Art of Clinical Care, Robert T. Sataloff. Raven Press, Ltd., New York © 1991.

11

Respiratory Dysfunction

*Joseph R. Spiegel, *Robert T. Sataloff, **John R. Cohn, and ***Mary Hawkshaw

*Department of Otolaryngology, Thomas Jefferson University, Philadelphia, Pennsylvania; **Thomas Jefferson University Hospital, Philadelphia, Pennsylvania; and ***American Institute for Voice and Ear Research, Philadelphia, Pennsylvania*

Anyone who works with singers and actors has encountered the term "support." Although the laryngologist, speech-language pathologist, voice scientist, singing teacher, acting teacher, and performer may have slightly different understandings of the word, virtually everyone agrees that support is essential to efficient, healthy, professional voice production. Although singers and actors frequently use the term "diaphragm" synonymously with support, it is actually a combination of thoracic, rib cage, and abdominal muscle function. This support mechanism constitutes the power source of the voice and should generate a vector of force in the direction of the air column passing between the vocal folds. The diaphragm is an inspiratory muscle, of course, and represents only a portion of the support mechanism. Practitioners in all fields recognize that proper training of the thoracic and abdominal support mechanism is essential. Deficiencies in anatomy or technique, or diseases undermining the effectiveness of the abdominal musculature and respiratory system often result not only in unacceptable vocal quality and projection, but also in abusive compensatory vocal behavior and laryngeal injury.

Breathing is a complex process. Voice scientists have struggled for years to break it down into component parts in order to study breathing more effectively. Basic research has provided insight into optimal methods of inspiration, prephonatory positioning of the chest and abdomen, and expiration. The knowledge acquired through scientific research has helped guide the speech-language pathologist, singing teacher, and acting teacher in modifying vocal behavior. It has helped reinforce some traditional practices and explained why others have often failed and should be abandoned.

Respiratory problems are especially problematic to singers and other voice professionals (1). They also cause similar problems for wind instrumentalists, also by interfering with support. The effects of severe respiratory infection are obvious and will be discussed only briefly in this chapter. Restrictive lung disease such as that associated with obesity may impair support by decreasing lung volume and respiratory efficiency. Even mild obstructive lung disease can impair support enough to result in increased neck and tongue muscle tension and abusive voice use capable of producing vocal nodules. This scenario occurs with unrecognized asthma. This may be difficult to diagnose unless suspected, because many such cases of asthma are exercise-induced. Performance is a form of exercise. Consequently, the singer will have normal pulmonary function clinically and may even have reasonably normal pulmonary function tests at rest in the office. He/she will also usually support well and sing with good technique during the first portion of a performance. However, as performance exercise continues, pulmonary function decreases, effectively impairing support and resulting in abusive technique. When suspected, this entity can be confirmed through a methacholine challenge test. Treatment of the underlying pulmonary disease to restore effective support is essential to resolving the vocal problem. Treating asthma is rendered more difficult in professional voice users because of the need in some patients to avoid not only inhalers, but also drugs that produce even a mild tremor, which may be audible during soft singing. A skilled pulmonologist can usually tailor a satisfactory regimen.

ASSESSMENT

The respiratory system consists of the nose, nasopharynx, oropharynx, larynx, trachea, lungs, musculoskeletal thorax, and abdominal musculature. Its function is influenced by the overall health and fitness of the individual. Assessment and care of the entire respiratory system are essential.

Assessment of a professional voice user's respiratory complaints begins with a complete history and physical examination and is followed by appropriate laboratory testing. It is particularly important to identify the correct diagnosis in a singer, since empiric trials of "shotgun" treatments may have deleterious effects on the voice (i.e., laryngeal inflammation encountered with some inhaled steroids, drying effects of antihistamines, etc.) and may adversely affect performance.

History

Evaluation begins with a complete history, emphasizing questions related to each portion of the respiratory tract. Symptoms may be constant or intermittent, have seasonal variation, be brought on or relieved by environmental changes (i.e., exposure to animals, plants, dusty environments, etc.), relieved by medication, or associated with other symptoms. Many singers and actors are symptomatic only when they perform outdoors or in dusty buildings.

Questions regarding respiratory complaints begin with the nose. Has the patient noted obstruction, congestion, epistaxis, rhinorrhea, or postnasal drip? Does he have a history of nasal trauma? Trauma that leads to nasal obstruction may not involve a significantly displaced nasal fracture. Minor nasal trauma, especially in early life, can lead to severe intranasal deformities as facial growth progresses.

Throat dryness and pain during performance may be noted by singers with nasal obstruction. Complaints of swelling in the throat, dysphagia, odynophagia, otalgia, and hyponasality are found with obstructing lesions. Such complaints may also be due to causes other than primary pathology in the respiratory system such as gastroesophageal reflux.

Laryngeal complaints may be due to either primary lesions that obstruct breathing or dysfunction of the lower respiratory tract. Mass lesions can cause stridor, hoarseness, breathiness, diplophonia, or pain with use of the singing or speaking voice. Symptoms such as loss of vocal range or vocal fatigue may be due to either primary laryngeal lesions or inadequate airflow being produced by the lungs. Singers and actors may complain of stiffness or pain in the neck during or after rehearsal and performance. These symptoms are usually secondary to tension and may result from changes in technique to compensate for inadequate respiratory function. A history of a neck mass may indicate infection, laryngocele, neoplasm, or other serious pathology. However, occasionally the "mass" will turn out to be severe spasm of neck muscles. This is especially common after trauma such as whiplash and is often associated with severe vocal dysfunction.

Questions regarding breathing strength, support, and control are critical. Does the vocalist feel short of breath, and, if so, is it related to performance? Is there wheezing or chest tightness related to dyspnea? Is there a cough, and is this cough productive? Is there hemoptysis? Chest pain can be related to dyspnea, hard coughing, improper vocal technique, or other causes.

The history also investigates the patient's overall health. Nutritional status is evaluated, remembering that the presence of obesity or anorexia can affect the bellows action of the chest. Recent changes in weight or bowel habits and the presence of symptoms such as headache, fever, and night sweats are noted. Allergies and asthma are especially important, because of their direct effect on breathing. A history of abdominal hernias, symptoms of gastroesophageal reflux (throat clearing, thick mucus, intermittent hoarseness, halitosis, prolonged warm-up time, dyspepsia), neurologic weaknesses, paresthesia, and lesions of the extremities may lead the physician to the cause of the voice complaint.

The past medical history is evaluated first for previous pulmonary diseases including tuberculosis (especially in recent immigrants to the United States and the inner city population), pneumonia, and environmental exposure to pulmonary irritants such as asbestos. Cardiac disease can directly influence respiratory function or can have indirect effects when it leads to exercise intolerance. Thyroid disease can have effects on both the general health of the patient and local compressive effects on the trachea.

The patient must be questioned about any drugs he/she is taking, including over-the-counter preparations. Propranalol, used by some performers to reduce anxiety, can exacerbate an underlying asthmatic condition (2). Long-term antibiotic use can cause secondary infections with opportunistic organisms. Antihistamines and decongestants produce drying of the upper airway that can alter respiratory function.

Alcohol and tobacco use and dietary and sleeping habits also give an indication of the patient's general and respiratory health status. Cigarette smoking is the leading cause of respiratory disease in the United States and should be avoided by all professional voice users! Cigarette smoking by family members or in the workplace may also cause symptoms. Marijuana and cocaine are especially deleterious.

Specific questions about vocal training and technique are helpful in determining the diagnosis and the most appropriate treatment for the professional voice user (3). The history and current level of vocal training, experience, and career goals provide an assessment of the patient's professional skill and needs. Particularly important is determining the date of the next critical performance or audition. Physicians who care for singers should also be aware of the basics of technique in both the singing and speaking voice.

Physical Examination

The patient is evaluated for obesity or lack of appropriate muscle mass. Affect is assessed for signs of anxiety or depression, which may affect breathing patterns.

A complete head and neck examination is required. The nose is examined during forceful inspiration for collapse of the critical nasal "valve" area, as well as for deformities that can lead to nasal obstruction. Mucosal inflammation, mass lesions, and the presence and quality of nasal secretions are noted.

Examination of the oral cavity reveals the level of dental hygiene, moisture of the mucosal surfaces, and motion of the tongue and soft palate. Mass lesions that can cause upper airway obstruction are noted. Patients with a history of adenoidectomy are evaluated for nasopharyngeal stenosis from excessive scar formation and for velopharyngeal incompetence.

The larynx is examined by indirect laryngoscopy, flexible laryngoscopy, or strobovideolaryngoscopy as the situation demands. Large obstructive mass lesions, severe mucosal edema, and recurrent nerve paralysis can usually be detected by mirror examination. Examination of the larynx in a singer is not complete without examination of the singing voice (3). Posture during singing or acting, abdominal support, breath control, and the development of dyspnea while performing are assessed, and the voice is evaluated for range, hoarseness, breathiness, and fatigue. Assessment of voice technique and efficiency often reveals the etiology of the performer's complaints.

The chest is examined to evaluate rales, wheezes, rhonchi, and areas of hyper- and hypoaeration. Auscultation of the chest with forced expiration may accentuate wheezing not apparent during quiet breathing. Auscultation of the heart is performed to determine rate, rhythm, the presence of murmurs, or a pericardial friction rub. The abdomen is examined for masses, hernias, and muscle tone. Extremities are evaluated for weakness, level of sensation, and deformities. The neurologic examination must be complete. Cranial nerve problems can affect the upper airway, while generalized problems of muscle weakness and loss of coordination can severely affect the thoracic and abdominal respiratory musculature.

Laboratory Tests

Rhinomonometry is considered the most useful test for quantifying nasal airflow before and after treatment (4, 5). However, variability among tests limits its clinical usefulness (6, 7). Additional research is needed to develop a more valid, reliable technique for assessing nasal function.

Airflow Rate Testing

Airflow rate testing determines the flow of air across the larynx during phonation. It is usually measured with a spirometer but can be evaluated more accurately with a pneumotachograph or hot-wire anemometer. The mean flow rate is defined as the total volume of air expired during phonation divided by the duration of the phonation. The average is 89 to 141 ml/sec and the normal range is 72 to 200 ml/sec (8). There is no significant difference noted between males and females or between older children and adults (9). The phonation quotient is defined as the vital capacity of the patient divided by the maximum time of phonation. The average for this test is 120 to 190 ml/sec with an upper limit of 200 to 300 ml/sec (8). Both these determinates are used to evaluate laryngeal lesions that affect upper respiratory function. Lesions that cause glottic incompetence, reducing laryngeal efficiency (i.e., vocal nodules, vocal fold paralysis), will lead to increased flow rates. Airflow testing is also useful for documenting the results of treatment for lesions such as nodules, a problem found frequently in professional voice users (9, 10).

Pulmonary Function Testing

The cornerstone of pulmonary function testing is spirometry. Various aspects of this important test are also discussed in Chapter 8. Spirometry is based on the measurement of the forced vital capacity (FVC) and its components (Fig. 1). The FVC is the quantity of air that is exhaled after the lungs are maximally filled (total lung capacity or TLC) and then forcefully emptied. This is plotted as a volume versus time curve. From this curve, the vital capacity (VC), forced expiratory volume in 1 sec (FEV_1), and maximal mid-expiratory flow rate (MMEFR, $FEF_{25-75\%}$) can be determined (Fig. 2). The MMEFR is the volume of air expired between the 25% point of the FVC ($FEV_{25\%}$) and the 75% point of the FVC ($FEV_{75\%}$) divided by the time it takes to expire that volume. This measurement is the single most sensitive value in diagnosing obstructive pulmonary disease that can be measured with simple equipment (11). The peak expiratory flow rate correlates well with functional limitations, but this is difficult to measure with conventional volume displacement spirometers (12). Others use the ratio of FEV_1/FVC to quantitate the degree of airflow obstruction.

The computer-generated flow versus volume loop has become popular as a more sensitive means of evaluating ventilatory impairment. The computer measures the instantaneous flow at multiple points during a forced expiration followed by a forced inspiration and plots the instantaneous flow against the volume expired or inspired at each point on a continuous graph (Fig. 3).

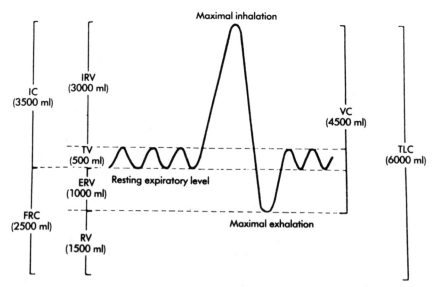

FIG. 1. Lung volumes (normal adult averages). TLC, total lung capacity; VC, vital capacity; IC, inspiratory capacity; FRC, functional reserve capacity; TV, tidal volume; IRV, inspiratory reserve volume; ERV, expiratory reserve volume; RV, reserve volume.

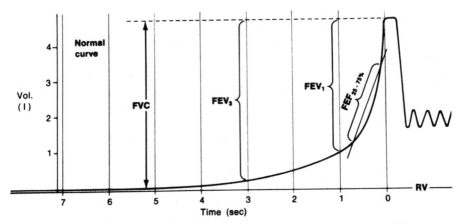

FIG. 2. Volume vs. time spirometric tracing. FVC, forced vital capacity; FEV$_1$, FEV$_3$, forced expiratory volume in 1 and 3 sec, respectively; FEF$_{25-75\%}$, ; RV, reserve volume.

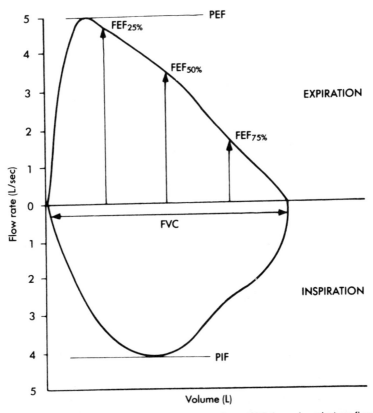

FIG. 3. Flow vs. volume loop. PEF, peak expiratory flow; FEF, forced expiratory flow; FVC, forced vital capacity; PIF, peak inspiratory flow.

This "loop" has a characteristic shape that can be useful in detecting and characterizing pulmonary and laryngeal pathology (13).

Spirometry is performed with the nose occluded and the patient making forceful expirations into the spirometer. The patient should complete three FVC trials with less than 5% variability in order to consider a test acceptable. Predicted normal values are determined from the height, weight, and sex of the patient. Blacks tend to have smaller lung volumes, so lower predicted values may be used. Normal values for the test subject are considered to be anything greater than or equal to 80%, or within 1.64 standard deviations of these predicted values (14).

Patterns of pulmonary disease can be determined from both the standard spirometric plot and the flow-volume loop (15). In obstructive disease, there are decreased flows represented by decreased FEV_1 and a decreased FEV_1/FVC ratio (Fig. 4). A flow-volume loop will initially show increased convexity of the expiratory phase, while, with more severe obstruction, there may be loss of expiratory volume and flattening of both the inspiratory and ex-

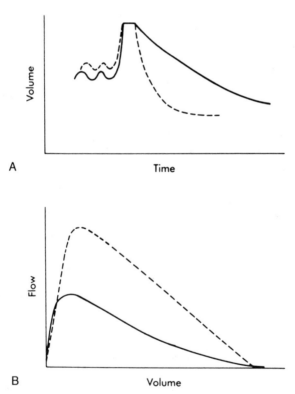

FIG. 4. Spirometric pattern in obstructive disease. **A:** Volume vs. time curve. **B:** Flow vs. volume curve, expiratory phase. Normal, dotted line; abnormal, solid line.

piratory phases. These characteristics can be variable, especially in the flow-volume loop, depending on the site and duration of the obstruction. Even when FEV_1 and FEV_1/FVC are normal, a decreased MMEFR can be noted in patients with asymptomatic asthma and in smokers. Patients with restrictive lung disease have decreased volumes but normal flow (Fig. 5). Thus, the FEV_1 and FVC are proportionately decreased, causing the FEV_1/FVC ratio to be normal or even increased.

Determination of reversible obstructive pulmonary disease can be made if an increase of 12% is noted in the FVC and FEV_1 or 25% in the MMEFR after treatment with inhaled bronchodilators (14). If the diagnosis is suspected but the test results are inconclusive or normal, a methacholine challenge may be performed using progressively greater concentrations of methacholine, with measurement of the FEV_1 and MMEFR after each dose. The test is completed when the FEV_1 is decreased by 20% or more (16). This dose is called the $PD_{20FEV/1}$. Generally, nonasthmatic subjects will have a PD_{20} greater than 8 mg/ml of methacholine (17). This measure of relative

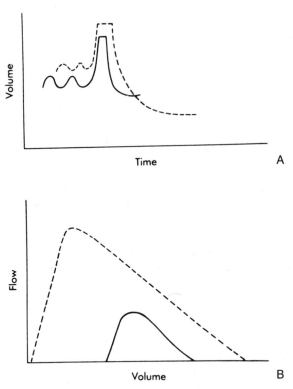

FIG. 5. Spirometric pattern in restrictive disease. **A:** Volume vs. time curve. **B:** Flow vs. volume curve, expiratory phase. Normal, dotted line; abnormal, solid line.

airway spasticity is particularly important in the diagnosis of exercise-induced asthma that is symptomatic under performance conditions (18).

Diffusing Capacity

Diffusing capacity is the relative ability of oxygen to diffuse across the arteriole-alveolar membranes in the lung, although the matching of ventilation and perfusion may be of equal or greater importance. It is tested by measuring diffusion of inhaled carbon monoxide into the blood (DLco). This determination is useful in the evaluation of patients with interstitial lung disease and correlates with oxygen desaturation during exercise (19).

Lung Volumes

TLC is measured indirectly by first determining functional reserve capacity (FRC) using an inert gas dilution technique, nitrogen washout, or body plethysmographic technique. Decreased TLC is the *sine qua non* of restrictive lung disease. Of interest, highly trained singers do not have substantially increased TLC but have improved their pulmonary efficiency by increasing FRC and reducing reserve volume (RV) (20).

Radiology

A chest radiograph should be obtained on every patient with persistent pulmonary complaints to rule out infectious or neoplastic disease. Patients with more common ailments such as asthma and bronchitis generally have normal chest radiographs. When mass lesions are identified, computerized tomography may be helpful in defining the extent of disease, although histologic correlation of radiographic abnormalities is frequently required. The ventilation/perfusion nuclear lung scan is used in the diagnosis of pulmonary embolism by defining areas of hypoperfusion.

Patients with nasal obstruction and acute or chronic sinonasal symptoms are evaluated first with plain radiographs of the sinuses. If extensive disease is suspected, computerized tomography using coronal sections will better define this region.

Other Tests

Arterial blood gas analysis (ABG) may be useful in the diagnosis of pulmonary disease. Appropriate stains of a sputum smear can provide important information in the diagnosis of infectious, allergic, and neoplastic pulmonary disease.

An electrocardiogram (ECG) assists in the diagnosis and evaluation of cardiac diseases that can be associated with dyspnea. A complete blood count (CBC) may demonstrate anemia, which contributes to dyspnea, an increased white blood cell count, which may be a sign of infection, or eosinophilia, suggesting allergy or other systemic disease.

Allergy Testing

Allergy tests are used to confirm the diagnosis and assist in the treatment of allergic disease. Problems of allergies in singers are discussed in greater length in Chapter 10. The most commonly used format is skin testing, which can be performed by scratch, prick, or intradermal technique (21, 22). Prick testing causes minimal discomfort and can be used to determine the presence of allergy to specific substances rapidly. The intradermal injection of antigens is the most sensitive test for allergy. When properly performed, either test, but particularly the intradermal technique, can be used to evaluate immediate and late phase allergic responses. Proponents of skin test–based therapy argue that this is the most sensitive and physiologically accurate way to determine the presence of allergy and plan treatment (23).

In recent years, a blood test for antigen-specific immunoglobulin E (IgE) to both inhaled and food antigens has become available. Originally done with a radioimmunoassay technique, the radioallergosorbent test (RAST) (24), it is now commonly performed as an enzyme-linked immunoabsorbent assay. These tests quantify the immunoglobulins responsible for the allergic reaction to each antigen. The proponents of RAST-based treatment contend that this precise measure of relative allergic response can be used to formulate individualized immunotherapy for the patient (25) and that RAST testing can be used to monitor the patient's response to therapy (26).

Endoscopy

Fiberoptic technology allows accurate visualization of the entire respiratory tract. Nasopharyngoscopy using a short, narrow fiberoptic endoscope is useful in defining internal nasal anatomy and in the diagnosis of pharyngeal and laryngeal obstruction. Mass lesions can be fully defined and their relationship to the vibrating edge of the vocal fold determined, especially when strobovideolaryngoscopy is also employed. Less obvious lesions such as arytenoid dislocation, vocal fold paresis, and scar are often much more apparent under stroboscopic light. Using bronchoscopy, mass lesions of the lower respiratory tract can be assessed clinically and, with the use of endobronchial biopsy, transbronchial biopsy, or brushings, can be identified pathologically.

DIAGNOSIS AND TREATMENT

Nasal Airway Obstruction

Obstruction of the nasal airway can be due to structural deformities, mass lesions, foreign bodies, or inflammation. Structural deformities usually involve deviation of the bony and/or cartilaginous nasal septum. Nasal deformity can also be complicated by inflammatory hypertrophy of the inferior turbinates and collapse of the external skeleton. Treatment of the obstructing nasal septum is surgical and involves resection and/or repositioning of the abnormal portions. It is suggested that the approach to surgery of the inferior turbinates be conservative in singers because long term drying effects have occurred secondary to mucociliary disruption when extensive resection is performed (27). Mass lesions are usually readily apparent on examination. After adequate radiologic assessment, sometimes including arteriography, most are removed surgically.

Inflammatory nasal obstruction may be infectious or allergic. Viral rhinitis is manifested by clear or mucoid rhinorrhea, postnasal drip, associated nasal obstruction, and other symptoms such as low-grade fever, sore throat, hoarseness, cough, myalgia, and malaise. Treatment is supportive with oral decongestants and hydration. When a patient has a crucial performance within 24 to 48 hr, intramuscular or oral steroids can be used to relieve many of the obstructive symptoms.

Allergic rhinitis usually involves the common "hay fever" symptoms of sneezing, itchiness, clear rhinorrhea, nasal obstruction, and associated complaints of allergic conjunctivitis. Symptoms may be related to geographical location, exposure to specific plants or wildlife, changes in diet, and the general environmental aspects and ventilation systems of lodgings and concert halls. The diagnosis is assisted by specific allergy testing (skin tests or RAST). When a single specific allergen can be defined, avoidance is the simplest solution. Removal of plants or pets, or taking precautions to avoid dust exposure within the home environment can yield dramatic improvement. Treatment of allergic rhinitis in a singer with multiple allergies by specific allergen immunotherapy is advisable. This involves weekly injections of increasing concentrations of a serum containing all the antigens to which the patient is allergic. This can provide relief from symptoms without the side effects from oral drug preparations or nasal sprays. Desensitization therapy is limited by variable patient compliance and failure to obtain a complete response in many cases.

Multiple pharamaceutical preparations are available to alleviate symptoms for patients who cannot fully avoid their allergic stimulus and are not candidates for immunotherapy. Topical steroid sprays (e.g., flunisolide, beclomethasone) can reduce nasal symptoms, and, in proper doses, these steroids are safe (28). Cromolyn sodium topical spray reduces allergic response in the mucosa, probably at least partly by stabilizing the mast cell membrane.

It is very effective in preventing allergic nasal symptoms and has few significant local side effects (29). Oral decongestant/antihistamine preparations can reduce most symptoms significantly, but the side effects of drying of the mucosal membranes and sedation, and the development of tolerance, limit the use of these medications in vocal performers. Parenteral and oral steroids rapidly reduce the edema associated with the allergic response without these side effects. In an acute obstructive phenomenon they are necessary to maintain the airway. However, long term use should be avoided because of the many potential serious side effects.

Sinusitis can cause partial or total nasal obstruction and can exacerbate an asthmatic condition (30). Major symptoms are mucopurulent rhinorrhea, postnasal drip, facial pressure, retro-orbital headache, and fever. Radiologic confirmation of chronic inflammatory changes or opacification of the paranasal sinuses and documentation of pathologic bacteria on culture of the sinus are helpful. Treatment of the acute phase of this illness includes antibiotics for two to three weeks, oral and topical decongestants, and steam inhalations. Performance can usually be permitted. In chronic conditions, long term antibiotics and treatment of any underlying conditions such as nasal obstruction blocking a sinus ostium, dental disease, or allergy are necessary. In persistent cases, surgical therapy of the paranasal sinuses may be required.

Pharyngeal Obstruction

Most cases of pharyngeal obstruction are due to adenoid and palatine tonsil hypertrophy in the adolescent or young adult. The patient usually complains of nasal obstruction and chronic mouth breathing and may have a significant snoring history. The source of the obstruction is usually apparent on physical examination and can be confirmed radiologically with lateral neck radiographs. When the obstruction is secondary to an acute infection, it is treated with high-dose oral or parenteral antibiotics. When rapid increase in the size of adenoids and tonsils is seen, mononucleosis should be considered, especially if there is associated cervical, axillary, or inguinal adenopathy. Adenoidectomy and tonsillectomy may be indicated in patients who have chronic symptomatic hypertrophy. Detailed examination of the palate is made prior to consideration of adenoidectomy. The presence of a submucous cleft, bifid uvula, or short palate can lead to significant hypernasality postoperatively (31).

Laryngeal Obstruction

Laryngeal lesions significant enough to cause respiratory impairment will cause changes in the voice. Edema secondary to infection, allergy, gastroesophageal reflux, and voice abuse can lead to partial upper airway obstruction in rare, severe cases. Anatomic defects, trauma, neoplasm, and epiglottitis are more likely to cause airway problems. Diagnosis is generally made by laryngeal examination, except in cases of epiglottitis. Radiographs are helpful in some patients. The degree of respiratory dysfunction is determined by airflow testing and pulmonary function testing. Steroids may be effective in reducing edema quickly in most of these conditions and should be accompanied by treatment of the underlying problem. Lesions that alter the respiratory function of the larynx such as vocal fold paralysis/paresis, laryngeal webs, and arytenoid dislocation usually cause vocal impairment to a far greater degree than they impair respiratory function. However, some patients elect improvement of their voices through compensatory vocal techniques or surgery, which leaves them with an adequate voice and impaired respiratory function. Treatment of the respiratory problems that these lesions cause in singers is extremely difficult. Surgical intervention to reduce the upper airway obstruction often disturbs vocal quality. Optimizing pulmonary function to overcome laryngeal inefficiency is often the best approach.

Most obstructing laryngeal lesions will not persist long enough to cause severe upper airway obstruction requiring tracheotomy, because vocal impairment occurs early in their course. When a laryngeal mass is found, endoscopic removal may be necessary if the lesion is not amenable to other therapy. These masses should be removed using an operating microscope and meticulous phonosurgical technique. Local anesthesia is used frequently in order to assess the surgical result during the procedure and avoid intubation, but excellent sedation by an anesthesiologist is necessary to keep the patient motionless even in cooperative patients. When general anesthesia is necessary, the laryngologist must take responsibility for protecting the larynx during intubation and extubation, and the most skilled anesthesiologist available should be used.

PULMONARY LESIONS

Obstructive Conditions

The most common obstructive airway disease is asthma, affecting approximately eight million people in the United States (32). It is defined as reversible obstructive airway disease, in the absence of an alternative explanation such as heart failure. Classic asthma is manifested by paroxysms of dyspnea, wheezy respirations, chest tightness, and cough, although a chronic cough can be the only presenting symptom (33). While it is usually allergic, the etiology can be nonallergic or mixed. Nonallergic groups of patients are usually older and may have symptoms associated with chronic infectious phenomena such as sinusitis or bronchitis. Symptoms can also be induced by exercise or exposure to cold air (34) or be associated with a triad including aspirin sensitivity and nasal polyps (35). The diagnosis of asthma is made by history or by demonstrating an obstructive pattern on pulmonary function testing that is reversible with bronchodilators either acutely or with chronic treatment. Bronchoprovocation with methacholine may be necessary to demonstrate the presence of asthma in patients with normal pulmonary function. Additional testing such as chest radiography, ABG, and bronchoscopy are useful in ruling out other conditions and diagnosing the long term sequelae of obstructive disease.

Airway reactivity induced asthma in singers (ARIAS) is a special form of exercise-induced asthma. Airway obstruction is caused by the exercise of singing performance. Decreased airflow undermines support, creating problems similar to those seen with improper abdominal muscle use. The singer may become short of breath, or may simply note voice fatigue, decreased range and impaired volume control. As in other conditions that impair the power source of the voice, compensatory efforts are common, including increased jaw tension, tongue retraction, and strap muscle hyperfunction. Treatment of the singing-induced asthma helps restore support for the singing voice and allows the singer to resume correct singing technique. In conjunction with singing lessons (and speech training when appropriate), voice symptoms usually disappear quickly.

The treatment of asthmatic conditions in singers is somewhat different from that of the general population. One must eliminate even mild airway reactivity in order to optimize respiratory function for performance. Inhaled steroids should be avoided entirely in singers because of the possibility of dysphonia from the propellant, steroid effects on the laryngeal musculature, or from Candida overgrowth (36–38). Mild asthma can usually be treated with sustained release oral theophylline with an inhaled beta-2 agonist for acute attacks. Inhaled sympathomimetics or cromolyn sodium may be useful in patients with exertion-induced problems just prior to strenuous voice use (39, 40). Appropriate allergen immunotherapy and inhaled cromolyn sodium are used in the care of allergic asthma and can reduce the need for bronchodilators. In more severe cases, an oral beta-2 agonist in addition to theophylline may be necessary. Steroids are effective in obtaining rapid control of asthmatic symptoms; however, they are usually reserved for severe acute exacerbations because of the side effects of prolonged use.

Chronic obstructive pulmonary disease (COPD) is a general term that is applied to airway obstruction that is not fully reversible. The most common cause of COPD is cigarette smoking. It is manifested by either bronchitis or emphysema, although many patients have elements of both diseases. Patients with bronchitis have a chronic productive cough. In emphysema, there is destruction of alveolar membranes. Patients with bronchitis or emphysema may have severe obstructive changes on pulmonary function testing and an abnormal radiograph with increased lung volume due to air trapping.

Exacerbations of bronchitis are treated with antibiotics. Otherwise, treatment is similar to that for asthma, but, because of the irreversibility of much of the airway disease, less response can be expected. In singers, hydration and cough suppressants reduce laryngeal trauma associated with coughing unless the pulmonary condition and need to clear secretions militate against the use of antitussives.

Another less commonly diagnosed cause of persistent pulmonary symptoms is gastroesophageal reflux (41). Chronic aspiration of gastric juice or particulate matter can result in chronic coughing, increased airway reactivity, or recurrent pneumonia (42). Diagnosis is made by noting arytenoid and posterior glottic inflammation on laryngeal examination, and reflux during radiologic upper gastrointestinal study with esophageal manometric testing by esophagoscopy and with 24-hr esophageal pH monitoring. Acid levels should be measured specifically during singing. Treatment includes antacids, elevation of the head of the bed, and histamine-2 antagonists (cimetadine, ranitidine) in severe cases. When medical treatment fails, surgical plication of the lower esophageal sphincter may be performed (43).

Pneumonia presents special problems for the singer. It often takes longer than a singer realizes for lung function to return to normal. Singing too soon after such infections may result in vocal difficulties as attempts are made to compensate for minor deficiencies in the power source of the voice.

Restrictive Conditions

Restrictive lung disease can be divided into two groups. The first involves restriction of the chest bellows function. Weakness of the musculoskeletal support system is found in myasthenia gravis, Guillain-Barré syndrome, poliomyelitis, multiple sclerosis, spinal cord injury, or diaphragmatic paralysis. Additionally, massive obesity, kyphoscoliosis, and flail chest from thoracic trauma impair the function of the chest wall. A second group of restrictive lesions affects the pulmonary parenchyma and includes hypersensitivity pneumonitis, atelectasis, sarcoidosis, pulmonary fibrosis, pulmonary edema, pneumonia, neoplasm, drug reactions, and congestive heart failure. The diagnosis of restrictive respiratory impairment is confirmed by pulmonary function testing. These patients have decreased lung volume with proportionately normal flow rates. The treatment of each of these syndromes is complex and not within the scope of this review. However, obesity is one cause of restrictive lung disease, and many singers have a significant weight problem. The effects of obesity on the voice have not been studied adequately; yet, there is no doubt that excessive weight can alter respiratory function. Restrictive pulmonary function due to excess weight has adverse effects on the endurance of a singer and probably on his/her longevity as a performer. Obesity is also related to hypertension, diabetes, and other conditions that may actually shorten the performer's life. Finally, a restrictive pattern of pulmonary function in a previously healthy singer may indicate early neurologic or neuromuscular disease, and comprehensive evaluation is warranted whenever this finding appears.

SUMMARY

Most singers and actors come to the laryngologist with complaints about changes in their voices; yet, many times the problem is not in the vocal folds but rather in the production of adequate airflow to drive the voice. Mild respiratory maladies such as cough or nasal congestion may not alter the voice primarily but can cause irritation or changes in technique that can impair vocal performance. Minor alterations in respiratory function that would go barely noticed in the general population can have significant effects on a professional voice user, causing vocal fatigue, loss of range, hyperfunctional abusive compensation, and other problems. Adequate knowledge of respiratory function and its disorders is essential to comprehensive care of the professional voice.

Much additional research about breathing and support is needed. Remembering that the end point of this research is the training and maintenance of healthy, beautiful professional voices, it is essential for voice scientists, voice teachers, and physicians to work together closely in clinical and basic research. Only through concerted efforts can we define the right questions and discover the right answers.

REFERENCES

1. Spiegel JR, Sataloff RT, Cohn JR, Hawkshaw M. *Respiratory dysfunction in singers: medical assessment, diagnoses and treatments. J Voice* 1988;2(1):40–50.
2. Thorn GW, Adams RD, Braunwald E, et al., eds. *Harrison's principles of internal medicine.* New York: McGraw-Hill, 1977;1215.
3. Sataloff RT. Professional singers: the science and art of clinical care. *Am J Otolaryngol* 1981;2:251–266.
4. Mertz JS, McCaffrey TV, Kern EB. Objective evaluation of anterior septal surgical reconstruction. *Otolaryngol Head Neck Surg* 1984;92:308–311.
5. Orgel HA, Meltzer EO, Kemp JP, Welch MJ. Clinical, rhinomanometric, and cytologic evaluation of seasonal allergic rhinitis treated with beclamethasone dipropionate as aqueous nasal spray or pressurized aerosol. *J Allergy Clin Immunol* 1986;77:858–864.
6. McCaffrey TV, Kern EB. Clinical evaluation of nasal obstruction. *Arch Otolaryngol* 1979;105:542–545.
7. Daubenspeck JA. Influence of small mechanical loads on variability of breathing pattern. *J Applied Physiol* 1981;50:299–306.
8. Hirano M. *Clinical examination of the voice.* New York: Springer-Verlagwein, 1981.
9. Shigemori Y. Some tests related to the air usage during phonation. *Clin Invest Otol (Fukuoka)* 1977;23:138–166.
10. Tanaka S, Gould WJ. Vocal efficiency and aerodynamic aspects in voice disorders. *Ann Otol Rhinol Laryngol* 1985;94:29–33.

11. Segall JJ, Butterworth BA. The maximal midexpiratory flow time. *Br J Dis Chest* 1968;62:139–145.
12. Despas PJ, Leroux M, Macklem PT. Site of airway obstruction in asthma determined by measuring maximal expiratory flow breathing air and a helium–oxygen mixture. *J Clin Invest* 1982;51:3235–3243.
13. Hyatt RE, Black LF. The flow-volume curve. *Am Rev Resp Dis* 1973;107:191–199.
14. Statement on spirometry: a report of the section on respiratory pathophysiology. *Chest* 1983;83:547–550.
15. Sackner MA, ed. *Diagnostic techniques in pulmonary disease.* New York: Marcel Dekker, 1980.
16. Chai H, Farr RS, Froehlich LA, et al. Standardization of bronchial inhalation challenge procedures. *J Allergy Clin Immunol* 1975;56:323–327.
17. Malo JL, Pineau L, Carter A, Martin RR. Reference values of the provocative concentrations of methacholine that cause 6% and 20% changes in forced expiratory volume in one second in a normal population. *Am Rev Resp Dis* 1983;128:8–11.
18. Chatham M, Bleeker ER, Smith PL, et al. A comparison of histamine, methacholine, and exercise airway reactivity in normal and asthmatic subjects. *Am Rev Resp Dis* 1982;126:235–240.
19. Martin L. *Pulmonary physiology in clinical practice.* St. Louis: C.V. Mosby, 1987.
20. Gould WT, Okamura H. Static lung volumes in singers. *Ann Otol Rhinol Laryngol* 1973;82:89–95.
21. Nelson HS. Diagnostic procedures in allergy. I. Allergy skin testing. *Ann Allergy* 1983;51:411–418.
22. Practice and Standards Committee. American Academy of Allergy and Immunology position statement. *J Allergy Clin Immunol* 1983;72:515–517.
23. Mangi RJ. Allergy skin tests: an overview. *Otolaryngol Clin NA* 1985;18:719–723.
24. Nalebuff DJ. An enthusiastic view of the use of RAST in clinical allergy. *Immunol Allergy Pract* 1981;3:77–87.
25. Fadal RG, Nalebuff DJ. A study of optimum dose immunotherapy in pharmacological treatment failures. *Arch Otolaryngol* 1980;106:38–43.
26. Ali M. Serum concentration of allergen-specific IgG antibodies in inhalant allergy: effect of specific immunotherapy. *Am J Clin Pathol* 1983;80:290–299.
27. Martinez SA, Nissen AJ, Stock CR, Tesmer T. Nasal turbinate resection for relief of nasal obstruction. *Laryngoscope* 1983;93:871–875.
28. Parkin JL. Topical steroids in nasal disease. *Otolaryngol Head Neck Surg* 1983;91:713–714.
29. Pelikan Z, Pelikan-Filipek M. The effects of disodium cromoglycate and beclomethasone dipropionate on the immediate response of the nasal mucosa to allergen challenge. *Ann Allergy* 1982;49:283–292.
30. McCaurin JG. A review of the interrelationship of paranasal sinus disease and certain chest conditions, with special consideration of bronchiectasis and asthma. *Ann Otol Rhinol Laryngol* 1935;44:344–353.
31. Croft CB, Shprintzen RJ, Ruben RJ. Hypernasal speech following adenotonsillectomy. *Otolaryngol Head Neck Surg* 1981;88:179–188.
32. Baum GC, Wolinsky E. *Textbook of pulmonary disease.* Boston: Little, Brown, 1983.
33. Corraa WM, Braman SS, Irwin RS. Chronic cough as the sole presenting manifestation of bronchial asthma. *N Eng J Med* 1979;300:633–637.
34. Strauss RH, McFadden ER, Ingram RH, Jaeger JJ. Enhancement of exercise-induced asthma by cold air. *N Engl J Med* 1977;297:743–747.
35. Spector SL, Wangaard CH, Farr RS. Aspirin and concomitant idiosyncrasies in adult asthmatic patients. *J Allergy Clin Immunol* 1979;64:500–506.
36. Watkins KL, Ewanowsk SJ. Effects of aerosol corticosteroids on the voice: triamcinolone acetonide and beclomethasone dipropionate. *J Speech Hearing Res* 1985;28:301–304.
37. Toogood JH, Jennings B, Greenway RW, Chuang L. Candidiasis and dysphonia complicating beclomethasone treatment of asthma. *J Allergy Clin Immunol* 1980;65:145–153.
38. Williams AJ, Baghat MS, Stableforth DE, et al. Dysphonia caused by inhaled steroids: recognition of a characteristic laryngeal abnormality. *Thorax* 1983;38:813–821.
39. Gimeno F, vanVeenen R, Steenhuis EJ, Berg WCH. Comparison of disodium cromogly-

cate, terbutaline and thiazinamium in the prevention of exercise-induced asthma and its relation to non-specific bronchial responsiveness. *Respiration* 1985;48:108–115.

40. Tullett WM, Tan KM, Wall RT, Patei KR. Dose-response effect of sodium cromoglycate pressurized aerosol in exercise induced asthma. *Thorax* 1985;40:41–44.
41. Davis MV. Relationship between pulmonary disease, hiatal hernia, and gastroesophageal reflux. *NY State J Med* 1972;72:935–938.
42. Mansfield LE, Stein MR. Gastroesophageal reflux and asthma: a possible reflex mechanism. *Ann Allergy* 1978;41:224–226.
43. Barish CF, Wu WC, Castell DO. Respiratory complications of gastroesophageal reflux. *Arch Intern Med* 1985;145:1882–1888.

Professional Voice: The Science and Art of Clinical Care, Robert T. Sataloff. Raven Press, Ltd., New York © 1991.

12

Reflux and Other Gastroenterologic Conditions That May Affect the Voice

Robert T. Sataloff

Department of Otolaryngology, Thomas Jefferson University, Philadelphia, Pennsylvania

GASTROESOPHAGEAL REFLUX LARYNGITIS

Reflux-induced otolaryngologic symptoms have been recognized for many years (1). Reflux is known to be responsible for many cases of "globus hystericus," laryngeal "spasms," cough, and other symptoms. Its association with Barrett's esophagus and esophageal carcinoma is established, and reflux is a suspected cofactor in laryngeal malignancy, especially in the postcricoid area. In professional voice users, gastroesophageal reflux laryngitis produces symptoms that might not be troublesome to other individuals but are very significant to the professional vocalist.

Gastroesophageal reflux laryngitis is endemic among singers. We have found it in 38% of patients undergoing strobovideolaryngoscopy (2), and it is present in many more of our professional voice patients, since strobovideolaryngoscopy is performed during only approximately 20% of professional singer visits, and reflux laryngitis alone is not a standard indication for strobovideolaryngoscopy. Several recent studies have documented the importance of this entity (3–5). Unfortunately, one recent study of a large number of patients reached conclusions contrary to those of previous studies and wide clinical experience (6). However, the methodology used in the study is open to criticism, and the conclusion cannot be accepted without confirmation. As discussed in Chapter 5, reflux is common among singers and other professional voice users for several reasons. First, their performance requires markedly increased abdominal pressure, which works against the esophageal sphincter. Second, many voice professionals perform without eating, because a full stomach interferes with abdominal support. In addition, they usually sing in the evening. Consequently, singers arrive home late at night, eat a large meal, and go directly to bed. This life-style combines with the stress of a performing career to produce the disproportionately high incidence of this condition. The most prevalent symptoms in professional voice users are hoarseness and low voice in the morning, prolonged warm-up time, halitosis and a bitter taste in the morning, a feeling of a lump in the throat, frequent throat clearing, chronic irritative cough, a "coated" mouth, and frequent tracheitis or tracheobronchitis. Any or all of these symptoms may be present. Classic dyspepsia is usually absent. Interestingly, after patients have been treated rigorously, dyspepsia often occurs when they relax their treatment regimens. It appears as if prolonged, chronic esophageal exposure to acid in patients who reflux through the upper sphincter may eventually dull the esophageal sensory response. However, the ability of the esophagus to produce discomfort usually returns within a month of treatment with H2 blockers and antacids. This phenomenon and the speculative explanation presented require further study.

Physical examination of the reflux patient usually reveals cherry red arytenoids and often erythema in the posterior third of the vocal folds. In severe cases, marked edema may be present, as well as granulomas or ulceration. In understanding the diagnosis and treatment of reflux laryngitis, it is helpful to review the most basic aspects of esophageal anatomy.

The esophagus is a tubular structure made of muscle and mucosa. Its primary function is to carry food from the mouth to the stomach. It starts at the upper esophageal sphincter (UES) and ends at the lower esophageal sphincter (LES). The UES and upper third are made of striated muscle, and the lower two-thirds and LES consist of smooth muscle. The outer layer is longitudinal, and the inner layer is circular. This striated muscle is innervated directly through fibers originating in the nucleus ambiguus, and the smooth muscle receives its nervous supply through the myenteric plexus from nerves originating in the dorsal motor nucleus of the vagus nerve. Swallowing involves oral (voluntary), pharyngeal (involuntary), and esophageal stages. Swallowing physiology is well covered in textbooks of gastroenterology, otolaryngology, and speech pathology and is not central to our considerations. However, it is important to understand the esophageal sphincters. The sphincters are designed to prevent abnormal movement of food upward from the stomach or esophagus and abnormal movement of air down. Atmospheric pressure in the mouth is ordinarily 0 mm Hg. The upper esophageal sphincter is ordinarily tonically contracted. Its normal pressure is roughly 80 mm Hg (about 50 mm Hg lateral and 100 mm Hg anterior/posterior). The intraesophageal pressure through the thorax is approximately -5 mm Hg. The tonically contracted lower esophageal sphincter usually has a pressure of approximately 20 mm Hg, and intragastric pressure is usually 5 mm Hg. In order to prevent gastroesophageal reflux, the LES must maintain a pressure higher than that in the stomach. Smoking, tranquilizers, some bronchodilators, nitrates, peppermint, alcohol, chocolate, and fat also decrease LES. LES is increased by antacids and protein ingestion. Its tone is caused by intrinsic muscle activity. Although it is not blocked by neuroinhibitors or vagotomy, it is decreased by drugs such as atropine and calcium channel blockers. Beta-adrenergic and dopaminergic neurotransmitters inhibit lower esophageal sphincter contraction, and cholinergic and alpha-adrenergic agents stimulate contraction. Various hormones alter lower esophageal sphincter pressure.

When gastric pressure becomes greater than LES pressure, reflux occurs. It must be remembered, however, that mechanical sphincter dysfunction is not the only cause of reflux symptoms. Gastric symptomatology (such as hypersecretion and alkaline gastroesophageal reflux), motility disorders, and other conditions must be considered. The mainstays of initial treatment for reflux laryngitis are elevation of the head of the vocalist's bed (not just sleeping on pillows), antacids, and avoidance of eating for three to four hours before going to sleep. This is often difficult for singers, but, if they are counseled about minor changes in eating habits (such as eating larger meals at breakfast and lunch), they can usually comply. Avoidance of alcohol and coffee is beneficial. For patients concerned with long-term consumption of some of the substances contained in specific antacids (such as aluminum), it is usually possible to select a medication that does not contain the chemical they wish to avoid (Tables 1 and 2). Cimetidine, ranitidine, or other H2 blockers are also often helpful, and we usually use an H2 blocker with the initial course of therapy. However, cimetidine has among its complications induction of male infertility. In this generally young population, it is probably best to avoid this drug, especially since the complication has not been

TABLE 1. *Contents of liquid antacids (in mg/tsp)*

	Aluminium hydroxide	Magnesium hydroxide	Calcium carbonate	Magnesium carbonate	Magaldrate	Simethicone	Sodium
Alternagel	600						<2.5
Aludrox	307	103					
Amphogel	320						
Camalox	225	200	250				
Delcid	600	665					≤15
Di-Gel	200	200				20	
Gaviscon (mg/tbsp)	95			412			
Gelusil	200	200				25	
Gelusil II	400	400				30	
Kolantyl	150	150					
Maalox	225	200					
Maalox Plus	225	200				25	
Mylanta	200	200				20	
Mylanta II	400	400				40	
Riopan					540		0.1
Riopan Plus					540	20	0.1
Riopan Plus E-S					1,080	30	0.3

TABLE 2. *Contents of antacids: tablets–chewables–gums (in mg)*

	Aluminium hydroxide	Magnesium hydroxide	Calcium carbonate	Simethicone	Dihydroxy-aluminium Na carbonate	Magnesium carbonate
Alka-Mints			850			
Algicon	360					320
Bisodol		178	194			
Calcitrel		120	585			
Chooz			500			
Remegel	Mg carbonate codried gel 476.4					
Rolaids (cherry)			550			
Rolaids (mint)					334	
Rolaids (plain)		64	317			
Tempo	133	81	414	20		
Titralac			420			
Tums			500			
Tums E-X			750			

reported with other H2 blockers. In selected cases, Omeprazole and related drugs may also be helpful, but they can only be used for short periods of time. When drugs of this class are necessary, consultation with a gastroenterologist is frequently helpful. If significant reflux problems are suspected, complete gastroenterological evaluation is advisable. Full work-up should be performed in all cases that do not respond dramatically to a three to four week therapeutic trial. If a patient complies strictly with treatment recommendations and does not show marked improvement within a month, either there is more significant gastrointestinal dysfunction, or the diagnosis is incorrect. Bulimia should also be considered in the differential diagnosis in such cases.

It is important to work with a skilled gastroenterologist who is sensitive to the special problems and critical self-assessment of professional voice users. Barium swallow, even with water siphonage, often does not detect significant reflux. Radionucleotide testing may be somewhat better. The best available test is a 24-hr pH monitor study. This is usually associated with manometry to rule out motility disorders and document sphincter function. A 24-hr test should be done in association with a timed log of activities performed while the monitor is in place. The interpretation of the 24-hr monitor test is different in professional voice users from standard interpretation in the gastroenterology literature. One must consider not only the amount of time that reflux occurs, but also its correlation with symptoms. Professional voice users may reflux in the upright position, even if they do not have significant reflux at night. Reflux may occur during exercise and particularly during singing or acting. If reflux is documented during these periods and is associated with symptoms, this finding is significant, even if all traditional criteria for abnormal 24-hr monitor studies are not met. In most cases, it is possible to control reflux medically. In rare instances, surgery is necessary. It should be performed by a surgeon with special interests and skill in performing antireflux procedures. Castell and his co-workers have highlighted the importance of this concept in the gastroenterology literature, describing a "symptom index," which needs to be considered in addition to other factors (7).

OTHER GASTROENTEROLOGIC PROBLEMS

The relevance of gastroenterologic dysfunction other than reflux is self-evident in most cases, and other gastrointestinal problems will not be discussed at length. Any condition that impairs abdominal function may interfere with the voice by undermining abdominal support. Diarrhea and constipation are notorious for causing such problems. When they are sporadic, they can usually be treated easily. When they are associated with more serious problems such as Crohn's disease or regional enteritis, treatment becomes more challenging. Physicians must try to select medications with the fewest side effects on the voice. For example, several of the more popular antidiarrheal agents contain atropine and may cause significant dehydration of the vocal folds and oral mucosa. Atropine also relaxes the lower esophageal sphincter and may aggravate reflux, if that problem is present concomitantly. It is important primarily to recognize that the conditions that produce abdominal pain or make a professional voice user limit abdominal muscle contraction (as happens with diarrhea) can cause voice dysfunction. They should be taken seriously and treated with due consideration for all consequences of treatment.

REFERENCES

1. Olson NR. The problem of gastroesophageal reflux. *Otolaryngol Clin North Am* 1986;19(1):119–134.
2. Sataloff RT, Spiegel JR, Carroll LM, et al. Strobovideolaryngoscopy in professional voice users: results and clinical value. *J Voice* 1988;1(4):359–364.
3. Koufman J, Wiener G, Wu W, Castel D. Reflux laryngitis and its sequelae: the diagnostic role of ambulatory pH monitoring. *J Voice* 1988;2(2):78–89.
4. Barish CF, William WC, Castell DO. Respiratory complications of gastroesophageal reflux. *Arch Int Med* 1985;145:1882–1888.
5. Murphy DW, Castell DO. Pathogenesis and treatment of gastroesophageal reflux disease. *Res Staff Physician* 1987;33(11):37–45.
6. Wilson JA, White A, von Haacke NP, et al. Gastroesophageal reflux and posterior laryngitis. *Ann Otol Rhinol Laryngol* 1989;98:405–410.
7. Wiener GJ, Richter JE, Copper JB, et al. The symptom index: a clinically important parameter of ambulatory 24 hour esophageal pH monitoring. *Am J Gastro* 1988;3:358–361.

Professional Voice: The Science and Art of Clinical Care, Robert T. Sataloff. Raven Press, Ltd., New York © 1991.

13

Halitosis

*Ronald S. Bogdasarian and **Robert T. Sataloff

*Department of Otorhinolaryngology, University of Michigan, Ann Arbor, Michigan; and **Department of Otolaryngology, Thomas Jefferson University, Philadelphia, Pennsylvania

In our society, halitosis, or "bad breath," is an embarrassing malady for the sufferer, his/her confreres, and even for physicians who are loath to mention the problem for fear of offending a patient. Nevertheless, it can be a serious condition for anyone who has to work face to face with other people. Otolaryngologists, dentists, barbers, beauticians, and others may suffer substantial loss of business because of this common, underappreciated problem. So may actors and singers! It is hard to play a romantic lead opposite someone with "fetor ex ore," or foul breath, and one's reputation for this problem spreads quickly. In addition to the social and professional implications, in some cases, halitosis may be a sign of a serious underlying systemic problem that warrants proper medical diagnosis and treatment. Consequently, it is useful for voice professionals and their health care providers to recognize the social and medical importance of halitosis, to admit its presence, to investigate it systematically, and to eliminate it whenever possible.

Many people with halitosis are unaware of the problem until they are informed by others. Most people who know they have a problem with malodorous breath have already consulted dentists and practice meticulous oral hygiene, often without adequate relief. The use of mouth sprays, mints, frequent tooth brushing, mouthwashes, and abusive vocal habits (such as talking with the jaw nearly closed or out of one side of the mouth) is common and may even become somewhat neurotically habitual. However, bad breath often does not originate in the mouth, and frequently it is not a hygiene problem at all. For example, all physicians are trained to recognize certain breath odors with diagnostic significance such as the acetone odor of a diabetic in ketoacidosis, the ammonia smell of people with uremia, or the rotten egg smell of a patient with liver failure. These are only a few of the conditions that may be detected on the breath.

The English language is somewhat weak in its descriptors of taste and smell. As Bogdasarian points out in his review of halitosis (1), the only way to assess expired air qualitatively is to smell it. The usual descriptive terms include "sweet, sour, pungent, garlicky, putrid, mousey, acrid, or stale." The quality of the breath may tell us a great deal about the problem. For example, the "rotten egg," musty breath associated with liver failure is due to bacterial action releasing dimethyl sulfide, which the damaged liver is unable to break down. Consequently, the sulfide is excreted through the lungs. Bacterial colonization elsewhere in the aerodigestive tract also produces a characteristic fetid odor associated with foreign bodies in the nose, upper airway cancers, oral cavity or tonsillar laceration or surgery, or severe necrotic tonsillitis.

Quantitative measurement of odors is not performed routinely under medical circumstances, although measurement is possible. The most common example is the alcohol breath analyzer used by police for people who are suspected of driving under the influence of alcohol. Such instruments are quite accurate. Devices to measure precisely expired hydrogen, as can be seen with malabsorption syndromes (2), and other odors are also available. An instrument called an osmoscope was developed to measure various breath odors quantitatively under experimental conditions (3), but the instrument was never widely accepted or used.

In evaluating halitosis, it is important to recognize the malodorous breath may arise from various anatomic locations from the mouth to the bloodstream. Recognizing potential sources for the problem is essential in guiding the history and physical examination that may lead to its identification and elimination. In some cases, knowledge of these conditions may permit successful self-diagnosis and cure, but persistent halitosis despite attempts at self-treatment warrants medical evaluation.

"NORMAL" BREATH

"Normal" breath varies in quality depending on a variety of factors including age, hunger, hydration, and others. Like many other things, breath seems to deteriorate with age (4). The poetic image "sweet as a baby's breath" has a physiologic basis. The breath of young children is generally sweet and pleasant. As Bogdasarian points out, this is also true of puppies and kittens (1). The breath becomes somewhat more pungent during adolescence, and definitely less pleasant during middle and later age, although the cause of these changes remains unknown. Breath also normally varies during the course of the day. It is often at its worst first thing in the morning for several reasons. Routinely, salivary flow decreases substantially during sleep. Normal saliva is slightly acidic and helps prevent the growth of gram-negative and anaerobic bacteria in the mouth. When salivary flow diminishes at night, the mouth becomes slightly alkaline, and these bacteria thrive. Amino acids and cellular proteins are broken down into sulfur-containing compounds such as hydrogen sulfide and methylmercaptan, which cause an objectionable odor (5). Dehydration contributes to a deficit in salivary flow and consequent increase in putrefaction of oral food particles or epithelial debris, with consequent halitosis. Ingestion of certain foods the previous day or evening may contribute to morning halitosis, particularly alcohol, onions, and garlic. The malodorous consequences of cigarette smoking are well known as well. Gastric reflux is also a common cause of morning halitosis, especially among singers in whom the condition is particularly prevalent. The halitosis is caused by reflux of gastric juice, bacteria, and partially digested food from the stomach into the pharynx. The odor is particularly unpleasant and generally controllable with reflux management. Hunger also produces an unpleasant breath odor. This is probably due to excretion of fat and protein metabolic breakdown products through the lungs. Hypoglycemia (low blood sugar) also produces a distinctive odor. Such odors are especially prominent in people who diet by skipping meals and they are often more noticeable in older individuals. "Hunger breath" disappears following ingestion of food. Chewing also increases salivary flow and helps clean the mouth of residual food products, epithelial debris, and bacteria that may contribute to halitosis. Dieters with particularly distressing halitosis problems may be helped by redesigning diet protocols to permit frequent small snacks rather than requiring long periods of starvation.

ORAL CAVITY ODORS

Oral hygiene problems are a common cause of halitosis and are usually easy to identify and cure. Food or epithelial debris may be trapped between teeth, in areas of periodontal disease, or in mucosal pockets or creases. Dental appliances such as dentures and bridges also frequently permit collection of such debris, which is broken down by anaerobic and gram-negative bacteria. Chronic periodontal disease (gingivitis) with bleeding from the gums produces a particularly unattractive odor that can be detected following oral bleeding from other causes such as trauma, bleeding disorders, tumors, and hemorrhage from the pharynx or tonsils. "Coated tongue" is also associated with bad breath. This is probably caused by interaction among food particles, bacteria, and a desquamated epithelium from the tongue. More serious oral infections such as Vincent's angina produce a repulsive, metallic odor. Interestingly, dental caries do not usually cause halitosis, unless there is a dental abscess or necrotic pulp space infection present. Any oral conditions that impair hydration also predispose to halitosis of oral origin. These include dehydration from insufficient fluid intake, chronic mouth breathing, medications such as antihistamines and diuretics, collagen vascular disease, sicca syndrome, aging, and radiation therapy. In most cases, excellent oral hygiene and dental and periodontal care can eliminate odors of oral origin.

NOSE AND SINUSES

Anything that causes infection in the nose or paranasal sinuses may produce a foul odor, particularly any infection involving anaerobic or gram-negative bacteria. Such conditions include acute or chronic sinusitis, nasal infections or tumors, or nasal foreign bodies. Destruction of normal mucosal function may lead to such infections. This is one of the potential consequences of rhinitis medicamentosa (nasal damage from overuse of nose sprays).

PHARYNX AND TRACHEA

Infections of the throat, pharynx, and tracheobronchial tree produce a putrid odor similar to that found with infections of the oral cavity or nose. In addition to acute infections and tumors, this unpleasant condition can be caused by chronic infection within tonsil or adenoid crypts. Food and desquamated epithelium trapped within these moist, warm spaces form an ideal medium for bacteria growth. This condition is usually curable without surgery, especially if the problem is located in the tonsils. Brushing the tonsils with a soft toothbrush or irrigating them with a water pick usually cleans the crypts effectively and controls the problem well.

THE LUNGS

Unpleasant odors from the lungs may arise either from diseases within the lungs themselves or from systemic problems with metabolic products excreted through the lungs. The lungs may produce unpleasant odors from conditions such as bronchiectasis, lung abscess, necrotic tumors or other ulcerative lesions such as may be seen with tuberculosis, and other conditions.

Many ingested or endogenously produced substances break down into metabolites excreted through the lungs and detectable on the breath. The quality of aromatic metabolites excreted through the lungs does not depend on the condition of the aerodigestive system. Studies of the mechanism have been performed using garlic, which can be ingested orally by capsule; placed in the stomach through gastrostomies, ileostomies, or colostomies; or rubbed on the skin. Regardless of its mode of entry, garlic produces its characteristic odor in the expired air (6). Like garlic, onions and various spices absorbed from the intestine are metabolized in the liver; their metabolic products are released into the bloodstream and excreted through the lungs. Anesthetic gases and other drugs such as paraldehyde follow a similar path of excretion and are also readily detectable on the breath.

Because of the obvious effects of inhaled and ingested substances on the breath through pulmonary excretion, many people believe that essential halitosis (bad breath of unknown cuase) is related to diet. Diets high in milk fat may produce halitosis, for example. It is not known whether this results from unidentified metabolites of fat ingestion or some other related condition. The stomach itself is not believed to play a primary role in causing halitosis unless vomiting, eructation, or reflux is present. Aromatic substances are generally absorbed from the small intestine, rather than the stomach or colon. Constipation also is not associated with halitosis.

SPECIAL ASPECTS OF THE HISTORY
AND PHYSICAL EXAMINATION

The specialized history used routinely for professional singers (7) and other voice users should provide initial information about many of the sources of halitosis and signal the direction for more in-depth inquiry. When halitosis is recorded in the history or noted on physical examination, specific questions should be asked to reveal the potential causes discussed above. Questions about dietary habits and gastroenterologic disorders should be included.

Ordinarily, the physician gets a fairly good idea of a patient's breath character during oral and laryngeal examination. If necessary, a piece of paper such as a 3 × 5 card can be waved in front of the patient's mouth or nose to direct the breath toward the examiner. When specific areas of the nose, pharynx, or oral cavity are suspected as a source for halitosis, debris from the area may be collected on a cotton tip applicator for olfactory examination by the physician and patient. To some extent, oral odors can be separated from odors originating elsewhere in the aerodigestive system by noting differences in expired air through the mouth versus through the nose. If an unpleasant odor is detected equally in expired oral and nasal air, it probably originates from lower in the aerodigestive system than the oral cavity, for example. Oral odors are treated best through meticulous oral hygiene and optimal dental care. Odors originating elsewhere are not improved by oral hygiene alone. If the problem is an infection in the nose, pharynx, or paranasal sinuses, appropriate antibiotic therapy is usually sufficient, occasionally supplemented by irrigation or surgery. Halitosis arising from severe reflux is improved substantially by the use of antacids, H2 blockers, appropriate changes in dietary habits, and elevation of the head of the bed. Halitosis associated with malabsorption may be eliminated with dietary changes with increases in the ingestion of fruits and vegetables and decrease in dietary fat intake to a maximum of 40 to 60 g. High roughage diets also aid oral hygiene. In all cases, hydration to optimize oral hygiene and salivary flow is essential.

Popular substances to mask breath odors are potentially helpful. In addition to routine mouthwashes and mints, it is interesting to note that oil of peppermint follows the same metabolic route as garlic. It is somewhat more potent than oil of wintergreen, although both may be helpful.

CONCLUSION

Halitosis is a common, perplexing, and often embarrassing problem. In professional singers, actors, or even voice teachers working in small studios, and other voice professionals, it may be unpleasant enough to interfere with a career. In most cases, it is caused by a minor medical problem that can be identified and eliminated. Both performers and physicians must be sensitive to the problem and its potential importance and patiently diligent in finding and eliminating its causes.

REFERENCES

1. Bogdasarian RS. Halitosis. *Otolaryngol Clin North Am* 1986;19(1):111–117.
2. Levine MD, Donaldson PM. Use of respiratory malabsorption. *J Lab Clin Med* 1970;75:937–945.
3. Morris PP, Read RR. Halitosis—variations in mouth and total breath odor intensity resulting from prophylaxis and anti-sepsis. *J Dent Res* 1939;28:324–333.
4. Castellani A. Fetor oris of tonsillar origin and certain bacilli causing it. *Lancet* 1930;1:623–624.
5. Tonzetich J, Ng SK. Reduction of malodor by oral cleansing procedures. *Oral Surg* 1976;42:172–181.
6. Blankenhorn MH, Richards CE. Garlic and breath odor. *JAMA* 1936;107:409.
7. Sataloff RT. Professional voice. I. Anatomy, function and general health. *J Voice* 1987;1(1):92–104.
8. Crohn BB, Drosd R. Halitosis. *JAMA* 1941;117:2242–2245.

Professional Voice: The Science and Art of Clinical Care, Robert T. Sataloff. Raven Press, Ltd., New York © 1991.

14

Obesity and the Professional Voice User

*Dahlia M. Sataloff and **Robert T. Sataloff

*Department of Surgery, University of Pennsylvania, Philadelphia, Pennsylvania; and **Department of Otolaryngology, Thomas Jefferson University, Philadelphia, Pennsylvania

"The opera's not over until the fat lady sings," is a well-known quip that makes most of us smile. However, it reveals a stereotype of opera singers that is common among audiences. Unfortunately, there has been some justification for this rather unflattering image. We are all familiar with a few great operatic stars who have indulged their love for a good meal far too often. We are also familiar with the stories of obese singers who "lose their voices" while losing 40 pounds in 30 days, conclude that they cannot sing when thin, and gain back 50 pounds. Today, most people involved in voice education and singing recognize that singing is athletic. As such, it requires good abdominal and respiratory conditioning, physical strength, and endurance. All these are undermined by significant obesity. Moreover, as classical music has moved from the opera stage to the movie and television screen, thin, attractive actor/singers have become essential for aesthetic and dramatic purposes, as well.

Nevertheless, singers, actors, and many other professional voice users are verbal, oral people. Most of us enjoy singing, talking, and a good bowl of pasta after the show. However, before indulging our passions for culinary excess, it is important to understand the impact of obesity not only on singing performance, but also on general health and longevity.

When obesity becomes extreme, serious measures may be necessary for medical reasons to accomplish weight loss. The most severely overweight patients have an entity called "morbid obesity." This condition is diagnosed when a person is more than 100 pounds or 100% over ideal body weight. Morbid obesity is a disease that is extremely common in our society. It is estimated that 34 million adult Americans (one of every five people over the age of 19) have significant obesity. As little as 20% excess over desirable body weight may be enough to constitute a health hazard. Doctors have long been aware of the difficulty in controlling weight problems with medical treatment alone. Of all patients who lose weight, 90% regain it at some point in their lives, and many even exceed their original weight. This led doctors to consider surgery as an option in treating this problem in selected cases.

In February 1985, a panel of experts from the National Institutes of Health looked at health problems associated with obesity. They concluded that obesity has adverse effects on health and longevity.

1. Obesity creates enormous psychological stress, which is a problem not well understood by the general population. Large people are unpopular, discriminated against in the workplace, and considered lazy.

2. Obesity is associated with high blood pressure. Obese people have high blood pressure three times more often than nonobese people.

3. Obesity is associated with higher levels of cholesterol.

4. Obesity is associated with diabetes. As with high blood pressure, this is seen three times more commonly in obese individuals.

5. Obesity is a factor in the development of heart disease.

6. Obesity increases the risk of developing certain cancers, specifically those of the uterus, breast, cervix, and gallbladder in women, and the colon, rectum, and prostate in men.

7. Obese individuals have a shorter life span.

8. Obesity is related to respiratory problems and arthritis.

With weight loss, all these problems can be significantly improved, and prolongation of life is possible.

Accepted ideal weights for men and women are summarized in Table 1.

The best treatment for obesity is avoidance of the problem. Early in training, singers should learn the importance of good physical and aerobic conditioning. This is important to the singer's general health, vocal health, and art. Even a moderate degree of obesity may adversely affect the respiratory system, undermining support. Weight reduction is recommended for people who are 20% or more above ideal weight. In the singer, weight should be lost slowly through modification of eating and life-style habits. Loss of 2 or 3 pounds per week is plenty. More rapid loss of weight causes fluid shifts that may result in changes in vocal quality and endurance. Although these appear to be temporary, the effects of weight on vocal function have not been studied adequately, therefore, we do not have answers to all the pertinent questions. It is certainly possible for a singer to lose weight too quickly, but we are not yet sure how much weight loss is too much. Studies are currently under way to learn more about this problem. However, it appears that maintenance of ideal body weight is probably as healthy for the voice as it is for the rest of the body. For people 20 to 100% above ideal body weight, weight loss can be accomplished with a medically supervised diet. However, people who are morbidly obese are frequently unable to lose weight by dietary or medical means alone.

Morbidly obese patients may be candidates for surgery to control their weight problems. At first, this seems like an extreme treatment. However,

TABLE 1. *Weight table*

Height	Inches	Weight for women	Weight for men
4'09"	57	90	95
4'10"	58	95	100
4'11"	59	100	105
5'00"	60	105	110
5'01"	61	110	115
5'02"	62	115	120
5'03"	63	120	125
5'04"	64	125	130
5'05"	65	130	135
5'06"	66	135	140
5'07"	67	140	145
5'08"	68	145	150
5'09"	69	150	155
5'10"	70	155	160
5'11"	71	160	165
6'00"	72	165	170
6'01"	73	170	175
6'02"	74	175	180
6'03"	75	180	185
6'04"	76	185	190
6'05"	77	190	195

the adverse effects of morbid obesity are often greater than the risks of surgery, even in singers. This is especially true in the presence of diabetes, high blood pressure, osteoarthritis, or respiratory problems. Weight loss after obesity surgery will significantly improve these health problems, and the medications required to control them before surgery (insulin and blood pressure medicines) may be stopped altogether in many cases. Certain patients are not candidates for surgery, even though they qualify on the basis of weight. These include people with psychoses or alcoholism, pregnant women, and others. In addition, women must plan not to become pregnant in the 12 to 18 months following obesity surgery. Although several kinds of obesity operations exist, the older procedures have resulted in significant problems. At present, the best method is vertical banded gastroplasty, commonly known as stomach stapling. Postoperatively, weight loss occurs over 12 to 18 months and stops as ideal body weight is approached. An individual may lose as much as several hundred pounds following this procedure, and most people are able to keep the weight off. Singing may be resumed 4 to 6 weeks following stomach stapling in most cases. Although the effects on the voice are not yet fully documented, there does not appear to be any significant problem associated with weight loss in patients with morbid obesity. Although further study is necessary to confirm these impressions, in singers or actors with this degree of weight problem, considerations of longevity, heart condition, blood pressure, and other critical health matters may out-weigh immediate vocal concerns.

For most singers, an extra 10, 20, or 30 pounds is not perceived as much of a problem. However, as 20 becomes 30, and 30 becomes 40, significant adverse effects occur in the body in general and the vocal tract specifically. In training, singers should be encouraged to treat their entire bodies with the same reverence with which they regard their vocal cords. Self-respect as a professional athlete is a sound basis for a longer life—and a longer vocal career.

Professional Voice: The Science and Art
of Clinical Care, Robert T. Sataloff.
Raven Press, Ltd., New York © 1991.

15

Stress, Anxiety, and Psychogenic Dysphonia

Robert T. Sataloff

*Department of Otolaryngology, Thomas Jefferson University,
Philadelphia, Pennsylvania*

In 2,286 cases of all forms of voice disorders reported by Brodnitz (1), 80% of the disorders were attributed to voice abuse or to psychogenic factors resulting in vocal dysfunction. Of the patients, 20% had organic voice disorders. Of women with organic problems, about 15% had identifiable endocrine causes. A somewhat higher incidence of organic disorders, particularly reflux laryngitis and acute infectious laryngitis, may be found more commonly. In fact, our clinical experience is currently being reviewed and will be reported in the near future. However, preliminary assessment indicates that our percentages of organic and psychogenic voice disorders are roughly the opposite of those reported by Brodnitz. Regardless of the incidence, it is clear that psychogenic and stress-related problems are important and common in professional voice users.

Stress pervades virtually all professions in today's fast-moving society. Whether one is a singer preparing for a series of concerts, a teacher preparing for presentation of lectures, a lawyer anticipating a major trial, a businessman negotiating an important contract, or a member of any other goal-oriented profession, each of us must deal with a myriad of demands on his/her time and talents. Such demands represent special problems for singers, because physiologic manifestations of stress may interfere with the delicate mechanisms of voice production. When most singers think of stress, stage fright comes to mind. This is only one of many stress scenarios.

Stress may be physical or psychological, and it often involves a combination of both. Either may interfere with performance. There are several situations in which physical stress is common and important. Generalized fatigue is seen frequently in hard-working singers, especially in the frantic few weeks preceding major performances. In order to maintain normal mucosal secretions, a strong immune system to fight infection, and the ability of muscles to recover from heavy use, one needs rest, proper nutrition and hydration, and appropriate exercise and muscular conditioning. When the body is stressed through deprivation of these essentials, illness (such as upper respiratory infection), voice fatigue, hoarseness, and other vocal dysfunctions may supervene.

Both physical and psychological stress may be either endogenous or exogenous in origin. Vocalists are hard-working, ambitious, conscientious professionals and are particularly prone to self-imposed (endogenous) stress. This may be associated with a singer's expectations of and demands on him/herself for performance quality, for example. Singers often create stressful situations for themselves by accepting performance commitments that place them under excessive pressure either through insufficient time for preparation or by involving material that they are not yet vocally prepared to sing. Even talented, well-developed singers may occasionally also create stress for themselves by failing to practice, exercise, prepare in advance, and rest sufficiently to allow comfortable performance. Exogenous stress is most commonly imposed by agents, conductors, theater management, parents, and teachers. When authority figures impose demands that exceed a professional voice user's ability under given circumstances, severe vocal problems may result. Such situations include pressure to rehearse or perform material during illness that would be within a vocalist's grasp if he/she were in good health.

Psychological stress is intrinsic to vocal performance. For most people, sharing emotions is stressful even in the privacy of our homes, let alone under spotlights in front of a room full of people. Under ordinary circumstances, during training, a singer or actor learns to recognize his/her customary anxiety about performing, to accept it as part of his/her instrument and to compensate for it. When psychological pressures become severe enough to impair or prohibit performance, careful treatment may be required. Such occurrences usually are temporary and happen because of a particular situation such as short notice for a critically important performance, a recent family death, etc. Chronic disabling psychological stress is a more serious problem. It may appear as incapacitating stage fright, repeated imaginary illnesses (hypochondriasis), or in even more serious psychological or physical guises discussed below. Psychiatric illness that requires treatment may also be associated with fatigue or difficulty concentrating, and may necessitate the use of psychotropic medications. Such conditions often interfere with optimal singing.

The special, comprehensive history and physical examination used for professional singers is usually sufficient to establish a diagnosis of stress-related dysfunction (2–4). Physicians must be careful in making this diagnosis, because it is much less common than might be imagined, particularly dysfunction from psychological stress in established performers. The diagnosis should be made only on the basis of positive evidence, not because "your vocal cords look fine; it must be stress."

Stress has numerous physical consequences. Through the autonomic nervous system, it may alter oral and vocal fold secretions, heart rate, and gastric acid production (stomach acid). Under acute, anxiety-producing circumstances, such changes are to be expected. When frightened, a normal person's palms become cold and sweaty, his/her mouth becomes dry, heart rate increases, pupils change size, and stomach acid secretions may increase. These phenomena are objective signs that may be observed by a physician, and their symptoms may be recognized by the performer as dry mouth, voice fatigue, heart palpitations, and "heartburn." More severe, prolonged stress is also commonly associated with increased muscle tension throughout the body (but particularly in the head and neck), headaches, decreased ability to concentrate, and insomnia (trouble sleeping). Chronic fatigue is also a common symptom. These physiological alterations may lead not only to altered vocal quality but also to physical pathology. For example, hyperfunctional, muscular tension dysphonia (usually excessive neck and tongue muscle activity) may lead to vocal nodules. Increased gastric acid secretion is associated with ulcers, as well as reflux laryngitis and arytenoid irritation. Chronic stress and tension may cause numerous pain symptoms, although headaches are most common. Stress is also associated with more serious physical problems such as myocardial infarction (heart attack). Thus, the constant pressure under which many performers live may be more than a modest inconvenience. Stress factors should be recognized, and appropriate modifications should be made to ameliorate them.

Medical treatment of stress depends on the specific circumstances. When the diagnosis is appropriate but poorly controlled anxiety, the singer can usually be helped by assurance that his/her voice complaint is related to anxiety and not to any physical problem. Under ordinary circumstances, once the singer's mind is put to rest regarding the questions of nodules, vocal fold injury, or other serious problems, his/her training allows him/her to compensate for vocal manifestations of anxiety, especially when the vocal complaint is minor. Slight alterations in quality or increased vocal fatigue are seen most frequently. These are often associated with lack of sleep, oversinging, and dehydration from the stress-producing commitment. The singer or actor should be advised to modify these and to consult his/her voice teacher. The voice teacher should ensure that good vocal technique is being used under performance and rehearsal circumstances. Frequently, young singers are not trained sufficiently in how and when to "mark." For example, many singers whistle to rest their voices, not realizing that active vocalization and potentially fatiguing vocal fold contact occur when whistling. Technical proficiency and a plan for voice conservation during rehearsals and performances are essential under these circumstances. A manageable stressful situation may become unmanageable if real physical vocal problems develop.

Several additional modalities may be helpful in selected circumstances.

Relative voice rest (using the voice only when necessary) may be important not only to voice conservation, but also to psychological relaxation. Under stressful circumstances, a singer needs as much peace and quiet as possible, not hectic socializing and parties with heavy voice use in noisy environments. The importance of adequate sleep and fluid intake cannot be overemphasized. Local therapy such as steam inhalation and neck muscle massage may be helpful in some people and certainly does no harm. The doctor may be very helpful in alleviating the singer's exogenous stress by conveying "doctor's orders" directly to theater management, etc. This will save the singer the embarrassment (and stress) of having personally to confront an authority and violate his/her "show must go on" ethic. A short phone call by the physician can be highly therapeutic. Singers should not hesitate to ask the doctor to make such a call. When stress is chronic and incapacitating, more comprehensive measures may be required. If psychological stress becomes so severe as to impair performance or necessitate the use of drugs to allow performance, psychotherapy may be indicated. In rare cases, expertly supervised biofeedback therapy may also be useful.

Tranquilizers and sedatives are rarely necessary and are undesirable, because they may interfere with fine motor control. Recently, beta-adrenergic blocking agents such as propranolol hydrochloride (e.g., Inderal by Ayerst) have achieved some popularity for treatment of preperformance anxiety. Beta-blockers are not recommended by this author for regular use. They have significant effects on the cardiovascular system and many potential complications including hypotension, thrombocytopenic purpura, mental depression, agranulocytosis, laryngospasm with respiratory distress, bronchospasm, and others. In addition, their efficacy is controversial. Although they may have a favorable effect in relieving performance anxiety, beta-blockers may produce a noticeable adverse effect on singing performance (5). As the blood level of drug established by a given dose of beta-blocker varies widely among individuals, initial use of these agents in preperformance situations may be particularly troublesome. In addition, beta-blockers impede increases in heart rate, which are needed as physiologic responses to the psychological and physical demands of performance. Although these drugs have a place under occasional extraordinary circumstances, their routine use not only is potentially hazardous, but also violates an important therapeutic principle. Performers have chosen a career that exposes them to the public. If such a person is so incapacitated by anxiety that he/she is unable to perform the routine functions of his/her chosen profession without chemical help, this should be considered symptomatic of a significant underlying psychological problem. It is not routine or healthy for a performer to be dependent on drugs in order to perform, whether the drug is benzodiazepine, a barbiturate, a beta-blocker, or alcohol. If such a dependence exists, psychological evaluation should be considered by an experienced arts-medicine psychologist or psychiatrist. Obscuring the symptoms by fostering the dependence is insufficient. However, if the singer is on tour and will only be under a particular laryngologist's care for a week or two, the physician should not try to make major changes in the singer's customary regimen. Rather, he/she should communicate with the performer's primary laryngologist or family physician and should coordinate appropriate long-term care through him/her.

Bulimia is a disorder associated with self-induced vomiting following episodes of binge eating. It may occur sporadically, or it may be a chronic problem. Vomiting produces signs and symptoms similar to severe chronic reflux as well as thinning of tooth enamel. Bulimia nervosa can be a serious disorder and may be associated with anorexia nervosa. Bulimia may be more common than most of us realize. It has been estimated to occur in as many as 2 to 4% of female adolescents and female young adults. Consequently, it is important for the laryngologist to recognize this condition not only because of its effects on the voice, but also on account of its potentially serious general medical and psychiatric implications. In addition to posterior laryngitis and pharyngitis, laryngeal findings associated with bulimia include subepithelial vocal fold hemorrhages, superficial telangiectasia of the vocal fold mucosa, and vocal fold scarring (6).

As with all medical conditions, the best treatment for stress in singers is prevention. Awareness of the conditions that lead to stress and its potential adverse effect on voice production often allows the singer to anticipate and avoid these problems. Stress is inevitable in performance and in life. Performers must learn to recognize it, compensate for it when necessary, and incorporate it into their singing as emotion and excitement—the "edge." Stress should be controlled, not pharmacologically eliminated. Used well, stress should be just one more tool of the singer's trade.

Psychogenic dysphonia may occur in anyone, but it is surprisingly uncommon in professional voice users. Since so much of their lives and egos are involved in their voices, one might expect the voice to fail for psychosomatic reasons much more frequently than it does. Psychogenic dysphonia often presents as total inability to speak, whispered speech, extremely strained or strangled speech, interrupted speech rhythm, or speech in an abnormal register (such as falsetto in a male). Usually, involuntary vocalizations during laughing and coughing are normal. The vocal folds are often difficult to examine because of supraglottic hyperfunction. However, if the patient whistles during flexible fiberoptic laryngoscopy, normal vocal fold mobility and closure can be seen. Electromyography may be helpful in confirming the diagnosis by revealed simultaneous firing of abductors and adductors. Psychogenic dysphonia is frequently misdiagnosed as spastic dysphonia, partially explaining the excellent spastic dysphonia cure rates in some series. In psychogenic dysphonia, it is often possible to elicit a history of stress, particular personal significance of the voice, or a family history of voice abnormality, although none of these conditions is present in all cases.

In addition to typical presentations of psychogenic dysphonia, it must also be recognized that voice quality is distinctly abnormal in various serious psychiatric conditions such as schizophrenia, which may be accompanied by strained speech initiation, primitive rhythms, faulty articulation, fixed vocal attitude, and other abnormalities. Severe depression is also typically accompanied by voice changes including reduced loudness, diminished inflection, and sometimes a rise in fundamental frequency. Physicians and other health care providers must remain alert to vocal manifestations of these and other serious diseases.

Functional dysphonia can often be eliminated by a speech-language pathologist, sometimes in one session. In several instances, successful restoration of normal voice has been achieved during fiberoptic laryngoscopy and stroboscopy. Even in such "easy" cases, additional therapy and counseling with an arts-medicine psychologist are usually indicated. Certainly, in all cases that do not respond promptly to traditional voice therapy, psychotherapy is the mainstay of treatment.

REFERENCES

1. Brodnitz F. Hormones and the human voice. *Bull NY Acad Med* 1971;47:183–191.
2. Sataloff RT. The professional voice. I. Anatomy and history. *J Voice* 1987;1(1):92–104.
3. Sataloff RT. The professional voice. II. Physical examination. *J Voice* 1987;1(2):191–201.
4. Sataloff RT. The professional voice. III. Common diagnoses and treatments. *J Voice* 1987;1(3):283–292.
5. Gates GA, Saegert J, Wilson N, et al. Effects of beta-blockage on singing performances. *Ann Otol Rhinol Laryngol* 1985;94:570–574.
6. Morrison MD, Morris BD. Dysphonia and bulimia: vomiting laryngeal injury. *J Voice* 1990;4(1):76–80.

Professional Voice: The Science and Art of Clinical Care, Robert T. Sataloff.
Raven Press, Ltd., New York © 1991.

16

Endocrine Dysfunction

Robert T. Sataloff

Department of Otolaryngology, Thomas Jefferson University, Philadelphia, Pennsylvania

Endocrine problems are worthy of special attention. The human voice is extremely sensitive to endocrinologic changes. Many of these are reflected in alterations of fluid content of the lamina propria just beneath the laryngeal mucosa. This causes alteration in the bulk and shape of the vocal folds and results in voice change. Hypothyroidism (1–5) is a well-recognized cause of such voice disorders, although the mechanism is not well understood. Hoarseness, vocal fatigue, muffling of the voice, loss of range, and a feeling of a lump in the throat may be present even with mild hypothyroidism. Even when thyroid function tests are within the low-normal range, this diagnosis should be entertained, especially if thyroid-stimulating hormone levels are in the high-normal range or are elevated. Thyrotoxicosis may result in similar voice disturbances (5).

Voice changes associated with sex hormones are encountered commonly in clinical practice and have been investigated more thoroughly than have other hormonal changes. Although there appears to be a correlation between sex hormone levels and depths of male voices (higher testosterone and lower estradiol levels in basses than in tenors) (6), the most important hormonal considerations in males occur during the maturation process. When castrato singers were in vogue, castration at about age 7 or 8 resulted in failure of laryngeal growth during puberty and voices that stayed in the soprano or alto range and boasted a unique quality of sound (7). Failure of a male voice to change at puberty is uncommon today, and usually is psychogenic. However, hormonal deficiencies such as those seen in cryptorchidism, delayed sexual development, Klinefelter's syndrome, or Frolich's syndrome may be responsible (8). In these cases, the persistently high voice may be the complaint that brings the patient to medical attention. Voice problems related to sex hormones are seen most commonly in female singers. Although vocal changes associated with the normal menstrual cycle may be difficult to quantify with current experimental techniques, there is no question that they occur (9–12). Most of the ill effects are seen in the immediate premenstrual period and are known as "laryngopathia premenstrualis." This condition is common and is caused by physiologic, anatomic, and psychologic alterations secondary to endocrine changes. The vocal dysfunction is characterized by decreased vocal efficiency, loss of the highest notes in the voice, vocal fatigue, slight hoarseness, and some muffling of the voice, and it is often more apparent to the singer than to the listener. Submucosal hemorrhages in the larynx are common (12). In many European opera houses, singers are excused from singing during the premenstrual and early menstrual days ("grace days"). This practice is not followed in the United States. Although ovulation inhibitors have been shown to mitigate some of these symptoms (11), in some women (about 5%), birth control pills may deleteriously alter voice range and character even after only a few months of therapy (13–16). When oral contraceptives are used, the voice should be monitored closely. Under crucial performance circumstances, oral contraceptives may be used to alter the time of menstruation, but this practice is justified only in unusual situations. Estrogens are helpful in postmenopausal singers but should be given alone. Sequential replacement therapy is the most physiologic and should be used under the supervision of a gynecologist or endocrinologist. It should be remembered that cessation of menstrual periods is often a late sign of menopause. In female singers and actresses over the age of 35 to 40, it is helpful to obtain baseline estrogen levels. They can then be monitored in consultation with an endocrinologist. In some cases, hypoestrogenic voice changes may precede interruption of menses, and it may be desirable to start estrogen replacement even before menstrual periods become irregular or stop. There is still controversy regarding the length of time that estrogen replacement can be used safely. There are many benefits of estrogen replacement including not only increased vocal longevity, but also avoidance of osteoporosis, cardiovascular disease and other systemic problems. However, there are also potential risks including a probable increased incidence of endometrial carcinoma, and a questionably increased incidence of breast cancer. Studies investigating the effect of prolonged hormone use on breast cancer are particularly contradictory and controversial. They should be interpreted with great caution, with particular attention to the kind of estrogen used, doses, and methods of maintaining hormone levels. Many women have used estrogen replacement for decades without adverse effect. If there are no medical contraindications to estrogen replacement, after the singer has been fully informed regarding risks and benefits, there does not appear to be sufficient evidence at present to justify withholding or discontinuing the drugs. Conjugated estrogens (such as Premarin) should be used, and estradiol should be avoided. Medication doses should be minimized and adjusted according to serum estrogen levels, and close medical follow up is mandatory.

Under no circumstances should androgens be given to female singers, even in small amounts, if there is any reasonable therapeutic alternative.

Clinically, these drugs are now used most commonly to treat endometriosis. Androgens cause unsteadiness of the voice, rapid changes of timbre, and lowering of fundamental voice frequency (17–22). The changes are irreversible. In the past, voices with androgenic damage have been considered "ruined." In our experience, voices are permanently altered, but not necessarily ruined. Through a patient, slow retraining process, it has been possible in some cases to return singers with androgenic voice changes to a professional singing career. However, their "new voice" has fewer high notes and fuller low notes than before androgen exposure. In rare instances, androgens may be produced by pathologic conditions such as ovarian or adrenal tumors, and voice alterations may be the presenting symptoms. Rarely, they may also be secreted during an otherwise normal pregnancy.

Pregnancy frequently results in voice alterations known as "laryngopathia gravidarum." The changes may be similar to premenstrual symptoms or may be perceived as desirable changes. In some cases, alterations produced by pregnancy are permanent (23–24). Although hormonally induced changes in the larynx and respiratory mucosa secondary to menstruation and pregnancy are discussed widely in the literature, the author has found no reference to the important alterations in abdominal support. Muscle cramping associated with menstruation causes pain and compromises abdominal contraction. Abdominal distension during pregnancy also interferes with abdominal muscle function. Any singer whose abdominal support is compromised substantially should be discouraged from singing until the abdominal disability is resolved. Hormonal disturbances in other segments of the diencephalic-pituitary system may also result in vocal dysfunction. In addition to the thyroid and the gonads, the parathyroid, adrenal, pineal, and pituitary glands are included in this system. Other endocrine disturbances may alter voice as well. For example, pancreatic dysfunction may result in xerophonia (dry voice), as in diabetes mellitus. Thymic abnormalities can lead to feminization of the voice (25).

Recently, we have seen increasing abuse of hyperbolic steroids. In addition to their many other hazards, these medications may alter the voice. They are (or are closely related to) male hormones; consequently, they are capable of producing masculinization of the voice. Lowering of fundamental frequency and coarsening of the voice produced in this fashion are generally irreversible.

ENDOCRINOLOGIC EVALUATION

Although the otolaryngologist can get a great deal of guidance from his/ her clinical impression, and from laboratory tests such as thyroid function test, dehydroepiandrosterone (DHEAS), androstenedione, cortisol, testosterone (total and free), estrogen, prolactin, 17-hydroxyprogesterone, and other tests, the value of a good endocrinologist interested in consulting in the care of professional voice users cannot be overestimated. As in other areas of professional voice care, recognizing abnormalities and titrating therapy can be tricky. The endocrinologist who understands arts-medicine concerns can help with diagnosis, adjusting postmenopausal sex hormone replacement by clinical and laboratory monitoring, optimizing thyroid replacement, stabilizing serum hormone concentrations in women prone to cyclical vocal fold hemorrhage, and in many other difficult situations. Otolaryngologists are strongly encouraged to enlist the services of an interested consultant and to assist in his/her education in the special problems of professional voice users.

REFERENCES

1. Ritter FN. The effect of hypothyroidism on the larynx of the rat. *Ann Otol Rhinol Laryngol* 1964;67:404–416.
2. Ritter FN. Endocrinology. In: Paparella M, Shumrick D, eds. *Otolaryngology*, vol. 1. Philadelphia: W.B. Saunders, 1973;727–734.
3. Michelsson K, Sirvio P. Cry analysis in congenital hypothyroidism. *Folia Phoniatr* 1976;28:40–47.
4. Gupta OP, Bhatia PL, Agarwal MK, et al. Nasal pharyngeal and laryngeal manifestations of hypothyroidism. *Ear Nose Throat* 1977;56(9):10–21.
5. Malinsky M, Chevrie-Muller, Cerceau N. Etude clinique et electrophysiologique des alterations de la voix au cours des thyrotoxioses. *Ann Endocrinol (Paris)* 1977;38:171–172.
6. Meuser W, Nieschlag E. Sexualhormone und stimmlage des mannes. *Deutsch Med Wochenschr* 1977;102:261–264.
7. Brodnitz F. The age of the castrato voice. *J Speech Hearing Disord* 1975;40:291–295.
8. Brodnitz F. Hormones and the human voice. *Bull NY Acad Med* 1971;47:183–191.
9. von Gelder L. Psychosomatic aspects of endocrine disorders of the voice. *J Commun Disord* 1974;7:257–262.
10. Schiff M. The influence of estrogens on connective tissue. In: Asboe-Hansen G, ed. *Hormones and connective tissue.* Copenhagen: Munksgaard Press, 1967;282–341.
11. Wendler J. Zyklusabhangige leistungsschwankungen der stimme und ihre beeinflussung durch ovulationshemmer. *Folia Phoniatr* 1972;24:259–277.
12. Lacina V. Der einfluss der menstruation auf die stimme der sangerinnen. *Folia Phoniatr* 1968;20:13–24.
13. Dordain M. Etude statistique de l'influence des contraceptifs hormonaux sur la voix. *Folia Phoniatr* 1972;24:86–96.
14. Pahn V, Goretzlehner G. Stimmstorungen durch hormonale kontrazeptiva. *Zentralb Gynakol* 1978;100:341–346.
15. Schiff M. "The pill" in otolaryngology. *Trans Am Acad Ophthalmol Otolaryngol* 1968;72:76–84.
16. Brodnitz F. Medical care preventive therapy (panel). In: Lawrence V, ed. *Transcripts of the seventh annual symposium, care of the professional voice.* New York: The Voice Foundation, 1978;3:86.
17. Damste PH. Virilization of the voice due to anabolic steroids. *Folia Phoniatr* 1964;16:10–18.
18. Damste PH. Voice changes in adult women caused by virilizing agents. *J Speech Hearing Disord* 1967;32:126–132.
19. Saez S, Francoise S. Recepteurs d'androgenes: mise en evidence dans la fraction cytosolique de muqueuse normale et d'epitheliomas phryngolarynges humains. *CR Acad Sci (Paris)* 1975;280:935–938.

20. Vuorenkoski V, Lenko HL, Tjernlund P, et al. Fundamental voice frequency during normal and abnormal growth, and after androgen treatment. *Arch Dis Child* 1978;53:201–209.
21. Arndt HJ. Stimmstorungen nach behandlung mit androgenen und anabolen hormonen. *Munch Med Wochenschr* 1974;116:1715–1720.
22. Bourdial J. Les troubles de la voix provoques par la therapeutique hormonale androgene. *Ann Otolaryngol (Paris)* 1970;87:725–734.
23. Flach M, Schwickardi H, Simen R. Welchen einfluss haben menstruation und schwangerschaft auf die augsgebildete gesangsstimme? *Folia Phoniatr* 1968;21:199–210.
24. Deuster CV. Irreversible stimmstorung in der schwangerscheft. *HNO* 1977;25:430–432.
25. Imre V. Hormonell bedingte stimmstorungen. *Folia Phoniatr* 1968;20:394–404.

Professional Voice: The Science and Art of Clinical Care, Robert T. Sataloff. Raven Press, Ltd., New York © 1991.

17

Bodily Injuries and Their Effects on the Voice

Robert T. Sataloff

Department of Otolaryngology, Thomas Jefferson University, Philadelphia, Pennsylvania

Professional voice users recognize routinely the ill effects of laryngitis, respiratory infections, direct trauma to the larynx, and other abnormalities in the head and neck. However, the relevance of injuries elsewhere in the body is not always so obvious. Such maladies may affect the voice by altering abdominal support, introducing excess tension, distracting the singer through pain, or by other means. Recognizing the potential hazard of injuries throughout the body often allows a singer or actor to compensate for them safely, preventing vocal stress and injury.

The anatomy of the singing voice involves the entire body. The larynx is inseparably interdependent with virtually all other body systems. The function of the vocal folds (oscillator), supraglottic vocal tract (resonator), and abdomen and thorax (power source) has been discussed in a previous chapter. The lower extremities (legs) and pelvis maintain a stable, balanced skeleton to optimize contraction of the abdominal and back musculature. While the arms are less intimately involved with voice production under normal, relaxed circumstances, their direct association with neck and shoulder muscles and their location adjacent to the chest allow them in abnormal use to introduce undesirable neck tension or constriction of respiration. The brain is responsible for fine motor control, expression of emotion and stress, control of secretions (including those on the vocal folds), and coordination of all bodily functions. Injury to any part of the body may impair optimal vocal function.

ANTERIOR NECK TRAUMA

Injury to the front of the neck or to the voice box itself can be devastating. Such injuries usually result from motor vehicle accidents in which the neck strikes the steering wheel or during altercations. Direct trauma to the voice box can produce hemorrhage into the vocal folds, dislocation of the arytenoid cartilages, and fracture of the other laryngeal cartilages. Depending on the severity of the injury and other factors, the outlook ranges from complete recovery to permanent ruination of the voice. Such injuries also have the life threatening potential of airway obstruction. They can be avoided in many cases by proper use of seat belts with shoulder restraints. However, when anterior neck trauma occurs, immediate visualization of the larynx by a skilled laryngologist is essential. Laryngeal injuries are frequently worse than they at first appear to be.

POSTERIOR NECK TRAUMA

The most common form of posterior neck trauma is "whiplash," although a direct blow to the back of the neck may produce similar effects. Whiplash is frequently much more trouble for singers than it is for nonprofessional voice users. This injury can result in neck muscle spasms, hyperfunctional vocal technique, and abnormal neck posturing secondary to pain. The injury is especially troublesome in singers who have already had to overcome a tendency for hyperfunctional voice abuse (such as singing with tight neck muscles or with the tongue pulled back). In such people, whiplash will often result in decompensation and return to previous "bad habits." If the whiplash is associated with jaw trauma or temporomandibular joint injury, these problems may be aggravated. Temporomandibular joint dysfunction and pain produce effects similar to those seen in whiplash.

HEAD TRAUMA

Serious injuries to the head producing unconsciousness may be fatal. However, even when people recover from skull fractures or closed-head injury, subtle brain dysfunction may persist for many months, or even permanently. This usually includes slight personality change, emotional lability, impaired memory, sometimes difficulty reading or speaking, and often a nonspecific loss of "sharpness." Such impairments may be serious impediments to healthy singing.

Head trauma may also be associated with hearing loss. This is most likely to occur if there is a blow directly to the ear or one severe enough to cause unconsciousness. Hearing should be checked after any serious head injury. If a hearing loss is found, counselling and rehabilitation usually avert problems. However, if hearing loss goes unrecognized, the singer may "over sing" in order to compensate for the hearing impairment (especially if it is sensorineural hearing loss or "nerve deafness"). Similar problems occur in actors or other professional speakers.

INJURY TO THE SUPRAGLOTTIC VOCAL TRACT

Injury to the nose such as nasal fracture can produce nasal obstruction. This alters the production of certain sounds (especially nasal consonants) and forces the singer to breathe unfiltered, unhumidified cold air through his mouth. This may result in voice irritation, especially in dusty or dry environments. Injury to the oral cavity including surgical injury such as tonsillectomy changes a singer's sound. The shape and vibration of the tongue, palate, and pharyngeal muscles are important. They are trained during vocal studies, just as laryngeal muscles are. Although voice alterations caused by minor swelling or scarring in these areas are often more obvious to the singer or actor than they are to listeners, they are hazardous, because performers (especially singers) tend to try to compensate for them. As these injuries produce structural changes in the anatomy of the vocal tract, there is no way to return the sound to "normal" while they are present. Many singers develop hyperfunctional technique in the vain attempt to overcome them. The close supervision of a teacher and learning to "sing by feel" rather than "by ear" usually avoid these problems.

CHEST AND ABDOMINAL INJURIES

Chest and abdominal injuries may occur through motor vehicle accidents, surgery, or other trauma. Usually, they result in temporary muscle dysfunction. In general, singing should be avoided until the support mechanisms are functional. A good rule of thumb is to require that the singer be able to do 10 sit-ups before resuming singing following chest or abdominal injury. This assumes reasonably good restoration of support muscle strength. It is generally safer not to sing at all than to sing without "support." Some less demanding vocal pursuits may be resumed sooner, with caution. However, some injuries leave residual problems. If all or part of one lung is lost, voice technique may need to be modified. The greatest tendencies to voice abuse often come as a singer is nearly out of breath. Such singers must be careful to alter their phrasing to permit extra breaths, rather than attempting to sing extended phrases as they had previous to the injury. In addition, a vigorous program of aerobic rehabilitation is advisable. Following abdominal injuries, weaknesses in the abdominal muscle wall may persist such as ventral hernias. These may interfere with the support mechanism and may require surgical repair.

INJURIES TO THE LOWER EXTREMITIES

Although singers do not regularly consider a sprained ankle or a broken leg as a voice complaint, vocal dysfunction frequently follows such injuries, especially in singers and actors. It is extremely difficult to maintain good abdominal-thoracic muscle support while balancing awkwardly on one foot. It is common for singers to present with voice fatigue and hoarseness while on crutches or limping. Damage from the undesirable posture is aggravated by the distractions of trying to keep one's balance and of pain associated with the injury. Usually, awareness of this potential hazard and the need for conscious attention to support will avert this problem.

INJURY TO THE UPPER EXTREMITY

A broken arm, dislocated shoulder, or other upper extremity injury usually produces pain and muscle tension. This tension is often reflected in excess, asymmetric neck muscle tension and in alterations of posture. Under most circumstances, awareness and special attention to these potential problems will avoid the hyperfunctional voice abuse that often supervenes.

SUMMARY

The voice mechanism is extremely sensitive to minor alterations anywhere in the body. Physicians must be alert for problems created not only by injuries to the larynx, but also by injuries elsewhere in the body. Helping the professional voice user to become aware of the problem, and to practice meticulous technique and good judgment, usually is sufficient to avoid serious or prolonged vocal disability from injuries with temporary effects. However, injuries that produce chronic pain or impairment frequently have chronic vocal consequences.

Professional Voice: The Science and Art
of Clinical Care, Robert T. Sataloff.
Raven Press, Ltd., New York © 1991.

18

Performing Arts-Medicine and the Professional Voice User

Risks of Nonvoice Performance

*Robert T. Sataloff and **Mary Hawkshaw

*Department of Otolaryngology, Thomas Jefferson University,
Philadelphia, Pennsylvania; and **American Institute of Voice
and Ear Research, Philadelphia, Pennsylvania

The developing specialty of arts-medicine is extremely valuable for voice professionals. It is useful for the physician caring for professional vocalists to be aware of developments in related fields (1). Through the National Association of Teachers of Singers (NATS) Journal, the Journal of Voice, The Voice Foundation Symposia, and many other sources, enlightened singing teachers have become familiar with recent advances in the care of professional voice users. Many of these arose out of interdisciplinary team work, and new insights have resulted in better methods of history taking, physical examination, objective voice measures, and wider availability of educational information about the voice. These have produced better informed, healthier singers. Although voice-medicine is the most advanced area of arts-medicine, there are several other specialties that may be helpful during a singing career. As singers must often be actors, dancers, pianists, and do other jobs as well, it is useful for singers and singing teachers to be aware of developments in related fields.

WHAT IS DIFFERENT ABOUT ARTS-MEDICINE?

For physicians, arts-medicine and sports-medicine pose special interests, challenges, and problems. Traditional medical training has not provided the background necessary to address them well. Consequently, development of both fields has required understanding and interaction among physicians, performers (or athletes), and members of other disciplines. Such cooperation and interaction have taken so long to develop because of language problems. For example, when a singer complains of a "thready midrange," most doctors do not know what he/she is talking about. To the traditional physician, if such a singer looks healthy and has "normal" vocal cords on mirror examination, he/she is deemed normal by the physician. Medicine in general enjoys a broad range of physical condition that is considered "normal." The biggest difference we encounter in arts-medicine and sports-medicine is the patient's sophisticated self-analysis and narrow definition of normal. In general, doctors are not trained to recognize and work with the last few percent of physical perfection. The arts-medicine specialist is trained to recognize subtle differences in the supranormal to near-perfect range in which the professional performer's body must operate. To really understand performers, physicians must either be performers themselves or work closely with performers, teachers, coaches, trainers, and specific paramedical professionals. In voice, this means a laryngologist working with a singing teacher, voice coach, voice scientist, speech-language pathologist, and often other professionals. In other fields, the specialties vary, but the principles remain the same.

HAND MEDICINE

After voice-medicine, hand-medicine is the most advanced specialty of arts-medicine. Like voice problems, problems of pianists, violinists, harpists, and other instrumentalists who depend on their hands are handled best by a team. An arts-medicine hand clinic usually includes a hand specialist (usually a surgeon), physical therapist, radiologist, and perhaps music coaches, teachers, and trainers. Facilities are available to observe the musician while playing his/her instrument, as many problems are due to subtle technical quirks. Hand-medicine really catapulted arts-medicine to public prominence. A great many musicians have health problems. A self-completion questionnaire study of the 48 affiliate orchestras of the International Conference of Symphony and Opera Musicians (ICSOM) (2) resulted in return of questionnaires by 2,212 of the 4,025 professional musicians studied. Of the musicians responding, 82% reported medical problems, and 76% had a medical problem that adversely affected performance. Many of these musicians have problems caused or aggravated by musical performance. Yet, until the past few years, this was not widely known, and musicians were afraid to admit their difficulties for fear of losing work. Moreover, those who did seek medical attention usually were disappointed with the evaluation and results. World-class pianist Gary Graffman changed all of that almost singlehandedly. When he developed difficulty controlling his right hand, he persevered until he found a physician who was willing to look at the possibility that his problem was caused by his piano playing. Together, they came to understand his overuse syndrome. When Graffman made his difficulties known to the general public and Leon Fleischer followed suit, thousands of musicians discovered they were not alone and began seeking help. Gradually, the medical profession has learned to provide the care they need. Moreover, far-sighted music schools like the Curtis Institute, which Graffman directs, are beginning to incorporate scientifically based practice and development techniques in their curricula.

Vague incomplete control over one's hands at the keyboard or on the strings is one of the primary symptoms of overuse syndrome. This often comes from excessive, ineffective practicing with unbalanced muscle development, which may result in nearly crippling problems that end an instrumentalist's career. Chronic pain is also a common concomitant symptom. In an early paper, Hochberg et al. (3) reported that the most common hand complaints among musicians were (in order): pain, tightening, curling (drooping or cramping), weakness, stiffness, fatigue, pins and needles, swelling, temperature change, and redness. They resulted in loss of control; decreased facility, endurance, speed, or strength; and tension. Many of the musicians with these problems had either stopped playing, altered their practice, or changed their fingering, technique, or repertoire. Some of them also had related problems in their forearms, elbows, upper arms, or shoulders. Arts-medicine centers now provide accurate diagnosis and helpful treatment for most of the conditions that cause these problems, if they are diagnosed early. Hand problems are not limited to pianists, violinists, and harpists, of course. For example, clarinetists often develop pain in the right thumb from the weight of the instrument and the position used to hold it up.

ORTHOPEDICS AND GENERAL ARTS-MEDICINE

Like swimmer's shoulder and tennis elbow in sports-medicine, many instruments produce localized pain. Among the most common are cymbalist's shoulder, flutist's forearm, and guitarist's nipple. Brass players may develop problems in their lips, jaws, tongue, and teeth. Changes in tooth alignment, which may follow dental wear, work, or injury, also present special and potentially disabling problems for wind players in whom embouchure is critical. There are arts-medicine specialists in the field of dentistry who are especially skilled at handling such problems. Wind players may also develop pharyngoceles or laryngoceles that present as large airbags, which stand out as they play. They sometimes interfere with performance and require treatment.

Performance-related problems may also occur in other parts of the performer's body. For example, neck and back problems are almost routine in violinists and violists. Skin abrasions and even cysts requiring surgery occur under the left side of the jaw at the contact point of the instrument in many string players. Dermatologic problems also occur in flutists. Lower back pain is also a problem in many instrumentalists, especially in pianists who sit on benches without back support for 8 hr of practice. In many performers, such problems exist throughout a career. In established performers, they are often precipitated by illness or slight changes in technique of which the performer may be unaware. Skilled analysis in an arts-medicine center can now usually help.

DANCE-MEDICINE

Ballet and modern dance are among the most demanding of all athletic pursuits. Various forms of popular and show dancing, and especially break dancing, also place enormous demands on the body. The stresses caused by unusual positions (such as dancing *sur les pointes*), hyperextension, and leaps and lifts result in injury. In young dancers, hip injuries are especially common. Ankle, foot, and lower leg problems are more common in older dancers. Even a mild muscle strain may interfere with performance for weeks or months and may produce minor technical changes that predispose to other injuries. Major injuries such as rupture of the Achilles tendon also occur. Stress fractures in the hips, legs, and feet, which cause persistent pain, are often missed on x-ray but can now be diagnosed early with computerized tomography or bone scan.

The aesthetic requirements of dance may result in other problems. Excessive weight loss, bulimia, and even anorexia are disturbingly common, although, in their most severe forms, they are usually encountered in students rather than in established dancers. However, the prevalence of malnutrition among classical dancers of all ages is most disturbing. Dancers also have other special problems that may be less obvious. Menarche (the age when the first menstrual period occurs) is approximately 2 years later among young dancers than it is in the general population. This is believed to be due to low body weight and extreme exercise and may be aggravated by malnutrition from weight loss. Amenorrhea (cessation of menstrual periods) is also common. The incidence of reversible infertility is also increased among female dancers. Vaginal yeast infections are also common because of the tights worn by ballet dancers. These and other problems of dancers are recognized immediately by physicians specializing in dance-medicine. Often, these are orthopedists who also are directors of sports-medicine centers. Participation by members of the arts-medicine clinic in the educational programs of dance schools and professional companies is already helping to avoid such problems for many dancers.

PSYCHIATRY

Performance careers are stressful. The demand for daily perfection, public scrutiny, constant competition, critics, and old-fashioned stage fright may all exact a heavy toll. The additional strain on the performer and his/her family that accompanies an extensive tour may be particularly trying and often results in marital strife and/or divorce. Such problems are shared by many successful performers, and usually they can be kept under control. However, when the stress has become unmanageable or interferes excessively with the performer's life or artistic ability, the intervention of a professional may be appropriate. Fortunately, there are now psychologists and psychiatrists who have special skills and insight into these problems. Many of them are performers themselves. They can be most helpful in controlling the effects of these stresses, managing stage fright, overcoming writer's block, and in teaching the performer to regain sufficient control over his/her life to permit continuation of his/her career. Most arts-medicine centers have access to psychological professionals with special interests in this area.

OTHER ARTS-MEDICINE PROBLEMS

Many other special problems occur in performers. For example, hearing loss may be an occupational hazard for musicians. This occurs not only in rock musicians, but also in members of symphony orchestras. Rock musicians help avoid the problem by standing behind or beside their speakers rather than in front of them. Satisfactory solutions in the orchestra environment have not yet been advanced. Instrumentalists sitting in front of the brass section have particular problems. Certain instruments may actually cause hearing loss in the performers who play them. For example, the left ear of a violinist is at risk. Occupational hearing loss in general is a complex subject, and the special problems of hearing loss in musicians require a great deal more study, as discussed in Chapter 19.

Bagpiper's disease, a little known problem within the medical profession, is also potentially serious. The skins used to make bagpipes are cured in glycerine and honey. Bags make an excellent culture medium for growth of bacteria and fungi. Chronic fungal pneumonias occur among bagpipers. They are usually caused by Cryptococcus, and occasionally by aspergillosis. Bagpipers may also develop a spastic, "hourglass" stomach, which makes frequent rumbling noises. Many other similar problems exist but are beyond the scope of this review. In addition to those already known, there is no doubt that many more will be recognized as sensitivity to performers increases.

IMPORTANCE FOR SINGERS

Singers are often called on for performance functions other than singing. Both singers and their teachers should be aware of the potential hazards of nonvocal performance and should recognize signs of problems early. Fortunately, they can usually be corrected. However, if left unattended, they may worsen and interfere not only with playing and dancing but also with a singing career. Help is usually available through arts-medicine centers, including the following centers:

Center for Performing Arts Medicine, Faculty of Health Sciences, McMaster University, 1200 Main Street, West, Hamilton, Ontario L8N 3Z5, Canada. (416) 525-9140, Ext. 2161. Director: Dr. John Chong.

Health Program for Performing Artists, San Francisco Medical Center, University of California, 400 Parnassus Avenue, 5th Floor, San Francisco, CA 94143. (415) 476-7373. Director: Dr. Peter F. Ostwald.

Colorado Clinic for Performing Artists, 1515 East Ninth Avenue, #314, Denver, CO 80218. (303) 837-0907. Director: Dr. Mary Poole.

University of Colorado Health Sciences Center, Department of Neurology, Campus Box B 183, 4200 East Ninth Avenue, Denver, CO 80262. (303) 270-7566. Contact: Dr. Stuart Schneck.

Medical Program for Performing Artists, Northwestern Memorial Hospital, 303 East Superior Street, Chicago, IL 60611. (312) 908-ARTS. Director: Dr. Alice Brandfonbrener.

Performing Arts Medicine Program, Indiana University School of Music, 541 Clinical Drive, Indianapolis, IN 46223. (317) 274-4225. Director: Dr. Kenneth D. Brandt.

Louisville Performing Arts Medicine Group, Department of Neurology, University of Louisville, Louisville, KY 40292. (502) 588-7981. Director: Dr. Jonathan Newmark.

Comprehensive Arts Medicine Program at Braintree Hospital, 250 Pond Street, Braintree, MA 02184. (617) 848-5353. Director of Clinical Services: Dr. Richard N. Norris.

Musical Medicine Clinic, Massachusetts General Hospital, Neurology Service, Boston, MA 02114. (617) 726-8657. Director: Dr. Fred Hochberg.

School of Medicine, St. Louis University, St. Louis, MO 63141. (314) 567-7366. Director: Dr. Simon Horenstein.

Kathryn and Gilbert Miller, Health Care Institute for Performing Artists, St. Lukes/Roosevelt Hospital, 428 West 59th Street, New York, NY 10019. (212) 554-6314. Director: Dr. Emil Pascarelli.

Performing Arts Center for Health, Mental Hygiene Clinic, Bellevue Hospital, 400 East 30th Street, New York, NY 10016. (212) 561-4073; messages (212) 561-4711. Director: Dr. Howard W. Telson.

Cleveland Clinic Foundation, Medical Center for Performing Artists, 9500 Euclid Avenue, Cleveland, OH 44106. (216) 444-5545. Director: Dr. Richard Lederman.

Clinic for the Performing Arts, 2651 Highland Avenue, Cincinnati, OH 45219. (513) 281-3224. Director: Dr. G. James Sammarco.

The Arts Medicine Center, Thomas Jefferson University Hospital, 1721 Pine Street, Philadelphia, PA 19103. (215) 955-8300. Director: Dr. Robert T. Sataloff.

The Medical Center for Performing Artists, Suburban General Hospital, Norristown, PA 19401. (215) 279-1060. Director: Dr. David Rosenfeld.

Arts Medicine Center, Austin Regional Clinic, 6835 Austin Center Boulevard, Austin, TX 78755. (512) 465-6631. Director: Dr. Stephen A. Mitchell.

Performing Artists Clinic, University of Texas Health Science Center, Houston, TX 77030. (713) 792-5777. Director: Dr. Alan Lockwood.

REFERENCES

1. Sataloff RT, Brandfonbrener AG, Lederman RJ. *Performing arts-medicine.* New York: Raven Press, 1991.
2. Fishbein M, Middlestadt SE, Ottati V, et al. Medical problems among ICSOM musicians: overview of a national survey. *Med Prob Perform Art* 1988;3:1–8.
3. Hochberg FH, Leffert RD, Heller MD, Merriman L. Hand difficulties among musicians. *JAMA* 1983;249(14):1869–1872.

Professional Voice: The Science and Art
of Clinical Care, Robert T. Sataloff.
Raven Press, Ltd., New York © 1991.

19

Hearing Loss in Singers

Robert T. Sataloff and Joseph Sataloff

*Department of Otolaryngology, Thomas Jefferson University
Philadelphia, Pennsylvania*

Singers depend on good hearing to match pitch, monitor vocal quality, and provide feedback and direction for vocal adjustments during singing. The importance of good hearing has been under-appreciated. While well-trained singers are usually careful to protect their voices, they may subject their ears to unnecessary damage and thereby threaten their musical careers. The ear is a critical part of the singer's "instrument." Consequently, it is important for singers to understand how the ear works, how to take care of it, what can go wrong with it, and how to avoid hearing loss from preventable injury.

CAUSES OF HEARING LOSS

The classification and causes of hearing loss, audiometric technique, and definitions of terms such as dB and dBA have been described in detail in standard textbooks of otolaryngology and previous works by the authors (1, 2), and they will be reviewed only briefly in this chapter. Hearing loss may be hereditary or nonhereditary, and either form may be congenital (present at birth) or acquired. There is a common misconception that hereditary hearing loss implies presence of the problem at birth or during childhood. In fact, most hereditary hearing loss occurs later in life. Otosclerosis, a common inherited cause of correctable hearing loss, often presents when people are in their 20s or 30s. Similarly, the presence of deafness at birth does not necessarily imply hereditary or genetic factors. A child whose mother had German measles during the first trimester of fetal life, or was exposed to radiation early in pregnancy, may be born with a hearing loss. Hearing loss may occur because of problems in any portion of the ear, the nerve between the

---

This chapter is republished with slight modification from Sataloff RT, Sataloff J. Hearing loss in musicians. In: Sataloff RT, Brandfonbrener A, Lederman R. *Performing arts-medicine*. New York: Raven Press, 1991.

ear and the brain, or the brain. Understanding hearing loss requires a basic knowledge of the structure of the human ear.

Anatomy and Physiology of the Ear

The ear is divided into three major anatomical divisions: (a) the outer ear, (b) the middle ear, and (c) the inner ear (Fig. 1).

The outer ear has two parts: (a) the trumpet-shaped apparatus on the side of the head called the auricle or pinna, and (b) the tube leading from the auricle into the temporal bone called the external auditory canal. The opening is called the meatus.

The tympanic membrane, or "eardrum," stretches across the inner end of the external ear canal separating the outer ear from the middle ear. The middle ear is a small cavity in the temporal bone in which three auditory ossicles—malleus (hammer), incus (anvil), and stapes (stirrup)—form a bony bridge from the external ear to the inner ear. The bony ridge is held in place by muscles and ligaments. The middle-ear chamber is filled with air

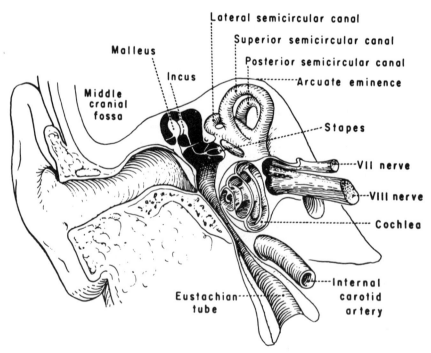

FIG. 1. Diagrammatic cross-section of the ear. The semicircular canals are connected with maintaining balance.

and opens into the throat through the eustachian tube. The eustachian tube helps to equalize pressure on both sides of the eardrum.

The inner ear is a fluid-filled chamber divided into two parts: (a) the vestibular labyrinth, which functions as part of the body's balance mechanism, and (b) the cochlea, which contains thousands of minute, sensory, hairlike cells (Fig. 2). The organ of Corti functions as the switchboard of the auditory system. The eighth cranial or acoustic nerve leads from the inner ear to the brain, serving as the pathway for the impulses the brain will interpret as sound.

Sound creates vibrations in the air somewhat similar to the "waves" created when a stone is thrown into a pond. The outer-ear "trumpet" collects these sound waves and funnels them down the external ear canal to the eardrum. The sound waves cause the eardrum to vibrate. The vibrations are transmitted through the middle ear over the bony bridge formed by the malleus, incus, and stapes. These vibrations, in turn, lead the membranes over the openings to the inner ear to vibrate, causing the fluid in the inner ear to be set in motion. The motion of the fluid in inner ear excites the nerve cells in the organ of Corti, producing electrochemical impulses that are transmitted to the brain along the acoustic nerve. As the impulses reach the brain, we experience the sensation of hearing.

ESTABLISHING THE SITE OF DAMAGE IN THE AUDITORY SYSTEM

The cause of a hearing loss, like that of any other medical condition, is determined by carefully obtaining a history, making a physical examination, and performing certain laboratory tests. In otology, hearing and balance tests parallel the function of clinical laboratory tests in general medicine. When a hearing loss is classified, the point at which the auditory pathway has broken down is localized, and it is determined whether the patient's hearing loss is conductive, sensorineural, central, functional, or a mixture of these.

Otologic Evaluation

Details of the otologic history, physical examination, and test protocols are available in many otolaryngology texts. Medical evaluation of a patient with a suspected hearing problem includes a comprehensive history; complete physical examination of the ears, nose, throat, head, and neck; assessment of the cranial nerves including testing the sensation in the external auditory canal (Hitzelberger's sign) and audiogram (hearing test); and other tests, as indicated. Recommended additional studies may include blood tests, computed tomography, magnetic resonance imaging, specialized hearing tests such as brainstem evoked response audiometry, tympanometry, and

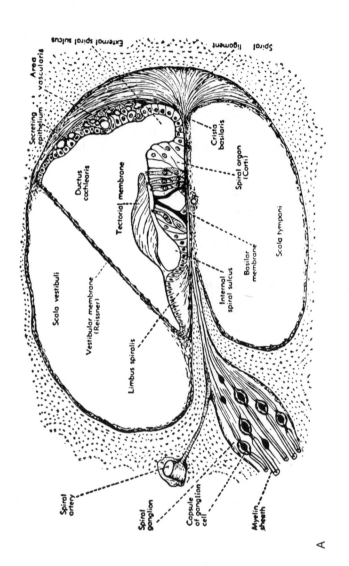

Spiral ligament

External spiral sulcus

Area vascularis

Secreting epithelium

Ductus cochlearis

Tectorial membrane

Crista basilaris

Spiral organ (Corti)

Scala tympani

Basilar membrane

Internal spiral sulcus

Scala vestibuli

Vestibular membrane (Reissner)

Limbus spiralis

Spiral artery

Spiral ganglion

Capsule of ganglion cell

Myelin sheath

A

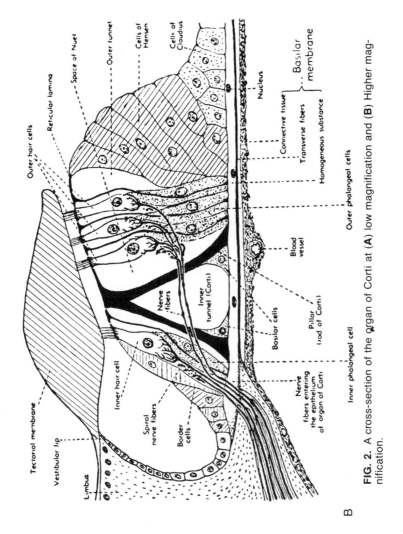

FIG. 2. A cross-section of the organ of Corti at (**A**) low magnification and (**B**) Higher magnification.

223

central auditory testing; balance testing; and a variety of blood tests for the many systemic causes of hearing loss. All patients with hearing complaints deserve a thorough examination and comprehensive evaluation to determine the specific cause of the problem and to rule out serious or treatable conditions that may be responsible for the hearing impairment. Contrary to popular misconception, not all cases of sensorineural hearing loss are incurable, so, "nerve deafness" should be assessed with the same systematic vigor and enthusiasm as conductive hearing loss.

Conductive Hearing Loss

In cases of conductive hearing loss, sound waves are not transmitted effectively to the inner ear because of some interference in the external canal, the eardrum, the ossicular chain, the middle ear cavity, the oval window, the round window, or the eustachian tube. For example, damage to either the middle ear, which transmits sound energy efficiently, or the eustachian tube, which maintains equal air pressure between the middle ear cavity and the external canal, could result in a mechanical defect in sound transmission. In pure conductive hearing loss, there is no damage to the inner ear or the neural pathway.

Patients diagnosed as having conductive hearing loss have a much better prognosis than those with sensorineural loss, because modern techniques make it possible to cure or at least to improve the vast majority of cases in which the damage occurs in the outer or middle ear. Even if they are not improved medically or surgically, these patients stand to benefit greatly from a hearing aid, because what they need most is amplification. They are not bothered by distortion and other hearing abnormalities that may occur in sensorineural losses.

Conductive hearing loss may result from anything that completely blocks the outer ear or interferes with sound transmission through the middle ear. Outer ear problems include birth defects, total occlusion of the external auditory canal by wax, foreign body (such as a piece of cotton swab or ear plug), infection, trauma, or tumor. Large perforations in the tympanic membrane may also cause hearing loss, especially if they surround the malleus. However, relatively small central perforations usually do not cause a great deal of hearing impairment. If someone with such a perforation has a 30-dB or 40-dB hearing loss, there is probably also a problem involving the ossicles. Middle ear dysfunction is the most common cause of conductive hearing loss. It may occur in many ways. The middle ear may become filled with fluid because of eustachian tube dysfunction. The fluid restricts free movement of the tympanic membrane and ossicles, thereby producing hearing loss. Middle ear conductive hearing loss may also be caused by ossicular abnormalities. These include fractures, erosion from disease, impingement by tumors, congenital malformations, and other causes. However, otosclerosis is among the most common. This hereditary disease afflicts the stapes and prevents it from moving in its normal pistonlike fashion in the oval window. Hearing loss from otosclerosis can be corrected through stapes surgery, a brief operation under local anesthesia, and it is usually possible to restore hearing.

Sensorineural Hearing Loss

The word "sensorineural" was introduced to replace the ambiguous terms "perceptive deafness" and "nerve deafness." It is a more descriptive and more accurate anatomical term. Its dual character suggests that two separate areas may be affected; actually, this is the case. The term "sensory" hearing loss is applied when the damage is localized in the inner ear. Useful synonyms are "cochlear" or "inner ear" hearing loss. The cochlea has approximately 15,000 hearing nerve endings (hair cells). Those hair cells in the large end of the cochlea respond to very high-pitched sounds, and those in the small end (and throughout much of the rest of the cochlea) respond to low-pitched sounds. Those hair cells, and the nerve that connects them to the brain, are susceptible to damage from a variety of causes. "Neural" hearing loss is the correct term to use when the damage is in the auditory nerve proper, anywhere between its fibers at the base of the hair cells and the auditory nuclei. This range includes the bipolar ganglion of the eighth cranial nerve. Other common names for this type of loss are "nerve deafness" and "retrocochlear" hearing loss. These names are useful if applied appropriately and meaningfully, but too often they are used improperly.

Although at present it is common practice to group both sensory and neural components, it has become possible in many cases to attribute a predominant part of the damage, if not all of it, to either the inner ear or the nerve. Because of some success in this area and the likelihood that ongoing research will allow us to differentiate between even more cases of sensory and neural hearing loss, we shall divide the terms and describe the distinctive features of each type. This separation is advisable because the prognosis and treatment of the two kinds of impairment differ. For example, in all cases of unilateral sensorineural hearing loss, it is important to distinguish between a sensory and neural hearing impairment, because the neural type may be due to an acoustic neuroma, which could become life-threatening. Those cases that we cannot identify as either sensory or neural and those cases in which there is damage in both regions we shall classify as sensorineural.

There are various and complex causes of sensorineural hearing loss, but certain features are characteristic and basic to all of them. Because the histories obtained from patients are so diverse, they contribute more insight into the etiology than into the classification of a case. Sensorineural hearing loss often involves not only loss of loudness, but also loss of clarity. The hair cells in the inner ear are responsible for analyzing auditory input and instantaneously coding it. The auditory nerve is responsible for carrying this complex coded information. Neural defects such as acoustic neuromas (tumors of the auditory nerve) are frequently accompanied by severe difficulties in discriminating words, although the hearing threshold for soft sounds may not be so severely affected. Sensory deficits in the cochlea are often associated with distortion of sound quality, loudness (loudness recruitment), and pitch (diplacusis). Diplacusis poses particular problems for musicians, because it may make it difficult for them to tell whether they are playing or singing correct pitches. This symptom is also troublesome to conductors. Keyboard players and other musicians whose instruments do not require critical tuning adjustments compensate for this problem better than singers, string players, etc. In addition, sensorineural hearing loss may be accompanied by tinnitus (noises in the ear), and/or vertigo.

Sensorineural hearing loss may be due to a great number of conditions including aging, exposure to ototoxic drugs (including a number of antibiotics, diuretics, and chemotherapy agents), hereditary conditions, systemic diseases, trauma, and noise, among other causes. Most physicians recognize that hearing loss may be associated with a large number of hereditary syndromes (2, 3) involving the eyes, kidneys, heart, or any other body system, but many are not aware that hearing loss also accompanies many very common systemic diseases. Naturally, these occur in musicians as well as others; and the presence of these systemic illnesses should lead physicians to inquire about hearing and perform audiometry to screen for hearing loss in selected cases. Problems implicated in hearing impairment include Rh incompatibility, hypoxia, jaundice, rubella, mumps, rubeola, fungal infections, meningitis, tuberculosis, sarcoidosis, Wegener's granulomatosis, vasculitis, histiocytosis X, allergy, hyperlipoproteinemia, syphilis, hypothyroidism, hypoadrenalism, hypopituitarism, renal failure, autoimmune disease, coagulopathies, aneurysms, vascular disease, multiple sclerosis, infestations, diabetes, hypoglycemia, cleft palate, and others (2). Prolonged exposure to very loud noise is a common cause of hearing loss in our society. Noise-induced hearing loss is seen most frequently in heavy industry. However, occupational hearing loss caused by musical instruments is a special problem, as discussed below.

Sensorineural hearing loss is one of the most challenging problems in medicine. A large variety of hearing impairments fall under this category. The prognosis for restoring a sensorineural hearing loss with presently available therapy is poor. Although some spontaneous remissions and hearing improvements with therapy have occurred, particularly in cases involving sensory loss. a great need for further research still exists.

Mixed Hearing Loss

For practical purposes, a mixed hearing loss should be understood to mean a conductive hearing loss accompanied by a sensory or a neural (or a sensorineural) loss in the same ear. However, the emphasis is on the conductive hearing loss, because available therapy is very much more effective for this group. Consequently, the otologic surgeon has a special interest in cases of mixed hearing loss in which there is primarily a conductive loss complicated by some sensorineural damage. In a musician, curing the correctable component may be sufficient to convert hearing from unserviceable to satisfactory for performance purposes.

Functional Hearing Loss

Functional hearing loss occurs as a condition in which the patient does not seem to hear or to respond; yet the handicap is not caused by any organic pathology in the peripheral or central auditory pathways. The hearing difficulty may have an entirely emotional or psychological etiology, or it may be superimposed on some mild organic hearing loss, in which case it is called a functional or psychogenic overlay. Often, the patient really has normal hearing underlying the functional hearing loss. A careful history usually will reveal some hearing impairment in the patient's family or some reference to deafness that served as the nucleus for the patient's functional hearing loss. The most important challenge in such a case is to classify the condition properly. Functional hearing loss occurs not only in adults, but also in children. This diagnosis should be considered when hearing problems arise in the musicians under great pressure, regardless of age, including young prodigies.

Central Hearing Loss (Central Dysacousis)

In central hearing loss, the damage is situated in the central nervous system at some point between the auditory nuclei (in the medulla oblongata) and the cortex. Formerly, central hearing loss was described as a type of "perceptive deafness," a term now obsolete.

Although information about central hearing loss is accumulating, it remains somewhat a mystery. Physicians know that some patients cannot interpret or understand what is being said and that the cause of the difficulty is not in the peripheral mechanism but somewhere in the central nervous system. In central hearing loss, the problem is not a lowered pure-tone threshold but is in the patient's ability to interpret what he/she hears. Obviously, it is a more complex task to interpret speech than to respond to a pure-tone threshold; consequently, the tests necessary to diagnose central hearing impairment must be designed to assess a patient's ability to handle complex information.

PSYCHOLOGICAL CONSEQUENCES OF HEARING LOSS

Singers are frequently sensitive, somewhat "high-strung" people who depend on physical perfection in order to practice their craft and earn their livelihoods. Any physical impairment that threatens their ability to continue as musicians may be greeted with dread, denial, panic, depression, or similar response that may be perceived as "exaggerated," especially by physicians who do not specialize in caring for performers. In the case of hearing loss, such reactions are common even in the general public. Consequently, it is not surprising that psychological concomitants of hearing loss in musicians are seen in nearly all cases.

Many successful professional voice users are communicative and gregarious. Naturally, anything that impairs their ability to interact with the world causes problems similar to those seen in nonmusicians. However, in addition, their vocational hearing demands are much greater than those required in most professions. Therefore, their normal reactions to hearing loss are often amplified by legitimate fears about interruption of their artistic and professional futures through hearing impairment. These concerns are encountered with hearing impaired musicians regardless of the cause. The problems involved in accurately assessing the disability associated with such impairments are addressed below in the discussion of occupational hearing loss in musicians.

OCCUPATIONAL HEARING LOSS IN SINGERS AND OTHER MUSICIANS

Occupational hearing loss is sensorineural hearing impairment caused by exposure to high intensity noise in the workplace, in the singer's case, music. Many singers perform with instruments, and many are also instrumentalists. It has been well established that selected symphony orchestra instruments, popular orchestras, rock bands, and personal stereo headphones produce sound pressure levels intense enough to cause permanent hearing loss. Such hearing loss may also be accompanied by tinnitus (ringing in the ears) and may be severe enough to interfere with performance especially in singers and violinists. The amount of hearing loss is related to the intensity of the noise, duration and intermittency of exposure, total exposure time over months and years, and other factors. Various methods have been devised to help protect the hearing of performers. For example, many musicians (especially in rock bands) wear ear protectors, at least during practice. They also stand beside or behind their speakers, rather than in front of them.

Attempts to solve similar problems in orchestras have included placement of plexiglass barriers in front of some of the louder brass instruments, rotating seating positions within orchestras, elevating sections, changing the space and height between players, and other measures. Noise levels in choral environments are also high, but their possible effects on hearing have not yet been studied. Singers should be aware of noise hazards and avoid them or use hearing protection in noisy surroundings whenever possible. They should also be careful to avoid exposure to potentially damaging avocational noise such as loud music through headphones, chainsaws, snowmobiles, motorcyles, and power tools.

For many years, people have been concerned about hearing loss in rock musicians exposed to intense noise from electric instruments and in audiences who frequently attend concerts of rock music. We have seen hearing loss in both of these populations, and similar problems in people who listen to music at very high volumes through earphones. Because of the obviously high intensity that characterizes rock music, hearing loss in these situations is not surprising. This situation raises serious concerns about prevention that are of compelling relevance to professional rock musicians whose livelihoods depend on their hearing. Clinical observations in the authors' practice suggest that the rock performing environment may be another source of asymmetrical noise-induced hearing loss, a relatively unusual situation, since most occupational hearing loss is symmetrical. Rock musicians tend to have slightly greater hearing loss in the ear adjacent to the drum and cymbal, or the side immediately next to a speaker, if it is placed slightly behind the musician. Various methods have been devised to help protect the hearing of rock players. For example, most of them stand beside or behind their speakers, rather than in front of them. In this way, they are not subjected to peak intensities, as are the patrons in the first rows.

The problem of occupational hearing loss among classical musicians is less obvious, but equally important. In fact, in the United States, it has become a matter of great concern and negotiation among unions and management. Various reports have found an increased incidence of high-frequency sensorineural hearing loss among professional orchestra musicians as compared with the general public; and sound levels within orchestras have been measured between 83 dBA and 112 dBA, as discussed below. The size of the orchestra and the rehearsal hall are important factors, as is the position of the individual instrumentalist within the orchestra. Players seated immediately in front of the brass section appear to have particular problems, for example. Individual classical instruments may produce more noise exposure for their players than assumed.

Because musicians practice or perform four to eight hours a day (sometimes more), such exposure levels may be significant. An interesting review of the literature may be found in the report of a clinical research project on hearing in classical musicians by Axelsson and Lindgren (4). They also found asymmetrical hearing loss in classical musicians, greater in the left ear. This is a common finding, especially among violinists. A brief summary of most of the published works on hearing loss in musicians is presented below.

In the United States, various attempts have been made to solve some of the problems of the orchestra musician, including placement of plexiglass barriers in front of some of the louder brass instruments, alteration in the orchestra formation such as elevation of sections or rotational seating, changes in spacing and height between players, use of ear protectors, and other measures. These solutions have not been proved effective, and some of them appear impractical and damaging to the performance. The effects of the acoustical environment (concert hall, auditorium, outdoor stage) on the ability of music to damage hearing have not been studied systematically. Recently, popular musicians have begun to recognize the importance of this problem and to protect themselves and educate their fans. Some performers are wearing ear protectors regularly in rehearsal and even during performance (5). Considerable additional study is needed to provide proper answers and clinical guidance for this very important occupational problem. In fact, review of the literature on occupational hearing loss reveals that surprisingly little information is available on the entire subject. Moreover, all of it is concerned with instrumentalists, and no similar studies in singers were found.

Study of the existing reports reveals a variety of approaches. Unfortunately, neither the results nor the quality of the studies is consistent. Nevertheless, familiarity with the research already performed provides useful insights into the problem. In 1960, Arnold and Miskolczy-Fodor (6) studied the hearing of 30 pianists. Sound pressure level measurements showed that average levels were approximately 85 dB, although periods of 92 to 96 dB were recorded. The A-weighting network was not used for sound level measurements in this study. No noise-induced hearing loss was identified. The pianists in this study were 60 to 80 years of age, and, in fact, their hearing was better than normal for their age. Flach and Aschoff (7), and later Flach (8), found sensorineural hearing loss in 16% of 506 music students and professional musicians, a higher percentage than could be accounted for by age alone, although none of the cases of hearing loss occurred in students. Hearing loss was most common in musicians playing string instruments. Flach and Aschoff also noted asymmetrical sensorineural hearing loss worse on the left in 10 of 11 cases of bilateral sensorineural hearing loss in musicians. In one case (a flutist), the hearing was worse on the right. In 4% of the professional musicians tested, hearing loss was felt to be causally related to musical noise exposure. Histories and physical examinations were performed on the musicians, and tests were performed in a controlled environment. This study also included interesting measurements of sound levels in a professional orchestra. Unfortunately, they are reported in DINPHONS, rather than dBA.

In 1968, Berghoff (9) reported on the hearing of 35 big-band musicians and 30 broadcasting (studio) musicians. Most had performed for 15 to 25 years, although the string players were older as a group and had performed for as much as 35 years. In general, they played approximately five hours per day. Hearing loss was found in 40- to 60-year-old musicians at 8,000 Hz and 10,000 Hz. Eight musicians had substantial hearing loss, especially at 4,000 Hz. Five of 64 (8%) cases were felt to be causally related to noise exposure. No difference was found between left and right ears, but hearing loss was most common in musicians who were sitting immediately beside drums, trumpets, or bassoons. Sound level measurements for wind instruments revealed that intensities were greater one meter away from the instrument than they were at the ear canal. Unfortunately, sound levels were measured in PHONS. Lebo and Oliphant (10) studied the sound levels of a symphony orchestra and two rock and roll orchestras. They reported that sound energy for symphony orchestras is fairly evenly distributed from 500 through 4,000 Hz, but most of the energy in rock and roll music was found between 250 and 500 Hz. The sound pressure level for the symphony orchestra during loud passages was approximately 90 dBA. For rock and roll bands, it reached levels in excess of 110 dBA. Most of the time, music during rock performance was louder than 95 dB in the lower frequencies, while symphony orchestras rarely achieved such levels. However, Lebo and Oliphant made their measurements from the auditorium, rather than in immediate proximity to the performers. Consequently, their measurements are more indicative of distant audience noise exposure than that of the musicians or audience members in the first row. Rintelmann and Borus also studied noise-induced hearing loss in rock and roll musicians, measuring sound pressure levels at various distances from five feet to 60 feet from center stage (11a). They studied six different rock and roll groups in four locations and measured a mean sound pressure level of 105 dB. Their analysis revealed that the acoustic spectrum was fairly flat in the low and mid-frequency region and showed gradual reduction above 2,000 Hz. They also detected hearing loss in only 5% of the 42 high school and college student rock and roll musicians they studied. The authors estimated that their experimental group had been exposed to approximately 105 dB SPL for an average of 11.4 hours a week for 2.9 years.

In 1970, Jerger and Jerger (11) studied temporary threshold shifts in rock and roll musicians. They identified temporary threshold shifts greater than 15 dB in at least one frequency between 2,000 and 8,000 Hz in eight of nine musicians studied prior to performance and within one hour after the performance. Speaks and co-workers (12) examined 25 rock musicians for threshold shifts, obtaining measures between 20 and 40 min following performance. In this study, shifts of only seven to eight dB at 4,000 and 6,000 Hz were identifed. Temporary threshold shifts occurred in about one-half the musicians studied. Six of the 25 musicians had permanent threshold shifts. Noise measurements were also made on 10 rock bands. Speaks et al.

found noise levels from 90 to 110 dBA. Most sessions were less than four hours, and actual music time was generally 120 to 150 min. The investigators recognized the hazard to hearing posed by this noise exposure. In 1972, Rintelmann, Lindberg and Smitley studied the effects of rock and roll music on humans under laboratory conditions (12a). They exposed normal-hearing females to rock and roll music at 110 dB SPL in a sound field. They also compared subjects exposed to music played continuously for 60 min with others in which the same music was interrupted by one minute of ambient noise between each three minutes musical selection. At 4,000 Hz, they detected mean temporary threshold shifts of 26 dB in the subjects exposed to continuous noise, and 22.5 dB in those exposed intermittently. Both groups required approximately the same amount of time for recovery. Temporary threshold shifts sufficient to be considered potentially hazardous for hearing occurred in slightly over 50% of the subjects exposed to intermittent noise, and 80% of subjects subjected to continuous noise.

In 1972, Jahto and Hellmann (13) studied 63 orchestra musicians playing in contemporary dance bands. Approximately one-third of their subjects had measurable hearing loss, and 13% had bilateral high-frequency loss suggestive of noise-induced hearing damage. They also measured peak sound pressure levels of 110 dB (the A scale was not used). They detected potentially damaging levels produced by trumpets, bassoons, saxophone, and percussion. In contrast, in 1974, Buhlert and Kuhl (14) found no noise-induced hearing loss among 17 performers in a radio broadcasting orchestra. The musicians had played for an average of 20 years and were an average of 30 years in age. In a later study, Kuhl (15) studied members of a radio broadcasting dance orchestra over a period of 12 days. The average noise exposure was 82 dBA. He concluded that such symphony orchestras were exposed to safe hearing levels, in disagreement with Jahto and Hellmann. Zeleny et al. (16) studied members of a large string orchestra with intensities reaching 104 to 112 dB. Hearing loss greater than 20 dB in at least one frequency occurred in 85 of 118 subjects (72%), usually in the higher frequencies. Speech frequencies were affected in six people (5%).

In 1976, Siroky et al. (17) reported noise levels within a symphony orchestra ranging between 87 and 98 dBA, with a mean value of 92 dBA. Audiometric evaluation of 76 members of the orchestra revealed 16 musicians with hearing loss, 13 of them sensorineural. Hearing loss was found in 7.3% of string players, 20% of wind players, and 28% of brass players. All percussionists had some degree of hearing loss. Hearing loss was not found in players who had performed for less than 10 years but was present in 42% of players who had performed for more than 20 years. This study needs to be reevaluated in consideration of aged-matched controls. At least some of the cases reported have hearing loss not causally related to noise (such as those with hearing levels of 100 dB in the higher frequencies). In a companion report, Folprechtova and Miksovska (18) also found mean sound levels of

92 dBA in a symphony orchestra, with a range of 87 to 98 dBA. They reported that most of the musicians performed between four and eight hours daily. They reported the sound levels of various instruments as follows [in dBA]:

Violin	84–103
Cello	84–92
Bass	75–83
Piccolo	95–112
Flute	85–111
Clarinet	92–103
French horn	90–106
Oboe	80–94
Trombone	85–114
Xylophone	90–92

A study by Balazs and Gotze (19), also in 1976, agreed that classical musicians are exposed to potentially damaging hearing levels. The findings of Gryczynska and Czyzewski (20) support the concerns raised by other authors. In 1977, they found bilateral normal hearing in only 16 of 51 symphony orchestra musicians who worked daily at sound levels between 85 and 108 dBA. Five of the musicians had unilateral normal hearing; the rest had bilateral hearing loss.

In 1978, Axelsson and Lindgren (21,22) published an interesting study of 83 pop musicians and noted a surprisingly low incidence of hearing loss. They reanalyzed previous reports investigating a total of 160 pop musicians, which identified an incidence of only 5% hearing loss. In their 1978 study (21), Axelsson and Lindgren tested 69 musicians, four disk jockeys, four managers, and six sound engineers. To have hearing loss, a subject had to have at least one pure-tone threshold exceeding 20 dB at any frequency between 3,000 and 8,000 Hz. Thirty-eight musicians were found to have sensorineural hearing loss. In 11, only the right ear was affected; in five, only the left ear was affected. Thirteen cases were excluded because their hearing loss could be explained by causes other than noise. Thus, 25% of the pop musicians had sensorineural hearing loss probably attributable to noise. The most commonly impaired frequency was 6,000 Hz, and very few ears showed hearing levels worse than 35 dB. After correction for age and other factors, 25 (30%) had hearing loss as defined above. Eleven (13%) had hearing loss defined as a pure-tone audiometric average greater than 20 dB at 3, 4, 6, and 8 kHz in at least one ear. Of these 11, seven had unilateral hearing loss (8%).

In 1981, Westmore and Eversden (23) studied a symphony orchestra and 34 of its musicians. They recorded sound pressure levels for 14.4 hr. Sound levels exceeded 90 dBA for 3.51 hr and equalled or exceeded 110 dBA for 0.02 hr. In addition, there were brief peaks exceeding 120 dBA. They interpreted their audiometric testing as showing noise-induced hearing loss in 23 of 68 ears. Only four of the 23 ears had a hearing loss greater than 20 dB at 4,000 Hz. There was a "clear indication" that orchestral musicians may be exposed to damaging noise. However, because of the relatively mild severity, they speculated that "it is unlikely that any musician is going to be prevented from continuing his artistic career." In Axelsson and Lindgren's 1981 study (4), sound-level measurements were performed in two theaters, and 139 musicians underwent hearing tests. Sound levels for performances ranged from 83 to 92 dBA. Sound levels were slightly higher in an orchestra pit, although this is contrary to the findings of Westmore and Enersden (23). Fifty-nine musicians (43%) had pure-tone thresholds worse than expected for their ages. French hornists, trumpeters, trombonists, and bassoonists were found to be at increased risk for sensorineural hearing loss. Asymmetric pure-tone thresholds were common in musicians with hearing loss and in those still classified as having "normal hearing." The left ear demonstrated greater hearing loss than the right, especially among violinists. Axelsson and Lindgren also found that the loudness comfort level was unusually high among musicians. Acoustic reflexes also were elicited at comparatively high levels, being pathologically increased in approximately 30%. Temporary threshold shifts were also identified, supporting the assertion of noise-related etiology.

In 1983, Karlsson and co-workers (24) published a report with findings and conclusions substantially different from those of Axelsson and others. Karlsson et al. investigated 417 musicians, of whom 123 were studied twice at an interval of six years. After excluding 26 musicians who had hearing loss for reasons other than noise, they based their conclusions on the remaining 391 cases. They concluded that there was no statistical difference between the hearing of symphony orchestra musicians and that of a normal population of similar age and sex. Those data revealed a symmetric dip of 20 dB at 6,000 Hz in flutist, and a 30-dB left high-frequency sloping hearing loss in bass players. Overall, a 5-dB difference between ears was also found at 6,000 and 8,000 Hz, with the left side being worse. Although Karlsson and co-workers concluded that performing in a symphonic orchestra does not involve an increased risk of hearing damage, and that standard criteria for industrial noise exposure are not applicable to symphonic music, their data are similar to previous studies. Only their interpretation varies substantially.

Johnson et al. (25) studied the effects of instrument type and orchestral position on the hearing of orchestra musicians. They studied 60 orchestra musicians from 24 to 64 years in age, none of whom had symptomatic hearing problems. The musicians underwent otologic histories and examinations and pure-tone audiometry from 250 through 20,000 Hz. Unfortunately, this study used previous data from other authors as control data. In addition to the inherent weakness in this design, the comparison data did not include thresholds at 6,000 Hz. There appeared to be a 6,000-Hz dip in the population studied by Johnson et al. (25), but no definitive statement could be made. The authors concluded that the type of instrument played and the position on the orchestra stage had no significant correlation with hearing loss, disagreeing with findings of other investigators. In another paper produced from the same study (26), Johnson et al. reported no difference in the high-frequency thresholds (9,000–20,000 Hz) between musicians and non-musicians. Again, because they examined 60 instrumentalists but used previously published reports for comparison, this study is marred. This shortcoming in experimental design is particularly important in high-frequency testing, during which calibration is particularly difficult and establishment of norms on each individual piece of equipment is advisable.

A particularly interesting review of hearing impairment among orchestra musicians was published by Woolford et al. (27) in 1988. Although this report presents only preliminary data, the authors have put forward a penetrating review of the problem and interesting proposals regarding solutions, including an international comparative study. They concluded that the presence of hearing loss among classical musicians from various etiologies including noise has been established, that some noise-induced hearing impairments in musicians are permanent (although usually slight), and that successful efforts to reduce the intensity of noise exposure are possible.

In addition to concern about hearing loss among performers, in recent years, there has been growing concern about noise-induced hearing loss among audiences. Those at risk include not only people at rock concerts, but also people who enjoy music through stereo systems, especially modern personal headphones. Concern about hearing loss from this source in high school students has appeared in the lay press and elsewhere (28,29). Because young music lovers are potentially performers, in addition to other reasons, this hazard should be taken seriously and investigated further.

Review of these somewhat confusing and contradictory studies reveals that a great deal of important work remains to be done in order to establish the risk of hearing loss among various types of musicians, the level and pattern of hearing loss that may be sustained, practical methods of preventing hearing loss, and advisable programs for monitoring and early diagnosis. However, a few preliminary conclusions can be drawn. First, the preponderance of evidence indicates that noise-induced hearing loss occurs among both pop and classical musicians and is causally related to exposure to loud music. Second, in most instances, especially among classical musicians, the hearing loss is not severe enough to interfere with speech perception. Third, the effects of mild high-frequency hearing loss on musical performance have not been established. Fourth, it should be possible to devise methods to conserve hearing among performing artists without interfering with performance.

LEGAL ASPECTS OF HEARING LOSS IN MUSICIANS

The problem of hearing loss in musicians raises numerous legal issues, especially the implications of occupational hearing loss, and hearing has become an issue in some orchestra contracts. Traditionally worker's compensation legislation has been based on the theory that workers should be compensated when a work-related injury impairs their ability to earn a living. Ordinarily, occupational hearing loss does not impair earning power (except possibly in the case of musicians and a few others). Consequently, current occupational hearing loss legislation broke new legal ground by providing compensation for interference with quality of life, that is, loss of living power. Therefore, all current standards for defining and compensating occupational hearing loss are based on the communication needs of the average speaker. Since music-induced hearing loss appears rarely to affect the speech frequencies, it is not compensable under most laws. However, although a hearing loss at 3,000, 4,000, or 6,000 Hz with preservation of lower frequencies may not pose a problem for a boilermaker, it may be a serious problem for a violinist. Under certain circumstances, such a hearing loss may even be disabling. Because professional instrumentalists require considerably greater hearing acuity throughout a larger frequency range, we must investigate whether the kinds of hearing loss caused by music are severe enough to impair performance. If so, new criteria must be established for compensation for disabling hearing impairment in musicians, in keeping with the original intent of worker's compensation law.

There may also be legal issues unresolved regarding hearing loss not caused by noise in professional musicians. Like people with other handicaps, there are numerous federal laws protecting the rights of the hearing impaired. In the unhappy situation in which an orchestra must release a hearing impaired violinist who can no longer play in tune, for example, legal challenges may arise. In such instances, and in many other circumstances, an objective assessment process is in the best interest of performers and management. Objective measures of performance are already being used in selected areas for singers, and they have proved very beneficial in helping the performer assess certain aspects of performance quality and skill development dispassionately. Such technological advances will probably be used in the future more frequently to supplement traditional subjective assessment of performing artists for musical, scientific, and legal reasons.

TREATMENT OF HEARING LOSS

For a complete discussion of the treatment of hearing loss, the reader is referred to standard otolaryngology texts. In general, conductive hearing loss can be cured medically or surgically. Some causes of sensorineural hearing loss are also amenable to treatment. For example, luetic labyrinthitis (syphilis) responds to medication. So does hypothyroidism. Meniere's disease may also respond to medication or surgery. However, most cases of sensorineural hearing loss produced by aging, hereditary factors, and noise cannot be cured. When they involve the speech frequencies, modern, properly adjusted hearing aids are usually extremely helpful. However, these devices are rarely satisfactory for musicians during performance. More often, appropriate counseling is sufficient. The musician should be provided with a copy of his/her audiogram and an explanation of its correspondence with the piano keyboard. Unless a hearing loss becomes severe, this information usually permits musicians to make appropriate adjustments. For example, a conductor with an unknown high-frequency hearing loss will call for violins and triangles to be excessively loud. If he/she knows the pattern of hearing loss, this error may be reduced. Musicians with or without hearing loss should also routinely be cautioned against avocational loud noise exposure without ear protection (hunting, power tools, motorcycles, etc.) and ototoxic drugs. In addition, they should be educated about the importance of immediate evaluation if a sudden hearing change occurs.

SUMMARY

Good hearing is of great importance to musicians, but the effects on performance of mild high-frequency hearing loss remain uncertain. It is most important to be alert for hearing loss from all causes in performers, to recognize it early, and to treat it or prevent its progression whenever possible. Musical instruments and performance environments are capable of producing damaging noise. Strenuous efforts must be made to define the risks and nature of music-induced hearing loss among musicians, to establish damage-risk criteria, and to implement practical means of noise reduction and hearing conservation.

CONCLUSION

Singers depend on their hearing almost as much as they do on their voices. It is important not to take such valuable and delicate structures as the human ears for granted. Like the voice, the ear must be understood and protected in order for a singer to enjoy a long, happy, and successful career.

REFERENCES

1. Sataloff J, Sataloff RT, Vassallo L. *Hearing loss*. Philadelphia and Toronto: J.P. Lippincott, 1980.

2. Sataloff RT, Sataloff J. *Occupational hearing loss.* New York: Marcel Dekker, 1987.
3. Konigsmark BW, Gorlin RJ. *Genetic and metabolic deafness.* Philadelphia: W.B. Saunders, 1976.
4. Axelsson A, Lindgren F. Hearing in classical musicians. *Acta Otolaryngol* 1981 suppl. 377:3–74.
5. Toufexis A. A fire hose down the ear canal. *Time,* Sept. 29, 1989;78.
6. Arnold GE, Miskolczy-Fodor F. Pure-tone thresholds of professional pianists. *Arch Otolaryngol* 1960;71:938–947.
7. Flach M, Aschoff E. Zur Frage berufsbedingter Schwerhorigkeit beium Musiker. *Ztschr Laryngol* 1966;45:595–605.
8. Flach M. Das Gehor des Musikers aus ohrenarztlicher sicht. *Msch Ohr.hk* 1972;9:424–432.
9. Berghoff F. Horleistung und Berufsbedingte Horschadigung des Orchestermusikers mit einem Beitrag zur Pathophysiologie des Larmtraumatischen Horschadens (dissertation) 1968. Cited in: Axelsson A, Lindgren F. Hearing in classical musicians. *Acta Otolaryngol* 1981 suppl. 377:3–74.
10. Lebo CP, Oliphant KP. Music as a source of acoustic trauma. *Laryngoscope* 1968;72(2):1211–1218.
11. Jerger J, Jerger S. Temporary threshold shift in rock-and-roll musicians. *J Speech and Hearing Res* 1970;13:221–224.
11a. Rintelmann, WF, Borus JF. Noise-induced hearing loss in rock and roll musicians. *Arch Otolaryngol* 1968;88:377–385.
12. Speaks C, Nelson D, Ward WD. Hearing loss in rock-and-roll musicians. *J Occup Med* 1970;12(6):216–219.
12a. Rintelmann WF, Lindberg RF, Smitley EK. Temporary threshold shift and recovery patterns from two types of rock and roll presentation. *J Acoust Soc Amer* 51;1249–1255.
13. Jahto K, Hellmann H. Zur Frage des Larm-und Klangtraumas des Orchestermusikers. Audiologie und Phoniatrie. *HNO* 1972;20(Heft 1):21–29.
14. Buhlert P, Kuhl W. Horuntersuchungen im freien Schallfeld zum Altershorverlust. *Acustica* 1974;31:168–177.
15. Kuhl W. Keine Gehorschadigung durch Tanzmusik, simfonische Musik und Maschinengerausche beim Rundfunk. *Kamp dem Larm* 1976;23(Heft 4):105–107.
16. Zeleny M, Navratilova, Kamycek Z, et al. Relation of hearing disorders to the acoustic composition of working environment of musicians in a wind orchestra. *Ceskoslov Otolaryngol* 1975;24(5):295–299.
17. Siroky J, Sevcikova L, Folprechtova A, et al. Audiological examination of musicians of a symphonic orchestra in relation to acoustic conditions. *Ceskoslov Otolaryngol* 1976;25(5):288–294.
18. Folprechtova A, Miksovska O. The acoustic conditions in a symphony orchestra. *Pracov Lek* 1976;28:1–2.
19. Balazs B, Gotze A. Comparative examinations between the hearing of musicians playing on traditional instruments and on those with electrical amplification. *Ful-orr-gegegyogyaszat* 1976;22:116–118.
20. Gryczynska D, Czyzewski I. Damaging effect of music on the hearing organ in musicians. *Otolaryngology (Pol)* 1977;31(5):527–532.
21. Axelsson A, Lindgren F. Hearing in pop musicians. *Acta Otolaryngol* 1978;85:225–231.
22. Axelsson A, Lindgren F. Horseln hos popmusiker. *Lakartidningen* 1978;75(13):1286–1288.
23. Westmore GA, Eversden ID. Noise-induced hearing loss and orchestral musicians. *Arch Otolaryngol* 1981;107:761–764.
24. Karlsson K, Lundquist PG, Olaussen T. The hearing of symphony orchestra musicians. *Scan Audio* 1983;12:257–264.
25. Johnson DW, Sherman RE, Aldridge J, et al. Effects of instrument type and orchestral position on hearing sensitivity for 0.25 to 20 kHz. in the orchestral musician. *Scand Audiol* 1985;14:215–221.
26. Johnson DW, Sherman RE, Aldridge J, et al. Extended high frequency hearing sensitiv-

ity: a normative threshold study in musicians. *Ann Otol Rhinol Laryngol* 1986;95:196–201.

27. Woolford DH, Carterette EC, Morgan DE. Hearing impairment among orchestral musicians. *Music Perception* 1988;5(3)(Spring):261–284.
28. Gallagher G. Hot music, high noise, & hurt ears. *Hearing J* 1989;42(3):7–11.
29. Lewis DA. A hearing conservation program for high-school-level students. *Hearing J* 1989;42(3):19–24.

Professional Voice: The Science and Art of Clinical Care, Robert T. Sataloff. Raven Press, Ltd., New York © 1991.

20

Common Infections and Inflammations and Other Conditions

Robert T. Sataloff

Department of Otolaryngology, Thomas Jefferson University
Philadelphia, Pennsylvania

UPPER RESPIRATORY TRACT INFECTION WITHOUT LARYNGITIS

Although mucosal irritation usually is diffuse, singers and actors sometimes have marked nasal obstruction with little or no sore throat and a "normal" voice. If the laryngeal examination shows no abnormality, a performer with a "head cold" should be permitted to perform. However, he should be advised not to try to duplicate his usual sound, but rather to accept the insurmountable alteration caused by the change in his supraglottic vocal tract. The decision as to whether it is advisable professionally for him to appear under those circumstances rests with the singer and his musical associates. He should be cautioned against throat-clearing, as this is traumatic and may produce laryngitis. If a cough is present, non-narcotic medications should be used to suppress it.

TONSILLITIS

Recurrent tonsillitis in professional singers seems particularly problematic. On the one hand, no one is eager to perform tonsillectomy on an established singer. On the other hand, a singer cannot afford to be sick for a week five or six times a year. Such incapacitation is too damaging to the singer's income and reputation. In general, the same conservative approach toward tonsil disease used in other patients should be applied to professional singers, and tonsillectomy should not be withheld if it is really indicated. It is particularly important to remove only the tonsil without damaging the surrounding tissues in order to minimize restriction of palatal and pharyngeal motion by scar. A singer must be warned that tonsillectomy may alter the sound of his voice, as discussed above. In addition to recurrent, acute tonsillitis, halitosis caused by uncontrollable tonsillar debris may be an appropriate indication for tonsillectomy, on rare occasion. Although we do not ordinarily consider halitosis a serious malady, it may be a major impediment to success for people who have to work closely with other people, as discussed in Chapter 13. If the problem cannot be cured with medication or with hygiene using a soft toothbrush or water spray to cleanse the tonsil, tonsillectomy is reasonable. When gastric reflux, dental disease, metabolic abnormalities and other causes of halitosis have been ruled out and chronic tonsillitis has been established as the etiology, treatment should be offered.

LARYNGITIS WITH SERIOUS VOCAL CORD INJURY

When laryngeal inflammation is accompanied by mucosal disruption or hemorrhage, voice performance is contraindicated until healing occurs. Initially, absolute voice rest may be advisable for up to one week. The management of vocal fold hemorrhage is discussed in Chapter 24.

LARYNGITIS WITHOUT SERIOUS DAMAGE

Mild to moderate edema and erythema of the vocal cords may result from infection or from noninfectious causes (Chapter 24, Fig. 8). In the absence of mucosal disruption or hemorrhage, they are not absolute contraindications to voice use. Noninfectious laryngitis commonly occurs in association with excessive voice use in preperformance rehearsals. It may also be caused by other forms of voice abuse and by mucosal irritation due to allergy, smoke inhalation, and other causes. Mucus stranding between the anterior and middle thirds of the vocal cords is often indicative of voice abuse. Laryngitis sicca is associated with dehydration, dry atmosphere, mouth breathing, and antihistamine therapy. Deficiency of lubrication causes irritation and coughing and results in mild inflammation. If there is no pressing professional need for performance, inflammatory conditions of the larynx are best treated with relative voice rest in addition to other modalities. However, in some instances, singing or acting may be permitted. The performer should be instructed to avoid all forms of irritation and to rest his voice at all times except during his warm-up and performance. Corticosteroids and other medications discussed in Chapter 22 may be helpful. If mucosal secretions are copious, low-dose antihistamine therapy may be beneficial, but it must be prescribed with caution and should generally be avoided. Copious, thin secretions are better for a singer than scant, thick secretions or excessive dryness. The singer or actor with laryngitis must be kept well hydrated to maintain the desired character of his mucosal lubrication.

Psychological support is crucial. It is often helpful for the physician to intercede on the singer's behalf and to convey "doctor's orders" directly to agents or theater management. Such mitigation of exogenous stress can be highly therapeutic. Infectious laryngitis may be caused by bacteria or viruses. Subglottic involvement is frequently indicative of a more severe infection which may be difficult to control in a short period of time (Chapter 24, Fig. 8). Indiscriminate use of antibiotics must be avoided. However, when the physician is in doubt as to the cause, and when a major performance is imminent, vigorous antibiotic treatment is warranted. In this circumstance, the damage caused by allowing progression of a curable condition is greater than the damage that might result from a course of therapy for an unproved microorganism while cultures are pending. When a major performance is not imminent, indications for therapy are the same as for the nonsinger.

Voice rest (absolute or relative) is an important therapeutic consideration in any case of laryngitis. When there are no pressing professional commitments, a short course of absolute voice rest may be considered, as it is the safest and most conservative therapeutic intervention. This means absolute silence and communication with a writing pad. The singer must be instructed not even to whisper, as this may be an even more traumatic vocal activity than speaking softly. Whistling through the lips also requires vocalization and should not be permitted. Absolute voice rest is *necessary* only for serious vocal cord injury such as hemorrhage or mucosal disruption. Even then, it is virtually never indicated for more than seven to 10 days. There are some excellent laryngologists who do not believe voice rest should be used at all. However, absolute voice rest for a few days may be helpful in patients with laryngitis, especially those gregarious, verbal singers who find it difficult to moderate their voice use to comply with relative voice rest instructions. Voice rest is discussed in greater detail in Chapter 21. In many instances, considerations of economics and reputation militate against a recommendation for voice rest.

Many factors must be considered in determining whether a given concert is important enough to justify the potential consequences. Steam inhalations deliver moisture and heat to the vocal cords and tracheobronchial tree and are often useful. Nasal irrigations are used by some people but have little proved value. Gargling also has no proved efficacy, but it is probably harmful only if it involves loud, abusive vocalization as part of the gargling process. Ultrasonic treatments, local massage, psychotherapy, and biofeedback directed at relieving anxiety and decreasing muscle tension may be helpful adjuncts to a broader therapeutic program. However, psychotherapy and biofeedback, in particular, must be expertly supervised if used at all. Voice lessons given by an expert teacher are invaluable. When there is any question of technical dysfunction, the singer should be referred to his teacher. Even when there is an obvious organic abnormality, referral to a voice teacher is appropriate, especially for younger singers. There are numerous "tricks of the trade" that permit a singer safely to overcome some of the disabilities of mild illness. If a singer plans to proceed with a performance during an illness, he should not cancel his voice lesson as part of his relative voice rest regimen. Rather, a short lesson to assure optimum technique is extremely useful.

INFECTION IN THE LOWER RESPIRATORY TRACT AND ELSEWHERE

Pulmonary infections may be as disruptive to voice performance as upper respiratory infections. While they will not be discussed at length in this chapter, close collaboration with a pulmonologist interested in singers is of great help in providing optimal treatment. In many cases, tracheal bronchitis or pulmonary infection is accompanied by a component of bronchospasm, for example. It is important to correct any treatable impediment to optimal respiratory infection in addition to treating the infection if voice performance is to continue during the illness. Infections elsewhere in the body (such as gastroenteritis) may also affect the voice by undermining support and should be treated in accordance with principles discussed elsewhere in this book.

AIDS

AIDS is a lethal disease that is becoming more and more common. Its incidence within the artistic community is probably somewhat higher than in the general public. Physicians should consider this diagnosis along with other causes of chronic debilitation and recurrent infections in the proper clinical setting in professional voice users. Dry mouth and hoarseness are common complaints in patients with HIV infection or Candida infection of the oral cavity or tracheobronchial tree and should make the clinician particularly suspicious. Recurrent respiratory tract infection and infection with unusual organisms also raise one's suspicions, but it should be remembered that infections with *Hemophilus influenzae, Streptococcus pneumoniae,* and common viruses are the most frequent pathogens in HIV-infected patients, just as they are in patients without the AIDS virus. Acute infectious laryngitis and epiglotitis may occur in AIDS patients, but they are less common than mild chronic laryngitis, dry mouth, and frequent or persistent symptoms of a "cold."

SYSTEMIC DISEASES THAT MAY AFFECT THE VOICE

There are numerous other conditions not covered in this book that may affect voices adversely. Most of them are not common problems among professional voice users, and they are discussed at length elsewhere (1). However, the laryngologist should remember that laryngeal manifestations of many systemic diseases may cause voice changes that bring the patient to medical attention for the first time. We must remain alert for their presence and think of them particularly when more common obvious etiologies are not identified, or when patients do not respond to treatment as expected. The voice may be affected by the following problems (among others): acromegaly, amyloidosis, Arnold–Chiari malformation, blood disgrasias, cardiac disease (vocal cord paralysis), collagen vascular diseases (including rheumatory arthritis, systemic lupus erythematosis, scleroderma, Sjogren's syndrome, and others), deafness, gout, Hodgkin's disease, leprosy, lymphoma, Madelung's disease, malignancies, myopathies, a myriad of infectious diseases (bacterial, viral, and fungal), mononucleosis, numerous syndromes (Basedow's, adrenogenital syndrome, Down's, hereditary angioedema, Klinefelter's, Melkersson–Rosenthal, pachyonychia congenita, short stature syndromes, Shy–Drager syndrome, and many others), syphilis, sarcoidosis, tuberculosis, Wegener's granulomatosis, Wilson's disease, and other chronic diseases.

REFERENCE

1. Gould WJ, Sataloff RT. *Diseases and surgery of the vocal tract.* St. Louis: CV Mosby, in preparation.

Professional Voice: The Science and Art of Clinical Care, Robert T. Sataloff. Raven Press, Ltd., New York © 1991.

21

Voice Rest

Robert T. Sataloff

Department of Otolaryngology, Thomas Jefferson University, Philadelphia, Pennsylvania

"Don't sing" is a common, overused, and often unnecessary prescription for vocal maladies. "Don't even speak" is less common a recommendation, but it is even more rarely justified. Certainly, voice rest is safe, conservative, and helpful to the ailing singer under many circumstances. It is also a comforting course for the laryngologist who is not intimately familiar with the techniques and latitude of singing demands, because the physician may be fairly certain that a prescription of voice rest will not result in injury to the voice. Of course, improper voice use under adverse circumstances may result in injury to the vocal folds. However, while canceling concert commitments may not damage a larynx, cancellations may damage seriously a performer's career, especially in the early years of a singer's professional exposure. Consequently, it is helpful for the laryngologist, performer, and teacher to understand various forms of voice rest, as well as the circumstances under which their prescription is reasonable.

"Absolute voice rest" means silence. The singer or actor is instructed to communicate with a writing pad. In the past, absolute voice rest has been prescribed for conditions ranging from vocal nodules to acute laryngitis. Sometimes it has been enforced for six weeks or more. Total silence is almost never necessary and is virtually never required for much more than 1 week. In fact, some excellent laryngologists no longer require absolute voice rest, even after vocal fold surgery. However, following acute vocal cord injury such as a mucosal tear, or a mucosal incision from vocal fold surgery, a short course of absolute voice rest is reasonable to minimize trauma while the mucosa repairs itself. Absolute voice rest is also reasonable following acute vocal fold hemorrhage, to minimize local trauma and the chances of recurrent bleeding. These are the only medical conditions that generally call for absolute voice rest, and even in these conditions its efficacy has not been proved convincingly. Nevertheless, extensive anecdotal experience supports its use under the circumstances mentioned. Voice rest may also be used in some people who find moderation difficult and are unable to comply with recommendations for relative voice rest. Some people find it easier not to speak at all than to speak infrequently and softly. If a singer is psychologically unable to comply with recommendations for voice conservation, not speaking at all is better than not resting at all.

"Relative voice rest" means using the voice only when absolutely necessary and vocalizing technically well while singing or speaking. In its most restrictive form, it is best summarized by Dr. Norman Punt's admonition: "Don't say a single word for which you are not being paid." Throughout the rest of this chapter, "voice rest" will mean relative voice rest or voice conservation unless "absolute voice rest" is stated specifically.

Voice rest is actually a helpful adjunct in the therapy of many voice problems. For example, acute inflammatory laryngitis or infectious laryngitis involves inflammation of the vocal cords. The redness seen by the laryngologist in examining the larynx is caused by dilated blood vessels. Laryngitis also involves other changes in the mucosal cover layer of the vocal cords and their lubrication. Singing or speaking in the presence of these alterations is always accompanied by an increased risk of further injury. Decisions on how much to speak and sing with laryngitis depend on the severity of the illness, importance and difficulty of vocal commitments, and the experience and proficiency of the vocalist. However, while absolute voice rest is generally not necessary, relative voice rest to avoid further injury and facilitate healing is always beneficial. Similarly, vocal nodules are products of voice abuse. Although absolute silence minimizes further abuse, it is unnecessary. Vocal nodules resolve with proper voice use and should be treated with voice modification and relative voice rest (in this case, avoidance of the abusive activities). Between the extremes of absolute silence and unrestricted voice use, many modifications of vocal behavior are possible. Some are practiced routinely by the singing community. Other techniques are utilized less frequently. The few suggestions for relative voice rest presented below should provide the laryngologist with practical and helpful guidelines for his/her professional vocalist patients.

MINIMIZE VOICE USE

Although it seems obvious, the importance of speaking or singing only when absolutely necessary cannot be overstressed. This is especially true for the singer or actor with laryngitis trying to get through a series of performances. He/she should avoid lengthy telephone conversations. It does not help to call all your friends on the telephone to tell them you have laryngitis! Staying out of school or work environment is occasionally helpful just to avoid the extreme temptation—almost need—to talk in these familiar surroundings. However, in the disciplined, committed professional, this crutch should not be necessary. It is reasonable for the singer to carry a note for his/her friends stating that "I have laryngitis," even though the singer knows that limited speech is permissible.

WARM-UP

Even during periods of voice rest, if the voice is used at all for speaking or for singing, a short period of controlled, soft vocal exercises first thing in the morning is invaluable. Even five minutes of gentle scales will allow the singer to analyze, place, and control the voice before using it even for speech. Besides improving vocal awareness, the physical benefits of such exercises are analogous to those experienced by runners and other athletes who stretch before exercising.

AVOID ABUSIVE ENVIRONMENTS

In addition to staying away from places filled with friends with whom one is tempted to converse, the sick singer should also try to avoid talking or singing in noisy situations. Cars, airplanes, choirs, parties, and other areas with excessive background noise lead a performer to speak or sing more loudly than desirable. The vocalist should also avoid as much as possible environmental irritants such as dry heat, air conditioning, dusty areas (e.g., rehearsal rooms undergoing construction), and similar abusive atmospheres.

OPTIMIZE GENERAL HEALTH

Dehydration, fatigue, and other general medical conditions may affect the mucosa covering of the vocal folds, may alter lubrication, and may decrease vocal efficiency. Optimizing physical conditions under the singer's control, such as sleep and nutrition, is an important part of any voice conservation regimen.

DO NOT CANCEL VOICE LESSONS

The injured voice benefits greatly from supervision. Voice lessons for a person on relative voice rest may consist of only 10 or 15 min of supervised vocal exercise, but they help assure proper placement and vocal technique. This may be especially useful if the vocal malady is associated with an upper respiratory infection and "stuffy ears." Such illnesses impair the performer's ability to hear him/herself, and feedback from a teacher familiar with the individual's voice may be invaluable. Many singing teachers are also sensitive to their students' use of a speaking voice. An alert teacher may detect deficits in support, breath control, pitch (usually too high), or other speaking habits that may produce voice fatigue and aggravate laryngeal injury. Singers should speak under all circumstances with the same control and awareness they use in singing, but this is particularly important during periods of illness.

LEARN TO MARK; BEWARE OF OCCULT VOICE ABUSE

Chapter 5, "Patient History," discussed various common forms of voice abuse that accompany choral conducting, cheerleading, voice teaching, singing with electric instruments, singing inappropriate or unfamiliar repertoire, and other conditions. Singers also often strain their voices unnecessarily even when they are trying consciously to protect them. "Marking," or modifying a rehearsal to conserve the voice, is a skill frequently neglected in routine voice teaching. A few particularly common errors are worth stressing. Many singers are under the mistaken impression that learning music (or "marking a rehearsal") by whistling is restful to the larynx. In fact, whistling is accompanied by vocal fold abduction and adduction (moving apart and coming together) that is hard to distinguish visually from actual singing. It is not a rest from the routine trauma of vocal cord contact. Furthermore, unconscious of his/her vocal activity, the singer in whistling is likely to whistle with poor breath and abdominal support, errors as potentially damaging as poorly supported singing. Even mere listening or silently reading along with one's vocal lines during a rehearsal can be abusive in some people. Subvocalizing is common among readers, especially when they are reading musical vocal lines. Subvocalization may also occur when reading novels and even when listening to emotionally charged dramatic material such as at movies or theatrical productions. There are several ways a singer can find out whether he/she subvocalizes. Subvocalization can be observed in some people with a fiberoptic laryngoscope, but a visit to one's laryngologist for this diagnosis is unnecessary and impractical. If a singer finds his/her neck muscles tight and throat tired at the end of a session of reading or listening, or if his/her reading speed drops when he/she tries to read and hum a steady tone simultaneously, subvocalization should be suspected. Environments associated with this occult and unsupervised vocal activity should be avoided, especially during periods of voice rest.

In the well-trained singer, marking is often accomplished best simply by singing reasonably softly in one's "normal" voice and by avoiding stressful notes at both extremes of vocal range. Special care should be taken to practice good support technique, even when singing softly and low in the singer's vocal range. Because singers mark in the "easy" part of their voices, and because they are singing softly and trying to "rest," there is a great temptation to rest abdominal and thoracic muscles as well. This is dangerous to vocal health. Proper marking requires technique as meticulously good as that practiced during unrestricted singing.

CANCEL NONESSENTIAL COMMITMENTS

Singers and actors are steeped in the "show must go on" philosophy. However, under conditions of vocal illness requirement in voice rest, the performer must exercise professional judgment in evaluating the risks and benefits of any given commitment. Frequently, canceling rehearsals is necessary in order to allow safe performances later in the week. Occasionally, when laryngeal inflammation is severe, and when difficult performance material cannot be modified, it may even be necessary to cancel an important concert. Although this form of voice rest always feels like a disaster at the moment, the professional voice user must remember that his/her responsibility is to preserve the instrument in optimum health for as many years as possible. Significant risks of severe vocal injury are rarely justified.

For the professional singer, voice rest is more complicated than simply keeping quiet. Like singing and speaking, it is a vocal skill that should be understood by the physician and patient, mastered, and used judiciously.

Professional Voice: The Science and Art
of Clinical Care, Robert T. Sataloff.
Raven Press, Ltd., New York © 1991.

22

Drugs for Vocal Dysfunction

Robert T. Sataloff

Department of Otolaryngology, Thomas Jefferson University
Philadelphia, Pennsylvania

ANTIBIOTICS

When antibiotics are given to professional voice users, high doses to achieve therapeutic blood levels rapidly are recommended, and a full seven- to 10-day course should be administered. Erythromycin and tetracycline may be particularly useful in managing respiratory tract infections (1). Although ampicillin is used commonly, amoxicillin may achieve higher tissue levels more rapidly (2) and may be advantageous, particularly when therapy is instituted shortly before a performance. It is often helpful to start treatment with an intramuscular injection.

ANTIHISTAMINES

Antihistamines may be used to treat allergies. However, because they tend to cause dryness and are frequently combined with sympathomimetic or parasympatholytic agents that further reduce and thicken mucosal secretions, they may reduce lubrication to the point of producing a dry cough. This dryness may be more harmful than the allergic condition itself. Mild antihistamines in small doses should be tried between performances, but, generally, they should not be used immediately before performances if the singer has had no previous experience with them. Newer antihistamines such as Seldane (Merrell Dow) produce less drowsiness and often less dryness; but, in many people, they also are less effective than drugs with more disturbing side effects. When a drug is needed for an acute allergic response shortly before a performance, corticosteroids usually accomplish the desired result without causing significant iatrogenic problems. The adverse effects of antihistamines may be counteracted to some extent with mucolytic agents.

MUCOLYTIC AGENTS

Iodinated glycerol [Organidin, (Wallace)] is an older mucolytic expectorant that helps liquify viscous mucus and increase the output of thin respiratory tract secretions. Entex (Baylor) is a useful expectorant and vasoconstrictor that increases and thins mucosal secretions. Guaifenesin also thins and increases secretions. Humibid (Adams) is currently the most convenient preparation available. These drugs are relatively harmless and may be very helpful in singers who complain of thick secretions, frequent throat clearing, or "postnasal drip." Awareness of postnasal drip is often caused by secretions' being too thick rather than too plentiful.

CORTICOSTEROIDS

Corticosteroids are potent anti-inflammatory agents and may be helpful in managing acute inflammatory laryngitis. Although many laryngologists recommend using steroids in low doses (methylprednisolone, 10 mg), the author has found higher doses for short periods of time more effective. Depending on the indication, dosage may be prednisolone (60 mg) or dexamethasone (six mg) intramuscularly once, a similar starting dose orally tapered over three to six days. Regimens such as a Decadron [dexamethasone (Merck, Sharp & Dohme)] dose pack or Medrol [methylprednisolone (Upjohn)] Dosepak may also be used. Physicians should be familiar with the dose relationship among steroids (Table 1). Adrenocorticotropic hormone (ACTH) may also be used to increase endogenous cortisone output, decreasing inflammation and mobilizing water from an edematous larynx (3), although the author has found traditional steroid therapy entirely satisfactory. Care must be taken not to prescribe steroids excessively. They should be used only when there is a pressing professional commitment that is being hampered by vocal fold inflammation. If there is any question that the inflammation may be of infectious origin, antibiotic coverage is recommended.

DIURETICS

In the premenstrual period, decreased estrogen and progesterone levels are associated with altered pituitary activity. An increase in circulating antidiuretic hormone results in fluid retention in Reinke's space as well as in other tissues. The fluid retained in the vocal fold during inflammation and hormonal fluid shifts is bound, not free, water (4). Diuretics do not remobilize this fluid effectively and dehydrate the singer, resulting in decreased lubrication and thickened secretions and persistently edematous vocal cords. If used at all, their effects should be monitored closely.

TABLE 1. *Steroid equivalency*

Adrenocortico-steroids	Common trade name	Glucocorticoid (anti-inflammatory potency) equivalent dose (mg)	Mineralocorticoid (sodium retention) relative potency
Betamethasone	Celestone (Schering)	0.60	0
Cortisone	Cortone (M-S-D)	25	0.8
Dexamethasone	Decadron (M-S-D)	0.75	0
	Deronil (Schering)		
	Dexameth (Major)		
	Gammacorten (CIBA)		
	Hexadrol (Organon)		
Fludrocortisone	Florinef (Squibb)	0.1	100
Fluprednisolone	Alphadrol (Upjohn)	2	0
Hydrocortisone	Cort-Dome (Dome)	20	1
	Cortef (Upjohn)		
	Cortenema (Rowell)		
	Cortril (Pfizer)		
	Hydrocortone (M-S-D)		
Methylprednisolone	Depo-Medrol (Upjohn)	4	4
	Medrol (Upjohn)		
	Solu-Medrol (Upjohn)		
Paramethasone	Haldrone (Lilly)	2	0
	Stemex (Syntex)		
Prednisolone	Delta-Cortef (Upjohn)	5	0.8
	Hydeltra T.B.A. (M-S-D)		
	Hydeltrasol (M-S-D)		
	Meticortelone (Schering)		
	Nisolone (Ascher)		
	Sterane (Pfizer)		
Prednisone	Delta Dome (Dome)	5	0.8
	Deltasone (Upjohn)		
	Deltra (M-S-D)		
	Meticorten (Schering)		
	Paracort (Parke-Davis)		
	Servisone (Lederle)		
Triamcinolone	Aristocort (Lederle)	4	0
	Aristospan (Lederle)		
	Kenacort (Squibb)		
	Kenalog (Squibb)		

M-S-D, Merck, Sharp & Dohme.

ANALGESICS

Aspirin and other analgesics frequently have been prescribed for relief of minor throat and laryngeal irritations. However, the platelet dysfunction caused by aspirin predisposes to hemorrhage, especially in vocal cords traumatized by excessive voice use in the face of vocal dysfunction. Mucosal hemorrhage can be devastating to a professional voice, and aspirin products should be avoided altogether in singers. Acetaminophen is the best substitute, as even most common nonsteroidal anti-inflammatory drugs such as

Ibuprofen may interfere with the clotting mechanism. Caruso used a spray of ether and iodoform on his vocal cords when he had to sing with laryngitis. Nevertheless, the use of analgesics is extremely dangerous and should be avoided. Pain is an important protective physiologic function. Masking it risks incurring significant vocal damage, which may be unrecognized until after the analgesic or anesthetic wears off. If a singer requires analgesics or topical anesthetics to alleviate laryngeal discomfort, the laryngitis is severe enough to warrant canceling a performance. If the analgesic is for headache or some other discomfort not intimately associated with voice production, symptomatic treatment should be discouraged until singing commitments have been completed.

SPRAYS, MISTS, AND INHALANTS

Diphenhydramine hydrochloride [Benadryl (Parke-Davis)], 0.5% in distilled water, delivered to the larynx as a mist may be helpful for its vasoconstrictive properties, but it is also dangerous because of its analgesic effect and is not recommended by this author. However, Punt (5) advocated this mixture and several modifications of it. Other topical vasoconstrictors that do not contain analgesics may be beneficial in selected cases. Oxymetazoline hydrochloride [Afrin (Schering)] is particularly helpful. Propylene glycol (5%) in a physiologically balanced salt solution may be delivered by large particle mist and can provide helpful lubrication, particularly in cases of laryngitis sicca following air travel or associated with dry climates. Such treatment is harmless and may also provide a beneficial placebo effect. Water or saline delivered via a vaporizer or steam generator is frequently effective and sufficient. This therapy should be augmented by oral hydration, which is the mainstay of treatment for dehydration. A singer can monitor his state of hydration by observing his urine color. Dr. Van Lawrence advises his singers to "pee pale."

Most inhalers are not recommended for professional voice users. Many people develop contact inflammation from sensitivity to the propellants used in many inhalers. Steroid inhalers used for prolonged periods may result in candida laryngitis. In addition, dysphonia occurs in up to 50% of patients using steroid inhalers, related to the aerosolized steroid itself and not to the Freon propellant (6). Prolonged steroid use such as is common in asthmatics also appears capable of causing wasting of the vocalis muscle.

OTHER DRUGS

The effects and side effects of various other medications are discussed in Chapter 5.

REFERENCES

1. Panckey G. Sinusitis, bronchitis, and mycoplasmal pneumonia. In: A symposium on the tetracycline: a major appraisal. *Bull NY Acad Med* 1978;54:156–164.
2. Neu HC, ed. International symposium on amoxicillin: clinical perspectives. *J Infect Dis* 1974;129(June)(suppl.):S123–S201.
3. Schiff M. Medical management of acute laryngitis. In: Lawrence V, ed. *Transcripts of the sixth symposium, care of the professional voice.* New York: The Voice Foundation, 1977;99–102.
4. Schiff M. Comment at the seventh symposium on care of the professional voice. New York: The Juilliard School, June 15 and 16, 1978.
5. Punt NA. Applied laryngology—singers and actors. *Proc R Soc Med* 1968;61:1152–1156.
6. Toogood JH, Jennings B, Greenway RW, Chuang L. Candidiasis and dysphonia complicating beclomethasone treatment of asthma. *J Allergy Clin Immunol* 1980;65(2):145–153.

Professional Voice: The Science and Art of Clinical Care, Robert T. Sataloff. Raven Press, Ltd., New York © 1991.

23

Medications for Traveling Performers

Robert T. Sataloff

Department of Otolaryngology, Thomas Jefferson University, Philadelphia, Pennsylvania

No physician likes treating patients without examining them. We like even less giving nonmedical personnel a collection of medications to take at their own discretion. However, we are frequently called on to care for actors and singers who must travel in foreign countries for prolonged periods of time. Many of these patients have been under our care for prolonged periods of time and are good judges of their health under most circumstances. In some instances, their health can be best served by providing them with a supply of medications and instructions on how to use them. This chapter constitutes not only suggestions on what medications to include, but also suggestions to the performer on how and when they should be used. As a convenience, a copy of this chapter may be given to a performer as a written guideline to safe use of medications in the travel kit (unless the performer has a copy of the book, of course).

RATIONALE AND WARNING FOR PERFORMERS

"Don't take medicine without consulting your doctor." That is standard, safe, sage advice. Whenever possible, it should be followed. Even the most experienced performer cannot accurately diagnose his own maladies consistently. Moreover, the wrong medication, or even the right medication taken the wrong way, can make an illness worse. However, having been a singer a lot longer than I have been a laryngologist, I must confess that I have never traveled anywhere without a "First Aid Kit" stocked with medications for every contingency. Many of my regular singer and actor patients are quite knowledgeable about their own health and recurrent maladies. Many of them, too, travel with a "bag of goodies," especially when they are touring outside the United States. In many foreign countries, it is particularly difficult to find a physician with whom a singer can communicate and in whom he has confidence. It is also sometimes difficult to know the contents of various European medications. This can be dangerous, especially if a performer has a known medication allergy. For this reason, and with all admonitions and warnings, this chapter provides a list of medications reasonable for a First Aid Kit and guidelines for their administration, but it must be emphasized that self-medication is fraught with hazards and should be avoided whenever a doctor is available. The price of the visit is less than the consequences of a medication error. Moreover, should a singer fail to respond favorably to any of these medications, or should he suffer a reaction, it is essential to obtain medical care promptly, no matter how inconvenient.

GROUND RULES

If carried at all, medications for a performer's First Aid Kit should be obtained through the performer's physician and with his approval. In addition to this chapter, consultation with one's personal physician will help guide the performer on appropriate conservatism in using the drugs, in their proper applications, and in avoiding allergic reactions. The singer or actor should be certain before each trip that all medications are fresh and their dates for safe use have not expired. Expiration dates are printed on the sides of the bottles. Medications should also be kept in the properly labeled bottles in which they are purchased. They should not be shared with friends and colleagues. Another person's medical condition and potential allergies may be much more complicated than either person knows. No professional voice user who is not a physician should assume the responsibility and liability for providing unlicensed medical or pharmaceutical help. What may seem like a simple act of friendship may be neither simple nor friendly. When a performer uses any of the medications in his First Aid Kit, he should keep a written record of what he used, when, and why. This information should be communicated to his physician to be kept as part of his permanent medical chart. This will also provide feedback for the singer on the appropriateness of his medicine use. At this time, the performer may also request a new prescription to replace the medication if another trip is planned in the near future. Medications should be packaged in a secure, padded, water-resistant container. If there is a lot of extra space in some of the bottles, this may be filled with clean cotton, so that the medications are not jostled or broken in travel.

INDIVIDUAL CUSTOMARY MEDICATIONS

A performer should bring an ample extra supply of any prescription medications used regularly such as thyroid pills, oral contraceptives, blood pressure medication, and heart medication. Even for a long trip, an extra month's supply is usually sufficient. If regular medications are lost, a month usually provides enough time to contact home and send for a new supply. The performer should check with his physician or pharmacist to be certain that his regular medications do not have adverse cross-reactions with any of the other medications in the First Aid Kit.

Analgesics

Aspirin is contraindicated in professional voice users because of its tendency to cause bleeding, particularly vocal fold hemorrhage. Many analgesics (pain medicines) and cold medications contain aspirin. Read the labels! Bring Tylenol (McNeil Consumer Products) or a similar medication that does not contain aspirin. This can be used for minor pain such as headache, back pain after long plane flights, or menstrual cramps. If there is sufficient throat pain associated with laryngitis to require medications in order to sing, the condition is probably too severe to allow safe performance. In any case, self-medicating for a laryngeal ailment without having the vocal cords visualized is extremely hazardous and should be avoided.

Antacids

Gastric reflux laryngitis is common among performers. This condition is aggravated by stress and eating late at night, both of which are common while traveling. Reflux may be aggravated in foreign countries by consumption of certain unfamiliar foods. While on tour, even people who do not regularly have problems with reflux may experience heartburn, a hoarse and low voice in the morning, bad breath in the morning, and prolonged warm-up time. A supply of liquid antacid or the newer chewable tablets designed to combat reflux [Algicon (Rorer) or Gaviscon (Marion), for example] may be helpful. Stronger antacid medications such as Tagamet (Smith Kline and French) and Zantac (Glaxo) may be included if the performer has had to use them in the past for significant reflux problems. Medication for reflux should always be supplemented by avoidance of eating for 3 to 4 hr before going to sleep and by elevation of the head of the bed.

Antibiotics

Antibiotics are among the most abused medications. Singers and actors must avoid the tendency to use them for every little cold or sore throat. They may produce adverse reactions, predispose to more severe infections, possibly impair the body's ability to fight off infections on its own, or produce other undesirable side effects. Performers should be extremely wary of packing any medication they have not used before, especially antibiotics that commonly produce allergic reactions. If a performer has had good experience taking a specific antibiotic on several occasions, it is reasonable to have one or two 10-day courses of the medication on hand during lengthy trips. Ampicillin, erythromycin, and tetracycline are relatively good broad-spectrum antibiotics that may be considered for inclusion in the First Aid Kit. Tetracyclines are inactivated by milk products and antacids. Consequently, they are not a good choice for anyone with reflux problems.

Antibiotics have no effect on viral infections, only on bacterial illnesses. If bacterial infection is suspected, it is best to consult a physician for examination and possibly for a culture. When this is not possible, antibiotic use is reasonable for severe sore throat, especially associated with white spots on the tonsils or a cough productive of yellow or green sputum, or for urinary tract infection with burning and frequency. A physician should be consulted as soon as possible. Once antibiotics are started, the 10-day course should be completed to avoid development of resistant organisms. In addition to allergic reactions, antibiotics may also cause nausea, diarrhea, abdominal cramping (which may interfere with singing or speaking), photophobia (hypersensitivity to sunlight), vaginitis, and other problems.

Antiviral Agents

A few antiviral agents are now available. However, they are generally not as effective as antibiotics, and they may produce side effects. For example, amantadine is useful against influenza A. If a performer has to work in a city in which there is a flu outbreak, it may be reasonable to use this drug. However, it can produce profound side effects including extremely dry mouth, agitation, and rapid heart beat; these side effects may be severe enough to require cancellation of a performance. We do not generally include this drug among travel medications.

Vaginal Medications

One of the most common complications of antibiotic use is vaginal candidiasis, or yeast infection. This is caused by overgrowth of yeasts that are normally present in the vagina but live in balance with other normal flora including bacteria that are killed by the antibiotics. When the bacteria are absent, the yeast grow unchecked. Especially in women who are prone to develop yeast infections, a supply of Monistat (Ortho Pharmaceutical) is prudent. It may be started for vaginal itching or cheesy discharge that occurs during antibiotic use. Early consultation with a physician is advisable to be sure that this is really the only problem. If vaginal symptoms develop independent of antibiotic use, a gynecologist should be consulted before any medication is started.

Nose Sprays

Nose sprays should generally be avoided and should rarely be used for more than three to five days. Afrin (Schering) is a good choice. It can be used in the morning and at night, or only at night. Prolonged use causes dependence and rebound congestion when the spray is stopped. Nose spray may be appropriate for an infection or allergy that causes enough congestion to block nasal breathing, especially shortly before performance. Breathing through the nose warms, filters, and humidifies air and saves a great deal of wear and tear on the larynx. It is a good idea to carry nasal spray and a decongestant with one's carry-on items on an airplane. On a poorly pressurized flight, the use of an oral decongestant and nasal spray an hour before landing helps prevent ear problems. However, decongestants may have side effects, including excessive drying of laryngeal mucosa, and should only be used in performers who have used the medication previously without difficulty.

Antihistamines and Decongestants

The use of antihistamines and decongestants in singers is very tricky, because the side effects are often worse than the problem they are supposed to treat. In a singer with true allergies, formal allergy evaluation and desensitization are often helpful. If the problems are minimal, through trial and error, performers can often find a mild antihistamine that controls the allergic symptoms adequately without producing too much dryness. If antihistamines are to be included, the performer should try them under a physician's supervision prior to traveling to choose the optimal medication. Decongestants without antihistamines (such as Sudafed (Burroughs Wellcome) have less drying effect but often produce a slight tremor (which may be heard in the voice), hyperirritability, and insomnia. They should also not be ingested for the first time shortly before a concert. However, they may be useful in some people to relieve the nasal congestion associated with a cold or mild allergy.

Mucolytic Agents

The drying effects of antihistamines may be partially counteracted by medications that increase or thin upper respiratory secretions. Such medications also help with the dryness from overuse of the voice and undesirable atmospheric conditions. However, they are no substitute for adequate hydration. The singer must be certain to drink enough liquid to keep his urine color extremely light and not try to compensate with medicines for insufficient fluid intake. This is the best way to be certain of adequate hydration.

Mucolytic agents are also useful to treat "postnasal drip," a condition caused by secretions that are too thick, rather than too copious. Mucolytic medicines thin the secretions and make them easier to handle. The most common medications in this category are Entex (Norwich Eaton), Organidin (Wallace), Robitussin (Robbins), and a new medication (perhaps the best) called Humibid (Adams).

Steroids

Avoid using steroids! They are commonly abused in singers and should be taken only for very specific indications, usually with a physician's guidance. They may be helpful in cases of acute inflammatory laryngitis associated with recent travel, smoke exposure, and oversinging. In this setting, they should be combined with hydration, relative voice rest, and sometimes other therapy. They are particularly helpful in combating acute allergic reactions to allergens in a new locale, medications, foods, or insect bites. I recommend including them in the First Aid Kit, especially for the latter indications. For example, if a performer develops acute nasal congestion, sneezing, and tearing and itching of the eyes immediately before a concert in a new city, steroids may be appropriate. They may also be helpful for a person who breaks out in hives after eating shellfish, for example. In either case, medical consultation is particularly important and should be obtained as soon as possible. Self-medication with steroids is strictly a last resort. A Medrol Dosepak (Upjohn) or Decadron dose pack (Merck, Sharp & Dohme) should suffice. An entire course of these drugs need not be taken as indicated on the dose pack. For inflammatory laryngitis, for example, two or three pills may be sufficient, rather than the six-pill first-day regimen suggested on the package. Each performer should seek advice from the doctor who prescribes the drug and should be particularly cautious about using these medications for the first time unsupervised. In some people, they aggravate stomach problems, and they also may cause hyperirritability and insomnia in larger doses. Antacids should generally be taken while steroids are being used. Prolonged use of steroids is almost never indicated, except for serious diseases, and should never be undertaken without close medical supervision.

Antidizziness Medications

Singers and actors who get seasick and perform on cruises have a special problem. Antivert (Roerig) and Dramamine (Searle Pharmaceutical), medicines for dizziness and motion sickness, are actually antihistamines that cause drying, as do scopolamine patches. Before leaving on a cruise, the performer should try wearing a patch and/or taking a dose or two of Antivert

(Roerig) to assess the side effects. In most of my patients, the patch has worked well. However, some people have excessive drying, as well as dilatation of the pupils with blurring of vision, and cannot tolerate the medication. It is best to find this out in advance.

Antidiarrheal Medications

Performers touring in certain parts of the world are likely to encounter traveler's diarrhea. This can often be avoided by taking Vibramycin (Pfizer) or Pepto Bismol (Procter & Gamble) prophylactically. The performer should consult his physician before leaving. Lomotil (Searle & Co.) should be included in the First Aid Kit in case severe diarrhea develops. However, this medication contains a small amount of atropine, which has a drying effect. Although it is usually tolerated well by most singers, it should be taken with caution. It should also not be taken more often than one pill every four to six hours. In higher doses, mucosal drying becomes a significant problem. Most other antidiarrheal medications also have potential side effects.

Ear Drops

"Swimmer's ear" is a common problem during travel, particularly in tropical climates. It usually follows exposure to water, especially if cotton swabs are used to dry the ears. Manipulation of the ears should be avoided. The old adage is a good one: "Put nothing smaller than your elbow in your ear." Otitis externa is characterized by pain and swelling of the ear canal. It is treated with ear drops such as Colymycin (Parke-Davis), Cortisporin (Burroughs Wellcome), Vasocidin (Iolab Pharmaceuticals), or Domeboro (Miles Pharmaceuticals). It is important to distinguish otitis externa from middle ear infection, which is usually associated with a cold. It is absolutely necessary to have the ear examined by a physician as quickly as possible after ear symptoms develop. However, in the healthy performer who develops ear pain, redness, and obvious swelling following water exposure, it is reasonable to start treatment with ear drops if a doctor is not immediately available. Nevertheless, a physician should definitely examine the ear as soon as possible. Allowing progression of this condition is not only potentially serious and painful, but it may also be associated with swelling in the face and jaw joint, which makes it difficult to open the mouth. This painful temporomandibular joint restriction can interfere with singing performance.

Sleeping Pills

In general, sleeping pills should not be necessary for healthy people. However, occasionally, the stresses of a tour and the aggravations of travel, along with frequent changes in time zone, can disturb sleep patterns. Sleeping pills should be used with great caution. However, especially when going on tour for the first few times, a small supply of mild sleeping medication such as Halcion (Upjohn) is not a bad idea. Performers should avoid using Benadryl (Parke-Davis), an antihistamine frequently also used as a sleeping medication. It is a safe drug and works well, but it produces excessive drying, which may hinder singing.

Nonmedicinal Items

Band-Aids (Johnson & Johnson), alcohol swabs, disinfectant, antibiotic ointment for superficial cuts, cotton and sterile gauze pads, and adhesive tape also come in handy.

Insect medicines are not included here.

Medications Intentionally Excluded

Diuretics are often prescribed by gynecologists to help alleviate premenstrual fluid bloating. Unfortunately, they diurese free body water, such as that needed for mucosal lubrication, but not protein-bound water, such as that in the vocal folds. Consequently, they produce a dry singer or actor with persistently boggy vocal cords, making matters worse.

Narcotics are strong pain killers. They should only be used under a physician's direct supervision. Moreover, they dull sensorium and interfere with good singing, making performance dangerous.

Valium (Roche), Inderal (Ayerst), and other medications for preperformance anxiety should generally be avoided. They are unnecessary in the healthy, well-trained performer, and they have side effects that can be dangerous not only to the voice, but also to the cardiorespiratory system.

CONCLUSION

Professional voice users should be extremely careful about self-medication and should avoid it whenever possible. However, during extended travel, particularly outside the United States, intelligent use of a properly stocked First Aid Kit with the consent of one's personal physician may be better than the available alternatives.

Professional Voice: The Science and Art of Clinical Care, Robert T. Sataloff. Raven Press, Ltd., New York © 1991.

24

Structural and Neurological Disorders and Surgery of the Voice

Robert T. Sataloff

Department of Otolaryngology, Thomas Jefferson University, Philadelphia, Pennsylvania

This chapter discusses selected common and/or important structural or neurological disorders that affect the voice. There are many others, of course, and they may be reviewed in standard texts of otolaryngology. Those discussed in this chapter have particular relevance to professional singers and actors by virtue of incidence, unusual presentation, or special rehabilitation problems.

Similarly, this chapter is not intended as a comprehensive review of modern vocal fold surgery. That, too, can be found elsewhere in the literature (1–3). Rather, specific surgical procedures are reviewed to highlight surgical principles and recent technical changes in the standard of surgical care. Modern microsurgery of the voice is referred to widely as "phonosurgery," although von Leden introduced that term originally for procedures that alter vocal quality or pitch. Voice surgery is usually performed with a microscope, small, modern instruments, and great respect for the induplicable anatomic complexity of the vibratory margin of the vocal fold.

VOCAL NODULES

Nodules are caused by voice abuse and are a dreaded malady of professional voice users (Fig. 1)* Occasionally, laryngoscopy reveals asymptomatic vocal nodules that do not appear to interfere with voice production. In such cases, the nodules should not be treated surgically. Some famous and successful singers have had untreated vocal nodules. However, in most cases, nodules are associated with hoarseness, breathiness, loss of range, and vocal fatigue. They may be due to abuse of the voice during speaking or singing. Caution must be exercised in diagnosing small nodules in patients who have been singing actively. Many singers develop bilateral, symmetri-

---

* See color plate that appears following page 276.

cal, soft swellings at the junction of the anterior and middle thirds of their vocal cords following heavy voice use. There is no evidence to suggest that singers with such "physiologic swelling" are predisposed toward development of vocal nodules. At present, the condition is generally considered to be within normal limits. The physiologic swelling usually disappears with 24 to 48 hr of rest from heavy voice use. Care must be taken not to frighten the patient or embarrass the physician by misdiagnosing physiologic swellings as vocal nodules. Nodules carry a great stigma among singers and actors, and the psychological impact of the diagnosis should not be underestimated. When nodules are present, the patient should be informed with the same gentle caution used in telling a patient that he/she has cancer. Voice therapy always should be tried as the initial therapeutic modality and will cure the vast majority of patients, even if the nodules look firm and have been present for many months or years. Even in those who eventually need surgical excision of their nodules, preoperative voice therapy is essential to help prevent recurrence of the nodules.

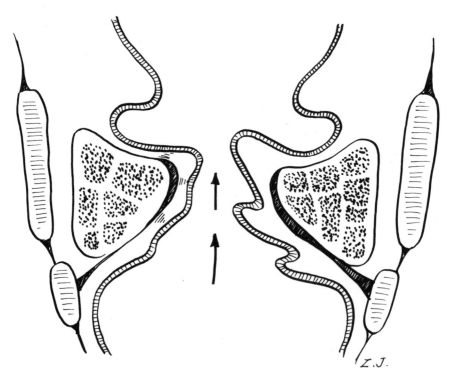

FIG. 2. The vocal fold on the **right** of the illustration shows normal free mobility of the cover over the body of the vocal fold as air flows (*arrows*) through the glottis. The drawing on the **left** of the figure illustrates scarring of the epithelium to the deeper layers of the lamina propria resulting in restriction of the mucosal wave and stiffness, as seen during stroboscopy. When the scarring is severe enough to stop vibration, the nonvibrating portion is known as an adynamic segment.

Surgery for vocal nodules should be avoided whenever possible and should virtually never be performed without an adequate trial of expert voice therapy *including patient compliance with therapeutic suggestions.* Surgical technique is discussed below. A minimum of six to 12 weeks of observation should be allowed while the patient is using therapeutically modified voice techniques, under the supervision of a speech-language pathologist and possibly a singing teacher. Proper voice use rather than voice rest (silence) is correct therapy. The surgeon should not perform surgery prematurely for vocal nodules under pressure from the patient for a "quick cure" and early return to performance. Permanent destruction of voice quality is not a rare complication. Even following expert surgery, this may be caused by submucosal scarring, resulting in an adynamic segment along the vibratory margin of the vocal fold. This situation results in a hoarse voice with vocal cords that appear normal with regular light, although under stroboscopic light the adynamic segment is obvious (Fig. 2). There is no reliable cure for this complication. Consequently, even large, apparently fibrotic nodules of long standing should be given a chance to resolve without surgery. In some cases, the nodules remain but become asymptomatic, with normal voice quality. Stroboscopy in these patients usually reveals that the nodules are on the superior surface rather than the leading edge of the vocal folds during proper, relaxed phonation (although they may be on the contact surface and symptomatic when hyperfunctional voice technique is used and the larynx is forced down).

VOCAL CYSTS

Submucosal cysts of the vocal folds are probably also traumatic lesions that result in blockage of a mucous gland duct. They can cause contact swelling on the contralateral side and are usually initially misdiagnosed as nodules. Often, they can be differentiated from nodules by strobovideolaryngoscopy when the mass is obviously fluid-filled. In other cases, they are suspected when the nodule (contact swelling) on the other vocal fold resolves with voice therapy, but the cyst does not resolve. Cysts may also be found on one side (occasionally both sides) when surgery is performed for apparent nodules that have not resolved with voice therapy. The surgery should be performed superficially and with minimal trauma, as discussed below.

VOCAL POLYPS

Many other structural lesions may appear on the vocal folds, of course, and not all respond to nonsurgical therapy. Polyps are usually unilateral, and they often have a prominent feeding blood vessel coursing along the superior surface of the vocal fold and entering the base of the polyp (Fig. 3).* The pathogenesis of polyps cannot always be proven, but the lesion is thought to be traumatic in many cases. At least some polyps start as vocal fold hemorrhages. In some cases, even sizable polyps resolve with relative voice rest and a few weeks of low-dose steroid therapy such as triamcinolone 4 mg twice a day. However, most of them require surgical removal. If polyps are not treated, they may produce contact injury on the contralateral vocal fold. Voice therapy should be used to assure good relative voice rest and avoid abusive behaviors before and after surgery. When surgery is performed, care must be taken not to damage the leading edge of the vocal fold, especially if a laser is used, as discussed below.

SURGERY FOR NODULES, CYSTS, AND POLYPS

When surgery is indicated for vocal cord lesions, it should be limited as strictly as possible to the area of pathology. There is virtually no place for "vocal cord stripping" in professional voice users with benign disease. Whenever possible, an incision should be made on the superior edge of the vocal fold and the lesion should be removed submucosally and superficially to avoid scarring. This is accomplished by staying superficial to the intermediate layer of the lamina propria (Fig. 4A–C). Preservation of the mucosa along the leading edge of the vocal cord seems to promote more rapid and better healing. When this is not possible, lesions such as vocal nodules should be removed to a level even with the vibratory margin rather than deeply into the submucosa (Fig. 5A–C). Naturally, if there is a question of serious neoplasm, proper treatment takes precedence over voice conservation.

Surgery should be done under microscopic control. The use of lasers is controversial at present. There is considerable anecdotal evidence suggesting that healing time is longer and the incidence of adynamic segment formation higher with the laser than with traditional instruments. Furthermore, two studies (4,5) raise serious concerns about dysphonia following laser surgery. It has been suggested that such complications may result from using too low a power density, causing dissipation of heat deeply into the vocal fold, and high-power density for short duration has been recommended. Nevertheless, many laryngologists caring for professional voice users avoid laser surgery along the vibratory margin in most cases. When the laser is used, a biopsy for evaluation by pathologists should be taken prior to vaporizing the lesion with the laser. If a lesion is to be removed from the leading edge, the laser beam should be centered in the lesion, rather than on the vibratory margin, so that the beam does not create a divot in the vocal fold (Fig. 6A and B). The CO_2 laser (at 1 watt, defocused) is particularly valuable for cauterizing isolated blood vessels responsible for recurrent hemorrhage.

---

* See color plate that appears following page 276.

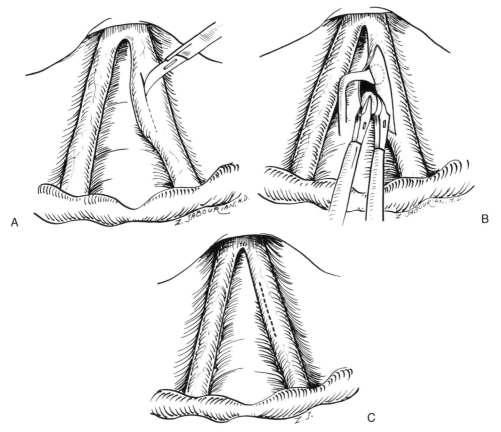

FIG. 4. A: Superficial incision is made in superior surface of true vocal fold. **B:** Blunt dissection is used to elevate mucosa from lesion (angled blunt dissector). Trauma to submucosal tissues is minimized, since they contain fibroblasts that produce scar. After the blunt dissector has been removed, only pathologic tissue is excised under direct vision. Mucosa and normal submucosal tissues are preserved. **C:** Mucosa is reapproximated. Leading edge has not been violated.

Such vessels are often found at the base of a hemorrhagic polyp (Fig. 7). At the suggestion of Jean Abitbol, M.D., Paris (*personal communication*), the author has recently been placing a small piece of ice on the vocal fold immediately prior to and following laser use to dissipate heat and help prevent edema. There are no studies on the efficacy of this maneuver, and we need more clinical experience before drawing final conclusions; but our preliminary impression is that the ice is helpful. Voice rest following vocal fold surgery is also controversial. Although some laryngologists do not consider it necessary at all, most physicians recommend voice rest for approximately one week, or until the mucosal surface has healed. Even following surgery,

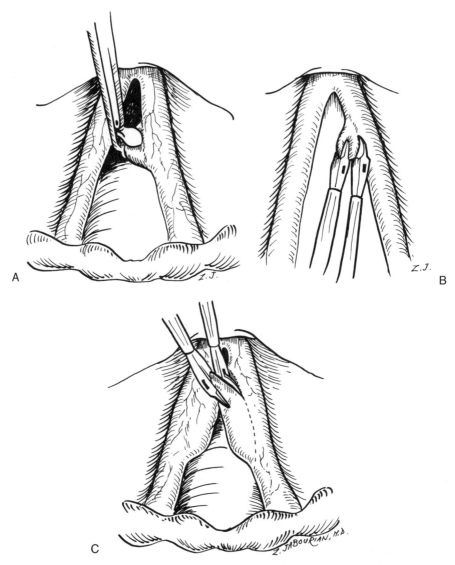

FIG. 5. The old technique of grasping the lesion with a cupped forceps and avulsing the lesion from the vocal fold is not sufficiently precise. It allows for tearing of mucosa beyond the necessary area of excision (**A**). Grasping the lesion with a delicate forceps and excising the pathologic tissue only (**B**) is the preferred technique. The lesion should not be retracted medially with the forceps, as this will tent the mucosa and often result in excessive excision. The mucosa is cut sharply, rather than ripped, as with cupped forceps. In resecting lesions the size of that illustrated in **B** or larger lesions, it is often helpful bluntly to separate the epithelium from the lamina propria (**C**). This should be done superficially, taking care not to traumatize the intermediate layer of the lamina propria. Reinke's space is not rich in fibroblasts, and utilizing this technique permits resection of the diseased tissue only, while minimizing the chance of initiating fibroblast proliferation in the intermediate and deep layers of the lamina propria.

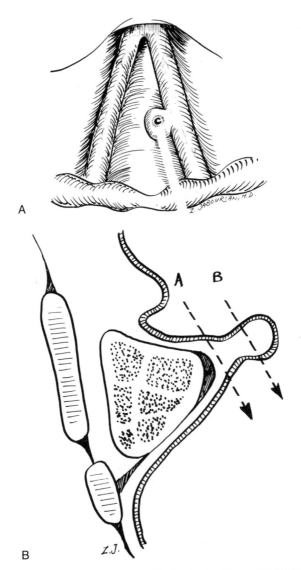

FIG. 6. The center of the laser beam is located in the body of the mass (**A**) in this view from above, and the zone of destruction (rather than the center of the laser beam) is approximately even with the vibratory margin. A cross-section of the vocal fold (**B**) illustrates the same principle. *Arrow B* represents the center of the laser beam. *Arrow A* represents the outermost region of the zone of destruction around the laser beam. The zone of destruction should be superficial to the intermediate layer of the lamina propria to prevent scar formation.

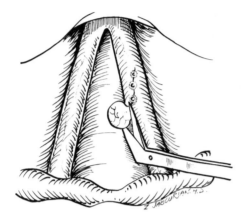

FIG. 7. The feeding vessel of a hemorrhagic polyp may be treated with 1-watt defocused laser bursts of short duration to cauterize the vessel and prevent recurrent hemorrhage. The polyp can then be removed from the leading edge with scissors, avoiding the risk of laser injury to the vibratory margin. Removal of the polyp using a laser is an acceptable alternative, although precautions must be taken as illustrated in Fig. 6.

silence for more than a week or 10 days is nearly never necessary and represents a real hardship for many patients.

CONTACT GRANULOMAS AND VOCAL PROCESS ULCERS

Granulomas usually occur on the posterior aspect of the vocal folds, sometimes in or above the cartilaginous portion (Figs. 1 and 3). Granulomas and ulcers in the region of the vocal processes have traditionally been related to trauma, especially intubation injury. However, they are also seen in young, apparently healthy professional voice users with no history of intubation or obvious laryngeal injury. Previous teachings have held that the lesion should be treated surgically but that the incidence of recurrence is high. In fact, the vast majority of granulomas and ulcerations (probably even those following intubation) are aggravated or caused by reflux. When the reflux is controlled, the lesions usually resolve within a few weeks. If they do not, they should be removed for biopsy to rule out other possible etiologies. So long as a good specimen is obtained, the laser is helpful in this surgery, because the lesions are usually not on the vibratory margin, and they are often friable.

REINKE'S EDEMA

The "elephant ear" floppy vocal fold appearance of Reinke's edema is uncommon among classical professional singers but is seen more frequently among pop singers, radio and sports announcers, attorneys, and other professional voice users (Fig. 8).* It is nearly always associated with cigarette smoking, although other factors such as hypothyroidism and voice abuse may be contributory. If it does not resolve after all irritants have been re-

---

* See color plate that appears following page 276.

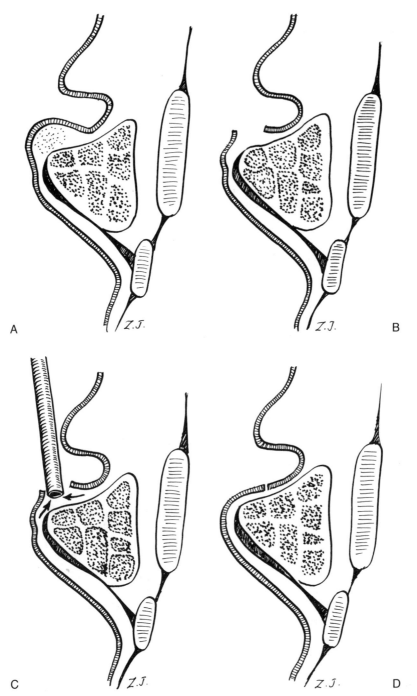

FIG. 9. Bulky vocal fold showing Reinke's edema (small dots) in the superficial layer of the lamina propria (**A**); incision in the superior surface opens easily into Reinke's space (**B**). Using a fine suction, the edema fluid is aspirated (**C,** *arrows*). The mucosal edges are reapproximated, trimming redundant mucosa if necessary (**D**).

moved and voice technique has been modified, surgery may be necessary in some cases. Only one vocal cord should be operated on at a sitting in most cases. The vocal fold may be incised along its superior surface and the edematous material removed with a fine suction (Fig. 9A–D). This often produces a very satisfactory voice, and it may be unnecessary to operate on the contralateral vocal cord even at a later date. Caution must be exercised in treating this condition, particularly in professional voice users. In an actor or radio announcer, for example, the edema may be partially responsible for the performer's voice "signature." Restoring a satisfactory cosmetic appearance and "normal" sound may damage or end a performer's career.

VOCAL FOLD HEMORRHAGE

Hemorrhage in the vocal folds and mucosal disruption are contraindications to singing and acting. When these are observed, the therapeutic course includes strict voice rest in addition to correction of any underlying disease. Vocal fold hemorrhage in skilled professionals may be seen commonly in premenstrual women using aspirin products. Severe hemorrhage or mucosal scarring may result in permanent alterations in vocal fold vibratory function. In rare instances, surgical intervention may be necessary. The potential gravity of these conditions must be stressed, for singers and actors are generally reluctant to cancel an appearance. As von Leden observed, it is a pleasure to work with "people who are determined that the show must go on when everyone else is determined to goof off" (6). However, patient compliance is essential when serious damage has occurred. At the present time, acute treatment of vocal fold hemorrhage is controversial. Most laryngologists allow the hematoma to resolve spontaneously. Because this sometimes results in an organized hematoma and scar formation requiring surgery, some physicians advocate incision along the superior edge of the vocal fold and drainage of the hematoma in selected cases. Further study is needed to determine optimum therapy.

Patients with recurrent vocal fold hemorrhage present special problems. Usually, they are due to repeated traumatic rupture of a varicose vein on the superior surface of the vocal folds, visible when the hemorrhage resolves. Although resolution may be complete, there is often a slight blush of the surrounding mucosa, extending to the vocal fold edge. Even when the patient feels that the voice has returned to normal, stroboscopy often indicates slight asymmetry of amplitude. If hemorrhage occurs repeatedly in the same area, it is usually treated best by vaporization of the offending vessel with defocused 1-watt CO_2 laser bursts. Care should be taken to keep the laser beam as far away from the lamina propria as possible. This sometimes requires everting the vocal fold slightly and stretching the mucosa laterally

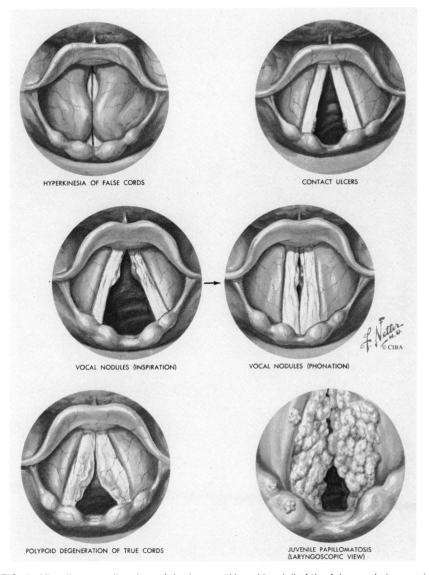

HYPERKINESIA OF FALSE CORDS

CONTACT ULCERS

VOCAL NODULES (INSPIRATION)

VOCAL NODULES (PHONATION)

POLYPOID DEGENERATION OF TRUE CORDS

JUVENILE PAPILLOMATOSIS
(LARYNGOSCOPIC VIEW)

FIG. 1. Miscellaneous disorders of the larynx. "Hyperkinesia" of the false cords is seen in hyperfunctional voice abuse. In its more severe form, phonation may actually occur primarily with the false vocal folds. This condition is known as dysphonia plica ventricularis. Contact ulcers occur in the posterior portion of the vocal folds, generally in the cartilagenous portion. They are thought to be caused by trauma from intubation and hyperfunction, but they are very frequently related to gastroesophageal reflux. Vocal nodules are smooth, reasonably symmetrical benign masses at the junctions of the anterior and middle thirds of the vocal folds. Although Netter's classic drawing is labeled "vocal nodules," the mass on the right appears hemorrhagic in origin. It may be a hemorrhagic cyst or fibrotic hematoma from hemorrhage of one of the prominent blood vessels on the superior surface. The mass on the left has the typical appearance of a vocal nodule. The illustration of vocal nodules during phonation shows failure of glottic closure anterior and posterior to the masses. This is responsible for the breathiness heard in the voices of patients with nodules. Polypoid degeneration, Reinke's edema, has a typical, floppy, "elephant ear" appearance. Juvenile papillomatosis is a viral disease. This disease and its treatment frequently result in permanent disturbance of the voice. From The Larynx. *Clinical Symposia,* Summit, New Jersey: CIBA Pharmaceutical Company, 1964;16(3): Plate VIII, with permission.

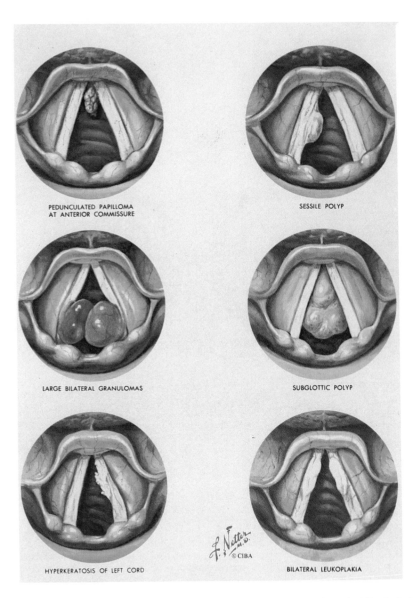

PEDUNCULATED PAPILLOMA
AT ANTERIOR COMMISSURE

SESSILE POLYP

LARGE BILATERAL GRANULOMAS

SUBGLOTTIC POLYP

HYPERKERATOSIS OF LEFT CORD

BILATERAL LEUKOPLAKIA

FIG. 3. Miscellaneous disorders of the larynx. An isolated papilloma such as that illustrated in the *top left* usually has less grave implications than the papillomatosis illustrated in Fig. 1. Nevertheless, careful removal with a laser is appropriate. The broad-based, sessile polyp illustrated has typically prominent vascularity at its base and along the superior surface of the vocal fold. The contact granulomas illustrated are considerably larger than those in Fig. 1. Even granulomas of this size sometimes resolve with antireflux therapy and low-dose steroids, although more often excision is required. Subglottic lesions such as the polyp illustrated can usually be removed safely without adverse effect on the voice. Potentially malignant or premalignant lesions such as the hyperkeratosis and leukoplakia illustrated may be encountered among professional voice users, particularly those who smoke. Malignant and premalignant lesions are not discussed in detail in this book. From The Larynx. *Clinical Symposia.* Summit, New Jersey: CIBA Pharmaceutical Company, 1964;16(3): Plate IX, with permission.

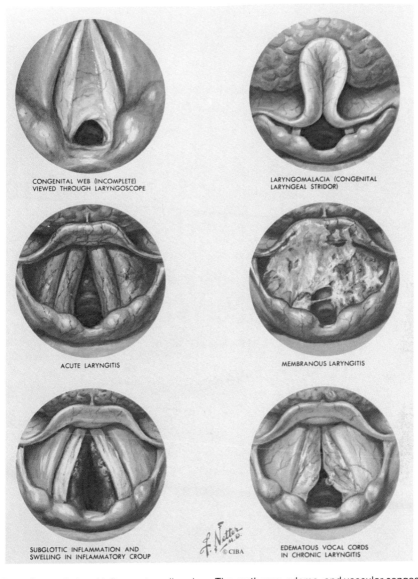

CONGENITAL WEB (INCOMPLETE)
VIEWED THROUGH LARYNGOSCOPE

LARYNGOMALACIA (CONGENITAL
LARYNGEAL STRIDOR)

ACUTE LARYNGITIS

MEMBRANOUS LARYNGITIS

SUBGLOTTIC INFLAMMATION AND
SWELLING IN INFLAMMATORY CROUP

EDEMATOUS VOCAL CORDS
IN CHRONIC LARYNGITIS

FIG. 8. Congenital and inflammatory disorders. The erythema, edema, and vascular congestion illustrated in the case of acute laryngitis are typical of a moderate to severe infection. With vocal folds this inflamed, performance could be justified only under most extraordinary circumstances. The subglottic inflammation illustrated from a case of croup is similar to that seen in adults with severe respiratory infections, which are difficult to control in short periods of time, although, in adult performers, a lesser degree of inflammation, swelling, and airway compromise is usually present. The edematous vocal cords seen in chronic laryngitis have fluid collections in Reinke's space. Vocal folds with this appearance may be diagnosed as edematous vocal cords, Reinke's edema, polypoid corditis, or polypoid degeneration. In some cases, the edema reverses when the chronic irritant is removed. The congenital web illustrated is extensive. Smaller webs may occur congenitally, or following trauma (including surgery). The illustration of laryngomalacia shows an omega-shaped epiglottis. This shape is common in normal larynges prior to puberty and may persist in some adults, making vocal fold visualization difficult. Membranous laryngitis is uncommon and severe, necessitating cancellation of performance commitments. From The Larynx. In: *Clinical Symposia,* Summit, New Jersey: CIBA Pharmaceutical Company, 1964;16(3): Plate VI, with permission.

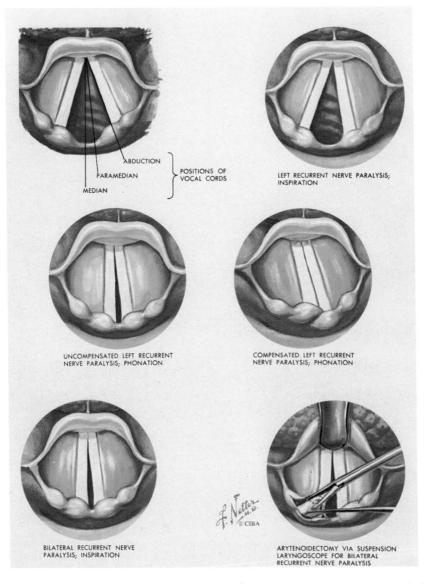

FIG. 10. Typical appearances of vocal fold in cases of recurrent laryngeal nerve paralysis. The illustration in the *lower right-hand corner* depicts endoscopic arytenoidectomy. This is one procedure to help reestablish an adequate airway for patients with bilateral vocal fold paralysis. However, it does so at the expense of vocal quality. From The Larynx. *Clinical Symposia.* Summit, New Jersey: CIBA Pharmaceutical Company, 1964;16(3): Plate VII, with permission.

with a cottonoid so that the vessel is over the muscle when the laser is used, even at such low-power densities. In patients with recurrent vocal hemorrhage clearly related to the menstrual cycle, hormonal manipulation may be tried instead of surgery. In some cases, the hemorrhages stop, and the prominent blood vessel even disappears. Care must be taken to monitor the voice carefully when hormones are used, and close collaboration with an endocrinologist is essential.

SULCUS VOCALIS

Sulcus vocalis is a ridge in the superior surface of the membranous portion of the vocal fold, usually extending throughout its length. The lesion is usually bilateral and involves primarily the superficial layer of the lamina propria. There are a deficiency of capillaries and increase in collagenous fibers in the region of the sulcus. Clinically, this structural abnormality is not diagnosed commonly, although it may be somewhat more frequent histologically. Sulcus vocalis increases the stiffness of the cover layer and is often associated with hoarseness, breathiness, and decreased vocal efficiency. Treatment is controversial.

SURGERY FOR POSTOPERATIVE VOCAL FOLD INJURY

Too often, the laryngologist is confronted with a desperate singer or actor whose voice has been "ruined" following vocal cord surgery, recurrent or superior laryngeal nerve paralysis, trauma, or some other tragedy. Occasionally, the cause is as simple as a dislocated arytenoid that can be reduced (6). However, if the problem is an adynamic segment, decreased bulk of one vocal cord following "stripping," bowing caused by superior laryngeal nerve paralysis, or some other serious complication in a mobile vocal cord, great conservatism should be exercised. None of the available surgical procedures for these conditions is consistently effective. If surgery is considered at all, it should be presented to the patient realistically and pessimistically. The patient must understand that the chances of returning the voice to professional quality are very slim and that there is a chance of making it worse. Zyderm Collagen (Xomed) injection is currently under investigation and shows promise of usefulness in some of these difficult cases (7). However, a great deal more research will be needed to determine not only the efficacy but especially the safety of this material before it can be recommended widely (8). It also appears possible that autologous fat may be useful in such cases, but research into this possibility has just begun.

VOCAL CORD PARALYSIS

Vocal cord paralysis may be unilateral or bilateral, central or peripheral, and it may involve the recurrent laryngeal nerve (Fig. 10)*, superior laryngeal nerve, or both. The physician's first responsibility in any case of vocal fold paralysis is to confirm the diagnosis (visually, radiographically, electromyographically, or in other ways), being certain that the laryngeal movement impairment is not caused by arytenoid dislocation, cricoarytenoid arthritis, neoplasm, or other causes, and to determine the etiology. Details of appropriate evaluation are available in any good otolaryngology text, and the otolaryngologist should be familiar with them. Briefly, if the paralysis appears to occur below the level of nodose ganglion, complete evaluation from the skull base through the chest (including the thyroid) is essential. This localization can usually be made reliably in isolated unilateral recurrent laryngeal nerve paralysis. If the paralysis is complete (recurrent and superior) or if there are other neurological findings, intracranial studies should be performed as well. Occasionally, central disease (especially multiple sclerosis) can produce unexpected neurologic symptoms, and, if no etiology is found after a recurrent laryngeal nerve paralysis has been worked up, addition of a magnetic resonance image (MRI) of the brain and other studies should be considered. Superior laryngeal nerve paralysis is suspected when one vocal fold lags in adduction and when the larynx is tilted. When it is complete, superior laryngeal nerve paralysis usually impairs volume and causes "threadiness" and crackling in the singer's midrange and loss of the highest notes and stability in the upper range. Paresis produces the same symptoms to a lesser degree. In addition to confirmation by electromyography, the author has found three clinical maneuvers particularly useful for making this condition more apparent. Repeated rapid phonation on /i/ with a complete stop between each phonation frequently causes increased vocal fold lag, as the pathologic side fatigues more rapidly than the normal side. This is sometimes easier to see during whistling. Laryngeal posture during this maneuver provides particularly good visibility of rapid vocal fold motions. The third maneuver is a glissando, asking the patient to slide slowly from his/her lowest to highest note. The vocal process should be observed under continuous and stroboscopic light. If a superior laryngeal nerve is injured, longitudinal tension will not increase as effectively on the abnormal side, disparities in vocal fold length will be apparent at higher pitches, and the vocal folds may actually scissor slightly with the normal cord being higher. Bilateral superior laryngeal nerve paralysis is often more difficult to diagnose and is probably frequently missed. Patients with this condition have a "floppy" epiglottis, rendering their larynges difficult to see. Their vocal quality, volume, and pitch range are impaired. It is often helpful to confirm a clinical impression of bilateral superior laryngeal nerve paralysis through electromyography.

---

* See color plate that appears following page 276.

SURGERY FOR VOCAL FOLD PARALYSIS

Surgery should not be performed for vocal fold paralysis until voice therapy has been tried. In many cases, strengthening vocal muscles and improving technique result in very good voice quality, and surgery is unnecessary. When the paralysis is idiopathic, or when the nerve is not known to be cut, approximately one year of observation and therapy should be completed to allow time for spontaneous return of function before performing any irreversible operation. Traditionally, most surgical procedures have worked best for unilateral recurrent laryngeal nerve paralysis. Unilateral vocal cord paralysis is common. It may be idiopathic, or it may occur following injury to the recurrent laryngeal nerve after neck or thoracic surgery, following neurosurgical procedures, or even following simple intubation. When the paralyzed cord remains in the partially abducted position, the functioning cord may be unable to cross the midline far enough to permit complete glottic closure. This will result in hoarseness, breathiness, ineffective cough, and, occasionally, in aspiration (especially following neurosurgical procedures or if other cranial nerves are also paralyzed). The most common treatment is injection of Teflon lateral to the paralyzed vocal fold. The Teflon paste pushes the paralyzed vocal fold toward the midline, allowing the nonparalyzed vocal cord to meet it more effectively (Figs. 11A and B). Various materials have been used for vocal fold injection since the technique was described by Brunings in 1911 (9). He used paraffin, which worked well but frequently extruded or resulted in a reactive paraffinoma. The technique was reintroduced in 1955 using diced cartilage particles (10). Since that time, various materials have been recommended including heterogeneous bovine bone paste (11), tantalum oxide (12), tantalum powder (13), silicon (14), and Teflon (15). Teflon paste is modified polytetrafluorethylene, 50% by weight in glycerine. Its density is 2.4, and it is the least reactive of known plastic materials.

The effects of Teflon injection can be predicted fairly well by prior injection with Gelfoam paste. This material is injected in the same position as Teflon, but it is temporary, resorbing in two to eight weeks. In professional voice users, periodic Gelfoam injections may also be appropriate early in the course of a recurrent laryngeal nerve paralysis, when recovery cannot be predicted and injection of permanent materials such as Teflon is not appropriate. For this technique, 1 g of sterile Gelfoam powder is mixed with 4 cc of physiologic saline. The saline must be added slowly, and the mixture should be stirred continuously. This produces 5 cc of thick paste, which can be transferred to a syringe and then into the Arnold-Brunings syringe. Injection technique is then identical to that for Teflon or other materials. The effects usually last for five to 10 weeks.

Correct technique involves injecting Teflon lateral to the thyroarytenoid

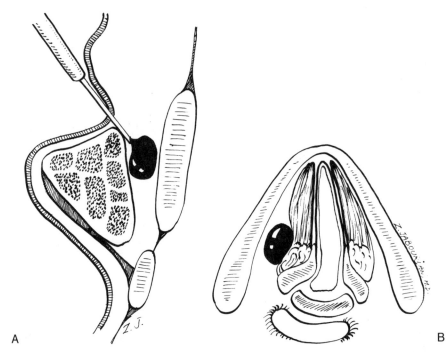

FIG. 11. Injection of Teflon lateral to the vocalis muscle (**A**). Seen from above (**B**), the collection of Teflon lateral to the vocalis muscle displaces the vocal fold medially. Moving the vocal fold toward the median position allows the mobile vocal fold to meet it. The depth of the injected Teflon depends on the size of the larynx, but the injection is usually 3 to 5 mm below the surface. Generally, 0.3 to 1.0 cc of Teflon plaste is required. Each click of the bruening syringe delivers approximately 0.2 cc of Teflon paste.

muscle. The quantity should be sufficient to move the vocal fold just to the midline. Most people inject Teflon or other materials for vocal fold paralysis endoscopically under local anesthesia. Transcutaneous injection with indirect mirror guidance is also possible. Injecting too much or injecting too superficially into the vocal fold mucosa often results in worsened voice quality. When properly placed, Teflon usually produces a minimal foreign body reaction locally, but no reaction in the surrounding cartilage and muscle (16). The Teflon is usually surrounded by a fibrous capsule, however, occasionally severe foreign body reaction and granuloma formation may occur. Preoperative and postoperative functional evaluation of the voice was advocated by von Leden et al. in 1967 and should now be standard practice (17).

Recently, several other materials have been injected. Collagen has been advocated, as discussed above in the section entitled "Surgery for Postoperative Vocal Fold Injury." Recently, Mikaelian et al. (18) have begun using autologous fat injections. Preliminary results have been promising. Various other techniques have been used and are valuable in selected circumstances.

REMOVAL OF TEFLON

One of the complications of Teflon injection is overinjection. If Teflon is injected in excessive amounts or too superficially, the voice must be substantially worse following surgery than it was prior to Teflon injection. Treating such complications and restoring satisfactory vocal quality are widely (and accurately) regarded as difficult. However, the otolaryngologist may be helped greatly by an accurate preoperative assessment of the problem.

Cross-sectional imaging using computed tomography (CT) of a larynx following Teflon injection documents the position of deposited Teflon easily, including its amount and depth. Although this high attenuation material (216 Houndsfield units) is easily seen, the value of radiologic assessment in these cases has been appreciated only recently (19).

In general, preoperative evaluation by strobovideolaryngoscopy, CT, and objective voice analysis allows reasonably accurate definition of the problem. If the Teflon has been incorrectly injected submucosally and the vibratory margin is adynamic, the patient should be advised that further surgical procedures are unlikely to produce improvement, especially if the vocal fold edge is smooth. If there are multiple lumps of superficial Teflon with failure of glottic closure between them, it is usually worthwhile to remove them and smooth the vibratory margin to improve glottic closure, even if vibration is not restored. If Teflon has been injected in a correct position, but vocal fold convexity exists because of excessive Teflon, results are more satisfactory. It should be noted that the "excess" may not be due to faulty technique on the part of the surgeon. Although Teflon should not ordinarily cause a reaction, some people do form a granulomatous response or thick capsule, thus increasing mass. Consequently, the amount of Teflon may have been correct at the time of surgery but become more than was necessary after the tissue response occurred. In the author's opinion, the best way to address this problem is with an incision with laser laterally over the collection of Teflon. The incision should be far from the vibratory margin. When the CO_2 laser touches the Teflon, a bright white glow is noted. If there is extensive granulomatous reaction around the Teflon, it may be necessary to excise the Teflon with the laser. In other cases, exposing a small portion of the Teflon allows it to be expressed and suctioned. Gentle pressure against the vocal fold edge is used to milk the desired amount of Teflon out of the vocal fold and to reestablish a smooth vocal fold margin. Slight overevacuation creating a minimal concavity of the vocal fold edge seems to produce the best results, although clinical experience has been insufficient for final conclusions or a formal report.

COLLAGEN INJECTION

Two specific advantages over Teflon were cited by Ford and Bless in their early work (20) and many subsequent publications. First, the substance is in liquid form, rather than a thick pastelike Teflon, and thus the ease and accuracy of injection are greatly enhanced. Second, long-term results from skin injections have shown a reduction of scar tissue in the treated areas. The combination of these two factors raises the possibility of using collagen injections in small segments of vocal cord scarring (such as after resolution of a vocal cord hemorrhage) or into adynamic segments of an otherwise normally moving vocal cord. Additionally, ease and accuracy of injection could allow attempts at augmentation for difficult problems such as persistent posterior glottic incompetence and combined recurrent and superior laryngeal nerve paralysis. Concerns have been raised about the safety of protocols designed to screen for reactions to collagen (8). More recent improvements in the collagen used and increasing clinical experience are encouraging. Although the risk of adverse reactions to collagen injected into the airway still raise concerns, the technique appears valuable in selected instances, as long as sufficient precautions are exercised.

THYROPLASTY

Another increasingly popular and very good approach is Type I thyroplasty. Although this procedure was proposed by Isshiki et al. in 1975 (21), it has been used widely in the United States only in the past few years. Thyroplasty is performed under local anesthesia. With the neck extended, a 4- to 5-cm incision is made horizontally at the midpoint between the thyroid notch and the lower rim of the thyroid cartilage. A rectangle of thyroid cartilage is cut out on the involved side. It begins approximately 5 to 7 mm lateral to the midline and is usually approximately 3 to 5 mm by 3 to 10 mm. Care must be taken not to carry the rectangle too far posteriorly, or it cannot be displaced medially. The cartilage is depressed inward, moving the vocal fold toward the midline. A wedge of silicone is then fashioned to hold the depressed cartilage in proper position (Figs. 12A and B).

ARYTENOID ADDUCTION/ROTATION

All the procedures discussed above work fairly well for recurrent laryngeal nerve paralysis but not nearly so well if the superior laryngeal nerve is

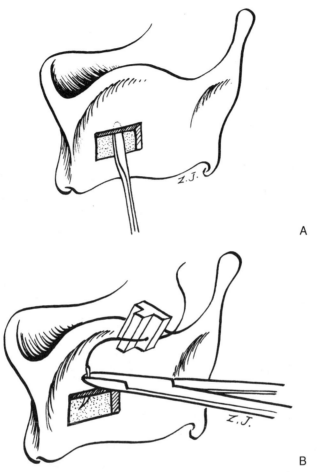

FIG. 12. In type I thyroplasty, a cartilage rectangle is cut beginning 5 to 7 mm lateral to the midline. It is 3 to 5 mm × 3 to 10 mm. After the cartilage cut has been completed, the inner perichondrium is elevated (**A**). A silicone block is used to depress the cartilage into proper position, displacing the vocal fold medially. The silicone is sutured to the cartilage (**B**).

involved or if the arytenoid is in abnormal position for some other reason. In these cases, arytenoid adduction/rotation procedures are preferable (22). Arytenoid adduction/rotation surgery is performed under local anesthesia. The thyropharyngeus muscle is divided, and the posterior margin of the thyroid cartilage is exposed. Subperichondrial elevation is carried onto the inferior surface of the thyroid ala. The cricothyroid joint is dislocated, and the pyriform sinus is protected. The muscular process of the arytenoid cartilage is identified, and the joint is opened through a small incision over the cri-

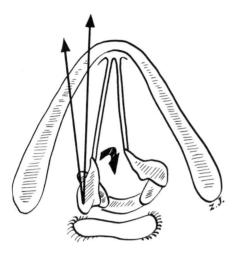

FIG. 13. In the arytenoid adduction/rotation procedure, directions of pull on the arytenoid cartilage are shown by *arrows.* Adjusting the two arytenoid sutures along the vectors shown permits medial and caudal rotation of the vocal fold.

coarytenoid muscle. Two 3-0 permanent sutures are fixed in soft tissue across the muscular process and tied in the directions of the lateral cricoarytenoid and lateral thyroarytenoid muscles, adjusting vocal fold position (Fig. 13).

NERVE ANASTOMOSIS AND NERVE–MUSCLE PEDICLE SURGERY

Reanastomosing divided or injured recurrent laryngeal nerve has not provided acceptable results. This may be due to abnormal intermingling of abductor and adductor fibers or to other causes, but the procedure has generally produced unsatisfactory vocal fold function in the voice. Attempts have been made to improve the results, optimizing abduction by dividing intralaryngeal adductor nerve branches (23). However, this technique has limited applicability. Procedures using various other nerves have been tried including vagus nerve bypass, split vagus nerve, phrenic nerve, and other nerves in the region. Results have been variable. Additional research on reinnervation is in progress, and the technique is probably valuable, at least under some circumstances.

Nerve muscle pedicle surgery involves implanting a portion of the sternohyoid muscle with its intact motor branch from the ansa hypoglossi into a paralyzed laryngeal abductor muscle, or a portion of the cricothyroid muscle with its motor branch of the superior laryngeal nerve into a paralyzed adductor muscle. Omohyoid muscle and others have also been used. The concept was originally reported by Takenouchi and Sato in 1968 (24) and was popularized by Tucker et al. in 1970 (25), and described in numerous publications thereafter. Reports of success rates have varied, and the operation certainly has not been universally satisfactory. Probably, the small improvement that is often seen results more from change in mass or position than from return of mobility. Failure of reinnervation after this procedure has been demonstrated histochemically (26).

OTHER TECHNIQUES

Numerous other techniques have been tried to restore voice quality in patients with vocal cord paralysis. They include switching of intact muscles, implantation of artificial muscles, cartilage implantation, and other methods. None of the techniques available is entirely satisfactory, although recent renewed interest in nerve anastomosis from adjacent nerves is encouraging.

ARYTENOID DISLOCATION

Arytenoid dislocation, although frequently unrecognized, is not a rare entity, although it is frequently mistaken for vocal fold paralysis. It is extremely important for the otolaryngologist to be aware of this condition, because it can usually be treated successfully if diagnosed promptly. When missed, or misdiagnosed as vocal cord paralysis, surgical repair becomes more difficult, although not impossible, as previously thought (27). Understanding the anatomy and embryology of this complex structure helps clarify the condition.

The primordium of the larynx, trachea, bronchi, and lungs arises as an outgrowth of the pharynx during the 3rd week of embryonic life, forming a laryngotracheal groove (28). This anterior groove lies immediately posterior to the hypobranchial eminence and becomes the primitive laryngeal aditus. The aditus lies between the sixth branchial arches. The laryngotracheal groove fuses in a caudal cranial direction at about the 4th week. The ventral ends of the sixth branchial arches grow and form the arytenoid eminences. During the 7th week, a fissure appears on each arytenoid eminence extending into the primitive vestibule. This is the laryngeal ventricle. The last portion of the laryngotracheal groove to be obliterated is the intra-arytenoid sulcus at about 11 weeks.

Laryngeal hyoid cartilages develop from branchial arch mesoderm, while elastic cartilages are derived from mesoderm of the floor of the pharynx (29). Most of the arytenoid is made of hyaline cartilage. However, the vocal processes are developed separately in association with the vocal folds and consist of elastic cartilage. The arytenoid cartilages (from the Greek word *arytainoeides* meaning ladle-shaped) are pyramidal in shape, consisting of an apex, base, and two processes. The base articulates with the cricoid cartilage. The apex attaches to the corniculate cartilage of Santorini and to the aryepiglottic fold. The vocal process projects anteriorly to connect with the vocal ligament, and the muscular process is the point of insertion for most of the muscles that move the arytenoid (30). The cricoarytenoid facets are well defined, smooth, and symmetrical. Each arytenoid articulates with an elliptical facet on the posterior superior margin of the cricoid ring. The cricoid facet is about 6 mm long and is cylindrical (31). Most of the cricoarytenoid motion is rocking; however, along the long axis of the cricoid facet, gliding also occurs (32). Limited rotary pivoting is permitted as well. The arytenoid cartilages and the cricoarytenoid facets are extremely symmetric and consistent (31). The cricoarytenoid joint is an arthrodial joint, supported by a capsule lined with synovium. The capsule is strengthened posteriorly by the cricoarytenoid ligament (33). This ligament is strong and ordinarily prevents anterior subluxation. The axis of the joint is at an angle of 45° from the sagittal plane and 40° from the horizontal plane. The cricoarytenoid joint controls abduction and adduction of the true vocal cords, thereby facilitating respiration, protection of the airway, phonation, and other laryngeal functions.

Arytenoid motion is controlled directly by intrinsic laryngeal muscles including the posterior cricoarytenoid, lateral cricoarytenoid, transverse arytenoid, oblique arytenoid, and thyroarytenoid. It is also affected by the cricothyroid muscle, which increases longitudinal tension on the vocal fold (which attaches to the vocal process of the arytenoid), and to a lesser degree by the thyroepiglottic muscle, which tenses the aryepiglottic fold.

Traditionally, arytenoid dislocation has been suspected on the basis of history and absence of the jostling phenomenon present in many cases of unilateral vocal fold paralysis (34). Often it is not diagnosed until direct laryngoscopy reveals impaired passive mobility of the vocal fold. Preoperative differentiation between vocal fold paralysis and arytenoid dislocation should be possible in virtually all cases. However, if not considered specifically, it will often be missed. Disparity in height between the vocal processes is much easier to see in slow motion under stroboscopic light at various pitches. In posterior dislocations, the vocal process and fold are usually higher on the dislocated side. In anterior dislocations, they are generally lower on the abnormal side. In either case, the injured vocal fold may move sluggishly or be immobile. Rarely, abduction and adduction may appear almost normal under continuous light. Video documentation of the preoperative and postoperative appearance can prove particularly helpful in cases of arytenoid dislocation, because many of them may involve litigation.

The most valuable tests are the stroboscopic examination to see differences in vocal process height, CT scan, which may image the arytenoid dislocation, and laryngeal electromyography to differentiate an immobile dislocated arytenoid joint from vocal fold paralysis. Airflow analysis is also helpful in documenting changes. Even though surgical reduction may be impossible even in rare early cases, it appears to be worth attempting reduction in all patients prior to treatment with vocal fold injection or other surgery. Even many months following injury, it has been possible to move the arytenoid enough to bring the vocal process back to normal height and allow good approximation with the mobile cord. We have found the anesthesiologist's straight Miller-3 laryngoscope blade the most useful instrument, especially in posterior dislocations (Fig. 14). The instrument is placed in the pyriform sinus with the rolled lip of the laryngoscope in the dislocated joint. An anteromedial lifting motion is applied. More force than expected is often necessary to reposition the cartilage. Anterior dislocations may be reduced with the tip of a Hollinger laryngoscope. More delicate instruments such as cupped forceps are not strong enough and are more likely to lacerate the mucosa and expose the cartilage to the risk of infection. Injection with Teflon, fat, or possibly collagen may be helpful in restoring glottic function. Implants and other techniques may also be appropriate.

Because of the value of early diagnosis in most cases, it is essential for otolaryngologists not only to be aware of arytenoid dislocation, but also to educate our anesthesiologist colleagues and other specialists about the importance of postoperative hoarseness. When severe dysphonia persists for more than two or three days after surgery, or when postoperative hoarseness is worse than expected, laryngoscopic examination by an otolaryngologist should be performed. The importance of prevention through extreme care at the time of intubation *and extubation* should be stressed. Additional stud-

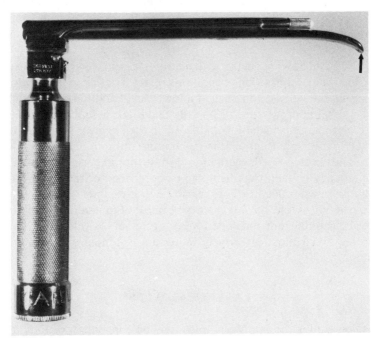

FIG. 14. Miller-3 laryngoscope blade was used for reducing posterior dislocations of the arytenoid. The raised tip (*arrow*) is especially helpful in lifting the joint into position.

ies to determine the true incidence of arytenoid dislocation following anesthesia and neck trauma should be encouraged.

"BOWED" VOCAL CORDS

The term "bowed" vocal cords is commonly applied when the vocal cords appear to be slightly concave and when glottic closure seems incomplete. Under stroboscopic light, most such cases reveal complete glottic closure but some thinning of the cover. Bowing of this sort is often associated with advanced age. In the past, many patients with this condition have been told either that it is incurable or that surgery to increase vocal cord bulk or tension is advisable. In the author's experience, neither statement is true for most patients. Unless there is neurological damage, the breathiness, slight hoarseness, and voice fatigue associated with apparent bowing in these patients can be corrected with specially designed voice therapy, ideally including both speaking and singing exercises. Such measures result in satisfactory improvement in the vast majority of cases. Injecting Teflon or other substances into mobile vocal folds is rarely advisable. Good results from vocal cord–lengthening phonosurgical procedures are generally short lived and are also rarely indicated. Senile vocal cord atrophy sufficient to prevent contact in a well-trained conditioned larynx is uncommon. However, the condition does occur occasionally. Similar laryngeal problems may occur in association with prolonged steroid use, debilitating illness, and similar medical problems.

True vocal fold bowing occurs with neurologic injury, particularly superior laryngeal nerve paralysis. This condition creates a deficit in longitudinal tension, causing the vocal fold to sag at a lower level and to bow laterally with increased subglottal pressure. When the condition is unilateral and incomplete, voice therapy is usually helpful. When the superior laryngeal nerve is completely paralyzed, treatment is much more difficult. Collagen injections have been advocated for this situation, but further experience is needed before the efficacy of such treatment can be confirmed or refuted. More invasive intralaryngeal procedures are usually not advisable.

When true vocal fold bowing occurs because of unilateral complete vocal cord paralysis (recurrent and superior laryngeal nerves), the voice can probably be improved most effectively using an arytenoid adduction/rotation procedure.

LARYNGEAL WEBS

Webs connecting the two vocal folds may be congenital, or they may follow trauma (Fig. 8). They are particularly apt to form when mucosa is disrupted in the anterior thirds of both vocal folds simultaneously, especially near the anterior commissure. Numerous otolaryngology texts and articles describe endoscopic and external surgical repair, which will not be reviewed in detail in this text on care of the professional voice. However, before deciding to operate on anyone, especially a professional voice user, it is essential for the surgeon to be certain that the web is symptomatic. Many anterior glottic webs, especially small ones, do not interfere with voice function. In fact, under stroboscopic light, many seem to disappear below the vocal folds, and vibratory activity may be normal. When the voice is hoarse and the web is caused by trauma, stroboscopy is essential. In some cases, the hoarseness is caused by scarring elsewhere in the vocal folds (an adynamic segment), and the web is not interfering with function. It is highly advisable to make such determinations before deciding whether to subject the patient to an operation that may not only fail to improve the voice, but may make it worse. Such cases can be complex medically, and patients with injuries resulting in hoarseness are frequently involved in litigation, as well; so it is clearly in the best interest of both the patient and the surgeon to take advantage of state-of-the-art technology for diagnosis and documentation before rendering a diagnosis and treatment recommendation.

LARYNGOCELE

A laryngocele is an air-filled dilatation of the laryngeal ventricle of Morgagni forming a sac with pseudostratified, ciliated columnar epithelium. The sac is usually connected to the ventricle by a narrow stalk. The ventricle is normally located between the true and false vocal folds. The anterior superior section of the ventricle is a blind pouch called the appendix of the ventricle of Morgagni. This is the region in which laryngoceles generally form. The appendix of the ventricle is considered abnormal if it extends above the upper border of the thyroid cartilage. Laryngoceles may cause a bulge in the neck during singing, and they may be seen more commonly in some instrumentalists, particularly in brass players (trumpeters). The laryngocele may be internal, external (outside the thyroid cartilage), or mixed. If the lesion is asymptomatic, treatment is not required. If the laryngocele produces symptoms, external support is unlikely to be satisfactory for a professional voice user, and surgery may be necessary.

LARYNGEAL TRAUMA

Laryngeal trauma may cause many problems in addition to the webs discussed above. Trauma may be internal or external. It may result in vocal fold hemorrhage or mucosal tears, either of which may produce permanent scars. Trauma may also fracture the laryngeal skeleton, dislocate the arytenoids, or paralyze the laryngeal nerves. The principles of treatment in a professional voice user are the same as those for anyone else. A safe airway should be assured. If intubation is required, immediate or early tracheotomy should be performed to minimize the risk of iatrogenic trauma to the vocal folds. Whenever possible, a complete diagnostic voice evaluation including strobovideolaryngoscopy and objective voice analysis should be carried out to map and document the injury as well as possible. High-resolution axial and coronal CT scans are often extremely helpful. At present, most of the scanners in common use have resolution limited to 11 line pairs. Higher resolution (16 line pairs or better) allows not only an excellent view of the larynx, but also clear visualization of the cricoarytenoid joints. Very high-quality computed tomography is helpful in many cases. When there is a question as to whether vocal fold motion is impaired because of paralysis or mechanical causes, laryngeal electromyography should be used. When major injuries occur in professional voice users, it is advisable to involve a speech-language pathologist in the patient's care as soon as the medical condition permits, preferably prior to surgery. Following surgery, the speech-language pathologist should participate in the patient's rehabilitation as soon as the patient is allowed to speak. Early involvement of the patient's professional voice teachers is also helpful, so long as the singing or acting teacher is interested in and comfortable with training of injured voices. Close collaboration among all members of the voice team is particularly important in rehabilitating such patients.

PAPILLOMA

Laryngeal papillomas are caused by viruses. Although they begin in the epithelium, they may invade deeply (Figs. 1 and 3). Although papillomas used to be seen primarily in children, the incidence in young adults (professional voice user age) appears to be increasing. There also seems to be a correlation between the increase in laryngeal papillomas and the increased prevalence of genital warts caused by the same virus. When papillomas interfere with airway or voice, surgery is the usual treatment. In general, it is performed with a continuous CO_2 laser beam taking care not to contaminate the lower airway with viral particles. Viral typing has been done on a small number of laryngeal papillomas, and virus infection was not identified in all cases (35). The relevance in the larynx of viral types associated with carcinoma of the uterine cervix (HPV 16 and 18) remains undetermined. There is also evidence that papilloma virus may be carried in the laser smoke and transmitted to the surgeon or operating room staff. So an intralaryngeal smoke evacuator should always be used during these procedures.

CARCINOMA OF THE VOCAL FOLD

Cancer of the larynx will not be reviewed in this book. There are many excellent references on the subject. When cancer occurs in professional voice users, obviously a great effort must be made to choose a treatment modality that preserves good voice function while providing the best chance for cure of the cancer. At present, there are no indisputable controlled studies on post-treatment vocal quality to help guide the laryngologist and patient. Initially, it may seem as if radiation therapy is "obviously" better for vocal quality than surgery. However, postradiation changes in the mucosa, lubrication, and muscle may be significant. Controlled studies comparing radiation with various surgical techniques are needed, and such studies must consider not only early results, but vocal quality five and 10 years after treatment. Laser surgery has become popular recently for treatment of selected vocal fold lesions. Hirano (36) et al. have pointed out that "tissue is much thicker after laser surgery than after radiation therapy," and critical comparisons of surgery with laser versus traditional instruments also require investigation.

SURGERY TO CHANGE VOICE QUALITY

Occasionally, singers and actors inquire about surgery for pitch alteration. Such procedures (37) have proved successful in specially selected patients (such as those undergoing sex-change surgery), but they do not consistently provide good enough voice quality to be performed on a professional voice user.

VELOPHARYNGEAL INSUFFICIENCY

Velopharyngeal insufficiency has also been suggested as a cause of problems for singers, actors, and instrumentalists. Damste (38) has described push back surgery for "congenital short palate" in a professional singer who presented with nodules and voice fatigue. The prevalence and importance of this problem await further clarification, and most of us who care for large numbers of singers and actors do not encounter it frequently.

OBSTRUCTIVE SLEEP APNEA SYNDROME IN PROFESSIONAL VOICE USERS

Snoring is a common problem of both adults and children. Forty-five percent of normal adults snore occasionally and 25% habitually (39).

Snoring may be the primary symptom of a potentially life-threatening condition called obstructive sleep apnea syndrome (OSAS). On the one hand, snoring that occurs intermittently and produces minor annoyance to others is rarely indicative of a serious airway obstruction and may be related to something as mild as nasal congestion. On the other hand, snoring that is so loud that it forces the snorer's spouse or roommate to sleep in another room and brings complaints from neighbors may be related to serious airway compromise. Such loud snoring is called "heroic snoring." In some cases, it may result in separation, divorce, or refusal to marry. It may reach 80 decibels when measured five feet from the source (40), as loud as a busy office with typewriters and tabulating machines. Habitual breath holding, flailing, sleep-walking, and noise frighten parents or family members. Often the "heroic snorer" is embarrassed, self-conscious, harassed, or ostracized; his/her snoring interferes with interpersonal relationships and normal daily activities. Obstruction of the airway, which causes the loud snoring, interferes with the restfulness of sleep and results in excessive daytime sleepiness (EDS) (41). The OSAS sufferer sleeps (and snores) at inappropriate times and frequently is asked to leave church, movies, concerts, or family gatherings. In addition, spontaneous sleeping may make it difficult for the snorer to drive or operate machinery safely.

Apnea is periodic cessation of breathing. In OSAS, episodes of apnea last 20 to 40 sec and may occur as frequently as 600 times per night (42). These interruptions in breathing deprive the body of oxygen (hypoxia) and can result in heart failure, irregular heart rhythm (arrhythmias), high blood pressure (hypertension), and reduced blood oxygenation (hypoxemia). In addition to the serious consequences that may follow cardiac arrhythmia and hypertension, chronic deprivation of oxygen during sleep results in clouded mental functioning when awake and can lead to accidental injury. Persons with chronic sleep apnea are so poorly rested that they frequently sleep spontaneously. For example, they can fall asleep while waiting at a red light in traffic.

Not all persons who snore experience apnea. Characteristically, those who do, snore "heroically." This snoring occurs virtually every time the person is asleep and is not relieved by position change. Sleep apnea may be evaluated by recording the snorer and observing him/her for episodes of silence (apneic periods), followed by a snorting sound as breathing resumes (resuscitative snort), abdominal and chest heaving, and flailing of the arms or legs. Although irregular breathing during sleep is normal, a period of four to five seconds or more between expiration and inspiration is abnormal. The observer should time the apneic episodes and determine how frequently they occur.

Sleep apnea is best evaluated by polysomnogram, a test performed in a sleep laboratory and that involves objective monitoring of cardiac and respiratory function, brain activity, and muscular activity. Polysomnogram and direct objective measurement in EDS determine the severity of OSAS.

Snoring occurs most commonly in males. In a study of 83 adult snorers, 82% were male. Obstructive sleep breathing worsens with age and is three times more common in obese subjects than in thin ones (43). OSAS has many causes. In children, it is associated with snoring, mouth breathing, daytime sleepiness, and poor performance in school and is most frequently caused by enlarged tonsils or adenoids. It can be associated with chronic upper respiratory infection (43). Consequently, tonsillectomy and/or adenoidectomy are curative in a high percentage of child snorers. In a recent study of children varying in age from three to 18, surgical treatments of this type successfully eliminated snoring in 100% of the cases (43). It must be remembered that these cases were carefully selected for surgery, however.

OSAS in adults has been associated with nasal abnormalities such as septal deformity and enlargement of the nasal bones (turbinate hypertrophy), malpositioning of the soft palate, swelling and bulkiness of the uvula and soft palate, anatomical narrowing of the nasopharyngeal space (usually due to excessive length of the soft palate), and redundancy of flabbiness of the pharyngeal mucosa (throat lining). As in children, significantly enlarged tonsils sometimes contribute to airway obstruction in adult patients. Adult patients with abnormalities of the soft palate or redundant boggy mucosa in the throat may appear to have a normal airway in the upright position. However, when supine (lying down) and relaxed, these structures may collapse into the airway and occlude it. In obese patients, a short, stocky neck, poor muscle tone, and the compressive weight of adipose tissue (fat) further contribute to the obstruction.

In adults, treatment of OSAS initially involves exercise; weight loss; avoidance of alcoholic beverages, tranquilizers, and sleeping pills; and elevation of the head of the bed. These treatments are only minimally helpful in many cases. Nonsurgical treatment may be inadequate for patients who experience compromise of heart and respiratory function as determined by polysomnogram. In order to maintain the airway and avoid dangerous complications, some patients undergo tracheotomy (44). Because this is a somewhat radical and disfiguring treatment, it is used only in potentially life-threatening situations documented by sleep studies. Clearly, it is a last resort for professional singers or actors.

In 1981, a surgical procedure to treat obstructive sleep apnea, called uvulopalatopharyngoplasty (UPPP), was devised (45). This procedure involves reshaping the uvula, palate, and pharyngeal space in order to enlarge the air space and reduce or eliminate obstruction during sleep. It involves a circumferential incision, which begins in the area of the tonsil on one side and extends across the back of the throat, involving the uvula, to the tonsillar area on the other side. During this procedure, an elongated uvula, redundant mucosa, a portion of the soft palate (if excessive in length), and tonsils (if present) are removed, enlarging the airway space at the back of the throat.

In order for a patient to be a candidate for this surgical procedure, he/she must have a history of loud habitual snoring and must have sleep apnea. Although the uvula, tonsils, and excessive mucosal tissue that are resected during UPPP are not necessary for normal functioning in the nonprofessional voice user (therefore usually causing no gross impairment when removed), all surgical procedures can result in complications such as blood loss, infection, and illness associated with general anesthesia. In professional voice users, there are special concerns. Even following tonsillectomy alone, scarring and restriction of palatal movement may alter the supraglottic vocal tract enough to change the sound of the voice substantially. Such procedures routinely change the singer's "feel" of his/her voice, at least for several months. Most doctors who care for singers and actors have seen cases where extensive scarring following tonsillectomy has caused long-term problems with voice performance. UPPP involves even more extensive surgery of the palate, tonsillar areas, and pharynx. We must anticipate the possibility of similar problems in some cases. However, like tonsillectomy, there are times when overriding health considerations justify the risks involved. Professional voice users should be careful to avoid unnecessary surgery, but, in the presence of severe OSAS unresponsive to medical treatments, surgery should be considered.

QUADRIPLEGIA

Abdominal muscle support is essential for singing and acting. Therefore, it would seem that quadriplegia following cervical fracture would end a professional singing career, and possibly an acting career. Sataloff et al. (46) described rehabilitation of a quadriplegic professional singer in 1984. Since that report, he has been able to continue a limited recording career and occasional public and television appearances, and he is now able to do so without the device we designed for him. In studying this patient and other quadriplegic people deprived of voice support, we have encountered frequent problems with voice fatigue and decreased volume, range, and projection. Additional activity in therapy and research should provide greater insights into the best methods to help the voices of quadriplegic patients in general and to restore performance ability to quadriplegic professional voice users. In addition, quadriplegic patients provide scientists with an opportunity to observe the consequences of consistent, drastic reduction in the support mechanism.

OTHER NEUROLOGIC PROBLEMS

Many other neurologic conditions such as Parkinson's disease, stroke, and dysarthria produce voice problems, as noted in Chapter 5. They may be helped by combined speech and singing therapy. However, these afflictions are not common in professional voice users and will not be discussed in detail in this book.

SPASMODIC DYSPHONIA

Spasmodic or spastic dysphonia is a term applied to patients with specific voice sounds. These patients have a variety of diseases that produce the same vocal result. There are also many interruptions in vocal fluency that are incorrectly diagnosed as spasmodic dysphonia. It is important to avoid this error, because different types of dysphonia require different evaluations and carry different prognostic implications. Spasmodic dysphonia is subclassified into adductor and abductor types.

Since spasmodic dysphonia is encountered only occasionally in professional voice users, the subject will be reviewed briefly in this chapter.

Adductor spasmodic dysphonia is characterized by hyperadduction of the vocal folds, producing an irregularly interrupted, effortful, strained staccato voice. It may be neurologic, psychogenic, or idiopathic in etiology, and its severity varies substantially among patients and over time. It is generally considered a focal dystonia. In many cases, the voice may be normal or more normal during laughing, coughing, crying, or other nonvoluntary vocal activities, or during singing. Adduction may involve the true vocal folds alone, or the false vocal folds and supraglottis may squeeze shut. Because of the possibility of serious underlying neurologic dysfunction or association with other neurologic problems as seen in Meige syndrome (blepharospasm, medical facial spasm, and spastic dysphonia), a complete neurologic and neurolaryngological evaluation is required. Adductor spastic dysphonia may also be associated with spastic torticollis and extrapyramidal dystonia, although the condition was previously believed to be psychogenic.

Abductor spasmodic dysphonia is similar to adductor spasmodic dysphonia except that voice is interrupted by breathy, unphonated bursts, rather than constricted and shut off. Like adductor spastic dysphonia, various causes may be responsible. The abductor spasms tend to be most severe during unvoiced consonants, better during voiced consonants, and absent or least troublesome during vowels. Both abductor and adductor spastic dysphonia characteristically progress gradually, and both are aggravated by psychological stress.

After comprehensive work-up to rule out organic causes, treatment for spasmodic dysphonia should include voice therapy. Adductor spastic dysphonia is much more common, and most therapy and surgical techniques have been directed at this form. Unfortunately, traditional voice therapy is often not successful. Speaking on inhalation has worked well in some cases. Patients who are able to sing without spasms but are unable to speak may benefit from singing lessons. We have used singing training as a basic approach to voice control and then bridged the singing voice into speech. In a few patients, medications such as baclofen or Dilantin (Parke Davis) have also been helpful, but these patients are in the minority. When all other treatment modalities fail, various invasive techniques have been used. Recurrent laryngeal nerve section produces vocal cord paralysis and improves spasmodic dysphonia initially in many patients. However, there is a high incidence of recurrence. Other surgical techniques that alter vocal fold length and modify the thyroid cartilage may also be efficacious. However, the most encouraging treatment for patients disabled by severe spasmodic dysphonia is botulinum toxin injection. At present, this is usually done with electromyographic guidance, and the technique produces temporary paralysis of selected muscles. This results in relief or resolution of the spastic dysphonia. However, the injections need to be repeated periodically in many patients.

STUTTERING

Stuttering is also not a common problem among professional voice users and is discussed widely in speech-language pathology and neurology literature. It is interesting to note, however, that stuttering rarely affects the singing voice. Consequently, even people with severe stuttering in speech have had successful professional singing careers. Botulinum toxin appears promising as a treatment for some stutterers.

VOCAL TREMORS

Voice tremors require comprehensive neurologic evaluation. One of the most common causes is essential tremor, also known as benign heredofamilial tremor. This may be associated with tremors elsewhere in the body, or it may involve the voice only. Although a small number of patients will improve somewhat with medication, in most instances, this tremor cannot be treated effectively. Before making a diagnosis of essential tremor, however, it is important to rule out more serious causes such as cerebellar disease, Parkinson's disease, psychogenic tremor, thyrotoxicosis, drug-induced tremor, neurologic disorders such as those discussed at the end of Chapter 7, and other causes.

MYASTHENIA GRAVIS

Myasthenia gravis is a disease of the myoneural junction. Ordinarily, nerve endings release acetylcholine, which depolarizes the end plate of the muscle fiber, causing excitation and muscle contraction. In myasthenia gravis, the muscle fails to depolarize either because of insensitivity of the muscle end plate, a defect in acetylcholine released from the nerve ending, or both. Ordinarily, acetylcholine is destroyed rapidly by acetylcholinesterase. Myasthenia gravis occurs most commonly in women in their 20s and 30s and in men in their 50s and 60s. The prognosis is better in young women. Although muscles of swallowing, respiration, the limbs, and ocular muscles are involved most commonly, virtually all areas of the body may be affected by myasthenia. Localized disease is well recognized and may involve only one eye, for example. Myasthenia gravis may also be isolated to the larynx. This results in rapid voice fatigue, breathiness, moderate hoarseness, and loss of range. In professional voice users, voice dysfunction may also be the first symptom the patient notices of more widely disseminated myasthenia.

Myasthenia gravis should be in the physician's differential diagnosis whenever the complaint of voice fatigue is present, although it is the cause only rarely. A history of weakness elsewhere in the body makes one more suspicious. Although our strobovideolaryngoscopic findings have not yet been reported in the literature, we have observed varying neurologic abnormalities in the larynx. For example, when the author suspects myasthenia, patients are examined early in the morning when they are well rested. A mild laryngeal asymmetry may be noted, such as a lag in adduction of one vocal fold. We then have the patient vocalize actively until marked fatigue develops and repeat the strobovideolaryngoscopic examination. We have noted changing abnormalities, such as markedly slow adduction on the opposite side, bilateral failure of complete adduction, and other changes from the time of the examination at rest.

Laboratory and other tests assist the diagnosis. Blood should be sent for levels of antistriatal antibody and antiacetylcholine receptor antibody. Electromyography with repetitive stimulation test often establishes the diagnosis. A tensilon test is helpful. The voice should be fatigued prior to the tensilon test and should be recorded before and during the test. Unless the consultant neurologist is used to working with the laryngologist in such cases, he/she should be warned that a tensilon test has been requested. Most laryngologists are not equipped to perform the test in the office routinely, although arrangements can be made easily with advanced warning. The disease can usually be treated well with Mestinon (Roche), and long-term steroid therapy can usually be avoided. Careful training in speech and singing is essential, because nearly all professional voice users with this problem develop undesirable vocal habits in vain attempts to compensate for vocal impairment before the diagnosis is made. Good technique must be established in conjunction with disease control. In some instances, thymectomy can be recommended. Because of the risk of injury to the recurrent laryngeal nerves, it is best to avoid this procedure in professional voice users when possible.

DOCUMENTATION

As has been noted elsewhere in this book, preoperative objective assessment and documentation are essential. As a bare minimum high-quality tape recording must be done before surgery. Photographs or videotapes of the larynx, and strobovideolaryngoscopy are extremely helpful. Ideally, complete assessment as described in Chapter 8 should be performed. Proper documentation is essential for assessing results. Even for the physician not interested in research or publication, accurate assessment is difficult without at least a tape recorder. Auditory memories of physicians and patients are not good in general, and both the doctor and postoperative professional voice user are often surprised when they compare postoperative and pre-operative recordings. Frequently, the preoperative voice is worse than either person remembers. In addition, such documentation is invaluable for medical–legal purposes.

REFERENCES

1. Gould WJ, Lawrence VL. *Surgical care of voice disorders.* New York: Springer-Verlag, 1984;1–105.
2. Isshiki N. *Phonosurgery: theory and practice.* New York: Springer-Verlag, 1989;1–227.
3. Gould WJ, Sataloff RT. *Diseases and surgery of the vocal tract.* C.V. Mosby, in preparation.
4. Abitbol J. Limitations of the laser in microsurgery of the larynx. In: Lawrence VL, ed. *Transactions of the twelfth symposium: care of the professional voice.* New York: The Voice Foundation, 1984;297–301.
5. Tapia RG, Pardo J, Marigil M, Pacio A. Effects of the Laser upon Reinke's space and the neural system of the vocalis muscle. In: Lawrence VL, ed. *Transactions of the twelfth symposium: care of the professional voice.* New York: The Voice Foundation, 1984;289:291.
6. von Leden H. Presentation at the seventh symposium on care of the professional voice. The Juilliard School, New York, June 16, 1978.
7. Ford CN, Bless DM. Collagen injected in the scarred vocal fold. *J Voice* 1988;1(1):116–118.
8. Spiegel JR, Sataloff RT, Gould WJ. The treatment of vocal fold paralysis with injectable collagen: clinical concerns. *J Voice* 1988;1(1):119–121.
9. Brunings W. Uber eine neue Behandlungsmethode der Rekurrenslahmung. *Verh Dtsch Laryngol* 1911;18:93–151.
10. Arnold GE. Vocal rehabilitation of paralytic dysphonia. I. Cartilage injection into a paralysed vocal cord. *Arch Otolaryngol* 1955;62:1–17.
11. Goff WF. Laryngeal adductor paralysis treated by vocal cord injection of bone paste: a preliminary investigation. *Trans Pac Coast Otophthalmol Soc* 1960;41:77–88.
12. Arnold GE. Vocal rehabilitation of paralytic dysphonia. VI. Further studies of intracordal injection materials. *Arch Otolaryngol* 1961;73:290–294.
13. Lewy RB. Glottic reformation with voice rehabilitation in vocal cord paralysis. *Laryngoscope* 1963;73:547–555.
14. Rubin HJ. Pitfalls in treatment of dysphonias by intracordal injection of synthetics. *Laryngoscope* 1965;75:1381–1395.
15. Arnold GE. Vocal rehabilitation of paralytic dysphonia. VIII. Phoniatric methods of vocal compensation. *Arch Otolaryngol* 1962;76:76–83.
16. Stone JW, Arnold GE. Human larynx injected with Teflon paste. *Arch Otolaryngol* 1967;86:550–561.
17. von Leden H, Yanagihara N, Kukuk-Werner E. Teflon in unilateral vocal cord paralysis. *Arch Otolaryngol* 1967;85(6):110–118.
18. Mikaelian DO, Lowry DL, Sataloff RT. Lipoinjection for unilateral vocal cord paralysis. *Laryngoscope,* in press.
19. Sataloff RT, Mayer DP, Spiegel JR. Radiologic assessment of laryngeal Teflon injection. *J Voice* 1988;2(1):93–95.
20. Ford CN, Bless DM. A preliminary study of injectable collagen in human vocal fold augmentation. *Otolaryngol Head Neck Surg* 1986;94:104–112.
21. Isshiki N, Okamura H, Ishikawa T. Thyroplasty type I (lateral compression for dysphonia due to vocal cord paralysis or atrophy). *Acta Otolaryngol* 1975;80:465–473.
22. Isshiki N, Tanabe M, Sawada M. Arytenoid adduction for unilateral vocal cord paralysis. *Arch Otolaryngol* 1978;104:555–558.

23. Murakami Y, Kirchner JA. Vocal cord abduction by regenerated recurrent laryngeal nerve. *Arch Otolaryngol* 1971;94:64–68.
24. Takenouchi S, Sato F. Phonatory function of the implanted larynx. *Jpn J Bronchoesophagol* 1968;19:280–281.
25. Tucker HM, Harvey JE, Ogura JH. Vocal cord remobilization in the canine larynx. *Arch Otolaryngol* 1970;92:530–533.
26. Rice DH, Owens O, Burnstein F, et al. The nerve–muscle pedicle: a visual electromyographic and histochemical study. *Arch Otolaryngol* 1983;109:233–234.
27. Sataloff RT, Feldman M, Darby KS, et al. Arytenoid dislocation. *J Voice* 1987;1(4):368–377.
28. Lee GJ. *Essential otolaryngology,* 3rd ed. New York: Medical Examination Publishing, 1983;246–247.
29. Langman J. *Medical embryology,* 3rd ed. Baltimore: Williams & Wilkins, 1975;269–272.
30. Hollinshead WH. *Anatomy for surgeons,* vol. 1, 3rd ed. New York: Harper & Row, 1982;423–427.
31. Maue WM, Dickson DR. Cartilages and ligaments of the adult human larynx. *Arch Otolaryngol* 1971;94:432–439.
32. von Leden H, Moore P. The mechanics of the cricoarytenoid joint. *Arch Otolaryngol* 1961;73:63–72.
33. Pennington CL. External trauma of the larynx and trachea. *Ann Otol Rhinol Laryngol* 1972;81:546–554.
34. Jackson C, Jackson CL. Disease and injuries of the larynx. New York: Macmillan, 1942;321.
35. Abitbol J, Mathae G, Battista C. Preliminary report on detection of papillomaviruses types 6, 11, 16, and 18 in laryngeal benign and malignant lesions. *J Voice* 1988;2(4):334–337.
36. Vaughan CW, Blaugrund SM, Gould WJ, et al. Surgical management of voice disorders. *J Voice* 1988;2(2):176–181.
37. Issiki N, Taira T, Tanabe M. Surgical alteration of the vocal pitch. *J Otolaryngol* 1983;12:335–340.
38. Damste PH. Shortness of the palate: a cause of problems in singing. *J Voice* 1988;2(1):96–98.
39. Zwillich CM. The clinical significance of snoring. *Arch Intern Med* 1979;139:24–26.
40. Seivert P. Snoring. *South Med J* 1980;73:1035–1036.
41. Guilleminault C, Cummiskey J. Progressive improvement of apnea index and ventilatory response to CO_2 after tracheostomy in obstructive sleep apnea syndrome. *Am Rev Resp Dis* 1978;126:14–20.
42. Fujita S, Conway WA, Zorick FJ, et al. Evaluation of the effectiveness of UPPP. *Laryngoscope* 1982;95:70–74.
43. Fairbanks DNF. Snoring: surgical versus non-surgical management. *Laryngoscope* 1984;94:1188–1192.
44. Guilleminault C, Dement W, eds. *Sleep apnea syndromes.* New York: Allen R. Liss (KROC Foundation Services), 1978.
45. Fujita S, Conway WA, Zorrick F. Surgical correction of anatomic abnormalities in obstructive sleep apnea syndrome: uvulopalatopharyngoplasty. *Otolaryngol Head Neck Surg* 1981;89:923–934.
46. Sataloff RT, Heuer RJ, O'Connor MJ. Rehabilitation of a quadriplegic professional singer. *Arch Otolaryngol* 1984;110:682–685.

Professional Voice: The Science and Art of Clinical Care, Robert T. Sataloff.
Raven Press, Ltd., New York © 1991.

25

Facial Plastic Surgery in Professional Voice Users

*Joseph R. Spiegel, *Robert T. Sataloff, **Mary Hawkshaw

*Department of Otolaryngology, Thomas Jefferson University,
Philadelphia, Pennsylvania; and **American Institute for Voice and Ear Research,
Philadelphia, Pennsylvania*

Plastic surgery refers to procedures that repair or reconstruct tissues. Cosmetic surgery encompasses any plastic surgical procedure or set of procedures utilized to enhance appearance. Performers, by the nature of their work, are in the public eye and thus are understandably concerned about their appearance. As cosmetic surgery has become more prevalent and safer in recent years, many performers consider it as a means to enhance their appearance and thus their careers. However, when considering any elective medical procedure, the performer must be able to evaluate fully any potential transient or permanent effects on his/her general health as well as on the ability to perform. Review of the general issues that any patient must consider in deciding about cosmetic surgery should be augmented, and emphasis must be placed on special considerations for professional performers. Because many singers also play musical instruments, a few additional comments are included in this chapter to highlight selected effects of facial plastic surgery on instrumental performance as well.

GENERAL CONSIDERATIONS

The first step any patient must make when considering cosmetic surgery is deciding what he/she wants to change. It is not necessary for a patient to know the specifics of which procedure or procedures are necessary. However, the ability to verbalize exactly what is making the patient unhappy and what is the most important change desired will make the initial evaluation much more productive. An important part of this process is ascertaining whether the patient's hopes are realistic. For this reason, some patients are well served by a preoperative psychological consultation.

The Surgeon

After the patient has a clear idea of the cosmetic problems to be approached, the next steps are to choose a surgeon, help in the choice of the correct procedure or combination of procedures, make the appropriate arrangements for surgery with regard to the patient's general medical condition, and make the necessary financial arrangements. As cosmetic surgery has become widespread in the United States, many physicians of varying specialties have become involved. The best advice to a patient considering cosmetic surgery is to research the reputation, skill, and experience of the surgeon in question, obtain information about his/her board certification, and check the surgeon's hospital affiliations. The first source of information is usually the family physician or some other physician in the community with whom the patient is familiar. Organizations such as the local medical society, the American Board of Plastic and Reconstructive Surgery, the American Board of Otolaryngology-Head and Neck Surgery, the American Academy of Facial Plastic and Reconstructive Surgery, and the American Board of Cosmetic Surgery will also be helpful in identifying surgeons who are qualified in specific areas of expertise.

Once it has been determined that the surgeon is qualified, reputable, and experienced, it is important to develop a dependable doctor/patient relationship. Cosmetic surgery in many cases is as much an artistic as a medical endeavor. A mutual understanding of both the patient's desires and the surgeon's concept of aesthetic beauty is crucial. The final consideration is cost. It is advisable to obtain a second opinion in planning cosmetic surgery. This is expected by most cosmetic surgeons and usually helps reinforce the patient's confidence when final decisions are made.

The Procedure(s)

The choice of which procedure or procedures will be performed results from the joint discussion and evaluation by the surgeon and patient. There are a myriad of procedures available to enhance physical appearance (Table 1), and, while a patient may have a specific idea about what is necessary,

TABLE 1. *Procedures of plastic surgery*

Rhinoplasty	Mentoplasty
Blepharoplasty	Chemabrasion
Rhytidectomy	Otoplasty
Collagen implant	Forehead lift
Dermabrasion	Liposuction
Submental lipectomy	

the experience of the surgeon is critical in determining exactly how to reach the desired goals. It is also important for the patient to understand the substantial limits of the surgeon's ability to predict the exact outcome of surgery. Many cosmetic surgeons now utilize computer imaging in their office to assist the patient's understanding of the surgical changes that can be accomplished. This is especially helpful in demonstrating the value of adjunct procedures to the patient (i.e., chin augmentations performed with rhinoplasty). However, it must be remembered that computer imaging provides only an estimate of the changes that can be made and does not represent a promise of the surgical result.

Limitations

All decisions regarding any surgical procedure must be made with consideration of the patient's general medical condition. Age itself is not a serious limiting factor in most cases. However, vascular and cutaneous changes that occur with age may make certain procedures more hazardous, delay the healing process, or reduce the time that a cosmetic procedure is effective. Except in cases of severe deformity, most young patients are advised to defer cosmetic surgery until full growth and maturation are achieved (15 to 20 years old). Chronic cardiac, pulmonary, or renal conditions may severely increase the risk of surgery, even when utilizing local anesthesia, and also may result in prolonged or suboptimal healing. A coagulopathy would severely restrict and perhaps contraindicate most cosmetic operations. Allergies to medications and environmental factors may limit the choice of perioperative drugs or influence the time of year during which certain procedures are scheduled. Finally, cigarette smoking has been proved to cause significant problems and delays in postoperative healing after many cosmetic procedures. Many surgeons will refuse to operate on patients who are actively smoking, especially when considering a procedure such as face-lift or blepharoplasty.

Finances

Costs should never be the major consideration influencing medical decisions. However, most cosmetic surgery is not covered by medical insurance; thus, the patient must bear most or all of the financial responsibility. Because of this, many plastic surgeons require payment of the surgery in advance. It is best if all discussions and arrangements regarding finances be completed with the surgeon or his/her staff prior to any detailed surgical planning so the patient is freed of these worries. At that point, all decisions can be made with only cosmetic and medical considerations in mind.

SPECIAL CONSIDERATIONS

When considering cosmetic plastic surgery, performers must evaluate not only all the factors discussed above, but must also consider any effects that these decisions will have on their careers in general. It is most important to avoid complications that would affect adversely the ability to sing or to make decisions with full knowledge as to how they might affect an artist's performance schedule.

The Surgeon

In addition to the desired attributes of the operating surgeon, the performers must look for a physician who is sympathetic to their special needs. The surgeon must be willing to make compromises in both surgical planning and operative technique to reduce the risk of damage to the performance apparatus. Additionally, the surgeon must be able and willing to provide detailed information about postoperative care and limitations and how these will affect the resumption of active performance. A cosmetic surgeon who has experience in caring for professional performers is optimal, but what is most important is the physician's willingness to work with the performer's teacher, coach, and other specialists involved, such as a laryngologist, voice teacher, and/or speech pathologist, if necessary, depending on the particular needs of the patient (1).

Anesthesia

The management of anesthesia is especially important. General anesthesia should be avoided whenever possible, especially in actors and singers, because of the need for endotracheal intubation in almost all cases. Interestingly, trained laryngeal activity is essential in playing many wind and brass instruments as well; these instrumentalists should be approached with the same caution used with professional singers. Complications of intubation include vocal cord edema, granuloma formation, arytenoid dislocation, vocal cord paralysis, and damage to teeth. Other serious voice impairments related to superior laryngeal nerve dysfunction, pulmonary complications of general anesthesia such as atelectasis and pneumonia, vocal fold hemorrhage, and gastroesophageal reflux laryngitis can also be incurred. While the risk of these potential complications is greater with prolonged intubation, they have all been noted after brief, "easy" intubation as well (2). However, certain cosmetic plastic surgical procedures outside the face such as abdominoplasty, many liposuction procedures, as well as augmentation and reduction mammoplasty require general anesthesia. When these procedures are desired, it is important to discuss the risks with the surgeon and the anesthesiologist so that intubation can take place under optimal conditions and be performed by the most skilled anesthesiologist. Additionally, an early postoperative laryngologic examination should be planned, so that any laryngeal lesions can be treated promptly. In certain patients, general anesthesia will be considered when multiple procedures are to be performed simultaneously (i.e., rhinoplasty and face-lift), and the time involved would not allow for comfortable local anesthesia. When possible, it is best for the performer to plan to undergo the procedures at different times, thus avoiding general anesthesia, though perhaps incurring some additional scheduling problems.

Effects on Voice and Instrumental Performance

Performers must also consider the specifics of the operative procedure when that procedure will alter the airway or vocal tract in any way. The most common cosmetic procedure performed in the United States is rhinoplasty, and this operation has probably led to more questions and anxiety among singers, other professional voice users, and instrumentalists than any other. Rhinoplasty can be performed safely and without adverse effect on performance in almost all cases. However, the operation must be meticulously planned, so that postoperative nasal airway obstruction and sinus obstruction can be avoided. In general, augmentation of the nose in order to attain a more pleasing appearance is safer than reduction. Excessive cartilage resection in the lower portion of the nose can lead to incompetence of the nasal valve, thus restricting nasal airflow on inspiration. Excessive removal of the dorsal hump and poorly controlled osteotomies of the nasal bones can lead to narrowing of the upper part of the nose, which may restrict both inspiration and expiration. Compromise of nasal breathing is extremely problematic for singers and wind players, especially those using double reed instruments such as oboe and bassoon. Singers ordinarily breath through their noses whenever possible, thus warming, filtering, and humidifying expired air. When forced to breath through their mouths, voice dysfunction often ensues. Double reed players practice circular breathing, a technique which allows them to play long, uninterrupted phrases without apparently taking a breath. Nasal obstruction is a severe problem for these performers and may disable them in some cases. Excessive and poorly controlled septal surgery can result in septal perforations, which can cause chronic irritation and obstruction that are very difficult to treat (3). Perforations may also cause whistling during respiration that is extremely problematic for vocalists and wind players. When evaluating a performing artist for rhinoplasty, these potential complications must be kept in mind and discussed. Compromises deviating from the ideal cosmetic result must be made in some cases in order to provide both an acceptable cosmetic result and a long and healthy performing career.

Most other considerations about specific surgical technique involve its influence on postoperative recovery. However, the surgeon must be very careful to explain all postoperative changes, even those considered minor in other patient populations. For example, tightness of the skin in the face and neck after such procedures as face-lift, chemical peel, and liposuction must be discussed in detail, so that a performer knows what to expect when he/she resumes performance. Such changes may be most unsettling to a singer, violinist or violist, or woodwind or brass player (if the embouchure is affected) and may lead to substantial deleterious changes in technique unless precautions are taken. Special care should also be taken when performing procedures in the neck or chin in violinists or violists. Procedures such as face-lifts or mentoplasty may cause alterations in the way the instrument is held, consequent neck and shoulder pain, and resultant performance impairment. In general, it is also not advisable to resect the skin irritation that occurs on the neck at the point of instrument contact. Neck surgery in singers and actors may also lead to slight changes in technique that can be quite problematic. A nurse in a cosmetic surgeon's office plays a critical role in assisting the patient through the postoperative recovery period. The nurse can be especially helpful if he/she has had experience in dealing with professional performers.

After all the decisions are made regarding the surgeon, anesthesia, and procedures to be performed, the performing artist must consider how surgery will affect the scheduling of future performances. Table 2 lists the most commonly performed cosmetic procedures and the average time of restrictions postoperatively. The first issue is whether hospitalization will be necessary. The great majority of cosmetic operations are performed on an outpatient basis, but a one- or two-day hospitalization is still occasionally required. The initial restrictions after surgery are no different from those in any other patient population. One to three days are usually necessary to recover general strength, appetite, and physical activity after any operation

TABLE 2. *Commonly performed cosmetic procedures*

Procedure	Anesthesia	Dressings[a]	Recovery time[a]	Voice restrictions[a]
Rhinoplasty	Local or general	1	1	2–6
Blepharoplasty	Local	None	1	2–7 days
Rhytidectomy	Local or general	1	2	2–6
Collagen implant	Local	None	2–3 hr	None
Dermabrasion	Local	1–2	1–2	1
Submental lipectomy	Local	1	1	1–2
Mentoplasty	Local	1	1	None
Chemabrasion	Local	1–2	1–2	1
Otoplasty	Local or general	1	1	None
Forehead lift	Local or general	1–2	2	None
Liposuction	General	1–2	1–2	1–2

[a]In weeks.

requiring general anesthesia or heavy sedation. The most critical risk in the immediate postoperative period is bleeding. Serious complications and poor cosmetic results can develop if bleeding occurs at this stage, especially in facial surgery (rhinoplasty, face-lift, and blepharoplasty). The patient is usually asked to avoid any strenuous activity, bending, or lifting for one week, and sometimes for as long as two weeks postoperatively, in order to reduce the risk of bleeding.

The appearance of the patient in the immediate postoperative period may also influence the ability to return to work. Ecchymosis, swelling, exposed suture lines, and open wounds are not uncommon in the weeks following facial plastic surgery and should be taken into account in making postoperative plans. Dressings may also be required for up to one week and create an appearance unsatisfactory for live performance, although radio or recording may be permitted in some cases. Again, a well-trained, experienced nurse working with the cosmetic surgeon will be invaluable in assisting the patient through these details of postoperative planning. The nurse should be familiar with what will be required in the day-to-day postoperative care and is usually best equipped to assist the patient in planning professional obligations.

Specific performance and practice restrictions must be discussed in detail preoperatively. The artist must be advised both of the routine restrictions that are necessary to ensure a smooth postoperative course and of any additional restrictions that would result from postoperative complications. If the patient undergoes general anesthesia, any resulting vocal cord swelling or irritation should be allowed to resolve before active voice use is resumed, for example. For most professionals, musical performance is an extremely energetic and physically demanding activity. Thus, it is usually restricted for one to two weeks postoperatively after such procedures as rhinoplasty, face-lift, and blepharoplasty, in which the strenuous activity could increase the risk of bleeding. This is also true of dancing. Total abstinence from music is rarely necessary, even in singers. Complete voice rest is not indicated. Speaking is not discouraged, and "light" singing can usually be attempted as early as 72 hr after most procedures.

The Rehabilitative Team

Following surgery, return to singing or instrumental playing should be done under the supervision of teachers, coaches, and knowledgeable physicians. This may also be advisable in dancers, even following facial cosmetic surgery; and it is essential for dancers following surgery elsewhere in the body.

For singers, once the surgery and the initial healing phase are complete, active vocalization may be resumed. Vocalists should work with their teacher or coach frequently in the postoperative period. This will assist resumption of voice use with optimal technique and assure that the vocalist does not rely on his/her own potentially altered perception of vocal quality. It is the experience of the authors that singers who feel that their voice has "changed" after facial surgery are usually noting a change primarily in their perception of their own voices rather than any objective alteration of its true quality. This is especially so after rhinoplasty. We have had similar experience with wind players. Observation and advice by the patient's vocal coach and laryngologist are critical in maintaining proper vocal technique in the face of both the perceived and any real changes in vocal quality. The patient should never be pressured by scheduling performances too soon after surgery. This requires detailed, realistic discussions between the patient, surgeon, and voice teacher and may also include the manager and laryngologist other than the cosmetic surgeon, so that appropriate postoperative planning is made.

A voice team consisting of a laryngologist, voice teacher, voice coach, speech pathologist, and nurse is a standard requirement now in the treatment of a singer or actor who requires care for an injured voice. The cosmetic surgeon must become part of this team or help assure that this support structure exists for the patient, especially if the patient is not involved with these professionals on a regular basis. This team can coordinate appointments and schedules, so that the patient has adequate vocal support both before and after surgery. Similar interdisciplinary support teams can be found through various arts-medicine centers and can be developed with interested specialists and performance teachers.

CONCLUSION

With proper knowledge on the part of both the surgeon and patient, safe and effective cosmetic surgery can be performed on the performer. If all the questions and concerns are dealt with preoperatively, safe and effective cosmetic surgery can be accomplished and can in fact be encouraged in this population. With the priorities of general health, performance health, and cosmesis kept in mind, the end result should be a happy, attractive, and content performing artist.

REFERENCES

1. Sataloff RT. Professional singers: the science and art of clinical care, *Am J Otolaryngol* 1981;2:251–266.
2. Gallivan GJ, Dawson JA, Robbins LD. Critical care perspective: videolaryngoscopy after endotracheal intubation: implications for voice. *J Voice* 1989;3:76–80.
3. Holt GR, Garner ET, McLarey D. Postoperative sequelae and complications of rhinoplasty. *Otolaryngol Clin North Am* 1987;20:853–876.

Professional Voice: The Science and Art of Clinical Care, Robert T. Sataloff.
Raven Press, Ltd., New York © 1991.

26

Introduction to Treating Voice Abuse

Robert T. Sataloff

*Department of Otolaryngology, Thomas Jefferson University,
Philadelphia, Pennsylvania*

ABNORMALITIES ASSOCIATED WITH VOICE DYSFUNCTION

As discussed in Chapter 5, a great number of physical and psychological problems may be responsible for voice dysfunction. These include derangements in virtually any body system. Most of the organic, psychological, and technical problems that may be related to voice complaints are discussed in detail in subsequent chapters. It is important for the physician to identify and sort out dysfunction in each category (organic, psychological, and technical); abnormalities in all three categories are frequently present simultaneously. For example, if the initial problem is an abnormality on the vocal fold, fear and psychological stress are normal reactions, and the performer frequently changes his technique (often subconsciously) in an effort to compensate for vocal impairment. Alternatively, technical dysfunction (such as hyperfunctional voice abuse or muscular tension dysphonia) may have been the initiating factor. This may have produced vocal fold pathology (such as nodules) and subsequent psychological reaction. In contrast, extreme, poorly compensated anxiety may have been the original culprit and caused laryngeal and technical problems. For each scenario, the treatment approach is different, and all appropriate members of the voice care team must understand the pathogenesis in order to design a treatment program that addresses not only immediate performance crises, but, moreover, long-term solutions to the principal problem. It is usually best to address all existing problems through a team approach. The team should include consultants in various specialties with special interest and knowledge regarding professional voice users. Because of the frequency and importance of voice abuse problems, the otolaryngologist must acquire extra training in technical aspects of voice production for speech and singing and should work particularly closely with a speech-language pathologist and singing voice specialist.

In this chapter, we shall briefly review selected conditions that are not covered in depth elsewhere in this book.

VOICE ABUSE

Vocal complaints are often due to abusive speaking or singing habits, especially hyperfunctional techniques. These problems and therapeutic approaches to them are discussed in detail later in this book. Laryngologists must be familiar with the specific techniques used by speech-language pathologists and singing teachers to diagnose and modify vocal abuses.

Physicians must be careful not to exceed the limits of their expertise or responsibility in applying this knowledge in the office. However, if the physician is trained in singing and notices a minor technical error such as isolated excess muscle tension in the tongue, this may be pointed out. Nevertheless, the singer should be referred back to his/her voice teacher or to a competent phoniatrist for management of these problems. Abdominal muscle problems should be noted and should also be referred back to the vocal teacher. Of course, any medical cause must be corrected.

Most of the important historical aspects and many treatment suggestions regarding voice abuse in speaking and singing are covered in Chapters 5, 28, and 31, although these later chapters concentrate on the responsibilities of the team members other than the laryngologists.

When voice abuse is due to extracurricular activities such as conducting, screaming during athletic events, or shouting at children, the physician should advise the patient about measures to protect the speaking voice and, consequently, the singing voice. However, if it is a matter of strain in the singing or speaking voice under ordinary circumstances, treatment should be deferred to a voice teacher or speech-language pathologist. In many instances, training the speaking voice will benefit the singer greatly, and physicians should not hesitate to recommend such training. Similarly, most singers benefit from formal training of the speaking voice. Surprisingly, most singers have not had such training, and they often speak much more abusively than they sing. The specially trained speech-language pathologist can be of great value to these singers, and usually only a few sessions are required.

SPEECH-LANGUAGE PATHOLOGY

An excellent speech-language pathologist is an invaluable asset in caring for professional voice users. However, laryngologists should recognize that, like physicians, speech-language pathologists have varied backgrounds and experience in treatment of voice disorders. In fact, most speech-language pathology programs teach relatively little about caring for professional speakers and nothing about professional singers. Moreover, there are few speech-language pathologists in the United States with vast experience in this specialized area. Speech-language pathologists often subspecialize. A person who expertly treats patients who have had strokes, stutter, have undergone laryngectomy, or have swallowing disorders will not necessarily know how to manage professional voice users optimally. The laryngologist must learn the strengths and weaknesses of the speech-language pathologist with whom he works. After identifying a speech-language pathologist who is interested in treating professional voice users, the laryngologist and speech-language pathologist should work together closely in developing the necessary expertise. Assistance may be found through laryngologists who treat large numbers of singers, or through educational programs such as the annual Voice Foundation's Symposium on Care of the Professional Voice. In general, therapy should be directed toward relaxation techniques, breath control, and abdominal support.

Speech-language pathology may be helpful, even when a singer has no obvious problem in his/her speaking voice but has significant technical problems singing. Once a person has been singing for several years, it is often very difficult for a singing teacher to convince him/her to correct certain technical errors. Singers are much less protective of their speaking voices. Therefore, a speech-language pathologist may be able rapidly to teach proper support, relaxation, and voice placement in speaking. Once mastered, these techniques can be carried over fairly easily into singing through cooperation between the speech-language pathologist and voice teacher. This "back door" approach has proved extremely useful in the author's experience. For the actor, it is often helpful to coordinate speech-language pathology sessions with acting lessons, especially with the training of the speaking voice provided by the actor's voice teacher or coach. Information provided by the speech-language pathologist, acting teacher, and singing teacher *should* be symbiotic and should not conflict. If there are major discrepancies, bad training from one of the team members should be suspected, and changes should be made.

SINGING TEACHERS

In selected cases, singing lessons may also be extremely helpful in non-singers with voice problems. The techniques used to develop abdomino-thoracic strength, breath control, laryngeal and neck muscle strength, and relaxation are very similar to those used in speech therapy. Singing lessons often expedite therapy and appear to improve the result in some patients.

Laryngologists who frequently care for singers are asked often to recommend a voice teacher. This may put the laryngologist in an uncomfortable position, particularly if the singer is already studying with someone in the community. Most physicians do not have sufficient expertise to criticize a voice teacher, and we must be extremely cautious about recommending that a singer change teachers. However, there is no certifying agency that standardizes or assures the quality of a singing teacher. Although one may be slightly more confident of a teacher associated with a major conservatory or music school or one who is a member of the National Association of Teachers of Singing, neither of these credentials assures excellence, and many expert teachers hold neither position. However, with experience, a laryngologist ordinarily develops valid impressions.

The physician should record the name of the voice teacher of each of his/her patients. He/she should observe whether the same kinds of voice abuse problems occur with disproportionate frequency in the pupils of any given teacher. He/she should also observe whose pupils usually have few technical problems and are only seen for organic disease such as colds. Technical problems can cause organic pathology such as nodules. So, any teacher who has a high incidence of nodules among his/her students should be viewed with careful concern. The physician should be particularly wary of teachers who are reluctant to allow their students to consult a doctor. The best voice teachers usually have a very low threshold for referral to a laryngologist if they hear anything disturbing in a student's voice. It is proper for the laryngologist to write a letter to the voice teacher (with the patient's permission) describing his findings and recommendations as he would to a physician, speech-language pathologist, or any other referring professional. A laryngologist seriously interested in caring for singers should take the trouble to talk with and meet local singing teachers. Taking a lesson or two with each teacher provides enormous insight as well. Taking voice lessons regularly is even more helpful. In practice, the laryngologist will usually identify a few teachers in whom he/she has particular confidence, especially for patients with voice disorders. He/she should not hesitate to refer singers to these colleagues, especially those singers who are not already in training.

Pop singers may be particularly resistant to the suggestion of voice lessons. Yet, they are in great need of training. It should be pointed out that a good voice teacher can teach a pop singer how to protect and expand his/her voice without changing its quality or making it sound "trained" or "operatic." The author finds it helpful to point out that singing, like other athletic activities, requires exercise, warm-up, and coaching for anyone planning to enter the "big league" and stay there. Just as no major league baseball pitcher would go without a pitching coach and warm-up time in the bull pen, no singer should try to build a career without a singing teacher and appropriate strength and agility exercises. This approach has proved palatable and effective.

Physicians should also be aware of the difference between a voice teacher and a voice coach. A voice teacher trains a singer in singing technique and is essential. A voice coach is responsible for teaching songs, language, diction, style, operatic roles, etc., but is not responsible for exercises and basic technical development of the voice.

More specific details of evaluation and treatment are included in Chapters 28 and 31.

VOICE MAINTENANCE

Prevention of vocal dysfunction should be the goal of all professionals involved in the care of vocalists. Good vocal health habits should be encouraged in childhood. Screaming, particularly outdoors during athletic events, should be discouraged. Promising young singers who join choirs should be educated to compensate for the Lombard effect. The youngster interested in singing or acting should receive enough training to avoid voice abuse and should receive enthusiastic support for singing works suitable for his age and voice. Singing advanced pieces and playing Metropolitan Opera stars should be actively discouraged. Training should be continued during or after puberty, and the voice should be allowed to develop naturally without pressure to perform operatic roles prematurely. Excellent regular training and practice are essential, and avoidance of irritants, particularly smoke, should be stressed early. Educating the singer with regard to hormonal and anatomic alterations that may influence the voice allows him/her to recognize and analyze vocal dysfunction, compensating for it intelligently when it occurs. Cooperation among the laryngologist, speech-language pathologist, acting teacher, and singing teacher provides an optimal environment for cultivation and protection of the vocal artist.

Professional Voice: The Science and Art of Clinical Care, Robert T. Sataloff. Raven Press, Ltd., New York © 1991.

27

Speech Pathology and the Professional Voice User

An Overview

Carol N. Wilder

Teachers College, Columbia University, New York, New York

The practice of speech pathology means the application of principles, methods, and procedures for measurement, testing, identification, prediction, counseling, or instruction related to development and disorders of speech, voice, and language. It may be used for identifying, preventing, managing, habilitating or rehabilitating, ameliorating, or modifying such disorders in individuals or groups of individuals (1). Although speech-language pathologists work with individuals with voice disorders, we do not diagnose or treat laryngeal disease or other physiological disorders, as does the laryngologist. Rather, speech-language pathologists are concerned with understanding, analyzing, and modifying vocal function, that is, with changing vocal behaviors. If the voice is within normal limits perceptually, and if it is being produced in a reasonably efficient, nonabusive manner, the speech-language pathologist does *not* seek to provide the special training that will develop the range, power, control, stamina, and esthetic quality of voice that are required for artistic expression, as does the singing or acting teacher. We are concerned primarily with the voice that presents a current problem or signs of a potential problem in one or more physical, perceptual, or behavioral dimensions. What happens when such a problem occurs in a professional voice user?

For the purposes of this chapter, the term professional voice user will be arbitrarily limited to individuals who use the voice extensively for some form of artistic expression, in other words, to performers. The definition includes professional singers and actors (e.g., those who earn their living by performing), those seeking to become professional singers or actors, and those for whom skilled amateur performance is a major, personally important activity. Excluded for the purposes of this chapter are those individuals who indeed rely heavily on their speaking voices in their professional activities, but who do not use their voices for artistic purposes (e.g., the classroom teacher, the trial lawyer, the clergyman, etc.).

Having said what speech pathologists do *not* do, let me give the briefest possible summary of what we *do* do. First, we analyze, systematically and sensitively the presenting vocal behaviors, both perceptually and with such objective measures as are clinically appropriate. Second, we analyze those vocational, educational, and psychosocial factors that may interact with vocal behaviors to precipitate, maintain, or exacerbate the voice problem. Finally, we design and implement an individualized program for modifying vocal behaviors and, insofar as is possible, any contributing factors. I stress the terms systematically and sensitively, because both need to be equally emphasized when we work with voice disorders. This is both a science and an art.

With this summary in mind, let us consider two questions: (a) When compared with voice disorders in a nonperformer, will the speech-language pathologist find that there is anything significantly different about evaluating and remediating voice problems in the performer? (b) Is any special knowledge needed in order to do so? The answer to both these questions is affirmative, because of the complexity of vocational, environmental, and psychosocial factors, which is unique to this population. These factors are so complex and interactive and beyond the scope of any single chapter, or even book. Nevertheless, I should like to highlight just a few of them that can be expected to have an impact on the activities of the speech-language pathologist.

The obvious factor that is special to this population is the way the voice is used. On the one hand, the range of vocal activities extends beyond the functional parameters we are used to dealing with in the nonprofessional voice patient, with respect to such things as pitch range, loudness extreme, control, and endurance. On the other hand, voice problems in the professional may be signaled by decrements in quality, sensation, or control, which are much more subtle than those we are used to working with. We cannot just sit back and be dazzled by the vocal displays in the cadenza or soliloquy, or be puzzled by the performer's intense concern about what might seem (in the nonprofessional) like a clinically insignificant change in voice control. It is our task to attempt to understand the physical processes that underlie both and to determine whether they relate to the presenting disorder. We must develop reasonable hypotheses about what is going on with respect to chest wall and laryngeal and supralaryngeal behaviors as these relate to lung volumes, pressure differentials, and the like, keeping firmly in mind the relationship of these hypotheses to our clinical purposes. Having made the hypotheses, we must test them. For these reasons, speech-language pathologists who want to work with the voice problems of the performer will find it useful to expand their knowledge of voice and speech science beyond the level that suffices for work with the nonperformer and to make a determined effort to keep abreast of the rapidly accumulating research on voice production.

To achieve a better understanding of the demands on the vocal mechanism of the performer, it is also useful to know something about music, if you are working with singers, or about the theater, if you are working with actors. One should develop an appreciation of the styles and vocal characteristics called for by different schools of performance or vocal training, or by specific composers and dramatists, because they may each call for very different kinds of vocal behaviors. Not only does this help us better understand the physical demands that may have contributed to the disorder, but it also helps us appreciate what kinds of vocal activities comprise the patient's hoped-for goals of therapy, to determine stepwise approximations toward the goals, and better to estimate whether these hoped-for goals are realistic.

The goals of therapy, by the way, are another feature that distinguishes our work with the performer from our work with the nonperformer. With performers, there are no degrees of freedom with respect to the desired outcome, whereas, with our other voice patients, there is much more latitude in the range of vocal behaviors that constitute an acceptable outcome.

For better understanding and for more effective communication with both the patient and the voice teacher or coach (with whom we want to cooperate closely), speech-language pathologists should also try to become familiar with some of the technical rudiments of these disciplines and with their terms of imagery and their technical vocabulary. For example, if a singer mentions problems with *tessitura* or *leggiero* passages, or with vibrato, it is helpful if the speech-language pathologist can appreciate the physical implications of these terms, which are not a part of our general professional lexicon. If an actor complains about being upstaged, the speech-language pathologist should be aware that the term is not just a cliché, but that it describes a specific physical situation that could be a potential contributor to vocal stress.

Speech-language pathologists are always concerned about environmental contributors to voice disorders. However, there are a number of special environmental factors in the performer's world with which many speech-language pathologists (or any other nonperformers, for that matter) may be unfamiliar. In order to get a better appreciation about conditions that may affect vocal behaviors, it is a good idea for the speech-language pathologist to visit a variety of performance environments (not just theaters and concert halls, but studios, rehearsal halls, and practice rooms) to experience first-hand the dust, fumes, temperature differentials, and ambient noise levels, as well as the general "feel" of the acoustic environment. The conditions are often far from ideal from the standpoint of what is good for the voice. See if you can arrange to visit sometime when you can have the place to yourself as well. Go ahead and sing a song or recite a speech; the insights you get from those few moments may be better than you get from hours of watching someone else do it.

When trying to delineate all those factors that may contribute to the voice problem, such things as stage direction, set design, and costume design should also be considered. Even an otherwise excellent vocal technique may be put under stress when the performer is in a situation that is physically awkward, uncomfortable, or even precarious. This is not at all uncommon. When some directors or designers are in hot pursuit of a particular artistic vision, concern about vocal stress is not exactly at the top of their priority list. A few years ago, I saw a Royal Shakespeare Company production in which a leading actor was required to deliver a long speech while hanging by his knees, upside down, from the top of a tall ladder. Fortunately, both his knees and his aplomb were equal to the task; but, not surprisingly, one heard signs of vocal tension that were never apparent when he was right-side up. In a memory that remains vivid after many years, I recall the awkwardness and discomfort I felt singing while wearing a costume that included a heavy pointed hat three feet long. It was the designer's idea of a medieval effect. I remember complaining that I had to tighten all the muscles of my neck in order to balance it so as to keep it from falling off. Looking back on it from my present perspective as a speech-language pathologist, it seems reasonable to assume that this feeling of tension reflected a degree of strap muscle tension that might well have contributed to vocal stress.

The voice may also be stressed if the performer gets so "carried away" by the emotional sweep of the performance that vocal techniques go by the boards, as it were. Muscles tighten; postures change subtly. These behaviors may not occur in any other vocal situation, making it useful for the speech-language pathologist to observe the patient in an actual performance situation whenever possible.

The essential point is that the performance environment is liberally endowed with "vocal ill-health potential." Some potential stressors are less obvious than others; some the performer may not be aware of and hence may not volunteer when you are taking a case history. If the speech-language pathologist is to understand what areas need to be explored as potential contributing factors to the voice disorder, he/she must become familiar with the full range of vocal stressors that may be found in the performance environment.

Now, back to that pointed hat. It might be asked why I simply did not refuse to wear it. It is in the answer to that question that the speech-language pathologist begins to encounter the unique psychosocial pressures experienced by the vocal professional, pressures that, indeed, make working with the professional different from working with other voice patients, pressures that may contribute to the development and maintenance of a voice disorder, pressures that can negatively influence the course of therapy if they are not taken into account by the speech-language pathologist.

A major and continuing source of pressure is the intense competition, the extent of which is sometimes difficult to appreciate unless you have experienced it. I did not refuse to wear the hat, because I was just beginning to develop as a performer, and I did not want to make waves. I knew full well that there were many competent replacements waiting in the wings who would have been only too happy to have a chance to sing the role—hat and all. Star level performers may be able to insist on certain performance conditions, but the great majority of performers cannot afford this luxury. Moreover, there is ample evidence in revealing remarks, publicized feuds, and sensitivity over prerogatives that even superstars are not immune to the pressure of competition. Having got to the top, there is pressure to stay there. The reality of this pressure must be acknowledged by the speech-language pathologist. There are times when the performer simply cannot follow your suggestions; cannot cancel a performance, audition, or competition; or cannot follow a therapeutic regimen that would change performance frequency, conditions, or style. It is up to us to understand and to adapt our therapeutic programs to this reality.

Another source of pressure is that the professional voice user is constantly on the line, with his/her performance judged not only by the audience, but by critics, conductors, managers, directors, producers, agents, teachers, and coaches. Most of us are not subject to such constant external scrutiny of our endeavors. The professional voice user lives with the realization that, if he/she makes even a minor goof during a performance, it will very likely be noticed, perhaps even pounced on. As if this were not a sufficient source of pressure, the standards of judgment to which the voice professional is held are frequently subjective, variable, and situation-bound. For example, two critics turn in such disparate reviews that you wonder if they went to the same concert, or contest judges disagree on a winner. After an audition, the performer may never find out *why* he/she did not get the contract or the part. Yet all these subjective, variable, and situation-bound judgments play major roles in determining the performer's career opportunities. No wonder there is performance anxiety; no wonder there are displays of insecurity or bravado. Clearly, this constellation of psychosocial pressures is also shared by instrumental musicians. However, the effect on vocal professionals may be even more profound because, for them, the instrument itself, the vocal mechanism, is known to be sensitive not only to stress-related muscle tension, but also to stress-related responses of the autonomic nervous system.

If there are all these pressures, if the rules of the game are so difficult, why is there so much competition? Why are there so many people out there doing everything they can to become professional users of the voice? What in the world possesses them? I am not sure there is any better answer to these questions than to say that they do, in fact, seem to be possessed (in some cases almost obsessed) by some sort of drive toward artistic vocal expression; and that brings me to the final area I should like to highlight as one that distinguishes our practice with this population.

If one is possessed by a drive toward artistic vocal expression, how devastating it is to develop any sort of a problem in the vocal mechanism, which is the foundation of one's endeavors. How frustrating it is if the problem develops at a pivotal or critical point in career development. How threatening for the established performer whose financial well-being rests on the condition of his/her vocal mechanism. As a consequence, speech-language pathologists who regularly work with professional voice users find that the response to the voice disorder is usually different from what we find with other types of voice patients—different not only in degree, but in kind. This response is a major consideration that must be factored into the management program. An experienced speech-language pathologist who has only relatively recently begun to work with the professional voice said to me that he had not entirely anticipated the intensity of the emotional reactions he has encountered with his professional voice patients. He described how one young woman's responses had ranged from shock at learning that she had a mass lesion of the vocal folds, to hope that it might be resolved through therapy, to tearful despair when she learned that, although the lesion was much smaller, it had not completely disappeared. This speech-language pathologist said that he had found the counseling of professional voice users to be a very heavy issue. Indeed, the ongoing education and counseling that are a part of our program with any voice patient must be handled with special thoroughness and exquisite sensitivity in the professional voice user.

These general highlights are intended for speech-language pathologists who have not yet had much clinical contact with professional voice users. Details of practice are discussed in another chapter. An active effort to become further acquainted with these special vocational, environmental, and psychosocial factors will help you to incorporate them—systematically and sensitively—into your evaluation and therapeutic procedures. Work with professional voice users is stimulating and enjoyable. Moreover, speech-language pathologists are not alone in this need to explore areas that were not included in their professional training curriculum. No single discipline adequately addresses in its present training program the totality of skills needed in the care of the professional voice. Therefore, all of us with a special interest in this area can profit from learning from each other in a spirit that will maximize cooperative efforts and optimize patient care.

REFERENCE

1. California Speech Pathologists and Audiologists Licensure Act, Chapter 5.3, Division 2 of the Business and Professions Code, as cited in Flower R. *Delivery of speech-language pathology and audiology services.* Baltimore: Williams & Wilkins, 1984;6.

Professional Voice: The Science and Art of Clinical Care, Robert T. Sataloff. Raven Press, Ltd., New York © 1991.

28

Voice Therapy

Kathe S. Darby and Rhonda K. Rulnick

American Institute for Voice and Ear Research, Philadelphia, Pennsylvania

Professional voice users who need voice therapy require special diagnostic and intervention strategies. Each of these individuals has a vested interest in preserving and protecting the voice. Singers and actors, in particular, differ from the general voice population because of the unusual demands placed on their voices. In many instances, therapy is indicated for voices that might generally be regarded as "normal." However, since their voice requirements are extraordinary, speech-language pathologists must learn to recognize and help restore optimal, not merely normal, voice. The voice therapist may acquire the necessary skills by learning to use instrumentation in therapy by studying singing, acting, and public speaking; by observing as many singing and acting teachers as possible to improve ear training; and through experience working with a voice care team.

In this chapter, we often refer to the singer, because the singer's need for flawless vocal technique is paramount. However, the vocal mechanism of the nonsinger should receive the same specialized care and training. Our approach to evaluating and treating singers is applicable to all professional voice users.

Classically trained singers are aware of the deleterious consequences of poor singing technique on the delicate tissues of the vocal folds. Even though they are usually conscientious in caring for their voices during singing, they often give little thought to how they use the same anatomy in speech. Appropriate speaking technique is just as important for singers as for other professional voice users. They have much to gain from voice therapy. The elimination of vocal abuse during speaking can have a dramatic and positive effect on the singing voice. The process of acquiring good speaking technique often facilitates singing training as well.

Many voice professionals have never received formal speech training. Hence, it is not surprising when vocal dysfunction occurs. This chapter outlines our approach to preventing voice problems and to treating injured voices. The approach is primarily behavioral, even though voice problems are not solely mechanical in nature. Voices have people attached to them; therefore, a myriad of personalities, stresses, and other mitigating circumstances can drastically affect one's voice, the therapy program, and the patient's ability to benefit from our approach. When the need arises, we solicit the assistance of other professionals (team members), so that each patient may be treated holistically.

The primary interdisciplinary team consists of the laryngologist, whose responsibility is diagnosing and restoring the structure of the larynx through medical/surgical means; the speech-language pathologist (voice therapist), whose responsibility is evaluating and treating specific abusing/misusing behaviors of the speaking voice; and the singing specialist/vocal teacher, whose province is singing technique and voice production during singing. Additional adjunct team members include the voice researcher or voice scientist, singing coach (involved primarily with repertoire and style), the speech/drama coach, psychologist, hypnotherapist, and others such as physicians in different specialties (especially pulmonology and neurology). It is important for all team members to understand the principles and approaches employed in voice therapy and for the voice therapist to understand the expertise of each of the other members of the team.

EVALUATION

When assessing singers and other voice professionals, our expectations of normal must be heightened, and stricter criteria must be used. State-of-the-art equipment and advanced techniques in voice analysis are routinely incorporated into the voice evaluation. They provide extremely valuable baseline information and documentation that help quantify and qualify the patient's voice problem. These instruments are important, but clearly our best clinical tools remain our own eyes and ears. With a few exceptions, this is especially true in recognizing degrees of high-level vocal function. Instrumentation is better at distinguishing abnormal from normal than at identifying differences between excellent and great voices.

The voice evaluation is divided into four parts: case history, examination, assessment, and recommendations. This chapter includes a brief overview of our evaluation procedures.

Case History

A careful case history involves a description of the circumstances leading to the development and maintenance of the present vocal problem. In a medical setting, where the patient is seen by all team members during the initial visit, the laryngologist and speech-language pathologist cooperate in gathering the background information. The information required is discussed in

Chapter 5. Additional history obtained by the speech-language pathologist is specific in exploring how vocal abuses and misuses affect the patient's voice on a daily basis. We focus particularly on the nature of the disorder, activities in daily professional or social life that may cause or aggravate the problem, voice patterns of other family members that may reinforce undesirable vocal behavior, daily vocal usage patterns, and details of previous speech therapy. In patients who have had previous voice therapy, asking them to demonstrate the techniques and exercises used may provide valuable insight. A complete inventory is made of voice abuse factors that may have contributed to the present voice problems, with special attention to smoking, passive smoking, caffeine consumption, alcohol consumption, poor rest/sleep patterns, environmental factors (dryness, chemicals), excessive talking, yelling, loud talking, throat clearing, coughing, whispering, poor hydration, and stress/tension.

Singers are asked additional questions regarding the type of music they sing (rock, popular, classical, show/night club, gospel, jazz/blues), the extent of their training, their present singing difficulties, and their professional career goals. This case history information is obtained in cooperation with the singing specialist. All singers also complete a written questionnaire (Appendix II).

The speech-language pathologist must do more than merely ask the usual questions and the special questions relevant to performers. The therapist must pay attention not merely to the content of the history, but also to the voice used by the patient in reporting it. In addition, selected questions should be explored in greater detail, looking for discrepancies between the history given to the otolaryngologist and that given to the speech-language pathologist. Occasionally, patients will reveal information to one team member that they are reluctant to reveal to another. Discrepancies in answers to questions from one team member to another are often closely related to the patient's underlying problem and deserve delicate but diligent scrutiny.

Examination

Objective Voice Measures

Data collection and the subsequent analysis furnish a detailed objective description of the voice. An audio recording is obtained using a high-quality reel-to-reel tape recorder. The protocol for the objective voice tasks is provided in Appendix IV, and details of the voice laboratory and therapeutic uses of laboratory equipment are discussed in other chapters. Briefly, a sample of sustained spoken and sung vowels, conversational speech, and reading is analyzed. The acoustic voicing parameters that are measured include speaking fundamental frequency (for conversation and reading), jitter, shimmer, harmonics/noise ratio, percent voicing (for a reading sample), physiological and musical frequency range, and maximum phonation or expiration time for /a/, /s/, and /z/. Respiration is measured with pulmonary function testing (PFT). Pulmonary function testing of all voice patients has proved beneficial in identifying singing-related respiratory dysfunction (i.e., exercise-induced asthma). Mean airflow rate (MFR) is an estimation of glottal efficiency and is calculated as milliliters of air over the time it took for that air to be expelled. Measures are compared with normative data, and judgments regarding the patient's phonatory ability are made. Measures are repeated for follow-up.

Subjective Evaluation

Respiration

Many vocal problems are the result of improper breathing technique. When evaluating respiration, the volume of air is important, but more critical is the manner in which the patient takes in the air (inhalation) and how the air is used to produce the voice (exhalation). Abdominal/diaphragmatic breath control and support are desirable and are the most efficient manner of providing the power source for the voice. The patient's respiration is observed in conversational speech and in reading. The following observations are made:

1. The pattern of breath support:
   [ ] Abdominal/diaphragmatic
   [ ] Upper thoracic
   [ ] Clavicular
   [ ] Combined or mixed (thoracic and abdominal)
2. Posture:
   [ ] Head/neck malalignment
   [ ] Improper sitting posture
   [ ] Improper standing posture
3. Phrasing:
   [ ] Too many words per breath
   [ ] Too few words per breath
   [ ] Failure to take appropriate pauses
   [ ] Excessive pauses
4. Respiration:
   [ ] Audible inspiration
   [ ] Forced exhalation
   [ ] Labored breathing

Phonation

Phonation refers to the production of sound at the level of the vocal folds. Judgments about the voice quality (hoarseness, breathiness), loudness (appropriate, too loud, too soft), and pitch are made during conversational speech and reading. The following characteristics are particularly important:

[   ] Hoarseness
[   ] Breathiness
[   ] Glottal fry
[   ] Diplophonia
[   ] Phonation breaks
[   ] Harsh glottal attacks

Harsh glottal attacks are counted during a standard reading passage and a percentage is calculated.

Measures of respiratory and phonatory efficiency are obtained using measurements of maximum exhalation or phonation for the following sounds:

/a/ _____   /i/ _____   /u/ _____   /s/ _____   /z/ _____

An s/z ratio is obtained, which provides a quick comparison of the patient's ability to control airflow for these voiceless and voiced speech sounds. While an s/z ratio is not necessarily a reliable assessment of phonatory ability or an indicator of laryngeal pathology, it provides useful information about the patient's ability to control exhalation in the presence or absence of voicing, that is, it is an indicator of *laryngeal efficiency*.

General observations are made regarding the patient's habitual speaking pitch. It is important to note whether the patient speaks too high (falsetto) or too low (glottal fry). The concept of "optimal pitch" is controversial, and "optimal" may not exist. More accurately, there is an optimal manner of vocal fold function that yields an appropriate pitch level. Generally, an inappropriate pitch level can be the effect of a mass lesion, which may lower the pitch or symptomatic of muscular tension, which may raise the pitch. Muscular tension dysphonia may also be present in association with a low-pitched voice, especially in a patient who forces his/her voice down near the lower end of the physiological frequency range.

Resonance

Resonance refers to the concentration of specific acoustic frequencies or harmonics within the cavities of the vocal tract (hypopharynx, pharynx, oral, nasal), as described in Chapter 4. Clinically, certain resonant patterns have been associated with specific anatomic areas. The terminology is useful, even if not entirely accurate. Excessive pharyngeal or "throaty" resonance is a common characteristic and can be associated with physical discomfort in speaking. Oral resonance is desirable and is affected by the size and shape of the oral cavity. Many patients exhibit mandibular restriction while speaking, which diminishes the effectiveness of the oral cavity as a resonator. The presence of hyper- or hyponasal speech is carefully assessed to rule out velopharyngeal incompetence. Functional or regional resonance deviations can be assessed using selected reading passages.

Tongue retraction occurs when the anterior portion of the tongue is pulled back from the lower incisors. The result is tongue muscle tension and a change in vocal tract shape that affects the resonance of the voice. Tongue position is observed during sustained production of /a/. Posterior tongue tension often cannot be directly observed without the use of objective instrumentation and may be present even if the anterior portion of the tongue is relaxed. Posterior tongue tension is often responsible for a pharyngeal resonance quality.

Articulation

A judgment is made regarding the patient's general ability to produce the sounds of the English language precisely. If English is not the patient's native language, comparisons are made between the patient's production in English and in his/her native language. The ability of the articulators (tongue, lips, teeth, jaw, and velum) to function in a smooth and connected manner is determined. Although articulation disorders are rare in this population, occasionally, a "lisp" has been identified. Particular attention is paid to any "hyperfunctional" articulation or tension sites in the articulators themselves. While tongue tension is common, it is addressed as a resonance imbalance and not an articulation problem.

Prosody

The prosodic features of speech (rhythm, fluency, timing, rate, pauses, and intonation or inflection patterns) are assessed very generally. These features often subtly affect the voice. The patient who demonstrates excessive laryngeal and strap muscle tension will often demonstrate faulty flow and blending of words in connected speech. A voice/speech pattern that lacks the normal prosodic features (stress, pitch variation, intonation, and loudness variation) may be perceived as monotonous. Further, a voice that lacks vocal variety may indicate that a patient is not gaining maximum flexibility from the voice, either physically or artistically.

Sites of Muscular Tension

Poor respiratory control and support can lead to muscle tension in specific muscle groups. While this tension is observed in association with poor breath control, it can be created for a variety of reasons. We observe these tension sites as we examine the levels of speech production, and have found a checklist helpful.

[   ] Tongue
[   ] Laryngeal rise or fall
[   ] Jaw or masseter muscle
[   ] Anterior or posterior neck
[   ] Shoulders
[   ] Upper chest wall cavity

Oral/Facial

A screening of the oral/facial mechanism should be included to rule out any abnormalities in the structure, symmetry, strength, range of motion or coordination that might impact on normal vocal function. This includes neurological problems.

Singing

The speech-language pathologist (unless specifically trained) is not qualified to evaluate the singer's technique in detail. However, observations are made that are extremely useful in determining the constancy of technique from one modality (singing) to another (speech). A checklist for observing the singer's technical misuses includes:

[   ] Sites of tension:
       face, neck, tongue, shoulders, forehead
[   ] Tongue retraction
[   ] Tone focus
[   ] Vocal placement
[   ] Poor breath support
[   ] Hoarseness following singing
[   ] Difficulties through the passaggio
[   ] Loss of upper/lower range

Trial Therapy

Various facilitating techniques are introduced on a trial basis during the evaluation. This gives the examiner an opportunity to observe how these changes affect vocal quality and whether the patient can feel and hear the difference in vocal production. Further, it enables the examiner to make inferences about the patient's learning ability and prognosis for remediation through therapy.

Assessment/Impressions

The voice evaluation, in addition to establishing baseline measures, affords the speech-language pathologist the opportunity to observe the patient and to formulate an impression of the factors that may have contributed to the voice problem. The speech-language pathologist assesses which modifications resulted in an immediate change in vocal quality or ease of production, and a therapy starting point is established.

The interpretation of what was observed about the patient's vocal production is discussed. Providing a clear picture of which factors have been most contributory to the voice problem is essential. The goals of therapy are enumerated, along with the procedures and their rationales.

There is no clear delineation between where evaluation ends and therapy begins. Evaluation occurs throughout the therapy process as the speech-language pathologist continually monitors the efficacy of treatment.

Recommendations

At the conclusion of the evaluation, recommendations are made regarding whether voice therapy is indicated, and goals are defined. Often, other referrals are made, such as specialized singing instruction. Occasionally, other testing is needed (i.e., articulation or motor speech function). The recommendations, including the anticipated duration of treatment (in weeks or months), approximate number of sessions, and how often the sessions are to be scheduled (weekly, biweekly, monthly), are reviewed. The patient is informed of the need for home practice and active participation, so that the goals can be met.

THERAPY

Voice therapy is designed to help the patient *feel* better and *sound* better. Most patients come to therapy with somatic complaints such as pain, tension, and vocal fatigue. Therefore, it is important that they begin to find relief quickly. This helps to elicit their cooperation and motivation early in the training process.

Initially, therapy focuses on speaking technique, with little regard to the quality of the tone that is produced. This is a difficult concept for many patients. Instead, singers and nonsingers are accustomed to concentrating on how they *sound* and pay little attention to how it *feels* to produce voice. Facilitating good vocal production can be achieved through "learning to speak by feel." Singers are often knowledgeable about their singing technique and are eager to correct any technical misuses in speech. They generally progress quickly and show rapid improvement in therapy because of their vocal sophistication and strong motivation.

While the major goal of voice therapy is to enhance vocal efficiency, the patient may need to make minor life-style changes to achieve this objective. High-achieving competitive professional voice users are especially vulnerable to speaking voice difficulties. We encourage them to look realistically at how their present life-style (touring, interviews, multiple performances per week) affects their general and vocal health.

The process of making changes begins with *identifying* the factors that have created the voice problem. The speech-language pathologist through history taking and observation has identified the vocal behaviors and abuses that contributed to the problem. The physician has identified contributory medical factors. Now it is the patient's responsibility to identify these factors by exploring them kinesthetically, tactilely, auditorily, and visually. Success in changing technical misuses occurs when the *patient* recognizes these problems. Many of our nonsingers have difficulty perceiving or understanding the concept of inappropriate tone focus. Exploration of the resonators using specific exercises is necessary so they can discern what they are doing to produce a particular resonance quality. Singers are more used to these concepts and catch on quickly. When they do not, problems with singing training or technique are suspect.

Therapy is also an *educational* process. When patients are provided with rationales and explanations, change occurs more readily. Often patients have an opinion regarding what caused their problem, but very few know "how" or "why." Even many experienced professional voice users have misconceptions about the size and location of the larynx and about the position of the vocal folds with the larynx. Therefore, a basic discussion of the anatomy and physiology of the voice and a description of speech production are provided.

The vocal hygiene discussion is usually the basis for much of the educational process. Many of our singers know that throat clearing and whispering are "bad for the voice," but many do not know why. It is our belief that naïveté contributes to many vocal problems.

The singer's own account of his/her medical diagnosis can be very revealing and often provides the therapist a point of reference with which to begin the reeducation. Following the doctor's examination, the patient is asked to explain what the doctor said. Any misconceptions or confusions are immediately clarified. Commitment to voice therapy is often facilitated when the patient is provided with clear, accurate information and effective approaches to vocal change.

Voice *modification* requires close attention to the interaction of each of the physiologic levels of speech production (respiration, phonation, resonation, articulation) and the prosodic features of speech. Interaction and integration of these systems create efficient use of the voice. The strength of the speech-language pathologist is in his/her ability to break down tasks of speaking into their component parts and develop hierarchies of learning that facilitate rapid behavioral changes using specific, carefully structured exercises and tasks. A sample outline of how to approach daily vocal exercises is provided (Appendix V). Additions and deletions to this outline are supplied as needed.

Retraining speaking technique for classically trained singers is accomplished in conjunction with their singing training. Singing teachers are traditionally skilled in their use of imagery, but their vocabulary is unfamiliar to many speech-language pathologists. For the voice therapist, developing a singer's vocabulary is helpful in working with singers. We hear phrases like brighter, depth, cover, and richness (to name just a few). Incorporating such terminology in voice therapy has been beneficial.

Carryover and stabilization of appropriate speaking technique are of premier importance. If we expect the speaking technique to be maintained long-term, the patient must be provided with specific training exercises in a variety of settings. Once the patient has developed consistent use of the therapy techniques in structured settings, strategies are needed to ensure long-term continuation of newly acquired technique. Since the specialized singing instruction is such an integral part of our approach, we have developed "bridging" techniques, which provide the patients with structured exercises in applying what they have learned with their singing voice to their speech. This bridging of one modality to another requires a specific plan. Stressing the unity of technique in speech and singing is one of several ways of maintaining good vocal habits over time, especially since many singers continue singing lessons throughout their lifetimes. The singing voice specialist and the speech-language pathologist cooperate closely to achieve this goal.

ESTABLISHING GOOD VOCAL HYGIENE

Voice professionals, singers, and nonsingers come to the speech-language pathologist with varying degrees of knowledge about which factors are responsible for their current problems. Positive alternatives to their vocally abusive behaviors are developed through a vocal hygiene program. Management of certain common problematic situations is stressed.

Throat Clearing

In some cases, excessive mucus is a problem (associated with gastric reflux; postnasal drip, and allergies). More often, patients clear their throats out of habit rather than need. This behavior, because it is traumatic to the vocal folds, should be eliminated. The following alternatives are useful:

1. Dry swallow. Swallowing closes the vocal folds and can help rid them of mucus. The action of swallowing can also relax the larynx (in the postadduction phase), helping to alleviate the perceived need to clear the throat.
2. Take small sips of water.
3. Use a "silent cough." This is achieved by using abdominal support to push air through the glottis as if producing an /h/ sound. The strong airflow blows mucus off the vocal folds.
4. Pant lightly, then swallow.
5. Hum lightly.
6. Laugh gently or "giggle" lightly, then swallow.
7. Talk *through* the mucus. The natural vibration of the vocal folds may rid them of any secretions.
8. For singers, vocalize lightly on five-note scales in a comfortable range on /a/, or slide up an octave softly on /a/, and crescendo (get louder).

Whispering

Many patients, especially singers, know that whispering should be avoided. During whispering, in many instances, the anterior two-thirds of the vocal folds approximate. Forced or "loud" whispering appears most harmful. The adverse effects of whispering have not been fully documented, but there is ample clinical experience to support the proscription. Although extremely soft whispering without vocal contact may be safe, few patients maintain this and resort to using a forced whisper so they can be heard. Therefore, patients are cautioned that all whispering should be avoided. Actors may need to make use of this type of vocal production in their work. In this case, specialized training is indicated.

Grunting/Noisy Vocalization

Grunting when lifting or exercising creates forceful, traumatic adduction of the vocal folds. Instead:

1. Exhale slowly on the exertion phase of any exercise (preferred method), or
2. Adduct the vocal folds gently, prior to initiating each exercise event (such as a sit-up or weight lift).

Yelling/Screaming or Loud Talking

Many performers and singers have gregarious, outgoing personalities. They commonly yell or scream as an expression of anger, frustration, elation, or joy. We advise them to "save it for the performance" and instead:

1. Use a whistle or bell.
2. Educate friends and family members about the harmful effects of yelling or screaming.
3. Engage the help of others for monitoring.
4. Use facial and other physical gestures to express emotions.
5. Use hissing as another nonvoiced outlet to express anger or frustration.
6. Know the limits of their vocal abilities. Be aware of how much loud talking can be tolerated before fatigue is experienced.
7. Cultivate the dramatic power of soft, articulated speech, which is often more effective than yelling.

Noisy Environments

Certain environments are inherently noisy (cars, airplanes, restaurants, social gatherings, night clubs). Special care needs to be taken not to speak over the noise level for long periods of time. Alternatives include:

1. Facing the listener.
2. Gently overarticulating rather than increasing loudness.
3. Slowing the speaking rate to avoid the need for repetition.
4. Speaking at a normal pitch. There is a tendency to raise pitch and loudness in background noise. A normal or slightly lower pitch often cuts through the ambient noise, naturally decreasing the need to speak more loudly. Training in the use of this technique is needed.

Excessive Talking

Gregarious patients find this a difficult habit to break. Modification can be facilitated using the following:

1. Schedule vocal "naps." Observe 20 min of silence, two to three times/day. Wear an alarm watch as a reminder to schedule a vocal nap.
2. Inexpensive digital watches are available with "time elapsed" functions that beep every 10 min or every hour. This signal can be used early in retraining as a reminder to check vocal behavior.

3. Limit the amount of time on the telephone.
4. Limit interrupting others in conversation. Be a good listener.

Caffeine Consumption

Excessive caffeine intake has a diuretic effect and depletes the vocal fold tissue of needed hydration. The patient should:

1. Avoid caffeinated beverages (coffee, soda, tea) especially before heavy voice use, dress rehearsals, performances, lectures, trials, sermons, or teaching.
2. Switch to decaffeinated beverages (water is a good substitute).
3. Drink a glass of water for every cup of coffee or soda, and follow the recommendations below for "systemic dryness."

Systemic Dryness

Good systemic hydration is necessary for all patients. They are instructed to:

1. "Sing wet—pee pale" (in the words of Dr. Van Lawrence). We have adapted this to "Speak wet—pee pale."
2. Drink water every time you eat.
3. Keep water at hand at all times.
4. If you absolutely "hate water," try bottled spring water or tap water with a "twist."

Environmental Dryness

Environmental factors can create a drying effect on the vocal mechanism. If the patient is singing or performing in geographical regions where relative humidity is low, special attention to improving environmental hydration is needed. The best way to humidify room air is controversial at present. There is no convincing evidence for or against the use of hot or cold steam or ultrasonic mist. Research is needed to answer the question of which is best. The relative humidity on airplanes is about 5%, as discussed in Chapter 5, and special precautions must be taken.

1. Superhydrate prior to and during air travel.
2. Use a humidifier and travel with it, if possible.
3. Minimize talking in the airplane.
4. Provide a moist environment in hotel rooms by running the hot water in the shower.

Inadequate Rest/Sleep Patterns

General body fatigue is reflected in the voice. Optimal vocal efficiency may not be achieved when the patient is tired.

1. Get more rest/sleep prior to heavy voice use.
2. Be particularly careful when traveling (jet lag).
3. Allow time for a short nap prior to important speaking commitments whenever possible.

Stress Management Strategies

Many voice patients experience tremendous stress/tension in their daily lives.

1. Talk and move more slowly. When you move slower, you tend to talk slower. You can control the pace of the situation.
2. Use physical exercise.
3. Read a familiar passage out loud. The passage may be recorded during a voice therapy session and the tape used to gauge and adjust the voice during stressful situations.
4. Use meditation or prayer when applicable.
5. Consider formal training in stress management with a specially trained psychologist.
6. Use techniques described in Chapter 29.

THERAPEUTIC APPROACH TO IMPROVING THE SPEAKING VOICE

Relaxation

Many voice therapy programs incorporate relaxation techniques. While this is useful for stress management, progressive or "deep" relaxation is not necessarily an integral part of voice therapy for all patients. We use relaxation techniques to reduce muscular tension and to energize those muscle systems used in voice production. We routinely use range of motion, muscle stretch, and physical energizing tasks. There are many popular techniques used to facilitate relaxation that we have found useful for muscular tension dysphonia and for some hyperfunctional voice users. However, carryover of this relaxed state to voice production is often difficult to achieve, and we find other techniques more effective and desirable.

The yawn-sigh technique has traditionally been a part of voice therapy and speech training. While it benefits some patients, it is not a technique that should be used indiscriminately. The initial inspiratory phase of a yawn creates a high soft palate position, a lowered vertical laryngeal position, and an open pharynx. However, once the yawn reflex is triggered, these same structures and muscles become tense. Phonating with this degree of tension is not desirable. The natural yawn may have some benefit in voice retraining, but the artificial yawn used as a therapy technique has many potential pitfalls. The yawn-sigh technique may be appropriate for:

1. Improving the patient's sensory awareness of the soft palate, muscles of the pharynx, and tongue.
2. Creating an open, relaxed pharynx.
3. Establishing a high soft palate position, useful for oral resonance improvement.

Relieving Specific Sites of Muscular Tension

Excessive muscular tension is observed in association with almost all voice problems. Developing tactile awareness of the muscles of voice and speech production is a supplemental goal of voice therapy and is facilitated through the muscle stretch exercises. Patients with a history of head/neck injuries or cervical arthritis are not candidates for these exercises.

Range of Motion

Again, we only recommend these exercises for those patients who do not have a history of head/neck injuries, back pain, spinal cord problems, or cervical arthritis. This exercise is designed to provide a complete stretch to isolated muscles of the neck, shoulders, and jaw. The instructions are routinely put on an audiotape, which allows for correct home practice. The following outline is provided:

1. *Head Forward and Backward.* The head comes forward and is held in that position for a count of 10. Slowly, the patient rotates the head from side to side as if watching a ball roll back and forth in his/her lap. The patient is then asked to open his/her mouth, look at the ceiling, and hold that position for a count of five. These steps are usually repeated twice, but more repetitions may be indicated for some patients.

2. *Head Side to Side.* The head rocks toward the right shoulder, as if the patient were trying to touch his/her right shoulder with his/her right ear. Instructions are provided to ensure that only the head moves and not the entire torso. While leaning toward the right, the head rocks forward and backward in one sweeping nod ("as if nodding yes"). The patient is asked to focus on the muscles on the left side of the neck as they stretch and elongate. The instructions are repeated with the head leaning to the left.

3. *Looking over Each Shoulder.* The patient is reinstructed regarding appropriate head and shoulder alignment. He/she is then asked to look over

the right shoulder as if something were behind him/her. This position is held for a count of 10, and the patient is instructed to feel the stretch of the sternocleidomastoid muscle. The same instructions are repeated for the left side.

4. *Shoulder Rolls.* The shoulders are rolled forward and backward, in isolation and then together. Specific instructions are provided to help the patient attend to the muscles he/she is stretching.

5. *Shoulder Shrugs.* The patient is asked to raise his/her shoulders, hold to the count of three, and then allow the shoulders to drop. Attention is directed to the contrast between tension and relaxation. As the shoulders drop, the patient is asked to feel the tension leave the shoulders through the fingertips.

6. *Jaw Relaxation.* The patient is asked to let the jaw drop open or down to create space between the back teeth. The therapist observes that the jaw is comfortably open and not hyperextended or "unhinged." This position is held for three seconds, then the jaw is closed. These steps are repeated five times.

7. *Tongue Stretch.* Posterior tongue tension is usually observed in association with pharyngeal or "throaty" resonance. The patient is asked to rest his/her tongue lightly against the bottom teeth or inside the lower lip. He/she is prompted to hyperextend the base of the tongue. This is repeated at least 10 times; 30 times is preferred. This repetition tires the posterior portion of the tongue and often has an immediate effect in producing a clearer resonant quality. Another approach consists of rapid repetitions of the same stretch. The patient is provided with the identical prompts, but using a "double time" pace. The therapist counts the rhythm (i.e., "1-2; 1-2; 1-2") to help the patient maintain this pace.

8. *Chewing.* A modified "chewing approach" is used to promote mobility and stretch of the muscles of the face, lips, jaw, and tongue. The patient is instructed to chew slowly with his/her mouth open and to make smacking noises "like a cow on a lazy summer afternoon." He/she is encouraged to use all the muscles of the lips, tongue, face, and jaw. When phonation is superimposed on the relaxed muscular complex, the result should be a clearer sound with more oral resonance. This technique should not be applied indiscriminately. Chewing is not a relaxing activity for all patients. Some patients are uncomfortable with the "crudeness" of chewing in such a socially unacceptable manner and, therefore, cannot relax with it. Chewing may also be contraindicated for patients with tempero-mandibular joint (TMJ) syndromes or pain.

Self-Massage

The face, temporal muscles, posterior neck, shoulders, and occasionally the anterior strap muscles are massaged by the patient.

1. *Facial Massage.* The masseter muscle is identified. The patient is

asked to press in firmly with his/her fingertips under the zygoma bones and to hold the press to the count of 10. The patient is always reminded to continue to breathe. Holding the breath can reinforce muscle tension. The fingertips are then released, and the patient is asked to go to the same spot and massage this muscle using a firm, slow circular motion. These same instructions are repeated along the jaw line, where the masseter muscle finishes its course. Massaging the temporal muscles (on both sides of the forehead) is extremely beneficial for relieving jaw tension. The same instructions of pressing, then massaging are provided.

2. *Posterior Neck and Shoulder Massage.* When excessive posterior neck muscle tension is observed, it is often created by inappropriate head/neck alignment. To massage the right side, the patient is asked to take the left hand, cross over to the right side, and press in on the trapezius muscle. The press is held for a count of 10 and is then released. The patient is instructed to keep breathing. Next, the instruction is given to go back to the same spot, press in firmly, then let the hand slide forward and down. These steps are repeated for two other places in the posterior neck and then two places on the shoulders. Both sides are massaged equally. The right hand is used to massage the left posterior neck and shoulder.

Body Posture and Head/Neck Alignment

Appropriate head and neck alignment and body posture are essential to developing efficient vocal production. Excessive anterior strap muscle and posterior neck tension is created when the head is tilted backward or the chin jutted forward. Suggestions and prompts are provided in conjunction with the other therapy techniques.

Breath Control and Support

We are born with an innate ability to breathe healthfully and appropriately for the production of normal speech. Watch a newborn during quiet (tidal) breathing: the abdomen expands while inhaling. During vocalizations such as screaming or crying, the abdominal muscles contract. Most adults have lost this natural habit of effortless breathing.

During the initial stages of therapy, difficulty arises when attention is called to breathing. Observe what often happens when a patient is asked to "take a nice deep breath." The abdomen is sucked in, the chest and shoulders rise, and the breath is held with the vocal folds tightly adducted. Obviously, this is not the desired behavior. There are certain maladaptive behaviors that are automatically exhibited in response to certain words (i.e., breathe, inhale, and exhale). Using appropriate vocabulary early in therapy facilitates the training of correct speech breathing. "Abdominal breathing" is referred to as "abdominal support." The terms "expansion" and "softening the belly" are used for the inhalation phase, and "pulling in" is used for the exhalation phase.

When explaining abdominal/diaphragmatic breathing, a description of the process is as follows (1):

"In deep inspiration, the diaphragm contracts and moves downward. This flattening of the diaphragm causes a protrusion of the belly and a relaxation of the abdominal muscles. During expiration, the diaphragm relaxes and the abdomen contracts, exerting upward pressure on the abdominal organs, thus squeezing air out of the lungs."

Our experience has shown that it is easier to teach a patient to "pull in" the abdominal muscles than to "expand" or "soften the belly." Therefore, we begin the process of training appropriate speech breathing from the exhalation phase. The patient uses his expiratory reserve volume to begin speaking as suggested by Boone (2). When the air is expelled, what follows is a spontaneous softening of the belly and concomitant, natural inhalation.

We provide an appropriate rhythm for this abdominal motion, which will be used extensively in later sessions. We explain that the rhythm is similar to a 3/4 time signature or slow waltz [58 or 62 beats per minute (bpm) on a metronome]. We count out the pace "1, 2, 3" as the patient pulls in the abdominal muscles, and "1, 2, 3" as he/she expands.

A discussion of the differences between support for speaking and support for singing is provided. Classically trained singers especially need the experience of adjusting the inspiratory phase of breathing. The respiratory needs for conversational speaking are considerably less than for singing. Although the basic principles are the same in both voice modalities, by taking the focus off "breathing" and providing experience in the abdominal "pump" using the 3/4 rhythm, the singer learns how to feel appropriate speaking support and avoids exerting so much muscular tension that his/her support efforts become counterproductive.

The beginning steps in establishing breath control are incorporated into the warm-up and cool-down routines discussed in a later section. For convenience, a step-by-step approach is presented. However, it must be emphasized that this outlines our customary therapeutic direction and is not a "cookbook" of techniques that can be applied indiscriminately without considerable clinical judgment and modification. This caveat applies not only to teaching breath control and support, but to all the other subjects covered in this chapter.

Step 1

We begin by introducing the concept of appropriate speech breathing for nonspeech tasks and isolated speech sounds.

Exercise 1. The patient is asked to pull in his/her abdominal muscles as if blowing out a candle. Once the air has been fully expelled, the abdominal muscles expand naturally, and the patient inhales spontaneously. This is repeated several times until it can be accomplished easily. During the process, the patient learns to sense and use abdominal and back muscles efficiently to support phonation.

Exercise 2. An alternative initial approach breaks down the abdominal breathing into muscular and respiratory components. The patient is asked to pull in his/her abdominal muscles and then to expand the abdomen as described above. However, an abdominal pump with special attention to rhythm is introduced. It is the rhythmic pattern and visual cuing that provide the patient with the appropriate mechanics of abdominal breath control and support. Once the rhythm of the pump is established, the breath is added. The patient is instructed to focus on blowing out. Once he/she is comfortable with the pump and blowing out, his/her attention is focused on the smooth and easy exchange of air. We describe this as a cycle of breathing and encourage the patient to feel breathing as a continuous action and motion.

Step 2

The transition from nonspeech tasks to speech tasks is accomplished systematically.

Exercise 1. We begin with monosyllabic words, starting with /h/ (i.e., hit, hot, hop). These words facilitate easy airflow through the glottis. The words are used individually and then combined in groups of two, three, or more words. We then progress through a series of words with varying initial phonemes. (See Frontal Placement Words, Appendix V.)

Exercise 2. The patient is asked to pull in and to count from one to 50, with five numbers to a support group (e.g., 1-2-3-4-5, expand, 6-7-8-9-10, expand, etc.). As always, attention to easy flow and support of the breath in connected speech are the objectives.

Exercise 3. The patient is asked to count again from one to 50, this time varying the breath support group. For example, the patient may choose to inhale after the fifth number or whatever feels comfortable. The goal of this exercise is to achieve a flow and rhythm of the breath for simple ongoing speech tasks.

Step 3

Phrasing is an important component of using appropriate breath control and support in ongoing speech.

Exercise 1. The patient is provided with a list of phrases from which to read (Appendix V). The phrases vary from three to 12 syllables per phrase. Typically, one or more sessions are spent training appropriate breath control and support at each specific phrase level. It is expected that the patient demonstrate competency at a particular phrase level before moving to the next. Onset and maintenance of breath control and support are monitored closely. The concept of rhythm and pacing the breath is of paramount importance. Imagery is helpful in establishing a relaxed easy speech breathing rhythm.

Exercise 2. The patient is provided with longer sentences and is asked to phrase appropriately. At this time, the patient begins to exercise spontaneity and freedom of where to plan the breath. If need be, visual cues can be provided as slash marks to denote where to breathe.

Exercise 3. Paragraphs are introduced. Phrases may be marked, or the patient may be asked to read the paragraph "cold," while it is being audiotaped. This allows the patient and therapist to critique the paragraph together, then mark phrases and repeat the reading. Additional markings may include cues for easy onset of troublesome words and attention to oral resonance or any other area in which the patient has been trained.

Exercise 4. The patient is provided with additional unmarked paragraphs for practice in breath control and support and phrasing.

Step 4

The transition from structured tasks to conversation is highly individualized. Some patients need very few techniques or strategies, while others require a very organized approach.

Exercise 1. Initially, the patient is asked to describe three things he/she will do during the rest of the day. Cues and prompts are provided as needed.

Exercise 2. Additional practice is gained by asking the patient to discuss specific topics and to read aloud on a daily basis from a newspaper or magazine. It may be helpful for the patient to tape record these practice sessions at home for review with the voice therapist at a subsequent therapy session.

Step 5

The patient is asked to pay attention to his/her quiet or tidal breathing.

Exercise. The patient is asked to begin the exercise with active breathing as in the "candle blowing" task using good abdominal support. The therapist provides the visual prompt to slow the breath, and the patient gradually changes the candle blowing to quiet breathing. He/she is asked to practice this exercise 10 times each day until a natural carryover of abdominal breathing for all quiet (nonspeech) breathing is established.

Reducing Harsh Glottal Attacks

The term harsh or hard glottal attacks refers to the forceful or abrupt approximation of the vocal folds on words that begin with vowels. The acoustic result is a sudden, sharp, or explosive sound often called a glottal click or glottal stroke. The onset of voicing or phonation for vowels should be initiated gradually and easily. The key to easing harsh glottal attacks lies in the timing of the airflow with phonation.

Easy Onset Exercises

Exercise 1. Negative Practice. The therapist contrasts for the patient an abrupt initiation of the vowel sound in single words. These same words are then produced with an easy onset. Discrimination of easy versus hard onset can be provided for home practice. This is especially useful for adolescents and children. Negative practice is limited to only a few trials. After the therapist demonstrates, the patient is asked to say a word "hard," then say it "easy." Instructions to produce the word easily include initiating the word with an /h/ sound.

Exercise 2. Single Words. Air naturally precedes vocal fold adduction when producing "h"-initiated words; therefore, easy vowel initiation can be shaped from such words. The word list (Appendix V) is used as stimulus material in a variety of ways. One alternative is asking the patient to produce a light /h/ sound before each word. It is discussed that using the /h/ to "slide" into the word helps to initiate an easy onset. In some cases, the patient is asked to produce a breathy quality to ensure an easy onset. It also is useful to encourage a slide into the word with a slight elongation of the initial vowel.

Exercise 3. Minimal Pairs. A list of minimal-paired words, e.g., hate/ate, high/I, etc., (Appendix V) is provided. The patient is directed to "feel" the openness of the glottis on the /h/ and the closure for the vowel-initiated pair.

Exercise 4. Long versus Short Vowels. It is helpful to begin with single words initiated with the long vowels in English, e.g., eat, ice (Appendix V). The practice material is structured so that words beginning with the same vowel shape are rehearsed in a string, e.g., are, art, arm. Minimizing change in oral cavity shape helps the patient focus his/her attention on the details of appropriate breathing, which assists in decreasing laryngeal tension. The task hierarchy proceeds from single words containing the long vowels to words beginning with short vowels, e.g., ill, it, is. Once easy onset is established, a hierarchical approach is employed moving from vowel-initiated words, to vowel-initiated phrases, to monitored reading, to conversational speech.

Exercise 5. Delay Approach. Timing the onset of breath support is the key to a soft onset for words that begin with vowels. Singers are asked to imagine a score of music that begins with an eighth-note rest. Visual cuing is provided to help with the slow onset time. The patient is asked to posture his/her mouth for the word that will be produced, but delay the onset of phonation until the air, which is achieved with good abdominal/diaphragmatic support, has reached the level of the vocal folds. Additional suggestions include "breath space between the vocal folds," "imagine that you are exhaling on the sound /h/ (an audible /h/ should not be produced for this exercise), wait for the air to reach the folds, then produce the word" (e.g., are).

Exercise 6. Downward Slide. Using a downward slide on the vowel sound that begins the word is another technique to reduce harsh glottal attacks. The patient is asked to expand his/her abdomen (to ensure a good supply of air), then slide down from a high pitch to a lower pitch on the vowel sound. Modeling is provided. It is important that the patient not think of this as singing.

Exercise 7. "Key Word" Approach. A "key word" carryover approach is used, with "I," "and," and other frequently occurring words in English. The patient may generate a list of vowel-initiated words (names of family members and friends) and practice using any of the other techniques described in this section.

Exercise 8. Blending. The above techniques pertain to vowel-initiated words that begin a breath group. For vowel-initiated words that do not begin a breath group, a "linking" technique is used. Vowel-initiated words are linked to the word that precedes them. Connecting vowel-initiated words in ongoing speech is generally an easy task for singers. They are reminded that the same connected ("legato") line and rules of phrasing in song apply to speech as well. A short list (Appendix V) of two-word combinations is used in which the first word is linked or "blended" to the second word.

Exercise 9. Conversation or Monologue. Conversation or a monologue is elicited. The patient's attention is directed to blending words and easing the onset of vowel-initiated words as they begin a breath group.

Oral Resonance

The distinction between oral resonance and tone focus is subtle. Speech-language pathologists use concepts of oral resonance as they are reported in therapy texts for the profession. Vocabulary, such as vocal placement or tone focus, is borrowed from the singing world. There are numerous techniques to improve the resonance quality of the voice such as exercises to increase oral cavity space. These include palatal, pharyngeal, and tongue exercises. The goal is to increase the oral cavity space anteriorly and posteriorly. We generally begin with awareness exercises, which are especially important for the nonsinger or those who have not had any formal voice or speech training.

Jaw and facial tension are commonly observed in hyperfunctional voice users. Tension is often expressed as "clenched teeth" posture, with little excursion of the jaw while speaking. By maintaining the jaw in a relatively fixed position, the tongue, pharynx, and other structures are forced to work harder to make the necessary adjustments for vowel differentiation. Further, the diminished space within the oral cavity compromises its effectiveness as a resonator.

In discussing the concept of jaw relaxation, it is preferable to use such words as "creating space" rather than "opening the mouth." Opening can be accomplished rather easily, but not necessarily in a relaxed position. Instructing the patient to feel space between the back teeth seems to achieve openness without tension.

Oral Resonance Exercises

Exercise 1. Palatal Awareness. This exercise is useful for patients with functional or regional nasality and is often used to shape resonance for the nonsinger. The patient is asked to stand and suggestions regarding appropriate head/neck position are provided as usual. The patient is asked to sustain an /ŋ/ using good abdominal/diaphragmatic breath support. Cues are provided to facilitate self-monitoring and to direct the patient's attention to the soft palate. Visual monitoring (using a hand mirror) is especially useful. The /ŋ/ is repeated at least 10 times. While continuing to use the mirror, the patient is asked to change the sustained /ŋ/ to /a/, and is guided to observe the movement of the soft palate and the tongue. The mirror is taken away, and the patient is asked to *feel* this action. The /ŋ/ to /a/ is repeated 10 times while sustaining one tone. Changing the tone by using an upward or downward slide is an option. However, this slide should be incorporated only after the patient has acquired good soft palate movement.

Exercise 2. Pharyngeal "Surprise." This exercise uses imagery to create an open pharynx and high soft palate position. The patient is asked to imagine that he/she has walked into a freezer and is surprised by the coldness. A gentle "gasp" is produced. We take care to instruct that the gasp be produced softly, without tension. The candle-blowing maneuver or any isolated speech sound may be used. The patient is asked to use the surprise on inhaling and observe the feeling of cool air as it touches the pharynx (back of the throat) and soft palate. We ask the patient to imagine that the cold air lifts the palate. This is incorporated into the cycle of breathing for the inspiratory phase.

Exercise 3. Tongue Protrusion. Hyperextending the position of the tongue for a simple task such as counting or reading short phrases is an extremely useful technique for finding immediate relief to tongue tension. This technique is often used when the patient feels vocally fatigued or in physical discomfort from speaking. The patient is asked to protrude the tongue so that it rests lightly on the lower lip (but not beyond the lip). Instructions are provided to ensure good speech breathing. The patient repeats one number per breath up to the number 10 then repeats the sequence. This sequence (counting from one to 10) is repeated three times to ensure that the posterior tongue muscles have stretched and relaxed. Essentially, the posterior tongue fatigues during this exercise, making hyperfunction more difficult. This is a useful technique for increasing patient awareness. When the tongue is placed back in the mouth, it is easier to maintain a comfortable, more forward tongue placement, and the tone quality that is produced is often strikingly free and clear.

Exercise 4. There are certain vowels and diphthongs that have an inherent "openness" to them (e.g., /a/, /θI/, /æ/, /au/) and naturally facilitate more vertical space within the oral cavity. The patient is provided with a practice list of words containing these vowels (Appendix V), which are used as targets in phrases to enable the patient to experience openness in connected speech. The patient is then asked to identify such words in longer phrases, paragraphs, and conversational speech.

Exercise 5. Increase the posterior dimension of the mouth space. Back vowel sounds such as /u/, /o/, and /ɔ/ are used in conjunction with a downward slide to increase posterior oral or pharyngeal dimension. The series of slides is practiced in consonant–vowel–consonant combinations. It is easier for a nonsinger to begin with a continuous consonant sound such as /ʃ/, /s/, /m/ and /l/. The combinations of sounds include /ʃ-u-t/, /s-u-t/, etc. The *pharyngeal surprise* can be incorporated into this exercise to maximize pharyngeal space.

Tone Focus/Vocal Placement in Speech

Incorrect vocal placement or tone focus is a common speaking error. The tendency to overuse the muscles of the pharynx and posterior tongue creates a distinct resonance quality. The terms used to describe this quality include: throaty, muffled, swallowing the words, heavy, guttural, and pressed. This excessive muscular tension can lead to physical discomfort and vocal fatigue.

The concept of "vocal placement" is a distinct entity and not synonymous with "pitch," even though changes in placement may concomitantly affect pitch. We usually avoid the use of the word pitch in therapeutic directions, as it carries with it certain preconceived ideas that can interfere with desirable behavioral change.

Vocal placement can be conceptualized as occurring along two axis: up/

down and front/back. A discussion of this two-axis theory, the difference between pitch and placement, and a heightening of awareness of articulatory placement within the oral cavity is provided. We begin with consonants because they are easier to conceptualize, having a definite point of contact or "placement." Any sound articulated on the alveolar ridge or anterior to that point is considered a "front sound," including /t/, /d/, /n/, /l/, /s/, /z/, /ʃ/, /tʃ/, /dʒ/, /Θ/ (voiced and voiceless), /f/, /v/, /p/, /b/, and /m/. "Middle sounds" include /r/ and /j/. "Back sounds" are represented by /k/ and /g/. Once frontal consonant placement is established, an attempt is made to create the image of vowels being carried forward with the consonants. A tape recorder is useful, so that the patient can hear as well as feel the difference in production.

We begin by having the patient contrast naturally front words (e.g., neat) with naturally back words (e.g., clock) to heighten awareness. A list of the front-placed words is provided to reinforce the feeling of the voice "buzzing" in the front of the mouth (Appendix V). The patient then produces these words followed by a phrase ending in that target word. If good placement is achieved at the beginning and end of the utterance, it can hopefully be maintained in between (e.g., neat—please be neat). The patient is then instructed to repeat and read sentences and short paragraphs, concentrating on the placement of the articulators and the focus of the voice. Conversational speech and short monologues are practiced in order to make the use of this technique more spontaneous.

Glottal Fry

Glottal fry (also called pulse register) occurs in the voice in the lowest frequency range (24–44 Hz). The tone that is produced in this range is perceived as "rough" or "gravelly." Glottal fry often occurs in association with inadequate breath support and/or pharyngeal vocal placement. Techniques to improve breath support, enhance appropriate vocal placement, negative practice, and attention to auditory feedback are particularly useful in eliminating this tonal quality.

Loudness versus Projection

The difference between loudness and projection is reviewed with each patient. We discuss the idea of "frivolous" loudness, which is most loud talking, yelling or screaming. Projection is defined as maximizing listener intelligibility with minimal speaker effort. Projection techniques are preferable to loud talking or yelling. While adjustments in breath support provide the foundation, making changes in the production of speech can enhance the perception of increased loudness. We suggest gentle overarticulation, which helps to maximize the production of words. These projection exercises are intended for conversational settings in the presence of loud background noise, for the telephone, for classroom teaching, and for some public speaking situations. They are not intended for the stage. Many years of training are required for stage projection. The patient's skills are developed using a hierarchy that begins with the breath support tasks.

Projection Exercises

Exercise 1. Single Words. Word lists (Appendix V) are presented that contain tongue-tip and other frontal consonant sounds, and we introduce a game of "baseball." Game rules: The therapist pitches a word (by swinging an arm toward the patient). A small arm swing indicates that the word is to be spoken at a comfortable loudness. Very gradually, the therapist increases the excursion of the arm swing, which is the patient's cue to use more breath support (by pulling in the abdominal muscles with more energy). The result is a naturally louder production of the word. It usually takes 10 trials for the patient to reach maximum loudness for a given word. Tactile-kinesthetic monitoring of the strap muscles and posterior tongue assures relaxation of these muscles.

Exercise 2. Using Speech Sounds in Phrasing. Often, the perception of loudness is related to the clarity of the tone, word, or phrase. We use diction exercises to enhance the listener's understandability and refer back to our lists of words and phrases. The patient is instructed to produce ending consonant sounds precisely. Care is taken to ensure that hyperfunctional over-articulation does not result.

Exercise 3. Combination. After the patient has had experience with the baseball game and improving diction for selected phrases, these two exercises are combined. The therapist pitches specific phrases to the patient. The phrases are usually kept short for this exercise (three, four, five, or six syllables per phrase). Again, the patient is instructed to use breath support more efficiently and not to focus on merely getting louder.

Exercise 4. Prosody. Prosody exercises also enhance loudness and projection in longer phrases. Patients are asked to decide which word or words carry the important content meaning of a phrase. They are then asked to accent that word by raising the intonation slightly and adding more breath support. If the selected word begins with a vowel, care is taken to ensure an easy onset.

Prosody

Major prosodic disturbances are not commonly observed in the professional voice population. However, a loss of "vocal variety" may occur during therapy as other aspects of speech/voice production are changed. In some cases, prosody exercises may be necessary.

Prosody Exercises

Exercise 1. Polysyllabic Words. Polysyllabic words are used, and the patient is instructed to exaggerate an upward inflection on the accented syllable (e.g., ed-u-**ca**-tion-al). The patient is taken through a hierarchy of tasks to establish this technique. The patient's conversational speech is taped. On playback, the patient and clinician mutually critique the patient's success in implementing this strategy. Improper responses are repeated in the correct form.

Exercise 2. Homographs. A list of words that differ in meaning depending on how they are contrasted is provided (**con**tent–con**tent**). A slightly exaggerated rising intonation for the accented syllable is demonstrated. These words are produced in a string of pairs. The patient's attention is directed to the intonation variation.

Exercise 3. Phrases. The patient is asked to use polysyllabic words in self-generated phrases while still using the exaggerated intonation.

Exercise 4. Reading. Identify the polysyllabic words in a reading paragraph. These words are used as the basis for the exaggerated intonation as the patient reads.

Exercise 5. Conversation. The patient's conversational speech is audiotaped. On playback, the therapist and patient mutually critique the patient's use of this exaggerated technique. Error responses are repeated in the correct form.

Pitch

Specific methods for changing pitch will not be addressed in this chapter. Inappropriate pitch is rarely the cause of a patient's vocal dysfunction. Rather, inappropriate vocal usage may cause a deviant pitch. When proper breath support and vocal placement are established, appropriate speaking pitch usually follows.

Bridging Exercises

Bridging exercises are used with all patients (singers and nonsingers) who receive jointly specialized singing instruction. These exercises are designed to bridge the gap (when one exists) between singing and speaking technique. The patient is provided with experience in maintaining appropriate tonal balance with breath control and support when the task changes from singing to speaking exercises. These techniques are especially useful for experienced singers who have not applied their trained vocal production and technique to speaking.

Exercise 1. Descending Slide on /m/. The patient is instructed to start in a high falsetto range and very slowly slide down on the /m/ sound. Care is taken to ensure good abdominal support, appropriate head/neck position, and appropriate tongue placement. This same slide is repeated five times, and the starting pitch is slightly lowered each time.

Exercise 2. Descending Slide for /m/ and /a/. The patient is asked to slide down on the /m/. About halfway down the slide, the patient is instructed to open his/her mouth. The resulting sound is an /a/. The important aspect of this exercise is the careful transition from the /m/ to the /a/. The patient is directed to feel the slow, gradual change to the /a/ sound.

Exercise 3. Sustained /m/ to Counting. The patient is asked to sustain an /m/ at a comfortable pitch and loudness. Cues are provided to help him/her focus on the sensory aspects that had been previously trained (i.e., open/relaxed pharynx, relaxed tongue position, etc.). The patient is requested to change from the /m/ to counting. The /m/ serves to bridge from a tone that sounds like light humming to speech.

Exercise 4. Lip Trills. The singing specialist and the speech-language pathologist incorporate the use of lip trills. For singers, this is often a familiar task, but nonsingers require careful instructions. Tactile monitoring of the strap muscles is needed to ensure that tension is not created as this task is learned. We begin with a silent lip trill, much like the sound a horse makes, which is sometimes referred to as a "flub." Visual prompts are provided, which help pace timing the breath. Following several trials, with the flub, voicing is added. It is helpful to have the patient initiate the flub first, then switch to the phonated lip trill. Lip trills are used on ascending and descending slides. It is important that the patient be producing a tone that is smooth and free of tension.

Exercise 5. /ŋ/ to /a/. Palatal awareness exercises are routinely incorporated in voice training. When used as a bridging exercise, the /ŋ/–/a/ is used during the production of ascending and descending slides.

Exercise 6. Ascending-Descending Slide on /m/. The patient is asked to slide up slowly then down in pitch on one breath for /m/. Modeling is provided, so that the higher pitch is not "pinched." Occasionally, a replenishing breath needs to be taken before the descending slide.

Exercise 7. Siren. The circular sound an emergency vehicle makes is used with isolated sounds such as /m/, /l/, and /v/, and for lip trills. The number of repetitions per breath depends on the patient's speech breathing ability. This is an excellent morning warm-up exercise.

Recitative

Classical singers are generally trained in recitative, a music cross between singing and speaking that occurs between arias in opera and oratorio. Singers who have mastered recitative can carry over good vocal technique by gradually dropping pitch specifically during recitative passages, letting them gradually convert to spoken dialogue. Similarly, singers may read passages as recitative on improvised notes, learning how to apply their musically trained breathing, support, and placement techniques to conversational speech. For singers who do not have an operatic background, patter songs (e.g., Gilbert and Sullivan) and rap are of similar value as bridging exercises.

Carryover Strategies

All the therapy techniques and exercises we have to offer are essentially worthless if the patient does not use them in his daily life. Carryover is the term used to describe the process of extending the use of new skills outside the speech-language pathologist's office.

Traditionally, carryover occurs toward the end of therapy and is accomplished by gradually changing the contexts in which desired behaviors are emitted. This is accomplished by changing the physical environment (e.g., moving from the therapy office to the waiting room and beyond) and expanding the social contexts in which the new behaviors are to be demonstrated (e.g., bringing significant others into the therapy office). However, we believe that carryover should begin in the early stages of therapy. Consistent practice on the patient's part may be the best way to facilitate this.

Carryover Exercises

Exercise 1. Greetings as Reminders. The patient is instructed to use all greetings and departures (hello, good-bye) as reminders to use appropriate support. These greeting words should be practiced in the studio and then serve to trigger the patient's awareness of speaking technique during face-to-face and telephone conversation.

Exercise 2. Telephone Strategies. Most professional voice users report some degree of vocal fatigue if extended telephone use is required. We routinely provide details in how to survive with the telephone. These suggestions include:

1. Observe appropriate head/neck position.
2. Use a slow speaking rate.
3. Make more effective use of pauses by stopping before or after important content words.

4. Hold each pause slightly longer than usual. This helps to give your listener more processing time.
5. Use projection techniques to get volume with ease.
6. Use projection techniques to maximize diction.
7. Switch which hand typically holds the receiver.

Exercise 3. People and Places/Situations. The patient is asked to identify three situations and persons with whom he/she will practice the speaking techniques. The three people consist of a personal relationship (spouse, child, parent), a social acquaintance (work colleague, neighbor), and a stranger (grocery clerk, bank teller). A hierarchy is developed, depending on the patient's feelings of comfort in each of these situations. Some patients report that it is easier to practice with a stranger. Others report that the techniques work best at work. This carryover strategy is highly individualized. The patient makes these active choices, and the therapist helps to guide their perceptions and practice.

Exercise 4. Daily Living Reminders. The patient is asked to describe his/her activities during the course of a typical day from the time the alarm clock rings until it is reset at night. A few events are selected as reminders to check vocal technique. These may include activities such as walking in the office door, taking a coffee break, coming through the door at home, as well as during each lunch hour, or at red lights when driving. The effectiveness of each of these activities as a vocal reminder is checked during subsequent therapy sessions.

Exercise 5. Key Word/Key Phrase. Beyond the carryover that occurs spontaneously with practice, there are other ways to encourage the use of newly learned behaviors in the patient's daily conversation. A key word/key phrase approach has been used successfully in facilitating the transfer of new skills. Patients tend to use certain words or phrases frequently in the course of their daily interactions, and they are encouraged to employ specific strategies on those specific words or phrases. For example, when working toward the elimination of harsh glottal attacks, ascertain the names of important people in the patient's environment that may be vowel-initiated. "I" and "and" are frequently occurring words in the English language and are good key words for most patients.

Exercise 6. Communicative Stress. Since the general approach is geared toward relaxation, specific practice in dealing with pressure situations is beneficial. The therapist will provide a series of rapid questions. These questions vary in the complexity of answers they require. A sample of questions includes:

1. What's your birthday?
2. What's your spouse's birthday?
3. What's your telephone number?
4. Why do we use napkins?

5. Why do we have traffic lights?
6. Why do we have income tax?
7. How do you make a bed?
8. How do you make your favorite meal?
9. What if a child was left unattended?

The therapist helps the patient identify vocal stress that develops in response to these questions, and instructions are given for identifying and ameliorating vocally abusive behavior in daily situations.

Exercise 7. Habituation and Maintenance. The patient is instructed to read aloud at least three to four times weekly. Tape recording these short paragraphs facilitates the patient's self-monitoring of vowel production.

Exercise 8. Professional Feedback. The patient is instructed to converse with the voice therapist or a similarly skilled listener periodically. (Timing depends on the stage of therapy.) While this is not exactly an exercise, the importance of skilled feedback cannot be overstressed.

ADDITIONAL THERAPY TECHNIQUES AND SUGGESTIONS

Negative Practice

Negative practice is one approach for directing the patient's exploration of specific misuses. The patient contrasts inappropriate (his/her present misuses) and appropriate productions (the target). Negative practice works well in helping the patient identify or contrast harsh glottal attacks from easy onset of the voice. One word of caution—since it is our goal to change muscle memory in a positive direction, we choose carefully and limit the number of trials used in negative practice exercises. For example, too much negative practice for harsh glottal attacks is inadvisable for some vocal fold pathologies (i.e., a vocal fold hemorrhage, contact ulcers, or a "fresh" mucosal tear).

Paired-Stimuli Approach

Another strategy that we find very useful is borrowed from articulation therapy. The paired-stimuli or key-word approach links one word that the patient can produce with ease and clarity 100% of the time to others that are more difficult. The patient is first asked to produce the key word at least 10 times. Target words that differ from the key word by only their initial phoneme (e.g., tip, chip) are paired with the key word, alternating between the key word and the target word. The patient is asked to produce these several times. The string of words may be changed so that the target word makes up the majority of the string and the key word is inserted occasionally. A new list may be compiled with words that differ from the key word by the vowel sound (e.g., beet-bit, beet-bought).

The patient is also presented with a list of mixed monosyllabic words. This list contains key words and target words. The patient is asked to alternate between the key word and the target. Reciting the list with and without the insertion of the key word is another possibility. By using the mixed list, the patient can gradually build on each word, moving into phrases and sentences of increasing length, and eventually to spontaneously produced sentences and conversation with the vocal quality established in the key word.

Tongue Tension in Speech

Ongoing observations of the patient's performance and reaction to the suggestions provided by the therapist is very important. During the warm-up/cool-down routine, watch the neck just under the chin for signs of tongue movement. Posterior tongue tension is especially obvious during production of /s/. To ensure good tactile monitoring, the patient is instructed to observe the difference in the tongue for /s/, and /ʃ/. If need be, a sloppy /s/ production will minimize tongue tension. Using a staccato rhythm challenges the patient and should be employed after success is achieved for the prolonged /s/.

Strap Muscle Hyperfunction

Using voiceless/voiced cognate pairs (i.e., f/v, s/z, ʃ/ʒ, θ/ð) facilitates "relaxed/easy" voicing. In making the transition from voiceless to voiced speech sounds, we often see the vertical laryngeal position shift upward, which squeezes the strap muscles and muscles of the pharynx. The result is a tight or pressed resonant quality. Occasionally, a downward shift of the larynx is observed. The patient is instructed to monitor neck tension (tactile-kinesthetic monitoring) and observe the transition from the voiceless sound to the voiced sound. The patient learns how to add voicing without the tension.

WARM-UP AND COOL-DOWN EXERCISES

The warm-up and cool-down routine is important in training the voice. Singers appreciate the need to exercise the voice before singing. Speaking exercises provide the patient with the equivalent of vocalises (singing scales) for the speaking voice. Consistent practice each morning prepares the vocal folds and muscles of the vocal mechanism for the demands of the day. The evening cool-down regimen is similar to the athlete's stretching and cooling down after running. An outline of the daily practice exercises (Appendix V) is provided on each visit. The routine includes a muscular stretch and range of motion exercises, which are useful for relaxation, but are specifically used to heighten the patient's tactile feedback system. The patient is then asked to vocalize scales that have been provided by the singing specialist and provide aerobic conditioning. If the patient does not receive concurrent singing instruction, this step is omitted. The speech-language pathologist does not provide instruction in this area. The final step in the daily routine is the speaking exercises. These usually include a variety of nonspeech tasks, voiceless speech, and voiced speech sounds, as well as bridging exercises. The therapist reviews each exercise and provides new tasks as the need arises. Any of the techniques described in this chapter may be suitable for warm-up/cool-down exercises.

CONCURRENT SPECIALIZED SINGING LESSONS

Most patients (singers and nonsingers) are routinely evaluated by the singing specialist. Singing provides the nonsinger exercises and training, which greatly enhance the speaking voice. Professional voice users find that the demands of speaking seem less when they have had the aerobic workout that the singing provides. The symbiotic techniques of the singing teacher are also very helpful in teaching breathing, support, placement, and other speaking techniques.

INTERRELATION OF VOICE FUNCTIONS

It is important to note that, although a number of common vocal misuses have been identified and their remediation discussed individually, deviant vocal behaviors do not occur in isolation. Therapy for one may obviate the need for specific, intensive work on another. For example, patients who speak too rapidly usually exhibit jaw tension. The reason for the association between the two is that, in order to speak at a rapid rate, the speaker cannot afford the time needed for the mandible to make the necessary excursion consistent with jaw relaxation. Breath support and vocal placement are similarly related. When a patient successfully achieves good abdominal breath support, the voice is naturally carried to a more frontal placement, on the well-sustained airflow. The importance of these examples is to emphasize the dynamic nature of vocal production.

VALUE OF INSTRUMENTATION IN VOICE THERAPY

Use of instrumentation for voice therapy will not be discussed in detail in this chapter. However, under special circumstances, voice therapy techniques in combination with instrumentation discussed in Chapter 8 such as the Visi-pitch, Sona-Graph, laryngograph, PM-Pitch Analyzer, flexible fiber-optic laryngoscope, or rigid endoscope can be helpful. For example, the laryngograph in combination with the Sona-Graph has been useful as biofeedback for such disorders as spasmodic dysphonia or muscle tension dysphonia. Following a brief training and orientation, the patient can visually monitor correct versus incorrect productions for specific tasks. The PM-Pitch Analyzer has a built-in program designed for use in direct therapy. Since it can interpret longer speech samples, it is ideal for monitoring speaking misuses such as harsh glottal attacks in ongoing speech.

MANAGING STRESS

For many singers, performers, and other voice professionals, voice problems present as a "hidden handicap." Often, families and friends do not share or empathize with the patient's frustrations, fears or anxieties associated with voice problems. The level of stress and its exacerbation of the present voice symptoms can interfere with therapy. When indicated, the speech-language pathologist may provide specific stress management strategies. A referral to a psychologist is made if these simple strategies alone do not provide relief from symptoms of stress. Occasionally, a singer will experience periods of significant stress when faced with vocal fold surgery. In this case, the patient is referred to the arts-medicine psychologist for counselling. Hypnotherapy for relaxation is another stress management tool. We have also found a support group to be helpful. It is important that the speech-language pathologist cooperate with the psychologist in structuring this group. The singing specialist's involvement in the voice support group is valuable. The singers in our voice support group have reported that they feel that there is no clear boundary between their voice, self-esteem, ego, and psyche. Many group sessions have been spent discussing their feelings of inadequacy and defectiveness because of their voice problems.

SHORT RELAXATION PRACTICE TECHNIQUES

The following exercises have been helpful for refocusing the patient's stress reaction. The exercises can be practiced routinely each day or used in times of high stress. Each of these exercises can be recorded on audiotape for playback at a later time. Many of our patients find it helpful to hear the therapist's voice to guide them through the relaxation protocol.

Two-Minute Spot Check

This short exercise is practical and easy. It is also extremely useful in reinforcing self-monitoring skills and facilitating the carryover phase of therapy.

1. Interrupt your thoughts—switch your thoughts to your breathing. Begin with the candle blowing, taking time to inhale and exhale fully. Take several cleansing breaths (quicker, fuller breaths), which require a more active exchange of air.
2. Scan your body for specific sites of tension (forehead, jaw, shoulders, neck, or tongue). Attempt to loosen this area (move gently, use the range-of-motion exercises, or self-massage).
3. Take two more cleansing breaths, then return to easy candle blowing, and return to your activity.

Range of Motion for Stress Management

This is similar to the range of motion provided as a daily warm-up exercise. For this purpose, more time is taken and more breathing is incorporated. On an audiotape, the patient is provided with instructions beginning with: "Find yourself sitting in a comfortable chair. Let your head come forward as if you wanted to place your chin on your chest. Let it remain there for a moment. The muscle you are now stretching is called your trapezius. Can you imagine the point where it begins at the base of your skull, and feel where it ends in the middle of your back?" The patient is lead on tape through a brief muscle relaxation program that helps dissipate stress.

The Quieting Response

This takes less than one minute to complete. It can be done in the midst of chaos, panic or stage fright.

1. Pant quickly using a forced expiration, gradually slow down your breathing, turn it into the candle blowing, then gradually return to quiet breathing.
2. Smile outwardly and inwardly. Suggest to yourself (silently or aloud) that you will be accepted and successful in what you are about to do. Imagine a positive outcome. Picture yourself being in a relaxed controlled state five minutes from now. Enjoy the feeling of accomplishment.
3. Resume your activity.

A Short Meditation (Five–10 Minutes)

The patient is provided with a tape of this relaxation exercise. The therapist guides the patient through each step, then finishes with the guided imagery.

1. Spot the body for muscular tension. Release specific areas of tension with the stretch and/or range-of-motion exercises. Focus on a warm, glowing feeling sweeping throughout your body.
2. Warm your hands by rubbing them together vigorously. Visualize the sun's warmth on your hands. Place them gently on your face and sweep downward and outward.
3. Focus now on your thoughts. Imagine a panel of switches. As you turn off each switch (one by one), your breathing slows and becomes very regular.
4. "Travel" to a place that is warm and safe and brings a smile to your face—the seashore, the country, your home, a good friend. Stay with this pleasant feeling.

Guided Imagery

Guided imagery works best once the patient is in a quiet/calm state with very slow, regular breathing. The patient is led through individualized images. The following is an example.

Imagine yourself lying on a carpet of soft grass in a shaded forest. It is a warm, pleasant day. The sky is a bright, clear blue. Sun rays filter through the leaves of the forest canopy above. The tree branches seem to embrace and protect this spot where you lie. A gentle breeze sings through the green grass and tickles the skin of your face. Imagine that there is a clearing in the branches and a shaft of yellow light is descending on you. Feel the warmth. Feel the warmth seeping onto your forehead, your cheekbones, your mouth, your chin. Feel the warmth flowing down your neck and into your chest. Take a deep breath . . . Smell the fragrant air . . . Hold the breath . . . Then, slowly let it go as you feel the tightness flow from your chest on down your arms and out your fingertips. Let the sun's rays warm your chest, your abdomen. Take a deep breath . . . Hold the warmth in your torso, then let it drift slowly down your legs and out your toes. You may stay in this moment and enjoy this perfect summer day and a feeling of deep contentment.

The patient is cued that the therapist will stop talking for a moment so he/she can enjoy the feeling. The patient is cued that he/she is brought back to that moment in time by counting from one to 10. Once the patient is accustomed to this technique, it can be used essentially as a form of self-hypnosis in times of stress (such as immediately before a performance).

CONCLUSION

The speech-language pathologist is an essential component of the voice care team for professional voice users, regardless of whether the primary voice problem occurred during speech or singing. Close collaboration among the voice therapist, laryngologist, singing teacher, and other members of the voice care team facilitates the development of optimal speaking technique in these patients. To many speech-language pathologists beginning therapy with professional voice users, the voices will initially sound normal. However, with increasing experience, one develops a great appreciation for the vocal disruption that may be caused by even minor misuses and abuses in voice professionals. Recognizing their need for near-perfection in vocal quality and endurance, and understanding the unusual stresses to which performers and their voices are routinely exposed, the speech-language pathologist will find exceptional gratification in working with this challenging group of patients. Professional voice users demand our most critical assessment acuity and therapeutic skills, excite our clinical imaginations, and achieve exceptionally gratifying (and appreciated) results.

REFERENCES

1. Aronson A. *Clinical voice disorders: an interdisciplinary approach.* New York: Thieme, 1985.
2. Boone D. *The voice and voice therapy.* Englewood Cliffs, New Jersey: Prentice-Hall, 1983.

SUGGESTED READING LIST

Andrews ML, Summers A. *Voice therapy for adolescents.* Boston: Little, Brown (College-Hill Press), 1988.

Aronson AE. *Clinical voice disorders,* 2nd ed. New York: Thieme, 1985.

Boone DR. *The voice and voice therapy.* Englewood Cliffs, New Jersey: Prentice-Hall, 1982.

Brubaker SH. *Workbook for aphasia.* Detroit: Wayne State University Press, 1978.

Brubaker SH. *Workbook for reasoning skills.* Detroit: Wayne State University Press, 1983, 1984.

Keith RL, Thomas JE. *Speech practice manual for dysarthria, apraxia, and other disorders of articulation: compare and contrast.* Toronto: B.C. Decker, 1989.

Kilpatrick K. *Therapy guide for the adult with language and speech disorders, vol. II.* Akron, Ohio: Visiting Nurse Service of Summit County, 1979.

Linklater K. *Freeing the natural voice.* New York: Drama Book Publishers, 1976.

Richards KB, Fallow M. *Workbook for the verbally apraxic adult: reproducibles for therapy and home practice.* Tucson: Communication Skill Builders, 1987.

Smith MC. *The phonemic speech workbook for dysarthria therapy.* Tucson: Communication Skill Builders, 1986.

Professional Voice: The Science and Art of Clinical Care, Robert T. Sataloff.
Raven Press, Ltd., New York © 1991.

29

Increasing Vocal Effectiveness

*Bonnie N. Raphael and **Robert T. Sataloff

*American Repertory Theater and Institute, Harvard University, Cambridge,
Massachusetts; and **Department of Otolaryngology, Thomas Jefferson
University, Philadelphia, Pennsylvania

PREPARATION FOR ORAL PRESENTATIONS

Physicians, speech-language pathologists, teachers, students, executives, and people in most walks of life are called on at some time or another to speak in public. Few people are naturally skilled, organized, comfortable public speakers. Most people are somewhat uncomfortable about speaking in public, some are petrified, and nearly all make less than optimal use of their vocal and dramatic skills without some instruction and preparation. While this book is not intended as a text to teach singing, conversational speech, or public speaking, we have selected this subject for our "example" chapter, because it is a common concern for most of our readers.

Not all considerations for voice preservation are "vocal." Many vocal stresses are controlled by eliminating psychological stress, understanding room acoustics, organizing material to be presented, and through other similar preparations. This chapter describes our basic initial approach to training someone such as a physician to present a paper or lecture. It includes a few vocal exercises, although they are rudimentary and no substitute for formal training with a speech-language pathologist, a singing or speech teacher, or an acting coach. It also includes descriptions of physical warm-up exercises used by many actors. Such exercises are frequently regarded as superfluous by the physician, but professional performers have found them extremely helpful. Use of appropriate preparation helps make a speaker appear relaxed, effective, and well-focused. Such preparation is also invaluable for controlling pre-performance anxiety. Most outstanding speakers do, in fact, work hard at making their presentations appear natural and unrehearsed.

All too often, talented and intelligent speakers will spend considerable time in preparing the content of upcoming presentations but will spend virtually no time preparing themselves for the most effective spoken presentation of their research or position papers. Content that is interesting, valuable to the listeners, and important to the profession is too often lost or short-changed because of ineffective presentation. Far too many speakers present what they have to say in a way that makes it either too difficult to grasp or too dull to have a favorable impact on a listening audience. This chapter outlines a methodical procedure through which oral presentations can be more effectively prepared. Various texts are available to supplement the material presented in this chapter (1–4).

PREPARATION OF WRITTEN MATERIALS

Ideally, the research should be completed and all materials to be presented should be available to the speaker no later than one month before the date of the presentation. This allows the speaker sufficient time to get the presentation into a form best suited to communicate the chief features of the research. Approximately one month before presentation, the speaker should write out as many drafts of the presentation as are necessary, until it expresses orally what he/she wishes to say in the clearest and most effective manner possible. Rather than simply reading from the same text submitted for publication, the speaker would do better to substitute words that are easier on the tongue and to use grammatical structure that is easier on the listener's ear. Sentences should be shorter and more concise for listeners than they might be for readers. The speaker should check the effectiveness of the presentation by reading the speech aloud a number of times, making certain that it fits easily into the time allotment assigned and that it is stylistically suited to the particular audience to be addressed. Effective speakers will prepare two drafts of a given presentation at this stage: one to meet the needs of the oral presentation and another that meets the needs of publication.

If the speaker is more experienced or more comfortable working in a somewhat but not totally structured manner, then he/she may decide to work from note cards or a simple outline of the presentation. Less experienced presenters or those dealing with a large amount of information that needs to be precisely stated may prefer to work from a written text of the speech. Even this written text, however, can be prepared in such a way that it does not intrude between the speaker and the audience.

One way in which the written presentation can be moved toward effective oral performance is via a *structural rewriting* of the speech. In a structural rewriting, the way in which the speech appears on the page to the reader's eye is the way he/she wishes to express it aloud. Use of a structurally rewritten text is particularly important to presenters for whom English is not their native language and to presenters inexperienced in formal speaking before large audiences. A structural version of a speech makes phrasing and

pausing at appropriate intervals far easier for the speaker, because it re-
places arbitrary paragraph form with functional form. In order to better
understand how this works, read aloud both versions of the Gettysburg
Address which follow. Most readers will find that, with virtually no preparation, the second rendering of the same written material is far easier to
deliver than the first, because the eye guides effective phrasing and pausing
choices.

The Gettysburg Address
by: Abraham Lincoln

Fourscore and seven years ago our fathers brought forth on this continent
a new nation, conceived in Liberty and dedicated to the proposition that all
men are created equal.

Now we are engaged in a great civil war, testing whether that nation, or
any nation so conceived and so dedicated, can long endure. We are met on
a great battlefield of that war. We have come to dedicate a portion of that
field, as a final resting-place for those who here gave their lives that this
nation might live. It is altogether fitting and proper that we should do this.

But, in a larger sense, we cannot dedicate—we cannot consecrate—we
cannot hallow this ground. The brave men, living and dead, who struggled
here, have consecrated it far above our poor power to add or detract. The
world will little note nor long remember what we say here, but it can never
forget what they did here. It is for us, the living, rather, to be dedicated here
to the unfinished work which they who fought here have thus far so nobly
advanced. It is rather for us to be here dedicated to the great task remaining
before us—that from these honored dead we take increased devotion to that
cause for which they gave the last full measure of devotion—that we here
highly resolve that these dead shall not have died in vain—that this nation,
under God, shall have a new birth of freedom—and that government of the
people, by the people, for the people, shall not perish from the earth.

The Gettysburg Address
by: Abraham Lincoln
(structurally rendered)

Fourscore and seven years ago
   our fathers brought forth on this continent
      a new nation,
         conceived in Liberty and dedicated to the proposition
           that all men are created equal.
Now we are engaged in a great civil war,
   testing whether that nation,
      or any nation so conceived and so dedicated,
         can long endure.
We are met on a great battlefield of that war.

We have come to dedicate a portion of that field as a final resting-place
    for those who here gave their lives that this nation might live.
It is altogether fitting and proper that we should do this.
But, in a larger sense,
    we cannot dedicate—we cannot consecrate—we cannot hallow this
    ground.
The brave men, living and dead, who struggled here,
    have consecrated it far above our poor power to add or detract.
The world will little note nor long remember what we say here,
    but it can never forget what they did here.
It is for us, the living, rather,
    to be dedicated here to the unfinished work
        which they who fought here have thus far so nobly advanced.
It is rather for us to be here dedicated to the great task remaining before us—
    that from these honored dead
    we take increased devotion to that cause
        for which they gave the last full measure of devotion—
that we here highly resolve
    that these dead shall not have died in vain—
    that this nation, under God, shall have a new birth of freedom—
    and that government of the people, by the people, for the people,
        shall not perish from the earth.

Just through this simple experiment the reader should be able to see the benefits of creating and rehearsing with a structured rendition of the presentation. The Gettysburg Address was, in fact, written as a speech rather than as an essay. Presenters who are both rewriting materials for oral presentation and restructuring their texts for more effective reading will find this technique of even greater value when dealing with materials that are more technical and less poetically phrased than this memorable address.

After creating the structural rendition of the presentation, the presenter can then spend the next week or so continuing the preparation process in one of two ways:

1. The speech can be read aloud about twice a day from the structural script until the phrasing and pausing seem very natural and comfortable to the presenter; or
2. The presenter can tape record the speech after just a few readings through of the structural script. This way, if rehearsal time is severely limited but commuting time to work or meetings is not, the tape can be played in a car, train, or airplane until it is virtually memorized as a result of the repeated listening.

If the presenter wishes to work from a written text of the speech but, because of excessive length, the structural version of it seems to involve too many pages, then it can be retyped into manuscript form, but with the following modifications:

1. The text should be double or triple spaced between lines.
2. The text should not extend lower than two inches from the bottom of any page, so that, if the podium has a "lip" to it, no lines are lost from view.
3. No sentence should begin on the bottom of one page and conclude on the top of the next page.
4. The speaker may choose to have the text of the speech photocopied in a way that the type is enlarged or darkened in the duplication process and, therefore, easier to read.
5. The text should be enclosed in some kind of cover or loose-leaf binder with the pages consecutively numbered, so that it is easier to handle and keep under control, in the days preceding delivery of the paper and while traveling to the performance site. However, the pages should be loose rather than bound or stapled during the presentation. This allows the speaker to slide them aside quietly during the talk.

If the speaker prefers to work from an outline or a series of note cards, then these can be prepared in a similar manner.

AUDIOVISUAL MATERIALS

The decision as to whether to use audiovisual aids and the specific aids selected depend on the speaker's style and subject. An exhaustive review of audiovisual devices to assist presentations is beyond the scope of this chapter. However, a few principles and suggestions warrant inclusion. Visual aids are used much more commonly than audio aids. The two most common types of visual aids are handouts and slides.

Handouts

Handouts vary from a brief outline of the material presented to a word-for-word transcription of the talk. They may include a bibliography of sources that amplify the material presented. All handouts should have a definite purpose. That purpose will determine the time of distribution, the length of the handout, and the size of the print. In general, if the speaker intends to refer to the handouts during the presentation, they should be prepared in large, bold type that can be read in dim light. Pages should be numbered, and each item should be marked for easy reference. Naturally, under these circumstances, handouts should be distributed prior to the presentation. It is often helpful to have figures in the handouts duplicated on slides for the speaker's use.

If the handouts will not be referred to, they will only distract the listener's attention away from the presentation. Under such circumstances, the handouts should be distributed after the presentation. This is also advisable when the handouts duplicate the speech. If handouts are distributed in advance by the host of a conference and a speaker wishes to prevent them from distracting his audience, the speaker should direct the room lights to be turned all the way down, so that the audience cannot see the handouts. This nullifies their potentially distracting effect and encourages the audience to focus its attention on the speaker. It is often helpful to supplement brief outlines with suggested readings. All handouts should include the speaker's name and address, so that listeners can write for additional advice, information, or to invite the speaker for future presentations.

Slides

Slide projectors are available in most lecture halls, and slides can be easily stored, transported, and seen when properly prepared. A well-organized slide lecture highlights important concepts for the audience, serves as an outline for the speaker, and projects figures important to the talk. Each slide projected should have a specific purpose. In general, a speaker can rarely use effectively more than approximately one slide per minute.

Slides should be prepared in bold type and are usually unreadable if they exceed six lines. Limiting each slide to four or five lines is recommended. As a rule of thumb, it should be possible for the speaker to read each slide held toward a room light at arm's length. If this is not possible, the slide will generally not project well in a large hall. In addition to being easy to read, slides generally should be easy to look at. Diazos, the standard white-on-blue slides, can be made inexpensively and are much easier on the eye than is typed print on a white background. Computer-generated slides are also relatively easy and inexpensive if the speaker has access to the necessary hardware and software. Slides should always be numbered, so that, if a slide tray is spilled at the last moment, the lecture can be reorganized. It is also advisable for the speaker to put his/her name on each slide, especially when the speaker does not use his/her own carousel. Whenever possible, the speaker should bring the slides already inserted in the carousel and checked in advance for order and position. In this case, the speaker's name should appear on the outside of the carousel. It is important to inquire in advance as to whether a standard carousel projector is available and whether front projection or rear projection will be used. In rear projection, the slides must be turned around from their usual position. When one is traveling, slides should always be carried with the speaker, not checked through airplane, ship, or train luggage. This is true for any important visual or auditory aid.

In some cases, dual projection (use of two projectors at the same time) may be desirable. When needed, both sets of slides should be numbered, so that the projectors can be easily coordinated (for example, slide 1A in one projector, 1B in the second projector). If slides will be shown on only one projector during the middle of the talk, it is advisable to match them with blank slides in the second projector. Keeping the same number of slides in both projectors decreases the risk of losing synchronization between the two projectors.

Transparencies

In general, transparencies are not as good as slides. They may work fairly well in a small classroom, but in large halls they are difficult to see and frequently look as if they have been made just moments before the lecture. If a speaker wishes to use transparencies to draw a figure and show the development of a concept or design, this can be done equally well (usually better) by a sequence of prepared slides. Transparencies are not significantly easier to make or cheaper than well-prepared slides, and their use should be discouraged.

Videotape

Videotape has become extremely popular and is a fine teaching tool. In order to be effective in a public presentation, it must be well-made, neatly edited, and self-sufficient. It is undesirable for the speaker to have to talk over the video in order for its message to be understood. In addition, there must be enough high-quality monitors in the auditorium to allow easy viewing by everyone in the audience. If the subject of the videotape is highly detailed, as may occur with microsurgery or histologic slides, numerous high-quality monitors often provide better resolution than projection video, and front projection usually provides better resolution than rear projection. It is important to be certain that the speaker's video format is compatible with the auditorium's equipment. This is a special concern if the speaker is presenting in a foreign country.

Film

With the advent of videotape, 16 mm sound movie projection has become less popular. However, this medium still provides excellent audio and video reproduction, and it may be preferable in some cases. Movie projection is especially useful if the speaker is required to use one central screen in a large room.

Audiotapes

Talks are often enhanced by the playing of audiotapes, but effective audio reproduction requires as much thought, planning, and equipment as videotape or film. Generally, playing an audio sample from a pocket cassette recorder through a podium microphone is ineffective. Such demonstrations are usually difficult to hear or understand, the sound is distorted, and they appear improvised. If audio samples are important to a talk, arrangements should be made in advance for high-quality audio playback equipment. The tapes should be cued for the sound engineer, and short leaders of known time duration should be placed between audio samples. If it will be necessary to turn tapes on and off several times during the presentation, it is helpful to put an audio signal (such as beep) at the end of each sample, so that the sound engineer will know when to turn the tape off. The next sample should come approximately 10 sec after the beep, allowing adequate time for the sound engineer to react and turn the tape recorder off, and for the tape recorder to be turned on and resume steady speed before the next example is heard. Either cassettes or reel-to-reel tapes may be used, but reel tapes can be repaired and played again more easily if they are damaged during a presentation. It is advisable to bring a backup copy and to bring both formats if equipment arrangements have not been confirmed.

WARM-UP AND PREPARATORY EXERCISES

Approximately one month before the presentation, effective presenters will begin an exercise regimen to get the voice primed for performance. A simple but demanding physical/vocal warm-up done on a regular basis (every day for at least three weeks before performance) will get body alignment, breathing, and voice in condition to present research and opinion in the manner they deserve. Use of such a warm-up can make the difference between a bland, forgettable rendering of a presentation and a dynamic delivery of the materials in a way that will more than do them justice.

The following series of exercises is divided into four parts. It is important that they are done regularly. Doing them all with attention to the sensations experienced as they are done will produce the most noticeable results. These exercises are very helpful if done correctly, but they may be difficult to master from written descriptions alone. Speakers interested in perfecting these skills will benefit from a few sessions with a performance coach or from a public speaking workshop such as those offered by Executive Performance in Training Centers (5). If pressed for time, the presenter should select and do at least one exercise in each of the four categories. As they are done, it is important to make them enjoyable rather than hard work.

I. General Relaxation and Energizing

The first category of exercises can serve to relax a speaker on days he/she is feeling tight or tense and to energize a speaker on days he/she is feeling weary or spent. If the speaker will take a moment to scan the body to ascertain physical and psychological state, then he/she will know best which exercises need to be emphasized and how much time to spend with each.

A. Full-body yawns, physically stretching out in all directions. Loosen belt and/or tie if necessary to give the stretches full excursion. Yawns should be genuine and not mere tokens.

B. Gentle shaking in many different areas of the body in order to loosen tension or to energize: hands, arms, shoulders, legs, small of the back, etc. (Some individuals prefer energetic dancing to music, jumping rope, yoga, or stair climbing.)

II. Breathing and Alignment

If there are any back problems that restrict flexibility or make certain movements uncomfortable, the exercises below can and should be modified accordingly.

A. Extended breathing out and then softening the belly to initiate effortless inhalation without any shoulder involvement. Allow the air out again easily and completely but without postural collapse. This can be done on just breath or with full sound (haaaaaaaahhhhhhh). Repeat slowly and enjoyably a half-dozen times and notice the calming and energizing effect.

B. Place the palms of the hands on the rib cage (without tensing the shoulders in order to do so) to encourage rib flexibility during inhalation and exhalation. During inhalation, allow the ribs to move out in the direction of the palms of the hands. During exhalation, use the palms of the hands to encourage the ribs to move back in, but without any postural collapse in the spine. Repeat slowly four to five times, then drop the arms and shoulders heavily at the sides and enjoy the free movement of the rib cage when not inhibited by the pressure of the hands.

C. Slowly roll down through the spine, leading with the head and relaxing over with knees slightly bent, going only as far down as is comfortable. Slowly and comfortably "rebuild" the spinal column, initiating the upward movement by pressing the soles of the feet into the floor and releasing the legs out of the hip joints, making sure that the head is the last thing to be added to the upright spinal column. Repeat three to four times until the body fully appreciates the connection between the feet and the head and moves as one connected and coordinated unit with no sharp division. Use full breaths to help maintain the sensation of internal space.

III. Top Quarter of the Body

A. Intertwine the fingers of both hands and place them on the back of the skull. Without tensing the shoulders or holding the breath, pull forward with the elbows and back with the head steadily for about 20 to 30 seconds. Release the isometric pull and enjoy the freedom that results in the cervical area of the spine.

B. With hands on shoulders, allow elbows to touch in front and to approach each other in back. Repeat until the muscles facilitating this activity fatigue just a bit. With hands on shoulders, "flap your wings" slowly until the muscles involved fatigue slightly. With hands on shoulders, allow elbows to make large, full circles first forward and then backward until muscles fatigue. Lift and drop shoulders easily until muscles fatigue somewhat. Notice any changes that may occur in your ability to breathe freely.

C. Stand tall through the spine with shoulders relaxed and spread. Reach your right hand across the chest to your left shoulder and firmly massage the band of muscles that extends from the shoulder to the base of the neck. If any knots are present, gently knead them and coax the tension to melt away, helping with free and easy breathing throughout. Repeat this activity on the other side.

D. With your face continuing to remain forward instead of facing either shoulder, use a slow, even count of 16 to complete one full head roll to the right, enjoying an easy relaxing stretch in each direction through which the head passes as it makes a single rotation. Reverse, making a full, slow rotation to the left. This can be repeated a few times, keeping the rolls slow and easy and the breath moving throughout.

E. With the heels of the hands, use even, steady pressure right in front of the ears as you make big circles releasing and relaxing the jaw on both sides. If the urge to yawn occurs, so much the better. Allow the hands to slide down the jaw on both sides, toward the chin, easing the jaw down as they do so. Yawn again to feel the deep relaxation. Use the thumbs on either side of the face, in the vicinity of the molars, to locate and firmly press into the masseter muscles. Continue the pressure while breathing deeply for about 30 sec before releasing the thumbs and enjoying the freedom and release in the jaw itself. (This exercise can be repeated anytime during the day when the jaw is feeling held and tight.)

F. Move the tongue around in the mouth to loosen it up. Use it to count the teeth, or stick it out in the direction of the nose, the right ear, the chin, and the left ear. With a loose, relaxed jaw, move just the tongue from top lip to bottom lip to top lip to bottom lip as you say or sing, la-la-la-la-la-la-la-la-la-laaaahhhh.

G. Move the different parts of the face around slowly and quickly. Stand in front of a mirror, if necessary, to make sure that movement is actually taking place: eyebrows, eyes, bridge of nose, nostrils, cheeks, lips. See whether you can appear very surprised, very happy, very angry. Repeat these manipulations easily, without holding the breath until, the muscles being used are a bit fatigued.

IV. Voice and Speech

A. Drop the jaw, take a breath, and release a long sigh, which starts high-ish and finishes lowish in the pitch range (haaaaaahhhh). Repeat three to four times, each time starting just a bit higher in pitch and finishing a bit lower without allowing the voice to either screech or growl. Explore the full extent of available range.

B. Use the fingers to rub and stimulate the face gently. Unfurrow the brow and relax the jaw. With the hands gently covering the cheeks and eyes and the lips gently touching, hum directly into the palms of the hands, feeling and enjoying the vibrations produced by the voice. Allow the pitches to move up and down while continuing to rub the face and hum. Then drop the hands and feel the vibrations in the bones of the face and skull instead of in the palms of the hands as the humming continues.

C. With the jaw relaxed (mouth open) and the tip of the tongue gently tucked behind the bottom front teeth, raise and lower the back of the tongue in order to move easily from "ng" (as in si*ng*) to "aaaahhhhh," keeping the sound forward. This combination can be either spoken or sung, but primary vibration of sound should ideally move from the nose to the mouth as the sounds alternate. Repeat enough times to make this comfortable.

D. Use full and steady breath from the midsection as you call out easily on full voice: "Hey, Joe! O.K.! Hello! How *are* you?"

E. Use a combination of different tongue twisters to help train the articulators to move more efficiently: red leather, yellow leather, blue leather; nuclear regulatory commission; blue-backed blackbird; delectable delicacy, etc. [A number of bookstores carry collections of enjoyable tongue twisters. Some children's books (e.g., the Dr. Seuss series) are quite useful in this regard as well.]

The more often these exercises are done attentively, the easier they become. They are representative of a far greater range of warm-up and developmental exercises available to the presenter who wishes to build the voice into an effective and expressive communication tool.

FINAL REHEARSAL AND PREPARATION

Approximately two weeks before performance, the opening sentence, the closing sentence, and any key ideas or quotations that would benefit from direct eye contact with the audience should be memorized.

The speech should be rehearsed at least once a day, until the presenter is very familiar and comfortable with its contents, its structure, and any accompanying visual materials to be included.

If possible in the final week of preparation, the presentation should be rehearsed with a podium, at a microphone, and/or to a camera. The more the presenter can simulate the actual conditions under which the speech will be delivered, the fewer surprises will occur when the speech actually takes place. If someone can videotape a performance of the presentation, the presenter can use it to make any necessary corrections or adjustments in either content or style.

About one week before the presentation, the speaker should add two important exercises to the warm-up regimen:

1. Visualization. Sit or lie down, do some deep breathing to relax your muscles, and focus your concentration; then imagine you are watching yourself giving the presentation *perfectly*—without a hitch from beginning to end. Include details, colors, emotions throughout; take your time. Get into the habit of envisioning it perfectly done so that the actual performance is a simple, direct repetition of a task already mastered.

2. Directing Energy. People who suffer "stage fright" often describe a sensation of self-consciousness. All those eyes focused right on the speaker can be intimidating if the presenter does not know how to direct that energy. As the speaker continues to practice the presentation, he/she should imagine the audience as a large slice of pie, which can be divided into six different sections. No matter how large an audience may be, it may help the speaker to remember that each person seated in that audience is only one human being. Instead of speaking to an undefined mass of faces, the speaker can think of presenting to a series of individuals seated in different locations throughout the audience. Figures 1 and 2 indicate possible "traffic patterns" for eye contact. If the speaker allows his/her gaze to linger with a specific

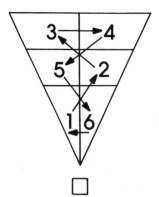

FIG. 1. Practiced, planned patterns of eye contact help assure that members of the audience will feel as if they are being spoken to personally. This figure contains one suggested eye-contact pattern that is particularly well suited to relatively narrow and/or deep auditoriums.

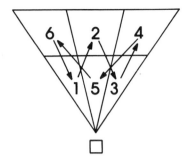

FIG. 2. This alternate pattern of eye contact may be better suited in a shallow and/or wide auditorium than that illustrated in Fig. 1.

individual for the length of a sentence or two and then to travel from section one to section two and so forth during transitions, then these individuals feel themselves an important part of the event rather than merely present. Any speaker who learns to make genuine rather than token eye contact with specific individuals in each section of the audience invites participation and interest in the presentation; he/she succeeds in making those present actual participants in the event. An act of communication demands not only a sender but an implied or actual recipient of the message.

Furthermore, stage fright and self-consciousness can be dramatically lessened if and when the speaker shifts attention away from the self and to the members of the audience. If the speaker gives full attention to the receivers (Are they paying attention? Are they understanding what I am saying? Do they need me to repeat that statement or to slow down a bit? Am I loud enough for the people in the back?), the focus of attention shifts from the self to them, and the task of communicating is that much more enjoyable.

During this final stage of rehearsal, a room of decent size should be used, in which should be placed three or four individual listeners, each sitting in a different section. After the presentation, the speaker can check with each listener to make sure he/she felt as though all present were being talked *to* rather than *at*. In the absence of cooperative helpers, the speaker can place specific objects in different locations in the room (a trash bin, a coffee mug on a seat, a sweater over another chair, etc.) and make sure really to see each object in turn.

READING THE ROOM

It is extremely helpful for any speaker to assess the room or hall prior to speaking. While this may not be quite so critical for the physician presenting research results through a microphone as it is for a singer presenting an unamplified recital, the comfort gained from the mistakes avoided is comparable. Whenever possible, the speaker should inspect the room before presenting: during a coffee break or lunch break or on a previous day. Any inconvenience is worth the effort. If this inspection is absolutely impossible, the speaker may gain some of the necessary information by observing and listening to earlier presenters.

In assessing a room, the speaker should investigate acoustics (Can speakers be heard well from all portions of the room?), type of microphones available, room temperature, availability of water, lighting on the podium, availability of a pointer, placement of projector controls, number and position of stairs leading to the stage, location of the nearest bathroom for possible use shortly before presentation, presence and quality of projectors, type of projection (front versus rear screen), location and operation of lighting controls, and presence or absence of a stage manager and projectionist. Familiarizing oneself with these matters can prevent numerous embarrassing moments. If the presentation is long and there is no water available, the speaker can place a glass of water under the podium before the audience arrives. If a fixed microphone is used, the speaker must be prepared to maintain a reasonably constant mouth-to-microphone distance and direction. With fixed microphones (such as those attached to a podium), the microphone needs to be adjusted immediately prior to the speech. It should be approximately at chin level (no higher) and should be no more than four to six inches away from the speaker's face. Whenever possible, it should be tested prior to the arrival of the audience.

If a lavaliere microphone is used, the speaker must remember not to brush the microphone cord by putting his/her hands into pockets and not to brush papers across the microphone. If a wireless microphone is used, the speaker should be certain to turn it off at the end of the presentation. There are many stories, humorous to everyone except the speaker, of presenters who have left microphones on during bathroom breaks or exceedingly frank conversations about previous speakers or hosts of the event. Many high-quality wireless microphones work well even through walls!

If a stage manager or projectionist is provided, the speaker should introduce him/herself ahead of time. These colleagues can greatly facilitate the smooth flow of the performance. They are used to being ignored by most speakers. However, they generally appreciate and deserve a little recognition. Taking a few moments prior to presentation to discuss one's needs or at least shake hands is worthwhile.

Occasionally, disasters occur. Some of them can be anticipated. For example, the author (RTS) depends heavily on slides for many presentations. Consequently, he generally travels with a carousel replacement bulb and pointer; sometimes with a remote slide changer; and with a projector when speaking in a nonacademic building where audiovisual arrangements are questionable. However, any speaker should be prepared, in the event of major problems, to proceed with no amplification or visual aids at all.

Room temperature can also be a potent detriment to good delivery. If the air conditioning is turned up so high that the speaker is shivering, the audience will perceive this as nervousness. Identifying this problem in advance allows the speaker to dress appropriately and/or have the room temperature adjusted. At the opposite extreme, a room that is too hot or stuffy can make the audience uncomfortable enough to lessen the effectiveness of even the best speaker; adequate ventilation may make all the difference to his/her success.

DELIVERING THE SPEECH

On the day of the performance, the speaker should make sure he/she is rested and physically comfortable. Shoes should be comfortable, breathing should not be restricted by either belt or collar, and even new clothing should have been tested in advance to ensure that the speaker will be comfortable performing whatever range of movement is called for during the presentation. Time should be allowed for a concentrated, uninterrupted warm-up and a visualization of the presentation perfectly performed. The speaker should make sure not to overeat before speaking and should drink enough water to maintain a good level of hydration without unduly taxing the kidneys and bladder in the process.

If there are a series of speakers in one program and/or the introduction is lengthy, there are some "hidden" warm-up activities that can be done in the interim: easy, gentle head and neck movement; small sips of water; moving the tongue easily around the mouth; releasing the jaw with lips closed; deep, easy breathing through the nose into the midsection of the body; finding supportive friends in the audience.

Finally, there is a "trick" that a number of successful speakers use in order to increase their degree of comfort during a presentation. They think of someone who loves their work, who thinks they can do no wrong; who is an ardent fan; and, in their imaginations, they bring this friend right into the audience they are about to address. It can be a young son, a grandmother who is no longer alive, or even a family dog. The speaker can just place this admirer in the audience and allow unqualified approval to inspire a confidence and ease that might otherwise be elusive.

During the presentation, the body should be fully erect but loose and easy rather than tight and held. Remembering to breathe easily and fully will be of great assistance in this regard. The speaker's feet should be slightly apart (one may be a few inches in front of the other), the weight should be forward over the metatarsal heads, the knees should be unlocked, and the speaker should be well balanced. This is an athletic "ready" stance, not far different from that seen in a shortstop or other athlete prepared to perform. It is also approximately the same position used in recital by classical singers.

The podium should not be used as a weight-bearing surface but rather as a script holder. A few gestures, all of which are directly related to the content of the material, are all that is needed. Constant shifting of weight from one leg to another and arbitrarily waving one's arms needlessly in the air simply serve to communicate the speaker's general discomfort and lack of real communication skills to the audience members. If the speaker makes genuine eye contact with specific people in different locations in the audience at the beginning of the speech, at key times during the speech, and again at the end, then there is a real sense of significant communication taking place.

Instead of simply twisting the head at the neck, if the speaker can face different sections of the audience at different times during the speech with the whole body (keeping the microphone between him/herself and the audience at all times), then a sense of real commitment to what one is saying is effectively and easily transmitted, and the head and trunk of the body are both in a better position to produce free breathing and a well-produced vocal sound. If the voice has been well prepared and exercised enough to respond easily and fully—in terms of pitch, loudness, rhythm, pause, quality—to the content of the speech, then what is being said by the speaker is wonderfully augmented by how the content is being transmitted. Finally, if the speaker can avoid any sense of collapse or visible relief when the speech is over— if, instead, he/she can make the final point, reestablish real eye contact with specific individuals, and then accept and acknowledge applause and reaction—then the delivery will be at least as remarkable as the content itself. Such techniques not only maximize a speaker's communicative impact but also help to minimize both the physical and the psychological stresses related to public speaking. Learning to present comfortably and effectively in person can make sharing one's research and opinions both healthy and enjoyable.

REFERENCES

1. Eisenson J. *Voice and diction: a program for improvement,* 5th ed. New York: Macmillan, 1985.
2. Fisher HB. *Improving voice and articulation,* 2nd ed. Boston: Houghton Mifflin, 1975.
3. Machlin E. *Speech for the stage.* New York: Theatre Arts Books, 1966.
4. Wilder L. *Professionally speaking.* New York: Simon & Schuster, 1986.
5. Executive Performance in Training Center (EPIC), 47 East 77th Street, New York, New York 10021.

Professional Voice: The Science and Art of Clinical Care, Robert T. Sataloff. Raven Press, Ltd., New York © 1991.

30

The Singing Teacher in the Age of Voice Science

Richard Miller

Oberlin College, Conservatory of Music, Oberlin, Ohio

What should a responsible voice teacher be teaching in a scientific age? Perhaps we should recall William Faulkner's opinion that the past is all that anyone living in whatever age actually has. What a responsible voice teacher does in this scientific age is not really different from what responsible voice teachers have been doing over several centuries, most of which have been replete with people who considered themselves enlightened and "scientific." Still, in light of recent expansion in knowledge and technology, it seems particularly important in the 1990s for singing teachers to be cognizant of developments in related fields and their potential to enhance teaching.

There is a prevalent opinion that, in past centuries, singers had little interest in science. That viewpoint is not supported by historical review. Consider, for example, the following description of respiration in singing:

> . . . the ribs raise outwardly, and . . . the diaphragm . . . descends and compresses the abdomen. . . . For good expiration . . . air must be made to leave with more or less force, with more or less volume, according to the character of the song (1).

Those words were written not by Bouhuys in the 1970s, nor by Hixon in the 1980s, but by Jean-Baptiste Berard in 1775. Similarly, current interests in the study of vowel tracking were preceded by generations of interest in acoustic adjustments, as expressed by Mancini in 1774 (2).

> If the harmony of . . . the mouth and "fauces" is perfect, then the voice will be clear and harmonious. But if these organs act discordantly, the voice will be defective, and consequently the singing spoiled.

Manual Garcia, inventor of the laryngeal mirror and a renown singing teacher, clearly appreciated the practical importance of scientific knowledge about the voice. His comments of 1847 could easily have been written today (3):

The capacity of the vocal cords to vibrate, the dimensions of the larynx, the thorax, the lungs, the pharyngeal, buccal and nasal cavities, the disposition of these cavities to resonate, constitute the absolute power of the voice of an individual. . . . The singer, in order to dominate the material difficulties of his art, must have a thorough knowledge of the mechanism of all these pieces to the point of isolating or combining their action according to the need.

A case could be made that teachers of singing have always wanted to know how the instrument functions. Certainly, both the great Lampertis made use of then-current scientific information. In the 20th century, such noted voice teachers as Marchesi, Shakespeare, Bachner, Herman Klein, Bartholomew, Mills, Curtis, Plunkett Greene, Witherspoon, Frank Miller, Clippinger, Martienssen-Lohman, Stanley, Westerman, Coffin, Appelman, and Vennard (the list could be greatly expanded) have called on factual information in support of pedagogical tenets. Rather than being a new idea, such interest in the available factual information characterizes the mainstream of historical vocal pedagogy.

We should not fool ourselves, however, into believing that what generally takes place today in vocal studios across America (or anyplace else) is based on intimate acquaintance with the current literature of science. Most teachers of singing still give a nod of approval to the helpful scientist, and we exhibit tolerance and indulgence toward those among us who want to play with machines, but, deep down in our hearts, we "know" that singing and teaching are matters of "instinct" and "artistry," and that there is no real possibility of improving on what Madame X handed down to Maestro Y, who in turn gave it unadulterated to my teacher.

Comparative vocal pedagogy reveals an immense stratified structure of both fact and nonsense. There exist systems of vocal technique built on assumptions without foundation in fact. Two brief current illustrations will suffice: a world-renowned premier tenor recently explained during a master class that the vowel /i/ was the only vowel narrow enough to enter the frontal sinuses, while a rival tenor who occupies the very pinnacle of the heap informed his master class participants (while demonstrating slight laryngeal descent on inspiration) that, for the "open throat," the epiglottis must be held low at all times. Results from students trying to apply either piece of advice were just short of disastrous.

What should today's voice teacher be doing in the studio? In any age, the main duties of a teacher of singing, with regard to technique, have always been chiefly two: (a) to analyze vocal problems and (b) to design proper solutions for them. It is a pleasure to have students who exhibit few vocal problems, but teaching such pupils is not really teaching voice so much as it is sophisticated coaching and performance preparation. The teacher who helps the less natural singer establish a solid technical basis is a real voice teacher. The potential of the student must be discovered and technical means offered for rectifying problems impeding fine performance. How can this be done?

One choice is to try to pass on to the student what the teacher has learned about his/her own instrument; we hope that knowledge is considerable. However, no teacher of singing has personally experienced all the possible forms of uncoordinated function that are exhibited daily in every active studio. In attempting to communicate impressions, instincts, and sensations through impressionistic, instinctive, and descriptive language, the teacher may not communicate all the concrete information that the student requires.

Another choice is teaching by modeling—by imitation. If a teacher can demonstrate a beautifully free vocal sound, one may gain some insight into how it is produced. If the teacher has been a great singer, an astute student may glean certain subtle aspects of style and even a little technique. If the teacher is an over-the-hill opera diva, one may also pick up some tendencies it might be better not to have picked up. If a teacher has never got his/her own instrument sufficiently mastered to be professionally useful, the student may be in real trouble when he/she models the master's voice!

It is important for the teacher to have a basic knowledge of bodily function and vocal acoustics and to be able to explain what students are doing wrong and why, in whatever language is necessary to reach any individual student. The *main* prerequisite for teaching singing today is none of the following: a fabulous ear, excellent musicianship, highly refined taste, a bubbling personality, good will, or a successful singing career, although *all* of these factors are helpful. The main prerequisite is to know what is malfunctioning in a singing voice and how to correct it. It is foolhardy to think one can reach a wise and consistently accurate assessment and resolution if one does not know something about how the vocal machine operates.

How much scientific information does the voice teacher need? As much as he/she can get. There is a growing, credible body of information to help the voice teacher understand what is really happening to a singer's voice, what various exercises can and should be done, and the real intent of the images used traditionally in voice teaching. In addition, learning such information increases the teacher's vocabulary, providing new language for those students in whom traditional constructs have not worked. There exists a fair battery of helpful scientific instrumentation that provides some exact information on singing. It includes a number of electronic devices. The spectrum analyzer tells us much about what singers describe as "resonance." The fiberscope and the electroglottograph also provide new possibilities (4). Studio uses of instrumentation are discussed in greater detail elsewhere in this book.

Unfortunately, much of the physiological explanations put forth in the voice studio are still surprising to all but those of us who are singers, and most "acoustic" explanations are pure fantasy. Yet, as soon as a teacher of singing requests alteration in vocal sound, he/she is dealing in physiology and acoustics. However, unlike the car mechanic, the voice teacher is not dealing simply with a mechanically complex instrument. Knowing how the voice functions has never yet produced a great teacher of singing. A fine teacher combines mechanistic information with the psychological and the aesthetic.

Once having chosen to pursue such a complex profession and accept the enormous responsibility (and liability) for a student's vocal health and longevity, to rely entirely on imagery is to saddle oneself with a serious handicap. For example, when the relative amplitudes of overtones in the voice do not produce the particular goal the teacher has in mind, how much helpful information is conveyed by requesting, "Put more space around the tone"? Although a teacher has a distinct tonal concept in mind, the student putting "space around the tone" may make alterations to the acoustic tract, to the laryngeal position, and in airflow rate that have no relationship to a teacher's tonal aesthetic. Trying to "sing on the breath," "spin the tone," "place the tone in the forehead," "send it up and over," etc., will, without doubt, have immediate influence on resulting timbre. By hit and miss, the teacher and student may finally get what the teacher wants. Persons using divining rods have also been known to locate underlying groundwater.

Today's singing teacher has access to a greater body of solid information and rational tools than ever before. We owe it to our students to be able to take advantage not only of everything that was known 200 years ago, but also of everything that is known today.

The advice of Bartholomew (5), a pioneer in the study of the acoustics of the singing voice, still is appropriate:

> . . . Imagery should be used merely to suggest indirectly through its psychological effects a certain muscular setting which is awkward for the beginner. The teacher, though using it, should bear in mind at all times the true facts, because when imagery becomes so vivid that it is transferred into the physical field and used to explain physiologic and acoustic phenomenon, it becomes extremely dubious, unreliable, and even false. It is this misuse which is largely responsible for the bitter controversies over vocal methods, as well as for their often comical explanations. Furthermore, since imagery is largely individual and thus variable, when it is trusted as a physical explanation, the so-called "True Method" becomes as variable as the individual temperament, instead of as stable as Truth is usually expected to be.

It is the responsibility of the singing teacher in a scientific age to interpret and expand vocal traditions through the means of current analysis so that the viable aspects of tradition can be communicated in a systematic way. The advantage of teaching singing in the era of the voice scientist is that today's teacher has the means of sorting through what is offered, both historically and currently, at the vocal pedagogy smorgasbord and choosing rationally what is most nutritious, while discarding the garbage, of which there is plenty.

How can emerging information for use in the studio be expanded? Singers of stature should be willing to cooperate in noninvasive investigations of the singing voice. To make such information useful, various schools and techniques of singing should be identified in research reports. Participants should not all be indiscriminately lumped together as "professional singers," nor should students, even at graduate level, be designated professional opera singers in published reports. The subtle individual properties that set apart one voice from another should not be averaged out. In order for scientific research to be valid and have practical value in the studio, teachers of singing must be involved, knowledgeable, and interested. Our input, in areas of expertise best understood by voice teachers, is essential.

Unless it is recognized that a number of separate techniques of singing exist, conclusions reached in studies about singers need to be read cautiously. There is little doubt, for example, that if five baritones studying with Dr. X have been taught to modify the vowel /a/ to the vowel /o/ at the pitch B_3, spectral analysis will reveal changes in the region of vowel definition at that point. It cannot, therefore, be concluded that professional baritones modify /a/ to /o/ at the pitch B_3, but only that baritones involved in the study who have been taught that particular method have learned their lesson well. Singing teachers must learn to read studies critically, so that the lessons they learn are the correct ones. They must also learn enough to know what kind of studies to seek out. For example, although perceptual studies are necessary, singing teachers really want to know more about *how* the vocal instrument produces the timbres singing voices are capable of making. They already hear those timbres. They need practical information on the mechanisms so it can be applied in the studio.

Much of what goes on in the vocal studio today is extraneous activity, or even counterproductive. This is true in the teaching of all athletic skills (of which singing is one). For example, in discussing sports biomechanics in 1984, Abraham (6) reported:

> Analysis of high-speed films of elite performers has led to many interesting observations. Baseball pitchers, for instance, have been apparently wasting much time in the past strengthening their wrist flexor muscles to improve speed of their pitches. Research at the University of Arizona has revealed that the wrist "snap," which does contribute heavily to the speed of the pitched ball, is actually caused by the sudden deceleration of the forearm and occurs so fast that the wrist flexor muscles cannot even keep up, much less contribute to the motion.

Many exercises thought to strengthen or relax the musculature of singing may have no more relationship to actual function than do those for the major league pitcher mentioned above. Learning to "relax," or to "energize," or to "strengthen" certain muscles of the face, neck, and torso may have little to do with singing, yet some vocal instruction is largely directed to such activities.

A main goal of teaching in this and any age should be to do no harm. Every aspect of vocal technique must be in agreement with what is known about healthy vocal function. Any teacher assuming responsibility for a student's artistic and vocal health (which we all do) is obligated to educate him/herself in the wisdom of a wide community of experts. There is no such thing as a unique vocal method or a unique teacher of singing. It is not necessary for each student and each teacher to rediscover the art of singing alone. There is a body of information that ought to be drawn on by anyone who claims to teach anything to anybody. No one can know it all, but we must be willing to modify what we do know as information expands. Demythologizing the language of vocal pedagogy is part of that process. Consultation with experts in related disciplines, through reading and offering our professional services to help discover new facts, is another. Above all, as teachers of singing in a scientific age, we must ask ourselves how much we really know about the subject matter we deal with. Do we have facts, or do we rely on anecdotal opinions? Do we know the literature of our own field, as well as that of related fields?

Singing today is not a dying art. It is very much alive and growing. At this moment, it occupies an advantageous position where the traditions of the past and the information of the present can be combined in an exciting way. The responsibility, excitement, and reward of our profession lie in rising to the challenges of our new opportunities to make the present and future of voice teaching even greater than the past.

REFERENCES

1. Berard JB. *L'Art du chant* (1775), translated and edited by Murray S. Milwaukee: Pro Music Press, 1969.
2. Mancini G. *Practical reflections on figured singing* (1774), translated by Foreman E. Champaign: Pro Music Press, 1967.
3. Garcia M. *A complete treatise on the art of singing, part one* (1847), translated by Paschke DV. New York: Da Capo Press, 1983.
4. Titze I. Instrumentation for voice research. *NATS Bull* 1983;38(5):29.
5. Bartholomew WT. *The role of imagery in voice teaching*. Proceedings of the Music Teachers National Association, 1935.
6. Abraham L. Sports Biomechanics: application of high tech to Olympic engineering. *Tex Prof Engineer* 1984;July–August:16–19.

Professional Voice: The Science and Art of Clinical Care, Robert T. Sataloff.
Raven Press, Ltd., New York © 1991.

31

The Singing Voice

*Linda M. Carroll and **Robert T. Sataloff

*American Institute for Voice and Ear Research, Philadelphia, Pennsylvania; and
**Department of Otolaryngology, Thomas Jefferson University,
Philadelphia Pennsylvania

The voice is a marvelous instrument. Singers are capable of bringing audiences to their feet or to tears. They are artists in the truest sense. They must combine concept, melody, text, and stage movement and make it all seem effortless. For most singers, this takes years of preparation. Still, even successful singers are often asked to sing under the worst of circumstances and the greatest stress. Dusty old theaters, smoky lounges, noisy parties, and cold rehearsal halls await those who dare to master this fine art. Nevertheless, how many people have wished "If only I could sing . . ."? The fact is, virtually everyone can. Anyone who has normal pitch variation in his/her speaking voice and can tell whether two musical tones are the same or different can be taught to sing. That does not mean that he will be the next Luciano Pavarotti, but such a person can probably develop the muscle strength, ear–voice coordination, and confidence to enjoy singing, and usually to be enjoyed by others.

TRAINING

There are basically two types of singing voice specialists: a voice teacher (or technician) and a vocal coach. The voice teacher works primarily on developing vocal technique and building coordination of musculature in the vocal mechanism. The vocal coach works primarily on repertoire (songs) and interpretation. Many singers work with both a voice teacher and a vocal coach. Singers need to be able to move on stage and feel comfortable with an audience, so some sort of dance training may be necessary. Singers with a desire to sing opera or musical comedy should take some acting and fencing training as well. Aspiring classical singers also require language courses in at least Italian, German, and French. Study of Russian, Spanish, and other languages is also recommended.

The beginning singer should, first and foremost, learn to omit any abusive vocal behaviors in both speaking and singing. Although many singing teachers work with the speaking voice, most are not formally trained speakers or teachers of speech. Speech-language pathologists are trained and licensed to work with the normal and pathological speaking voice. Many, however, have little training (if any) in the professional voice. Those speech-language pathologists who have a particular interest in the professional voice attend special symposia, obtain internships, and seek mentors. Fortunately, there are some speech-language pathologists who have a great deal of experience and knowledge in voice, and it is ideal (but unusual) for a singing teacher to affiliate with such a colleague. Voice trainers also exist, but there is no licensing or quality control for people who designate themselves in this category. In addition, there is no set of requirements that must be fulfilled in order for one to call himself or herself a singing teacher. Consequently, it is essential for other professionals to investigate the quality, training, experience, and reputation of singing teachers with whom they anticipate collaborating in patient care. Membership in the National Association of Teachers of Singing (NATS) is an encouraging sign, but the requirements for membership are certainly not rigorous enough to assure that all members are high quality teachers. At present, it is illegal in most states for anyone but a licensed speech-language pathologist to treat a pathological speaking voice. Pathology, of course, is diagnosed only by a laryngologist.

There are nearly as many methods of teaching singing as there are singing teachers. Over the years, many approaches have become popular enough to be known as "schools." There are German, French, Italian, and Russian schools, schools that follow the tenets of various famous teachers, and countless articles and books on teaching methodology. Many of the ideas and principles of one school of thought conflict with those of others. In this chapter, we make no effort to define good singing teaching, or to promulgate any one technique as *the* correct way. Rather, we present a few basic principles that can be used to assess singing teaching in general and the summary of our basic approach to teaching voice. Naturally, many details are omitted. However, for the reader who is not a voice teacher, this chapter should provide a basic idea of what a singing teacher does; and for the singing teacher, we have included information on documentation of voice lessons, correspondences with other professionals, and approaches to teaching people with injured voices. These topics are frequently not included in routine training for singing teachers. Our approach is presented not as the definitive method, but rather as an example and guideline for singing teachers who may be interested in understanding the care and treatment of people with vocal health problems and in collaborating in an arts-medicine setting.

In general, singing teaching begins with an assessment of the student. This leads to a "diagnosis" of the singer's talent and problems, which guides the development of a lesson (or treatment) plan. Specific exercises are designed to correct problems and improve vocal control and eventually artistry. There are many differences between singers and typical speakers. For example, conversational speech usually encompasses about a major sixth. Most singers possess a 2-octave range. Interestingly, physiological frequency range is about 3 ½ octaves in both singers and nonsingers, so most people have more potential than they realize. Pulmonary demands are also much greater during singing than speaking. In speech, we typically use 10 to 25% of vital capacity. The singer frequently uses closer to 65% of vital capacity.

Training occurs in all areas of the singer's anatomy. Abdominal exercises, pulmonary control, and correct alignment of posture cultivate the power sources of voice. Vocal exercise increases neuromuscular strength and coordination at the laryngeal level, improving not only range, quality, and vibratory symmetry, but also smooth control over changes in subglottal pressure, registers, and other variables. The supraglottic vocal tract is also trained, developing optimal vocal tract position and shape to create the desired harmonics without unnecessary muscle tension and with improved resonance. In general, principles of artistic economy apply. That is, if a good sound can be made without involving a specific muscle group (such as those muscles that retract the tongue), then using those extraneous muscles is generally wrong and deleterious to vocal health and performance. In most cases, voice lessons result in steady, gradual improvement in voice quality, range, efficiency, and endurance. Voice lessons should not end in hoarseness or physical discomfort in the neck or throat (although abdominal and back muscles are often fatigued and ache). The principles of proper voice production are largely the same in speaking and singing. In fact, many people believe that the singing voice is simply a natural extension of a good speaking voice. In any case, training supplied by a singing teacher and a speech-language pathologist should be compatible and symbiotic. If a singer is receiving contradictory information from these two voice professionals (and is correctly interpreting their instructions), this is usually indicative of incorrect training from one of them. Close scrutiny is warranted.

ASSESSMENT

In evaluating a potential new student, most singing teachers listen to a song or two, ask the singer to sing a few specific exercises, and discuss the singer's previous training. This procedure (history, diagnosis, treatment) is the same as that used by physicians and speech-language pathologists. More enlightened singing teachers also discuss matters of vocal health and hygiene in greater detail. Our assessment protocol is more involved, not only because we work with singers with vocal problems, but, moreover, because we believe that the singing teacher should have extensive knowledge of the student's experience, habits, and health and should have the knowledge to use this information effectively in the training program. Good singing teachers who hear anything abnormal in a voice (hoarseness, breathiness) routinely refer the prospective student for a laryngologic evaluation. In some music schools, medical assessment and vocal cord visualization are required of all voice majors prior to matriculation. In an arts-medicine setting, the laryngologist has usually examined the patient before the singing teacher begins the evaluation. Regardless of these circumstances, we find value in a systematic, comprehensive assessment of each singer.

The questions asked in the history are the same as those asked by the physician and are summarized in Appendix II. If a history form has not been completed for the laryngologist, the singing teacher asks the student to complete a similar questionnaire. If a patient history form has already been completed for the physician, the singing teacher reviews this information and asks additional questions about previous teachers and training, specific techniques used, and other singing experience. The teacher also inquires about the singer's goals. In some cases, he or she is aspiring to a Metropolitan Opera career; in others, he or she is taking a few singing lessons only to develop techniques to improve the speaking voice. The teacher then assesses the student's knowledge of voice function.

If the student is a singer, the next portion of the evaluation involves listening to a song of the singer's choice. The entire evaluation is taperecorded, and videotaped, if possible, as are subsequent lessons. Such tapes are good not only for documenting progress, but also for feedback for teaching purposes. In addition to the tape recorder and video camera, basic equipment for a voice studio includes a piano (or keyboard), full length mirror, handheld mirror, and good lighting. The studio should have reasonably "live" acoustics, with a minimum of sound-treatment materials. It should also be properly heated and humidified, and drinking water should be readily available. The singer then sings a series of scales, while they are played on the piano. The singing evaluation is done with the student standing. The singer is assessed for stance/posture, breath control, support, jaw and oral cavity position, general tension, range, and quality of sound. Range should be assessed with a series of scales, beginning approximately at the natural pitch of the speaking voice. The scales should proceed past the upper passaggio (including the falsetto in men) up to the highest musically acceptable note and descend to the lowest musically acceptable note. The voice should not be strained, and it is the teacher's responsibility to decide when the patient has reached his or her limit. We use a form for the singing teacher to record observations conveniently (Fig. 1). Specific characteristics are assessed in each area, and a training program is designed to correct any errors observed.

Stance/Posture

The head, neck, and shoulders should be in neutral position. The shoulders should not be elevated, rolled forward, or held back, as these maneuvers introduce unnecessary tension. The singer should stand comfortably straight, but not in a stiffly erect, military fashion. Knees should be slightly bent and flexible, not locked, and weight should be centered over the meta-tarsal head (balls of the feet), not the heels. The feet should be apart, but not more apart than the width of the shoulders. Many singers prefer to have one foot slightly forward. This athletic, well-balanced stance optimizes breathing and support. It behooves the singing teacher to acquire special knowledge of posture analysis and muscle conditioning. In many cases, it is advisable for the student to include physical exercises to improve posture and strengthen support muscles. Basic principles of posture analysis and exercise programs can be found in the literature[1], and consultation with a skilled physiatrist or physical therapist may be valuable in selected cases.

Breathing

The rib cage should be erect, so that the upper thorax appears slightly more full than during comfortable speech, but it should not rise excessively or cause muscle distension in the upper thorax, supraclavicular area, or neck. Most of the active breathing is abdominal, and distension should occur in the front, back, and sides. Breathing should be relatively relaxed, quiet, and nasal breathing is preferable when time between phrases permits. High thoracic breathing patterns, rapid intake, and noisy inspiration frequently indicate tension, which is carried over into vocalization. Abdominal move-ment during inspiration and expiration should be efficient. Excessive ab-dominal activity may occur in singers consciously struggling to optimize breathing and support. Such excessive inflection, contraction, and disten-sion of abdominal muscles undermine the adjustment process between breathing and initiating effective support.

Support

Support is a difficult concept for many singers, and various constructs are used to teach it. The fundamental principle is to generate a vector of force under the airstream, supporting it upward between the vocal folds. Support should be continuous, not static. Reasonably good abdominal and thoracic support occurs spontaneously in most people while singing a rolled /r/, and singing scales on /v/. Good support is also experienced during various spon-taneous maneuvers such as yelling (although this is frequently accompanied by other abuses). Muscles in the lower abdomen, upper abdomen, and lower thorax and back are actively involved. Their movement should be inward and slightly upward. Support should be initiated before a tone is heard. In many cases, if teachers advise a student to bring abdominal muscles in and up, the student will also raise his or her shoulder, chest, and neck muscles. Consequently, many teaching constructs have been created including one

TAPE # _____

SUBJECTIVE EVALUATION:*
SINGING VOICE

NAME: _____

DATE OF EVALUATION: _____

AGE: _____ DATE OF BIRTH: _____

SEX: ☐ MALE ☐ FEMALE

OTOLARYNGOLOGIST: _____

MEDICAL DIAGNOSIS: _____

SPEECH-LANGUAGE PATHOLOGIST: _____

☐ PROFESSIONAL VOICE USER
☐ NONPROFESSIONAL VOICE USER
☐ CLASSICAL SINGER
☐ NON-CLASSICAL SINGER
☐ NONSINGER

OCCUPATION: _____

YEARS VOICE STUDY: _____

VOICE TEACHERS: _____

LONGEST TEACHER: _____

LAST VOICE LESSION: _____

CHARACTERISTIC	CORRECTS TECHNIQUE		
	+ CUES	+ + CUES	UNABLE

STANCE/POSTURE:
    FEET POSITION
    WEIGHT FORWARD
    KNEES UNLOCKED
    UPPER TORSO/STERNUM
    SHOULDERS
    STRAP MUSCLES
    LARYNGEAL MOVEMENT
    FOREHEAD TENSION
    HEAD/NECK PROTRUSION
    HEAD/NECK ELEVATION

BREATH:
    ABDOMINAL/DIAPHRAGMATIC
    THORACIC
    CLAVICULAR
    SHALLOW
    RAPID
    AUDIBLE
    EXCESSIVE ABDOMINAL MOVEMENT

SUPPORT:
    EFFECTIVE
    DEFICIENT
    INEFFECTIVE
    LATE
    INVERSE PRESSURE

FIG. 1. Evaluation form used by singing voice specialists. +, minimal cues; + +, considerable tactile and visual cues required.

ORAL CAVITY:

REDUCED OPENING	
RISORIUS TENSION	
JAW JUTTING	
ANTERIOR JAW TENSION	
POSTERIOR JAW TENSION	
ANTERIOR TONGUE RETRACTION	
ANTERIOR TONGUE CURL	
POSTERIOR TONGUE ELEVATION	
POSTERIOR TONGUE DEPRESSION	

RESONANCE: _____

FOCUS: _____

RANGE: SCALES:

QUALITY:

PLAN:

FIG. 1. *Continued.*

including one in which students are advised to think of their support as going "down and out" (the inverse pressure approach), rather than "inward and upward." Any teaching imagery can be effective, so long as the student and teacher understand the difference between the language of the imagery and the physical effect they are really trying to achieve. Good support should be present not only when singing high notes, but also in lower ranges. Singers frequently support well going up a scale but relax excessively during descending passages and have virtually no effective support in portions of their mid and lower ranges.

Laryngeal Position

For most classical Western singing, the larynx is usually slightly below its neutral vertical position. The larynx should remain relatively stable and should not rise appreciably with ascending pitch or fall with descending pitch. These caveats are not necessarily true in other styles such as pop music (for intermittent special effects), Oriental music, and certain other cultural and ethnic styles.

Jaw Position

Jaw position is assessed while singing /a/. The jaw should be allowed to open to its maximum, relaxed position, but it should not be forced open excessively. Appropriate jaw position is similar to that seen in most people just before the initiation of a yawn. It is generally close to a two-finger span, although no one should be forced to meet this guideline if this degree of opening introduces jaw tension. The corners of the mouth should not be tensed, and the jaw should not quiver or change position with changes in pitch. The posterior jaw should also be relaxed for all vowels.

Tongue Position

Tongue position is also assessed on /a/. The tip of the tongue should rest in a relaxed posture against the mandibular central incisures. It should not retract, curl anteriorly, or rise posteriorly. The pharynx should generally be visible, not obscured by arching of the posterior aspect of the tongue. It is important to assess visually and by listening to the sound of the voice not only the anterior tongue position, but also the posterior position of the tongue. Most well-trained singers note that the tongue is supposed to be relaxed and should not pull back from the teeth. However, it is possible (especially for the more advanced singer) to maintain the anterior tongue in good position and still introduce excessive posterior tongue tension. This excessive tension results in voice fatigue and sometimes also limitation of range. In addition to the criteria noted, tongue position should not change with alterations in pitch, and there should be no tongue activity apparent during routine five-note scales on /a/.

Face

While singing scales on /a/, virtually no facial muscle activity should be required. Excessive tension in the corners of the mouth, lips, corrugation of the chin, forehead tension, or other extraneous muscle use indicates hyperfunction and may be associated with deficient support. The facial expression should be pleasant, but no specific facial muscle gestures should be *required* to produce an /a/. Eliminating dependence on facial hyperfunction is important not only to optimize technique, but also because the singer needs to be able to use facial muscles independently to show expression and emotion without affecting voice production.

Summary

At the completion of the assessment process, observations and findings are reviewed with the student. Fatigue, nervousness, and other variables must be taken into account during the first lesson, but an experienced teacher can usually draw accurate conclusions during the initial evaluation. Specific deficiencies are explained, and plans to remedy them are established. Specific exercises are selected, and the singing teacher teaches them to the student or patient in the singing studio. A specific practice schedule is assigned, and arrangements for follow-up and further lessons are made.

EXERCISES

Singing lessons involve selected exercises to build muscle strength, coordination, and efficiency. Throughout training, a combination of tactile (hands), verbal, visual, and auditory (live and recorded) feedback is used to correct errors and assure that the singer can tell which techniques and sounds are correct and which are not. The exercises are designed to develop all parts of the vocal mechanism. Like other muscle building exercises, it is often better to structure such exercises in short sessions to be repeated a few times throughout the day. In beginners, such sessions should rarely be more than 20 minutes in length until muscle strength is developed and technique becomes consistent. Exercises to warm up the voice first thing in the morning, and to warm down the voice following each practice session, rehearsal, performance, and in the evening are especially important.

General Body Exercises

The singing teacher must make an assessment of the student's general physical condition. Good aerobic conditioning, abdominal muscle strength, and back muscle development are particularly important. In any student with health problems, or in older students, exercise programs should always be developed in conjunction with medical supervision. Vocal development should include some form of aerobic activity (such as jogging, fast walking, swimming, aerobic dance, etc.), abdominal muscle exercises (such as sit-ups), and exercises that affect the back and lower abdomen (such as leg lifts). Singers must be instructed to avoid forceful glottic closure and other forms of voice abuse while exercising. Groaning during sit-ups or weight lifting, or counting numbers during aerobic dance can cause vocal injury (in fact, hoarseness and vocal nodules are seen commonly in aerobics instructors). Nevertheless, if a singer cannot run up a couple of flights of stairs without getting winded, poor physical conditioning is likely to compromise vocal technique.

Breathing

There are many exercises that work well for teaching breathing. In some cases, the teacher simply explains thoracic and abdominal breathing and the desired principles and helps the student experiment with correct and incorrect breathing techniques and postures, pointing out which techniques are correct. In most students, some sort of tactile feedback helps. Placing a student in unusual positions frequently helps him or her sense aspects of breathing technique that are harder to feel in normal positions. Such exercises may be done with the student lying on the floor with a small book under his or her head. Another useful technique is to ask the student to bend from the waist and place his or her hands laterally on the waist. The student is then instructed to take a full breath and feel rib expansion. The breath is taken slowly, avoiding elevation of the shoulders and maximizing expansion of the lower portion of the rib cage. The singer then exhales slowly and repeats the exercise several times. The student then inhales and stands one-third to one-half the way up, maintaining proper balance. The exercises are repeated, trying to maintain the same abdominal and lower back sensations. They are then repeated while standing erect. Many alternate exercise regimens are also effective. The student may stand with arms perpendicular to the floor, palms upward, and sense upper torso alignment, ease of breath, and efficiency of support. Students are also instructed to practice breathing and combining relaxed breathing with flexion, and relaxation of support musculature, periodically during the day, not only during practice sessions, but also while speaking or simply walking from place to place.

Support Exercises

It is important for each student to realize that it is possible to vocalize without hyperfunctional muscle activity. Many students, especially those with previous singing experience, habitually engage superfluous muscle groups in preparation for each sung phrase. For such students, it is often best to start teaching support by eliminating as much extraneous muscle activity as possible, teaching the student simply to breathe in a relaxed fashion, and then add support and sound. For other students with fairly good technique and no significant hyperfunctional abuse, it may be appropriate to proceed directly to discussions of improving support musculature strength and coordination. The latter group of students is easier to teach, and the exercises listed below are examples of the kind of approach used for the former group. Such students may be advised to:

1. Take slow, deep breaths in and out through the mouth, eliminating all muscle tension in the oral cavity, head, and neck. These exercises are done facing a mirror.
2. Take a slow, deep breath, and exhale slowly for as long as possible on "wh," being careful to maintain good posture and not allow the chest to collapse.
3. Take a slow, deep breath, and exhale on /s/, /z/, and /ʃ/, being careful to maintain good posture and slow exhalation.

FIG. 2. Five-note ascending/descending scale.

4. Take a slow breath, and initiate a descending sigh on /u/, /o/, and /a/. These vowels are then repeated but initiated with the consonants used in the previous exercise. In particular, /s/ has a tendency to help support. The student is instructed to maintain the same abdominal and lower back sensations during the vowel as initiated during the consonant. The student should not be afraid if this exercise encompasses more than one register. Smooth transition between registers in the long descending sigh should be encouraged.

5. Take a slow breath, and exhale, permitting a gently voiced sigh during the exhalation. The exercise is then repeated, and the singer is asked to sustain the sigh on a descending scale.

6. Take a slow, deep breath, drop the jaw, engage the support musculature as previously explained, and sustain the vowel /a/. Observe the tongue and neck closely. Abdominal support should not create any visible change in the oral cavity, head, or neck.

7. Take a deep breath, initiate support, and sing five-note ascending and descending scales beginning on the note identified during deep sigh exercises. The scales should be done on /a/, and later on /o/ and other vowels (Fig. 2). Initially, the notes should be connected (legato), and the student should take care to avoid laryngeal rise and fall while changing pitch. For some beginners, even five notes is too great a range to sing with improper techniques such as tongue retraction. However, for most students, five-note scales can be performed throughout low and high ranges. Later, when technique is more consistent, more advanced exercises are used.

8. Rolled /r/, /v/, /ʃu/ and lip trills (continuous "br") in descending passages are also good for developing breath management and increasing consciousness of correct skeletal posture (Fig. 3). The student must be monitored carefully for laryngeal and throat tension. Students who cannot

FIG. 3. Descending slide.

FIG. 4. Repeated ascending/descending scales.

FIG. 5. Slow ascending/descending slide of major third interval.

produce a rolled /r/ or lip trills without considerable effort should avoid these exercises until later in training.

Technical Exercises

Technical exercises are used to develop agility, increase range, and improve pitch accuracy. Such exercises include (among others):

1. Rapid and slow five-note ascending/descending scales while humming and on various vowels (Fig. 4). This exercise is good for virtually all patients. It may be preceded by a descending five-note slide.
2. Slow sliding scales ascending and descending a major third on /a/ and on /o/ → /a/ (Fig. 5). This exercise is applicable for all patients and is especially helpful for patients with scar tissue, vocal fold masses, superior laryngeal nerve paresis and paralysis, significant breaks between registers, and when singing is resumed following vocal fold surgery.
3. Arpeggio scales on /a/ and /o/ → /a/, slowly, with careful legato connection from note to note (Fig. 6). This exercise is good for the intermediate singer and for those with technical weaknesses.
4. Slowly descending five-note scale, beginning on /u/ and changing to /a/ on the last note, with a trill (Fig. 7). This exercise should be used in the lower part of the voice to increase vocal control and effective use of support in the lower register. The trill should be a true half-step or whole-step trill, not simply excessive vibrato.
5. Lip vowel variation (/a/ to /o/ to /u/ to /o/ to /a/) exercises sung on a sustained tone (Fig. 8). Tongue vowels may also be approached in this manner. This exercise may be done with tactile cues to keep the sound from "spreading." The vowel variation exercises are good for focusing the voice, particularly with recurrent laryngeal nerve paralysis and following vocal fold surgery.

FIG. 6. Arpeggio scales.

FIG. 7. Descending scale with trill on last note.

6. A great number of additional exercises are used during the training process. They involve connected and disconnected scales, patterns of scales involving various intervals rather than adjacent notes, exercises at different dynamics, exercises bridging different registers (e.g., crescendo/dimminuendo singing from falsetto to modal register and back), and many other patterns. Such vocalises may be found in numerous published collections and texts on vocal pedagogy.

PLACEMENT, RESONANCE, AND PROJECTION

Detailed discussion of placement, resonance, and projection is bound to be controversial. For the purposes of this chapter, suffice it to say that, as respiratory control, muscle strength, and laryngeal coordination improve, various techniques are used to optimize the shape of the vocal tract. The tongue, soft palate, pharynx, jaw, and other regions of the supraglottic vocal tract are trained to generate with minimal effort the desired harmonic spectrum. In particular, the resonators enhance the desirable formant, as discussed in Chapter 4. Exercises to accomplish these goals include use of vowels, consonants, songs, ear training, and a considerable amount of trial and error with feedback from the teacher. Feedback from instrumentation such as spectrographs may also be helpful in selected cases.

Carryover Exercises

Singing teachers who collaborate with speech-language pathologists and laryngologists sometimes teach patients for short periods of time solely to assist with development of the speaking voice. In these patients, and in trained singers who develop speaking voice problems, it is often possible to establish a singing technique that is far superior to habitual speaking technique. Several methods are helpful in bridging the gap between song and speech. A few are listed below.

1. Descending five-note scales on /o/ are sung, changing to counting with the speaking voice on the last note, concentrating on maintaining an up-

FIG. 8. Vowel variation exercise.

FIG. 9. Carryover exercise from singing voice to speaking voice.

ward lilt to the speaking voice (Fig. 9). This is a particularly good carryover exercise into the speaking voice. It encourages the use of abdominal support from the /o/ to be maintained in the speaking voice, and it facilitates speaking pitch variability. It is also good for helping the speaker to find a comfortable habitual pitch. If the exercises are performed too low, the beginning of each count (1, 2, 3, etc.) typically has roughness and hesitation. When appropriate habitual pitch is approached, the transition from song to speech becomes easier and smoother. When the appropriate pitch range is exceeded, the speaking voice sounds strained, and counting is again difficult to initiate or maintain.

2. The relationship between recitative and speech can be very useful. For a good speaker, singing teachers frequently teach recitative by having the student speak the words in rhythm and then adding notes in a natural fashion. The connection can be bridged in the opposite direction as well. Opera and oratorio singers skilled in recitative can start a familiar recitative passage with notes and gradually eliminate specific pitches, slipping into speaking voice. Such exercises often expedite traditional voice therapy. However, they are always done in conjunction with therapy provided by a speech-language pathologist.

3. Rap music works well for nonclassical singers with speaking voice problems. Rap music provides bridging materials similar to recitative. When using rap music, the rhythm track may be gradually faded out during the rap. It is surprising how many singers can sing and rap with appropriate technique, but who speak poorly and have trouble grasping traditional speech therapy approaches. Like recitative, rap exercises can be combined with instruction from a speech-language pathologist to facilitate therapy.

SONGS

Building repertoire may begin when the student has mastered several of the vocalises and has developed voice control over a large enough range to permit comfortable singing of the vocal literature. Singers who wish to sing classical repertoire do well to begin with an anthology of early Italian songs and arias, and with simple English and American songs. Nonclassical singers should start with standard lyric-legato songs. Rock singers should also begin with slow lyric rock songs, not hard rock, and use songs that vary between modal and falsetto register, if possible. It is usually easier to begin with new repertoire, rather than trying initially to relearn old material in a technically correct fashion. Active performers should concentrate on incorporating the new technique into slower songs, gradually building the repertoire into an entire set or concert. If the student has been performing actively prior to studying with the teacher, it is especially important for the teacher to see the singer in performance. This allows a much deeper understanding of the singer's vocal needs, problems, and progress. Technical aspects of singing are the singing teacher's domain. Many singing teachers also provide training in interpretation, staging, and other artistic aspects of performance, although these matters can be relegated to voice coaches, acting teachers, and other professionals.

FREQUENCY OF LESSONS

Voice lessons should be given every week when possible, and every 10 to 14 days, at least, if weekly sessions are not possible. Frequent lessons are especially important early in training to be certain that techniques are being implemented correctly in practice sessions between lessons. If the student is working with a singing teacher and speech-language pathologist, it is particularly helpful if he or she can see both of them on the same day. Ideally, they should be in the same location. The combined team approach is highly effective for singers and speakers, and it is often helpful for the singing teacher and speech-language pathologist to work together with the student part of the time. This provides an opportunity to be certain that singing lessons and speech therapy are coordinated and that any potential misconceptions in the student's mind are resolved.

SPECIAL ASPECTS FOR SINGERS WITH VOCAL INJURIES

The singing teacher who works in an arts-medicine setting encounters several differences from routine studio work. The range of student potential is enormous. Some students have great potential talent; others may already be world-class professional singers but require special instruction while recovering from an injury. Still others have no interest in singing but benefit from support, relaxation, and musical training in an effort to improve their speaking voice. Such a variety of students provides a great many challenges, and even teachers who have spent their lives preparing opera students for major careers find teaching most patients challenging and rewarding. The excellent, experienced teacher who is interested and willing to learn about anatomy, physiology, laryngology, and speech pathology will have no difficulty applying previous experience and common sense in order to function successfully in this setting. However, the problems encountered with injured voices require greater flexibility than most teachers exercise routinely in terms of teaching style, varieties of language and imagery, and tailoring programs and expectations for the patient.

Special problems arise in patients who have had injuries to the true vocal folds. These may include nodules, cysts, polyps, hemorrhages, scars, trauma, recent surgery, or other afflictions that have serious implications for vocal fold fragility. Training a voice with skillfully chosen techniques in this setting provides invaluable rehabilitation. Incorrect exercises can result easily in serious or permanent injury.

In order to work well with these patients, the singing teacher must have a clear understanding of the anatomy and pathology involved, the natural course of the pathological process, and a good working relationship with the laryngologist and speech-language pathologist. Specific exercises are designed for each patient that minimize vocal fold trauma, but avoid muscle disuse atrophy, while increasing vocal strength, endurance, and efficiency. The exercises may include three- or five-note scales sung softly and with the notes connected, slightly more complex vocalises, or muscle exercises without phonation or vocal fold contact. The singer must be taught to sing "by feel," relying on tactile, proprioceptive, and visual feedback. Emphasis should be on using correct technique, not on imitating a perfect sound. The timing of initiation of singing lessons following vocal injury is determined by the laryngologist. The timing of advancement in vocal training for such patients is determined by the singing teacher in collaboration with the laryngologist and speech-language pathologist. In order to avoid reinjury in the course of normal speech, singers with vocal injury will find it advantageous to initiate specially designed voice training as soon as medically safe after the injury. Although it might seem that singing should be eliminated until total healing occurs, this is appropriate in only a few circumstances, such as early, acute vocal fold hemorrhage.

TRAINING OF THE SINGING VOICE SPECIALIST FOR THE MEDICAL SETTING

Singing voice specialists must be excellent singing teachers to begin with. They should have extensive training in the singing voice and ideally have personal experience as professional singers. Being able to relate to performance demands on the basis of personal experience is most helpful. It is also desirable (but not essential) for the singing voice specialist to have reasonably good keyboard skills. He or she should be able to play scales with the student, accompany simple songs, and make individualized practice tapes. It is not essential that the singing voice specialist be a highly skilled pianist. However, it is essential that he or she has an exceptional ability to hear minute changes in vocal quality and be an astutely critical perfectionist. In addition to these basics, the singing voice specialist must acquire knowledge of anatomy and physiology of the voice, including neuroanatomy, familiarity with objective voice measurement equipment, a basic understanding of the principles of laryngology and medications, and a fundamental knowledge of the principles and practices of speech-language pathology.

At present, there are no formal training programs in the United States that teach singing voice specialists to work with injured voices. In fact, there are very few programs to train interested persons in "how to teach singing" in general. Certainly, a degree in music education does not assure that a person is a good voice teacher. Similarly, a degree in voice performance does not necessarily mean that the graduate is a good singer, or that he or she has impeccable technique. Likewise, a highly successful, famous singer with impeccable technique is not necessarily a good teacher. In fact, many great singers who have been blessed with naturally good technique and have very few vocal problems themselves are not good teachers, since they have had little experience in the complexities of correcting vocal difficulties. It is illegal in most states for a singing teacher to provide therapy for an injured or pathological voice unless he or she meets licensure requirements, most of which are equivalent to membership in American Speech-Hearing Association (ASHA).

As mentioned earlier, speech-language pathologists do not generally receive training on care of the professional speaking voice, either. There are no speech-language pathology training programs that provide instruction on care of the professional singer, and most have no training in the singing voice at all. There is, however, a joint committee of ASHA and NATS that has compiled a list of those professionals who have partially or fully met requirements for interdisciplinary training. Information on this joint committee may be obtained by contacting either ASHA or NATS. At present, if a voice teacher accepts a student for voice *therapy* without having the student work concurrently with a licensed speech-language pathologist, that teacher may be subject to litigation, even if the student is referred by a laryngologist. A good interdisciplinary team not only provides optimal patient care, but also obviates potential legal problems of this sort.

In order to acquire the necessary knowledge, it is helpful for the interested singing teacher to take advantage of available graduate level courses in speech science, neuroanatomy, neurophysiology, and speech-language pathology. There are also an increasing number of symposia dedicated to the professional voice. These offer additional training by practitioners skilled in the field. The Voice Foundation offers the most extensive annual symposium on care of the professional voice. Information may be obtained by writing to The Voice Foundation, 1721 Pine Street, Philadelphia, Pennsylvania 19103. Important information can also be gleaned from many of the publications listed as suggested reading near the end of this book. In addition, even for experienced voice teachers, a professional internship of some sort is almost imperative. The duration varies with the teacher's experience and need, and it may be broken up into short observation periods. However, a singing teacher interested in becoming active in caring for the injured voice needs to observe the laryngologist in the office and operating room, speech-language pathologists specializing in professional voice care, and other singing teachers working with injured voices, and become skilled in voice laboratory instrumentation. Access to such opportunities is limited, but they are available.

REPORTS AND DOCUMENTATION

It is necessary for the singing voice specialist to communicate in writing with the laryngologist and speech-language pathologist. An initial report should be sent to the referring professional and should include the behaviors exhibited, exercises used, effectiveness of therapeutic intervention, and treatment plan. If the singer-patient is from a distant area, this report (along with the reports of the laryngologist, speech-language pathologist, and voice laboratory) will serve as a guideline for the voice teacher in the patient's locality. If the patient intends to continue studying with the singing voice specialist, each session is documented on audio (and often video) tape and with progress notes similar to those used by physicians and speech-language pathologists. In our office, these progress notes are kept in the medical chart, along with notes by the other team members. Periodically, progress reports are prepared as well. Record keeping is not traditionally a requirement of the singing teacher. However, professional standards have been established in a medical milieu, and singing voice specialists must observe them like any other medical professional. Such documentation may be useful for students without health problems in private studios, as well. A sample initial report is provided in Appendix IV.

CONCLUSION

Teaching singing is a complex and challenging process. Through exercises that build body strength, finely tuned neuromuscular control, and artistic taste, most people can be trained to sing at least better, if not well. The skills acquired during voice training are directly applicable to good speaking technique. Singing teachers who acquire special skills in training patients with vocal injuries provide invaluable help in the medical setting. One hopes the current great demand, along with increasing interest among singing teachers, will result in high quality, interdisciplinary training programs to make it easier for voice teachers to enter this exciting new field.

REFERENCE

1. Kendall FP, McCreary EK. *Muscles: Testing and function.* Baltimore, Maryland: Williams and Wilkins, 1983:269–320.

Professional Voice: The Science and Art of Clinical Care, Robert T. Sataloff. Raven Press, Ltd., New York © 1991.

32

Use of Instrumentation in the Singing Studio

Robert T. Sataloff

Department of Otolaryngology, Thomas Jefferson University, Philadelphia, Pennsylvania

VOICE TRAINING APPLICATIONS OF MEDICAL TECHNOLOGY

For generations, both medical care and voice teaching have been hampered by the need to rely on subjective assessment of the voice. On those fortunate occasions when the doctor or teacher has a skilled, unbiased ear and excellent auditory memory, subjective assessment may work fairly well. However, the health and safety of patients and students in general are better served by more objective methods of voice assessment. For voice teachers, dependence on the ear alone gives rise to special problems. For example, there is sometimes disagreement as to which vocal productions are good and which are bad; whether a voice is the same, better, or worse after a year or two of training, what exactly is meant by "good" or "bad," etc. Consequently, it would be valuable for a singing teacher or music department to be able accurately to assess the vocal performance and progress of each student through objective measures of voice function repeated over time. Such technology is no substitute for traditional, excellent voice training. Rather, it provides an extra set of tools for the voice teacher to help identify specific problem areas and to assure steady progress. Physicians have been faced with the same needs in diagnosing voice abnormalities and assessing the results of treatment. Consequently, instrumentation has been developed for medical voice assessment, and much of this instrumentation has potential application in the studio.

While instrumentation to perform all the tests is not widely available, much of it can be found in large cities with medical schools, especially if there is a laryngologist specializing in voice in the area. All the relevant tests are painless, and occasionally they have the added advantage of detecting an unsuspected and treatable medical problem that may affect vocal training and performance. Even the singing teacher who is not in the position to

403

utilize such technology regularly should be familiar with it, because such analysis may prove extremely revealing and helpful in selected students with special problems that do not respond to a teacher's usual approach.

Without restating information discussed in Chapter 31 on each of the six components of objective voice assessment, a few additional comments are worthwhile to shed light on potential teaching applications of medical instrumentation.

VOCAL FOLD VIBRATION

For the purposes of vocal training, we include in the category Vocal Fold Vibration not only true measures of vocal fold vibration, but also visual evaluation of laryngeal posture. The flexible fiberoptic laryngoscope has revolutionized our ability to visualize the larynx. It is small (about 3.5 mm in diameter) and passes painlessly through one nostril. Occasionally, a gentle topical anesthetic is placed in the nose, but most people do not find the tube uncomfortable in the nose, even with no anesthetic at all. When connected to a video camera, the flexible fiberoptic laryngoscope allows the student, teacher, and physician to watch the position of the palate, pharynx, tongue base, epiglottis, false and true vocal folds, and other vocal tract structures during speech and singing. At some institutions such as the Academy of Vocal Arts in Philadelphia, recordings of this sort have been made routinely for several years, prior to each student's matriculation as a freshman. Laryngeal posture, degree of tongue retraction, signs of strain, and other factors can then be compared with future recordings over the course of training. Such recordings are not only instructive for the student and teacher, but they may also provide invaluable feedback in selected cases. For example, occasionally, teachers are faced with a student with extremely "throaty" production, marked tongue retraction, and markedly excessive tension during singing. Most such students can have their techniques improved through traditional exercises, but an occasional student finds it very difficult to change technique to a more relaxed posture. Some such students do extremely well when the usual constructs and abstractions of the studio are supplemented by visual feedback. The student can watch his or her vocal folds and tongue base during singing and eliminate the hyperfunction and tongue retraction. While such situations do not occur often, it is useful for the voice teacher to know that such assistance is available for special cases. In a great many more cases, students and teachers find visual inspection of the larynx and pharynx during singing interesting and useful, although not essential.

Vocal fold vibration can be assessed by several means, as discussed above. The most common and best is strobovideolaryngoscopy. It allows detection of scars, small masses, subtle neurologic weaknesses, and other problems that may be heard in the voice as hoarseness, breathiness, or weakness. It is invaluable for a singing teacher to have such information so that the teacher and student know whether the vocal problems they are hearing are merely training deficits, or whether they are the result of a physical problem that requires special training methods.

PHONATORY ABILITY

Objective measures of phonatory ability are easily and readily available. Maximum phonation time is measured using a stopwatch, as discussed in Chapter 8, along with physiological frequency range and musical frequency range, which can be measured at the piano. These and other tests of phonatory ability should theoretically improve during vocal training, except for physiologic frequency range (which probably remains about the same). The student or patient is instructed to sustain the vowel /a/ for as long as possible on deep inspiration, vocalizing at a comfortable frequency and intensity. Ideally, the frequency (pitch) and intensity are controlled using inexpensive equipment that can be purchased at a local radio electronics store. Physiological frequency range of phonation disregards quality and measures the lowest and highest notes that can be produced. Musical frequency range of phonation measures the lowest and highest musically acceptable notes. Such tests can be performed into a high quality tape recorder and sent to a laboratory for formal analysis, including spectrographic analysis. Frequency limits of vocal registers may also be measured, as well as several other parameters. Combinations of tests of phonatory ability allow measures of glottal efficiency that may be valuable and should theoretically improve during vocal training.

AERODYNAMIC MEASURES

The aerodynamic tests discussed above may be especially valuable to the professional voice user and teacher. In some singers and actors, lung capacity may be substantially less than expected. It is especially important to identify such vocalists and optimize their pulmonary function through aerobic exercise and other means. In other singers and actors, initially good lung function gets progressively worse during singing or other exercise. Such singers may have unrecognized asthma induced by the exercise and performance. It is essential to identify such singers and treat them, or they will usually develop the same kinds of hyperfunctional voice abuse problems seen in people with poor support technique, even if they are well trained.

In addition to measures of lung function, airflow can be measured across the vocal folds. This provides a good measure of glottal efficiency and an objective way to identify voices that are excessively breathy, pressed, or well adjusted. These parameters should also improve during training, and this should be especially noticeable with many beginner students.

ACOUSTIC ANALYSIS

The best acoustic analyzers are still the human ear and brain. Unfortunately, they are still not very good at quantifying the information they perceive, and we cannot communicate it accurately. The acoustic analysis equipment discussed above is expensive and not needed very frequently in routine voice teaching. However, since most of the tests performed require only a good quality tape recording, they are always at a singing teacher's disposal. It is sometimes useful to document progress in vocal stability, vibrato regularity, pitch accuracy, or development of desirable harmonics (the singer's formant). In nonvoice majors required to study singing, visual feedback instruments are available to assist students in learning to match pitches.

LARYNGEAL ELECTROMYOGRAPHY AND PSYCHOACOUSTIC EVALUATION

Laryngeal electromyography and formal psychoacoustic evaluation have relatively little applicability in routine voice teaching. However, the principles of psychoacoustics may provide useful guidance for school faculty juries judging singers, actors, and other speakers. Traditionally, such juries are composed of people with differences in opinion, taste, and sometimes personality, and the biases inevitably introduced in such situations are very difficult to identify and negate. Most music and acting schools handle this problem simply by trying to have enough people on each jury to have such problems "even out." However, study of formal techniques of psychoacoustic evaluation would probably lead to improvements in the jury system.

DISCUSSION OF STUDIO APPLICATIONS

Currently available techniques for looking at, analyzing, and documenting voice function have been used successfully by physicians and a few farsighted voice teachers. They are not substitutes for good studio teaching technique but are rather extra tools in the teacher's armamentarium. As such, it behooves the modern voice teacher to become familiar with available technology that may enhance teaching efficiency and consistency.

There are other reasons, however, why singing and acting teachers should be familiar with and concerned about objective voice assessment. Political and legal developments over the past several years have made it clear that voice teachers are eventually (and probably soon) going to have to introduce the same kind of peer review and quality control practiced in other professions such as medicine and speech-language pathology. At present, most teachers and music schools rely on very little beyond personal opinion to define good singing, healthy singing, successful training progress, or even a "good voice." In modern times, such subjective vagaries may be insufficient for the individual voice teacher and especially for the music school trying to assess voice teachers and select an optimal voice faculty. Objective voice analysis may help. Not only can it define parameters and progress for individual students, but it can also help teachers in self-assessment and improvement, and music schools in faculty assessment. Any good teacher is eager to identify his or her own strengths and weaknesses, so the introduction of objective assessment should be viewed as a blessing by most high quality people in the profession. For example, consider the school with four voice faculty members each of whom is assigned 15 freshmen. Each freshman can be recorded on high quality audio and video tape singing standardized scales and an audition aria and can undergo comprehensive objective voice analysis. Such recordings can be repeated at the end of the first and second semesters, and annually (or more often) thereafter. Assume in each studio there are four new students with the same technical problems: tongue retraction, ineffective support, poor soft singing, and slight tremolo. Assume further that students of three of the teachers have these problems disappear within the first year, but the students of the fourth teacher have their problems get worse, and two or three students of that teacher who didn't have those problems initially develop them. Objective voice assessments detect such patterns early, document them in a clear, scientific fashion that eliminates the perceived personal persecution with which such information is often greeted and allows the teacher, students, and administration to make appropriate adjustments before significant (and possibly compensable) harm is done to the students.

Clearly, objective voice assessment has been a boon to laryngologists and can be a valuable adjunct to the individual singing and acting teacher. Moreover, it may provide our first real means to define good, healthy singing, acting, and teaching and to help promulgate high standards of practice among those who choose to call themselves "voice teacher."

Professional Voice: The Science and Art of Clinical Care, Robert T. Sataloff. Raven Press, Ltd., New York © 1991.

33

Physicians Studying the Voice and the Arts

Robert T. Sataloff

Department of Otolaryngology, Thomas Jefferson University, Philadelphia, Pennsylvania

Much has been said in this book about the necessity for interdisciplinary education. Speech-language pathologists and singing teachers clearly need to study anatomy, physiology, and basic health maintenance of the voice. Singing teachers need to learn about the singing voice. Speech-language pathologists benefit from singing study, voice scientists need to understand clinical problems and priorities, and so forth. At the most practical level, the reasons why a laryngologist should study voice are obvious. Through singing lessons, speech lessons, and personal performance experience, we acquire terminology experience, and understanding that cannot be achieved in other ways; this makes us better doctors. Without such training, the laryngologist can compensate to some degree by reading and study, but he or she never acquires quite the same expertise or patient rapport as the physician who has also experienced the discipline of musical development and the ecstasy and terror of public performance.

However, there may be even more compelling reasons for physicians to study the arts in general. Many of the most rewarding joys of subspecializing in voice or other areas of arts-medicine come from the interdisciplinary opportunities for creativity and the philosophical influence of our colleagues in the humanities. It is wise and rewarding for physicians to recognize the importance of the study of the arts in making us not only better doctors, but better people as well.

A modern poet has characterized the personality of art and the impersonality of science as follows: "Art is I: Science is We" (1). Since its earliest days, medicine has concerned itself with refining its understanding of the truths of science and art and applying their universal wisdom to the care of people. This implies an obligation for the physician to understand more about life than just the particulars of body function with which our science is concerned. We must expand our parochial vision into a broad understanding of humanity. One of the most obvious and accessible avenues to such philosophical breadth is the combination of medical studies with the study of the arts.

"Only through art can we get outside ourselves and know another's view of the universe which is not the same as ours and see landscapes which would otherwise have remained unknown to us like the landscapes of the moon. Thanks to art, instead of seeing a single world, our own, we see it multiply until we have before us as many worlds as there are original artists" (2). David, daVinci, Shakespeare, Bach, and others of their stature have remained vital because of the depth and universality of their visions of life. Understanding their messages enriches our entire being and gives new light to our own vision. Moreover, the process of learning to understand their wisdom teaches us how to perceive another's view—the art of understanding. As physicians, we must believe that there are as many "original artists" as there are people in the world; and it is the art of our profession to see what they see and to care for them accordingly.

"The principal complaint which patients make about 'modern scientific medicine' is the failure of physicians to communicate with them adequately" (3). What they are trying to tell us is not that they want more information, but that they want more humanity. "Art is the human activity having for its purpose the transmission to others of the highest and best feelings to which men have risen" (4). This fundamental caring is what we fail to communicate. This is especially curious, since it is the emotion that draws so many of us to medicine and makes it so much more fulfilling for us than the laboratory sciences. As Hippocrates observed: "Where there is love of man, there is also love of the art" (5). If we are to master the art of medicine, study of the arts may provide invaluable help, for to have the love is not enough. We must learn to understand it and to communicate it to our patients so that they feel it. This is where our science fails; and without this art, we are about as comforting as a well-programmed computer—and not nearly so efficient.

In addition to more abstract wisdom, study of the arts reveals a rather reassuring similarity of methods among the arts and sciences, as well as a similarity of goals.

"He who would do good to another must do it in minute particulars:

General good is the plea of the scoundrel, hypocrite and flatterer,

For art and science cannot exist but in minutely organized particulars" (6).

Both science and art seek universal truths; both seek the "I" and "We," and both recognize that the substance of great truths is smaller truths. Only their perspectives differ. Moreover, mastery of these differences may well be the substance of the genius that allows a few people occasionally to see that what has been before all of us all of the time has been missed.

We swear in the Hippocratic Oath: "I will keep pure and holy both my life and my art." In our quest to master the science and art of healing, we will do well to pay attention to the nature of the lives and world with which we live and especially to art, the science of the study of that nature. "It is art that makes life, makes interest, makes importance, for our consideration and application of these things, and I know no substitute whatever for the force and beauty of its process" (7).

It is somewhat comforting, somewhat humbling to consider one final truth:

All nature is but art unknown to thee,

All chance, direction which thou canst not see;

All discord, harmony not understood;

All partial evil, universal good;

And, spite of pride, in erring reason's spite,

One truth is clear, Whatever is, is right. (8)

REFERENCES

1. Bernard C. *Bull NY Acad Med IV* 1928;IV:997.
2. Proust M. O'Brien J, ed. *The maxims of Marcel Proust.* New York: Columbia University Press, 1948;XXIV,235.
3. Harvey AM, Johns RJ, Owens AH, Ross RS. *The principles and practice of medicine,* 18th ed. New York: Appleton-Century-Crofts, 1972;2.
4. Tolstoy L. *What is Art?* 1898, Chapter 8.
5. Hippocrates. *Precepts.* Chapter 1.
6. Blake W. *Jerusalem.* Chapter 3, Sec. 55.
7. James H. Letter to H.G. Wells, July 10, 1915.
8. Pope A. An essay on man. Epistle I. 289.

Appendix I

International Phonetic Alphabet

	English	Italian	Latin	French	German
Vowels					
[i]	meet, key	chi	Filio	qui, cygne	liebe, ihn, wir
[e]	—	—	—	parlé, nez, parler, parlerai	Seele, geben, Weh
[I]	mitt, hit	—	—	—	mit, sitzen
[e²]	chaotic	vero	—	—	Tränen
[ɛ]	bed	bello	requiem	belle, avait, mai, tête seine	Bett, hätte
[ɛ̃]	—	—	—	sein, pain, fin, faim, thym	—
[a]	—	—	—	voilà la salade	—
[ɑ]	father	alma	mala	âme	Vater, Mahler
[ɑ̃]	—	—	—	enfant, champ, Jean, paon	—
[ɔ]	jaw	morte	Domine	sortir, aura	Dorn
[o²]	rowing	nome, dolce	—	—	—
[ʊ]	foot	—	—	—	Mutter
[o]	—	—	—	rose, ôter, pot, beau, faut, écho	Rose, tot, froh
[õ]	—	—	—	fond, ombre	—
[u]	moon	luna	unum	fou	Uhr, Buch, tun
[y]	—	—	—	tu, flûte, eût	früh, Tür
[ʏ]	—	—	—	—	Glück
[ø]	—	—	—	peu, berceuse	schön
[œ]	—	—	—	coeur, fleur	können
[œ̃]	—	—	—	parfum, défunt	—
[ə]	Rita, oven	—	—	je, faisant, parlent (forward— use lips)	lieben
[ɛ̃]	—	—	—	—	Liebe
[æ]	cat	—	—	—	—
[ɜ]	first	—	—	—	—
[ʌ]	cup	—	—	—	—
Consonants: Fricatives					
[f]	father, physic	fuori	fecit	fou, phare	Vater, Phantasie
[v]	visit	vecchio, Wanda	vestrum	vent, wagon	Weg
[ʃ]	shine (bright)	lascia (bright)	scitote	charme (dark)	schön, Stadt, Spass (dark)
[ʒ]	Asia (bright)	—	—	je, givre (dark)	—
[s]	simple, receive	seno, questo	salutare	soixante, cent, leçon, jasmin	essen, Fenster, Haus
[z]	roses, zoo	rosa, sdegno	—	rose, azure	Seele, unser, Rose
[θ]	three	—	—	—	—
[ð]	this	vado	—	—	—
[ʕ]	human	—	—	—	ich, recht
[x]	—	—	—	—	Nacht, doch, such
[h]	house, who	—	—	—	Haus, lebhaft

413

	English	Italian	Latin	French	German
Consonants: Nasals					
[m]	mother	mamma	mortuus	maman	Mutter, nahm
[n]	nose	naso	nescio	nez	nein, Nase (dental)
[ɲ]	onion	ognuno	agnus	oignon, agneau	—
[ŋ]	ring, thank	sangue, anche	—	—	Ring, Dank
Consonants: Lateral and trilled					
[l]	liquid	largo, alto	alleluia	large, fatal	links, alte, also
[ɫ]	milk	—	—	—	—
[r]	three	rosa, orrore	rex	roucoule	Retter, irre
Consonants: Affricates					
[tʃ]	cheer, pitch	cielo, cenere	cibo, coelo, caeca	—	plätschert
[dʒ]	joy, George	gioia, gemo	pange, regina	—	—
[ts]	cats	zio, senza	gratias, justitia	—	Zimmer, Spitz
[dz]	leads	azzuro, bonzo	azymis	—	—
Consonants: Plosives					
[p]	pepper (explosive)	papa (dry)	peccata (dry)	papa, absent (dry)	Paar, lieb (explosive)
[b]	bow	bada	beata	bas	Bett
[t]	tent (sharp, alveolar)	tutto (dry, dental)	terra, catholicam (dry, dental)	tantot (dry, dental, palatalized before [i] [y] [j] [ɥ]) tire, tu tiens, tuer	Tante, Grund, Thau (sharp, alveolar)
[d]	dead (alveolar)	doppio (dental)	Domine (dental)	dindon (dental; palatalized before [i] [y] [j] [ɥ]) dire, dure, Dieu, réduit	decken (alveolar)
[k]	cat, chorus, quick (explosive)	come, ecco, chioma, che questo (dry)	credo, bracchio (dry) mihi	comment, qui, choeur (dry, except before [i] [y] [j] [ɥ])	Kunst, Qual, chor, Tag (explosive)
[g]	give	gamba, grande, gonfia	gaudebit	gauche, grande	geben, General
Glides, diphthongs, and triphthongs					
[j]	yes (no buzz)	ieri (no buzz)	ejus (no buzz)	bien, moyen	Jahr
[w]	west	guarda	qui, linguis	oui	—
[ɥ]	—	—	—	nuit	—
[ʎ]	lute	gl'ochhi	—	—	—
[ɑːi]	mine, high	mai	Laicus	—	—
[ɑːl]	mine, high	—	—	—	mein, Hain
[aj]	—	—	—	corail	—
[ɛːi]	say, mate	sei	mei	—	—
[ɛːl]	say, mate	—	—	—	—
[ɛj]	—	—	—	soleil	—
[œj]	—	—	—	denuil	—
[uj]	—	—	—	fenouil	—
[oːu]	grow	—	—	—	—
[ɔːi]	boy	poi	—	—	—
[ɔːl]	boy	—	—	—	—
[ɔːy]	—	—	—	—	treu, träumen
[ɑːu]	cow	aura	laudamus	—	—
[ɑːʊ]	cow	—	—	—	Tau
[ɑːo]	—	—	—	—	Tau
[ɛːə]	air	—	—	—	—
[Iːə]	ear	—	—	—	—

	English	Italian	Latin	French	German
[ɔːə]	ore	—	—	—	—
[ʊːə]	sure	—	—	—	—
[ɑːiə]	fire	—	—	—	—
[ɑːuə]	our	—	—	—	—
[ɔːyə]	—	—	—	—	Feuer

Modified from Moriarty J. *Diction.* Boston: E.C. Schirmer, 1975, 257–263.

Appendix IIa

PATIENT HISTORY: SINGERS
Robert Thayer Sataloff, M.D., D.M.A.
1721 Pine Street
Philadelphia, PA   19103

NAME _____ AGE _____ SEX _____ RACE _____
HEIGHT _____ WEIGHT _____ DATE _____
VOICE CATEGORY: _____ soprano   _____ mezzo-soprano   _____ alto
                  _____ tenor   _____ baritone   _____ bass

(If you are not currently having a voice problem, please skip to Question #3.)

PLEASE CHECK OR CIRCLE CORRECT ANSWERS
1. How long have you had your present voice problem?

   Who noticed it?

   [self, family, voice teacher, critics, everyone, other _____]

   Do you know what caused it? Yes _____ No_____

   If yes, what?

   Did it come on slowly or suddenly? Slowly _____ Suddenly _____
   Is it getting: Worse: _____ , Better _____ , Same _____
2. Which symptoms do you have? (Please check all that apply.)
   _____ Hoarseness (coarse or scratchy sound)
   _____ Fatigue (voice tires or changes quality after singing for a short
         period of time)
   _____ Volume disturbance (trouble singing) softly _____
                                              loudly _____
   _____ Loss of range (high _____ low _____)
   _____ Change in classification (example: voice lowered from soprano to
         mezzo)

417

_____ Prolonged warm-up time (over ½ hr to warm up voice)
_____ Breathiness
_____ Tickling or choking sensation while singing
_____ Pain in throat while singing
_____ Other: (Please specify) _____

_____

_____

3. Do you have an important performance soon? Yes _____ No _____
   Date(s): _____
4. What is the current status of your singing career?
   Professional _____   Amateur _____
5. What are your long-term career goals in singing?
   [ ] Premiere operatic career
   [ ] Premiere pop music career
   [ ] Active avocation
   [ ] Classical
   [ ] Pop
   [ ] Other (_____)
   [ ] Amateur performance (choral or solo)
   [ ] Amateur singing for own pleasure
6. Have you had voice training? Yes _____ No _____ At what age did you
   begin?
7. Have there been periods of months or years without lessons in that
   time? Yes _____ No _____
8. How long have you studied with your present teacher?

   Teacher's name:
   Teacher's address:

   Teacher's telephone number:
9. Please list previous teachers and years during which you studied with
   them.

10. Have you ever had training for your speaking
    voice?   Yes _____   No _____
    Acting voice lessons? Yes _____   No _____
    How many years?
    Speech therapy?   Yes _____   No _____
    How many months?

11. Do you have a job in addition to singing?
   Yes _____   No _____

   If yes, does it involve extensive voice use?
   Yes _____   No _____

   If yes, what is it? [actor, announcer (television/radio/sports arena), athletic instructor, attorney, clergy, politician, physician, salesperson, stockbroker, teacher, telephone operator or receptionist, waiter, waitress, secretary, other _____]
12. In your performance work, in addition to singing, are you frequently required to speak?   Yes _____ No _____
   dance?   Yes _____ No _____
13. How many years did you sing actively before beginning voice lessons initially?
14. What types of music do you sing? (Check all that apply.)
   _____ Classical   _____ Show
   _____ Nightclub   _____ Rock
   _____ Other: (Please specify.) _____
   _____
15. Do you regularly sing in a sitting position (such as from behind a piano or drum set)?   Yes _____ No _____
16. Do you sing outdoors or in large halls, or with orchestras?
   (Circle which one.)   Yes _____ No _____
17. If you perform with electrical instruments or outdoors, do you use monitor speakers?   Yes _____ No _____
   If yes, can you hear them?   Yes _____ No _____
18. Do you play a musical instrument(s)?   Yes _____ No _____
   If yes, please check all that apply:
   _____ Keyboard (piano, organ, harpischord, other _____)
   _____ Violin, viola
   _____ Cello
   _____ Bass
   _____ Plucked strings (guitar, harp, other _____)
   _____ Brass
   _____ Wind with single reed
   _____ Wind with double reed
   _____ Flute, piccolo
   _____ Percussion
   _____ Bagpipe
   _____ Accordion
   _____ Other: (Please specify.) _____

19. How often do you practice?
    Scales: [daily, few times weekly, once a week, rarely, never]

    If you practice scales, do you do them all at once, or do you divide them up over the course of a day?
    [all at once, two or three sittings]

    On days when you do scales, how long do you practice them?
    [15,30,45,60,75,90,105,120,more] minutes

    Songs: [daily, few times weekly, once a week, rarely, never]

    How many hours per day?
    [½,1,1½,2,2½,3,more]

    Do you warm up your voice before you sing?   _____ Yes _____ No

    Do you warm down your voice when you finish singing?
                                                       _____ Yes _____ No
20. How much are you singing at present (total including practice time) (average hours per day)?
    Rehearsal:
    Performance:
21. Please check all that apply to you:
    _____ Voice worse in the morning
    _____ Voice worse later in the day, after it has been used
    _____ Sing performances or rehearsals in the morning
    _____ Speak extensively (e.g., teacher, clergy, attorney, telephone work)
    _____ Cheerleader
    _____ Speak extensively backstage or at postperformance parties
    _____ Choral conductor
    _____ Frequently clear your throat
    _____ Frequent sore throat
    _____ Jaw joint problems
    _____ Bitter or acid taste, or bad breath first thing in the morning
    _____ Frequent "heartburn" or hiatal hernia
    _____ Frequent yelling or loud talking
    _____ Frequent whispering
    _____ Chronic fatigue (insomnia)
    _____ Work around extreme dryness
    _____ Frequent exercise (weight lifting, aerobics)
    _____ Frequently thirsty, dehydrated
    _____ Hoarseness first thing in the morning

_____ Chest cough
_____ Eat late at night
_____ Ever used antacids
_____ Under particular stress at present (personal or professional)
_____ Frequent bad breath
_____ Live, work, or perform around smoke or fumes
_____ Traveled recently: When: _____
                   Where: _____

Eat any of the following before singing?

_____ Chocolate	_____ Coffee
_____ Alcohol	_____ Milk or ice cream
_____ Nuts	_____Spiced foods

Other: (Please specify.)
_____ Any specific vocal technical difficulties?
[trouble singing soft, trouble singing loud, poor pitch control, support problems, problems at register transitions, other] Describe other:
_____ Any problems with your singing voice recently prior to the onset of the problem that brought you here?
[hoarseness, breathiness, fatigue, loss of range, voice breaks, pain singing, others] Describe others:
_____ Any voice problems in the past that required a visit to a physician? If yes, please describe problem(s) and treatment(s): [laryngitis, nodules, polyps, hemorrhage, cancer, other] Describe other:

22. Your family doctor's name, address, and telephone number:

23. Your laryngologist's name, address, and telephone number:

24. Recent cold?   Yes _____   No _____
25. Current cold?   Yes _____   No _____
26. Have you been exposed to any of the following chemicals frequently (or recently) at home or at work? (Check all that apply.)

_____ Carbon monoxide	_____ Arsenic
_____ Mercury	_____ Aniline dyes
_____ Insecticides	_____ Industrial solvents
_____ Lead	(benzene, etc.)
_____ Stage smoke	

27. Have you been evaluated by an allergist?   Yes _____ No _____

If yes, what allergies do you have:
[none, dust, mold, trees, cats, dogs, foods, other _____]
(Medication allergies are covered elsewhere in this history form.)
If yes, give name and address of allergist:

28. How many packs of cigarettes do you smoke per day?

Smoking history
_____ Never
_____ Quit. When?
_____ Smoked about __ packs per day for __ years.
_____ Smoke __ packs per day. Have smoked for __ years.
29. Do you work or live in a smoky environment?   Yes _____ No _____
30. How much alcohol do you drink? [none, rarely, a few times per week, daily] If daily, or few times per week, on the average, how much do you consume? [1,2,3,4,5,6,7,8,9,10, more] glasses per [day, week] of [beer, wine, liquor].

Did you formerly drink more heavily?   Yes _____ No _____
31. How many cups of coffee, tea, cola, or other caffeine-containing drinks do you drink per day?
32. List other recreational drugs you use [marijuana, cocaine, amphetamines, barbiturates, heroin, other _____]:
33. Have you noticed any of the following? (Check all that apply)
_____ Hypersensitivity to heat or cold
_____ Excessive sweating
_____ Change in weight: gained/lost _____ lb in _____
                        weeks/ _____ months
_____ Change in skin or hair
_____ Palpitation (fluttering) of the heart
_____ Emotional lability (swings of mood)
_____ Double vision
_____ Numbness of the face or extremities
_____ Tingling around the mouth or face
_____ Blurred vision or blindness
_____ Weakness or paralysis of the face
_____ Clumsiness in arms or legs
_____ Confusion or loss of consciousness
_____ Difficulty with speech
_____ Difficulty with swallowing
_____ Seizure (epileptic fit)

_____ Pain in the neck or shoulder
_____ Shaking or tremors
_____ Memory change
_____ Personality change

For females:

Are you pregnant?	Yes _____ No _____
Are your menstrual periods regular?	Yes _____ No _____
Have you undergone hysterectomy?	Yes _____ No _____
Were your ovaries removed?	Yes _____ No _____
At what age did you reach puberty?	
Have you gone through menopause?	Yes _____ No _____
If yes, when?	

34. Have you ever consulted a psychologist or psychiatrist?
    Yes _____   No _____
    Are you currently under treatment?   Yes _____ No _____
35. Have you injured your head or neck (whiplash, etc.)?
    Yes _____   No _____
36. Describe any serious accidents related to this visit.
    None _____

37. Are you involved in legal action involving problems with your voice?
    Yes _____   No _____
38. List names of spouse and children:

39. Brief summary of ear, nose, and throat (ENT) problems, some of which
    may not be related to your present complaint.

PLEASE CHECK ALL THAT APPLY

_____ Hearing loss	_____ Ear pain
_____ Ear noises	_____ Facial pain
_____ Dizziness	_____ Stiff neck
_____ Facial paralysis	_____ Lump in neck
_____ Nasal obstruction	_____ Lump in face or head
_____ Nasal deformity	_____ Trouble swallowing
_____ Mouth sores	_____ Excess eye skin
_____ Jaw joint problem	_____ Excess facial skin
_____ Eye problem	
_____ Other: (Please specify.)	

40. Do you have or have you ever had:

_____ Diabetes

_____ Hypoglycemia

_____ Thyroid problems

_____ Syphilis

_____ Gonorrhea

_____ Herpes

_____ Cold sores (fever blisters)

_____ High blood pressure

_____ Severe low blood pressure

_____ Intravenous antibiotics or diuretics

_____ Heart attack

_____ Angina

_____ Irregular heartbeat

_____ Other heart problems

_____ Rheumatic fever

_____ Tuberculosis

_____ Glaucoma

_____ Multiple sclerosis

_____ Other illnesses: (Please specify.)

_____ Seizures

_____ Psychiatric therapy

_____ Frequent bad headaches

_____ Ulcers

_____ Kidney disease

_____ Urinary problems

_____ Arthritis or skeletal problems

_____ Cleft palate

_____ Asthma

_____ Lung or breathing problems

_____ Unexplained weight loss

_____ Cancer of (_____)

_____ Other tumor (_____)

_____ Blood transfusions

_____ Hepatitis

_____ AIDS

_____ Meningitis

41. Do any blood relatives have:

_____ Diabetes

_____ Hypoglycemia

_____ Cancer

_____ Heart disease

_____ Other major medical problems such as those above. Please specify:

42. Describe serious accidents *unless* directly related to your doctor's visit here.

_____ None

_____ Occurred with head injury, loss of consciousness, or whiplash

_____ Occurred without head injury, loss of consciousness, or whiplash Describe:

43. List all current medications and doses (include birth control pills and vitamins).

44. Medication allergies
    _____ None
    _____ Penicillin
    _____ Sulfa
    _____ Tetracycline
    _____ Erythromycin
    _____ Keflex/Ceclor/
    Ceftin
    _____ Other: (Please
    specify.)

    _____ Novocaine
    _____ Iodine
    _____ Codeine
    _____ Adhesive
    tape
    _____ Aspirin
    _____ X-ray dyes

45. List operations
    _____ Tonsillectomy
    (age _____)
    _____ Appendectomy
    (age _____)
    _____ Other: (Please
    specify.)

    _____ Adenoidectomy
    (age _____)
    _____ Heart surgery
    (age _____)

46. List toxic drugs or chemicals to which you have been exposed:
    _____ Lead   _____ Streptomycin, neomycin, kanamycin
    _____ Mercury   _____ Other: (Please specify.)

47. Have you had x-ray *treatments* to your head or neck (including treatments for acne or ear problems as a child, treatments for cancer, etc.)?
    Yes _____   No _____

48. Describe serious health problems of your spouse or children.

    _____ None

Appendix IIb

PATIENT HISTORY: PROFESSIONAL VOICE USERS
Robert Thayer Sataloff, M.D., D.M.A.
1721 Pine Street
Philadelphia, PA   19103

NAME _____ AGE _____ SEX _____ RACE _____
HEIGHT _____ WEIGHT _____ DATE _____

1. How long have you had your present voice problem? _____

   Who noticed it?

   Do you know what caused it? Yes _____ No _____

   If so, what?

   Did it come on slowly or suddenly? Slowly _____ Suddenly _____
   Is it getting: Worse _____, Better _____, Same _____
2. Which symptoms do you have? (Please check all that apply.)
   _____ Hoarseness (coarse or scratchy sound)
   _____ Fatigue (voice tires or changes quality after speaking for a short
   period of time)
   _____ Volume disturbance (trouble speaking) softly _____
                                                         loudly _____
   _____ Loss of range (high _____ , low _____)
   _____ Prolonged warm-up time (over ½ hr to warm up voice)
   _____ Breathiness
   _____ Tickling or choking sensation while speaking
   _____ Pain in throat while speaking
   _____ Other: (Please specify.) _____
   _____
   _____

3. Have you ever had training for your speaking voice?
          Yes _____   No _____
4. Have there been periods of months or years without lessons in that
   time?   Yes _____   No _____

5. How long have you studied with your present teacher?
   Teacher's name:
   Teacher's address:
   Teacher's telephone number:
6. Please list previous teachers and years during which you studied with them:

7. Have you ever had training for your singing voice?
   Yes _____   No _____
   If so, list teachers and years of study:

8. In what capacity do you use your voice professionally?
   _____ Actor
   _____ Announcer (television/radio/sports arena)
   _____ Attorney
   _____ Clergy
   _____ Politician
   _____ Salesperson
   _____ Teacher
   _____ Telephone operator or receptionist
   _____ Other: (Please specify.)
9. Do you have an important performance soon?   Yes _____ No _____
   Date(s): _____
10. Do you do regular voice exercises?   Yes _____ No _____
    If yes, describe:
11. Do you play a musical instrument?   Yes _____ No _____
    If yes, please check all that apply:
    _____ Keyboard (piano, organ, harpischord, other _____)
    _____ Violin, Viola
    _____ Cello
    _____ Bass
    _____ Plucked strings (guitar, harp, other _____)
    _____ Brass
    _____ Wind with single reed
    _____ Wind with double reed
    _____ Flute, piccolo
    _____ Percussion
    _____ Bagpipe
    _____ Accordion
    _____ Other: (Please specify.) _____
12. Do you warm up your voice before practice or performance?
    Yes _____ No _____
    Do you warm down after using it?
    Yes _____ No _____

13. How much are you speaking at present (average hours per day)?
_____ Rehearsal   _____ Performance   _____ Other

14. Please check all that apply to you:
_____ Voice worse in the morning
_____ Voice worse later in the day, after it has been used
_____ Sing performances or rehearsals in the morning
_____ Speak extensively (e.g., teacher, clergy, attorney, telephone, work)
_____ Cheerleader
_____ Speak extensively backstage or at postperformance parties
_____ Choral conductor
_____ Frequently clear your throat
_____ Frequent sore throat
_____ Jaw joint problems
_____ Bitter or acid taste; bad breath or hoarseness first thing in the morning
_____ Frequent "heartburn" or hiatal hernia
_____ Frequent yelling or loud talking
_____ Frequent whispering
_____ Chronic fatigue (insomnia)
_____ Work around extreme dryness
_____ Frequent exercise (weight lifting, aerobics)
_____ Frequently thirsty, dehydrated
_____ Hoarseness first thing in the morning
_____ Chest cough
_____ Eat late at night
_____ Ever used antacids
_____ Under particular stress at present (personal or professional)
_____ Frequent bad breath
_____ Live, work, or perform around smoke or fumes
_____ Traveled recently: When: _____
                                   Where: _____

15. Your family doctor's name, address, and telephone number:

16. Your laryngologist's name, address, and telephone number:

17. Recent cold?   Yes _____   No _____
18. Current cold?   Yes _____   No _____
19. Have you been evaluated by an allergist?   Yes _____ No _____
    If yes, what allergies do you have:
    [none, dust, mold, trees, cats, dogs, foods, other, _____]
    (Medication allergies are covered elsewhere in this history form.)
    If yes, give name and address of allergist:

20. How many packs of cigarettes do you smoke per day?
    Smoking history
    _____ Never
    _____ Quit. When?
    _____ Smoked about __ packs per day for __ years.
    _____ Smoke __ packs per day. Have smoked for __ years.
21. Do you work or live in a smoky environment?   Yes _____ No _____
22. How much alcohol do you drink? [none, rarely, a few times per week, daily] If daily, or few times per week, on the average, how much do you consume? [1, 2, 3, 4, 5, 6, 7, 8, 9, 10, more] glasses per [day, week] of [beer, wine, liquor]
    Did you formerly drink more heavily?   Yes _____ No _____
23. How many cups of coffee, tea, cola, or other caffeine-containing drinks do you drink per day?
24. List other recreational drugs you use [marijuana, cocaine, amphetamines, barbiturates, heroin, other _____]
25. Have you noticed any of the following? (Check all that apply)
    _____ Hypersensitivity to heat or cold
    _____ Excessive sweating
    _____ Change in weight: gained/lost _____ lb in _____
                                weeks/ _____ months
    _____ Change in your voice
    _____ Change in skin or hair
    _____ Palpitation (fluttering) of the heart
    _____ Emotional lability (swings of mood)
    _____ Double vision
    _____ Numbness of the face or extremities
    _____ Tingling around the mouth or face
    _____ Blurred vision or blindness
    _____ Weakness or paralysis of the face
    _____ Clumsiness in arms or legs
    _____ Confusion or loss of consciousness
    _____ Difficulty with speech
    _____ Difficulty with swallowing
    _____ Seizure (epileptic fit)
    _____ Pain in the neck or shoulder
    _____ Shaking or tremors
    _____ Memory change
    _____ Personality change
    For females:
    Are you pregnant?   Yes _____ No _____
    Are your menstrual periods regular?   Yes _____ No _____
    Have you undergone hysterectomy?   Yes _____ No _____
    Were your ovaries removed?   Yes _____ No _____

At what age did you reach puberty?

Have you gone through menopause?   Yes _____ No _____

26. Have you ever consulted a psychologist or psychiatrist?

    Yes _____   No _____

    Are you currently under treatment?   Yes _____ No _____

27. Have you injured your head or neck (whiplash, etc.)?

    Yes _____   No _____

28. Describe any serious accidents related to this visit.

    None _____

29. Are you involved in legal action involving problems with your voice?

    Yes _____   No _____

30. List names of spouse and children:

31. Brief summary of ear, nose and throat (ENT) problems, some of which may not be related to your present complaint.

    _____ Hearing loss   _____ Ear pain

    _____ Ear noises   _____ Facial pain

    _____ Dizziness   _____ Stiff neck

    _____ Facial paralysis   _____ Lump in neck

    _____ Nasal obstruction   _____ Lump in face or head

    _____ Nasal deformity   _____ Trouble swallowing

    _____ Nose bleeds   _____ Trouble breathing

    _____ Mouth sores   _____ Excess eye skin

    _____ Excess facial skin   _____ Eye problem

    _____ Jaw joint problem

    _____ Other. (Please
    specify.)

32. Do you have or have you ever had:

    _____ Diabetes   _____ Seizures

    _____ Hypoglycemia   _____ Psychiatric therapy

    _____ Thyroid problems   _____ Frequent bad
                                         headaches

    _____ Syphilis   _____ Ulcers

    _____ Gonorrhea   _____ Kidney disease

    _____ Herpes   _____ Urinary problems

    _____ Cold sores (fever   _____ Arthritis or skeletal
    blisters)   problems

    _____ High blood pressure   _____ Cleft palate

    _____ Severe low blood   _____ Asthma
    pressure

    _____ Intravenous antibiotics _____ Lung or breathing problems
    or diuretics   _____ Unexplained weight loss

    _____ Heart attack   _____ Cancer of (_____)

    _____ Angina   _____ Other tumor (_____)

    _____ Irregular heartbeat   _____ Blood transfusions

    _____ Other heart problems   _____ Hepatitis

_____ Rheumatic fever   _____ AIDS
_____ Tuberculosis   _____ Meningitis
_____ Glaucoma
_____ Multiple sclerosis
_____ Other illnesses: (Please
    specify.)

33. Do any blood relatives have:
    _____ Diabetes   _____ Cancer
    _____ Hypoglycemia   _____ Heart disease
    _____ Other major medical problems such as those above.
        Please specify:

34. Describe serious accidents *unless* directly related to your doctor's visit here.
    _____ None
    _____ Occurred with head injury, loss of consciousness, or whiplash
    _____ Occurred without head injury, loss of consciousness, or whiplash
        Describe:

35. List all current medications and doses (include birth control pills and vitamins).

36. Medication allergies
    _____ None   _____ Novocaine
    _____ Penicillin   _____ Iodine
    _____ Sulfa   _____ Codeine
    _____ Tetracycline   _____ Adhesive tape
    _____ Erythromycin   _____ Aspirin
    _____ Keflex/Ceclor/   _____ X-ray dyes
        Ceftin
    _____ Other: (Please
        specify.)

37. List operations:
    _____ Tonsillectomy   _____ Adenoidectomy
        (age _____)   (age _____)
    _____ Appendectomy   _____ Heart surgery
        (age _____)   (age _____)
    _____ Other: (Please
        specify.)

38. List toxic drugs or chemicals to which you have been exposed:
    _____ Lead   _____ Streptomycin, Neomycin, Kanamycin
    _____ Mercury   _____ Other: (Please list.)

39. Have you had x-ray *treatments* to your head or neck (including treatments for acne or ear problems as a child), treatments for cancer, etc.?
    Yes_____ No _____

40. Describe serious health problems of your spouse or children.
    _____ None

Appendix IIc*

PATIENT HISTORY: SINGERS
Robert Thayer Sataloff, M.D., D.M.A.
1721 Pine Street
Philadelphia, PA   19103

NAME _____ AGE _____ SEX _____ RACE _____
HEIGHT _____ WEIGHT _____ DATE _____
VOICE CATEGORY: _____ soprano   _____ mezzo-soprano   _____ alto
                  _____ tenor   _____ baritone   _____ bass

(If you are not currently having a voice problem, please skip to Question #3.)

PLEASE CHECK OR CIRCLE CORRECT ANSWERS
1. How long have you had your present voice problem?

[1,2,3,4,5,6,7,8,9,10, more]
[hours, days, weeks, months, years]

Who noticed it?

[self, family, voice teacher, critics, everyone, other _____]

Do you know what caused it?
[Yes _____ No_____]

If yes, what? [a cold, yelling, excessive talking, singing, surgery, other _____]

Did it come on slowly or suddenly?
[Slowly _____ Suddenly _____]

Is it getting: Worse _____ , Better _____ , Same _____

---

*English language questionnaire was modified to a yes/no and circled answers format to allow comparison with foreign language translations that follow.

2. Which symptoms do you have? (Please check all that apply.)
   _____ Hoarseness (coarse or scratchy sound)
   _____ Fatigue (voice tires or changes quality after singing for a short
   period of time)
   _____ Volume disturbance (trouble singing) softly _____
   _____ loudly _____
   _____ Loss of range (high _____ low _____)
   _____ Change in classification (example: voice lowered from soprano to
   mezzo)
   _____ Prolonged warm-up time (over ½ hr to warm up voice)
   _____ Breathiness
   _____ Tickling or choking sensation while singing
   _____ Pain in throat while singing
   _____ Other: (Please specify.) _____
   _____
   _____

3. Do you have an important performance soon?   Yes _____ No _____
   Date(s): _____

4. What is the current status of your singing career?
   Professional _____   Amateur _____

5. What are your long-term career goals in singing?
   [   ] Premiere operatic career
   [   ] Premiere pop music career
   [   ] Active avocation
   [   ] Classical
   [   ] Pop
   [   ] Other (_____)
   [   ] Amateur performance (choral or solo)
   [   ] Amateur singing for own pleasure

6. Have you had voice training?   Yes _____ No _____ At what age did
   you begin? (Circle)
   [2,3,4,5,6,7,8,9,10,11,12,13,14,15,16,17,18,19,20,
   21,22,23,24,25,26,27,28,29,30,35,40,45,50,55,60,65,70,75,80,85]

7. Have there been periods of months or years without lessons in that
   time?   Yes _____ No _____

8. How long have you studied with your present teacher?

   [1,2,3,4,5,6,7,8,9,10,11,12,13,14,15,16,17,18,19,20,
   21,22,23,24,25, more]

   [weeks, months, years]

   Teacher's name:

Teacher's address:

Teacher's telephone number:

9. Please list previous teachers and years during which you studied with them:

10. Have you ever had training for your speaking
    voice?   Yes _____   No _____
    Acting voice lessons? Yes _____   No _____
    How many years?   [Less than one, 1–5,6–10, more]
    Speech therapy?   Yes _____   No _____ How many months?
                           [1,2,3,4,5,6,7–12, more]
11. Do you have a job in addition to singing?
    Yes _____   No _____

    If yes, does it involve extensive voice use?
    Yes _____   No _____

    If yes, what is it? [actor, announcer (television/radio/sports arena), ath-
    letic instructor, attorney, clergy, politician, physician, salesperson,
    stockbroker, teacher, telephone operator or receptionist, waiter, wait-
    ress, secretary, other _____]
12. In your performance work, in addition to singing, are you frequently
    required to speak?   Yes _____ No _____
    dance?   Yes _____ No _____
13. How many years did you sing actively before beginning voice lessons
    initially?
    [2,3,4,5,6,7,8,9,10,11,12,13,14,15,16,17,18,19,20,21,22,23,24,25, more]
14. What types of music do you sing? (Check all that apply.)
    _____ Classical   _____ Show
    _____ Nightclub   _____ Rock
    _____ Other: (Please specify.) _____
    _____

15. Do you regularly sing in a sitting position (such as from behind a piano
    or drum set)?   Yes _____ No _____
16. Do you sing outdoors or in large halls, or with orchestras?
    (Circle which one.)   Yes _____ No _____
17. If you perform with electrical instruments or outdoors, do you use mon-
    itor speakers?   Yes _____ No _____
    If yes, can you hear them?   Yes _____ No _____

18. Do you play a musical instrument(s)?   Yes ____ No ____
    If yes, please check all that apply:
    ____ Keyboard (piano, organ, harpischord, other ____)
    ____ Violin, viola
    ____ Cello
    ____ Bass
    ____ Plucked strings (guitar, harp, other ____)
    ____ Brass
    ____ Wind with single reed
    ____ Wind with double reed
    ____ Flute, piccolo
    ____ Percussion
    ____ Bagpipe
    ____ Accordion
    ____ Other: (Please specify.) _____
19. How often do you practice?
    Scales: [daily, few times weekly, once a week, rarely, never]

    If you practice scales, do you do them all at once or do you divide them
    up over the course of a day?
    [all at once, two or three sittings]

    On days when you do scales, how long do you practice them?
    [15,30,45,60,75,90,105,120, more] minutes

    Songs: [daily, few times weekly, once a week, rarely, never]

    How many hours per day?
    [½,1,1½,2,2½,3, more]

    Do you warm up your voice before you sing?   ____ Yes ____ No

    Do you warm down your voice when you finish singing?
                                          ____ Yes ____ No
20. How much are you singing at present (total, including practice time)
    (average hours per day)?
    Rehearsal: [½,1,1½,2,2½,3,4,5,6,7,8,9,10]
    Performance: [½,1,1½,2,2½,3,4,5,6,7,8]
21. Please check all that apply to you:
            ____ Voice worse in the morning
            ____ Voice worse later in the day, after it has been used
            ____ Sing performances or rehearsals in the morning
            ____ Speak extensively (e.g., teacher, clergy, attorney, telephone
            work)

_____ Cheerleader
_____ Speak extensively backstage or at postperformance parties
_____ Choral conductor
_____ Frequently clear your throat
_____ Frequent sore throat
_____ Jaw joint problems
_____ Bitter or acid taste, or bad breath first thing in the morning
_____ Frequent "heartburn" or hiatal hernia
_____ Frequent yelling or loud talking
_____ Frequent whispering
_____ Chronic fatigue (insomnia)
_____ Work around extreme dryness
_____ Frequent exercise (weight lifting, aerobics)
_____ Frequently thirsty, dehydrated
_____ Hoarseness first thing in the morning
_____ Chest cough
_____ Eat late at night
_____ Ever used antacids
_____ Under particular stress at present (personal or professional)
_____ Frequent bad breath
_____ Live, work, or perform around smoke or fumes
_____ Traveled recently: When: _____
                          Where: _____

Eat any of the following before singing?
          _____ Chocolate   _____ Coffee
          _____ Alcohol   _____ Milk or ice cream
          _____ Nuts   _____ Spiced foods

Other: (Please specify.)
          _____ Any specific vocal technical difficulties?
          [trouble singing softly, trouble singing loudly, poor pitch con-
          trol, support problems, problems at register transitions,
          other] Describe:
          _____ Any problems with your singing voice recently prior to the
          onset of the problem that brought you here?
          [hoarseness, breathiness, fatigue, loss of range, voice
          breaks, pain singing, others] Describe:
          _____ Any voice problems in the past that required a visit to a phy-
          sician? If yes, please describe problem(s) and treatment(s):
          [laryngitis, nodules, polyps, hemorrhage, cancer, other]
          Describe:

22. Your family doctor's name, address, and telephone number:

23. Your laryngologist's name, address, and telephone number:

24. Recent cold?   Yes ____   No ____
25. Current cold?   Yes ____   No ____
26. Have you been exposed to any of the following chemicals frequently (or recently) at home or at work? (Check all that apply.)
     ____ Carbon monoxide   ____ Arsenic
     ____ Mercury   ____ Aniline dyes
     ____ Insecticides   ____ Industrial solvents
     ____ Lead   (benzene, etc.)
     ____ Stage smoke
27. Have you been evaluated by an allergist?   Yes ____ No ____
    If yes, what allergies do you have:
    [none, dust, mold, trees, cats, dog, foods, other ____]
    (Medication allergies are covered elsewhere in this history form.)

    If yes, give name and address of allergist:

28. How many packs of cigarettes do you smoke per day?

    Smoking history
    ____ Never
    ____ Quit. When?
    ____ Smoked about [less than ½, ½, 1, 1½, 2, 2½, 3, more] per day for [1,2,3,4,5,6,7,8,9,10,11–15,16–20,21–25,26–30,31–35,36–40,41–45,46–50, more] years
    ____ Smoke [less than ½, ½, 1, 1½, 2, 2½, 3, more] per day for [1,2,3,4,5,6,7,8,9,10,11–15,16–20,21–25,26–30,31–35,36–40,41–45,46–50, more] years
29. Do you work in a smoky environment?   Yes ____ No ____
30. How much alcohol do you drink? [none, rarely, a few times per week, daily] [1,2,3,4,5,6,7,8,9,10, more] glasses per [day, week] of [beer, wine, liquor]

    Did you formerly drink more heavily?   Yes ____ No ____
31. How many cups of coffee, tea, cola, or other caffeine-containing drinks do you drink per day? [0,1,2,3,4,5,6,7,8,9,10]
32. List other recreational drugs you use [marijuana, cocaine, amphetamines, barbiturates, heroin, other ____]:

33. Have you noticed any of the following? (Check all that apply)
   _____ Hypersensitivity to heat or cold
   _____ Excessive sweating
   _____ Change in weight: gained/lost _____ lb in _____
                     weeks/ _____ months
   _____ Change in skin or hair
   _____ Palpitation (fluttering) of the heart
   _____ Emotional lability (swings of mood)
   _____ Double vision
   _____ Numbness of the face or extremities
   _____ Tingling around the mouth or face
   _____ Blurred vision or blindness
   _____ Weakness or paralysis of the face
   _____ Clumsiness in arms or legs
   _____ Confusion or loss of consciousness
   _____ Difficulty with speech
   _____ Difficulty with swallowing
   _____ Seizure (epileptic fit)
   _____ Pain in the neck or shoulder
   _____ Shaking or tremors
   _____ Memory change
   _____ Personality change

For females:

Are you pregnant?   Yes _____ No _____
Have you undergone hysterectomy?   Yes _____ No _____
Were your ovaries removed?   Yes _____ No _____
Are your menstrual periods regular?   Yes _____ No _____
At what age did you reach puberty?
[7,8,9,10,11,12,13,14,15,16,17,18,19,20]
Have you gone through menopause?   Yes _____ No _____
If yes, when? [presently; 1,2,3,4,5,6,7,8,9,10, more] years ago
34. Have you ever consulted a psychologist or psychiatrist?
            Yes _____   No _____
   Are you currently under treatment?   Yes _____ No _____
35. Have you injured your head or neck (whiplash, etc.)?
            Yes _____   No _____
36. Describe any serious accidents.

37. Are you involved in legal action involving problems with your voice?
            Yes _____   No _____

38. List names of spouse and children:

39. Brief summary of ear, nose, and throat (ENT) problems, some of which may not be related to your present complaint.

Please check all that apply:

_____ Hearing loss   _____ Ear pain
_____ Ear noises   _____ Facial pain
_____ Dizziness   _____ Stiff neck
_____ Facial paralysis   _____ Lump in neck
_____ Nasal   _____ Lump in face
        obstruction   or head
_____ Nasal deformity   _____ Trouble
_____ Mouth sores   swallowing
_____ Jaw joint   _____ Excess eye
        problem   skin
_____ Eye problem   _____ Excess facial
_____ Other: (Please   skin
        specify.)

40. Do you have or have you ever had:

_____ Diabetes   _____ Seizures
_____ Hypoglycemia   _____ Psychiatric therapy
_____ Thyroid problems   _____ Frequent bad
_____ Syphilis   headaches
_____ Gonorrhea   _____ Ulcers
_____ Herpes   _____ Kidney disease
_____ Cold sores (fever   _____ Urinary problems
        blisters)   _____ Arthritis or skeletal
_____ High blood pressure   problems
_____ Severe low blood   _____ Cleft palate
        pressure   _____ Asthma
_____ Intravenous antibiotics _____ Lung or breathing
        or diuretics   problems
_____ Heart attack   _____ Unexplained weight
_____ Angina   loss
_____ Irregular heartbeat   _____ Cancer of (_____)
_____ Other heart problems   _____ Other tumor (_____)
_____ Rheumatic fever   _____ Blood transfusions
_____ Tuberculosis   _____ Hepatitis
_____ Glaucoma   _____ AIDS
_____ Multiple sclerosis   _____ Meningitis
_____ Other illnesses: (Please
        specify.)

41. Do any blood relatives have:
    _____ Diabetes   _____ Cancer
    _____ Hypoglycemia   _____ Heart disease
    _____ Other major medical problems such as those above.
    Please specify:

42. Describe serious accidents *unless* directly related to your doctor's visit here.
    _____ None
    _____ Occurred with head injury, loss of consciousness, or whiplash
    _____ Occurred without head injury, loss of consciousness, or whiplash
    Describe:

43. List all current medications and doses (include birth control pills and vitamins).

44. Medication allergies
    _____ None   _____ Novocaine
    _____ Penicillin   _____ Iodine
    _____ Sulfa   _____ Codeine
    _____ Tetracycline   _____ Adhesive
    _____ Erythromycin   tape
    _____ Keflex/Ceclor/   _____ Aspirin
          Ceftin   _____ X-ray dyes
    _____ Other: (Please
          specify.)

45. List operations:
    _____ Tonsillectomy   _____ Adenoidectomy
          (age _____)   (age _____)
    _____ Appendectomy   _____ Heart surgery
          (age _____)   (age _____)
    _____ Other: (Please
          specify.)

46. List toxic drugs or chemicals to which you have been exposed:
    _____ Lead   _____ Streptomycin, neomycin, kanamycin
    _____ Mercury   _____ Other: (Please specify.)

47. Have you had x-ray *treatments* to your head or neck (including treatments for acne or ear problems as a child, treatments for cancer, etc.)?
    Yes _____   No _____
48. Describe serious health problems of your spouse or children.

_____ None

French Translation of Appendix IIc.

PASSE MEDICAL : CHANTEURS
Robert Thayer Sataloff, M.D., D.M.A.
1721 Pine Street
Philadelphia, PA. 19103

NOM _____ AGE _____ SEXE _____ NATIONALITE _____
TAILLE _____ POIDS _____ DATE _____
TYPE DE VOIX : soprano _____ mezzo soprano _____ alto _____
              tenor _____ baryton _____ basse _____

(Si vous n'avez pas de problème de voix courant, veuillez passer à la question n° 3)

VEUILLEZ COCHER OU ENTOURER LA REPONSE
CORRESPONDANT A VOTRE CAS:
1. Depuis combien de temps avez-vous votre problème de voix actuel?
   1, 2, 3, 4, 5, 6, 7, 8, 9, 10, plus
   heure(s), jour(s), semaine(s), mois, an(s)

   Qui l'a remarqué?
   Moi-même, ma famille, le professeur de vocalises, les critiques, tout le monde, autre _____

   En connaissez-vous la cause?
   Oui _____ Non _____

   Si oui, donnez la cause : vous avez attrapé froid, crié, trop parlé, chanté, subi une intervention chirurgicale, autre _____

   Est-ce arrivé progressivement ou subitement?
   Progressivement _____ Subitement _____

   Quelle est la situation actuelle? Pire _____, meilleure _____ , sans changement _____

443

2. Quels sont vos symptomes? (Veuillez indiquer tout élément se rapportant à votre cas)
   _____ Enrouement (sons rauques ou grêles)
   _____ Fatigue (la voix se fatigue ou sa qualité change après avoir chanté pendant une courte période de temps)
   _____ Trouble du volume sonore (difficulté pour chanter: doucement _____ , fort _____)
   _____ Perte d'intensité dans les gammes hautes _____ basses _____
   _____ Changement de classification (par exemple: la voix passe de soprano à mezzo)
   _____ Allongement de la période de mise en train vocale (plus d'une demi-heure pour préparer la voix)
   _____ Problème de respiration
   _____ Sensations de chatouillement ou d'étouffement en chantant
   _____ Douleur dans la gorge en chantant
   _____ Autre (veuillez préciser: _____)
3. Avez-vous un important tour de chant bientôt? Oui _____ Non _____
   Date(s): _____
4. Quel est votre statut habituel de chanteur?
   Professional _____ Amateur _____
5. Quels sont vos objectifs de carrière à long terme?
   _____ Chanteur d'opéra de premier rang
   _____ Chanteur de musique populaire de premier rang
   _____ Activité secondaire régulière
   _____ Chanteur classique
   _____ Chanteur populaire
   _____ Autre (précisez: _____)
   _____ Tours de chant amateurs (chorale ou solo)
   _____ Chanteur amateur pour la satisfaction personnelle
6. Avez-vous suivi une formation pour développer la voix?
   Oui _____ Non _____
   A quel âge l'avez-vous commencé? (Entourez:)
   2, 3, 4, 5, 6, 7, 8, 9, 10, 11, 12, 13, 14, 15, 16, 17, 18, 19, 20, 21, 22, 23, 24, 25, 26, 27, 28, 29, 30, 35, 40, 45, 50, 55, 60, 65, 70, 75, 80, 85
7. Y avait-il des mois ou des années sans leçons pendant?
   Oui _____ Non _____
8. Depuis combien de temps étudiez-vous avec votre professeur actuel?
   1, 2, 3, 4, 5, 6, 7, 8, 9, 10, 11, 12, 13, 14, 15, 16, 17. 18, 19, 20, 21, 22, 23, 24, 25, plus
   [semaine(s), mois, an(s)]

   Nom du professeur:
   Adresse du professeur:

   N° de téléphone du professeur: _____

9. Veuillez énumérer, ci-dessous, le nom des professeurs précédents et les années pendant lesquelles vous avez étudié avec eux:

10. Avez-vous déjà reçu un entraînement pour votre voix de conversation?
Oui _____ Non _____
Cours de voix pour la comédie ? Oui _____ Non _____
Combien d'années? Moins d'une, 1–5, 6–10, plus
Séances pour trouble de la langue? Oui _____ Non _____
Combien de mois? 1, 2, 3, 4, 5, 6, 7–12, plus

11. Avez-vous un autre métier en parallèle à votre activité de chanteur?
                          Oui _____ Non _____

Si oui, cette autre occupation nécessite-t-elle un emploi intensif de la voix?
                          Oui _____ Non _____

Si oui, quel métier est-ce ? Acteur, présentateur (de télévision, à la radio, sur les terrains de sport), professeur d'éducation physique, avocat, prêtre, politicien, médecin, représentant, agent de change, professeur, standardiste ou réceptionniste, serveur, serveuse, secrétaire, autre: ___

12. Lors de vos tours de chant, en plus de votre chant, vous est-il fréquemment nécessaire de parler? Oui _____ Non _____ De danser?
Oui _____ Non _____

13. Pendant combien d'années avez-vous chanté régulièrement avant de commencer les cours pour la voix?
2, 3, 4, 5, 6, 7, 8, 9, 10, 11, 12, 13, 14, 15, 16, 17, 18, 19, 20, 21, 22, 23, 24, 25, plus

14. Quelle type de musique chantez-vous? (Veuillez indiquer tout élément se rapportant à votre cas)
_____ pour des représentations   _____ pour des spectacles
       classiques
_____ pour les discothèques   _____ pour le rock
_____ autre (veuillez préciser: _____)

15. Chantez-vous généralement en position assise (comme derrière un piano ou une batterie)? Oui _____ Non _____

16. Chantez-vous à l'extérieur, dans de grandes salles, ou avec des orchestres? (Entourez)   Oui _____ Non _____

17. Si vous effectuez votre tour de chant avec des instruments électriques ou à l'extérieur, utilisez-vous des haut-parleurs? Oui _____ Non _____
Si oui, pouvez-vous les entendre? Oui _____ Non _____

18. Jouez-vous d'un ou de plusieurs instruments de musique?
Oui _____ Non _____

Si oui, veuillez cocher le ou les instruments:

_____ instruments à touche (piano, orgue, clavecin, autre: _____)

_____ violon, alto

_____ violoncelle

_____ basse

_____ instruments à cordes non frottées (guitare sèche, harpe, autre: _)

_____ cuivres

_____ instruments à vent à une anche

_____ instruments à vent à double anche

_____ flûte, piccolo

_____ percussions

_____ corneumuse

_____ accordéon

_____ autre (veuillez préciser: _____)

19. Quand faîtes-vous des gammes?

_____ quotidiennement

_____ quelques fois par semaine

_____ une fois par semaine

_____ rarement

_____ jamais

Si vous faîtes des gammes, les faîtes-vous toutes en une fois ou bien les répartissez-vous tout au long de la journée?
[Toutes en une fois, en deux ou trois parties]

Les jours pendant lesquels vous faîtes des gammes, pendant combien de temps le faîtes-vous?
[15, 30, 45, 60, 75, 90, 105, 120, plus minutes]

Quand pratiquez-vous le chant?
[Quotideiennement, quelques fois par semaine, une fois par semaine, rarement, jamais]

Combien d'heures par jour?
[0,5, 1, 1,5, 2, 2,5, 3, plus]

Faîtes-vous des exercices de voix avant de chanter?
Oui _____ Non _____

Faîtes-vous des exercices de voix après le chant? Oui _____ Non _____

20. Combien de temps consacrez-vous au chant actuellement (en comprenant l'entraînement, en temps moyen par jour)?

Répétitions : 0,5, 1, 1,5, 2, 2,5, 3, 4, 5, 6, 7, 8, 9, 10

Tours de chant : 0,5, 1, 1,5, 2, 2,5, 3, 4, 5, 6, 7, 8

21. Veuillez indiquer, ci-après, tout élément vous concernant:

_____ voix plus mauvaise le matin

_____ voix plus mauvaise en fin de journée, après pratique vocale

_____ effectue répétitions et tours de chant la matin

_____ parle beaucoup (professeur, prêtre, avocat, au téléphone, au travail, etc.)

_____ animateur

_____ parle beaucoup en coulisses ou aux soirées après les tours de chant

_____ chef de chorale

_____ râcle souvent ma gorge

_____ fréquents maux de gorge

_____ problèmes articulaires de la mâchoire

_____ goût amer ou aigre, mauvaise haleine au réveil

_____ fréquentes brûlures d'estomac ou hoquets

_____ crie souvent ou parle fort

_____ chuchotement souvent

_____ fatigue chronique (insomnie)

_____ travail en des lieux très secs

_____ fais de l'exercice physique régulièrement (poids, aérobic, etc.)

_____ souvent assoiffé, déshydraté

_____ enrouement au réveil

_____ toux venant de la poitrine

_____ mange tard le soir

_____ ai pris des remèdes contre les acidités

_____ suis particulièrement tendu(e) en ce moment (pour des raisons personnelles ou professionnelles)

_____ ai souvent mauvaise haleine

_____ vis, travaille, ou chante en des lieux avec fumée ou vapeur

_____ ai voyagé récemment, quand: _____ , où: _____

Avant de chanter, mange du _____ chocolat

_____ des noisettes

_____ de la glace

_____ de la nourriture épicée

_____ de l'alcool

_____ du café

_____ du lait

autre: _____

Avez-vous des difficultés vocales techniques quelconques?

Difficulté à chanter doucement, difficulté à chanter fort, difficulté à contrôler un accord, problèmes de soutien, difficultés avec les modulations, autre (décrivez): _____

Avez-vous eu des problèmes récemment avec votre voix de chanteur, préalablement au problème qui vous amène?
Enrouement, problème de respiration, fatigue, perte d'intensité, voix cassée, douleur en chantant, autre (décrivez): _____

Avez-vous déjà eu des problèmes de voix qui vous ont amené(e) à voir un médecin? Si oui, veuillez décrire le ou les problème(s) et son ou leur traitement(s): laryngite, nodules, polypes, hémorragie, cancer, autre (décrivez): _____

22. Nom, adresse et téléphone de votre médecin traitant:

23. Nom, adresse et téléphone de votre laryngologiste:

24. Avez-vous attrapé froid récemment? Oui _____ Non _____
25. Avez-vous un rhume actuellement? Oui _____ Non _____
26. Avez-vous déjà été exposé(e) à l'un des produits chimiques suivants fréquemment ou récemment à la maison ou au travail (veuillez indiquer tout élément vous concernant)?
    _____ monoxyde de carbone   _____ arsenique
    _____ mercure   _____ colorants azoïques
    _____ insecticides   _____ solvants industriels (benzine, etc.)
    _____ plomb
    _____ fumées de scène
27. Avez-vous reçu le diagnostic d'un spécialiste des allergies?
    Oui _____ Non _____

Si oui, quelles sont vos allergies? Aucune, à la poussière, à la moisissure, aux arbres, aux chats, aux chiens, à certains aliments, autre: _____
(Les allergies à certains médicaments sont traitées ultérieurement dans ce questionnaire médical)

Si oui, veuillez indiquer le nom et l'adresse du spécialiste des allergies:

28. Combien de paquets de cigarettes fumez-vous par jour?
    Histoire de votre consommation de cigarettes:
    _____ jamais
    _____ ai arrêté, quand? _____
    _____ fumais environ: moins d' 0,5, 0,5, 1, 1,5, 2, 2,5, 3, plus par jour
          pendant 1, 2, 3, 4, 5, 6, 7, 8, 9, 10, 11–15, 16–20, 21–25, 26–30,
          31–35, 36–40, 41–45, 46–50, plus an(s)
    _____ fume moins de 0,5, 0,5, 1, 1,5, 2, 2,5, 3, plus par jour pendant 1,
          2, 3, 4, 5, 6, 7, 8, 9, 10, 11–15, 16–20, 21–25, 26–30, 31–35, 36–40,
          41–45, 46–50, plus an(s)
29. Travaillez-vous dans un entourage de fumeurs? Oui _____ Non _____
30. Dans quelle mesure buvez-vous de l'alcool?
    Pas du tout, plusieurs fois par semaine, tous les jours
    1, 2, 3, 4, 5, 6, 7, 8, 9, 10, plus verres par jour, semaine
                          de bière, vin, liqueurs

    Vous est-il arrivé de boire davantage dans le passé d'une façon
    habituelle?
                          Oui _____ Non _____
31. Combien de tasses de café, thé, ou de verres de coca-cola ou autre bois-
    son contenant de la caféine buvez-vous par jour? 0, 1, 2, 3, 4, 5, 6, 7, 8,
    9, 10
32. Veuillez énumérer ci-après les autres drogues auxquelles vous vous
    adonnez: marijuana, cocaïne, amphétamines, barbituriques, héroïne,
    autre: _____
33. Avez-vous remarqué l'un des phénomènes suivants (indiquez tout élé-
    ment vous concernant):
    _____ hypersensibilité au froid ou à la chaleur
    _____ transpiration excessive
    _____ changement de poids: preudre/perte du poids: _____ kilos
                          en _____ semaines,
                          _____ mois
    _____ changement observé au niveau de la peau, des cheveux
    _____ palpitations cardiaques
    _____ trouble de l'équilibre émotionnel (changements d'humeur)
    _____ vision double
    _____ insensibilité du visage ou des extrêmités
    _____ picotement de la bouche ou du visage
    _____ vision trouble ou cécité
    _____ faiblesse ou paralysie du visage
    _____ maladresse des bras ou des jambes
    _____ troubles de la conscience ou perte de conscience
    _____ problèmes d'élocution
    _____ difficulté à avaler

_____ crises (crises d'épilepsie)
_____ douleur dans le cou ou dans l'épaule
_____ tremblements ou frémissements
_____ troubles de la mémoire
_____ changement de personnalité
Pour les femmes:

Etes-vous enceinte? Oui _____ Non _____

Avez-vous eu une hystérectomie? Oui _____ Non _____
Vous a-t-on enlevé les ovaires? Oui _____ Non _____
Avez-vous un cycle régulier? Oui _____ Non _____
A quel âge avez-vous atteint la puberté? 7, 8, 9, 10, 11, 12, 13, 14, 15,
    16, 17, 18, 19, 20
Avez-vous eu votre ménopause? Oui _____ Non _____
    Si oui, quand? En ce moment _____
    ou y-a-t-il 1, 2, 3, 4, 5, 6, 7, 8, 9, 10, plus   an(s)
34. Avez-vous déjà consulté un psychologue ou un psychiatre?
                    Oui _____ Non _____
    Etes-vous actuellement sous traitement? Oui _____ Non _____
35. Vous êtes-vous blessé(e) à la tête ou au cou (coup du lapin, etc.)?
                    Oui _____ Non _____
36. Veuillez décrire tout accident sérieux qui vous serait arrivé:

37. Etes-vous en procès pour des problèmes de voix? Oui _____ Non _____
38. Nom de votre conjoint(e) et enfant(s):

39. Bref résumé de vos coordonnées médicales, dont certains aspects peu-
    vent n'avoir aucune relation avec votre problème actuel:

VEUILLEZ COCHER TOUT ELEMENT VOUS CONCERNANT:

_____ perte de l'ouïe   _____ prolème ophtalmologique
_____ sons dans l'oreille   _____ autre (précisez: _____)
_____ vertiges   _____ douleur dans
_____ paralysie faciale   l'oreille
_____ obstruction nasale   _____ douleur de la
_____ plaies buccales   face
_____ problème articulaire de la   _____ cou raide
    mâchoire

_____ ganglion dans le
cou
_____ ganglion sur le
visage ou la tête
_____ difficulté
d'absorption

_____ excès de mem-
brane oculaire
_____ excès épider-
mique sur le
visage

40. Avez-vous ou avez-vous eu:
_____ du diabète
_____ de l'hypoglycémie
_____ des problèmes de
thyroïdes
_____ la syphilis
_____ des gonorrhées
_____ de l'herpès
_____ des gerçures ou des bou-
tons de fièvre
_____ de l'hypertension
_____ une baisse importante de
tension
_____ des injections intravei-
neuses d'antibiotiques ou
de diurétiques
_____ une crise cardiaque
_____ une angine
_____ un battement cardiaque
irrégulier
_____ d'autres problèmes
cardiaques
_____ une fièvre rhumatismale
_____ la tuberculose
_____ un glaucome
_____ une sclérose multiple
_____ autre(s) problème(s)?
Précisez:

_____ des crises
_____ des soins psycho-
thérapiques
_____ des ulcères
_____ une maladie rénale
_____ de l'arthrose ou des
problèmes de
squelette
_____ des blessures du
palais
_____ de l'asthme
_____ des problèmes de respiration ou de
poumons
_____ une perte de poids
inexpliquée
_____ un cancer de _____
_____ autre tumeur _____
_____ une hépatite
_____ des transfusions de
sang
_____ le SIDA
_____ la méningite

41. Est-ce que l'un de vos parents a:
_____ du diabète   _____ un cancer
_____ de l'hypoglycémie   _____ une maladie cardiaque
_____ un autre problème médical évoqué dans la liste précédente,
précisez:

42. Décrivez les accidents sérieux dont vous avez été victime, à moins qu'il ne soit directement liè au problème qui vous amène ici:
    _____ aucun
    _____ est arrivé avec blessure à la tête, perte de conscience ou "coup du lapin"
    _____ est arrivé sans blessure à la tête, perte de conscience, ni "coup du lapin"
    Décrivez:

43. Enumérez tous vos médicaments en cours, ainsi que leur quantité (y compris la pillule contraceptive et les vitamines):

44. Allergies médicamenteuses:
    _____ aucune   _____ novocaïne
    _____ pénicilline   _____ iodine
    _____ sulfamides   _____ codéïne
    _____ tétracycline   _____ aspirine
    _____ érythromycine   _____ colorants pour les
    _____ Keflex, Ceclor,   rayons X
    Ceftine   _____ sparadrap
    _____ Autre, précisez:

45. Enumérez les interventions chirurgicales:
    _____ amygdalectomie (âge: _____)   _____ enlèvement d'une tumeur
    _____ appendicite (âge: _____)   _____ des glandes (âge: _____)
    _____ opération cardiaque (âge: _____)
    _____ Autre, précisez:

46. Enumérez les drogues toxiques ou les produits chimiques auxquels vous avez été exposé(e):
    _____ plomb   _____ streptomycine, néomycine, kanamycine
    _____ mercure   _____ Autre, précisez: _____

47. Avez-vous eu des traitements aux X-rays pour votre tête ou votre cou (y compris les traitements pour l'acné ou les problèmes d'oreilles en tant qu'enfant, les traitements pour le cancer, etc.)? Oui _____ Non _____

48. Décrivez les problèmes médicaux importants de votre conjoint(e) ou de votre ou vos enfant(s), s'il y a lieu:

German Translation of Appendix IIc.

PATIENTENANAMNESE: SÄNGER
Robert Thayer Sataloff, M.D., D.M.A.
1721 Pine Street
Philadelphia, PA   19103

Name _____ Alter (i.J.) _____ Geschlecht _____
Rasse _____ Grösse _____ Gewicht _____ Datum _____
Stimmlage: ____ Sopran ____ Mezzosopran ____ Alt
            ____ Tenor ____ Bariton ____ Bass

(Wenn Sie derzeit kein Stimmproblem haben, gehen Sie bitte direkt zur
Frage Nr. 3.)

BITTE KREUZEN ODER UMKREISEN SIE DIE FÜR SIE
ZUTREFFENDEN ANTWORTEN:

1. Wie lange haben Sie Ihr derzeitiges Stimmproblem schon?
   (1, 2, 3, 4, 5, 6, 7, 8, 9, 10, länger)
   (Stunden, Tage, Wochen, Monate, Jahre)

   Wer hat es zuerst bemerkt?
   (Sie selbst, Familie, Gesangslehrer, Kritiker, alle, andere Personen)

   Kennen Sie die Ursache?
   (Ja ____ Nein ____)

   Wenn ja welche? (Erkältung, Schreien, exzessives Sprechen,
   Singen, Operation, andere Ursachen _____)

   Begann Ihr Stimmproblem langsam oder trat es plötzlich auf?
   (langsam ____ , plötzlich ____)

   Wie ist der Verlauf bisher?: Schlechter ____ Besser ____ Gleich ____

453

2. Welche Symptome haben Sie? (Bitte kreuzen Sie alle für Sie zutreffenden Antworten an.)

_____ Heiserkeit (rauhe oder kratzige Stimme)

_____ Ermüdungszeichen (Stimme ermüdet oder ändert sich in der Qualität, nachdem Sie kurze Zeit gesungen haben.)

_____ Volumenprobleme (erschwertes Singen) bei _____ leisem Singen
_____ lautem Singen

_____ Verlust der stimmlichen Rangskala(hohe Töne _____ , tiefe Töne _____)

_____ Änderung der Stimmlage (Bsp.: Stimmlage verändert sich von Sopran zu Mezzosopran)

_____ Verlängerte Aufwärmphase (über ½ Stunde)

_____ Kurzatmigkeit

_____ Kratzen im Hals oder Engegefühl beim Singen

_____ Halsschmerzen beim Singen

_____ Andere Symptome (Bitte beschreiben Sie sie): _____

_____

3. Haben Sie in Kürze ein wichtiges Konzert? Ja _____ Nein _____
Termindaten: _____

4. Singen Sie derzeit professionell _____ oder als Amateur _____?

5. Was sind die langfristigen Ziele Ihrer Gesangskarriere?

_____ Opernsänger mit Premierenvorstellungen

_____ Popsänger mit Premierenvorstellungen

_____ nebenberufliche Gesangstätigkeit

_____ Klassischer Gesang

_____ Popmusik

_____ Andere Ziele (_____)

_____ Amateurveranstaltungen (Chor oder Solo)

_____ Amateursingen zum eigenen Vergnügen

6. Hatten Sie Gesangsunterricht? Ja _____ Nein _____
In welchem Alter haben Sie damit begonnen? (Bitte zutreffendes umkreisen)
(2, 3, 4, 5, 6, 7, 8, 9, 10, 11, 12, 13, 14, 15, 16, 17, 18, 19, 20, 21, 22, 23, 24, 25, 26, 27, 28, 29, 30, 35, 40, 45, 50, 55, 60, 65, 70, 75, 80, 85)

7. Gab es monate- oder jahrelange Unterbrechungen des Gesangsunterricht? Ja _____ Nein _____

8. Wie lange arbeiten Sie mit Ihrem jetzigen Lehrer zusammen?
(1, 2, 3, 4, 5, 6, 7, 8, 9, 10, 11, 12, 13, 14, 15, 16, 17, 18, 19, 20, 21, 22, 23, 24, 25, länger)
(Wochen, Monate, Jahre)

Name Ihres Gesangslehrers:
Adresse:

Telefonnummer:

9. Bitte geben Sie Ihre früheren Lehrer an und wieviele Jahre Sie mit ihnen studiert haben:

10. Hatten Sie jemals Sprachunterricht ? Ja _____ Nein _____
Aktiven Sprachunterricht ? Ja _____ Nein _____
Wieviele Jahre? (weniger als 1 Jahr, 1–5 Jahre, 6–10 Jahre, länger)
Hatten Sie jemals eine logopädische Behandlung? Ja _____ Nein _____
Wenn Ja, wieviele Monate? (1, 2, 3, 4, 5, 6, 7–12, länger)

11. Üben Sie einen Beruf zusätzlich zu Ihrer Gesangstätigkeit aus?
Ja _____ Nein _____

Wenn ja, wird Ihre Stimme dabei sehr beansprucht?
Ja _____ Nein _____

Wenn ja, welchen Beruf üben Sie aus ? (Schauspieler/in, Ansagesprecher/in - in TV, Radio, Sportarena), Sportlehrer/in, Rechtsanwalt/wältin, Sekreträr/in, Politiker/in, Arzt/Ärztin, Verkäufer/in, Makler/in, Lehrer/in, Telephonist/in, Kellner/in, anderer Beruf _____)

12. Müssen Sie bei Ihrem Auftreten, neben dem Gesang, vermehrt Sprechen? Ja _____ Nein _____   Tanzen? Ja _____ Nein _____

13. Wieviele Jahre haben Sie aktiv gesungen, bevor Sie Sprachunterricht genommen haben ?
(1, 2, 3, 4, 5, 6, 7, 8, 9, 10, 11, 12, 13, 14, 15, 16, 17, 18, 19, 20, 21, 22, 23, 24, 25, mehr)

14. Welche Musikrichtungen singen Sie?
(Bitte kreuzen Sie alle zutreffenden an)
__ Klassik   __ Showmusik   __ Nachtklub   __ Rockmusik
_____ Andere (Welche? : _____
_____)

15. Singen Sie regelmässig in einer sitzenden Position (wie z.B. am Klavier oder Schlagzeug)? Ja _____ Nein _____

16. Singen Sie im Freien, in grossen Hallen oder mit Orchester?
Ja _____ Nein _____ (Bitte umkreisen Sie das Zutreffende)

17. Wenn Sie Auftritte mit elektronischen Instrumenten oder im Freien haben, benützen Sie einen Lautsprecher? Ja _____ Nein _____
Wenn ja, können Sie ihn hören? Ja _____ Nein _____

18. Spielen Sie ein Musikinstrument? Ja _____ Nein _____
Wenn ja, bitte kreuzen Sie alle für Sie zutreffenden Instrumente an:
_____ Tasteninstrument (Piano, Orgel, Cembalo, andere _____)
_____ Violine, Viola
_____ Cello
_____ Bass
_____ Saiteninstrument (Gitarre, Harfe, andere _____)

_____ Blechinstrument
_____ Blasinstrument mit einem Blatt
_____ Blasinstrument mit zwei Blättern
_____ Querflöte, Piccoloflöte
_____ Schlagzeug
_____ Dudelsack
_____ Akkordeon
_____ Andere Instrumente (welche?: _____)

19. Wie oft üben Sie?
Tonleitern : (täglich, mehrmals in der Woche, einmal in der Woche, selten nie)

Wenn Sie Tonleitern üben, üben Sie alle auf einmal oder verteilen Sie sie über die gesamte Übungsdauer?
(alle auf einmal, in 2 oder 3 Teilen)

Wenn Sie Tonleitern üben, wie lange?
(15, 30, 45, 60, 75, 90, 105, 120, mehrere Minuten)

Lieder : (täglich, mehrmals in der Woche, einmal in der Woche, selten, nie)

Wieviele Stunden am Tag üben Sie ?
(½, 1, 1-½, 2, 2-½, 3, mehr)

Wärmen Sie Ihre Stimme auf, bevor Sie singen? Ja _____ Nein _____

Wärmen Sie Ihre Stimme ab nach dem Singen? Ja _____ Nein _____

20. Wieviel singen Sie zur Zeit (einschliesslich der Übungszeit, Durschnittliche Stundenanzahl/Tag)?
Übung: (½, 1, 1-½, 2, 2-½, 3, 4, 5, 6, 7, 8, 9, 10)
Aufführungen: (½, 1, 1-½, 2, 2-½, 3, 4, 5, 6, 7, 8)

21. Bitte kreuzen Sie alles an, was auf Sie zutrifft:
_____ Stimme ist besonders am Morgen schlecht
_____ Stimme ist schlechter später am Tag (nach Gebrauch)
_____ Gesangsaufführungen- oder proben am Morgen
_____ Vermehrtes Sprechen (z.B., Lehrer, Sekretär, Anwalt, Telephon, Arbeit, etc.)
_____ Anführer beim Anfeuern (z.B. Sportveranstaltungen)
_____ Vermehrtes Sprechen hinter der Bühne oder auf Parties nach der Vorstellung
_____ Chorleiter
_____ Häufiges Räuspern im Hals

_____ Häufige Halsschmerzen

_____ Kiefergelenksprobleme

_____ Bitterer, sauerer Geschmack, oder schlechter Atem nach dem Aufwachen

_____ Häufiges Sodbrennen oder Hiatushernie

_____ Häufiges Schreien oder lauteres Sprechen

_____ Häufiges Flüstern

_____ Chronische Müdigkeit (Schlaflosigkeit)

_____ Arbeit unter extremer Trockenheit

_____ Häufige sportliche Tätigkeit (Gewichtheben, Aerobic, etc.)

_____ Häufiges Durstgefühl, Dehydratation

_____ Heiserkeit am frühen Morgen

_____ Husten

_____ Mahlzeiten in den späten Abendstunden

_____ Einnahme von Antazida

_____ Besondere Belastungssituation zum jetzigen Zeitpunkt (persönlich oder beruflich)

_____ Häufig schlechter Atem

_____ Ständig verräucherte Umgebung - Rauchen oder sonstige Abgase - (privat, beruflich, bei Aufführungen)

_____ Sind Sie jüngst verreist?: Wann?: _____
Wohin?:

Nehmen Sie vor dem Singen etwas zu sich, z.B.:

_____ Schokolade   _____ Kaffee

_____ Alkohol   _____ Milch oder Eiskrem

_____ Nüsse   _____ Scharf gewürzte Speisen

_____ andere Speisen (welche?): _____

Haben Sie bestimmte technische Schwierigkeiten beim Singen? (erschwertes Singen an leisen Stellen, erschwertes Singen an lauten Stellen, schwache Tonhöhenkontrolle, Atemstützeprobleme, Probleme bei Tonlagenübergang, andere Probleme?) _____

Haben Sie jüngst noch andere Probleme beim Singen bemerkt, abgesehen von dem Problem, das Sie hierherführte? (Heiserkeit, Luftnot, Ermüdung, Verlust der stimmlichen Rangskala, Stimmzusammenbruch, schmerzhaftes Singen, andere Probleme, (welche? _____)

Hatten Sie gesundheitliche Probleme in der letzten Zeit, die einen Arztbesuch erforderten? Wenn ja, bitte beschreiben Sie die Probleme und ggf. Behandlungen: (Laryngitis, Knötchen, Polypen, Blutungen, Krebs, andere Probleme: _____)

22. Name, Adresse and Telefonnummer Ihres Hausarztes:

23. Name, Adresse, und Telefonnummer Ihres Hals, Nasen, Ohren - arztes:

24. Waren Sie jüngst erkältet? Ja _____ Nein _____
25. Sind Sie zur Zeit erkältet? Ja _____ Nein _____
26. Waren (oder sind) Sie häufiger den folgenden Chemikalien ausgesetzt? (zuhause oder beruflich)

    _____ Kohlenmonowasserstoffen   _____ Arsen
    _____ Quecksilber   _____ Anilinfarbstoffen
    _____ Insektizide   _____ Industrielle Lösungsmittel
    _____ Blei   _____ (Benzol, etc.)
    _____ Bühnenrauch

27. Wurden Sie bei einem Allergologen ausgetestet? Ja _____ Nein _____

    Wenn ja, welche Allergien haben Sie?:
    (keine, Staub, Schimmelpilze, best. Baumarten, Katzen, Hunde, Lebensmittel, andere _____)
    (Die Medikamente werden später im Fragebogen erfasst werden)

    Wenn ja, bitte geben Sie den Namen und die Adresse des Allergologen an: _____

28. Wieviel rauchen Sie täglich?

    Raucheranamnese:
    _____ Garnicht
    _____ Aufgehört. Wann? _____
    _____ Habe geraucht (Packungen: weniger als ½, ½, 1, 1-½, 2, 2-½, 3, mehr) pro Tag über (Jahre: 1, 2, 3, 4, 5, 6, 7, 8, 9, 10, 11–15, 16–20, 21–25, 26–30, 31–35, 36–40, 41–45, länger)
    _____ Rauche derzeit (Packungen: weniger als ½, ½, 1, 1-½, 2, 2-½, 3, mehr) pro Tag über (Jahre: 1, 2, 3, 4, 5, 6, 7, 8, 9, 10, 11–15, 16–20, 21–25, 26–30, 31–35, 36–40, 41–45, 46–50, länger)

29. Arbeiten Sie in einer Umgebung, in der geraucht wird? Ja _____ Nein _____
30. Wie oft und wieviel Alkohol trinken Sie?
    (garnicht, selten, ein paar Mal/Woche, täglich)
    (1, 2, 3, 4, 5, 6, 7, 8, 9, 10, mehr) Gläser (Bier, Wein, Likör) pro (Tag, Woche)

    Haben Sie früher einmal mehr getrunken? Ja _____ Nein _____

31. Wieviele Tassen Kaffee, Tee, Cola oder anderer koffeinhaltiger Getränke trinken Sie pro Tag? (1, 2, 3, 4, 5, 6, 7, 8, 9, 10)
32. Welche Entspannungsmedikamente nehmen Sie ein? (Marihuana, Kokain, Amphetamine, Barbiturate, Heroin, andere _____)
33. Haben Sie folgende Zeichen an sich selber festgestellt?
    (Bitte kreuzen Sie alle zutreffenden an)
    _____ Überempfindlichkeit gegunüber Hitze oder Kälte
    _____ Verstärktes Schwitzen
    _____ Gewichtsänderung: zugenommen/abgenommen _____ Pfund in __
    Wochen/ _____ Monaten
    _____ Haut- oder Haarveränderung
    _____ Herzflattern oder -rasen
    _____ Emotionale Labilität (Stimmungsschwankungen)
    _____ Doppeltsehen
    _____ Taubheitsgefühl im Gesicht oder an den Extremitäten
    _____ Kribbeln um dem Mund herum oder im Gesicht
    _____ Unscharfes Sehen oder Blindheit
    _____ Schwäche oder Lähmung im Gesicht
    _____ Schwerfälligkeit in Armen oder Beinen
    _____ Bewusstseinsverwirrung oder - verlust
    _____ Sprachschwierigkeiten
    _____ Schluckbeschwerden
    _____ Schwindelattacken (epileptischer Anfall)
    _____ Nacken- oder Schulterschmerzen
    _____ Zittern oder Tremor
    _____ Gedächtnisveränderung
    _____ Persönlichkeitsveränderung

    Spezielle Fragen für Frauen:

    Sind Sie schwanger? Ja _____ Nein _____
    Hatten Sie eine Hysterektomie? Ja _____ Nein _____
    Wurden bei Ihnen die Eierstöcke entfernt? Ja _____ Nein _____
    Ist Ihre Periode regelmässig? Ja _____ Nein _____
    In welchem Alter erreichten Sie die Pubertät?
    (7, 8, 9, 10, 11, 12, 13, 14, 15, 16, 17, 18, 19, 20)
    Sind sie in der Menopause? Ja _____ Nein _____
    Wenn ja, seit wann? (jüngst, seit 1, 2, 3, 4, 5, 6, 7, 8, 9, 10, mehr Jahren)
34. Haben Sie jemals einen Psychologen oder Psychiater aufgesucht?
    Ja _____ Nein _____
    Befinden Sie sich zur Zeit in Behandlung?
    Ja _____ Nein _____
35. Haben Sie eine Kopf- oder Halsverletzung durchgemacht?
    Ja _____ Nein _____
36. Beschreiben Sie ggf. durchgemachte ernstere Unfälle.

37. Sind sie in ein Gerichtsverfahren verwickelt, bezüglich Ihrer Stimme? Ja _____ Nein _____

38. Name des Ehegatten/gattin und der Kinder:

39. Kurze Zusammenstellung der Hals-, Nasen- oder Ohrenprobleme, welche möglicherweise nicht mit Ihren derzeitigen Beschwerden zusammenhängen:

BITTE KREUZEN SIE ALLE ZUTREFFENDEN ANTWORTEN AN:

_____ Hörverlust

_____ Ohrgeräusche

_____ Schwindel

_____ Gesichtslähmung

_____ Obstruktion im Nasenbereich

_____ Nasenverformung

_____ Wunden oder Entzündungen im Mundbereich

_____ Kiefergelenksprobleme

_____ Augenprobleme

_____ Andere Probleme (welche?)

_____ Ohrschmerzen

_____ Gesichtsschmerzen

_____ Steifer Nacken

_____ Schwellung im Nacken

_____ Schwellung im Gesicht - oder Kopfbereich

_____ Erschwertes Schlucken

_____ Überhäug Augeulider

_____ Vermehrte Falteubildung im Gesicht

40. Haben oder hatten Sie jemals:

_____ Diabetes

_____ Unterzucker

_____ Schilddrüsenprobleme

_____ Syphilis

_____ Gonorrhoe

_____ Herpes

_____ Erfrierungen (Fieberblasen)

_____ Bluthochdruck

_____ Ausgeprägte Hypotonie

_____ Intravenöse Behandlung mit Antibiotika oder Diuretika

_____ Herzanfall

_____ Angina

_____ Unregelmässiger Herzschlag

_____ Andere Herzprobleme

_____ Rheumatisches Fieber

_____ Tuberkulose

_____ Glaukom

_____ Multiple Sklerose

_____ Andere Erkrankungen (welche?):

_____ Schwindelattacken

_____ Psych. Behandlung

_____ gehäuft starke Kopfschmerzen

_____ Geschwüre

_____ Nierenerkrankung

_____ Harnblasenproblem

_____ Gelenkbeschwerden

_____ Kiefer-Gaumenspalte

_____ Asthma

_____ Lungen-oder Atemproblem

_____ Ungeklärter Gewichtsverlust

_____ Krebs (welchen? _____)

_____ Anderer Tumor (_____)

_____ Blutübertragung

_____ Hepatitis

_____ AIDS

_____ Meningitis

41. Haben Ihre Blutsverwandten Erkrankungen?:
_____ Diabetes   _____ Krebs
_____ Unterzucker   _____ Herzerkrankung
_____ Andere grössere gesundheitliche Probleme (welche?)

42. Bitte beschreiben Sie schwere Unfälle, sofern sie nicht direkt mit Ihrem heutigen Arztbesuch zusammenhängen.
_____ Keine
_____ Unfälle mit Kopfverletzungen, Bewusstseinsverlust oder Halswirbelsäulenverletzungen
_____ Unfälle ohne Kopfverletzungen, Bewusstseinsverlust oder Halswirbelsäulenverletzungen (welche?: _____)

43. Bitte geben Sie alle Medikamenten in der derzeit eingenommenen Menge an (einschliesslich Antibabypille und Vitaminpräparaten)

44. Bestehen bei Ihnen Allergien auf bestimmte Medikamente:
_____ keine   _____ Novokain
_____ Penizillin   _____ Jod
_____ Sulfonamid   _____ Kodein
_____ Tetracyclin   _____ Pflaster
_____ Erythromycin   _____ Aspirin
_____ Cefalosporin   _____ Röntgenkontrastmittel
_____ Andere Medikamente (welche?):

45. Geben Sie Operationen an:
_____ Tonsillektomie (im Alter von _____ Jahren)
_____ Appendektomie (im Alter von _____ Jahren)
_____ Adenoidektomie (im Alter von _____ Jahren)
_____ Herzoperationen (im Alter von _____ Jahren)
_____ Andere Operationen (welche?):

46. Listen Sie die Medikamente oder Chemikalien auf, denen Sie ausgesetzt waren:
_____ Blei   _____ Streptomycin, Neomycin, Kanamycin
_____ Quecksilber   _____ Andere (welche):

47. Hatten Sie eine Strahlenbehandlung im Kopf- oder Halsbereich (eingeschlossen Aknebehandlung, Bestrahlung bei Ohrprobleme im Kindesalter, Krebstherapien, etc.)?
Ja _____ Nein _____

48. Bitte beschreiben Sie ernsthafte gesundheitliche Probleme Ihres Ehegatten/gattin oder Ihrer Kinder.

_____ keine

Italian Translation of Appendix IIc.

STORIA DEL PAZIENTE: CANTANTI
Robert Thayer Sataloff, M.D., D.M.A.
1721 Pine Street
Philadelphia, PA   19103

NOME _____ ETÀ _____ SESSO _____ RAZZA _____
STATURA _____ PESO _____ DATA _____
CATEGORIA DELLA VOCE:
_____ Soprano _____ Mezzo Soprano _____ Alto
_____ Tenore   _____ Baritono   _____ Basso

(Se non ha problemi di voce in questo momento, risponda incominciando dalla domanda #3)

CERCHIA LA RISPOSTA CORRETTA:
1. Da quanto tempo ha questo problema di voce?
   [1, 2, 3, 4, 5, 6, 7, 8, 9, 10, più a lungo]
   [ore, giorni, settimane, mesi, anni]

   Chi notò il problema?
   [lei, un familiare, il maestro di voce, critici, tutti, altri _____]

   Sa da cosa è causato?
   [si _____ no _____]

   Se la risposta è si, qual'è la causa? [raffreddore, gridare, parlare troppo, canto, chirurgia, altro _____]

   Il problema si manifestò con l'andar del tempo o sull'istante?
   [andar del tempo _____ sull'istante _____]

   Sta: Peggiorando _____ , Migliorando _____ , Rimane lo stesso _____

2. Che sintomi ha? (Marchi tutti i sintomi.)

_____ Voce rauca

_____ Fatica (la voce si stanca oppure cambia di qualità dopo aver cantato per un corto periodo di tempo)

_____ Problemi di volume (problemi mentre canta

a voce soffice _____

a voce piena _____

_____ Perdita di banda di frequenze (alta _____

bassi _____)

_____ Cambio di voce (per esempio: voce abbassata da soprano a mezzo soprano)

_____ Prolungamento del tempo necessario per riscaldare la voce (più di mezz'ora)

_____ Mancanza di fiato

_____ Solletico o sensazione di strangolamento mentre canta

_____ Dolore mentre canta

_____ Altri sintomi (per favore specifichi): _____

_____

_____

3. Deve dare un concerto? Si _____ No _____

Data: _____

4. Lei è un cantante?

Professionale _____ Dilettante _____

5. A lungo termine, quali sono le sue mete?

[ ] Carriera lirica

[ ] Carriera nella musica pop

[ ] Vocazione attiva

[ ] Classica

[ ] Pop

[ ] Altro (_____)

[ ] Prove dilettanti (corale o solo)

[ ] Canto dilettante per piacere personale

6. Ha avuto lezioni di voce? Si _____ No _____ A che età incominiciò?

[2, 3, 4, 5, 6, 7, 8, 9, 10, 11, 12, 13, 14, 15, 16, 17, 18, 19, 20, 21, 22, 23, 24, 25, 26, 27, 28, 29, 30, 35, 40, 45, 50, 55, 60, 65, 70, 75, 80, 85]

7. Ci son stati periodi di mesi o anni senza lezioni durante questo tempo?

Si _____ No _____

8. Quanto tempo ha studiato con il suo corrente maestro?

[1, 2, 3, 4, 5, 6, 7, 8, 9, 10, 11, 12, 13, 14, 15, 16, 17, 18, 19, 20, 21, 22, 23, 24, 25, di più]

[settimane, mesi, anni]

Nome del maestro:

Indirizzo:

Numero di telefono:
9. Altri maestri con i quali ha studiato e le date:

10. Ha avuto lezioni di voce parlata?

                   Si _____ No _____

Lezioni di voce da teatro? Si _____ No _____

Quanti anni? [Meno di uno, 1–5, 6–10, di più]

Logoterapia? Si _____ No _____ Quanti mesi?

            [1, 2, 3, 4, 5, 6, 7–12, di più]

11. Ha un altra professione?

Si _____ No _____

Se si, usa la voce molto?

Si _____ No _____

Se si, che professione? [attore, annunciatore (televisione/radio/campi sportivi), istruttore atletico, avvocato, prete, politico, dottore, venditore, venditore di azioni, maestro, telefonista, cameriere, cameriera, segretaria, altro _____]

12. Nel suo lavoro in oltre al canto, deve parlare frequentemente?

Si _____ No _____

Ballo? Si _____ No _____

13. Per quanti anni ha cantato prima di iniziare lezioni?

[2, 3, 4, 5, 6, 7, 8, 9, 10, 11, 12, 13, 14, 15, 16, 17, 18, 19, 20, 21, 22, 23, 24, 25, di più]

14. Che tipo di musica canta?

_____ Classica   _____ Show

_____ Nightclub   _____ Rock

_____ Altro (per favore specificare): _____

15. Regolarmente canta seduto (per esempio al pianoforte)?

Si _____ No _____

16. Canta all'aperto, in saloni, o con orchestra?

(cerchia la parola corrispondente) Si _____ No _____

17. Se canta all'aperto o con accompagnamento di strumenti amplificati, usa altoparlanti di monitoraggio? Si _____ No _____

Se si, li può sentire? Si _____ No _____

18. Suona un strumento musicale? Si _____ No _____
    Se si, indichi quale o quali strumenti:
    _____ strumenti a tastiera (piano, organo, arpicordo, altro _____)
    _____ Violino, viola
    _____ Cello
    _____ Basso
    _____ Chitarra, arpa, altro _____
    _____ Ottoni
    _____ Strumenti a fiato a singola canna
    _____ Strumenti a fiato doppia canna
    _____ Flauto, piccolo
    _____ Strumenti di percussione
    _____ Zampogna
    _____ Fisarmonica
    _____ Altro (specifichi): _____

19. Con che frequenza si esercita?
    Scale musicali: [giornalmente, qualche volta alla settimana, una volta
    alla settimana, raramente, mai]

    Se si esercita mediante le scale musicali, queste vengono effettuate in
    una sessione oppure vengono divise durante il corso della giornata?
    [tutte insieme, due o tre sedute]
    Nei giorni in qui si praticano le scale musicali, per quanto tempo ven-
    gono effettuate?
    [15, 30, 45, 60, 75, 90, 105, 120, di più] minuti

    Canzoni: [giornalmente, qualce volta alla settimana, raramente, mai]

    Quante ore al giorno?
    [½, 1, 1½, 2, 2½, 3, di più]

    Effettua il riscaldamento della voce prima di cantare?
    _____ Si _____ No

    Viene effettuato un periodo di raffreddamento al termine?
    _____ Si _____ No

20. Quanto tempo canta in questo periodo (totale, incluso il tempo di eser-
    cizio) (media giornaliera)?
    prova: [½, 1, 1½, 2, 2½, 3, 4, 5, 6, 7, 8, 9, 10]
    esibizione: [½, 1, 1½, 2, 2½, 3, 4, 5, 6, 7, 8]

21. Segni tutto ciò che le si addice:
    _____ Voce peggiore al mattino
    _____ Voce peggiore più tardi nel giorno, dopo averla usata
    _____ Prove o esibizioni canore nel mattino

_____ Parla per periodi di tempo prolungati (i.e. maestro, prete, avvocato, telefono, lavoro)

_____ Cheerleader (sostenitore)

_____ Parla a lungo dietro le quinte o a riunioni dopo l'esibizione

_____ Direttore del coro

_____ Frequentemente schiarisce la gola

_____ Mal di gola frequente

_____ Problemi alla giontura delle mascelle

_____ Palato amaro o acido, o alito cattivo di prima mattina

_____ Frequente acidità di stomaco o ernia iatale

_____ Grida o parla ad alta voce frequentemente

_____ Sussurra frequentemente

_____ Affaticamento cronico (insonnia)

_____ Lavora in luoghi secchi

_____ Esercizio fisico di frequente

_____ Assetato di frequente, desidratato

_____ Rauco al primo mattino

_____ Tosse bronchiale

_____ Mangia tardi la sera

_____ Ha usato antiacidi

_____ È stressato (per ragioni personali o professionali)

_____ Alito cattivo con molta frequenza

_____ Vive, lavora o si esibisce in locali dove c'è fumo

_____ Ha viaggiato recentemente: Quando: _____
        Dove: _____

Mangia una o più delle seguenti cose prima di cantare?

_____ Cioccolata   _____ Caffe

_____ Alcoolici   _____ Latte o geleto

_____ Noci   _____ Alimenti piccanti

Altro (specifichi): _____

_____ difficoltà tecniche vocali specifiche?
        [problema con il canto sotto voce, problema con il canto a piena voce, poco controllo del "pitch", problema nell'accompagnamento vocale, problema alla trasposizione del registro, altro]
        Descriva:

_____ Ha recentemente avuto dei problemi di voce prima dell'inizio del disturbo che l'ha condotta qui?
        [voce rauca, mancanza di fiato, affaticamento, perdita di "range", interruzzione della voce, dolore mentre canta, altro] Descriva:

_____ Ha avuto problemi nel passato per i quali ha dovuto consultare ad un medico? se si, descriva il problema e la terapia:
[laringite, noduli, polipi, emorragia, cancro, altro]
Descriva:

22. Indichi nome, indirizzo e numero di telefono del suo medico di famiglia:

23. Indichi nome, indirizzo e numero di telefono del suo otorino:

24. Ha avuto recentemente un raffreddore? Si _____ No _____
25. Ha attualmente il raffreddore? Si _____ No _____
26. È stato frequentemente (o recentemente) esposto a qualcuna delle seguenti sostanze chimiche: (segni tutte ciò che si applichino)

_____ Monossido di carbonio   _____ Arsenico
_____ Mercurio   _____ Coloranti di anilina
_____ Insetticidi   _____ Solventi industriali
                                             (benzene, etc.)
_____ Piombo   (benzene, etc.)
_____ Fumo

27. Si è sottoposto alla visita di un allergologo?
Si _____ No _____

Se si, di quali allergie lei soffre:
[nessuna, polvere, muffa, piante, gatti, cani, cibi, altro _____]
(le allergie ai farmaci sono trattate in un altro punto di questo questionario)

Se si, indichi nome ed indirizzo dell'allergologo a cui si è rivolto:

28. Quanti pacchetti di sigarette fuma al giorno?

Sua storia come fumatore
_____ Mai
_____ Ha smesso, quando?
_____ Fumava circa [meno di metà, metà, una, una e mezza, due, due e mezza, tre, tre e mezza, di più) al giorno per [1, 2, 3, 4, 5, 6, 7, 8, 9, 10, 11–15, 16–20, 21–25, 26–30, 31–35, 36–40, 41–45, 46–50, di più) anni.

_____ Fuma [meno di metà, metà, una, una e mezza, due, due e mezza, tre, di più] al giorno per [1, 2, 3, 4, 5, 6, 7, 8, 9, 10, 11–15, 16–20, 21–25, 26–30, 31–35, 36–40, 41–45, 46–50, di più] anni.

29. Lavora in un ambiente dove si fuma? Si _____ No _____

30. Quanti alcolici mediamente beve? [mai, raramente, qualche volta alla settimana, giornalmente] [1, 2, 3, 4, 5, 6, 7, 8, 9, 10, di più] bicchieri al [giorno, settimana] di [birra, vino, liquori]

   Beveva in misura maggiore? Si _____ No _____

31. Quante tazze di caffè , tè, cola, o altre bevande contenenti caffeina beve in un giorno? [0, 1, 2, 3, 4, 5, 6, 7, 8, 9, 10]

32. Elenchi eventuali droghe o farmaci che lei usa
   [mariuana, cocaina, amfetaminici, barbiturici, eroina, altro _____]

33. Ha notato alcune delle seguenti manifestazioni? (Segni quello che descriva le sue manifestazioni)
   _____ Ipersensibilità al caldo o al fredda
   _____ Sudore eccessivo
   _____ Cambiamenti in peso aumento/diminuizione _____ Kg in _____ settimane/ _____ mesi
   _____ Cambiamenti della pelle o dei capelli
   _____ Palpitazioni cardiache
   _____ Labilità emozionale (cambi di umore)
   _____ Sdoppiamento della vista
   _____ Intorpidità della faccia o delle estremità
   _____ Formicolio alla bocca o alla faccia
   _____ Visione sfuocata o cecità
   _____ Debolezza o paralisi della faccia
   _____ Goffagine nelle braccia o nelle gambe
   _____ Sintomi di confusione o perdita di consapevolezza
   _____ Difficoltà nel parlare
   _____ Difficoltà in inghiottire
   _____ Attacchi epilettici
   _____ Dolori al collo o alle spalle
   _____ Tremori
   _____ Perdita di memoria
   _____ Cambiamenti di umore

Per le donne

È incinta? Si _____ No _____
Si è sottoposta ad isterectomia? Si _____ No _____
Si è sottoposta ad intervento di rimozione delle ovaia?
                              Si _____ No _____
Ha un ciclo mestruale regolare? Si _____ No _____

A quanti anni ha avuto la prima menstruazione?
[7, 8, 9, 10, 11, 12, 13, 14, 15, 16, 17, 18, 19, 20]
È già in menopausa? Si _____ No _____
Se si, da quanti anni? [adesso; 1, 2, 3, 4, 5, 6, 7, 8, 9, 10, di più] anni fa.
34. È mai ricorso ad un psicologo o ad un psichiatria?
    Si _____ No _____
    È attualmente in cura? Si _____ No _____
35. Ha avuto danni alla testa o al collo?
    Si _____ No _____
36. Desriva ogni incidente serio che ha avuto.

37. Ha qualche azione legale in atto a causa di problemi connessi alla sua voce?
    Si _____ No _____
38. Elenchi il nome del suo coniuge e dei figli:

39. Breve sommario di problemi otorinolaringoiatrici, alcuni dei quali possono anche non essere collegati al suo attuale disturbo.

    Segni tutto ciò che è applicativo

    _____ Perdita uditiva
    _____ Sensazione di rumore nelle orecchie
    _____ Vertigini
    _____ Paralisi facciale
    _____ Ostruzione nasale
    _____ Deformità nasale
    _____ Piaghe alla bocca
    _____ Problemi alla Giunzione mandibolare

    _____ Problemi agl'occhi
    _____ Altro (specifichi):
    _____ Dolore alle orecchie
    _____ Dolore facciale
    _____ Collo rigido
    _____ Gromulo al collo
    _____ Gromulo in faccia o testa
    _____ Problemi con l'ingoire
    _____ Pelle agl'occhi in eccesso
    _____ Pelle facciale in eccesso

40. Soffre o ha mai sofferto di:
    _____ Diabete
    _____ Ipoglicemia
    _____ Problemi alla tiroide
    _____ Sifilide
    _____ Gonorrea

    _____ Epilessia
    _____ Ricorso a terapia psichiatrica
    _____ Frequenti attacchi di cefalea

_____ Herpes   _____ Ulcere
_____ Piaghe   _____ Artrite o problemi
_____ Ipertensione arteriosa   ossei
_____ Ipotensione arteriosa   _____ Cleft palate
_____ Assunzione di antibiotici   _____ Asma
  o diuretici in vena   _____ Problemi respiratori
_____ Attacchi cardiaci   o polmonari
_____ Angina   _____ Inspiegabile perdita
_____ Battito cardiaco irregolare   di peso
_____ Altri problemi cardiaci   _____ Cancro a (_____)
_____ Febbre reumatica   _____ Altri tumori
_____ Tubercolosi   _____ Trasfusioni sanguigne
_____ Glaucoma   _____ Epatite
_____ Sclerosi multipla   _____ AIDS
_____ Problemi di reni   _____ Menengite
  urinario
_____ Problemi all'apparato
_____ Altre malattie (si prega di specificare):

41. Ha storia di familiari consanguigni di:
    _____ Diabete   _____ Cancro
    _____ Ipoglicemia   _____ Problemi cardiaci
    _____ Altri gravi problemi medici di entità para a quelli precedentemente
    indicati. si prega di specificare:

42. Descriva incidenti gravi da lei avuti, eccetto quelli direttamente riferibili
    alla sua attuale visita medica.
    _____ Nessuno
    _____ Incidente con trauma cranico, perdita di coscienza o contusione
    al collo
    _____ Incidente senza trauma cranico, perdita di coscienza o contusione
    al collo
    Descriva:

43. Elenchi tutte le medicine che attualmente assume e le relative dosi (in-
    cludere la pillola anticoncezionale e le vitamine):

44. Allergie farmacologiche:
    ____ Nessuna   ____ Novocaina
    ____ Penicillina   ____ Iodina
    ____ Sulfamidici   ____ Codeina
    ____ Tetraciclina   ____ Cerotti
    ____ Eritromicina   ____ Aspirina
    ____ Keflex/ceclor/ceftin ____ Coloranti radiologici
    ____ Altro (si prega di specificare):

45. Interventi chirurgici
    ____ Tonsillectomia (età ____)   ____ Adenoidi (età ____)
    ____ Appendicite (età ____)   ____ Chirurgia cardiaca (età __)
    ____ Altro (si prega specificare):

46. Elenchi le sostanze tossiche o gli agenti chimici a cui è stato esposto:
    ____ Piombo   ____ Streptomicina, neomicina, canamicina
    ____ Mercurio   ____ Altro (specifichi):

47. Si è mai sottoposto a terapio radiante per problemi alla testa o all collo (incluse cure per l'acne, problemi uditivi infantili, terapia per il cancro, ecc.)?
    Si ____ No ____
48. Descriva seri problemi di salute del suo coniuge o dei suoi figli.

    ____ Nessuno

Spanish Translation of Appendix IIc.

Historia del paciente: Cantantes
Robert Thayer Sataloff, M.D., D.M.A.
1721 Pine Street
Philadelphia, PA   19103

NOMBRE _____ EDAD ____ SEXO ____ RAZA ____
ESTATURA _____ PESO _____ FECHA _____
CATEGORIÁ DE LA VOZ:

_____ Soprano ____ Mezzo Soprano ____ Alto
_____ Tenor   ____ Baritono   ____ Bajo

(Si actualmente usted no tiene ningún problema vocal, por favor omita la pregunta #3.)

MARQUE LA RESPUESTA CORRECTA

1. ¿Por cuánto tiempo ha venido padeciendo su problema vocal?
   [1, 2, 3 . . . . 10, más]
   [horas, días, semanas, meses, años]

   ¿Quién le dió a conocer el problema?
   [usted mismo, su familia, su profesor, críticos, otros ____]

   ¿Conoce usted qué pudo causar esto?
   [Sí ____ No ____]

   Si la respuesta es sí, ¿qué cree usted pudo causardo?
   [un resfriado, gritar, hablar en exceso, cantar, cirugía, otros ____]

   ¿Comenzó a sentir estos síntomas de repente o gradualmente?
   [De repente ____ Gradualmente ____]

   ¿Cómo se siente ahora?: Peor ____ , Mejor ____ , Igual ____ ?

2. ¿Qué síntomas usted presenta? (Por favor marque todos los que se relacionen con su estado.)

_____ Ronquera (áspera o irregular emisión)

_____ Fatiga (cansancio vocal o cambios de cualidad después de haber cantado por un corto periódo de tiempo)

_____ Cambios en el volumen de la voz (Problemas al contar)

Bajo _____

Fuerte _____

_____ Pérdida del registro (alto _____ bajo _____)

_____ Cambios de clasificación (por ejemplo: de Soprano a mezzo)

_____ Tiempo prolongado de vocalización o calentamiento de la voz (más de media hora)

_____ Voz con mucha pérdida de aire

_____ Sensación de cosquiello o obstrucción mientras está cantando

_____ Dolor en la garganta mientras está cantando

_____ Otros: (Especifique.) _____

3. ¿Tiene usted una actuación importante próximamente?

Sí _____ No _____

Fecha(s): _____

4. ¿A qué nivel está su entrenamiento como cantante?

Profesional _____ Amateur _____

5. ¿Cuáles son sus aspiraciones como cantante?

[ ] cantante operístico

[ ] Cantantede música moderna

[ ] Como pasatiempo

[ ] Popular

[ ] otros

[ ] Actuaciones no profesionales (coral o solista)

[ ] Canta para su propia distracción

6. ¿Ha recibido usted entrenamiento vocal?

Sí _____ No _____. A qué edad usted comenzó?

(Encierre en un círculo.)

[2, 3, 4, 5, 6, 7 . . . . . 20 . . . más]

7. ¿Ha tenido usted periódos de tiempo en los cuales mo ha recibido lecciones de canto?

Sí _____ No _____

8. ¿Por cuánto tiempo ha estado usted estudiando con su profesor actual?

[1, 2, 3, 4, 5, 6, 7 . . . . 25, más]

[semanas, meses, años]

Nombre de su professor:

Dirección de su profesor:

Número de Teléfono:
9. Por favor escriba el nombre de sus previos profesores y los años que usted estudió con ellos:

10. ¿Ha tenido usted entrenamiento para su voz hablada?
    Sí _____ No _____
    ¿Lecciones de voz para actuación?
    Sí _____ No _____
    Cuántos años? [menos de uno, 1–5, 6–10, más]
    ¿Terapia de hablar? Sí _____ No _____ ¿cuántos meses?
    [1, 2, 3, 4, 5, 6, 7–12, más]
11. ¿Además del canto; desempeña usted otro tipo de trabajo?
    Sí _____ No _____

    Si su respuesta es sí, qué tipo de trabajo? [Actor, anunciador, locutor (T.V./radio/deportes), instructor deportivo, abogado, religioso, político, vendedor, corredor de bolsa, profesor, telefonista o recepcionista, camarero, camarera, secretaria, otros _____]
12. ¿En el desempeño de su trabajo, además de cantar, utiliza su voz con mucha frecuencia?
    Sí _____ No _____
    ¿usted baila? Sí _____ No _____
13. ¿Cuántos años estuvo usted cantando activamente antes de comenzar sus lecciones de canto?
    [2, 3, 4, 5 . . . . . . 25, más]
14. ¿Qué tipo de música usted canta?
    _____ Clásica   _____ Presentaciones públicas
    _____ Club Nocturno   _____ Rock (música moderna)
    _____ Otros: (Especifique.)
15. ¿Canta used regularmente sentado (detrás de un piano, o instrumentos de percusión)?
    Sí _____ No _____
16. ¿Canta usted en espacios abiertos o en grandes salas de concierto o con orquesta?
    Sí _____ No _____
17. ¿Si usted realiza sus presentaciones con instrumentos eléctricos o en espacios abiertos, usa usted monitores? Sí _____ No _____
    Si su respuesta es sí, puede usted escucharlos?
    Sí _____ No _____

18. ¿Ejecuta usted algún instrumento musical?
    Si su respuesta es afirmativa por favor marque cuál o cuales:
    _____ Teclados, (piano, organo, clavicordio, otros _____)
    _____ Metales
    _____ Violin, Viola
    _____ Violoncello
    _____ Contrabajo
    _____ Instrumentos de cuerda (guitarra, arpa, otros _____)
    _____ Instrumentos de viento de caña sencilla
    _____ Instrumentos de viento de caña doble
    _____ Flauta, piccolo
    _____ Percusión
    _____ Fagot
    _____ Acordión
    _____ Otros: (Especifique.) _____

19. ¿Cuánto a menudo usted práctica?
    Escalas: [diariamente, algunas veces a la semana, una vez a la semana,
    esporadicamente, nunca]

    ¿Si usted práctica escalas, las hace todas a lavez o las divide en el trans-
    curso del día?
    [todas a la vez, dos o tres sesiones]

    ¿En los diás que usted hace escalas, cuánto tiempo las práctica?
    [15, 30, 45, 55, ... más] minutos

    Canciones: [diariamente, algunas veces a la semana, una vez a la se-
                mana, esporadicamente o nunca]

    ¿Cuántas horas al día?
    [½, 1½, 2, 2½, 3, más]

    ¿Vocaliza usted antes de cantar? _____ Sí _____ No

    ¿Vocaliza usted ligeramente su voz cuando termina de cantar?
    _____ Sí _____ No

20. ¿Actualmente cuánto tiempo usted canta? (tiempo de práctica en horas
    por día)
    Ensayos: [½ . . . . 10]
    Funciones: [½ . . . . 8]

21. Por favor marque los item con los cuales usted se sienta relacionado (a):
    _____ muy mala voz en la mañana
    _____ muy mala voz en el transcurso del diá, después de haberla usado

_____ Funciones o ensayos en la mañana
_____ Hablar continuamente (profesor, clerigo, abogado, telefonista, trabajo, etc.)
_____ Jefe de Barra (escuela, universidad, etc.) en deportes
_____ Hablar excesivamente fuera del escenario o en fiestas después de haber terminada la función
_____ Director de Coro
_____ Frecuentemente trata de limpiar la flema en la garganta
_____ Frecuente mal de garganta
_____ Problemas con la mandíbula
_____ Siente sabor amargo y ácido, o mal aliento al levantarse en las mañanas
_____ Frecuente ácides estomacal o hernia en el hiato
_____ Frecuentemente grita o habla muy fuerte
_____ Frecuentemente habla susurrando
_____ Fatiga crónica (insomnia)
_____ Trabaja en un ambiente extremadamente seco
_____ Realiza ejercicios físicos con mucha frecuencia, Clevantamiento de pesas, aeróbicos, etc)
_____ Frecuente resesquedad y deshidratación
_____ Ronquera en la mañana
_____ Tos de pecho
_____ Comer a altas horas de la noche
_____ Uso de Antiácidos
_____ Se encuentra bajo alta tension nerviosa o presiones (personal o profesional)
_____ Mal aliento frecuentemente
_____ Vive, trabaja, o canta en lugares donde se fuma, o presencia de vapores
_____ Recientes viajes: Cuándo: _____
Dónde: _____

¿Come o bebe cualquiera de los siguientes productos antes de cantar?
_____ Chocolate   _____ Café
_____ Alcohol   _____ Leche o helados
_____ Mani   _____ Comidas con muchos condimentos
Otros: (Especifique.)

_____ ¿ Cualquier dificultad o problema técnico vocal?
[problemas al cantar suave, problemas al cantar a plena voz, pobre control de la entonación probleman de apoyo, problemas de cambio de registros, otros] describa:

_____ ¿Cualquier malestar vocal reciente antes de comenzar el problema que lo trajo a usted aquí?
[ronquera, aire en la voz, fatiga, pérdida de (registro, la voz se corta, dolor al cantar, otros] Describa:

_____ ¿Cualquier otro problema vocal que requirió su vista a un médico o especialista? Si la respuesta es sí, por favor describa el (o los) problema(s) y el tratamiento(s).
[laringitis, nodulos, pólipos, hemorragias, cancer, otros] Describa:

22. Nombre del médico familiar, dirección, y número telefónico:

23. Nombre de su otorringolaringologo, dirección, y número telefónico:

24. ¿Reciente resfriado? Sí _____ No _____
25. ¿Actual resfriado? Sí _____ No _____
26. ¿Ha estado usted, reciente o frecuentemente en su trabajo o en su casa, expuesto a cualquiera de los siguientes productos guímicos?
    _____ Monoxido de carbono   Arsénico _____
    _____ Mercurio   Anilina _____
    _____ Insecticidas   Solventes industriales _____
    _____ Gasolina (con plomo)   (benzina, etc)
    _____ Humo de cigarrillo
27. ¿Ha sido usted evaluado por un especialista en alergias?
                      Sí _____ No _____

Si responde afirmativamente, a qué cosa es usted alergico:
[ninguno, polvo, moho, árboles, gatos, perros, comidas, otros _____]
(Medicamentos a los cualdes es usted alergico y están incluidos en la historia médica de su especialista.)

Si responde afirmativamente, por favor escriba el nombre y la dirección de su alergista:

28. ¿Cuántas cajas de cigarrillos usted fuma al día?

Historia del furmador

_____ Nunca

_____ Por untiempo. ¿Cuándo?

_____ Fumada cerca de [menos de la mitad, la mitad, una, una y media, dos, dos y media, tres, más] al día por [1, 2, 3, 4, 5, 6, 7, 8, 9, 10, 11–15, 16–20, 21–25, 26–30, 31–35, 36–40, 41–45, 46–50, más] años

_____ Fuma cerca de [menos de la mitad, la mitad, una, una y media, dos, dos y media, tres, más] al día por [1, 2, 3, 4, 5, 6, 7, 8, 9, 10, 11–15, 16–20, 21–25, 26–30, 31–35, 36–40, 41–45, 46–50, más] años

29. ¿Trabaja usted en un lugar donde se fuma?

Sí _____ No _____

30. ¿Cuánto alcohol usted bebe? [nada, raramente, algunas veces por semana, diariamente] [1, 2, 3, 4, 5, 6, 7, 8, 9, 10, más] vasos al [día, semana] de [cerveza, vino, licor]

¿Acostumbra usted beber mucho? Sí _____ No _____

31. ¿Cuántas tazas de café, té, cola, o otras bebidas que contienen cafeina, usted toma al día?

[0, 1, 2, 3, 4, 5, 6, 7, 8, 9, 10]

32. Señale otras drogas que usted usa [marihuana, cocaina, anfetaminas, barbituricos, heroina, otros _____]:

33. ¿Ha observado en usted cualquiera de los siguientes cambios? (Marque todas las que se relacionen con usted)

_____ Hipersensibilidad al calor o frío

_____ Transpiración excesiva

_____ Cambios en el peso: ganancia/perdida _____ libras

en _____ semanas/ _____ meses

_____ Cambios en la piel o el pelo

_____ Rápida palpitación de el corazón

_____ Cambios de estados emocionales

_____ Doble visión

_____ Entumecimiento o insensibilidad en la cara o en las extremidades

_____ Comezón alrededor de la boca o la cara

_____ Visión borrosa o poca visión

_____ Parálisis facial

_____ Pesadez en brazos o piernas

_____ Pérdida del conocimiento

_____ Dificultad al hablar

_____ Dificultad al tragar

_____ Ataque epiléptico

_____ Dolor en el cuello y los hombros

_____ Espasmos o temblores

_____ Cambios en la memoria
_____ Cambios en la personalidad

Para el sexo femenino:
¿Está usted embarazada? Sí _____ No _____
¿Ha sufrido una histerectomía? Sí _____ No _____
¿Sus ovarios fueron removidos? Sí _____ No _____
¿Es regular su periódo menstrual? Sí _____ No _____
¿A qué edad usted alcanzó la pubertad?
[7, 8, 9, 10, 11, 12, 13, 14, 15, 16, 17, 18, 19, 20]
¿Está usted en periódo menopausico? Sí _____ No _____
¿Si su respuesta es afirmativa, cuándo ocurrió?
[ahora; 1, 2, 3, 4, 5, 6, 7, 8, 9, 10, más] años

34. ¿Ha usted consultado un psiquiatra o psicólogo?
                    Sí _____ No _____
    ¿Está usted actualmente en tratamiento?
                    Sí _____ No _____
35. ¿Se ha lastimado usted su cuello o su cabeza?
                    Sí _____ No _____
36. Describa cualquier serio(s) accidente(s).

37. ¿Está usted embrollado en acciones legales relacionadas con su pro-
    blema vocal?
                    Sí _____ No _____
38. Escriba los nombres de su esposa e sus hijos:

39. Resumen de problemas relacionados con Oídos, Nariza, y garganta, al-
    gunos de los cuales puedan no estar relacionados con su presente
    malestar.

    Por favor marque todos con los que usted se sienta relacionado:

_____ Pérdida de la audición	_____ Exceso de piel en la cara
_____ Ruidos en el oído	_____ Otros: (Especifique.)
_____ Vértigos	_____ Problemas en la mandíbula
_____ Parálisis facial	_____ Problemas Oculares
_____ Obstrucción Nasal	_____ Dolor en los oídos
_____ Deformidad Nasal	_____ Dolor en la cara
_____ Dolor en la boca	_____ Cuello rígido
_____ Problemas para tragar	_____ Hinchazón en el cuello
_____ Exceso de piel en los ojos	_____ Hinchazón en la cara o la cabeza

40. Padece usted o padeció de algunas de los siguientes problemas:

_____ Diabetes
_____ Hipoglicemia
_____ Problemas con la
        Tiroides
_____ Sífilis
_____ Gonorrea
_____ Herpes
_____ Ampollas causador por
        alta fiebre
_____ Alta presión circulatoria
_____ Severa baja presión
        circulatoria
_____ Antibióticos intravenosos
        o diuréticos
_____ Ataque al corazón
_____ Angina
_____ Latidos irregulares del
        corazón
_____ Otros problemas
        cardíacos
_____ Fiebre reumática
_____ Tuberculosis
_____ Glaucoma
_____ Esclerosis multiple
_____ Otras enfermedades:
        (Especifique.)

_____ Convulsiones
_____ Psicoterapia
_____ Frecuentes dolores de cabeza
_____ Úlceras
_____ Enfermedades en los riñones
_____ Artritis o problemas en los huesos
_____ Palatosquisis
_____ Asma
_____ Problemas pulmonarios o
        respiratorios
_____ Inexplicable pérdida de peso
_____ Cancer de (_____)
_____ Otros tumores (_____)
_____ Transfusiones de Sangre
_____ Hepatitis
_____ SIDA
_____ Meningitis

41. Algunos de sus familiares tienen:
_____ Diabetes   _____ Cancer
_____ Hipoglicemia   _____ Enfermedades cardiovasculares
_____ Otras enfermedades o graves problemas médicos:
        (Por favor especifique)

42. Describa serios accidentes que usted no halla relatado en su visita al doctor.
_____ Ninguno
_____ Daños en la cabeza, o pérdida del conocimiento
_____ No daños en la cabeza o pérdida del conocimiento
Describa:

43. Escriba los nombres y las dosis de los medicamentos que actualmente está usando (incluya pastillas anticonceptivas y vitaminas).

44. Alergia a medicaciones.

_____ Ninguna   _____ Novocaina
_____ Penicilina   _____ Iodina
_____ Sulfatos   _____ Codeina
_____ Tetraciclina   _____ Cinta adhesiva
_____ Eritromicina   _____ Aspirina
_____ Keflex/Ceclor/Ceftin   _____ Rayos X
_____ Otros: (Especifique.)

45. Operaciones a las que ha sido sometido(a):
_____ Extracción de las amigdalas (edad _____)
_____ Extracción del apéndice (edad _____)
_____ Extracción de adenoides (edad _____)
_____ Cirugía del corazón (edad _____)
_____ Otros: (Especifique.)

46. Marque las drogas tóxicas o químicos a los cuales usted halla sido expuesto:
_____ Plomo   _____ Estreptomicina, neomicina, kanamicina
_____ Mercurio   _____ Otras: (Especifique.)

47. ¿Ha sido usted tratado con rayos X en su cabeza o cuello. (incluya tratamientos por acne o problemas del oído cuando era niñi, tratamientos por cancer, etc)?

Sí _____ No _____

48. Describa serios problemas de salud de su esposa e sus hijos.

Additional translations of this form are available in Portuguese, Swedish, Romanian, Polish, Greek, Russian, Chinese, Japanese, Korean, Arabic, Hebrew, and Yiddish. Please contact the author directly at the following address:

Robert T. Sataloff, M.D., D.M.A.
1721 Pine Street
Philadelphia, PA   19103

Appendix III

Laryngeal Examination

SPEAKING VOICE

Range: _____ Soprano _____ Alto _____ Tenor _____ Baritone _____ Bass

Pitch variability: _____ Normal _____ Decreased _____ Increased

Excess tension: _____ Normal _____ Minimal _____ Moderate _____ Severe

_____ Tongue

_____ Neck

_____ Face

Support: _____ Good _____ Deficient

Volume: _____ Appropriate _____ Soft _____ Loud

Volume variability: _____ Appropriate _____ Diminished _____ Excessive

Quality: _____ Normal _____ Hoarse _____ Breathy

_____ Fatiguable _____ Diplophonic

Rhythm: _____ Normal _____ Slow _____ Fast _____ Spasmodic

_____ Stuttering _____ Dysarthric

Habits: _____ Throat clearing _____ Coughing

Other:

SINGING VOICE

Stance: _____ Balanced, proper _____ Balanced, weight back _____ Unbalanced

_____ Knees locked

Breathing: _____ Nasal, unobstructed

_____ Nasal partially obstructed

_____ Oral

_____ Chest (excessive)

_____ Abdominal (proper)

Excess tension: _____ Face _____ Lip _____ Jaw _____ Neck

_____ Shoulders _____ Tongue

Tongue tension: _____ Corrects easily _____ Does not correct easily

Support: _____ Present   _____ Practically absent

_____Effective   _____ Ineffective

_____Initiated after the tone

Laryngeal position: _____ Stable   _____ Alters   _____ High   _____ Low

Mouth opening: _____ Appropriate   _____ Decreased   _____ Excessive

Vibrato: _____ Regular   _____ Irregular   _____ Rapid   _____ Tremolo

Range: _____ Soprano   _____ Alto   _____ Tenor   _____ Baritone   _____ Bass

Register changes: _____ Controlled   _____ Uncontrolled

Quality: _____ Premier   _____ Professional   _____ Amateur   _____ Pathologic

_____Hoarse   _____ Breathy   _____ Fatiguable   _____ Diplophonic

Technical errors present: _____ In all registers   _____ Low   _____ Middle

_____High

Pitch: _____ Accurate   _____ Inaccurate

Appendix IVa

Sample Letter to Referring Physician

I examined John Doe, M.D. (fictional name), on April 12, 1990. He is a prominent physician and professional baritone who had an active singing career and no voice problems until seven years ago. At that time, he had been singing actively in oratorio, opera, and cantorial literature. Dr. Doe also plays the trumpet. While driving, he had a sudden, violent sneeze followed by severe hoarseness. A colleague diagnosed right vocal fold hemorrhage. In three to four weeks, he resumed singing and was able to sing "almost as well" as before, but with slightly decreased brightness. He continued extensive performance until approximately one year later. At that time, he sang a dress rehearsal of "Elijah" well. However, the next day, he developed sudden hoarseness, which resulted in a poor performance. His voice has never returned completely to normal, and he has had difficulties of varying degrees in singing and speech. In the last two years, he has had difficulty in his midrange and especially at his upper passaggio (E flat, E, and F). He has lost his ability to sing high notes consistently, and his voice cracks periodically. He is troubled by voice fatigue, breathiness, and trouble singing softly, as well. Dr. Doe has studied with two well-known voice teachers. However, in recent years, he has been working more on interpretation than technique. He has had no training for his speaking voice. His vocal peak was between 1977 and 1982. At present, his vocal problems have become so severe that he has decided to give up singing in public, including his cantorial position. He is most eager to restore his voice, if possible. Dr. Doe admits to intermittent reflux symptoms and frequent throat clearing. He uses antacids but has not tried more rigorous antireflux therapy. He exercises regularly and is in good physical condition. His past medical history includes hiatal hernia, spinal stenosis with two degenerative lumbar discs, and a history of arrhythmia. He has no medication allergies and uses Xanax 0.5 mg twice daily. He smoked one-third pack of cigarettes per day for 10 years, but quit in 1970. He rarely consumes alcohol.

Otoscopic examination is normal. Nasal examination is within normal limits, although there is slight septal spurring, especially on the right. His oral cavity and neck are normal. Attached is a copy of his strobovideolaryngoscopy report. His singing voice revealed balanced stance with his weight intermittently too far back over his heels, oral breathing, limited posterior expansion with inspiration, firm abdominal contraction with questionably effective support especially on lower notes, slight tremolo, and increased tension in the strap muscles, jaw, and especially tongue. He is not able to correct the increased tongue tension easily. Reports of his objective voice analysis and the assessments by my speech-language pathologist and singing voice specialist are attached, along with his stroboscopy report and video tape.

Dr. Doe has several problems. First, there is a red, firm mass in the middle of the membranous portion of his right vocal fold, which prevents glottic closure. Second, there is stiffness along the vibratory margin deep to the mass, probably secondary to injury rather than mass effect. Third, there are diffuse hypervascularity of the right vocal fold, and small varicosities and a prominent blush along the posterior aspect of the superior surface on the right. Fourth, there are marked technical abuses in speech and singing. Fifth, there is evidence of gastroesophageal reflux laryngitis. I have placed Dr. Doe on a therapeutic trial of antireflux therapy. Speech therapy and singing training have also been initiated. We have discussed the options of voice modification alone and voice modification in association with surgery. He is well aware of the potential risks and complications of surgery, especially the possibility of permanent hoarseness. However, in light of the size, apparent texture, and nature of the mass, along with its position, which prevents complete glottic closure, he has elected to proceed with surgical excision of the mass and possible laser vaporization of feeding or varicose vessels. He will continue voice training until he is able to arrange surgery and will cancel or limit his performance commitments.

If I may provide further information, please do not hesitate to contact me.

Sincerely,

Robert Thayer Sataloff, M.D., D.M.A.
Professor of Otolaryngology
Thomas Jefferson University
Philadelphia, Pennsylvania

Appendix IVb

Report of Operation: John Doe

April 12, 1990

Preoperative diagnosis: 1. Old right vocal fold hemorrhage 2. Reflux laryngitis

Postoperative diagnosis: Same, plus vocal fold scar, mass, and vascular varicosities of the right vocal cord. Small prominent vessel on the left vocal cord

Procedure: Laryngoscopy with magnification, strobovideolaryngoscopy, and complex voice analysis including synchronized electroglottography

Surgeon: Robert Thayer Sataloff, M.D., D.M.A.

The patient was taken to the special procedure room and prepared in the usual fashion. Topical anesthesia was used. In addition to the rigid laryngoscope, flexible laryngoscopy was included to permit dynamic voice assessment. The laryngoscope was inserted, suspended, and connected to the video system for magnification and documentation. Initial examination was performed using continuous light. The voice was slightly breathy. There was moderate supraglottic hyperfunctional activity, with decrease in anterior/posterior diameter during phonation at the patient's habitual pitch. The appearance of the patient's supraglottic architecture improved with voluntary increase in pitch. Abduction and adduction were normal. The arytenoids were erythematous in color. True vocal fold color was normal on the left. The right vocal fold had a diffuse blush. There were prominent vessels along the superior surface of the right cord, with dilatations and a more prominent blush posteriorly. There was also a tiny varicosity on the vibratory margin of the left vocal fold at the posterior aspect of the area of contact with the mass on the right vocal fold. The right vocal fold mass was red, rounded on its medial surface but irregular at its base, and firm in appearance. It was unchanged from my observations of approximately two months ago. Under stroboscopic light, the mass appeared solid, rather than fluid-filled.

The procedure was continued using stroboscopic light. Observations were made at several frequencies and intensities. Vibrations were slightly asymmetric in amplitude and asymmetric in phase. Periodicity was fairly regular. Glottic closure was incomplete, anterior and posterior to the mass. The mass interfered not only with glottic closure but also with the vibratory pattern of the right vocal fold. However, there appeared to be stiffness underlying the base of the mass, and the traveling wave stopped and altered character just posterior to the mass. Under stroboscopic light, it was apparent that the mass extended much more deeply into the vocal fold than it had appeared to under continuous light, and it probably involves the deeper layers of the lamina propria. Amplitude of the right vocal fold was decreased. Amplitude of the left vocal fold was normal. Wave form of the right vocal fold was decreased. Wave form of the left vocal fold was normal. There were no adynamic segments.

Simultaneous synchronized electroglottography was performed in conjunction with strobovideolaryngoscopy. The electroglottograph revealed a wave form nearly within normal limits. Synchronized electroglottography was also used to assess periodicity.

The procedure was concluded without complication.

Robert Thayer Sataloff, M.D., D.M.A.
Professor of Otolaryngology
Thomas Jefferson University
Philadelphia, Pennsylvania

Appendix IVc

Speaking Voice Evaluation

HISTORY

Dr. John Doe has been experiencing vocal difficulty, primarily in singing, over the past seven to eight years. He complained of vocal fatigue, breathiness, and mild hoarseness. The problem is consistent and seems to be worse in the morning (the voice is lower in pitch). Dr. Doe suspected that he had something on his vocal cord. The patient has sought the attention of Dr. Robert Sataloff, who evaluated him today and diagnosed right vocal fold scar, mass and vascular varicosities, and a small left prominent vessel. Dr. Sataloff recommended speech therapy, singing lessons, and surgery.

Dr. Doe is a practicing physician and an excessive voice user. He admits to smoking five to 10 cigarettes per day during his late teens and early adulthood. However, he has not smoked at all in the past 20 years. The patient denies alcohol and caffeine intake, yelling, loud talking, or whispering. He reportedly gets five to six hours of sleep per night. He denies environmental dryness. Dr. Doe engages in exercise on a daily basis including back exercises, bicycling, and weights three times per week. He is well aware of his breathing during exercise. Dr. Doe admitted to frequent throat clearing, and he was observed to do it excessively during the course of the evaluation. The patient drinks only two to three glasses of water per day. He is under a fair amount of stress both occupationally as a practicing physician and researcher, and personally.

Dr. Doe is a serious avocational singer. He began training in 1972 and accomplished his first opera in 1975. He trained with two teachers. He studied singing weekly for seven to eight years and then less frequently. He is currently not training.

Between 1975 and 1982, Dr. Doe did a lot of singing, including cantorial work for four years. While driving to a musical Sabbath service, he reportedly sneezed and hemorrhaged into his right vocal cord. He canceled a concert and did not sing for three weeks, but when he went back to singing his voice was only "okay." His primary complaint about his singing voice is a loss of upper range and cracking on top notes.

Dr. Doe reported his medical health to be generally good. He has a history of a single episode of cardiac arrhythmia, which lasted for five hours. He denies any history of high blood pressure, frequent bouts of pneumonia or bronchitis, asthma, frequent sore throats, thyroid problems, postnasal drip, or any neurogenic symptomatology. He denies any head or neck injury. He currently takes Xanax (0.5 mg bid).

EXAMINATION

Dr. Doe presents with generally good vocal quality. However, there are an "edge" to the voice and some inconsistent breathiness and slight hoarseness. Hard glottal attacks were excessive with 39% of the vowel-initiated words in a reading passage judged to be "hard." Vocal placement was inadequate, with a pharyngeal resonance predominating. Articulation was within normal limits. The patient's rate of speech was adequate, but his loudness level was excessive at times. Dr. Doe exhibited a mixed breathing pattern. He appeared to use good abdominal/diaphragmatic breath support in reading and singing. However, in conversational speech, his pattern of support was primarily thoracic and clavicular in nature. He was able to prolong the sound /ʃ/ for a maximum of 26.2 sec, the unvoiced /s/ for a maximum of 31.2 sec, and the voiced /z/ for a maximum of 22.2 sec. This yielded an s/z ratio of 1.4. Habitual pitch was judged to be slightly low. Mandibular excursion during speech production was somewhat limited, contributing to jaw and facial tensions. On manual manipulation of the head and neck, a moderate to extreme amount of resistance was encountered.

A cursory examination of the oral/facial mechanism revealed all structures (including the face, lips, tongue, jaw and velum) to be intact for symmetry, strength, range of motion, speed of movement, and coordination. No fasciculations were noted of any of these structures. The patient denied any TMJ symptomatology or swallowing difficulties.

The patient was observed in singing and was noted to have a very powerful voice. However, he exhibited inconsistent abdominal/diaphragmatic breath support and facial tension.

Dr. Doe responded well to the facilitating techniques presented during the course of the evaluation including techniques of abdominal/diaphragmatic breath support, easy onset of voice, forward placement, and increased mandibular excursion.

ASSESSMENT/RECOMMENDATIONS

Dr. Doe presents with symptoms consistent with hyperfunctional voice usage. He does not necessarily abuse his voice (with the exception of throat clearing). However, he does not use his speaking voice optimally. It is quite possible that his present manner of voice usage developed compensatorily following his initial vocal fold hemorrhage and has been habituated over the past seven to eight years. The manner in which he is currently using his speaking voice may be putting undue strain on his vocal mechanism.

It is recommended that Dr. Doe undergo voice therapy to modify the manner in which he uses his voice. It is further recommended that he continue working with a singing voice specialist to be sure that his singing technique is not the major contributor to his vocal complaints and to enable him to reach his maximum singing potential.

The specific goals of voice therapy are suggested as follows:

1. Establish a good program of vocal hygiene (including the elimination of throat clearing)
2. Establish consistent abdominal/diaphragmatic breath support.
3. Promote greater mandibular excursion during speech (thus decreasing jaw and facial tension).
4. Eliminate hard glottal attacks.
5. Promote a more forward oral vocal placement.

Respectfully submitted,

Rhonda K. Rulnick, M.A., CCC-Sp/L
Certified Speech-Language Pathologist

Appendix IVd

Singing Voice Evaluation

PATIENT: John Doe, M.D.
DATE: April 13, 1990

Dr. Doe is a 54-year-old physician and cantor. He has had approximately nine years of formal voice training with three teachers. He also has training as a trumpeter. He has been diagnosed by Dr. Robert Sataloff with vocal fold hemorrhagic mass. During his initial evaluation session (4/13/90), Dr. Doe exhibited the following technical deficits: weight shifting from side to side while singing, tense upper torso, shallow and slightly high abdominal-diaphragmatic breathing patterns, slightly rigid support, excessive tongue tip retraction, slight posterior tongue tension, wide oral opening, and jaw tension. His placement was "spread," and he tended to push his voice at the beginning of the upper passaggio. His range was D2–G4.

The lesson concentrated on improving his stance, upper torso positioning, use of abdominal-diaphragmatic breathing pattern, initiating effective abdominal-diaphragmatic support before and throughout vocal line, and using a relaxed oral cavity position. He was able to improve his stance, breathing pattern, and support with increased visual or tactile cuing but continued to require greater concentration for improved oral cavity position. Dr. Doe tended to overcorrect his stance at times. The following exercises were used: descending slides, descending slides to five-note scales, ascending/descending scales, sliding "block" scales, "/i/ → /a/" exercises, and breathing/support exercises.

I have recommended that Dr. Doe warm up and warm down his voice daily, and that he practice throughout the day for short periods to increase his vocal strength. I have asked him to concentrate on the exercises used during the lesson and to sing by "feel" rather than sound. We also discussed the acoustic effects of the mass and postoperative rehabilitation. I plan to see him in follow-up in one month and will keep you advised of his progress. Thank you again for your referral of this delightful patient.

Linda M. Carroll, B.M., B.S.
Singing Voice Specialist

Appendix IVe

Objective Voice Measures

NAME: John Doe, M.D.   DOB: 7/7/35   AGE: 54
DATE: 4/12/90   HEIGHT: 69″   WEIGHT: 202 lb
MEDICAL DIAGNOSIS: hemorrhagic mass

RESULTS

Conversational SFF: 123.7 Hz
Reading SFF: 115–118 Hz
FRP: 32 semitones (88.7–542 Hz)

MPT: 27.70 sec

MFR: 117 ml/sec

s/z ratio: 1.27
Percent voiced: 94%

NORMATIVE DATE

Age norms:
Male: 118.4 Hz

Male: 36 semitones (Range 80.1–
   674.6 Hz)
Male: 34.6 sec (confidence limits
   30.2–39.4)
Male: 101 ml/sec (confidence limit
   86–117)
1.0 (confidence limit 0.8–1.299)
Marvin Williams: 94.5–100%

SPECTROGRAPHIC ANALYSIS

The voicing parameters listed below were averaged over five trials for spoken and sung vowels.

SPOKEN	/a/	/i/	/u/
Fo (Hz)	121.87	120.29	121.9
Jitter	1.19	1.04	1.31
Harmonics/noise (dB)	8.59	19.16	17.08
Percent voiced	100%	100%	100%

SUNG	/a/	/i/	/u/
Fo (Hz)	123.27	154.27	144.06
Jitter	1.76	4.26	1.77
Harmonics/noise (dB)	11.35	9.42	21.04
Percent voiced	100%	100%	100%

Narrow and wide-band spectrographs for spoken /a/ are found in Fig. 1 and 2. Presence of Singer's formant at 2,580 Hz was evident, as well as "ring" for the speaking voice at 2,640 Hz (Fig. 3). Formant strengths with Fo = 100 Hz were as follows: Sung /a/ 560, 980 2,580, 3,220, 3,580 Hz; Spoken /a/ 640, 1,700, 2,120, 2,640, 3,200, 3,960 Hz. Formants also remained strong during long-term averaging (Fig. 4). A tracing of the waveform is also attached (Fig. 5).

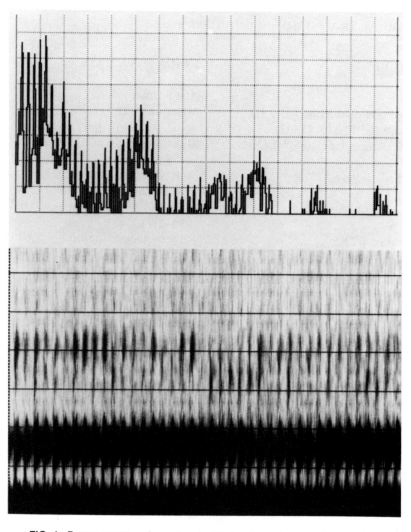

FIG. 1. Power spectrum (upper) and wide-band spectrogram (lower) of /a/.

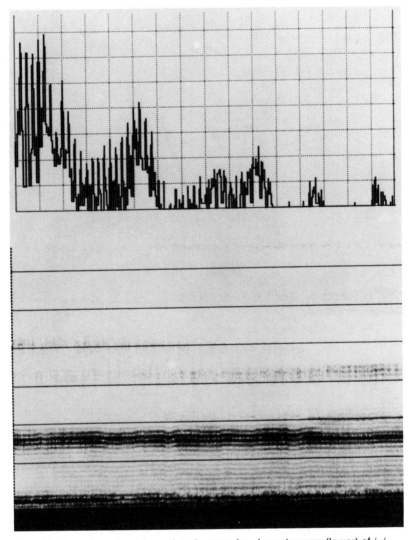

FIG. 2. Power spectrum (upper) and narrow-band spectrogram (lower) of /a/.

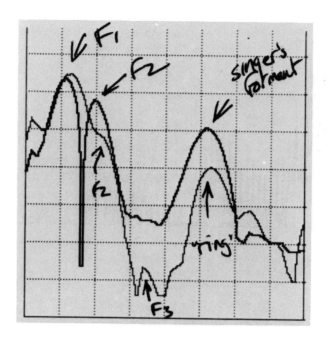

FIG. 3. Singer's formant versus speaker's "ring" on /a/.

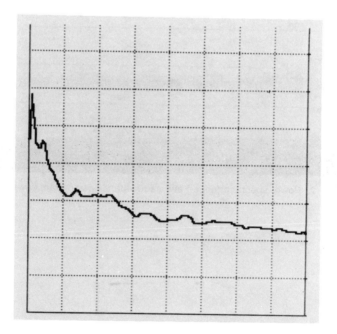

FIG. 4. Long-term averaging of formants.

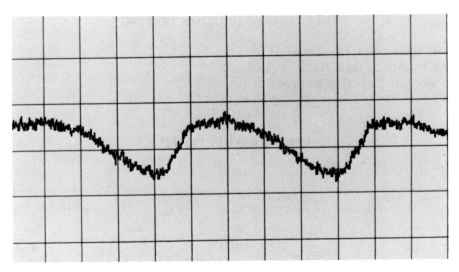

FIG. 5. Lx waveform electroglottogram (EGG) display of /a/.

PULMONARY FUNCTION TESTING

Normative data: (Knudson)
FEV 1.0: 3.51 liters (102% of predicted)
FVC: 4.36 liters (100% of predicted)
FEF 25–75: 3.52 liters (81% of predicted)

PERTURBATION PROFILE

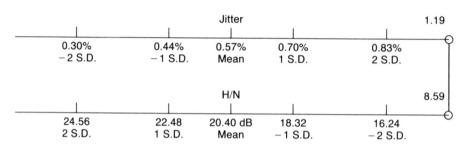

GLOTTAL EFFICIENCY PROFILE

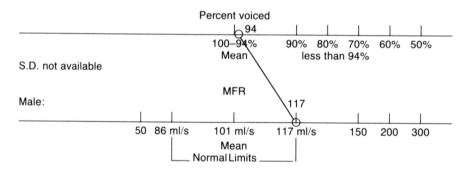

RECORDING/ANALYSIS EQUIPMENT

Recordings were made on a 7½″ reel-to-reel Nagra (E) tape recorder. A Beyer Dynamic microphone (M88N-C) was used to record from a distance of 10 cm. Analysis of the recorded sample was performed using the Kay Elemetrics Visi-Pitch (SE 6095) and Voice Identification PM Pitch Analyzer. Spectrographic analysis was performed using the Kay Elemetrics DSP Sona-graph (model 5500). The Kay Elemetrics Laryngograph was used in conjunction with the sonograph to measure additional voicing parameters. Mean flow rate was obtained using the S&M Instrument Company Pulmo-Screen. Pulmonary function measures were obtained through the Infomed Remote Field Unit (5000-C3). The recording room met or exceeded the ANSI S3.1 (1977) standards.

SUMMARY AND COMMENTS

Dr. Doe demonstrated normal speaking fundamental frequency, s/z ratio, long-term averaging of formants, singer's formant and speaker's "ring," and pulmonary function testing. Percent voiced for longer reading passages and mean flow rate were borderline. Physiological frequency range, maximum phonation, harmonic:noise, and jitter fell outside the expected ranges.

Linda M. Caroll, B.M., B.S.
Voice Technologist

Appendix Va

Outline for Daily Practice

I. Warm-up and cool-down routine
   A. Stretch/relaxation exercises:
      1. Head/neck range of motion
      2. Shoulder rolls and shrugs
      3. Facial massage
      4. Tongue stretch
   B. Vocalises (which are provided by the singing specialist)
   C. Speaking exercises:
      1. Easy speech breathing exercises:
         "Candle blowing," /s/, /ʃ/, /h/-/a/, /m/, /a/
      2. Oral resonance warm up:
         "ng-ah"
      3. Connected speech:
         Counting
      4. Monitoring sites of tension:
         /f-v/, /s-z/, /θ-ð/, /ʃ-ʤ/
      5. Bridging exercises:
         a) sliding block scale for /m/
         b) spoken "vocalises"
         c) Lip trills
      6. Quiet breathing exercise
II. Additional daily practice:
   The target areas are addressed systematically.
   A. Breath control and support
   B. Phrasing
   C. Easy onset and blending techniques
   D. Oral resonance
   E. Tone focus and vocal placement
   F. Loudness/projection
   G. Speaking rate, rhythm, and intonation
III. Carryover practice:
   A. Application of specific goals in ongoing speech
   B. Transition from structured to spontaneous
   C. Stress management strategies

Appendix Vb

Sample Phrases

THREE SYLLABLES IN LENGTH

Put it on.
Tell me how.
Walk around.
Did you know?
Juicy peach.
Yes and no.
Do you know?
Crunchy apple.
Put them down.
What's your name?
Come over here.
Not right now.
Time to go.
Close your eyes.
Fine report.
Read the book.
Who is it?
Pick it up.
Take a nap.
Good evening.

FOUR SYLLABLES IN LENGTH

Pleased to meet you.
You'd like it there.
The sun was bright.
Fill it up, please.
How much is it?
He knows the way.
The train was late.
Maybe later.
Cream and sugar.
Bread and butter.
Salt and pepper.
Toast and butter.
Pie and coffee.
Needle and thread.
Turkey and cheese.
Nice to meet you.
That's fine for now.
Don't tease the dog.
Beth arrived late.
This is enough.

FIVE SYLLABLES IN LENGTH

Where are they going?
The concert was great.
Turn off the iron.
The book was stolen.
Tip the waiter well.
When is he finished?
Flowers need water.
Will she be here soon?
The oven is on.

SIX SYLLABLES IN LENGTH

That's a good idea.
Ted wants to come along.
Put everything away.
He can phone us later.
She bought it somewhere else.
Leave the window open.
Place it down carefully.
Come over and see us.
The children were playing.

FIVE SYLLABLES IN LENGTH

The tea is steeping.
Yes, that's fine with me.
The phone is ringing.
Play the clarinet.
Let's consider it.
They enjoyed the song.

SIX SYLLABLES IN LENGTH

The fire alarm rang.
The switch is over there.
Let me know when he calls.
They moved to the mountains.
The spectators were pleased.
The puppy is playful.

SEVEN AND EIGHT SYLLABLES IN LENGTH

The weather in August is hot.
I love sleeping late on Sundays.
What time can you come for dinner?
We will probably start at six.
The top of this jar is stuck.
Would you help me open it, please?
I can't remember the number.
Please give it to me again.
What shall we have for dessert?
Pie and ice cream sound delicious.
What are you doing after work?
Be careful not to go too fast.
The snowfall was light that year.
Our guests will arrive at nine.

NINE AND TEN SYLLABLES IN LENGTH

Lisa bought some vegetables for dinner.
He wears a 16 and a half collar.
I will be happy to meet with you.
They all went skiing for the holiday.
The bakery smells simply delicious.
There are four bedrooms on the top floor.
After the rain, the air smelled earthy.
Have you been to the theater lately?
Summer at the seashore is popular.
They ate breakfast at the diner.

TEN, ELEVEN, AND TWELVE SYLLABLES IN LENGTH

City buses are often crowded and noisy.
He avoided making eye contact while riding on the bus.
Don't forget to turn off the lights and lock the door.
Oh no, I think I left my keys inside.
We usually go boating each summer.
The car was badly damaged by the crash.
Fortunately, there were no injuries.
Sally loves to go swimming in the lake.
She was reminded not to go too far.
Distilled water tastes much better than tap.

Appendix Vc

Frontal Placement Words

till	town	teal
tot	test	tips
lash	style	still
tall	team	hall
ten	mile	Bill
leash	swell	toad
much	lot	tell
tie	tip	net
latch	least	leap
dial	bell	top
smile	loft	loud
snowfall	town hall	distill
livid	low tide	windmill
tinfoil	vowel	man-made

Appendix Vd

H/Vowel Minimal-Pairs

had–add	hall–all	hold–old
head–Ed	hit–it	home–ohm
hone–own	ho–oh	his–is
hay–ay	hat–at	hand–and
hear–ear	hitch–itch	hi–I

Appendix Ve

Vowel-Initiated Words

LONG VOWELS IN ENGLISH

/a/	/o²/	/a:I/	/i/
odd	oath	aisle	eat
octet	oat	eye	east
object	oak	ice	each
obtuse	old	idle	eek
octopus	oboe	I've	eager
operate	okay	Irish	Ethan
otter	only	iota	enough
obligate	overt	item	even

SHORT VOWELS IN ENGLISH

/æ/	/ɛ/	/I/	/ʌ/
as	end	in	up
at	ever	is	ugh
ask	effort	if	ugly
after	educate	ill	uplift
apple	elephant	id	upset
attitude	enemy	image	utmost
avenue	elegant	issue	under
accident	envy	inactive	unlock
accent	entertain	indent	usher

Appendix Vf

Phrases for Blending

fall over	go into	put upon
leave on	the only	lose it
see it	the other	win it
do it	not even	that's enough
put on	not any	leave open
down under	cold as	one of
not old	the ice	she's ill
look at	he's ill	then add
the end	yes and	so it
high up	one at	Sue is

Appendix Vg

Phrases to Practice Easy Onset and Blending

Elliot ate an apple and allowed Andrew another.

Each and every avenue is open at eight o'clock.

Over on Aston Avenue is an open air amphitheater.

I am in agreement in every aspect of our association.

Alan's attitude is overly obnoxious.

In April, Addle always attends an extravaganza in Aerobe.

Alice openly acknowledges an aversion to avocados.

Exercise is an important and energizing activity.

Amanda is in Alabama at an annual event.

It is eleven o'clock already, and all of us are anxiously awaiting Ellen's arrival.

Eliminating additives is advisable.

Is Emily afraid of an eery effigy?

Eddie is outdoors on an icy evening.

Actually, I am aware of all errors in Adam's arithmetic assignment.

Every evening in autumn our area orchestra attempts to entertain an uninterested audience of adolescents.

Appendix Vh

Homographs

refuse–refuse
compound–compound
converse–converse
console–console
project–project

contrast–contrast
content–content
commune–commune
minute–minute
object–object

Appendix Vi

Open-Vowel Words

/a/	/æ/	/a:I/	/au/
top	map	tie	power
hot	match	reply	town
pocket	hot	side	found
deposit	flag	fire	coward
probable	sad	line	tower
knock	bag	fine	without
shot	cash	confide	house
doctor	cast	tired	how
father	happen	height	loud
garage	mash	rhyme	flower

Suggested Reading List

See also "Suggested Reading List" at the end of Chapters 3 and 28.

1. Appleman DR. *The science of vocal pedagogy.* Bloomington, Indiana: Indiana University Press, 1967.
2. *ASHA.* American Speech-Language Hearing Association, Rockville, Maryland 20852.
3. Baken RJ. *Clinical measurement of speech and voice.* Boston: College Hill Press, Little, Brown and Company, 1987.
4. Borden G, Harris K. *The speech primer.* Baltimore: Williams & Wilkins, 1980.
5. Brodnitz F. *Keep your voice healthy.* Boston: College Hill Press, Little, Brown and Company, 1988.
6. Bunch M. Dynamics of the singing voice. *Disorders of human communication 6.* New York: Springer-Verlag, 1982.
7. Colton R, Casper J. *Understanding voice problems.* Baltimore: Williams & Wilkins, 1990.
8. Crelin EF. *The human vocal tract.* New York: Vantage Press, 1987.
9. Fried M. *The larynx, multidisciplinary approach.* Boston: College Hill Press, Little, Brown and Company, 1988.
10. Gould WJ, Lawrence VL. *Surgical care of voice disorders. Disorders of human communication 8.* New York: Springer-Verlag Wien, 1984.
11. Gould WJ, Sataloff RT. *Diseases and surgery of the vocal tract.* St. Louis: C.V. Mosby Company, in preparation.
12. Hirano M. *Clinical examination of the voice. Disorders of human communication 5.* New York: Springer-Verlag Wien, October, 1981.
13. Hixon T. *Respiratory function in speech & song.* Boston: College Hill Press, Little, Brown and Company, 1988.
14. Issihiki N. *Phonosurgery: theory and practice.* New York: Springer-Verlag, 1989;1–227.
15. *Journal of Voice.* Raven Press, 1185 Avenue of the Americas, New York, New York 10036 (a quarterly publication).
16. *Medical Problems of Performing Artists.* Journal. Philadelphia: Hanely & Belfus.
17. Moriarty J. *Diction.* Boston: E.C. Schirmer Music Company, 1975;257–263.
18. The *NATS* Journal. Oberlin, Ohio: National Association of Teachers of Singing (a bi-monthly publication).
19. Peacher G. *Speak to win.* New York: Bell Publishing, 1985.
20. Pickett JS. *The sounds of speech communication.* Baltimore: University Park Press, 1980.
21. Sataloff RT, Brandfonbrener A, Lederman R. *Performing arts medicine.* New York: Raven Press, 1991.
22. Sundberg J. *The science of the singing voice.* De Kalb, Illinois: Northern Illinois University Press, 1987.
23. Titze IR. *The principles of voice production,* in preparation.
24. Vennard W. *Singing: the mechanism and the technic.* New York: Carl Frisher, Inc., 1967.
25. Zemlin WR. *Speech and hearing science: anatomy and physiology.* Englewood Cliffs, New Jersey: Prentice-Hall, 1988.

Educational Video Tapes

1. The Voice Foundation, 40 West 57th Street, Room 300, New York, New York 10019.
2. AIVER, 1721 Pine Street, Philadelphia, Pennsylvania 19103.

(A video tape companion to this book is in preparation.)

Subject Index

Subject Index